UNITED STATES ARMY IN WORLD WAR II

The Army Ground Forces

THE ORGANIZATION OF

GROUND COMBAT TROOPS

*by Kent Roberts Greenfield, Robert R. Palmer
and Bell I. Wiley, of the Historical Section
Army Ground Forces*

HISTORICAL DIVISION

UNITED STATES ARMY

WASHINGTON, D.C.   1947

This volume is the first to be published in the series THE UNITED STATES ARMY IN WORLD WAR II, and the first in the subseries THE ARMY GROUND FORCES. All the volumes will be closely related, and the series will present a comprehensive account of the activities of the Military Establishment during World War II. The order in which future volumes and subseries are to appear will be determined later. A tentative list of subseries is appended at the end of this volume.

Library of Congress Catalog Card Number: 50–14024

Reprinted 1970

For sale by the Superintendent of Documents, U.S. Government Printing Office
Washington, D.C. 20402 - Price $6.75

. . . to Those Who Served

Foreword

The conflict with the Axis Powers confronted the United States Army with problems on a scale never faced before—problems as great in administration, training, supply, and logistics as in strategy and tactics. THE UNITED STATES ARMY IN WORLD WAR II sets forth in detail the nature of the problems faced, the methods used to solve them, and the mistakes made as well as the success achieved. The object is to provide a work of reference for military and civilian students as well as a record of achievements which deserve an honorable place in the pages of history. Its value to the thoughtful citizen as an aid to his comprehension of basic problems of national security has been a major consideration. Its preparation has also been prompted by the thought that in a faithful and comprehensive record all who participated in the Army's vast effort would find a recognition merited by their service and sacrifice.

The advantage to the Army and the scholar has been the decisive factor in proceeding with the least possible delay to the publication of such a series. No claim is made that it constitutes a final history. Many years will pass before the record of the war can be fully analyzed and appraised. In presenting an organized and documented narrative at this time, the Historical Division of the War Department has sought to furnish the War Department and the Army schools an early account of the experience acquired, and to stimulate further research by providing scholars with a guide to the mountainous accumulation of records produced by the war.

The decision to prepare a comprehensive account of military activities was made early in the war. Trained historians were assigned to the larger units of the Army and War Department to initiate the work of research, analysis, and writing. The results of their work, supplemented by additional research in records not readily available during the war, are presented in this series. The general plan provides for a division into subseries dealing with the War Department, the Army Air, Ground, and Service Forces, the technical services, and the theaters of operations. This division conforms to the organization of the Army during World War II and, though involving some overlapping in subject matter, has the advantage of presenting a systematic account of developments

v

in each major field of responsibility as well as the points of view of the particular commands. The plan also includes volumes on such topics as statistics, order of battle, military training, the Women's Army Corps, and other subjects that transcend the limits of studies focused on an agency or command. The whole project is oriented toward an eventual summary and synthesis.

The studies in this volume were written during the war in the Historical Section of Headquarters, Army Ground Forces, where the authors had free access to the records and experience of the command. The Historical Division of the War Department has confined material changes to such additions of information, approved by the authors, as seemed necessary to round out the picture presented. The full and frank presentation of the wartime point of view of the Army Ground Forces, which has not been affected by the changes made, is regarded as one of the most valuable features of this particular series of studies.

E. FORREST HARDING
Major General, U. S. A.
Chief, Historical Division
War Department Special Staff

Washington, D. C.
1 July 1946

Preface

The series of historical studies of the Army Ground Forces, 1942–45, of which the present volume is the first to be published, was prepared during the course of the war or immediately thereafter on the responsibility of the Commanding General, Army Ground Forces.[1] The headquarters studies in the series were written by professional historians, of whom three were officers of the Army of the United States and one a civilian. These historians were members of a historical office of Headquarters, Army Ground Forces, at first a part of the G–2 Section, but on 25 June 1943 organized as a separate Historical Section. Histories of subordinate commands were prepared under the supervision of this Section by a historical officer in each command, who, except in the Second Army, acted as such in addition to other duties.

The studies were designed primarily for the use of the Army and were planned to be completed by the time the Army Ground Forces had discharged its war mission or shortly thereafter. Their object is to state not only what was done, but also why and how the actions recorded were taken and what lessons were learned. The judgments expressed are those of the officers concerned, not those of the historical officers. The function conceived as proper for the historical officers was to find and state the facts which seemed to have a bearing on the major problems that faced the Army Ground Forces, in the belief that in this context of facts the decisions of its commanders and the consequences of these decisions could be best understood.

In general, effort was concentrated on doing what could probably not be done as well, if at all, after the war. Concretely, this meant exploiting the advantage of access to the records while these were being made, and of access to the officers of the command while the problems they faced and the solutions proposed were in the foreground of their thought and interest. The subjects chosen for intensive study comprised the major activities of the Army Ground Forces and the major problems which it faced in organizing, equipping, and

[1] Established by WD ltr AG 210.31 (6–26–42) MR–F–PS–M, 15 July 42, sub: Appointment of Historical Officers.

training the ground forces for combat. Inevitably this choice made the survey primarily a history of high command and not of tactical units.

The present volume consists of six studies dealing with basic organizational problems of the ground forces. The first study concerns the antecedents of the Army Ground Forces, during the years 1940–42, as represented by General Headquarters, U. S. Army, from which the Army Ground Forces and its policies in respect to the organization and training of the ground troops developed. Given the limited objective inherent in the mission of the authors as members of the Historical Section, Army Ground Forces, the study of General Headquarters is not an exhaustive treatise on that organization, but emphasizes its exercise of those functions and activities which were later assumed by the Army Ground Forces. Nevertheless, such subjects as the activities of GHQ in planning and directing operations and the steps involving GHQ which led to the reorganization of the Army high command in March 1942 are included, not only to round out the picture, but also to contribute to the understanding of larger questions the information found in the records of GHQ.

The next four studies in this volume give an account of the principal problems and decisions of the Army Ground Forces regarding the size, internal organization, and armament of the ground troops deployed in World War II. The last study explains the part played by the Army Ground Forces in the redeployment and reorganization of the ground forces for the final assault against Japan.

The point of view represented in the studies is that of General Headquarters and of the Army Ground Forces, and only their decisions are fully documented. In general, research was carried beyond the records of these two organizations only so far as seemed necessary to explain their views and decisions. No effort was made to explore facts not known to them at the time when action was recommended or taken. It is recognized that a knowledge of other facts and circumstances is necessary for a balanced judgment of their recommendations and decisions, a knowledge which will be attainable only when the history of the war, and of the part played by the War Department and the U. S. Army in winning it, has been written.

The study of General Headquarters was written by the undersigned and by Dr. Robert R. Palmer, now Professor of History in Princeton University. In its preparation helpful, in some instances invaluable, information or criticism was obtained from Maj. Gen. H. J. Malony, Maj. Gen. C. L. Bolte, Maj.

Gen. C. L. Hyssong, Maj. Gen. F. A. Keating, Maj. Gen. A. R. Bolling, Maj. Gen. F. L. Parks, Maj. Gen. W. F. Dean, Brig. Gen. J. M. Lentz, Brig. Gen. P. McD. Robinett, Brig. Gen. W. G. Walker, Brig. Gen. J. S. Winn, Jr., Brig. Gen. R. F. Ennis, Col. J. W. Wurts, Lt. Col. George Seleno, and Maj. K. W. Hechler.

The second, third, fourth, and fifth studies of this volume were prepared by Dr. Palmer, and the sixth study by Maj. Bell I. Wiley, now Professor of History in Louisiana State University. All were prepared with the advice and collaboration of officers of the Army Ground Forces. Materials obtained from records and interviews in Washington were supplemented by observations in the field. The officers consulted furnished in many cases oral information on points not fully covered in the records. Special acknowledgment is due the officers of the Mobilization Division of the G–3 Section and the Organization Division of the Requirements Section for their collaboration in connection with this volume. Mrs. Ida M. Elmquist, Administrative Assistant to the Chief of the Organization Division, gave most helpful assistance in finding necessary data in the files of that Division. The following officers gave particularly valuable information on one or more of the studies: Maj. Gen. J. G. Christiansen, Chief of Staff, Army Ground Forces; Col. H. T. Todd, Chief, and Lt. Col. W. W. Johnson, Lt. Col. J. W. H. Lusby, Lt. Col. W. G. Bartlett, and Lt. Col. J. M. Cummins, Jr., members of the Mobilization Division, G–3 Section; Col. L. H. Frasier, Chief of the Organization Division, Requirements Section, and Col. J. S. Sauer, his Executive Officer; Lt. Col. John Lemp and Lt. Col. Forsyth Bacon, Special Projects Division, G–3; Brig. Gen. A. W. Waldron, Chief of the Requirements Section; Brig. Gen. A. D. Warnock, Assistant Division Commander, 5th Infantry Division; Col. S. L. Weld, Mobilization Division, G–3 Section; Col. A. L. Harding, Operations Branch, G–3 Section; Col. L. H. Schrader, G–3 Section, Col. P. J. Kopcsak, Personal Affairs Division, G–1 Section; Col. W. M. Breckinridge, Commanding Officer, 10th Regiment, 5th Infantry Division; Lt. Col. M. F. Brennan, Training Division, G–3 Section; Lt. Col. J. A. Hanson, Task Force Division, G–4 Section; Lt. Col. G. T. Petersen, Ordnance Section; Lt. Col. J. U. Parker, Control Division, G–3 Section; Lt. Col. M. L. Rosen, Assistant Ground Liaison Officer, New York Port of Embarkation.

The photographs included in the volume were taken by the U. S. Army Signal Corps, except that opposite page 42, which was kindly furnished by Representative Thomas E. Martin.

At the end of the volume, certain aids to the reader have been added: a glossary covering numerous abbreviations appearing in the text; a footnote guide explaining the system of documentation employed; and a bibliographical note to guide future students of the problems treated in the studies through the archival materials which have been used. For the benefit of the general reader it may be stated that "G–1," "G–2," "G–3," and "G–4" have been used to designate staff sections as follows: G–1, *personnel;* G–2, *intelligence;* G–3, *operations and training;* and G–4, *supply.*

KENT ROBERTS GREENFIELD
Lieutenant Colonel, Infantry
Chief, Historical Section
Headquarters, Army Ground Forces

Washington, D. C.
1 April 1946

Contents

Origins of the Army Ground Forces:

General Headquarters

United States Army, 1940–42

by

Kent Roberts Greenfield and Robert R. Palmer

Contents

Charts

Illustrations

I. The Development of General Headquarters, United States Army

With the outbreak of hostilities in Europe in September 1939, the War Department, already alerted by the activities of the Axis in Europe and the Far East, intensified its preparations for the possibility of war. Through the winter of 1939–40 Great Britain and France held the line of the Rhine, and the American public found it difficult to see the danger. In April and May the dam broke. Denmark, Norway, the Netherlands, Belgium, and France were overrun by the German armies, and in June Italy declared war. With the Axis in control of western Europe Great Britain faced immediate invasion. The threat to the security of the United States could no longer be disregarded, and public opinion rallied to the support of extraordinary measures to meet it. Mobilization and intensive training began during the early summer of 1940 on the basis of agencies and plans which had been elaborated within the framework of the National Defense Act of 1920.

One of the first steps toward mobilization, taken 26 July 1940, was the activation of a "nucleus of General Headquarters." [1] To understand this measure it is necessary to have in mind the organization of the military establishment in 1940 and the general plan of mobilization then in effect.

Organization of the Military Establishment in 1940

The field forces of the United States in being and on paper in 1940 were composed of the Regular Army, the National Guard, and the Organized Reserves. The Regular Army, with an actual enlisted strength of 243,095 in July 1940, was a standing army, based on short-term enlistments and led by a corps of professional officers, approximately 14,000 in number. The National Guard, with an

---

[1] WD ltr AG 320.2 (7–25–42) M (Ret) M–OCS, 26 Jul 40, sub: GHQ. 320.2/3. The basic WD memo is OCS 21152–2 OCS–OW to TAG GHQ, 25 Jul 40, sub not given. AGO Records. Other background papers in AGO Classified Records, WPD 3209–10. For the general defensive measures taken by the Army, see *Biennial Report of the Chief of Staff of the U. S. Army, July 1, 1939, to June 30, 1941, to the Secretary of War,* pp. 1–2. (Cited hereafter as *Biennial Report, CofS, 1941.*)

actual enlisted strength of 226,837, was a force of civilian volunteers trained by the States in accordance with standards set by the War Department and put through field exercises for two weeks each summer under Federal direction. The units of the Organized Reserve existed only in the blueprints for mobilization. A reservoir of trained officers, 104,228 in number was available in the Organized Reserve Corps, which by 1940 was made up chiefly of graduates of the Reserve Officers' Training Corps and of Citizens' Military Training Camps.[2]

Behind the field forces stood the arms and services, whose function was to develop and supply personnel and equipment and to formulate the tactical and training doctrines embodied in their technical and field manuals, the bible of the Army. These branches were responsible for what may be termed the "developmental" functions of the military establishment—the preparation of personnel, equipment, and doctrine which the field forces were to employ. Their relation to the General Staff was not well defined. Their chiefs, having direct access to the Chief of Staff, could bypass the General Staff in its advisory capacity, and exercised a very considerable influence. In 1940 the branches commonly regarded as combat arms were seven in number: Infantry, Cavalry, Field Artillery, Coast Artillery, the Air Corps, Corps of Engineers, and Signal Corps. This distribution of "developmental" functions reflected the art of warfare as understood in 1921, but technology was rapidly producing new potentialities and arms. The need for exploring the military potentialities of the airplane had been recognized after the war of 1917–18 in the creation of the Air Corps, and experiments in mechanization and with new weapons were being continuously carried on in the established arms.

Each of the traditional arms and services had a standard institutional pattern. Each operated a service school and a board. The schools not only provided professional training but also developed the doctrine and training literature of the several branches. The boards developed and tested equipment. The school system of the branches was supplemented by general service schools operated by the War Department for the Army as a whole—the United States Military Academy at West Point, the Army Industrial College, the Command and General Staff School at Fort Leavenworth, Kans., and finally the Army War College in Washington, the postgraduate school of the Army, where officers were trained in the staff work incident to high command.

[2] (1) *Annual Report of the Secretary of War, 1940*, pp. 26, 27, and 40. The enlisted strength of the Regular Army as given does not include some six thousand Philippine Scouts. (2) *Annual Report of the Chief of the National Guard Bureau, 1940*, p. 6.

At the top of the structure stood the War Department General Staff, directed by the Chief of Staff who acted as adviser to the Secretary of War and as head of the military establishment. Gen. George C. Marshall held this position in July 1940. The War Department General Staff, the offices of the Chiefs of Arms and Services, and those of the Secretary of War and the Assistant Secretary of War constituted the War Department.

The administration of the Army within the continental limits of the United States, the Zone of Interior, was conducted in peacetime through nine territorial commands, known as corps areas. The corps area commanders administered the "housekeeping" of the Army stationed in the United States. They were also responsible for the execution of the training program of the arms and services. Until 1932 they directed the tactical training of the Regular Army and the National Guard units stationed in the United States.

In 1932, under the direction of Gen. Douglas MacArthur as Chief of Staff, a stride was made toward preparing the field forces of the Army "to take to the field and execute the plans prepared for them." [3] The tactical units in the United States, both those in being and those planned for activation in an emergency, were brought together into the First, Second, Third, and Fourth Armies. Their commanders took over from the corps area commanders responsibility for the tactical training of the field forces, concentrated in quadrennial maneuvers of the Regular and National Guard units assigned to each. [4] By exercising this responsibility the headquarters of each army would be training for its planning, tactical, and administrative duties in time of war. The four armies were also designed to provide a large tactical framework for mobilization. [5]

[3] WD ltr OCofS, 9 Aug 32, sub: Establishment of the Fld Armies.

[4] Brief histories of the Second, Third, and Fourth Armies in the period preceding mobilization were prepared by the AGF Historical Section. Copies of all narratives prepared by the AGF Historical Section are on file in the Historical Division, WDSS.

[5] General MacArthur explained the purpose in view: "Heretofore the War Department has never been linked to fighting elements by that network of command and staff necessary to permit the unified tactical functioning of the American Army." Before World War I "the military force then existing was conceived of and administered as a collection of infantry, cavalry and artillery regiments." By establishing the "skeletonized Army Group on a satisfactory basis," and by decentralizing certain responsibilities to army commanders, General MacArthur believed that the War Department was providing "a suitable framework for the assimilation of the thousands of recruits who will, almost simultaneously with the declaration of war, volunteer for service with the colors." Without the constitution of such an authority, existing units would be swamped and immobilized with the organizational and training detail. "The four Field Army organization . . . constitutes a logical and definite basis for initial expansion." WD ltr OCofS to CGs four Fld Armies, 22 Oct 32, sub: Development of the Four Fld Armies. AGO Records, 320.2 (8–6–32) Sec 1A.

After this change, as before, corps area commanders were responsible for supply, the special training of officers and enlisted men in the arms and services, and the mobilization training of recruits. The change was not as great in fact as in principle. Means were not provided to effect a physical separation of the armies from the corps areas. The senior corps area commander in the territorial area assigned to each army was designated as the commanding general of that army, and his headquarters staff was drawn from the corps area staff, whose members now acted in a double capacity. But the training functions of the four army commands created in 1932 contained, in germinal form, the primary mission which was centralized in GHQ in July 1940 and in Army Ground Forces after 9 March 1942.

Reduced to the simplest general terms, the main features of the plan of mobilization and expansion of the field forces, within the organization of the Army just outlined, were as follows:

1. The units of the Regular Army would be brought to full strength.

2. The National Guard would be inducted into Federal service and its units brought to full strength.

3. Units of the Organized Reserve would be activated, according to plan, as needed.

4. The training nucleus of each of these new units would be a cadre of officers and enlisted men drawn from existing units.

5. Fillers, to bring enlisted units to full strength and new units from cadre to authorized strength, would be obtained by voluntary recruitment or draft, and, before assignment, be put through a course of basic training in replacement training centers.[6] These centers would be operated by the corps area commanders under the supervision of the chiefs of the arms and services concerned, except for the "branch immaterial" centers, which were to be directly under the War Department.

6. Officers for new units, in addition to cadre officers, would be drawn in large part from the Officers' Reserve Corps.

7. Preparation of tactical units for combat would be conducted by the armies created in skeleton form in 1932, which would be brought to full strength and activity.

[6] The replacement training centers were not set up until the spring of 1941, and their output was never sufficient for the purpose stated. From the beginning, many of the fillers went directly to tactical units and received in these their training in Mobilization Training Programs which were programs for basic training in the various arms and services. In the actual process of expansion the tactical unit became the school of the individual soldier.

8. A General Headquarters, United States Army, would be activated as the high command of the field forces.

GHQ in the Mobilization Plan of 1940–42

Into this plan of mobilization "a nucleus of GHQ" was injected on 26 July 1940. Its mission was to facilitate and speed up the process of mobilization by taking over the direct supervision of the huge task of organizing and training the field forces within the continental United States.

A GHQ had been one of the capital features of the reorganization of the War Department effected in 1921, a reorganization based on the lessons of World War I as read and digested by the Harbord Board.[7] It had been expected that in the next war a GHQ such as that of the American Expeditionary Force of 1917–18 would be required. To prepare staff officers of this headquarters as completely as possible for their grave responsibilities in war, a War Plans Division (WPD) was included in the War Department General Staff as reorganized in 1921. This division was given the responsibility for drawing the strategic plans for the employment of the field forces, and upon the mobilization of the Army it was to take the field as the staff of GHQ to put these plans into effect.[8] In 1936 this feature of the plan was extended by designating certain officers of the General Staff for future duty with GHQ when it took the field. It was expected that other officers needed would be drawn from the Army War College, which would be suspended for the duration of the war. Originally the Chief of Staff of the War Department was to become the commanding general of this expeditionary force, but in 1936 it was decided that, while the Chief of Staff would automatically become commanding general of the field forces and of GHQ units when mobilization began, the final choice of the commander of the expeditionary forces must be left to the decision of the President.[9]

[7] The deliberations and report of this Board will be found in *The National Defense: Historical Documents Relating to the Reorganization Plans of the War Department and to the Present National Defense Act, Hearings before the Committee on Military Affairs, House of Representatives, 69th Congress, 2d Session* (1927), pp. 568–648. (Hereafter cited as *Historical Documents.*)

[8] (1) Preliminary Rpt of Committee on "Nucleus for General Headquarters in the Field in the Event of Mobilization," 11 Jul 21, especially par 9. *Historical Documents,* pp. 571ff. (2) Par 15, sec IV, GO 41, WD, 16 Aug 21.

[9] (1) *Historical Documents,* p. 576. (2) AR 10–15, 25 Nov 21, with changes of 1933. (3) The changes made in 1936 included the designation of officers in each General Staff Division to reinforce WPD when it took the field as the staff of GHQ. Memo OCS 15313–5 of DCofS USA for CofS USA, 16 Apr 36, sub:

The "nucleus of GHQ" activated on 26 July 1940 consisted of a Chief of Staff and a small group of officers selected to perform the only function which was given to it initially, namely, the supervision of the training of tactical units of the Army in the continental United States. It was under the command of General Marshall, the Chief of Staff, acting as the commanding general of the field forces. In its function as a training agency, GHQ was a headquarters inserted between the War Department and the four armies. As such it put a capstone on the four-army plan.[10] The training supervision given GHQ went further: it included, in addition to the four armies, "GHQ Aviation," which comprised the tactical air forces then existent, the Armored Force (constituted 10 July 1940), harbor defense troops, and "other GHQ reserves." In short, administration of the training of the field forces, as distinct from planning and policy decisions, was decentralized in July 1940 by transferring this function of the War Department General Staff to the staff of GHQ. The reason stated for the activation of GHQ was "to decentralize the activities of the War Department," thereby assisting General Marshall "in his capacity as Commanding General of the Field Forces."

General Marshall was the commanding general. His Chief of Staff was Brig. Gen. Lesley J. McNair, who became Major General in September 1940 and Lieutenant General in June 1941. He had been Commandant of the Command and General Staff School since April 1939 and reported for duty in his new assignment on 3 August 1940. General Marshall freely delegated authority over training to General McNair. Though in constant communication with his Chief of Staff, he saw him infrequently and actually visited GHQ, located at the Army War College, for the first time on 13 May 1941.[11] General McNair directed GHQ.

Separation of the Field Armies from the Corps Areas

The activation of GHQ was a first step toward concentration of effort on training. Another major step was taken in October, when the command of corps areas was separated from that of the four armies.[12] On 19 July 1940 G–3 had made a modest proposal that, as a means of establishing more effective control

---

Reorgn of GHQ, approved the same date by the CofS, and memo of the Sec WDGS for ACofS WPD, 17 Apr 36, sub as above. OPD Records 3209.

[10] The directive of 26 July 1940 stated that the jurisdiction of GHQ was to be "similar in character to that of Army Commanders."

[11] Notes (C) on a talk at GHQ by Gen Marshall, 0930 13 May 41. 337/4 (C).

[12] Corrected WD ltr AG 320.2 (9–27–40) M–C, 3 Oct 40, sub: Orgn, Tng, Adm of Army. 320.2/8.

over training, "tactical headquarters" should be set up "at convenient locations" to assist corps area commanders in their training duties.[13] General McNair, four days after reaching his desk at GHQ, pointed out that the activation of GHQ called for more radical action. "The establishment of GHQ," he remarked, "amounts in principle to superimposing a theater of operations on the Zone of Interior." He therefore recommended that the existing territorial organization, the corps area system, "be used for Zone of Interior functions *only*," and that troop units be organized, trained, and administered by armies, corps, divisions, and similar tactical units as though in a theater of operations.[14] General Marshall directed that a reorganization be worked out along the lines indicated by General McNair.[15]

The effect of the reorganization adopted was to implement the four-army plan of 1932. Army commanders were designated whose staffs, now distinct from those of any corps area headquarters, were henceforth to concentrate on training. The armies, though still in the United States and based while training on the posts, camps, and stations of the corps area commands, were to be "in the field." When on maneuvers they would, "insofar as practicable, assume supply functions comparable to those of an Army Commander in a Theater of Operations where supplies are received direct from Zone of Interior supply points." [16] The object was to set the stage for bringing the units of the field forces, including the armies, to maximum readiness for combat before they left the United States. Always desirable, this objective had now become necessary. In 1917–18 it had been possible for American troops to undergo or complete their training and have much of their equipment produced behind the lines in France. In June 1940, when the Axis acquired possession of all accessible beachheads on the European Continent, this possibility was excluded from plans for the impending conflict. A vastly more ambitious objective had to be envisaged. When the proposal to separate the armies from the corps areas and place them under the command of GHQ was under discussion, General McNair stated that "the ultimate and essential result of these measures would be to develop the field forces into a united whole—GHQ troops and four

[13] Memo G–3/42980 for CofS USA, 19 Jul 40, sub: Div Tng. AGO Records, AG 353 (12–28–39), Tng Dir 1940–41 (2).

[14] GHQ 1st ind, 7 Aug 40, to above.

[15] Sec V of memo G–3/42980 for CofS USA, 19 Jul 40, cited in footnote 13.

[16] WD ltr AG 320.2 (10–14–40) M–C–M, 19 Oct 40, sub: Change in Dir on Orgn, Tng, and Adm of the Army. 320.2/18.

armies—free to move strategically and capable of prompt and effective tactical action. Thus it would be possible to move an army when and where directed by a simple order." [17]

This ideal was not completely implemented by the measures actually taken. General McNair had envisaged the establishment of GHQ as amounting "in principle to superimposing a theater of operations on the Zone of Interior." [18] The measures taken in July and October 1940 did not in fact produce this result. They failed to complete either the delegation of authority over the training of the field forces or the liberation of the army commanders from responsibility for the administration of posts. In short, GHQ was not vested with the full authority of a theater headquarters. Though its jurisdiction was described "as similar in character to that of Army Commanders," [19] GHQ was never vested with the administrative authority even of an army commander, but was subject in logistical matters to G–4 of the War Department. In principle the respective authority of army and corps area commanders was clearly delimited. Corps area commanders, operating under G–4 of the War Department, remained responsible for the system of supply and for the construction, maintenance, and repairs of fixed installations, specifically of posts, camps, and stations, and harbor defense projects, as well as for the training of service troops assigned to their stations. On the other hand, to give the armies and their staffs full training for field duty, army commanders were not only to take over at once from corps area commanders their training functions as far as tactical units were concerned, but to the extent of their facilities and personnel to provide medical care and evacuation for the field forces and in periods of maneuvers, "insofar as practicable, assume supply functions." The chain of command,

[17] 3d ind, 16 Sep 40, to memo G–3/42980 for CofS USA, 19 Jul 40, cited in footnote 13.

[18] GHQ 1st ind, 7 Aug 40, to above.

[19] WD ltr AG 320.2 (7–25–40) M (Ret) M–OCS, 26 Jul 40, sub: GHQ. 320.2/3. The basic memo is OCS 21152–2 OCS–OW, 25 Jul 40. AGO Records.

GENERAL McNAIR AND GENERAL MARSHALL
The "situation map" shows the positions of the Second and Third Armies in the Louisiana Maneuvers, 26 September 1941.

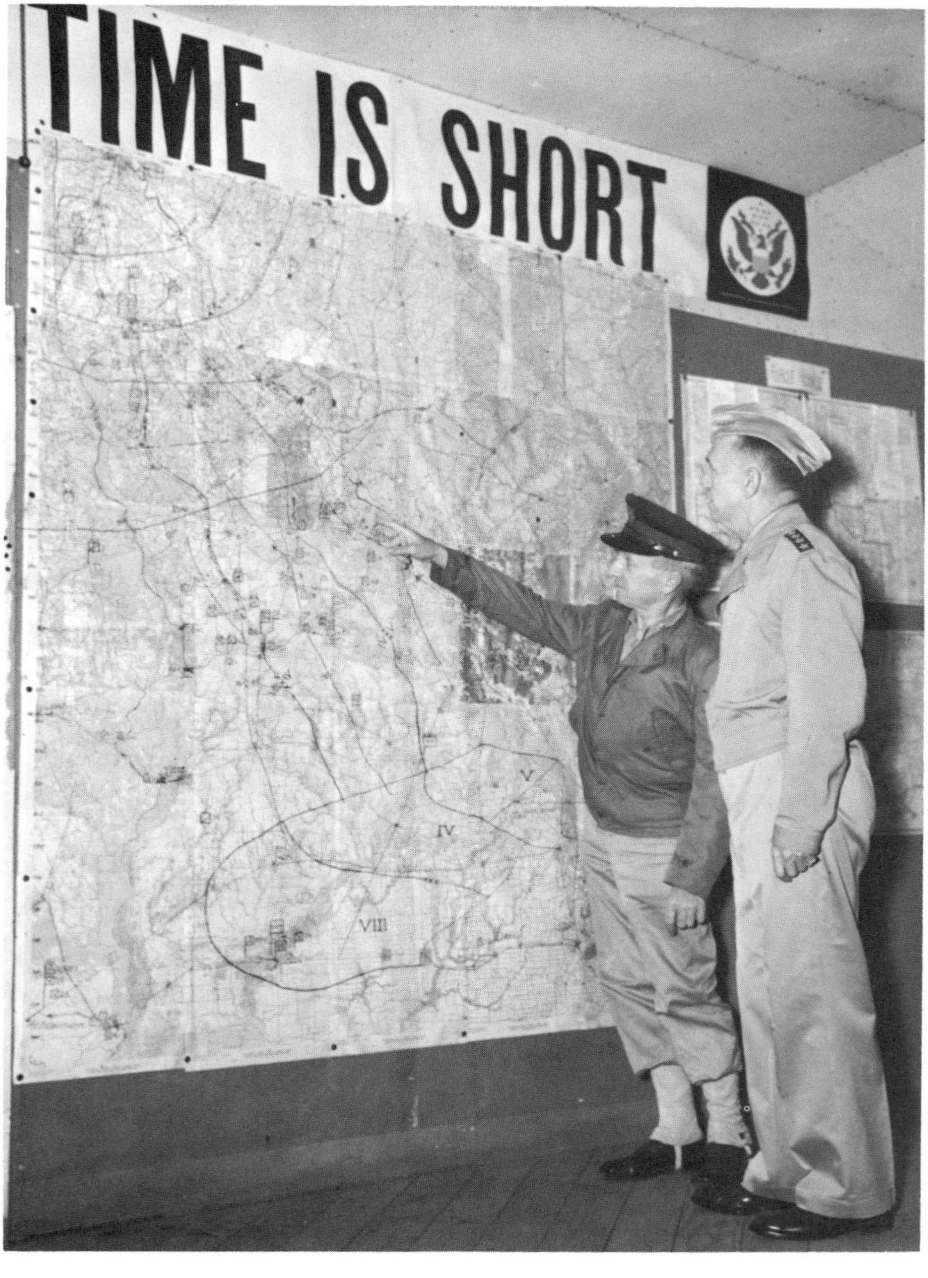
TIME IS SHORT
IV
V
VIII

nevertheless, remained tangled. In supply matters army commanders were under the corps area system and G–4, not GHQ. When a tactical commander on a post, camp, or station was senior to the representative of the corps area commander, he became post commander. The expedient adopted to relieve him of post duties in such cases was to instruct him to appoint a "post executive" and delegate to him the routine administration of the post.[20] As noted above, General McNair's concept was that GHQ, to accomplish its training mission effectively and with complete realism, should have essentially the organization of a theater of operations. The link in the chain of command necessary to complete this concept would have been a communications zone placed under its authority. This link was not provided. The need for it was felt even more sharply later when the authority of GHQ was extended to include base and defense commands.

Nevertheless, in the establishment of GHQ and the reorganization of October 1940 important steps had been taken to limber up a peacetime system which had been largely occupied with routine housekeeping functions and to put the Army into the field under centralized direction to train for combat.

Training Tasks of GHQ

The magnitude of the training tasks confronting GHQ in August 1940 was staggering. The tactical units whose preparation for war it was to direct and energize existed for the most part only on paper. All planning and preparation had been hampered by lack of money and manpower. Eight infantry divisions, one cavalry division and elements of a second, and one armored division had been activated, but in August 1940 these divisions were far from full strength. Only enough corps troops had been brought together to activate one corps and sketch another. The four armies consisted only of skeleton headquarters and 4,400 troops. The units of the Regular Army in the United States, located at widely scattered posts, had not been assembled except in quadrennial maneuvers directed by each army in turn. The eighteen divisions of the National Guard had had only such training in the field as could be acquired in a two-week period each summer. The field training of corps and armies had had to be limited largely to command-post exercises. Not until 1940 had it been possible

---

[20] Par 11*b* corrected WD ltr AG 320.2 (9–27–40) M–C, 3 Oct 40, sub: Orgn, Tng, and Adm of the Army. 320.2/8. The arguments for this device are fully set forth in a memo of G–3 WD for CofS USA, 24 Aug 40, sub: Adm of Posts. AGF Records, G–3/43332.

to stage what General Marshall described as "the first genuine corps and army maneuvers in the history of this Nation." [21]

GHQ had the twofold task of completing the imperfect training of the forces in being and at the same time of using such experience and military skill as these had to train for imminent war the mass of units and fresh recruits that were then being mobilized. On 13 June 1940 the authorized enlisted strength of the Regular Army had been expanded from 227,000 to 280,000 and on 26 June to 375,000. On 16 September the induction of National Guard units began, continuing until November 1941 as housing and equipment became available. These units brought 278,526 enlisted men into active service.[22] They had had more and better training than in 1917, thanks to the program authorized in 1920. But their training was far from complete, and the National Guard, no less than the mass of raw recruits, had to be taught tactics and the use of weapons which were revolutionizing the art of warfare. On the date when induction of the National Guard began, the Selective Service Bill became law, and, by July 1941, 606,915 selectees had been inducted.[23] These selectees were used to bring existing units up to authorized strength or as fillers for new units. Beginning 1 March 1941 large numbers of them were sent to the replacement training centers of the arms and services for basic training.

Meanwhile new units were being constructed around cadres drawn from units of the Regular Army and National Guard. The ground forces, as they expanded under GHQ, were organized into 27 infantry divisions (9 Regular Army, one of which was motorized, and 18 National Guard), 4 armored divisions, 2 cavalry divisions, and 1 cavalry brigade. Enough corps units were assembled or activated to set up nine army corps.[24] Before the end of 1941 the organization of the four armies had been brought to a point which made it possible to put all of them through maneuvers and in September of that year to pit two of them, fully organized, against each other in the field. By 1 July 1941 the strength of the field forces had reached a total of 1,326,577 officers and enlisted men.[25] The training of this huge force, and more to come, had

---

[21] (1) *Annual Report of the Chief of the National Guard Bureau, 1941*, pp. 6–9. The period of field training for the Guard was increased to three weeks in 1939–40 and to four in the summer of 1941. (2) *Biennial Report, CofS, 1941*, p. 3.

[22] *Annual Report of the Chief of the National Guard Bureau, 1941*, p. 27.

[23] *Annual Report of the Secretary of War, 1941*, p. 101.

[24] *Biennial Report, CofS, 1941*, Chart 4.

[25] This figure is given in the *Annual Report of the Secretary of War, 1941*, p. 96.

to match or excel the preparation of enemy forces known to be thoroughly trained and, in the case of Germany, magnificently equipped.

To provide the military leadership for this great task GHQ had immediately available its share of the 13,797 Regular Army officers then on active duty. The National Guard was to bring into active service 21,074 officers.[26] But only 6,800 of these had completed a course of instruction in a service school.[27] An officer pool existed, consisting of approximately 33,000 Reserve officers and 104,228 graduates of the ROTC in the Officers' Reserve Corps.[28] By 1 July 1941, 56,700 Reserve officers in these two categories had been called to extended active duty; at that date they already constituted from 75 to 90 percent of the officers of the Regular Army divisions.[29] Commissioned personnel was currently being supplemented by graduates of West Point and of ROTC units and, after August 1941, by graduates of the officer candidate schools set up in July of that year.

Men and means having been provided, work had to be done in haste and distraction which could be done with maximum efficiency only in the leisure of peace. The basic training of soldiers, the advanced training of many officers of all grades, and the tactical training of units of all sizes up to armies had to be carried on simultaneously, with officers and men in every degree of proficiency or lack of it and with only a thin line of Regular Army officers and noncommissioned officers to take the lead.

The task was made immensely more difficult because it had to be prosecuted in the midst not only of an unprecedented expansion but also of continual and rapid changes imposed by the overwhelming successes of the German Army. Arms and equipment were being changed, and the new types could not be made available in quantities adequate for training. Many units were being converted; the Cavalry was being mechanized; the motorized division was being developed. At the same time the basic organization of the infantry division was undergoing a radical reform while the Army was being assembled. The "triangular" division was being substituted for the "square" division, to provide the flexibility required by the concept of the combat team. This process of change began in the winter of 1939–40,[30] but as late as September 1940 the Tables of

---

[26] *Annual Report of the Secretary of War, 1941*, p. 96.

[27] Draft memo (S) of CofS USA for USW, 30 Sep 41, sub: Morale of the Army. AGO Records, 352 (9–19–40) (1) (Morale of the Army) (S).

[28] *Annual Report of the Secretary of War, 1940*, pp. 35–36, 40.

[29] *Annual Report of the Secretary of War, 1941*, p. 110.   [30] *Biennial Report, CofS, 1941*, p. 2.

Organization for the triangular division were still not ready. In August preliminary charts were issued, to which nine Regular Army infantry divisions, the 1st through the 9th, were ordered to conform by 1 October.[31] The eighteen National Guard divisions remained square divisions during the first year of their field training and were reorganized on the triangular pattern only during January and February 1942.[32] Meanwhile, all through the period of GHQ's existence new types of units were being formed or multiplied: armored divisions, parachute troops, mountain troops, antitank and antiaircraft units, and the service and maintenance units required to support these specialized troops.[33] As organization changed, doctrine and rules of procedure as set forth in technical and field manuals had to be kept up to date, and the staff of GHQ, as the group in charge of training operations, was called on to give much thought and time to the necessary revisions. These were only some of the changes that were taking place in the GHQ period, but they provide a rough measure of the magnitude of the job which General McNair was given in the summer of 1940.

The GHQ Staff

General McNair performed his task with a staff whose maximum strength by 31 May 1941 was only twenty-one commissioned officers. To get officers who had "an open mind with reference to innovations," General Marshall directed that those assigned to GHQ should be under fifty years of age. General McNair reported to the Army War College from Fort Leavenworth on 3 August 1940. By the end of the month his staff was composed of seven officers. The Infantry, the Field Artillery, the Cavalry, the Coast Artillery Corps, the Armored Force, the Corps of Engineers, and the Signal Corps were each represented by one officer. In September G-1, G-2, G-3, and G-4 functions were assigned, and an Adjutant General, an Air officer, and a National Guard officer were brought in. In October a representative of the Organized Reserves was added, in November

[31] WD ltr AG 320.2 (8-31-40) M (Ret) M-C, 10 Sep 40, sub: Reorgn of Triangular Divs. 320.2/6. The charts had been issued with WD ltr AG 320.2 (8-12-40) P (C), 23 Aug 40, sub: Charts for Orgn of the Triangular Div, the Type Army Corps, and Army Trs of a Type Army of Three Corps. (As approved 8 Aug 40.) 320.2/4. An example of the achievement of the Army in bringing an army to life in spite of insufficient personnel and funds is recorded in AGF Historical Section, The Third Army.

[32] The 32d, 34th, and 37th Divisions were triangularized in January, and all of the others except the 27th in February 1942. The 27th, which had been sent to Hawaii, was reorganized on 24 August. Directives in 322, 322.13, and 320.2 (S).   [33] *Biennial Report, CofS, 1941,* p. 10.

ARMY WAR COLLEGE

a Medical officer, and in January 1941 an officer from the Quartermaster Corps. In January the officer who had represented the National Guard was redesignated as representative of the Civilian Component, and in April the Coast Artillery officer became the Antiaircraft officer.[34]

During this first year the line between general and special staff functions was not sharply drawn. Business was carried on in an informal manner, largely by consultation.[35] The staff met for work under Stanford White's Roman vaults in the Army War College building, where the last graduating exercises of the War College "for the duration" had been held on 20 June.[36] On the breezy point between two rivers, at the end of the campus-like parade ground of the Army War College post, the officers reported for duty in civilian clothes, as they continued to do until Pearl Harbor. The civilian guard at the main door recalls not recognizing General McNair and other generals and challenging them to show their identification cards. General McNair's little staff of officers had anything but a martial aspect, in spite of the warlike concentration and energy with which they devoted themselves to their task.

GHQ as a Training Division of the General Staff

During the first year of its existence GHQ was virtually a division of the War Department General Staff, although it was located outside the General Staff and was itself organized as a complete staff in embryo. As Chief of Staff

---

[34] For General Marshall's policy for the selection of officers, see p. 48 below and also minutes of his talk at GHQ, 13 May 1941. 337/4 (C). The other statements in this paragraph were obtained from 330.3 (Monthly Rosters–Strength Returns), checked with Lt Col Seleno, Ground AG Sec.

The officer personnel of the staff on 31 May 1941 was as follows:

Maj Gen Lesley J. McNair	Lt Col Morris Handwerk	Lt Col Charles B. Spruit
Col William E. Lynd	Lt Col Vernon K. Hurd	Maj James G. Christiansen
Lt Col Lloyd D. Brown	Lt Col Clyde L. Hyssong	Maj Thomas E. Lewis
Lt Col Mark W. Clark	Lt Col Allen F. Kingman	Maj Hammond McD. Monroe
Lt Col Frederick J. de Rohan	Lt Col Jerry V. Matejka	Maj William D. Old
Lt Col Charles H. Gerhardt	Lt Col Bryan L. Milburn	Maj Julian E. Raymond
Lt Col Farragut F. Hall	Lt Col Richard B. Moran	Col Kenneth Buchanan (attached)

[35] This statement is based on the recollections of staff officers on duty at Hq AGF in May 1943, notably General Hyssong and Colonel Seleno, and par 1, ltr of Gen McNair to TAG, 9 Jan 41, sub: Enl Pers for Duty at GHQ USA (AGO Records, OCS 21152–2) stating that all officers at present, except the AG, are assigned to the General Staff and perform the dual function of general and special staff officers.

[36] The Army War College was suspended by WD ltr AG 352.01 (6–11–40) M–MC, 11 Jun 40, sub: Courses at AWC and C&GS Sch, 1940–41. AGO Records.

Chart No. 1

Organization of the War Department, June 1941

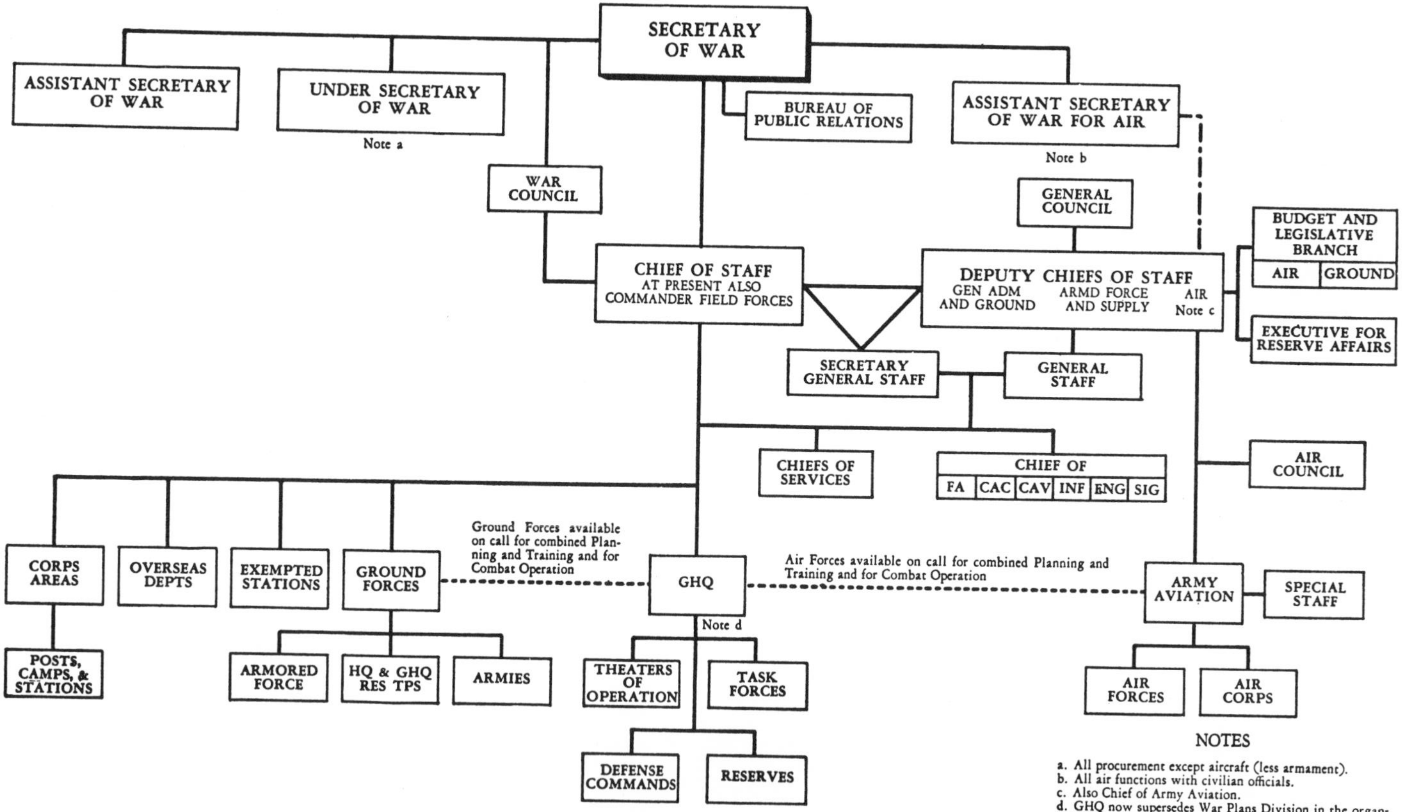

SECRETARY OF WAR

ASSISTANT SECRETARY OF WAR

UNDER SECRETARY OF WAR — Note a

WAR COUNCIL

BUREAU OF PUBLIC RELATIONS

ASSISTANT SECRETARY OF WAR FOR AIR — Note b

BUDGET AND LEGISLATIVE BRANCH — AIR | GROUND

EXECUTIVE FOR RESERVE AFFAIRS

CHIEF OF STAFF — AT PRESENT ALSO COMMANDER FIELD FORCES

DEPUTY CHIEFS OF STAFF — GEN ADM AND GROUND | ARMD FORCE AND SUPPLY | AIR — Note c

GENERAL COUNCIL

GENERAL STAFF

SECRETARY GENERAL STAFF

CHIEFS OF SERVICES

CHIEF OF — FA | CAC | CAV | INF | ENG | SIG

AIR COUNCIL

ARMY AVIATION — SPECIAL STAFF

AIR FORCES

AIR CORPS

Air Forces available on call for combined Planning and Training and for Combat Operation

GHQ — Note d

THEATERS OF OPERATION

TASK FORCES

DEFENSE COMMANDS

RESERVES

Ground Forces available on call for combined Planning and Training and for Combat Operation

CORPS AREAS

POSTS, CAMPS, & STATIONS

OVERSEAS DEPTS

EXEMPTED STATIONS

GROUND FORCES

ARMORED FORCE

HQ & GHQ RES TPS

ARMIES

NOTES

a. All procurement except aircraft (less armament).
b. All air functions with civilian officials.
c. Also Chief of Army Aviation.
d. GHQ now supersedes War Plans Division in the organization and control of task forces and operations. It will continue to direct the training of the Ground Forces and combined air-ground training.

reporting directly to General Marshall, General McNair was drawn into the staff discussion of all major issues. Usually he consulted his own staff before making recommendations. At the same time GHQ became a living presence to the commanders under its supervision by going to the field and making itself known. It met their desire for a single command post in the War Department capable of representing their needs and of initiating expeditious action. In December 1940 the War Department found it necessary to remind the commanders of units placed under GHQ for training that only those communications which dealt with training should pass through the Chief of Staff, GHQ. "In the past," the letter ran, "the Chief of Staff has exercised his functions as commander of the Field Forces through the War Department. GHQ is the agency through which he would exercise command over such forces in an emergency. For the present, however, the recently formed GHQ will be concerned only with the direction and supervision of training of the Field Forces, exclusive of overseas garrisons. The War Department will continue to be the agency through which command, except for training, will be exercised." [37] It seemed necessary to General McNair himself, a month later, to keep his staff within bounds by cautioning it against initiating projects not directly concerned with training. The War Department had been referring many matters other than training to GHQ for comment and recommendation, and the staff was therefore encouraged to include in its training contacts observations of conditions other than training. "But such side issues," General McNair declared, "must not weaken the main effort—training—nor create the impression among troop units that this staff is interested more than casually in other activities." [38] These two directives indicate both General McNair's concentration on training and the importance which GHQ had already acquired by the early weeks of 1941 in the eyes both of its staff and of the commanders under its supervision.

Expansion of the Functions and Authority of GHQ, 3 July 1941

The critical international situation required not only intensive and rapid training of the U. S. Army but also the development of definite plans for the defense of the United States. When Dunkerque and the air bombing of England

---

[37] WD ltr AG 320.2 (12–5–40) M–P–M, 13 Dec 40, sub: GHQ Trs and Armies. 320.2/87.
[38] Memo of CofS GHQ for Staff GHQ, 15 Jan 41. 320.2/3/3.

threatened the security of the country, measures had to be concerted for the defense of the continental United States and Alaska as well as the Atlantic approaches to the United States and the Panama Canal.

On 17 March 1941 the United States was divided into four defense commands.[39] If invasion threatened, these defense commands were to become theaters of operations. Each was put under the authority of the commanding general of one of the four field armies. The immediate duty of the commander and his army staff, given an augmentation of personnel for the purpose, was to plan the measures necessary to repel invasion. Since it was expected that an initial attack on the United States would have to be met first in the air, air planning and organization figured prominently in these measures for defense. The order of 17 March 1941, creating the defense commands, activated four air forces, located in "districts" roughly coterminous with those of the four defense commands. The commander of GHQ Aviation, after 20 June 1941 the Air Force Combat Command, in which the four air forces were united, was made responsible for "the aviation and air defense plans for Defense Commands." [40]

Meanwhile preparation had also been made for strengthening an outer ring of defenses toward Europe. On 3 September 1940, the President had announced the lease from Great Britain of additional bases in the Atlantic, in exchange for fifty destroyers, and in the spring of 1941 agreed to replace British troops in Iceland with U. S. forces. Detailed plans for garrisoning Iceland, the new bases, and a cordon of defense commands in the Atlantic and Caribbean had to be made.

But while the necessary defensive measures were being taken, plans for an eventual offensive also had to be prepared. The traditional doctrine of the Army and Navy placed the emphasis on crushing the enemy's attack far from our shores and on launching an offensive at the earliest possible moment.

The existing organization of the War Department (see Chart No. 1) was put under an enormous strain by the burden and multiplicity of all these demands for planning and administration. The danger of war was increasing rapidly. The destroyer-bases exchange in September 1940 and the passage of the Lend-Lease Act in March 1941 had committed the United States to supporting Great Britain openly in order to stave off attack while arming and to maintain positions from which to strike the potential enemy. As war came swiftly nearer, a group of officers in the General Staff, alarmed by the delays involved in existing proce-

---

[39] WD ltr AG 320.2 (2–28–41) M–WPD–M to CGs, CofS GHQ, etc, 17 Mar 41, sub: Defense Plans—Continental US, with atchd charts. AGO Records.

[40] For a discussion of these measures see below, Section VIII.

AIR VIEW OF THE ARMY WAR COLLEGE

dures, became convinced that the War Department must freely delegate some of its responsibilities to speed up action and to lighten the burden which was mounting on the shoulders of the Chief of Staff. A step toward this end was taken on 3 July 1941, when the authority of GHQ was extended to include, in addition to training, the planning and command of military operations.[41]

"GHQ now supersedes War Plans Division in the organization and control of task forces and operations. It will continue to direct the training of the Ground Forces and combined air-ground training." Such was the statement of policy approved by General Marshall on 17 June.[42] By this decision GHQ was advanced closer toward assuming the role for which it had been cast by the Harbord Report in 1921. GHQ was to plan operations as well as direct them. It was to "prepare theater of operations plans prescribed in Army Strategic Plans and such other operations as may be directed by the War Department." [43] GHQ was secretly informed that it would shortly be directed to prepare, in a given order of priority, four such plans.[44]

Behind this decision lay the recognition of the imminence of war for the United States. It was stated that "military combat operations may be required in the near future." Effective "coordination, conduct and control" of operations "in a number of minor and widely separated theaters" would be "an extremely difficult task," requiring "an executive organization capable of prompt decision and expeditious action." Since it was recognized that there was "no agency of the War Department now organized to meet this requirement," the powers of GHQ were enlarged to meet it.[45]

The new mission of GHQ was defined as "planning, initiation and execution of such military operations as may be directed by the War Department." Specifically, the mission consisted of the following duties: [46]

[41] WD ltr (R) AG 320.2 (6–19–41) MC–E–M, 3 Jul 41, sub: Enlargement of the Functions of GHQ. 320.2/3/34.

[42] Note, 17 Jun 41. AGO Records, WPD 3209–11 (S).

[43] Par 1b (1), WD ltr, 3 Jul, cited in footnote 41 above.

[44] Pars 2 and 3, Sec I, WPD memo (S) for CofS USA, — Jun 41, sub: Enlargement of the Functions of GHQ. 320.2/1 (S). This GHQ copy bears the following note, initialed "F. L. P(arks)": "This staff was approved and promulgated by restricted letter AG 320.2 (6–19–41) MC–E–M, Subject: 'Enlargement of Functions of GHQ.' Parts were not put in letter to avoid classification of 'Secret' (verbally from Gen. Malony to Col. Parks)."

[45] Pars 1–4, Sec I, WPD memo, Jun 41, cited in footnote 44 above.

[46] WD ltr (R) AG 320.2 (6–19–41) MC–E–M, 3 Jul 41, sub: Enlargement of the Functions of GHQ. 320.2/3/34 (R).

Chart No. 2

GHQ in the Chain of Command after 3 July 1941

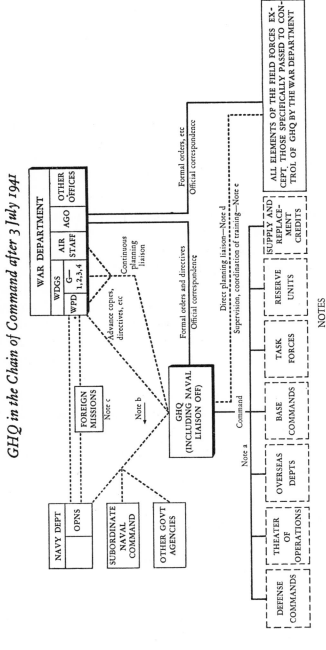

NOTES

a. Except for certain restrictions stated below, GHQ exercises command over the forces and supplies shown when these are specifically passed to its control by the War Department. Thereafter GHQ is responsible for the execution of the War Department directive relating to such forces. Certain actions desired by GHQ which require coordination by the War Department will be executed on orders of the War Department upon approval of requests of GHQ submitted directly through pertinent divisions of the War Department General Staff. These actions include movements of units or supplies which have been passed to GHQ command but which are still in the Zone of Interior, transportation to the Theater of Operations, purchase of special equipment, creation of special units, concentration of troops in staging areas, and similar matters.

b. GHQ participates in joint planning necessary to the execution of directives assigned to it by War Department.

c. Essential GHQ contact with foreign mission by liaison officer through WPD.

d. GHQ delegates planning responsibility to commands and units which subsequently, by War Department order, pass to its command for execution of plans. It also supervises preparation of plans of defense commands. To facilitate planning, direct correspondence with subordinate planning agencies and issue of necessary travel orders are authorized.

e. GHQ, functioning as G–5, WDGS, supervises and coordinates training of ground elements of the Field Forces and combined air-ground training in the continental U. S. except—

  (1) Services and other ground units allocated to Air Force.

  (2) Air defense, continental U. S.

1. GHQ will prepare theater of operations plans for those operations prescribed in Army Strategic Plans and such other operations as may be directed by the War Department . . . .

2. It will coordinate and control military operations in those theaters assigned to its command, to include such overseas departments, bases, and other military means as are made available to it by the War Department.

3. It will exercise command over task forces set up for and required in the execution of a prospective operation from the date specified by the War Department for the assumption of such command.

4. It will exercise command over such combat or other units, in the continental United States, both air and ground, as shall hereafter, from time to time, be designated to it as a reserve by the War Department.

5. It shall have under its direct control such credits in supplies, ammunition and equipment as may, from time to time, be specifically allotted to it by the War Department.

By a directive of 25 March GHQ had been empowered to supervise and coordinate the planning activities of the four defense commands in the continental United States, but not "until such time as the staff of GHQ had been expanded to undertake these additional responsibilities." That time had now come. GHQ was given "full authority for the employment of the means available to it, including designated reserves, in the execution of the task in each of the theaters assigned to it for command, and authority for the transfer of units and means between theaters under its control," with the proviso, of course, "that such transfer falls within the framework of the strategic directive issued by the War Department." [47]

Under the terms of the new directive GHQ shared the planning of operations with WPD, with the Chief of the Army Air Forces, and with the commanders of bases and defense commands. Theoretically the division of functions (see Chart No. 2) was as follows: WPD drafted strategic plans; GHQ, in collaboration with the commanders of bases and defense commands, elaborated theater plans which fitted into these; the Chief of the Army Air Forces, maintaining contact with GHQ by means of an Air Support Section located in that headquarters,[48] made air plans which became air annexes of theater plans

---

[47] (1) WD ltr AG 320.2 (3–24–41) M–WPD–M, 25 Mar 41, sub: Defense Plans—Continental US. 320.2/158/3. (2) See footnote 46 above.

[48] This was a staff section of the Air Force Combat Command. Its chief was Colonel Lynd, who had been General McNair's Air officer from the beginning. The Air Annexes were prepared in this section. Statement to AGF Hist Off by Mrs. Naomi Allen, who was in charge of the Records Section, Army War College, as well as the processing of war plans framed by GHQ.

after approval by the theater commander and the concurrence of the Chief of Staff, GHQ. When execution of a theater plan was ordered, GHQ was drawn into the chain of command between the theater commander and the War Department to supervise, to coordinate, to inspect, and to share the burden of administration at Washington. But even at this stage full command was withheld, since GHQ was not given control over supply.

Such an organization was obviously not "functional" in the sense of conferring clear-cut authority commensurate with responsibility. It remained to be seen whether it would stand up under the stress of impending events, which were to include the outbreak of war on 7 December.

Although the charter received in July was somewhat restrictive, extensive assignments were given GHQ in the following eight months.

Planning Activities

GHQ prepared in whole or part sixteen detailed operational plans for task forces, including those for the U. S. forces which relieved the British in Iceland and in British and Dutch Guiana, and for the forces sent to the British Isles in the spring of 1942. At the beginning plans for reconnaissance and occupation of protective bases in the Atlantic were in the foreground. Other plans were prepared for expeditionary forces which seemed likely to be required by the rapidly changing situation in Europe and the Western Hemisphere but which were not launched. The plans nevertheless had to be worked up in detail and under high pressure. One of these, SUPER-GYMNAST, prepared in January 1942, laid the basis for TORCH, the plan for the operation launched in North Africa on 8 November 1942.[49] In addition, GHQ had to work out operational plans for the base commands in Bermuda, Greenland, Newfoundland, Iceland, and Alaska and to supervise and coordinate the theater plans submitted by the commanding generals of the Caribbean Defense Command and of three of the four defense commands in the United States—the Northeastern, Southern, and Western.[50]

---

[49] Memo (S) of Gen McNair for CG FF, 15 Jan 42, sub: Future Operations. McNair Correspondence with CofS (S).

[50] This summary is based on (1) the Diary (S) of GHQ, 314.81 (S); (2) Minutes (S) of Staff Conferences, GHQ, 337 (S); (3) 381 General (S), all in GHQ Records; (4) various papers filed under the names of pertinent "color" plans and base and defense commands in AGO Classified Records Section, and in the Combined Subjects file of OPD records, where they were consulted through the courtesy of Miss

A highly efficient routine was worked out for processing through the GHQ staff the "operations plans" which that headquarters was directed to prepare. The first step, taken whenever feasible, was to send a party to the area in question to make spot reconnaissance. On its return, a general conference of the staff for "orientation" was held in the War College Auditorium. The next step was for the "G's" in a standard order—G–2, G–3, G–1, and G–4—to work up all the basic data for a plan framed within the strategic directive handed down by WPD. A draft was then blocked out under the headings: "Situation," "Missions and Organization," "Operations," "Supply," "Command." [51] The draft was presented to the entire staff for discussion. Details were provided in "annexes" worked out by the general and special staff sections. All parts of the plan were prepared and assembled in conformity with a dummy model.[52] When completed, the plan was submitted to WPD for approval.

Meanwhile, the commander and his staff assigned for a particular operation were ordered to the War College, where the approved plan was laid before them for study. They were instructed to ask no questions for two days, after which they were free to discuss it in detail with the officers who had drafted it.

The whole task required the management and coordination of a complicated mass of details in the form of factual information, men, and things. In the drafting stage each section and annex of a plan had to be coordinated not only with numerous agencies located in the complex organization of the War Department, but with agencies of the Navy Department as well. Nevertheless, plans were worked up with conspicuous speed and economy of effort. The first of these, the plan for Iceland, was completed in seven days after the reconnoitering party had reported. The Diary and Minutes of GHQ from September 1941 until the following March show that headquarters preparing plans and dispatching them with a speed comparable to that of an assembly plant under rush orders. One secret of the efficiency displayed was a compact staff, located apart from the maze of offices in the Munitions Building and under the direction of a leader, the Deputy Chief of Staff, Brig. Gen. Harry J. Malony, who

---

Alice Miller; (5) the file "Status, War Plans," AWC Records 111–55c, a ledger of the plans prepared by GHQ, in the custody (1945) of Mrs. Naomi Allen. The assistance of Miss Miller and Mrs. Allen, supported by their recollections, has been of great value. No evidence has been found that the Central Defense Command submitted a plan to GHQ.

[51] (1) Min (S) of Staff Conferences, GHQ, 17 Sep 41. 337 (S). (2) GHQ memo (S) for all Staff Secs GHQ, 10 Oct 41, sub: Preparation of Plans, Rainbow 5. 381 R–5/3 (S)

[52] *Ibid.* See also mimeographed model of operations plan, Cpy 3. AWC Records, 111–55B.

inspired them with his sense of the urgency and importance of their task. Another was the presence under a single roof, and in a single organization, of representatives of the arms and services, who could furnish both technical information and quick contact with these agencies. The isolated location of GHQ made it easier to enforce security. The standard operating procedure developed was so effective that it continued to be employed by the Operations Division of the War Department General Staff, which in March 1942 took over the planning functions of GHQ.[53]

Command Problems

Meanwhile, GHQ was also exercising its command functions over task forces and theaters successively placed under its authority. In July 1941 it organized and dispatched the first echelon of the force sent to Iceland. On 13 August it was given control of the second echelon, which sailed on 5 September. This force was, the report stated, "the first United States Expedition to depart with a complete plan and all means necessary to implement it." [54] On 2 January 1942 GHQ was put in command of the forces in the British Isles, and in the following weeks it organized and dispatched the units sent to Northern Ireland and England. It also planned and prepared those designated for the relief of the garrisons in Dutch Guiana and those which it was believed might be needed to reinforce other strategic points on the coasts of Central and South America.

At the same time the responsibilities of GHQ gradually came to include an ever greater number of new bases and defense commands which were being activated in 1940–41 in the Atlantic, the Caribbean, and Alaska to give additional protection to the approaches to the United States and the Panama Canal. On 15 July 1941 the Bermuda Base Command and on 19 July the Newfoundland Base Command were transferred from the First Army to GHQ.[55] On the latter date United States Army units in Greenland were attached to GHQ for tactical command only; on 26 November they were constituted under

---

[53] The information in this and the foregoing paragraph was drawn largely from interviews of the AGF Historical Officer with Maj. Gen. Harry J. Malony, formerly DCofS GHQ, 10 Jan 44, and with Brig. Gen. Paul McD. Robinett, formerly ACofS G–2 GHQ, 5 Feb 44.

[54] GHQ Quarterly Rpt (S), 15 Sep 41. 320.2/1 (S).

[55] (1) WD telg (S) AG 320.2 (7–8–41) MC–E to First Army, 8 Jul 41. AGO Records, 320.2 (4–28–41) (Comd of US Units in Newfoundland) (S). (2) WD ltr AG 320.2 (7–8–41) MC–E–M to CofS GHQ, sub: Comd of US Army Units in Bermuda. AGO Records, 320.2 (BBC) (7–8–41).

GHQ as the Greenland Base Command.[56] In the previous February a Caribbean Defense Command had been established with headquarters at Quarry Heights, Panama Canal Department, embracing all bases under United States control in the Atlantic approaches to the Panama Canal.[57] On 1 December 1941 command of this critically important area was vested in GHQ.[58]

Then came Pearl Harbor and war. On 14 December the Western Defense Command, with Alaska included, was made a theater of operations under the command of GHQ.[59] On 24 December the Northeastern Defense Command, extended to embrace Newfoundland, was similarly converted into the Eastern Theater of Operations under GHQ.[60] The responsibilities of GHQ for the control of operations had now reached their peak. In the summer and fall of 1941 the eventual transfer of Hawaii and the Philippines, indeed of "all projects and outlying bases," had been expected by the GHQ staff.[61] These expectations were not realized. Indeed the command responsibilities of GHQ were eventually contracted. On 19 December 1941 control of army as well as naval forces assigned for operations to the Caribbean Coastal Frontier, the seaward sector of the Caribbean Defense Command, passed despite the protests of GHQ to the Navy under the principle of "unity of command." On 31 January 1942 operational forces assigned to Bermuda were also transferred to the control of the Navy Department.[62] Control of operations in the Pacific area beyond the western coast line were not delegated by the War Department to GHQ.

[56] (1) WD ltr (S) AG 320.2 (7-10-41) MC–E–M, 10 Jul 41, sub: Comd of US Army Units in Greenland. AGO Records, 320.2/7 (Greenland) (S). (2) WD ltr (C) AG 320.2 (11-5-41) MC–C–M, 26 Nov 41, sub: Activation of Greenland Base Comd. AGO Records, WPD 4173–126 to Greenland, sec 5 (S).

[57] WD rad (S) to Lt Gen Voorhis, SC PCZ, 10 Feb 41, sub: Caribbean Defense Comd. AGO Records, 320.2 (1-8-41) (S).

[58] Telg No 7 (S), CG GHQ to CG CDC, 28 Nov 41. AGO Records, 320.2/3 (CDC) (S).

[59] (1) WD ltr (S) AG 320.2 (12-11-41) MC–F to CG WDC, 11 Dec 41, sub: Supplementary Directions for WDC. (2) Telg No 10 (S) to CG WDC, 14 Dec 41, signed Marshall "Official, Hyssong," no sub given. Both in AGO Records, 320.2/34 (WDC Str) (S).

[60] WD ltr (C) AG 371 (12-19-41) MSC–E–M, 20 Dec 41, sub: Creation of ETO. AGO Records.

[61] (1) Min (S) of Staff Conferences, GHQ, 6 Aug 41. 337 (S). (2) Memo (S) for all Staff Secs GHQ, 7 Aug 41, sub: Expansion of GHQ. 320.2/22 (S). (3) "We have advance copies of directive of tasks to be turned over to GHQ. In general all projects and outlying bases are to be ours." Min (S) of Staff Conferences, 9 Aug 41. 337 (S). On 15 November the DCofS reported that Alaska and the Philippines would be transferred "when construction was in better shape and further advanced, and when equipment and supply matters were in better shape in the Philippines." 337, 5 Nov 41 (S).

[62] (1) WPD memo (S) for TAG, 19 Dec 41, sub: Unity of Comd in the Caribbean Coastal Frontier. AGO Records, 381 (Unity of Comd) (12-17-41) (S). (2) A telegram (S), Andrews to GHQ, 20 Dec 41, reported assumption of command by the Navy on that date. 320.2/90 (CDC) (S). (3) The protest of GHQ

Expansion and Reorganization of the GHQ Staff

In response to the new demands made on General McNair and his staff after 3 July 1941, GHQ underwent a transformation. Its strength, which stood at 29 officers and 64 enlisted men in the latter part of June, was considerably more than doubled by 1 December 1941 (76 officers, 178 enlisted men). Before the dissolution of GHQ on 9 March 1942 it had increased to 137 officers and 327 enlisted men.[63] This expansion created new administrative burdens. Officers had to be procured and office space had to be found for them. The War College building overflowed, and a new office building, "T–5," and additional living quarters were authorized, designed to accommodate an anticipated strength of approximately 300 officers and 1,000 enlisted men.[64] At the beginning of December 1941 the staff was reorganized for the more effective discharge of its dual function of training on the one hand and operations and planning on the other. The little group of officers in mufti, consulting informally in the big spaces of the War College and frequently absent on inspection tours, was converted into a highly organized planning and administrative machine, which crowded all the available space on the Army War College post. Measures had to be taken to maintain the expeditious action characteristic of the original "nucleus." [65]

As late as January 1941 the staff had been organized only to the extent of having on it officers representing arms and services and "G" functions essen-

---

is recorded in memo (S) of Gen McNair for CofS USA, 18 Dec 41, sub: Unity of Comd in Caribbean and Panama Coastal Frontiers. 320.2/93 (CDC) (S). (4) For Bermuda: WPD memo (S) for CofS USA, 6 Feb 42, sub: Unity of Comd in Bermuda. Same file as (1) this note.

[63] The figures given are drawn from the following sources: (1) For officers on 24 June, immediately after the increase of strength on 18 June, par 2, memo (S) of Lt Col Carrington, ACofS G–1 GHQ for Sec GS GHQ, 28 Aug 41, sub: Resumé of the Orgn and Opns of GHQ. 320.2/1 (S). (2) For enlisted men, same date, par 1a, GHQ ltr to TAG, 15 Jul 41, sub: Pers Asgd to Hq Sp Trs GHQ and Hq and Hq Co GHQ. (3) For the other dates the figures are compiled from GHQ Rosters. 330.3.

[64] Memo of CofS GHQ for CG FF, 23 Jan 42, sub: Construction of Additional Office Space for GHQ. 680.341/23. The additional office space immediately needed was created by clearing the cavalry stable of the AWC post. The new building, T–5, was not ready for occupancy by 9 Mar 42. The strength requested on 27 Jan 42 was 212 officers and 489 enlisted men. The actual strength on that date was 146 officers and 266 enlisted men. Ltr 320.3/4 GHQ–A to TAG, 27 Jan 42, sub: Revised T/O. AGO Records.

[65] The Secretary (Col Floyd L. Parks) "recommended to the Staff that in view of the limited time of the Chief of Staff and the Deputy Chief of Staff in offices, the Staff take final action whenever possible and avoid references to the Deputy or the Chief of Staff except when policy or matters of major importance were involved. To keep the Chief of Staff and the Deputy Chief of Staff informed by short memos in matters they should know about to maintain a general background of current business." Min (S) of Staff Conferences, GHQ, 17 Oct 41. 337 (S).

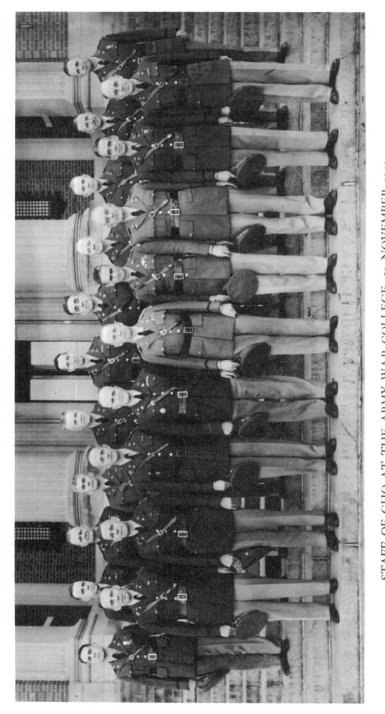

STAFF OF GHQ AT THE ARMY WAR COLLEGE, 29 NOVEMBER 1940.

Front row, left to right: Lt. Col. Morris C. Handwerk, Lt. Col. Vernon K. Hurd, Lt. Col. William C. Crane, Col. Kenneth Buchanan, Maj. Gen. Lesley J. McNair, Col. William E. Lynd, Lt. Col. Charles B. Spruit, Lt. Col. Allen F. Kingman, Lt. Col. Charles H. Gerhardt.

Back row, left to right: Maj. Julian E. Raymond, Lt. Col. Farragut F. Hall, Lt. Col. Frederick J. de Rohan, Lt. Col. Lloyd D. Brown, Lt. Col. Bryan L. Milburn, Lt. Col. Mark W. Clark, Lt. Col. Clyde L. Hyssong, Lt. Col. Jerry V. Matejka, Maj. Hammond McD. Monroe, Maj. Thomas E. Lewis, Maj. James G. Christiansen.

tial to its training mission. In that month foundations for seven special staff sections, "to facilitate their immediate organization when necessary," were laid by obtaining the assignment to GHQ of specially qualified enlisted men.[66] As soon as the new role of GHQ was determined, on 17 June, six officers reported to General McNair from WPD, War Department, led by General Malony, who was made Deputy Chief of Staff.[67] In the months following, the staff was expanded and its organization was pushed to completion under the twofold stress of new duties growing out of the great GHQ-directed maneuvers in Louisiana and Carolina in September and November and of the mounting pressure of events abroad.[68] Much energy was expended in overcoming the difficulties and delays attending the procurement of a large number of specially qualified officers within the policy set by General Marshall of not assigning to GHQ officers over fifty years old. The events of 7 December added the problems of open warfare. The next day GHQ was put on a 24-hour basis, and in the following months a fresh effort was made to bring the staff up to its full complement.[69]

With increase in numbers came a sharper division of labor. On 14 July GHQ was given a Headquarters Company and Special Troops.[70] The four "G" sections and the following special sections were built up out of the previously informal organization: the Adjutant General, Antiaircraft, Aviation, Engineers, Quartermaster, Medical, and Signal. No organized staff sections for the Armored Force, Cavalry, Field Artillery, or Infantry were ever activated, and Chaplains, Civilian Affairs, and Provost Marshal General sections were not

---

[66] Pars 1 and 3, ltr of CofS GHQ to TAG, 9 Jan 41, sub: Enl Pers for Duty at GHQ USA. AGO Records, OCS 21152–2. Chief Clerks were requested for the following special sections: Armd Force, CA, Engrs, FA, MC, QMC, and Sig C. The special sections represented by officers, in addition to the seven just named, were, at that time: Avn, Cav, Inf, Med, NG, and Organized Res. GHQ off memo, 10 Jan 41. 312/2 (Correspondence, Methods, Forms, etc).

[67] (1) GHQ memo (S) to CG FF, 15 Sep 41, sub: Quarterly Rpt of Planning and Opns Activities GHQ, to include 10 Sep 41. 320.2/1 (S). (2) The officers reporting were Brig Gen H. J. Malony, Lt Col G. De L. Carrington, Lt Col George P. Hays, Lt Col E. N. Harmon, Maj L. L. Lemnitzer, Maj A. M. Gruenther, Memo (S) of ACofS G–1 GHQ for the Sec GS GHQ, 28 Aug 41, sub: Resumé of the Orgn and Opns of GHQ. 320.2/1 (SS). (3) On 18 Jun Gen Malony was made DCofS, Col Carrington G–1, Col Clark G–3, Col Harmon G–4. GHQ SO 66, 18 Jun 41. 320.2/3/9. Shortly afterward Col Paul McD. Robinett, formerly Secretary of the War Department General Staff, became G–2.

[68] For section chiefs of the staff as reorganized after 3 July 1941, see roster at end of this study.

[69] "4.31 A. M. [Dec 8] . . . This headquarters is open on a 24-hour basis." Diary (S), 8 Dec 41. The whole effort to expand the staff to authorized strength can be followed in 320.2/3, binders 1 and 2.

[70] WD ltr AG 320.2 (6–28–41) MR–M–C, 8 Jul 41, sub: Activation of Hq Co GHQ and Sp Trs GHQ 320.2/3/16.

deemed necessary.[71] Representation of the Civilian Component was discontinued, and Finance, Ordnance, and Judge Advocate General sections were set up. In December a representative of The Inspector General was introduced and in January 1942 a Chemical Warfare Section was added. Liaison officers from the Marine Corps and Navy were attached to the staff and close relations with the Army Air Forces were maintained by the Aviation Section, GHQ, and through the Air Support Section of the Air Force Combat Command, initially located in GHQ.

GHQ Activities

How busy and many-sided General Headquarters, with all its responsibilities and interests in training, planning, and operations, had become by the fall of 1941 can be illustrated by a sketch of its activities during the last two weeks of September. By that date the headquarters had a strength of 64 officers and 145 enlisted men. Even this expanded staff, despite long hours, found it hard to meet the requirements of the diverse missions with which the headquarters had been charged.

The activity of GHQ as a training headquarters was at the moment dominated by the Louisiana maneuvers. General McNair and his G–3, Brig. Gen. Mark W. Clark, had already departed before 15 September to direct these great inter-army maneuvers on which so much preparatory work undertaken at GHQ converged. They were joined on 24 September by General Malony, Deputy Chief of Staff, and were reinforced during the following days by some thirty officers from the headquarters in Washington.[72] On 15 September GHQ was directed to prepare recommendations in the light of the maneuvers for the Field Manual on Air Support of Ground Forces, and by 19 September the G–3 Section was hard at work on this assignment. On 25 September General McNair, from Director Headquarters, issued instructions that the 1st, 2d, and 3d Antitank Groups tested in the Louisiana maneuvers be sent on about 1 November for the Carolina maneuvers.

On 22 September GHQ reported on the deficiencies in landing operations shown in tests of the Carib amphibious force. On the next day it was directed to prepare the Army components for an amphibious operation planned by the

---

[71] GHQ Monthly Rosters. 330.3 (Str Returns).

[72] GHQ memos for Lt Col E. H. Brooks, ODCofS USA, 16 and 23 Sep, 7 Oct 41, sub: Summary of Activities, GHQ. 319.1/31, /33, and /34 (Wkly Rpts of GHQ Activities).

Joint Strategic Committee of the Army and Navy. During these weeks GHQ was frequently in communication with the Marine Corps regarding arrangements for the joint amphibious exercises planned for November.[73]

Meanwhile the staff officers left behind at the War College were busily occupied with details of the operational responsibilities of GHQ in Newfoundland, Greenland, and Iceland. Its first major task as an operational headquarters was completed with the safe arrival of Maj. Gen. Charles H. Bonesteel's "Indigo" Force in Iceland on 15 September. But matters such as additional supplies, mail service, radio frequencies, and hospital facilities for the troops in Iceland and elsewhere required attention from day to day. Beginning 24 September GHQ had to initiate arrangements for a gradual increase of the Army garrison in Iceland, as ordered by the President on 22 September. On 24 September GHQ became responsible for a pool of twelve counter intelligence officers trained by the War Department for eventual transfer to bases under GHQ. In the meantime arrangements were being worked out with the British for the establishment of a U. S. garrison in Bermuda.[74]

While handling such administrative details GHQ was pushing forward its work on war plans. On 17 September the basic Joint Board operations plan adopted to meet the eventuality of war was turned over to GHQ to be worked out in detail. Instructions were issued at the staff conference on that date. The next day the whole staff assembled in the auditorium to be oriented, and a procedure was worked out to reduce the necessary planning to routine.[75] At the same time plans for relieving the British garrisons at Curaçao, Aruba, and Surinam were in preparation, preliminary plans for the Caribbean Defense Command were being drawn, and the plans for a major amphibious operation in the Atlantic, prepared at GHQ in August, then expanded by the War De-

---

[73] (1) WD ltr AG 062.11 FM (9–9–41) PC–C, 15 Sep 41, sub: Combined Tests to Develop Doctrine and Methods for Avn Support of Grd Trs. 461/179. (2) Min (S) of Staff Conferences, GHQ, 19 Sep 41. 337 (S). (3) Ltr of Gen McNair to CG Third Army, 25 Sep 41, sub: GHQ Provisional Antitank Trs. 353/15 (AT). (4) GHQ ltr (C) to ACofS WPD, 22 Sep 41, sub: Correction of Deficiencies in Landing Opns. 354.2/37 (Carib) (C). (5) WD ltr (S) AG 353 (9–3–41) MC–E, 23 Sep 41, sub: Tng of 1st Div and Supporting Army Units for Landing Opns. 353/1 (AFAF) (S). (6) Diary (S) GHQ. 314.81 (S). (7) Min (S) of Staff Conferences, 23 Jul–31 Oct 41. 337 (S).

[74] These statements are based on the Diary, GHQ (S) (314.81 (S)) and Min (S) of Staff Conferences, GHQ, 23 Jul 41 to 31 Oct 41 (337) (S).

[75] (1) Diary (S), 17 Sep 41. 314.81 (S). (2) Min (S) of Staff Conferences, GHQ, 17 Sep 41. 337 (S). (3) GHQ memo (S) of Lt Col Lemnitzer for the Sec GS GHQ, 17 Dec 41, sub: Major Activities of the G–3 Sec during Period 10 Sep–10 Dec 41. 320.2/1 (S).

Chart No. 3

Organization of GHQ after 3 July 1941

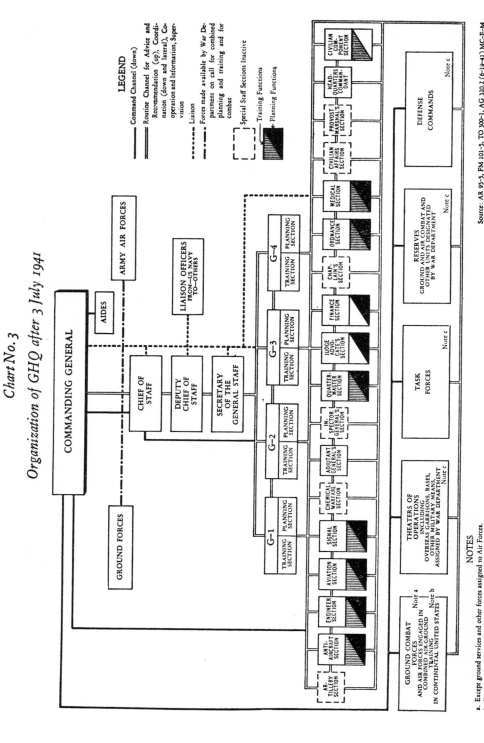

LEGEND

Command Channel (down)

Routine Channel for Advice and Recommendation (up), Coordination (down and lateral), Co-operation and Information, Supervision

Liaison

Forces made available by War Department on call for combined planning and training and for combat

Special Staff Sections Inactive

Training Functions

Planning Functions

COMMANDING GENERAL

AIDES

ARMY AIR FORCES

GROUND FORCES

CHIEF OF STAFF

DEPUTY CHIEF OF STAFF

SECRETARY OF THE GENERAL STAFF

LIAISON OFFICERS FROM—U.S. NAVY TO—OTHERS

G-1   G-2   G-3   G-4

PLANNING SECTION
TRAINING SECTION

SIGNAL SECTION
AVIATION SECTION
ENGINEER SECTION
ANTI-AIRCRAFT SECTION
AR-TILLERY SECTION
CHEMICAL WARFARE SECTION
ADJUTANT GENERAL'S SECTION
IN-SPECTOR GENERAL'S SECTION
QUARTER-MASTER SECTION
JUDGE ADVO-SECTION
FINANCE SECTION
CHAP-LAIN'S SECTION
ORDNANCE SECTION
MEDICAL SECTION
CIVILIAN AFFAIRS SECTION
PROVOST MARSHAL'S SECTION
HEAD-QUARTERS COMMAN-DANT
CIVILIAN COM-PONENT SECTION

GROUND COMBAT FORCES AND AIR FORCES ENGAGED IN COMBINED AIR-GROUND TRAINING IN CONTINENTAL UNITED STATES
Note a
Note b

THEATERS OF OPERATIONS INCLUDING OVERSEAS GARRISONS, BASES, OTHER MILITARY MEANS, ASSIGNED BY WAR DEPARTMENT
Note c

TASK FORCES

RESERVES GROUND AND AIR COMBAT AND OTHER UNITS DESIGNATED BY WAR DEPARTMENT
Note c

DEFENSE COMMANDS

Note c

NOTES

a. Except ground services and other forces assigned to Air Forces.

b. Except active air defense by interceptor command.

c. GHQ exercises superior command of Theaters of Operation, Task Forces, Defense Commands, Base Commands, Overseas Garrisons, and Reserves after there are passed to its control by War Department.

Source: AR 95-5, FM 101-5, TO 300-1, AG 320.2 (6-19-41) MC-E-M

partment, were completed and distributed.[76] On 17 September GHQ was directed to cooperate in the execution of Navy Western Hemisphere Plan No. 4, issuing appropriate instructions to the commanders in Bermuda, Greenland, Newfoundland, and Iceland.[77] On 20 September a plan for reorganizing the antiaircraft installations in Greenland was completed, and on 1 October a directive was issued to the commanding officer, Col. Benjamin F. Giles, who had been at GHQ on special duty since 15 September.[78] On 26 September plans for using the United States Army Moving Picture Service in all the bases but Iceland were finished.[79]

In these weeks GHQ still anticipated that the Caribbean Defense Command, the Alaskan Defense Command, the Hawaiian Department, and the Philippines would be put under its jurisdiction. Although it had been expected since August that these transfers would be made before the end of September, the dates were undetermined on the 15th.[80] Consequently the staff worked in a state of uncertainty as to when the scope of its duties might be greatly extended.[81] Short of personnel, with many officers absent on maneuvers, and having to be prepared for the contingency of expansion, GHQ was engaged in a continuous search for additional officers—an effort attended by delays and disappointments.[82] On the other hand, during these same weeks a WPD study proposing to reduce the responsibilities of GHQ was being debated. The records leave an impression of urgent activity accompanied by a growing sense of instability.

The busiest period for GHQ came after Pearl Harbor. At that time, in addition to its other duties, GHQ had the task of deploying available forces to secure the continental United States, Alaska, and the Panama Canal Zone against

[76] Min and Diary cited above.

[77] WD ltr (S) AG 381 (9–15–41) MC–E–M, 17 Sep 41, sub: Navy Western Hemisphere Defense Plan No 4. AGO Records, 381 (NWHD Plans) (S).

[78] (1) Memo (S) 319.1–Gen–F of Gen McNair for CG FF, 21 Dec 41, sub: Quarterly Rpt of Planning and Opns Activities, GHQ, to include 10 Dec 41. 320.2/1 (S). (2) GHQ ltr (S) 320.2 CBC–C to Col. B. F. Giles, 4 Oct 41, sub: Comd of USA Units in Greenland. AGO Records, WPD 4173–126 (S). (3) GHQ memo for Lt Col Hyssong, 23 Sep 41, sub: Activities of GHQ for Week Ending 23 Sep 41. 319.1/32 (Wkly Rpts of GHQ Activities).

[79] Diary (S), GHQ, 23 Sep 41. 314.81 (S).

[80] Min (S) of Staff Conferences, GHQ, 6 and 7 Aug, 4 and 15 Sep 41. 337 (S).

[81] See below, Section X. General Malony reported to the GHQ staff on 8 Sep: "I am urging quick decision on the paper, Subject: 'Enlargement of the Functions of GHQ' before the Chief of Staff departs on maneuvers." Min (S) of Staff Conferences, GHQ. 337 (S).

[82] (1) GHQ memo to TAG, 17 Sep 41, sub: Additional Offs for GHQ. (2) GHQ memo for ACofS G–1 WD, 6 Sep 41, sub: Additional Offs for GHQ. (3) WD ltr AG 210.61 Gen Staff (9–18–41), 2 Oct 41, sub: Additional Offs for GHQ. 320.2/3/68.

another Pearl Harbor. It also had to take up the redoubled burden of training under the January 1942 program, which was to bring the strength of the ground forces alone to 1,760,000 by December 1942.[83] To meet the immediate danger of attack, airplanes, antiaircraft units, and ground troops were rushed under GHQ direction to the Pacific Coast and Panama.

The movement of three infantry divisions to the West Coast was started on 14 December. Air reinforcements were flown through Mexico, and antiaircraft units were moved by sea to strengthen the Panama Canal Zone. Alaska was reinforced to frustrate a possible Japanese attack on Dutch Harbor. By 17 December the critical areas on both the Atlantic and Pacific Coasts had been covered with a reasonable degree of protection against air attack. The relation of GHQ to this effort was regularized with the activation of the Western and Eastern Theaters of Operations on 14 and 24 December under GHQ control. During the spring of 1942 GHQ was more active than ever in planning and organizing task forces for immediate offensives that might be undertaken and busy preparing units to reinforce the British Isles and the outposts of the Caribbean Defense Command. Despite these added burdens GHQ had to devote more and more of its energies to the task of expanding the armies at home for the eventual offensive against the Nation's enemies in Europe and the Far East.

The Split within GHQ between Training Functions and Operational Functions

Because of the twofold nature of the responsibilities delegated to GHQ, almost all sections of its staff had both training functions and planning and operational functions after 3 July 1941. Each section was in effect, as General Malony remarked, "split down the middle" into a training branch and an operational branch. (See Chart No. 3.[84]) This split threatened to destroy the solidity of the organization.[85] On 8 December 1941 a reorganization was effected which gave formal recognition to the division within each section. At the same time a G–5 Section of eleven officers was added to devote its whole attention

---

[83] Recapitulation (C), Troop Unit Basis for Mobilization and Training, Jan 42, p. 48. AGF Plans Sec Records (C).

[84] Chart found in 320.2/3/43.

[85] General Malony's memo on the subject read: "Consequently there is no solidity in the organization. There are no promotional prospects for staff heads. G–3 (Operations) is the worst sufferer." Par 2b, memo of Gen Malony, DCofS GHQ for CofS GHQ, 5 Dec 41, sub: GHQ Orgn. 320.2/3/108.

to training. General Clark, until then G–3, was made chief of this section and also Deputy Chief of Staff for Training.[86] General Malony retained his title of Deputy Chief of Staff.

The separation of training and operational personnel was made to increase the functional efficiency of the staff. It was represented as a step taken in compliance with the directive that GHQ should be so organized that its training function could be readily transferred to the War Department.[87] It was also designed to ease a tension developing within the staff between General Malony and General Clark and those who represented their respective points of view. Undoubtedly, personalities and the strain of a crisis that seemed desperate played their part. But the conflict was fundamentally one of views regarding the primary mission of GHQ. General Malony was intent on making GHQ the agency which the expanding War Department needed for "quick action" in directing the forces it was deploying.[88] General Clark, who had distinguished himself as Deputy Director of the great army maneuvers in Louisiana, was intent on developing the original mission of GHQ as the means of training the ground forces for future offensives. The two Deputies had growing as well as diverse responsibilities which tended to make heavy demands on the resources of the whole staff. General McNair's deep interest in training eventually combined with the reorganization which the War Department was planning to determine the fate of GHQ. When this reorganization went into effect on 9 March 1942, it was not the training functions but the operational functions of GHQ that were transferred to the War Department. The functions of GHQ as an agency for training the ground army were delegated to General McNair as commander of the Army Ground Forces.

---

[86] GHQ GO 2, 8 Dec 41, sub: Change in Orgn of GHQ USA. 320.2/3/119. The creation of G–5 Sec was authorized 2 Feb. 1st ind TAGO, 2 Feb 42, to CG FF AWC on GHQ memo for ACofS G–1 WD, 11 Dec 41, sub: Expansion of GHQ. 320.2/3/140. The division of duties between G–3 and G–5 is defined in memo for all Staff Secs GHQ, 31 Jan 42, sub: Staff Functions G–3, G–5, with background recommendations from G–3, G–5, and Gen McNair. 320.2/3/153.

[87] GHQ off memo, 18 Dec 41, sub: Operating Procedure with Respect to the Increased Functions and Responsibilities of GHQ. 312.11/15. See also par 2, WD ltr (R) (6–19–41) MC–E–M, 3 Jul 41, sub: Enlargement of Functions of GHQ. 320.2/3/34.

[88] "Gen Marshall wants GHQ to be an agency for quick action." Min (S) Staff Conferences, GHQ, 17 Oct 41. 337 (S).

II. The Administration of Training

Authority of GHQ over Training

The directive of 26 July 1940 establishing GHQ assigned to it "supervision and direction" over the training of all tactical elements in the Army. This responsibility was retained even after the reorganization of 3 July 1941, when its supervision over air training was limited to combined air-ground training exercises. While command and planning functions after July 1941 were supervised mainly by the Deputy Chief of Staff, General Malony, the attention of General McNair remained centered on training. This training mission was the task left for the Army Ground Forces to carry forward after 9 March 1942.[1]

GHQ, as the agency charged with the training of the tactical forces, carried out its program in cooperation with the arms and services, the corps areas, and other agencies created from time to time after its activation. Important among these new agencies were the replacement training centers, which began to receive and train selectees on 1 March 1941 under the supervision of the chiefs of arms and services;[2] the officer candidate schools, ten of which were opened in July 1941, under the same supervision;[3] the Antiaircraft Training Center, activated 14 February 1941;[4] the Provisional Parachute Group, set up in the summer of 1941; the Tank Destroyer Tactical and Firing Center, activated 1 December 1941; and the Amphibious Force, Atlantic Fleet, and the Amphibious Force, Pacific Fleet, which took shape in the latter half of 1941.

GHQ, unlike Army Ground Forces, did not, strictly speaking, exercise command over training. It supervised, directed, interpreted, and coordinated. But General McNair, though merely acting for General Marshall, the Commanding General of the Field Forces, and consequently only a staff officer, was invested

---

[1] (1) WD ltr AG 320.2 (7–25–42) M–Ret–M–OCS, 26 Jul 40, sub: GHQ. 320.2/3/1. (2) WD ltr AG 320.2 (6–19–41) MC–E–M to CofS GHQ, 3 Jul 41, sub: Enlargement of Functions of GHQ. 320.2/3/34. (3) Memo of DCofS GHQ for CofS GHQ, 5 Dec 41, sub: GHQ Orgn. 320.2/3/108.

[2] ". . . under present plans, . . . reception and training of the Selective Service personnel will commence about March 1, 1941." Par 1, WD ltr AG 320.2 (12–13–40), 31 Dec 40, sub: Activation of Hq Repl Centers. 320.2/99. For the types and locations of these Centers, see Chart 7, *Biennial Report, CofS, 1941.*

[3] Chart 8, *Biennial Report, CofS, 1941.*   [4] See 420.2/16.

with authority that goes with command. He was made responsible for the success or failure of the training program.

When GHQ was created it took over the administration of the established training program as outlined in the War Department Training Directive for 1940–41, published on 2 March 1940.[5] This directive announced that "the primary objective is to prepare units to take the field on short notice at existing strength, ready to function effectively in combat." Among the subjects specified for emphasis were leadership, mobility, teamwork by combined arms, and defense against aircraft and mechanized troops, together with training of the National Guard and Organized Reserves. GHQ accepted this program and at first exercised little influence on the elaboration of new plans. For example, when the Office of the Chief of Staff asked General McNair on 17 August 1940 to suggest additions to a list of subjects proposed for study in the light of the military crisis in Europe, the list was already so complete in the opinion of General McNair that he added only remarks on equipment.[6]

State of Training in August 1940

The first coordinated staff work of GHQ developed out of the August maneuvers of 1940. The whole staff of seven officers prepared detailed criticisms of the maneuvers for General McNair,[7] who combined them into a draft letter to the army commanders, submitted to General Marshall on 5 September 1940 [8] and published 7 January 1941 in substantially its original form. This letter described the condition of the Army as General McNair saw it shortly after taking charge at GHQ. He summarized the shortcomings in training as follows:

  1. Obviously deficient training of small units and in minor tactics.

  2. Faulty employment of the infantry division and of its combat teams.

  3. Failure fully to appreciate the purpose of motor vehicles and exploit their capabilities.

  4. Inadequate reconnaissance and lack of contact between adjacent units.

  5. Inadequate support of infantry by division artillery.

  6. Faulty signal communications.

  7. Too passive employment of antitank guns.

[5] WD ltr AG 353 (12–28–39) M–MC, 3 Mar 40, sub: WD Tng Dir for 1940–41. 353/1.
[6] (1)- Memo OCS 21157–3 of Lt Col Orlando Ward for Gen McNair, 17 Aug 40, sub: Suggested Studies for Tng. 353/35. (2) Memo of Gen McNair for Col Ward, 5 Sep 40.353/36.
[7] See 354.2/1–8.
[8] GHQ draft of ltr to Army Comdrs, 5 Sep 40, sub: Comments on Army Maneuvers 1940. 354.2/17.

8. Improper employment of horse cavalry.

9. Neglect of ammunition supply and evacuation of wounded.

10. Unreal situations due to faulty umpiring.

Except for points 8 and 9, these proved to be persistent faults, to be repeatedly pointed out as time went on. Their correction became a major concern of GHQ in its supervision of training.

Observers from the National Guard Bureau at the August maneuvers agreed fully with the conclusions of GHQ.[9] Moreover, speaking of the National Guard divisions, they added that 20 percent of the staff and divisional officers were not qualified, that the troops needed squad and platoon problems rather than division and corps problems, and that all troops required at least three months' basic training. It was evident that little progress had yet been made toward fulfillment of the broad aims of the War Department Training Directive of 2 March. Much work remained to be accomplished.

Preparation for the Citizen Army

Imperfect as they were, these units had to serve as a nucleus for the future Army of the United States. With the adoption of Selective Service and the induction of the National Guard, GHQ faced the problem of turning the able-bodied male population of the country into soldiers. Existing field service regulations provided the tactical doctrine to which the new men were to be introduced. Technical manuals described the care and employment of equipment. On 9 August 1940 the War Department initiated a series of training circulars to keep the Army abreast of current developments pending the publication of new or reedited training and technical manuals.[10] Training Circular No. 2, dated 10 September 1940, briefly outlined the instruction to be given to inducted men. Mobilization Training Programs (MTP's) specified in more detail the 13-week basic training to be given in various branches of the service.

GHQ interpreted these directives to army commanders and provided means to facilitate and coordinate the execution of the policies laid down. The initial GHQ training directive,[11] which remained basic until January 1941, was sent to the army commanders on 16 September 1940, the day on which President Roose-

[9] Ltr Natl Guard Bur to TAG, 20 Sep 40, sub: Report of Observers Attending August Maneuvers. 354.2/12.

[10] Tng Cir 1, WD, 9 Aug 40.

[11] Ltr of Gen McNair to Army Comdrs, 16 Sep 40, sub: Tng. 353/1(Tng Dirs).

velt signed the Selective Service Bill and the first National Guard units were inducted. The GHQ directive combined the ideas of the dozen officers who by that time composed the GHQ staff, but in its final form it bore the strong imprint of General McNair. It stated in substance:

1. The Army, to prepare for national defense, justify Selective Service, and win the respect of selectees and the confidence of the public, must give the best possible training in the year allowed without compromise as to quality.

2. Leadership must be demonstrated by success in the training of individuals and units and be recognized by promotion.

3. Centralization of training methods, because of the shortage of qualified instructors, would be necessary and would be achieved through

   a. Replacement Training Centers prescribed by the War Department, where selectees would normally receive their basic training according to MTP's.

   b. Divisional troop schools, in which battalion and company instructors would first learn what they had to teach.

4. Responsibility for the results of training and for planning of details in applying general directives or adapting them to local conditions rested directly upon commanding officers of all units. "Planning and preparation of training is a function of command."

5. Tests of results would be given "in appropriate form by higher commands of all echelons up to and including General Headquarters."

For further coordination of the training program General McNair directed in letters of 26 and 29 September that copies of training directives issued by subordinate units be submitted to GHQ.[12]

The National Guard divisions presented a special problem. Inducted into Federal service between September 1940 and March 1941, they varied greatly in quality, but all needed assistance. They swamped the training centers, where firing ranges, maneuver areas, and other facilities were inadequate for the increased demands. To help adjust the old installations to the new manpower, GHQ sent out on 15 October a chart modifying the MTP's, showing alternative sequences for the 13-week basic program.[13] In addition, General McNair established a policy of visiting in person, accompanied by members of his staff, the commanding officer and the staff of each National Guard division at the time of its induction.[14]

---

[12] (1) GHQ ltr to CGs, 26 Sep 40, sub: Tng Dirs. (2) GHQ ltr to Army Comdrs, 29 Oct 40, sub: Tng Programs. Both in 353/47.

[13] Ltr of Gen McNair to Army Comdrs, 15 Oct 40, sub: Tng under MTP's. With attached charts. 353/3 (Tng Dirs).

[14] Ltr of Gen McNair to First (Second, Third, Fourth) Army, 10 Dec 40, sub: Contacts with Non-Inducted Divs. 353/123.

On these occasions he discussed frankly the problems facing the Army and pointed out shortcomings. For example, during the visit to the 30th Division on 27–28 September, General McNair and his staff were favorably impressed by the personal qualities of the commanding general, but found the chief of staff unqualified and G–3 in a temporary daze. "We devoted our time actively," wrote General McNair a few weeks later, "to showing the division staff and subordinate commanders how to start in planning training . . . . The idea of centralized training, with special instruction of instructors beforehand was entirely new to them, so that it was impossible to ascertain how effectively they would be able to institute and execute such a system. During our visit they were simply at 'Drill'— blind leading the blind, and officers generally elsewhere." [15] Experience of this kind led General McNair to recommend on 9 November that National Guard units train for at least two months before receiving selectees.[16] Such a procedure was necessary in view of the extreme inadequacy of provisions made for the field training of the larger units of the National Guard in time of peace.

For the education of divisional staff officers, present and prospective, the Command and General Staff School at Fort Leavenworth opened the first of a series of special 2-month courses on 2 December 1940. The first class consisted of 54 National Guard, 11 Reserve, and 31 Regular Army officers. Instruction was carried on in conferences centering around staff problems. Each student specialized in that section of the General Staff for which his commanding officers had designated him.[17]

General McNair indicated his conception of general staff work for a division in training in a letter, dated 9 December, to Brig. Gen. Edmund L. Gruber, his successor as Commandant at the Command and General Staff School. Citing experience already gained with newly inducted divisions, he inclosed detailed comments on the functions of staff officers. The "G's" of National Guard divisions had had little chance to do their work in peacetime. G–1, said General McNair, should know the published Army doctrine on personnel and morale and should perform in person such duties as the inspection of divisional post offices and kitchens. The job of G–2 was to supervise public relations, provide maps, etc., but principally to train the division in combat intelligence. To G–3 fell the administration of the training program, the supervision of physical con-

---

[15] Personal ltr of Gen McNair to Maj Gen W. C. Short, 23 Oct 40. 320.2/21 (GHQ Army and Corps).

[16] Memo of Gen McNair for G–3 WD, 9 Nov 40, sub: Period between Induction and Receipt of Trainees. 324.71/8 (SS Men).

[17] Ltr of Comdt C&GSS to TAG, 4 Feb 41, sub: Rpt Sp Course End 1 Feb 41. 352/2 (C&GSS).

ditioning, the assignment of new weapons, the operation of divisional troop schools, and the conduct of tests set by the commanding general. G–3 was advised to get into the field, not stay at the office. G–4 was urged to learn thoroughly the procedure for obtaining supplies at all levels and from all agencies. Lack of knowledge in this field might easily become a frequent cause of shortage, waste, and delay.[18]

The basic training of recruits under Selective Service did not, as such, come under the direct supervision of GHQ, which dealt with organized tactical units of the field forces. This division of labor, however, could not be carried out at first because of the shortage of Army housing. Before April 1941, when the construction program caught up with the plans of the War Department, selectees were assigned immediately to tactical units.[19] After that date they received their thirteen weeks' basic training at replacement training centers, which were outside the jurisdiction of GHQ, being under the corps area commanders and the chiefs of branches. From April until after the declaration of war, divisions and other units filled their ranks with enlisted men from replacement training centers.[20] Most of the officers came from the National Guard and Officers' Reserve Corps, since the output of the officer candidate schools, established in July 1941, remained quantitatively negligible until 1942.

In the closing months of 1940 General McNair began to make clear the spirit in which his headquarters interpreted the training of the Army. His desire to keep the troops active became evident in his opposition to the reduction of the 44-hour training week, which was nevertheless decided upon by the War Department, and in his order of 25 November that men lacking new equipment should train with such equipment as they had.[21] His insistence on "pick-and-shovel work" was illustrated by his comments on a 3-volume manuscript on infantry tactics. While he considered this lengthy manual to be of long-run educational value, he called it "a book for the study, not the field," inappropriate

---

[18] "Comments Concerning Staff Functioning," 9 Dec 40, enclosed with ltr of Gen McNair to Gen Gruber, same date, same sub. 352/1 (C&GSS).

[19] (1) WD ltr AG 324.71 (8–28–40) M–A–M, 10 Sep 40, sub: Reception of SS Men. 324.71/1 (SS Men). (2) Memo of G–1 GHQ for CofS GHQ, 23 Oct 40, sub: Recpn Cens. 320.2/24 (GHQ Armies and Corps).

[20] (1) WD ltr AG 320.2 (12–13–40) M (Ret) M–C, 31 Dec 40, sub: Activation of Hq, Rcpl Cens. 320.2/99. (2) WD ltr AG 324.71 (8–20–41) ER–A to CofS GHQ, 12 Sep 41, sub: Policy for the Procurement of Pers for RTC's. 324.71/89 (SS Men).

[21] (1) Memo of Gen McNair for ACofS G–3 WD, 7 Nov 40, sub: 44–Hour Week of MTP's. 353/59. See also 353/83,/84,/99. (2) Ltr of Gen McNair to CGs, 25 Nov 40, sub: Tng with the M–1 Rifle. 356/6 (Tng Dirs).

in the circumstances.[22] The views that were to govern his policy toward army schools were expressed in his nonconcurrence with a War Department proposal of territorial schools for motor mechanics. "Under present conditions," he wrote, "the primary objective must be the development of field force units, trained and ready for field service, in a minimum of time. The detachment of officers and enlisted men for special schooling must be held to a minimum— which is not the case at present." He added that existing units, posts, and quartermaster depots afforded adequate means for the training of motor mechanics.[23] He was willing to make use of existing schools in what he considered their appropriate functions, as shown by his interest in the new staff officer course at Fort Leavenworth. Again, when the question arose of preparing a typical standard operating procedure for the guidance of newly inducted divisions, he recommended that the matter be turned over to the service schools.[24]

General Proficiency versus Specialism in the New Army

The ever increasing threat to national security raised the question whether the Army should be immediately trained to form task forces for special missions. Special training programs, projected or in progress at the end of 1940, included amphibious training, air-ground tests, and training for operations in mountain, jungle, and arctic conditions. General McNair consistently opposed these forms of specialism if they were carried to a point where they might endanger the unity of the Army or its fundamental soldierly fitness. On 10 March 1941 he wrote to the commanding general of the 3d Division, which for some time had been practicing amphibious operations at Fort Lewis, advising the division commander not only to continue with basic training but also to consider it more important than amphibious specialization. "Even though landing is the first step, success presumably will come only from skill in combat." [25]

A memorandum of 16 January 1941 to General Marshall made the same point in more general terms.[26] It is quoted in full as an explicit statement of governing policies at GHQ in an early and formative period in the creation of the national army.

---

[22] Personal ltr of Gen McNair to Col W. R. Wheeler, 5 Dec 40. 353/116.

[23] Memo of Gen McNair for ACofS G–3 WD, 5 Nov 40, sub: Territorial Sch for Motor Mechanics. 352.01/8.

[24] Memo of Gen McNair for ACofS G–3 WD, 6 Dec 40, sub: SOP. 353/118.

[25] Personal ltr (C) of Gen McNair to Maj Gen C. F. Thompson, 10 Mar 41. 353/1 (C).

[26] Memo of Gen McNair for Gen Marshall, 16 Jan 41, sub: Specialized Tng. 353/136.

Memorandum for General Marshall:

My reactions to the inclosed discussion, "Specialized Training in the Training Phase of the Military Program," are:

1. If it is to be inferred from this paper that our organization is obsolete, that we should be concentrating on specialized task forces rather than integrated large units—I disagree. Our Army "on order" is modern according to current lessons—except for its antitank defense.

2. The first phase stated—expansion—now is conflicting with the second phase—training—but nevertheless expansion should go on until we have an adequate force in being. Interference with training must be accepted as unavoidable now, although it will diminish later as adequate zone of interior establishments are developed.

3. Training must be progressive. *Basic and small-unit* training can not be slighted. *Combined* training in its many modern forms is essential for all units. Finally the coordinated and smooth action of *large units* is indispensable if we envision decisive operations on a National scale. These steps are the foundation of military efficiency—today even as yesterday. They can be hurried and slighted only at a price. Germany devoted years to this phase. Her special training for Norway probably was given last winter, after thorough general training as a foundation.

4. The need for specialized training such as recommended is not questioned, but it should follow—not precede—the basic and general training indicated. Exceptions of course would be those cases of special training demanded by the international situation, such as the occupation of outlying air bases.

5. I incline to criticize, however, the present test at Fort Benning of air-ground cooperation, as being premature. It interrupts current and essential training and no air units will be available to carry it out on a full scale earlier than August 1941. Again, stationing divisions in cold climates at this time is open to question, since general training is retarded. The National Guard divisions particularly would be better off in the South, where they could train effectively. It is believed now that next winter would have been a better time for such special training, although it is appreciated that the situation may have appeared quite different six months or more ago.

6. Subject to compelling international developments, I favor the following general policy:

a. The most rapid possible expansion of our armed forces to a size adequate for our prospective role in world affairs.

b. Then a sound, methodical program of basic and general training at least through the summer of 1941 to include inter-army maneuvers.

c. Then, for those units which demonstrate satisfactory general training, special training to meet the various missions set up by the color plans of the War Department.

7. In other words, I do not question the need of special training, but believe that in general its priority is below both expansion and sound general training, and that such special training should be minimized until the fall of 1941, perhaps later.

The principles announced in paragraphs 3, 6a, and 6b were being worked out at GHQ at the time this memorandum was written. A "sound, methodical program," a sequence of basic and small-unit training, combined training, and large-unit training, was ready for promulgation in January 1941.

Large-Unit Training and Testing

With the turn of the year GHQ discussed the program which was to follow the basic training nearly completed by some of the troops. On 4 January 1941 a letter was sent to the army commanders prescribing after basic training thirteen to sixteen weeks of combined training, i. e., coordination of the various weapons of the regiment and the division. Command post exercises, field exercises, and field maneuvers were ordered. All field maneuvers were to be free. The commander was given only the objectives and was made responsible for achieving them with the means at his disposal. Avoidance of artificiality was recommended for all exercises. An immediate critique of each exercise was required of each commanding officer as a necessary step in instruction. Definite problems were set for the training of regimental and brigade combat teams and for the field exercises and maneuvers of divisions.[27]

In World War I American troops had received no training in units higher than the division before going overseas. The establishment in 1932 of four armies comprising nine army corps furnished the framework for training above the division level. In January 1941 General McNair made plans to complete the conversion of these large but shadowy bodies into effective combat organizations. On 7 January he sent to the army commanders his comments on maneuvers, drafted in the preceding September and summarized above. He chose this moment because he judged that his views would make their maximum impression with the entrance upon large-unit training. He continued on 15 January with another letter to army commanders on "Corps and Army Training," which was to be put into effect after the combined training order on 4 January. Each corps was to train for a period of one to two months under direction of its army commander. After command post and field exercises, the corps was to engage in a field maneuver against either another corps or one of its own divisions. It was hoped that this corps training might be finished by June 1941. Armies would then train as units. Army training remained under army com-

[27] Ltr of Gen McNair to Army Comdrs, 4 Jan 41, sub: Combined Tng. 353/13 (Tng Dirs).

COMMANDERS AND STAFF OFFICERS, LOUISIANA ARMY MANEUVERS, SEPTEMBER 1941

Left to right: Brig. Gen. Mark W. Clark, Maneuver Director; Brig. Gen. Harry J. Malony, Deputy Chief of Staff, GHQ; Col. Dwight D. Eisenhower, Chief of Staff, Third Army; Lt. Gen. Ben Lear, Commander, Second Army; Lt. Gen. Walter Krueger, Commander, Third Army; Lt. Gen. Lesley J. McNair, Chief of Staff, GHQ.

manders, except that the final field maneuvers of entire armies would be directed by GHQ. General McNair stipulated that corps training should be, and army training might be, interrupted by periods of training for divisions and smaller units.[28]

The necessity of maintaining the integrity of the tactical unit in training, in maneuvers, and in battle was frequently emphasized at GHQ. Integrity of the unit heightened morale, clarified responsibility, and preserved maximum striking power. One danger to unit integrity was the detachment of personnel for attendance at schools. General McNair therefore favored a maximum use of troop schools within divisional and other units. Another danger to unit integrity was the recent tendency to employ infantry-artillery combat teams as quasi-permanent tactical bodies instead of as temporary groupings for specific missions. This tendency threatened to disintegrate the division. General McNair protested that the division was itself the paramount combat team and chief fighting unit of the Army. When it was brought to his attention that faulty combat-team doctrine was taught in the course at Fort Benning, he arranged through the Chief of Infantry to have the matter corrected. He attributed the excessive use of combat teams to the inability of higher commanders to manage as large an organization as the division. In 1941 he noted some improvement in this respect.[29]

It was a policy of GHQ that all units should be tested as they completed successive stages of their training. For armies and corps the tests took the form of maneuvers directed by higher headquarters. In lower units General McNair found a persistent disinclination of higher commanders to administer the necessary tests. "The troops suffer correspondingly," he wrote. "We now have plenty of money and plenty of higher commanders, and it is time to bestir ourselves in this connection." On 4 March 1941, referring back to the principle of command responsibility set forth in the directive of 16 September 1940, GHQ instructed army and corps commanders to conduct tests of their divisions and separate units and to report the findings to GHQ.[30]

[28] (1) Ltr of Gen McNair to Army Comdrs, 7 Jan 41, sub: Comments on Army Maneuvers, 1940. 354.2/17. (2) Ltr of Gen McNair to CGs, 15 Jan 41, sub: Corps and Army Tng. 353/15 (Tng Dirs).

[29] (1) Memo of Gen McNair for ACofS G–3 WD, 4 Nov 40. Tab B in AGO 353 TC 10, WD, 26 Nov 40. AGO Records. (2) Memo of Gen McNair for CofInf, 10 Apr 41, sub: Teaching of the Inf Sch, with related documents. 352/6 (Inf). (3) Memo of Gen McNair for CofS USA, 21 Oct 41, sub: Rpt by CofFA. 354.2 (Rpts 1941) (S). (4) Memo of Gen McNair for ASW, 12 Feb 42, sub: Tng Sch for the Combined Arms. McNair Correspondence.

[30] (1) Personal ltr of Gen McNair to Brig Gen E. L. Gruber, 1 Mar 41. 354.2/18. (2) Ltr of Gen McNair to Army Comdrs, 4 Mar 41, sub: Tng Tests. 353/1 (Tng Dirs).

GHQ itself was not sedentary. Weekly reports running from 19 February 1941 to 9 March 1942 show that officers from GHQ were at all times in the field, to lend assistance, inspect, and exercise supervision. General McNair set the example. In the nine months preceding the declaration of war, he spent 111 days on tours of inspection, four times reaching the Pacific Coast. War changed his habits. He is not reported to have left his headquarters, except once to address the graduating class at Fort Leavenworth, in the three months from Pearl Harbor to the dissolution of GHQ. Staff officers, however, continued their tours. For example, in the year preceding 9 March 1942, Fort Lewis, Wash., was visited five times by officers from GHQ; Fort Bragg, N. C., seven times; Fort Knox, Ky., seven times. Inspecting officers from GHQ were present at all large maneuvers and at field exercises and tests at which significant features of the training program were under trial.[31]

Field exercises, maneuvers, tests, and inspections brought to light grave deficiencies in the progress of training. In April 1941 the War Department proposed that expert "demonstration cadres" tour the training centers to exhibit the methods of modern war. General McNair replied that such devices had been used in the Second Army without notable success and that the trouble was not lack of knowledge in the field units, which were amply supplied with training literature and materials, but in the inability of officers to make use of what was put into their hands. The cure, he said, was improvement in command, not "artificial respiration."[32] By June 1941 it was becoming doubtful whether many units would be well enough prepared to participate in the army and corps training scheduled for the summer. The failures were attributed by GHQ to undue haste and to the assigning of teaching functions to officers and noncommissioned officers not competent to give instruction. Higher commanders were blamed for permitting such conditions. They were directed on 7 July to institute an intensive review of basic and small-unit training, to give close supervision to troop schools for officers and noncommissioned officers, to administer more training tests, to secure reassignment of commanders found unsatisfactory, and to report to GHQ units not yet qualified to participate in further corps and army training.[33]

---

[31] "Weekly Reports of GHQ Activities." GHQ 319.1, 319.1 (C), and AGF 319.1/1.

[32] Memo of Gen McNair for CofS USA, 22 Apr 41, sub: Demonstration Cadres. 320.2/153.

[33] GHQ ltr to CGs Second, Third, and Fourth Armies, 7 Jul 41, sub: Review of Tng Prior to Further Corps and Army Tng. 353/164 (Second Army).

The War Department Training Directive for 1941–42, prepared in June but not issued until 19 August 1941, gave expression to some of the doctrines developed at GHQ in the past year. On General McNair's recommendation, in view of current changes in the air forces a clear distinction was drawn between air and ground troops. GHQ was to be responsible for the training of ground forces only and was to prepare them for eventual employment as task forces with flexible organization. The need of progression in training was emphasized. Each step in the training process was to be mastered and tested before the next step was undertaken. The directive reiterated the importance of thorough grounding in the elements of small-unit training and of energetic leadership at subordinate levels of command as prerequisites to success in combined operations and in the training of task forces.[34]

GHQ-Directed Army Maneuvers, 1941

The results achieved by all this detailed work in supervision and direction were to receive their most decisive training test in the maneuvers of the four field armies in the summer and fall of 1941.[35] In August elements of the Fourth Army opposed each other in the State of Washington. In September the Second and Third Armies were pitted against each other in Louisiana. In November the First Army opposed the IV Corps, reinforced by the I Armored Corps, in the Carolinas. GHQ directed the Louisiana and Carolina maneuvers. All maneuvers were free. Each commanding general, after receiving a broad tactical mission from Director Headquarters, operated at his own discretion in response to changing battle conditions. At the close of each maneuver a critique was immediately given by General McNair as Director of the maneuvers and General Clark as Deputy Director. These critiques were mimeographed and circulated to the higher echelons of all armies. On returning to Washington, General McNair also sent extensive private comments to Red and Blue commanders.[36] General Marshall had warned against unfavorable criticism of commanding generals in the presence of their subordinates.[37]

[34] (1) Memo of CofS GHQ for ACofS G–3 WD, 16 Jun 41, sub: WD Tng Dir 1941–42. 353/340. (2) WD ltr AG 353 (6–16–41) MT M–C to CGs, CofS GHQ, etc, 19 Aug 41, sub: WD Tng Dir 1941–42.

[35] Table, "Army Training, August–November, 1941," GHQ, dated 15 Aug 41. 353/34 (Tng Dirs).

[36] Mimeographed copies of the critiques and carbon copies of the private comments are to be found in the 353 and 354.2 series in the GHQ file for the First, Second, and Third Armies and the IV Corps.

[37] Memo OCS 14440–363 of CofS USA for CofS GHQ, 18 Jun 41, sub not given. 354.2/269.

One of the most important tasks in free maneuvers was umpiring, which was made especially difficult in 1941 by peacetime safety regulations, lack of equipment, and shortage of aviation and armored elements in proportion to the number of troops engaged. These maneuvers were to have all the realism of actual warfare except destruction and casualties, but without full equipment for the troops the task of umpiring was harder than ever before.

A year earlier General McNair had ascribed many of the disappointing features of the August 1940 maneuvers to inadequate umpiring.[38] At that time G–3 of the War Department prepared a draft for a new umpire manual, but General McNair found this publication unsatisfactory.[39] He himself took over the responsibility of providing adequate instructions and with the aid of his staff sections produced a GHQ Umpire Manual in February 1941. The new manual eliminated most umpires at headquarters above the battalion. Umpires were placed in the field, accompanying moving units and marking artillery fires. An Aviation Supplement was added in August. Umpires for the army maneuvers were trained in the preceding division and corps maneuvers. Amendments to the manual were continually made, and it was expected that the army maneuvers would produce further suggestions for improvements.[40]

General McNair insisted at all times that the maneuvers should be carried out in an atmosphere resembling actual battle as nearly as possible. The new umpire manual represented only one step in this direction. "The truth is sought," General McNair wrote to the army commanders, "regardless of whether pleasant or unpleasant, or whether it supports or condemns our present organization and tactics."[41] To promote antitank training, when enough real tanks could not be obtained, General McNair ordered the simulation of tanks in sufficient quantity to give an accurate test. Troops had to be inured to the noise of modern battle, and though it was feared at GHQ that artificial noise-making might distract attention from basic training, five sound-trucks were dispatched for this purpose to the GHQ-directed maneuvers in Louisiana.[42] To achieve realism in

---

[38] Memo of Gen McNair for Gen Marshall, 5 Sep 40, sub: Comments on Army Maneuvers, 1940. 354.2/8.

[39] Memo of Gen McNair for Sec WDGS, 13 Feb 41, sub: Draft of FM 105–5 Umpire Manual. 461/57.

[40] "Umpire Manual, General Headquarters, U. S. Army, February 1941," with supporting documents. 353/19 (Tng Dirs).

[41] Ltr of Gen McNair to CGs, 15 May 41, sub: Antitank (AT) Defense. 353/25 (Tng Dirs).

[42] (1) Memo of Gen McNair for Col Godfrey, WD, 1 Apr 41, sub: Simulating Battlefield Noises in Tr Tng. 353/146. (2) Memo of Gen McNair for ACofS G–3 WD, 25 Apr 41, sub: Realism in Tng.

combat intelligence, army commanders were cautioned against using any sources of information except those available under battle conditions.[43] The commander of the Third Army was criticized for allowing his signal officers to plan a $200,000 telephone pole line in preparation for maneuvers. "I submit that such stuff is artificial," wrote General McNair, "and suggest that you ask your staff, in substance, how the German army made such preparations for their campaign in Poland." [44]

The Second vs. Third Army maneuvers, held in Louisiana in September, involved over 350,000 men and were the largest ever conducted in the United States in time of peace. The Inspector General, in his report to General Marshall, gave a favorable verdict: "The soundness of the establishment of GHQ to supervise training and to plan and conduct large maneuvers was definitely proved by the results obtained during the recent GHQ maneuvers. The officers assigned to GHQ are keen, energetic and efficient. Their work in the planning and handling of maneuvers was outstanding in comparison with similar groups at other maneuvers, and it is my belief that the policy of assigning staff officers not in excess of fifty years of age to that headquarters has been justified. I was particularly impressed with the efficiency, balance and judgment displayed by General Clark." The Inspector General especially commended GHQ for its policy of holding a free maneuvers, which, emancipating GHQ from the details of tactical planning, had allowed it to concentrate upon the essentials of training, and which also, far better than a controlled maneuver, made participants feel their own responsibility for results and allowed GHQ to appraise aptitude for command. "In my opinion," The Inspector General concluded, "General McNair and his headquarters have accomplished, and are continuing to accomplish, an outstanding job in the supervision of training of the Army." [45]

The success of these maneuvers consisted largely in the accuracy with which they drew attention to failures in training that required correction. It was General McNair's responsibility to point out these failures to the army commanders, and his observations on what had passed were less favorable than The Inspector General's. In the detailed written comments sent to the com-

---

353/155. (3) WD ltr AG 451 (9–9–41) MO–C to CofS GHQ, 10 Sep 41, sub: Use of Sound Trucks to Provide Realism in Maneuvers. AGO Records.

[43] GHQ ltr to CG First Army, 4 Sep 41, sub: Intel Procedure during Maneuvers. 354.25/66. Similar letters to CGs Second, Third, and Fourth Armies. 354.25/67–69.

[44] Personal ltr of Gen McNair to Lt Gen Krueger, 5 Jun 41. 354.25/2.

[45] Memo of TIG for CofS USA, 16 Oct 41, sub not given. 333/6.

manding generals of the Second and Third Armies, faults were pointed out in the tactics of both, especially the committing of troops to action before reconnaissance had located the enemy strength. Inadequate combat intelligence, poor liaison and communications, dispersion of effort, and underestimation of danger from the air were held to be common failings. The shortcomings peculiar to each arm and service in both armies were noted, and suggestions were offered for their amendment.[46]

This procedure was repeated at the close of the Carolina maneuvers. On 30 November General McNair delivered the final address at the oral critique. The date is significant, for his talk came after a year of Selective Service, at the completion of the first training cycle, and a week before Pearl Harbor. He said:

> As I look back on the nation-wide series of maneuvers such as these here, and review the mass of comments of all kinds which have been made, certain features of the picture stand out, among them:
>
> The irrepressible cheerfulness, keen intelligence, and physical stamina of the American soldier. He is indeed an inspiration and a challenge to his leaders. He will follow them anywhere, and asks only that they bring him success and victory.
>
> Imperfect discipline of the type which makes the individual subordinate himself to the advantage of his unit, be it large or small; that is, the type which is vital for success in war.
>
> Disregard of the air threat. Columns moved closed up when experience shows beyond question that disaster would result under war conditions. It is clear that revision of the umpire manual must include putting vehicles out of action as a penalty for air attack and artillery fire.
>
> Inadequate reconnaissance and security, although there is slow improvement.
>
> The small proportion of units which is brought to bear against the enemy, due to reluctance to leave roads and column formation.
>
> The question is asked repeatedly, "Are these troops ready for war?" It is my judgment that, given complete equipment, they certainly could fight effectively. But it is to be added with emphasis that the losses would be unduly heavy, and the results of action against an adversary such as the German might not be all that could be desired.

He added that the faults which persisted showed that finished troops could not be trained in one year.[47]

---

[46] (1) Ltr of Gen McNair to CG Second Army, 11 Oct 41, sub: Comments on Second vs. Third Army Maneuvers, Sept 15–30, 1941. 353/466 (Second Army). (2) Ltr of Gen McNair to CG Third Army, 10 Oct 41, sub as in (1) above. 353/595 (Third Army).

[47] "Critique of Second Phase of GHQ-directed Maneuvers, Carolina Area, November 25–28, 1941, by Lt. Gen. L. J. McNair, GSC, Director." 354.2/20 (First Army).

Morale

The maneuvers provided an occasion for observing the morale of the Army, which by the summer of 1941 was causing anxiety to the public and becoming a serious problem to the higher commands. The building of a high morale and sound discipline had been emphasized by General Marshall on 16 October 1940 as a principal aim in the year's training of men about to be inducted by Selective Service.[48] This aim had not been adequately fulfilled.[49] Part of the difficulty was political, arising from disagreement among selectees on the national foreign policy and a resulting failure to see military training as a necessity.[50] Such political difficulties lay beyond the power of military action to remove. Other sources of trouble, not easy to correct, were of a military nature. Letters complaining of conditions in the Army, written by soldiers or their parents and friends, were forwarded by the War Department to GHQ. General McNair sent extracts from these letters to army commanders and summarized the most frequent subjects of complaint: waste of training time through idleness or delay; poorly planned exercises; inadequately explained maneuvers; lack of confidence in officers and of respect for noncommissioned officers who were illiterate and unintelligent; lack of opportunity for promotion; and assignment to duty not in keeping with special civilian experience. He commended these criticisms to the serious consideration of army commanders, noting that they often were written by educated and patriotic selectees with constructive intent.[51] Later, on 18 December, army commanders were directed to prevent such misassignments as those by which clerks became laborers or truck drivers hospital orderlies, a practice held by GHQ to be both injurious to morale and wasteful of the training given in replacement centers.[52]

[48] WD ltr AG 324.71 (9–3–40) M–A of Gen Marshall to Lt Gen Hugh A. Drum, 16 Oct 40, sub: Morale and Discipline. 324.71/5 (SS). Same letter to CGs other Armies, all Corps Areas, and Overseas Departments.

[49] See the 2-volume report (S) made in September 1941 by N. H. Railey, "Morale in the U. S. Army." AGO Records, 353.8 (10–14–41) (Morale in the Army), Bulky Package, Cabinet No. 10, Shelf 4 (S).

[50] (1) Memo (C) MID 353.8 Welfare Activities 9–4–41, 3 Sep 41. 353.8/1 (C). (2) Memo (C) MID 250.1 of Lt Col R. C. Smith, G–2 WD for TAG, 26 Aug 41, sub: Morale. 353.8/3 (C).

[51] Ltr of Gen McNair to all Army Comdrs and CofArmd F, 8 Sep 41, sub: Complaints from Soldiers, with copies of sample letters. 330.14/12 (Criticisms).

[52] Ltr of Gen McNair to all Army Comdrs and CofArmd F, 18 Dec 41, sub: Misassignment of Selectees from RTCs. 324.71/135 (SS Men).

Observers of maneuvers agreed that what the troops needed was meaningful activity and dynamic leadership. In the presence of a real opponent, troops on maneuvers were found to show an improvement of morale, largely because they were kept busy in operations in which they sensed a purpose. In fact, the zeal of troops on maneuvers was noted as a cause of tactical faults, leading to a neglect of precautions of reconnaissance and concealment that would be fatal in combat. But maneuvers could not supply dynamic leadership. Instead, they exposed its absence.[53]

Leadership—the Officer Problem

The unfitness for combat leadership of many officers of all components was a fact well known to the War Department. In the early part of 1941 General McNair frequently expressed the opinion that many officers neither had nor deserved the confidence of their men.[54] To this fact the defects in morale were mainly ascribed. General Marshall gave this explanation in a report on morale, dated 30 September 1941, to the Under Secretary of War.[55] Junior officers, lacking experience, had little confidence in themselves and hence failed to assume or discharge their proper responsibilities. The same was often true of noncommissioned officers. Senior officers were often deemed unqualified for large commands. The opportunities to test the capacity even of senior Regular Army officers to command large units had been limited in the period of lean appropriations since World War I. The problem of obtaining officers trained for combat command was complicated by the fact that a large proportion of those available were officers of the National Guard, who had been called to duty with the mobilization of their units. Many of these were over-age in grade. In June 1941 General McNair found that 22 percent, or 771, of the first lieutenants ordered to active duty in the National Guard were over 40 years old; 919 captains were over 45; 100 lieutenant colonels were over 55.[56] Of 17,752 officers of the National Guard or on duty with the National Guard units in September 1941,

---

[53] (1) Memo MB 353 (9–18–41) WR of Capt F. H. Weston for Lt Col Montgomery, 8 Sep 41, sub: Rpt of Observations Made at the Third Army Maneuvers for Period Aug 16–25, 1941. 353.8/1 (Third Army). (2) Memo of TIG for CofS USA, 10 Sep 41, sub: Morale. 330.14/16 (Criticisms).

[54] For example, see personal ltr of General McNair to Col H. D. Chamberlin, 14 Mar 41. 353/144.

[55] Memo (C) of CofS USA for USW, stamped 30 Sep 41, sub: Morale of the Army. 353.8/1 (Morale) (C).

[56] Memo (C) of Gen McNair for Gen Marshall, 18 Jun 41, sub: TIG—Leadership in the Army, with cpy of TIG memo. 320.2/30 (GHQ Army and Corps) (C).

only 6,800 had had the opportunity to complete a course in one of the service schools, some of them many years in the past.[57] The initial problem was to remove from key positions of command officers of all components who were too old or lacked the necessary training and standards to meet the exacting requirements of leadership in the field. As early as January 1941, a new procedure had been provided for the reclassification of commissioned officers.[58] But reclassification was a slow process, humiliating to the officer concerned. On 7 May 1941, General Marshall sought General McNair's advice.[59] The problem, as General Marshall saw it, was to rid the field forces of misfits, while preserving the reputation and self-respect of officers, particularly in the civilian components, who very often through no fault of their own found themselves in positions which they could not fill. General McNair, like General Marshall, was determined that the field forces should have the best possible leadership. He favored a sweeping policy of maximum age in grade.[60] After consulting his G–1, he immediately advised that more use be made of reassignment and resignation. By this plan, the talents of senior officers regarded as unfit for command in the field could be utilized to the advantage of the service in administering fixed installations, or such officers might honorably resign from the service if their higher commanders certified that there was no vacancy in which they were needed.[61]

At first General McNair thought existing regulations sufficient to bring about the desired result and blamed army commanders for failure to enforce them. "The principal obstacle now," he wrote on 18 June to General Marshall, "is that commanders lack either the guts or the discernment to act." General McNair wrote to Lt. Gen. Walter E. Krueger, Commander of the Third Army, that General Marshall had made

crystal-clear that the reclassification of incompetent officers, regardless of grade, was exactly what he was exerting every effort to bring about . . . . He made no distinction at all as between the Regular Army and the National Guard—both should be given a thorough overhauling. In short, you certainly are free to handle all cases of this kind on their merits without fear of embarrassing the War Department. I may go further and say that the War Department emphatically urges such action by army commanders.

[57] See footnote 55.   [58] AR 605–230, 22 Jan 41, sub: Commissioned Offs: Reclassification.

[59] Personal ltr (C) of Gen Marshall to Gen McNair, 7 May 41. 210.01/1 (C).

[60] See footnotes 55 and 56.

[61] (1) Memo (C) of Gen McNair for Gen Marshall, 21 May 41, sub: Reclassification of Offs. (2) Memo (C) of Lt Col L. D. Brown for Gen McNair, 20 May 41, sub as in (1). Both in 210.01 (C).

Again, speaking of a particular case: "If such action is inadequate, it will then be a question what action is in order with respect to the Army commander." He noted that the problem was not confined to the civilian components. There were also unfit Regular officers, who could be dealt with only by very cumbersome methods. "Possibly G–1 can suggest simpler procedure, or, if necessary, a new law." [62]

By September General McNair had come to regard the system as at fault and exonerated the army commanders. "To lay the blame for failure in the present system upon the field commanders or on the War Department is a fallacy." He repeated General Marshall's observations of the preceding May that reclassification was too slow for the good of the Army and unfair to officers from the civilian components. He renewed his recommendation for the use of resignation.[63] After the September maneuvers and before leaving the maneuver area, he obtained from the War Department authorization for the army commanders to speed up this process and avoid as far as possible embarrassment to the officers concerned.

He shared, however, the anxiety of The Inspector General regarding the effect of a sweeping policy of relieving officers who were over-age or fell short of the desired standards of efficiency. Such a policy would retire from active duty "some Regular and a large number of National Guard officers." He did not approve immediate wholesale relief of National Guard officers. He observed that qualified Regular officers would soon be used up as replacements and doubted the wisdom of removing old officers before the supply of competent new ones was assured.[64] The dilemma presented was difficult to solve. Officers of moderate capacity had to be kept on pending the training of better ones, but, if war should come quickly and make these officers combat leaders, disaster might result. To put it another way, new officers had to be trained along with the new troops whom they were eventually to lead in battle, but meanwhile they could not exercise mature leadership in training. At Fort Leavenworth in February 1942 General McNair stated that in his view "the outstanding generalization" of a year of training experience was "that we did not have in fact the great mass of trained

    [62] (1) See footnote 56. (2) Personal ltr of Gen McNair to Lt Gen Walter Krueger, 28 Aug 41. McNair Correspondence.

    [63] Memo (C) of Gen McNair for CofS USA, 25 Sep 41, sub: Reclassification. 210.01/2 (C).

    [64] (1) Telg, McNair to ACofS G–1 WD, 27 Sep 41. Misc Journal, G–1 GHQ. (2) Memo of Gen McNair for Gen Marshall, 20 Oct 41, sub: Leadership Deficiencies—Repls. 333/5. (3) Memo of TIG for CofS USA, 9 Oct 41, sub and location as in (2) above.

officers that were carried on the books . . . . Inadequately trained officers cannot train troops effectively." [65]

Reemphasis on Essentials

Training operations after the September maneuvers were prescribed in a letter of 30 October 1941 on "Post-Maneuver Training." [66] While the training of "task forces with flexible organizations" was indicated for the future as in keeping with the War Department Training Directive of 19 August, for the immediate present General McNair demanded a return to fundamentals. "Recent maneuvers and field exercises have shown glaring weaknesses in basic and small-unit training. . . . It is apparent that mobilization training as covered in mobilization training programs has not been mastered." He ordered, therefore, that after a short period of furloughs a four months' review of basic and small-unit training be held. Combat firing was to be emphasized, with observers from GHQ in attendance. Army and corps commanders were to conduct field-exercise tactical tests of infantry battalions and cavalry squadrons, with artillery delivering actual overhead fire when feasible. Command post exercises were ordered for the training of headquarters and communications units and troop schools to prepare officers and noncommissioned officers for current training. With this directive were enclosed exact stipulations of the tests prescribed, from the platoon up to the battalion.

War Plans for the Creation of New Divisions

The gross result of the GHQ-directed training program culminating in the army maneuvers of 1941 is reflected in General McNair's report to the War Department on 20 December 1941. Of the 34 divisions under GHQ control, 14 infantry divisions, 2 armored divisions, and 1 cavalry division were ready for combat. He stated that 3 more infantry divisions would be ready by 1 February 1942; 8 more infantry divisions, 1 more cavalry division, and 1 cavalry brigade by 1 March; the rest—2 infantry divisions and 2 armored divisions—by

[65] GHQ Pub Relations Off copy of speech delivered by Gen McNair, 14 Feb 42. 210.693/3.

[66] GHQ ltr to all Army Comdrs and CofArmd F, 30 Oct 41, sub: Post-Maneuver Tng. 353/652.

1 April.[67] But the fresh expansion of the armored forces after 7 December 1941 made radical changes in these dates necessary.[68]

When war came on 7 December, it found the United States after a year of Selective Service with an army of 1,638,086 men in various stages of military proficiency,[69] but with no more infantry divisions than had existed, inactive or understrength, in the peacetime Army.

That GHQ had anticipated the needs of war is apparent from its reaction on 6 December to a War Department plan calling for the creation of twenty-seven reserve divisions in three years.[70] The question, which had been under consideration since the early days of Selective Service, was the peacetime question of disposal of selectees after their period of military training. It had been decided to place them in new Regular Army reserve units. The purpose was to increase the number not only of trained men but also of trained or partly trained divisions and other units available for immediate call in an emergency.[71]

General McNair viewed this 27-division plan with disfavor. He pointed out that twenty-seven divisions comprised only 430,000 men out of 2,700,000 to be made available in three years under existing Selective Service legislation and that most selectees would therefore return to their homes as individuals, without divisional experience or adequate unit training. This outcome he called "unreasonable." "I do not profess to understand," he wrote on the day before Pearl Harbor, "the precise military objective of our Army, but assume as obvious that it must be more than a passive hemispherical defense." He estimated that operations would require 200 divisions and that their training could not begin too soon.[72]

With the declaration of war the War Department produced a plan for the activation of three or four divisions a month beginning with March 1942 and

[67] Memo (S) of Gen McNair for ACofS G–3 WD, 20 Dec 41, sub: Readiness of Divs for Combat. 314.7 (AGF Hist) (S).

[68] See AGF Historical Section, The Building and Training of Infantry Divisions, and "Mobilization of the Ground Army," in this volume.

[69] Tabular Rpt (S) of 30 Nov 41. 320.2/57 (Gen Str) (S).

[70] Memo (S) of Gen. McNair for ACofS G–3 WD, 6 Dec 41, sub: Organized Res. 320.2/58 (S).

[71] GHQ had long advised the creation of Regular Army Reserve units. See: (1) Memo of Gen McNair for ACofS G–3 WD, 27 Nov 40, sub: Sources of Units for Activation. 320.2/56. (2) Memo of Gen McNair for Gen Bryden, 14 Dec 40, sub: Additional Defense Plans. 320.2/56. (3) Ltr of CofS GHQ to CGs all Armies, 15 May 41, sub: Unit Tng of Newly Activated RA Units. 353/24 (Tng Dir). (4) Memo of Gen McNair for ACofS G–3 WD, 12 Aug 41, sub: Pers Policies and Priorities Affecting Tng and Orgn. 320.2/456.

[72] See footnote 67.

proceeding until the number of divisions reached 100 by the end of 1943. Asked for a recommendation, General McNair advised that 20 percent of these divisions be armored.[73] He strongly opposed the proposal that, under war conditions of accelerated expansion, divisions be filled directly from reception centers, not from replacement training centers. He objected on the ground that the best combat divisions could not be produced in minimum time if filled initially with raw recruits. "It is the belief of this headquarters," wrote General McNair on 29 December 1941, "that the providing of new divisions with replacement center personnel is of the highest priority and should take precedent over practically all other requirements."[74] GHQ urged repeatedly, but without success, that replacement training centers be expanded to keep pace with the expansion of the Army.

For creating new divisions the War Department prescribed the cadre system, whereby a group of experienced officers and enlisted men withdrawn from a "parent" division became the organizing and training element of the new division, which was to draw most of its officers from officer candidate schools and the service schools, and the overwhelming mass of its enlisted men directly from reception centers. The system threw a heavy burden on the cadre, and General McNair on 20 December 1941 submitted to General Marshall a plan for the training of cadres.[75] He proposed that:

1. The commanding general and the two brigadiers of each division be appointed two and a half months before the date set for activation of the division.

2. That they report immediately to GHQ for instruction in the training program.

3. That GHQ assist the division commander in the selection of his general and special staff.

4. That

a. The commander and his staff take refresher courses at the Command and General Staff School, and

b. The officers and enlisted men of the cadre report to service schools and Replacement Training Centers respectively for special instruction.

[73] Memo (S) of Gen McNair for Gen Moore, DCofS WD, 23 Dec 41, sub: Command Set-up of Armd Units. 320.2/58 (Gen Str) (S).

[74] (1) Memo (S) of Gen McNair for ACofS G-3 WD, 29 Dec 41, sub: Mob and Tng Plan Revised. 320.2/58 (Gen Str) (S). (2) Memo (S) of Gen McNair for ACofS G-3 WD, 30 Dec 41, sub: Mob and Tng Program Prepared by your Office Dec. 27, 1941. 320/58 (Gen Str) (S). (3) Ltr of CG FF to First Army, 31 Jan 42, sub: Tng of Enl Repl Reporting Directly from RCs. 353/763 (First Army). Same letter to other CGs.

[75] Memo (S) of Gen McNair for CG FF, 20 Dec 41, sub: Expansion of the Army. 320.2/58 (Gen Str) (S).

This plan was accepted. Details were worked out at GHQ in the following weeks. On 17 January 1942 the first in a long series of charts, entitled "Building an Infantry Triangular Division," was completed. Its main outlines were only slightly modified in later charts, for the Army Ground Forces continued to create new divisions on the principles devised at GHQ immediately after the outbreak of war.[76]

Additional guidance for the training of new infantry divisions was provided in a letter from GHQ forwarded to army commanders on 16 February 1942, after advance notification to the Chief of Infantry.[77] This directive laid down in principle a period of ten to twelve months as the time needed to prepare a newly activated division for combat. It specified seventeen weeks for the accomplishment of the 13-week Mobilization Training Programs, allowing an initial four weeks to smooth out the confusion attendant upon activation. Then were to follow thirteen weeks of unit training, chiefly regimental, and fourteen weeks of combined training to include at least one maneuver of a division against a division. For combined training the directive of 4 January 1941 remained basic. As "points of special importance" it was stipulated that field maneuvers should be free, that exercises should be repeated, if necessary, until establishment of proficiency, that tests and critiques should be given, and that training in air and antimechanized security measures should be continuous. Combat conditions were to be simulated with increasing realism. This is evident from a proposal by the Chief of Infantry for the liberalization of safety precautions and greater use of actual fire, in which GHQ concurred on 8 January.[78]

Except for the organization of new units, the more rapid influx of recruits, and the increased realism in training which war made acceptable to the public, the training program was not much affected by the declaration of war. Essentials remained as worked out in the past year. Principles already adopted were applied on a larger scale. Though a large Army was not ready for combat on 7 December 1941, the United States entered the war, thanks to the establishment of General Headquarters and of Selective Service more than a year before, with a training program carefully thought out and in full operation. This was a great gain over 1917.

[76] See AGF Historical Section, The Building and Training of Infantry Divisions.

[77](1) Ltr of CG FF to CGs all Armies, 16 Feb 42, sub: Tng of Newly Activated Inf Divs. 353/21 (Inf). (2) GHQ memo (C) for CofInf, 8 Jan 42, sub: Training Programs (TPs) for New Inf Divs. 353/1 (Inf) (C).

[78] Ltr of CofInf, CI 300.3/AR 750–10 (11–29–41) to TAG, 31 Dec 41, sub: Liberalization of Safety Precautions, AGO Records.

Summary of Training Principles under GHQ

The principles developed by GHQ during 1940 and 1941 emphasized thorough training of the soldier and his unit in fundamentals and might be summarized as follows:

1. A *progression* in training through a 4-phase sequence of individual basic training, small-unit training, combined training, and large-unit maneuvers.

2. *Tests* of these successive phases, given in each case by the next higher headquarters.

3. Emphasis and reemphasis on *elementary training,* with frequent review, when tests showed unsatisfactory results.

4. *Free,* as opposed to controlled, *maneuvers* with realistic umpiring.

5. Immediate *critiques* of performance in maneuvers.

6. *General soldierly proficiency,* as a necessary preliminary to training for special operations.

7. Instruction given in *troop schools,* as opposed to detachment of officers or enlisted men from their units for attendance at schools elsewhere.

8. *Integrity of the tactical unit,* as shown in the criticism of combat-team tactics, in the preparation of reserve units for the peacetime army, in the policy toward special schools, and in the principle of command responsibility.

9. *Responsibility of commanding officers* of all echelons for the planning, conduct, and results of training of their units, with consequent high valuation on leadership and officer quality.

10. *Realism,* or the simulation of combat conditions.

All these principles were carried over from GHQ into the administration of the Army Ground Forces, where General McNair continued to apply them in the training of the millions of men eventually assigned to ground combat.

III. GHQ and the Armored Force

Establishment of the Armored Force

The Armored Force was established on 10 July 1940, sixteen days before the activation of General Headquarters. For more than twenty years United States Army officers had worked hard to develop tanks, and their achievement compared favorably with that of the British and the French. Their work had been severely limited by lack of funds and by difficulties in coordinating the armored activities of Infantry, Cavalry, and other arms and services concerned with tanks. The German victories of May–June 1940 made the tank question more urgent than ever. The Germans had used large armored formations for deep penetration and wide encirclement of hostile positions. This conspicuous success in armored warfare strengthened the arguments of those officers who had long advocated a new armored tactics and organization. The result was the creation of an Armored Force. But because of continuing differences of outlook and the limitation on the creation of new arms imposed by the National Defense Act of 1920, the new force was set up only provisionally, "for purposes of service test." [1]

Though at first provisional, the Armored Force was from the beginning a strong autonomous organization. It received control of all tank units already existing in the Infantry and Cavalry and of certain Field Artillery and service units as well. It was to include, as they were activated, "all armored corps and divisions, and all GHQ Reserve tank units." At its head was a Chief of the Armored Force, Brig. Gen. Adna R. Chaffee, who was also Commanding General of the I Armored Corps. The status of an "arm," which could be conferred only by an Act of Congress, was withheld from the new force, but the functions of its

---

[1] (1) WD ltr AG 320.2 (7–5–40) M (Ret) M–C, 10 Jul 40, sub: Orgn of the Armd F. 320.2/1 (Armd F). (2) Background papers in AGO Records 320.2 (6–5–40) (3) Sec 1; also in G–3/41665 and in G–3/41665 (C), Secs 1 and 2.

chief were described in the original directive as "essentially those of a chief of a combatant arm" with respect to all tank elements in the Army. In addition, the Armored Force soon obtained a temporary authority to train all nontank elements of large armored units, mainly the infantry, artillery, and service components of armored divisions.[2]

Under the vigorous and able leadership of General Chaffee and his associates, and later of Maj. Gen. Jacob L. Devers, the Armored Force rapidly expanded. Within a few weeks it had formed from existing elements two armored divisions, which were to be followed by three more in 1941, the only strictly new divisions created in the United States Army before Pearl Harbor. An Armored Force School and an Armored Force Board were set up immediately and in 1941 an Armored Force Replacement Training Center and an Armored Force Officer Candidate School were established. On 23 November 1940 the Armored Force published its own Mobilization Training Program, which prescribed the hours and subjects for thirteen weeks of basic individual and small-unit training not only for tank personnel, but also for the infantry, field artillery, ordnance, signal, quartermaster, engineer, and medical units comprised in the Armored Force.[3]

Freed in large measure from dependence on other branches, controlling its own schools and replacement system, formulating its own tactical doctrine, shaping its own personnel through successive phases of training, organizing and directing units as high as divisions and corps, possessing an intense group spirit and a strong enthusiasm for its special weapon, the Armored Force tended to become an autonomous and self-contained element in the Army. This tendency raised a basic problem of military organization for the War Department, which had to integrate the development of the new Armored Force with the training activities of the old arms and services. The development of the tank since 1916 had in effect produced a new technique of warfare. An answer had to be found to the question whether emphasis should be placed on specialization in its use, resulting in a relatively independent organization to meet the new need, or whether the new organization should be kept within the established framework, acting interdependently with the older parts. In other words, how far, if at all, should the Armored Force develop in the direction of autonomy which the Air Corps was taking?

[2] See footnote 1 (1) above, and WD immediate action ltr AG 320.2 (11–8–40) M–C, 13 Nov 40, sub: Tng of Components of Armd F. 320.2/11 (Armd F).

[3] Armd F, "Mobilization Training Program," 23 Nov 40. 322.091/2 (Armd F).

Relation of GHQ to the Armored Force

Relations between GHQ and the Armored Force were always somewhat distant and unclear. As a headquarters concerned with training of units, GHQ had no authority on questions of Armored Force organization. General McNair's views on this subject were nevertheless often requested by the War Department, as were his opinions on questions of Air Corps and tank destroyer organization. He exerted a personal, not an official, influence. He expressed reluctance to deal with the question of Armored Force organization, possibly because his ideas on this subject were generally shared and expressed by G–3 of the War Department.

For training, GHQ had direct supervision only over the field forces, i. e., organized tactical units. Its authority therefore stopped short of the schools and replacement activities of the Armored Force, but embraced the I Armored Corps, the armored divisions, and the separate tank battalions which were designed to reinforce infantry or other elements at the discretion of higher commanders and which were known as GHQ tank battalions. To assist in the discharge of these responsibilities, General McNair included an Armored Force officer, Lt. Col. Allen F. Kingman, in his original small "nucleus" of a staff. But even in the training of tactical units General McNair was disposed to leave the Armored Force to its own devices, though representatives of GHQ frequently visited Fort Knox and submitted reports. The main part played by GHQ was to employ armored units produced by the Armored Force in the GHQ-directed maneuvers of 1941.

Training Directives and Maneuvers

GHQ issued no major training directives specifically to the Armored Force. Even the general training directives issued at intervals to army commanders laying down broad training policies for the field forces were not at first addressed to the Chief of the Armored Force. Copies, however, were sent to Fort Knox for information, and the Armored Force showed a willingness to conform to them. When the Armored Force published its Mobilization Training Program in November 1940, it listed among its references General McNair's first training directive, i. e., his letter of 16 September 1940 to army commanders. Neither the GHQ directive of January 1941 on "Combined Training," nor the one of March

1941 on "Training Tests," nor any equivalent was addressed to the Armored Force. The letter of 30 October 1941 on "Post-Maneuver Training" was the first major training directive sent both to army commanders and to the Chief of the Armored Force.

This reluctance to interfere in the training of the Armored Force can probably be ascribed to its peculiar situation during its first year. Training had to be sacrificed to expansion. Hardly were the 1st and 2d Armored Divisions organized when they were required to produce cadres for the 3d and 4th. From February to May, 1941, the 2d Armored Division was needed for air-ground tactical tests. In November 1940 the GHQ tank officers reported that basic training was being neglected, but that the Armored Force authorities were aware of the problem; in January 1941, that training within divisions suffered from the creation of new units and that the Armored Force was expanding before any of its existing units were properly trained; in March, that expansion was still proceeding, but was handicapped by the failure of the War Department to activate new divisional headquarters in advance.[4] In these circumstances it was not until late 1941 that Armored Force units were ready to profit fully by directives laid down by GHQ for ground troops at large.

Sometimes inspections resulted in attempts to bring Armored Force methods into greater harmony with the policies of GHQ. On one occasion it was found that training tests were so arranged that a battalion virtually tested itself. General McNair wrote to General Chaffee that the battalion should be tested by its next higher headquarters.[5] Again, after his representative had attended a field exercise of the 1st Armored Division, General McNair wrote that in such exercises the enemy should be represented at least by umpires and that a brief oral critique should immediately follow.[6] But, in general, few such letters were written, and in all phases of training short of maneuvers for corps and armies the Armored Force went its way with little direction from GHQ.

Armored divisions appeared for the first time in U. S. Army maneuvers in the summer of 1941; the 2d Armored Division, in June; and the 1st, a few

---

[4] Memos of Lt Col A. F. Kingman for CofS GHQ, 15 Nov 40, 22 Jan 41, and 28 Mar 41. 333.1 (Ft Knox), items 1, 2, and 3.

[5] Ltr of Gen McNair to CofArmd F, 22 Apr 41, sub: Training Tests. 353/43 (Armd F).

[6] Ltr of Gen McNair to CofArmd F, 19 May 41, sub: Training Tests, 1st Armd Div, May 12–14, 1941. 333.1/5 (Ft Knox). Other GHQ reports on Fort Knox may be found in this file and in 319.1 (Weekly Rpts of GHQ Activities).

weeks later. Various corps and army headquarters had the opportunity, through attachment, to employ them in the field.[7] The main test came in the GHQ maneuvers of November 1941 in the Carolinas. The I Armored Corps, comprising the 1st and 2d Armored Divisions, was attached to the IV Army Corps under Maj. Gen. Oscar W. Griswold, in opposition to the First Army under Lt. Gen. Hugh A. Drum. General Griswold's numerical inferiority (100,000 against 195,000) was to be compensated for by massing under his command 865 tanks and armored scout cars. Against him the First Army had 4,321 guns which might be effective against tanks, and, of these, 764 were capable of mobile concentration against tank assault.

As director of the maneuvers, General McNair judged that General Griswold employed his tank strength prematurely and piecemeal, losing the opportunity to use the I Armored Corps as a whole for a concentrated blow at the critical time. He also thought that armored units had on occasion been used where other types of units, easier to replace, might have accomplished the same objective. In general, the maneuvers were inconclusive as to the effects of massed tank action at a decisive moment.

They confirmed, however, certain developments which had been growing more evident since the great German armored offensives of May–June 1940. Antitank guns proved themselves highly effective. Umpires ruled that 983 tanks had been put out of action—91 percent by guns, 5 percent by grenades, 3 percent by mines, and 1 percent by air. The 1st Armored Division was destroyed, after its line of communications was severed at the beginning of the attack. It was agreed that tanks needed the strong support of infantry to hold ground and neutralize antitank guns. A much improved warning system against mobile antitank guns was found to be necessary. Better radio discipline in tank units was recommended in the interest of security. General Griswold noted a tendency on the part of the I Armored Corps "to operate independently and without too much regard for other members of the team."[8]

---

[7] See (1) 1st ind Hq Armd F to CofS GHQ, 7 Apr 41. 353 (2d Armd Div). (2) 353.28 (VII Corps). (3) GHQ ltr to CGs all Armies and CofArmd F, 16 Jul 41, sub: Assumed and Simulated Weapons during GHQ-directed Maneuvers. 353/130 (Armd F). (4) GHQ memo for ODCofS USA, 2 Sep 41, sub: Summary of Activities, GHQ, for Week Ending 2 Sep 41. 319.1/29 (Wkly Rpts).

[8] The preceding four paragraphs are based on mimeographed reproductions of oral comments made at the critique following the maneuvers by (1) Gen McNair (354.2/20 (First Army)) and (2) Gen Griswold (354.2/10 (First Army)), and on Gen McNair's subsequent written criticisms, ltr of Gen McNair to CG IV Corps, 7 Jan 42 (354.2/1 (IV Army Corps)).

But, at the same time, the staff of the I Armored Corps distinguished itself in intelligence work and by its skill in withdrawing the two armored divisions and the 4th Motorized Division over limited road nets. The armored units showed themselves able to move effectively at night. The willingness and endurance of the troops were noted by General McNair, and General Griswold observed that no one should be misled by the success of antitank weapons into underestimating the power of tanks.

Thus the Armored Force, in somewhat over a year and in spite of the drains caused by expansion, had performed the important task of putting two competent armored divisions into the field. At the end of 1941 three additional armored divisions were in less advanced stages of training.

Organizational Problems

Since the Armored Force was at first established provisionally, the question soon arose of its more permanent organization. The issues raised were of the highest importance to the Army, and in the ensuing discussion GHQ played a substantial, though largely unofficial, part. The organizational question was brought up by the Armored Force on 2 October 1940 and was temporarily resolved by a War Department directive of 3 April 1941. During these six months four proposals were made, two by the Armored Force and two by G–3 of the War Department General Staff.

The first proposal of the Armored Force, that of 2 October 1940, made four recommendations: (1) That the Armored Force receive a headquarters and headquarters company of its own, instead of using those of the I Armored Corps. Over this request no controversy developed, though action on it was delayed until the general settlement of 3 April 1941. (2) That three GHQ Reserve Group headquarters be activated to command the fifteen GHQ tank battalions contemplated by the War Department. Only the timing, not the substance, of this request became an issue. (3) That a II Armored Corps be activated, since the War Department planned to create a third and a fourth armored division. (4) That a large and varied assortment of organic corps troops be assigned to each armored corps.

The third and fourth recommendations raised considerable difficulties. They posed the question whether the War Department should create a "type" armored corps so fully provided with its own supporting troops as to constitute a small independent army. The requested corps troops included military police and signal units; corps artillery, medical, ordnance, and quartermaster units; one decontaminating company; an antiaircraft regiment and an antitank battalion; five kinds of engineers; four replacement battalions; and, for air support, an armored observation squadron, a composite pursuit group, and an entire wing of light bombers.[9]

To these plans G–3 responded with a proposal of its own, dated 19 November 1940. It rejected the idea of a heavily equipped "type" armored corps and saw no need of a second armored corps until the following fiscal year. Organic corps troops were to be held to a minimum—a headquarters and headquarters company and a signal battalion. All other types of troops in the Armored Force list, according to G–3, should be supplied to armored corps from GHQ reserves as determined by higher command. In this respect the G–3 proposal tended to check the development of the Armored Force in the direction of independence, but, in another respect, it encouraged it. Continuing to support a policy for which it had failed to obtain acceptance in the preceding July, G–3 recommended that the Armored Force be set up as a fully recognized separate arm.[10]

This suggestion revived an old controversy. The Chiefs of Infantry and of Cavalry strongly dissented. The Chief of Infantry felt that the severance of tanks from foot troops had already gone too far and that the development of tank tactics and training of tank personnel should be a responsibility of his office. The Chief of Cavalry, in a long memorandum, chiefly historical in nature, contended that the Cavalry had long led the way in mechanized developments, but that lately the views of his office had been persistently disregarded. On the War Department General Staff, G–1 and G–2 expressed nonconcurrences less emphatic than those of the two Chiefs. General approval of the plan was given by WPD, the Armored Force, and GHQ. The War Plans Division concurred without comments. The Armored Force accepted the G–3 proposal with reservations on the matter of corps troops. GHQ was in favor of establishing the Armored Force as a separate arm and wanted the II Armored Corps set up before the 4th Armored Division in accordance with its principle of activating headquarters before receipt of subordinate units.[11]

---

[9] Ltr of CG Armd F to TAG, 2 Oct 40, sub: Orgn of the Armd F. AGO Records, 320.2 (6–5–40) (3) Sec 1.

[10] Memo G–3/41665 of Gen F. M. Andrews, ACofS G–3 for CofS USA, 19 Nov 40, sub: Orgn of the Armd F. AGO Records, 320.2 (6–5–40) (3) Sec 1.

[11] Memos for ACofS G–3 WD, sub: Orgn of the Armd F, as follows: (1) CI 322/9816 from Gen G. A. Lynch, 7 Dec 40; (2) from Gen G. K. Herr, CofCav, 7 Dec 40; (3) G–1/16249 from Gen W. E. Shedd,

In view of these extremes of disagreement, the Office of the Chief of Staff decided to postpone an immediate decision on the basic question and issued on 21 January 1941 a compromise directive. The G–3 proposal was rejected. Divisions and corps containing armored units were to be considered as tactical units of combined arms, not as units of a separate arm or branch, and officers of such units were to come from all arms and services. If a separate Armored Force branch were established, officers would be detailed to it for limited periods from other combat arms. But, like the other combat arms, this separate Armored Force would become responsible for developing the tactics and technique of its units, including the largest.[12]

G–3 responded to these instructions by what seems to have been a delaying action, merely recommending on 27 February that, if a separate arm were created, officers should be commissioned in it permanently.[13] On this problem GHQ continued to stand with G–3, approving fully the suggestion made.[14] War Plans Division took an ambiguous position, agreeing with G–3 in principle but suggesting that, if the compromise plan of detailing officers temporarily to the Armored Force should prove successful, then all "arms" and "branches" might well be abolished. G–1 objected to the G–3 proposal, fearing that officers commissioned in an armored arm would become too specialized. It recommended temporary detail of officers to the Armored Force, as the Navy detailed officers to its air force without loss of efficiency in aviation. G–4 agreed with G–1. The views of the Chiefs of Infantry and Cavalry were not sought at this stage.

Meanwhile, the Armored Force itself was willing to let the separate-arm question wait but pushed forward its campaign for autonomy of command. A study of armored organization in European armies was made at Fort Knox.

---

9 Dec 40; (4) G–2/2045–1510 from Gen Sherman Miles, 16 Dec 40; (5) from Gen L. T. Gerow, WPD, 9 Dec 40; (6) from Gen C. L. Scott, CG Armd F, 26 Nov 40; (7) from Gen L. J. McNair, CofS GHQ, 3 Dec 40. All in AGO Records 320.2 (6–5–40) (3) Sec. 1.

[12] Memo OCS 21149–20 of Col Orlando Ward for ACofS G–3 WD, 21 Jan 41, sub: Orgn of the Armd F. 322.091/10 (Armd F).

[13] Memo (C) of ACofS G–3 WD for CofS USA, 27 Feb 41, sub: The Establishment of the Armd F as a Separate Arm. 322.091/10 (Armd F).

[14] Memos for ACofS G–3 WD, sub: Establishment of the Armd F as a Separate Arm, as follows: (1) G–1/16249–33 from Gen W. H. Haislip, 10 Mar 41; (2) G–4/32714 from Gen E. Reybold, 12 Mar 41; (3) WPD 4334–8 from Col J. W. Anderson, 18 Mar 41. All in AGO Records, 320.2 (6–5–40) (3) Sec 1. The concurrence of GHQ is indicated by the initials "LJM" in the appropriate place on the G–3 memo, 27 Feb 41, in this file.

This report stressed the fact that the Germans, whose superiority in this respect was unquestioned early in 1941, had a more independent armored organization than the British or French and that in the Battle of Flanders they had employed an armored army consisting of four armored corps.[15]

Fortified by these findings, the Armored Force submitted on 22 February 1941 its second proposal for permanent organization. Maj. Gen. Charles L. Scott, commanding in General Chaffee's absence, pointed out the similarity of the organization recommended to that already in effect in the Air Corps.[16] The Armored Force was to be headed by a commanding general whose rank, it might be inferred from the study, was to be that of a full general. Under him were to be two subdivisions: an administrative division under a major general comparable to a chief of arm, and a field headquarters under a major general as chief of staff. Through this staff the commander of the Armored Force would control the several armored corps, each under a lieutenant general, and the tank groups under which the separate tank battalions were placed.[17] A letter of 1 March from General Chaffee to the Armored Force liaison officer in Washington, the contents of which had also been forwarded to General Marshall, made the meaning of the proposal clear:[18]

The Armored Force should be placed on the status of an Armored Army Headquarters capable of operating the force as a whole or of detaching any part of it, Corps, Division, Group or Battalion, as is the GHQ Air Force. It should have the same relation to GHQ as has the GHQ Air Force. GHQ couldn't possibly operate it with a staff alone; it has too many other things to do.

The questions of the Chief of Arm should be set up as Scott has them, capable of being separated and left in the zone of interior or SOS should Force Headquarters be in the zone of the Armies.

In a letter of 18 March to General McNair, General Chaffee developed his ideas and requested support.[19] According to General Chaffee the Armored Force, because of its peculiar mobility, its peculiar problems of supply, the special knowledge required of its officers, and its considerable size could not successfully

---

[15] (1) Armd F, "Orgn for Command of Large Armd Units in European Armies," 18 Jan 41. 322.091/8 and /11 (Armd F). (2) Personal ltr of Gen McNair to Gen C. L. Scott, 24 Jan 41. 322.091/8 (Armd F).

[16] Armd F ltr to TAG, 22 Feb 41, sub: Orgn of the Armd F to Meet Proposed Expansion. 322.091/11 (Armd F).

[17] Chart, incl 2 to ltr cited in footnote 16.

[18] Personal ltr (C) of Gen Chaffee to [Lt Col G. X.] Cheves, 1 Mar 41. G–3/41665 (C) Sec 4.

[19] Personal ltr of Gen Chaffee to Gen McNair, 18 Mar 41. 322.091/12 (Armd F).

be operated through the ordinary channels of command and staff. Above the armored corps, therefore,

is needed a headquarters which thoroughly understands and is trained and equipped to handle the problems of concentration, supply, replacement, field equipment, and maintenance of masses of armored troops. . . . GHQ may wish to employ more than a corps of two divisions, and if so it should have the trained organization available.

Even with the small 7th Cavalry Brigade, Mechanized, I have never attended a maneuver . . . where I did not have to take over from Army or Corps headquarters all the questions of supply including gasoline and oil, maintenance, and evacuation, etc. Staffs which are not trained in large armored units have not sufficient appreciation of their detailed requirements to be able to give good service.

If you should set up in GHQ an Armored Force section to take over the details of movement, operation, supply, maintenance, and evacuation of several detached and separate armored corps and several separate GHQ tank groups, I believe it would break down, and one of your earliest steps would be to set up a command group for this similar to that of the GHQ Air Force which can take care of all these matters, and make available to you for operations at any time and place a separate battalion or division corps or any larger part of the Armored Force that may be necessary in your plan. . . .

I therefore hope that you will nonconcur strongly in the G–3 memorandum which I mentioned and insist on a proper, adequate and forward-looking organization.

The G–3 memorandum referred to by General Chaffee was a G–3 proposal drawn up on 13 March in answer to the second proposal of the Armored Force. G–3 was not convinced of the need of an armored army. The new G–3 proposal recommended instead (1) that the office of the Chief of the Armored Force be organized like that of any other chief, not under a tactical commander of the arm; (2) that the largest armored tactical unit be a corps, not an army; and (3) that control of armored units in operation be through Armored Force staff sections at the headquarters of field armies, theaters of operations, and GHQ, not through a special commanding general of the whole Armored Force.[20]

General McNair was now forced to choose between G–3 and the Armored Force, both of whom sought his support, but since he seemed not yet to have reached a clear decision in his own mind he wrote rather noncommittally to General Chaffee. To General Scott he observed: "I, myself, will not tangle in this matter, since my job is training and not organization." [21] He inclined far enough to Armored Force views to express a mild nonconcurrence in the second

[20] Memo of ACofS G–3 WD for CofS USA, 13 Mar 41, sub: Orgn of the Armd F to Meet Proposed Expansion. 322.091/12 (Armd F).

[21] Personal ltr of Gen McNair to Gen Chaffee, 24 Mar 41. 322.091/12 (Armd F); and to Gen Scott, 10 Mar 41. 353/28 (Armd F).

and third points of the G–3 proposal, which opposed the establishment of an armored army and the appointment of a full general for the whole Armored Force.[22]

"In my view," wrote General McNair to G–3, "the essential element of armored action is a powerful blow delivered by surprise. While the armored units may be broken up and attached to division and army corps, it is readily conceivable, and indeed probable, that the entire force, under a single command, may be thrown against a decisive point."

In other words, in March 1941 GHQ not only favored the establishment of the Armored Force as a separate arm but was willing to see further consideration of the idea of an armored army.

Other influences, however, were at work to keep armored units within the older framework of the field forces. It was believed in Armored Force circles that Maj. Gen. William Bryden, Deputy Chief of the War Department General Staff, was among them.[23] The identity of others may be conjectured from the records of nonconcurrences in the earlier recommendations of G–3. All that can be said on the basis of evidence examined is that on 25 March the Office of the Chief of Staff issued instructions which, if carried out, would have given less autonomy to the Armored Force than G–3 recommended and even less than it had possessed up to that date. The Armored Force was to remain on a provisional basis, "for purposes of service test," under a chief who would exercise the same functions in training, inspection, and development as other chiefs of arms. Officers would be detailed to, not commissioned in, the Force. The I Armored Corps would continue, but the activation of a second would be deferred. Though these provisions left the Armored Force about the same as the directive of July 1940 had created it, two other provisions reduced its powers. It was stipulated that the 3d and 4th Armored Divisions, when organized, should not be included in the Armored Force but placed as separate divisions under GHQ for training, subject to attachment to the Third and First Armies. All GHQ reserve tank battalions were to be transferred from the Armored Force to GHQ. G–3 was instructed to incorporate these principles in a directive within two days.[24]

[22] Memo of Gen McNair for ACofS G–3 WD, 24 Mar 41, sub: Orgn of Armd F to Meet Proposed Expansion. 322.091/12 (Armd F).

[23] Memo of Lt Col F. R. Waltz, Armd F liaison off to CofArmd F, 5 Mar 41, sub not given. 353/28 (Armd F). Cf. Gen McNair's ltr to Gen Scott cited in footnote 21 above.

[24] Memo OCS 21149–30 for ACofS G–3 WD, 25 Mar 41, sub: Armd F. AGO Records, 320.2 (6–5–40) (3) Sec 1.

As the result of a protest from General Chaffee to General Marshall, the Office of the Chief of Staff almost immediately reversed itself. Acting on oral instructions which superseded those of both 25 March and 21 January from the Office of the Chief of Staff, G–3 prepared a directive to be issued as an immediate action letter by The Adjutant General. General Marshall wrote "O. K., GCM" on the G–3 paper. Published on 3 April 1941, the directive was as significant in its silences as in its statements.[25]

Nothing was said on the problem of the Armored Force as a separate arm, or on the related questions of the detailing or commissioning of its officers. Nothing was said of an armored army, or of a second armored corps, or of the organic constitution of an armored corps, or of the corps as the largest permissible armored tactical unit. At the same time no more was said of removing the separate tank battalions from Armored Force jurisdiction.

Those who had feared the growth of an independent Armored Force could feel that the directive killed the movement to create a new arm as well as a new army. They could point to certain provisions as safeguards for their views. All armored units were declared to be subject to attachment to existing field armies for combined training. In establishing doctrine for the use of GHQ tank battalions in armored support of infantry, the Chief of the Armored Force was to share the responsibility with the Chief of Infantry. The Chief of Staff, GHQ, was to have authority over the Chief of the Armored Force during combined training. General McNair noted that this provision had no significance.

The Armored Force retained the powers granted to it in the preceding July. It obtained a distinct Force headquarters and headquarters company, "constituted on the active list," under command of General Chaffee. The I Armored Corps was continued, under command of General Scott. The 3d and 4th Armored Divisions, and by implication all future armored divisions, would be organized and trained as separate divisions by the Armored Force. Leaders of the Armored Force could feel that they had at least won an established status and that some of their larger proposals, while now passed over in silence, might be reopened in the future.

---

[25] (1) Memo of Gen Adna R. Chaffee for CofS USA, 27 Mar 41. Personal Files of General Chaffee. See AGF Historical Section, The Armored Force, Command, and Center, Sec VI. (2) Memo of ACofS G–3 WD for TAG, 31 Mar 41, sub: Armd F. AGO Records, 320.2 (6–5–40) (3) Sec IA. (3) WD ltr AG 320.2 (1–21–41) M (Ret) M–C to CofArmd F, CG I Armd Corps, CofInf, and CofS GHQ, 3 Apr 41, sub: Armd F. 320.2/1 (Armd F).

Status of the Armored Force

Fundamentals of Armored Force organization did not again become an issue until after Pearl Harbor. Meanwhile the Armored Force organized its headquarters, as authorized by the directive of 3 April, and initiated studies looking toward an extensive reconstruction of the armored divisions to increase flexibility of striking power. This reconstruction became effective 1 March 1942. On both matters the plans were produced at Fort Knox and accepted by the War Department with the concurrence of GHQ.[26]

Two developments before Pearl Harbor tended to limit the self-sufficiency of the Armored Force. By the first its replacement training center lost the function, temporarily granted in the preceding November, of training enlisted men of various arms and services. Henceforth, with its own replacement center confined to the training of tank and headquarters personnel, the Armored Force was to receive infantry, signal, medical, and other replacements from centers conducted by their respective branches. Specialization for armored operations was restricted. This action, in which GHQ had played no part, came as a result of a query raised by General Marshall.[27]

In the other development GHQ, as the agency directing the field operations of large units, was directly concerned. The Armored Force, in planning the participation of its tactical units in the summer and fall maneuvers, asked for the control during the maneuver period of two quartermaster gasoline companies of a special highly mobile type, and of one heavy ponton engineer battalion equipped to build bridges that could carry tanks. It was argued that an armored corps or division, in executing one of its characteristic deep penetrations or wide flanking movements, would outrun the supply facilities of higher headquarters and must therefore have its own means of bridge building and refueling. But, of the units asked for, few existed, and these few might be needed for various missions. Consequently GHQ decided that the units concerned should be attached to army or army corps headquarters, which could make them available to armored or other elements as changing conditions might

---

[26] For the concurrences of GHQ and related papers, see 320.3/11 and /25.

[27] (1) Memo OCS 21149–35 of GCM[arshall] for ACofS G–3 WD, 14 Apr 41, sub not given. AGO Records, 320.2 (6–5–40) (3) Sec 1A (Armd F). (2) Memos G–3/6541–Gen 647 for CofS USA, 16 Apr 41 and 9 Jun 41, sub: Functions of Armd F RTC, Ft Knox, Ky. AGO Records, 320.2 (6–5–40) (3) Sec 6, (Repl Cen). (3) WD ltrs, both to CofArmd F, AG 320.2 (8–21–41) MT–C, 26 Aug 41, sub: Function of AFRTC Ft Knox, Ky, and AG 320.2 (9–12–41) MT–C, 19 Sep 41, sub: Tng of Armd F Repls. AGO Records, 320.2 (6–5–40) (3) Sec 6, (Repl Cen).

require. The principle of armored self-sufficiency was sacrificed to the principle of economy of force under centralized command.[28] Still General McNair foresaw trouble in the employment of armored forces if higher commanders were not schooled in their use. When General Devers became Chief of the Armored Force in August 1941, General McNair promised his help in getting Armored Force doctrine understood in the higher ranks of the field forces. At the same time he reaffirmed his disinclination to discuss Armored Force policies, declaring that such policies "are out of our line." [29]

The declaration of war raised again the question of the over-all composition of the Armored Force. The rapid expansion of the Army now proposed required a decision on the proportional increase of armored divisions. GHQ was called on to make a recommendation.[30] After reviewing the experience of the 1941 maneuvers General McNair recommended a 20-percent proportion of armored to infantry divisions. According to the plans then under consideration, this meant an increase in authorized strength from six to twenty armored divisions by the end of 1943.[31]

On the value of constituting new armored corps, varying conclusions were drawn from the maneuvers. The Armored Force, believing that armored divisions required higher headquarters specially prepared in armored work, requested that at least two new armored corps be established.[32] General Marshall, on the other hand, was understood to desire a system by which army and army corps commanders could be trained in the handling of armored divisions. General McNair suggested a solution between these two views. He saw the need for only one new armored corps, and G–3, of the War Department, acting on his recommendation, authorized the II Armored Corps on Christmas Day, 1941.[33] To implement what he believed to be General Marshall's policy and "to

---

[28] (1) Ltr of CG Armd F to CofS GHQ, 12 Apr 41, sub: Allocation of Gasoline Companies and Engineer Troops to Armd F during 1941 Maneuvers. 353/42 (Armd F). (2) Ltr of CofS GHQ to CG Armd F, 26 Apr 41, sub: Function of AFRTC at Ft Knox, Ky. Located as in footnote 27 (2).

[29] Personal ltr of Gen McNair to Gen Devers, 15 Aug 41. 353/197 (Armd F).

[30] Memo (S) of Col E. N. Harmon, CofS Armd F for Gen McNair, 23 Dec 41, sub not given. 320.2/58 (Gen Str) (S).

[31] Memo (S) of Gen McNair for Gen Moore, DCofS USA, 23 Dec 41, sub: Command Set-up of Armd Units. 320.2/58 (S).

[32] Armd F memo (C) for CofS USA, 12 Dec 41. G–3/41665 (C) Sec 4.

[33] (1) Memo (C) of ACofS G–3 WD for TAG, 25 Dec 41, sub: Activation of Headquarters & Headquarters Company, II Armd Corps. G–3/41665 (C) Sec 6. (2) WD ltr AG 320.2 (12–17–41) MR–M–C to CofArmd F, 14 Jan 42, sub as above. AGO Records, 320.2 (6–5–40) (3) Sec 1B.

obtain experience and new ideas as to both organization and employment of armored units," General McNair recommended an assortment of command arrangements. He proposed that the I and II Armored Corps and the III and VI Army Corps, all under separate higher commands, should each operate with a different mixture of infantry, armored, and motorized divisions.[34] For a time he doubted the need of even one armored corps, since the only trained armored divisions, the 1st and 2d, were already earmarked to take part in different overseas missions.[35] An important use was soon found, however, for the I Armored Corps in the establishment and organization of the Desert Training Center.[36]

In its attempt to enlarge the organic composition of an armored corps the Armored Force was even less successful. As a result of experience with the I Armored Corps in the November 1941 maneuvers, General Devers considered the current composition of an armored corps, including only two armored divisions, a signal battalion, and headquarters troops, insufficient. He proposed to add, as organic elements, a motorized infantry division, an armored military police company, an armored engineer battalion, an armored medical regiment, and an armored light maintenance company.[37] Both GHQ and G–3 thought it premature to accept a "type" armored corps, i. e., one with an elaborate permanent organization. Both disapproved of the creation of specialized armored service units, and GHQ believed in addition that infantry divisions should not be organic in armored corps but attached as needed.[38] General McNair noted "a definite tendency to make the armored corps an administrative rather than a tactical unit, as though the armored corps would operate independently of an army."

The combined views of G–3 and GHQ were presented to the Chief of the Armored Force in a War Department letter rejecting General Devers' proposal.[39]

[34] Memo of Gen McNair for CofS USA, 17 Dec 41, sub: Gen Devers' Memorandum of Dec 12. 320.2/39 (Armd F).

[35] Memo (C) of Gen. McNair for ACofS G–3 WD, 22 Jan 42, sub: Proposed Orgn of Armd Corps. 320.2/1 (Armd F) (C).

[36] AGF memo (C) for G–3 WD, 5 Mar 42, sub: Orgn of 1st and 2d Armd Corps. 320.2/3 (Armd F) (C).

[37] Ltr of CG Armd F to TAG, 20 Dec 41, sub: Supporting Elements for Armd Div and Corps. AGO Records, 320.2 (6–5–40) (3) Sec 1B.

[38] (1) Memo of ACofS G–3 WD for CG FF, 28 Jan 42, sub: Orgn of an Armd Corps and Supporting Elements for Armd Divs & Corps. AGO Records, 320.2 (6–5–40) (2) Sec 1B. (2) Memo of Gen McNair for ACofS G–3 WD, 4 Feb 42, sub as above. AGO Records, 320.2 (6–5–40) (2) Sec 1B.

[39] WD ltr AG 320.2 (12–30–42) MR–C to CofArmd F, 14 Feb 42, sub as in footnote 38 (1). AGO Records, 320.2 (6–5–40) (2) Sec 1B.

The following reasons were given:

2. . . . The War Department view is influenced by considerations which affect the Army as a whole and by appreciation of estimated needs for the next eighteen months. It is believed that armored corps will usually be employed as part of an army and will have available the reinforcing elements of such command. Simplicity and standardization of these elements is greatly desired, and the urge to create special armored units should be resisted unless no satisfactory substitute can be made available.

3. It is believed unnecessary to assign motorized divisions organically to armored corps, as attachment at appropriate times should serve the purpose economically.

4. It is thought that at this time the organic set-up for an armored corps should be a trim tactical organization, comprising a small headquarters with a minimum of corps troops and a minimum of administrative activity.

5. If and when plans call for the independent operation of armored corps, there would then be no question as to setting up appropriate reinforcements. This, however, is not regarded as an immediate problem.

6. It is considered satisfactory procedure, therefore, to attach the standard type motorized, Engineer, Military Police, Medical and light maintenance units to armored corps when needed.

Meanwhile the Armored Force, somewhat inadvertently, stirred up the old issue of an armored army. It submitted proposed Tables of Organization for the enlargement of Armored Force headquarters. Five supporting charts were included, showing the functions of each general staff section and of the Adjutant General.[40] The functions of G–1 were stated to include the responsibility for casualty reports, prisoner of war reports, relations with civilian government in the theater of operations, graves registration, burials, and other matters unmistakably suggesting combat. The charts for G–2 and G–3 showed fewer such indications and those for G–4 and the Adjutant General none at all. Apparently the work had been imperfectly coordinated. G–3 of the War Department took alarm, suspecting that the Armored Force had ambitions to move bodily into theaters of operations as a tactical command, and requested the comments of GHQ. GHQ replied that the Armored Force was indeed understood to be a Zone of Interior establishment only and that no armored units larger than the corps would be required in the foreseeable future, but that the proposed Tables of Organization in themselves seemed reasonable in the strength requested.[41] A demand by G–3 that the Armored Force revise its tables was stopped by action

[40] Five charts, filed in "Bulky Package," AGO Records, 320.2 (10–30–41) (2) Sec 12.

[41] (1) Memo of ACofS G–3 WD for CG FF, 17 Jan 42, sub: Table of Orgn, Hq Armd F. 320.3/55. (2) Memo of Gen McNair for ACofS G–3 WD, 23 Jan 42, sub as above. 320.3/55.

of General Bryden, and the new Tables of Organization were published in their original form. They gave the Armored Force a headquarters comparable in size to those of the field armies or the Air Force Combat Command.[42]

By the time of the dissolution of GHQ, the net effect of War Department policy had been to check the acquisition by the Armored Force of the degree of independence achieved by the Army Air Forces. The over-all unity of the Army was broken as little as possible by special treatment accorded the Armored Force. Armored divisions or armored corps were to be placed under the higher control of commanders of combined arms. Tanks were to be supported largely by standard units rather than by specialized armored units of engineers, ordnance, and other branches of the Army. In the interest of flexibility, economy, and centralization of command, the principle of standard interchangeable parts was carried as far as was practicable. The Armored Force itself contributed to the application of this principle by reorganizing the GHQ tank battalions to make them identical, and hence interchangeable, with the tank battalions found in armored divisions. The Armored Force also pioneered in experimenting with tactical group headquarters, a necessary corollary to the principle of interchangeable battalions.[43] The War Department decided that, in dealing with armored matters, the organic elements of a corps should be held to a minimum and the corps made adaptable to contingencies through attachment of troops as needed. This principle, like the principle of interchangeable standard parts was to assume greater importance in the U. S. Army as the war proceeded.[44]

The failure of the Armored Force to follow the path of the Air Corps, to which at first it compared itself, might possibly be ascribed to the fact that in the year and a half after June 1940 more effective defense was found against tanks than against aircraft. Moreover, it was generally agreed by all concerned that tank action, to be successful, required close coordination with other arms. These developments may also explain the changes observable in the attitude at GHQ, which was less inclined to favor armored army and corps commands at the end of 1941 than at the beginning of that year.

[42] (1) Memo of ACofS G–3 WD for TAG, 26 Jan 42, sub: Proposed Orgn for Hq Armd F. Marked "not used." G–3/42117. (2) Memo of ACofS G–3 WD for TAG, 3 Feb 42, sub as above. G–3/42117. (3) T/O 17–200–1, 3 Feb 42.

[43] Memo of CG Armd F for ACofS G–3 WD, 22 Jan 42, sub: Orgn for New GHQ Tk Bns. AGO Records, 320.2 (6–5–40) (3) Sec 1B.

[44] See below, "Reorganization of Ground Troops for Combat."

IV. GHQ and Tank Destroyer Elements

In the summer of 1940 a most urgent problem was presented by the demonstration in Europe of the offensive capabilities of the tank. The shockingly sudden collapse of France had been brought about by fast-moving German armored divisions used in conjunction with dive bombers and infantry. Even in some military circles the air-tank team was considered invincible, and many Army officers, working independently, turned their attention to the problem of stopping the armored force attack. Consideration had been given before 1940 to antitank tactics and equipment, but after the disaster in Europe this field of military study became widely active. In the development of initial doctrine, organization, and training of tank destroyer elements GHQ was to play an important part.

The subject bristled with disputed questions. Could tanks best be stopped by guns or by other tanks? Assuming that antitank guns were extensively developed, how much of the strength of the Army should be used for this purpose? How heavy a caliber should be adopted in view of the concurrent need of mobility? Should mobile antitank guns be towed or self-propelled? Should they be regarded as weapons to be used by the several arms, or organized and administered as if constituting a new arm? In battle, should they await the appearance of enemy tanks or aggressively search out and locate enemy tanks? Should they maneuver freely during the fire fight or should they fire only from previously selected concealed positions?

Combat experience of United States forces in later years helped to clarify some of these questions, but preparedness required that decisions be made before combat. On all questions concerning antitank artillery many shades of opinion could be found at all times. In general there were two schools: those who believed in intensive tank destroyer development and those who were skeptical of such development. Both schools could eventually point to ways in which their anticipations had proved correct and those of their opponents mistaken. In such an atmosphere of controversy there was a tendency for all concerned to think that they had been right all the time—to feel that what they believed in 1943 or 1945 was what they had believed in 1940 or 1941.

Views at GHQ on Antitank Measures

General McNair was one of the most aggressive advocates of the movement to develop tank destroyers. Though the tank destroyers developed did not turn out as at first expected, the primary contention of their proponents, that tanks could be stopped by guns, was fully confirmed by experience. The tank terror of 1940 was overcome. Some of the views which General McNair held in 1940, 1941, and 1942 required modification when the destroyers had been used in battle. Through 1942 he urged an expansion of the tank destroyer program which by 1943 was generally regarded as excessive. In his desire to overcome a defensive psychology he stated his beliefs in unqualified terms which may have contributed, during the period extending through 1942, to an employment of tank destroyers which he himself believed to require correction in 1943. Then the doctrine was promulgated that, while tank destroyers must be aggressive in reconnaissance and selection of concealed positions, they must not "chase" tanks or maneuver aggressively within range of enemy armor.[1]

General McNair came to GHQ in August 1940 with his views on antitank measures well developed. He had experimented with antitank organization in 1937 at San Antonio. He had studied the problem in 1940 while Commandant of the Command and General Staff School. He refused to believe that tanks could be beaten only by other tanks. He had faith in the antitank mine and the antitank gun. He declared in a visit to the War Department General Staff on 29 June 1940 that the big problem before the War Department was to find means of stopping armored divisions and that for this purpose flat trajectory guns, with a range of at least 1,500 yards and of heavier caliber than either the 37-mm. or the 75-mm. then in use, would be required.[2]

General McNair continued to make these views known after arriving at GHQ. Called upon in August 1940 to comment on a list of subjects proposed for staff study in the War Department, he recommended the further develop-

---

[1] For a discussion of this development, see "Organization and Training of New Ground Combat Elements" in this volume.

[2] (1) Memo (C) G-3/41665 I for ACofS G-3 WD, 29 Jun 40, sub: Gen McNair's Visit. (2) "With reference to antitank defense, it has been a matter of keen interest to me for over ten years, but it took the present European War to bring action." Ltr of Gen McNair to Col A. U. Faulkner, 7 Aug 40. McNair Correspondence.

ment of antitank guns. He declined to concur in a subsequent War Department study of antitank measures on the ground that it was grossly inadequate. In remarks on a third War Department proposal he protested that only passive antitank defense was provided, except in the armored divisions, and expressed his preference for antitank "groups" of three battalions, rather than single antitank battalions, "in order to afford a better control of large numbers of guns concentrated at a threatened point." The same ideas were repeated in his comments on the maneuvers of August, 1940: "There were few if any instances of the employment of antitank guns other than passively. Such methods are effective only against mechanized reconnaissance vehicles. A mechanized attack invariably will be concentrated, calling for a concentration of antitank weapons. The smaller the number of antitank guns the greater is the need of holding them as a mobile reserve, ready instantly to rush to the point of mechanized attack." On 23 September the War Department in Training Circular No. 3, superseding instructions dating from March 1938, directed that a minimum of antitank guns should be placed in fixed initial positions and a maximum held as a mobile reserve.[3] This was the first break in a doctrine of passive defense but was still defensive in character and scope.

Delay in Preparing Antitank Measures

The effort to incorporate the new doctrine in training was attended with difficulties. When in the alarm over events in Europe antiaircraft artillery regiments were directed on 16 August 1940 to practice antitank fire,[4] few antitank guns existed in divisional artillery. Most antitank weapons were at this time organized in antitank companies in infantry regiments. Such decentralization ran contrary to the principles favored by GHQ.

On the matter of antitank mines delays were also unavoidable. In February 1941 the War Department initiated a study looking toward modifications in

---

[3] (1) Memo of Gen McNair for Col Ward, 5 Sep 40, sub: Studies by General Staff Divs. 353/36. (2) Memo G–3/43107 for CofS USA, 18 Nov 40, sub: Antitank (AT) Defense, and memo of Gen McNair for DCofS USA, 30 Dec 40, sub as above. 322.091/3 (Armd F). (3) Ltr of Gen McNair to Maj Campbell, 4 Sep 40, sub not given. 320.2/20 (GHQ Armies and Corps). (4) Par 33 of draft of Gen McNair submitted to Gen Marshall for ltr to Army comdrs, sub: Comments on Army Maneuvers, with pencilled "LJM 9/5." 354.2/8. Par 34 of final copy of same, dated 7 Jan 41. 353/14 (Tng Dirs). (5) Tng Cir 3, WD, 23 Sep 40, sub: Antimechanized Defense.

[4] WD ltr AG 353 (8–14–40) M–C to CGs all Corps Areas and Depts and CofCA, 16 Aug 40, sub: Tng of AAA Regts in Antimechanized Defense. AGO Records.

published doctrine. GHQ was requested to assemble data from experience in the field and to prepare a report, which, however, was not completed until January 1942, when evidence was at hand from the large fall maneuvers.[5]

Meanwhile, little progress was made. In April 1941, so far as was known at GHQ, of all the armies and corps only the VI Corps and the Armored Force had issued any instructions on antitank defense.[6] "It is beyond belief," wrote General McNair on 12 April 1941, "that so little could be done on the question, in view of all that has happened and is happening abroad. I for one have missed no opportunity to hammer for something real in the way of antitank defense, but so far have gotten nowhere. I have no reason now to feel encouraged but can only hope this apathy will not continue indefinitely." [7]

Discussions on this problem were in fact taking place at this time in the War Department General Staff, both in G–2 and in G–3. Brig. Gen. Sherman Miles, G–2, produced a memorandum on 1 March 1941 entitled "Evaluation of Modern Battle Forces," based upon military experience in France and Libya. He affirmed that the air-tank combination, having rendered ineffective the old infantry-artillery combination, had revolutionized warfare as much as the battles of Adrianople and Crécy, and concluded that either the air-tank combination would become the nucleus of the army of the future or the infantry division must develop means to repel tank assaults.[8]

General McNair, asked for his comments, found General Miles' position extreme. He preferred a middle-of-the-road interpretation of European events. This same tendency had been apparent in his directive of 4 January on "Combined Training," in which he prescribed that the full strength of aviation and armored elements should be carefully simulated in all combined exercises, but that exaggeration of the menace should be avoided and the troops not left with a sense that effective defense was impossible. Commenting on General Miles' study, he observed that the Germans had used twenty infantry divisions in France. Rather than revolutionize the infantry division, he proposed the formation of strong air and tank units and the creation of mobile masses of antiaircraft

[5] (1) WD ltr AG 353 (1–25–41) P–C to CofS GHQ, 14 Feb 41, sub: Tactics and Technique for the Use of AT Mines. With supporting documents. 479.1/1. (2) Ltr (C) of CofS GHQ for TAG, 20 Oct 41, sub as above. 353/3 (AT) (C). (3) Ltr of Gen McNair to TAG, 21 Jan 42, sub as above. 479.1/20.

[6] Memo of Lt Col F. J. de Rohan, Inf Sec GHQ for CofS GHQ, 10 Apr 41, sub: Tk Hunting. Incls filed separately. 353/34 (AT).

[7] Personal ltr of Gen McNair to Lt Col R. T. Heard, 12 Apr 41. 470.71/2.

[8] WD memo G–2/2016–1297 of Gen Miles for CofS USA, 1 Mar 41, sub: Evaluation of Modern Battle Forces. 059/1 (Mil Stats).

and antitank guns to cope with the air-tank menace: "The need of a greatly expanded *mobile* force of suitable antitank guns has been pointed out repeatedly, but is not being procured." In further memoranda of 9 May and 1 July 1941 General McNair reiterated his faith in the standard infantry division, once an adequate antitank force, distinct from the infantry, had been created.[9]

The action initiated by G–3 of the War Department led to a series of conferences on the antitank question. In the first, occurring on 15 April 1941, the War Plans Division of the War Department General Staff, GHQ, and the Chiefs of Infantry, Cavalry, Field Artillery, Coast Artillery, and the Armored Force were represented.[10] No general conclusions on antitank doctrine could be reached, though all present expressed approval of offensive tactics. Disagreement appeared over the organization and command of antitank units. In general, the chief of each arm favored the placing of antitank means in units of his arm. It was finally decided to retain the antitank companies in infantry regiments—GHQ alone not concurring. Divisional antitank battalions were to be created and antitank 37's to be transferred from the Field Artillery—the Chief of Field Artillery disapproving. A central reserve of GHQ antitank battalions was formed, though in smaller numbers than desired by GHQ. The Chiefs of Infantry and of Cavalry both offered reasons why the responsibility for developing antitank defense should be entrusted to his branch. On branch responsibility no conclusion was reached, nor was provision made for establishing an antitank force distinct from the older branches. The GHQ representative at the conference concluded his report to General McNair in these words: "It is therefore recommended that GHQ attempt to get the War Department promptly to place the development of antitank defense under the commander of a tentative Antitank Force set up at a center reasonably close to the station of the First or Second Armored Division." [11]

A second antitank conference on 10 May was attended only by representatives of the War Department General Staff and by Colonel Kingman of GHQ. The discussion turned chiefly on material, G–3 favoring self-propelled mounts for antitank guns against the fears of GHQ that guns so mounted might prove

[9] (1) Memo of Gen McNair for CofS USA, 12 Mar 41, sub as in footnote 8 above. With supporting documents. 059/1 (Mil Stats). (2) Par 10, ltr of Gen McNair to Army Comdrs, 4 Jan 41, sub: Combined Tng. 353/13 (Tng Dirs).

[10] For steno record of meeting 15 April see Tab B to memo G–3/43107 for CofS USA, 28 May 41, sub: Defense against Armd Fs. AGO Records, 320.2 (6–5–40) Sec 1A (Orgn and Expansion of the Armd F).

[11] Memo of Lt Col A. F. Kingman for CofS GHQ, 17 Apr 41, sub: WD Conference on AT Defense, 15 Apr 41. 337/11.

inaccurate in fire. General McNair's representative reported that he had brought up the question of organization and continued: [12]

> On the basis of the agreement arrived at in the meeting of April 15 that antitank weapons should be withdrawn from the Field Artillery and placed in divisions and higher antitank units, I suggested that this be done at once and that provisional antitank organizations be formed, including division battalions as well as units of higher echelons, so as actually to test your scheme of mobile antitank defense in the coming maneuvers. I pointed out that despite their summary dismissal of GHQ's recommendations for the setting up of an antitank center and the centralization under one headquarters of antitank development, and their favoring of tank-chaser units, that there are no such units in existence and that the coming maneuvers afford an opportunity to test GHQ's recommendations. The suggestion apparently fell on fertile ground . . . .

Creation of the Planning Branch, G–3, WDGS

At this point, in mid-May 1941, the influence of General Marshall made itself felt. In a talk at GHQ on 13 May he observed that there had been much opposition in the War Department to the establishment of GHQ in the preceding summer and that there had been practically a solid front against the adoption of new ideas. He went on to say that GHQ should "retain an open mind with reference to innovations." On the next day, 14 May, he directed G–3 of the War Department to take immediate action on antitank measures and to create a Planning Branch whose sole function would be to devise new methods of warfare. On 15 May such a Planning Branch was established under Lt. Col. Andrew D. Bruce, an active sponsor of antitank development and soon to be the first commander of a new Tank Destroyer Center.[13]

Creation of the Provisional Antitank Battalions

A third conference, held in Colonel Bruce's office on 26 May with GHQ represented, adopted conclusions generally in accord with the stand taken by GHQ. To win concurrence from the Chief of Infantry, antitank companies were

---

[12] Memo of Lt Col A. F. Kingman for CofS GHQ, 10 May 41, sub: Rpt on Meeting Called by Gen Bryden on Branch Responsibility for AT Defense. 337/17. On GHQ preference for towed guns, see also GHQ 1st ind to G–3 WD, 16 Jan 41, on GHQ ltr, Col Kingman to CofS GHQ, 13 Jan 41, sub: Mechanized Antitank Orgn. 322.091/5 (Armd F).

[13] (1) "Notes on Gen Marshall's Talk to GHQ, 9:30 A. M. 13 May." 337/2 (C). (2) Memo OCS 21103–6 for ACofS G–3 WD, 14 May 41, sub: Defense against Armd Fs. 353/15 (AT, Tab A). (3) Memo G–3/311 of Ex Off G–3 WD, 15 May 41, sub: Planning Branch. 337/17.

left with the infantry regiments, against the policy preferred both by GHQ and by Colonel Bruce, but in each divisional and higher headquarters an antitank officer was to be appointed. The new provisional antitank battalions were to be organized at once. Those for divisions would take their weapons from divisional artillery; those for GHQ reserve and for some divisions would obtain theirs from corps and GHQ field artillery brigades. To facilitate this decision, a recommendation on the subject from the Chief of Field Artillery was removed from discussion by order from the Chief of Staff of the War Department. It was decided also to establish before the end of 1941 a "large antitank unit" along the line of the antitank force long recommended by GHQ.[14]

Though the provisional antitank battalions were activated by War Department letter on 24 June 1941, they were not tested until the maneuvers in September. The antitank assistant G–3's were appointed.[15] The Tank Destroyer Center was not set up until 1 December.

The Antitank Conference of July 1941

In June 1941 advocates of a strong and rapid development of antitank units found encouragement in two events which made that month a turning point in the development of antitank preparations. The vulnerability of tanks was demonstrated by the Germans, who managed to destroy over 200 British tanks on the Egyptian–Libyan frontier. G–2 of the War Department found this to be "one of the first cases in this war when a tank attack has been definitely stopped." Antiaircraft and other artillery had been used by the Germans most effectively against tanks, and orders went out immediately to units of this type in the U. S. Army to intensify their antitank training. General McNair, agreeing that all possible types of cannon should be employed against tanks, warned that their use should not delay the development of a series of special antitank guns.[16]

[14] Memo of Lt Col A. F. Kingman for CofS GHQ, 26 May 41, sub: G–3 Planning Br Conference on AT Defense, 26 May. 337/17.

[15] WD ltr AG 320.2 (6–19–41) MR–M–C to CGs all Armies, 24 Jun 41, sub: Orgn of Provisional Div and GHQ AT Bns for Use in Current Maneuvers. AGO Records.

[16] (1) Memo (C) G–2/2016–1348 for CofS USA, 26 Jun 41, sub: Use of AAA Against Tks. 353/1 (AT)(C). (2) Memo of GCM[arshall] for Gen McNair, 25 Jun 41, sub not given. 353/12 (AT). (3) Ltr of CofS GHQ to CGs All Armies and Def Comds, 17 Jul 41, sub: Tng of Mobile CA Units in Antimechanized Defense and Firing on Landing Boats. 353/22 (AT). (4) Memo (C) of Gen McNair for CofS USA, 10 Jul 41, sub: Use of AAA Against Tks. 353/1 (AT) (C).

The second source of encouragement was found in the June maneuvers of the Second Army in Tennessee. General McNair found the antitank action, while still too passive, more effectively handled than he had anticipated and confirmatory of his own views on antitank organization and tactics. From the maneuvers he wrote: "It can be expected that the location of hostile armored elements will be known practically constantly, thus permitting antitank opposition to be moved correspondingly, and massed at the proper point. This is the question which has raised doubt in the minds of those who incline toward dissipating our antitank means by organic assignment to units all over the Army." [17]

To prepare for the fall maneuvers and to promote education in antitank measures, the recently appointed antitank officers of divisions and higher units were assembled in a great antitank conference called by G–3 of the War Department and held at the Army War College from 14 to 17 July 1941. A feeling of confidence and enthusiasm prevailed. Colonel Bruce and others active in antitank planning explained the current program. Brig. Gen. Harry L. Twaddle, G–3, who opened the meeting, and General McNair, who made the closing remarks, agreed that smashing the tank was the most urgent problem before the Army, that progress toward its solution was being made, and that the main task of the antitank officers on returning to their units must be to overcome the excessive fear of armored attack felt by the troops since the fall of France. [18]

Testing of Antitank Weapons in GHQ-Directed Maneuvers

It was the intention of GHQ to test out, in the GHQ-directed fall maneuvers, its policies of aggressive use and centralized control of antitank guns. The umpire manual had been carefully revised to give an accurate picture. New rules were prescribed for the laying of dummy mine fields. [19] The antitank officers of field units were informed of developments in the conference just past. The provisional antitank battalions were available. They were to be attached to the Third Army in the September maneuvers for use against the armored elements of the Second. On 8 August 1941 GHQ issued a directive to the commanding general

[17] Personal ltr of Gen McNair to Col J. A. Consadine, 7 Jul 41. 353/18 (AT).

[18] (1) "Notes on G–3 Antitank Conference, Jul 14–20, 1941, War College, Washington, D. C." Separately filed in 353/98 (AT). (2) Memos of Lt Col A. F. Kingman for CofS GHQ, 16, 17, 18, 22 Jul 41, sub: WD AT Conference. 334.8/9.

[19] Ltr of CofS GHQ to CGs All Armies and CofArmd F, 6 Aug 41, sub: Use of Dummy AT Mines in Maneuvers. 479.1/10.

of the Third Army on the tactical employment of antitank battalions.[20] He was instructed to organize nine battalions into three "groups" of three battalions each and to have in addition a headquarters company, ground and air reconnaissance elements, and intelligence, signal, engineer, and infantry units, all fully motorized. Both offensive and defensive tactics were outlined, with preference expressed for a speedy and aggressive action to search out and attack opposing tanks before they had assumed formation. The ideas championed by General McNair were finally to be tried, though the War Department Training Directive for 1941-42 issued at this time still reflected a defensive conception of antitank operations.[21]

After the September maneuvers General McNair expressed satisfaction with the way in which the antitank units had been handled, pointing only to a persisting tendency to commit them to positions prematurely and to dissipate them. The provisional battalions with their group organization were continued in being and used in the Carolina maneuvers in November.[22] On this occasion, as noted above, 983 tanks were ruled put out of action—91 percent by guns—and the 1st Armored Division was ruled by the umpires to have been destroyed.

Progressive Acceptance of Principles Favored at GHQ

The elaboration of long-range plans on the organization of antitank units progressed simultaneously with these tests in the field, and the principles favored by GHQ found increasing acceptance. In answer to General Marshall's request of 14 May, G-3 of the War Department produced a detailed memorandum on 18 August 1941. It was designed for an army of 55 divisions, now envisaged by the War Department, and proposed a ratio of 4 antitank battalions per division: 55, or 1 each, for the divisions, 55 for armies and corps, and 110 for GHQ. General Marshall had stipulated in May that the question of a new branch or arm should not be raised. The old arms—Infantry, Field Artillery, etc.— were therefore given by G-3 responsibility for creating the new antitank bat-

---

[20] Ltr of CofS GHQ to CG Third Army, 8 Aug 41, sub: GHQ AT Units in GHQ-Directed Maneuvers. 353/30 (Tng Dirs).

[21] WD ltr AG 353 (6-16-41) MT M-C to CofS GHQ, CGs, etc, 19 Aug 41, sub: WD Tng Dir, 1941-42. AGO Records. Par 8 g: "While the offensive spirit and offensive tactics are fundamental doctrine in American training, antiaircraft and antimechanized defense must receive constant special attention in view of the experiences of the present war."

[22] (1) Ltr of Gen McNair to CG Third Army, 10 Oct 41, sub: Comments on Second vs Third Army Maneuvers. 353/595 (Third Army). (2) Ltr of Director Hq GHQ to CG Third Army, 25 Sep 41, sub: GHQ Provisional AT Gps. 353/15 (AT). (3) WD ltr AG 320.2 (9-29-41) MR-M-C to CGs all Armies, 2 Oct 41, sub: Orgn of Provisional Div and GHQ AT Bns for Use in Current Maneuvers. 353/15 (AT).

talions, and the antitank center, on whose establishment all were agreed, was to be put under the authority of the Chief of the Armored Force.[23]

On 2 September General McNair, praising the boldness of the proposals, found them in keeping with the urgency of the situation but withheld his concurrence. He preferred a separate antitank force, to include all antitank guns except those in infantry regiments. He objected to the subordination of the antitank force to the Armored Force, thinking the two should be rivals. He objected to the organic inclusion of antitank battalions in divisions, corps, and armies, believing that they should be massed for attachment when and where needed. He considered 220 antitank battalions more than were necessary for an Army of 55 divisions, and on the question of self-propelled versus towed guns he called for further investigation, recommending that whichever type was found to be better should be adopted for all antitank battalions. G–1 and G–4 of the War Department Staff concurred in his comments.[24]

General McNair's recommendations were embodied, step by step, in the decisions reached by the War Department, except for his view on the total number of battalions. This exception, however, was not of immediate practical importance since the production rate of equipment made possible the training of only 63 battalions in the near future.

The Office of the Chief of Staff acted on the G–3 memorandum on 8 October. The provisions for dividing antitank responsibility among chiefs of branches were rescinded. The antitank center, made independent of the Armored Force, was to be established under War Department control. This much was consistent with the recommendations of GHQ. But the action of 8 October provided for organic antitank battalions in divisions, corps, and armies and for the continued association of battalions already provisionally organized with the Infantry, Field Artillery, or other arm in which they originated.[25]

The Tank Destroyer Center and the Tank Destroyer Battalions

A War Department letter of 27 November 1941 officially ordered the activation on or about 1 December of a Tank Destroyer Tactical and Firing Center at

---

[23] WD memo G–3/43107 for CofS USA, 18 Aug 41, sub: Orgn of AT Units in the Army. 353/15 (AT).

[24] Tab E, memo of Gen McNair for ACofS G–3 WD, 2 Sep 41, sub: Orgn of AT Units in the Army. 353/15 (AT). Tabs F and G give the concurrences of G–1 and G–4.

[25] WD memo OCS 21103–20 for ACofS G–3 WD, 8 Oct 41, sub: Orgn of AT Units in the Army. 353/15 (AT).

Fort Meade, Md. It was to include a Tank Destroyer Board. Colonel Bruce of the Planning Branch of G–3 was to command the new center. The letter of 27 November made no provision for antitank battalions in divisions, corps, or armies. The fifty-three antitank battalions whose immediate activation was ordered were all to be under GHQ, but they might be attached to lower echelons for training.[26]

A War Department order of 3 December reduced the connections still existing between antitank battalions and the several arms. "Antitank battalions" were redesignated "tank destroyer battalions," the old term savoring too much of defensive tactics. All tank destroyer battalions, it was repeated, were allotted to GHQ. Antitank units in cavalry divisions and in field artillery battalions and regiments in the continental United States were to be inactivated. Infantry anti-tank battalions were to lose the name "infantry," be renumbered, and be redesignated as "tank destroyer battalions." The net effect was to create a new homogeneous tank destroyer force, composed of battalions only nominally connected with the older arms. Of these battalions only the 893d was complete from the first, with full reconnaissance and other supporting elements. It was assigned on 30 January as a school unit to the Tank Destroyer Tactical and Firing Center.[27]

The higher organization of the tank destroyer battalions remained to be settled. As early as August 1940 General McNair had wished the battalions to be combined into groups, which had been provisionally organized for the fall maneuvers of 1941. By the end of 1941, however, the component battalions, not the groups, had been shifted from a provisional to a permanent basis. On 24 January 1942 the commanding general of the Western Defense Command again raised the question by pointing out that all tank destroyer battalions at the moment were separate GHQ units. He recommended that one light battalion be organically included in each infantry division and that a tank destroyer group headquarters be assigned to each army corps to which two or more heavy battalions were attached. The reply of the War Department followed the recommendations of GHQ. No tank destroyer battalions were to be organically included in divisions. Group headquarters were to be organized, but on the

---

[26] WD ltr AG 320.2 (11–5–41) MR–M–C to CO TD Tactical and Firing Center, 27 Nov 41, sub: Orgn of TD Tactical and Firing Center. 320.2/736. Supporting documents in 680.1/31.

[27] (1) WD ltr AG 320.2 (11–17–41) MR–M–C to CGs All Armies and Corps Areas and CofArmd F, 3 Dec 41, sub: Orgn of TD Bns. 320.2/736. (2) WD ltr AG 320.2 (1–24–42) MR–M–C to CGs All Armies and Corps Areas and CofArmd F, 30 Jan 42, sub: Orgn of TD Bns. 320.2/736.

insistence of General Clark they were to remain directly under GHQ, not assigned to army corps.[28]

Thus antitank policies favored at GHQ at the time of its establishment were, on the eve of its dissolution, the accepted policies of the War Department. These policies called for a separate antitank force, distinct from the several arms, with tank destroyers removed from organic assignment to divisions, corps, and armies and concentrated under the commanding general of the field forces in order to allow quick massing of mobile antitank power, preferably for offensive action. In 1942 the tank destroyer establishment underwent a tremendous expansion under the guidance of the Army Ground Forces.[29] Some of the principles agreed upon in March 1942 had to be revised in the light of combat experience, but the insistence of GHQ upon a strong antitank force had helped to bring into existence an organization well fitted to meet future demands.

---

[28] (1) Ltr of CG WDC to CG FF, 24 Jan 42, sub: Control of TD Bns. 320.2/5 (TD Units). (2) 1st, 2nd, and 3d ind on above. (3) GHQ disposition sheet, 9 Feb 42, with Gen Clark's "Memo for G-5," 14 Feb 42, on reverse of page. 320.2/5 (TD).

[29] For this development see AGF Historical Section, The Tank Destroyer History, and "Organization and Training of New Ground Combat Elements," in this volume.

V. The Relation of GHQ to Amphibious Training

Provision for amphibious training of Army ground units antedated the activation of GHQ on 26 July 1940. On 26 June 1940 the 1st and 3d Divisions were directed to practice landing operations.[1] This order followed shortly upon the German occupation of western Europe, which closed all friendly ports on the European Continent and threatened to bring the French West Indies and other French possessions in the Western Hemisphere under Axis control. In October 1940 the War Department General Staff initiated the organization of "emergency expeditionary forces"; GHQ concurred on 4 December 1940, and by July 1941 three task forces had been constituted for action in the Caribbean and Newfoundland.

Though the need of amphibious training was recognized, training in this form of combat remained limited in scope for a year after June 1940. Sufficient special equipment was not available. Moreover, the training policies of GHQ prescribed that special training, such as amphibious, should not seriously interrupt the development of general soldierly fitness. Of the three task forces provided for after October 1940, only Task Force 1, designed for a mission in the Caribbean, required the occupation of a hostile shore against probable opposition. For this task the 1st Division was selected in November 1940. It was chosen because it had received more amphibious training up to that time than any other division. Even its training had not been extensive, reaching the maneuver stage only in February 1941. At that time only 10 percent of the personnel of the division took part in the amphibious maneuver at Culebra, and in June 1941 only 20 percent of the divisional personnel engaged in a second amphibious maneuver.[2]

---

[1] (1) WD ltr (C) AG 353 (6–17–40) M–C to CG First Army, 26 Jun 40, sub: Tng of 1st and 3d Divs in Landing Operations. 353/4 (C). (2) Similar ltr (C) to CG Fourth Army. 353/4 (S). (3) WD memo (S) WPD 4161–3 for CofS USA, 12 Nov 40, sub: Emergency Expeditionary Forces. With related documents. 381/4 (S).

[2] (1) Personal ltr (C) of Gen McNair to Gen Thompson, CG 3d Div, 10 Mar 41. 353/1 (C). (2) Ltr (S) of CG 1st Div to CG AFAF, 28 Jan 42, sub: Rpt on January Amph Exercise. 353/24 (AFAF) (S).

In the summer of 1941 the amphibious training program was expanded. Some of the War Department's stategic plans included amphibious operations, and the War Department Training Directive for 1941–42, compiled in June 1941, specified the preparation of task forces as one of the objectives of the coming year. The Joint Army-Navy Board issued training plans for both coasts. The Carib Plan of 21 June 1941 organized the 1st Division and the 1st Marine Division into a 1st Joint Training Force, which subsequently developed into the Amphibious Force, Atlantic Fleet. The Pearl Plan of 9 September 1941 designated the 3d Division and the 2d Marine Division as the Second Joint Training Force, subsequently known as the Amphibious Force, Pacific Fleet. Each Joint Training Force—a term by which only the landing force was meant—was put under command of a Marine general, and in each case command of the whole enterprise rested with the Navy.[3]

The Role of GHQ

The role of GHQ in amphibious training was at first very ill-defined. The Carib Plan made no mention of GHQ, and the 1st Joint Training Force began operations late in June 1941 before the staff at GHQ had received definite instructions regarding its responsibilities in the matter. The War Department directive of 3 July, enlarging the functions of GHQ, made no specific reference to amphibious training, though it indicated that the command of certain task forces would be assigned to GHQ. A War Department directive of 8 July, citing the directive of 3 July, was the first step in this direction. It instructed General McNair "to take over, at once, the functions of GHQ in connection with the Carib training operation." The nature of these functions was not made clear. The directive merely observed that, with "all responsibility for training" resting with the Navy, the Army's responsibility was "principally to make available, at the proper time and place, the Army units involved, and the use of Army facilities as called for." How these Army responsibilities were to be divided between the GHQ staff and the War Department staff was not stated.[4]

Correspondence between GHQ and War Plans Division relieved some of the uncertainty. On 7 July GHQ, in a memorandum to WPD, requested a clari-

[3] (1) The Carib Plan (C) J. B. 350 (Serial 698), 21 Jun 41, is on file in AWC Records 242–16. (2) Pearl Plan (C) J. B. 350 (Serial 705), 9 Sep 41. 353/1 (AFPF) (C).

[4] (1) WD ltr AG 320.2 (6–19–41) MC–E–M to CofS GHQ, 3 Jul 41, sub: Enlargement of the Functions of GHQ. 320.2/3/34. (2) WD ltr (S) AG 353 (7–5–41) MC–E to CofS GHQ, 8 Jul 41, sub: Responsibility of GHQ for CARIB Tng Opns. 353/6 (Tng Force CARIB) (S).

fication of its relationship with the Navy and made two recommendations: first that WPD confer with GHQ in formulating joint plans with the Navy Department, and second that GHQ be authorized to confer directly with Maj. Gen. Holland M. Smith, U. S. M. C., Commanding General of the First Joint Training Force. WPD on 9 July accepted both recommendations. The first was met by WPD's promise to consult GHQ. The second was not merely accepted, but was broadened in scope. WPD stated that "subordinate planning, and operations in connection with the execution of the basic joint directive and subordinate plans will be a responsibility of GHQ. In this connection, GHQ should deal directly with Navy echelons subordinate to the Chief of Naval Operations." [5]

The principles of administration worked out in connection with the Carib Plan became somewhat more explicit in the preparation of the Pearl Plan. GHQ recommended, and the War Department designated, the 3d Division and supporting units as the Army component of the Second Joint Training Force. [6] The completed plan, issued on 9 September, named GHQ as the agency charged with "the execution of all Army responsibilities under this plan." But "execution" meant in practice only the administration of certain details, for the War Department continued to act without consultation with GHQ, and the Navy Department had charge of training, which was the essence of the operation. [7]

The Amphibious Force, Atlantic Fleet

The first phase of the Carib Operation was executed as planned, but the site of the second phase was changed from Puerto Rico to the New River area, North Carolina. General McNair and eight members of his staff witnessed the landing exercises. They found that the 1st Division, which had practiced amphibious movements for a year, showed considerable proficiency, [8] but on the whole the operation was not considered satisfactory at GHQ. General Malony, Deputy Chief of Staff, in a memorandum for General Marshall dated 29 October 1941, [9]

[5] (1) Memo (S) of CofS GHQ for WPD, 7 Jul 41, sub: Tng for Joint O'seas Opns. 353/7 (Tng Force CARIB) (S). (2) WD memo (S) WPD 4232–33 for CG GHQ, 9 Jul 41, sub as above. 353/7 (S).

[6] Memo (C) of Gen McNair for WPD, 19 Jul 41, sub: Amph Tng for Army and Marine Trs on West Coast. 353/34 (C).

[7] For Pearl Plan see footnote 3 (2).

[8] GHQ memo for DCofS USA, 5 Aug 41, sub: Summary of Activities, GHQ, for Week Ending Aug 5, 1941. 319.1/25 (Wkly Rpts of GHQ Activities).

[9] GHQ memo (S) for CofS USA. 29 Oct 41, sub: Preparation for Amph Opns. 353/2 (AFAF) (8).

listed four major causes of the deficiencies shown: lack of time for preparation, inexperience, lack of planning, and complicated channels of command. He especially emphasized the last, pointing to poor coordination within the Army and among the Army, Navy, and Marine Corps. He enumerated eleven remedial measures already taken and made six further recommendations. To these proposals no definite answers were received.[10]

When during the summer of 1941 the threat of Axis control over the Atlantic increased, additional amphibious assault forces seemed to be needed to forestall potential enemy moves. The Joint Strategic Committee of the War and Navy Departments worked out basic plans for the possible occupation of Atlantic islands by United States forces,[11] and between 18 August and 2 September the staff sections at GHQ developed a corresponding theater of operations plan.[12] The First Joint Training Force, disbanded after the Carib exercise except for the joint staff, was in effect reconstituted as the Amphibious Force, Atlantic Fleet, comprising the 1st Division and the 1st Marine Division with supporting units, and was again put under command of General Smith of the Marine Corps. Unity of command was vested in the Navy.

The selection of Army units to take part in the proposed operation brought to light a division of authority in the War Department. Designation of such units was clearly understood to rest with the General Staff of the War Department, but recommendation of units for designation, i. e., their actual selection from among all units in the Army, was a power exercised by both GHQ and the General Staff. As a result, proposed troop lists for the force down to station hospitals and platoons of bakers passed back and forth, amended and counteramended, between GHQ and the War Department from September on into December.[13]

[10] WD ltr (S) AG 320.2 (11–29–41) MSC–C to CofS GHQ, 19 Dec 41, sub: Preparation for Amph Opns. 353/2 (AFAF) (S). This letter, written in another connection, gives an indirect and casual reply.

[11] WD ltr (S) AG 353 (9–3–41) MC–E to CofS GHQ, 23 Sep 41, sub: Tng of 1st Div and Supporting Army Units for Landing Opns. 353/1 (AFAF) (S).

[12] Memo (S) of Gen McNair for CG FF, 15 Sep 41, sub: Quarterly Rpt of Planning and Opns Activities, GHQ, to include Sept. 10, 1941. 320.2/1 (GHQ) (S).

[13] (1) See footnote 11 above. (2) GHQ memo (S) for ACofS WPD, 9 Oct 41, sub: Units of 1st Div and Supporting Army Units for Landing Opns. (3) WD ltr (S) AG 354.21 (10–7–41) MC–E to CofS GHQ, 29 Oct 41, sub: Joint Exercise in Forced Landings against Opposition. (4) Memo (S) WPD 4232–62 for CofS GHQ, rubber-stamped 29 Nov 41, sub: Amph Tng in New River Area. (5) GHQ distribution sheet (S) attached to preceding with pencilled note signed L[emnitzer] G–3. (6) GHQ ltr (S) to TAG, 1 Dec 41, sub: Gray–2 Force and Joint Exercise in Forced Landings. (7) TAG 1st ind (S), 23 Dec 41, on preceding. (8) Incl 4 (S) to preceding ind. All these documents are in 353/1 and /2 (AFAF) (S).

The training exercise of the force, first planned for December, was post-poned in October until January 1942 since naval commitments elsewhere made impracticable the initial idea of a dress rehearsal in Puerto Rico. With the declaration of war and the appearance of danger from submarines, the landing operations scheduled for the New River area were hastily shifted to Cape Henry. By a last-minute change of command General Smith became director of ma-neuvers instead of commanding general of the operation. Finally, from 12 to 14 January, a little more than half the personnel of the 1st Division carried out a landing maneuver against opposition simulated by the 116th Regimental Combat Team. Three officers from G–5, GHQ, observed the action, in which the GHQ umpire manual was used. The results of the exercises were hardly encouraging. General Smith's director headquarters adjudged all landings unsuccessful.[14]

After the Cape Henry maneuver General Smith requested that the 1st Division, together with the 70th Tank Battalion and the 36th Engineers, con-tinue training at their home station, Fort Devens, according to training direc-tives supplied by the Amphibious Force, Atlantic Fleet. GHQ declined the request for the 1st Division but approved it for the 70th Tank Battalion and the 36th Engineers. Its basic policy toward amphibious training became evident in the directive to these two units, which were ordered to devote two-thirds of their time to the general program outlined in the directive of 31 October 1941, entitled "Post-Maneuver Training," and only one-third to the continuation and development of special amphibious skills.[15]

Two reasons chiefly influenced GHQ in its nonconcurrence in General Smith's request. One was the need for reassembling the 1st Division as a tactical unit. In the past year this division had engaged in five amphibious maneuvers, in each case with only a fraction of its personnel. In view of this fact the divisional commander now strongly recommended a future course of training in which the division could act as a whole. The second reason for not accept-ing General Smith's request was the sudden need of the 1st Division for other duties. GHQ had been called upon to suggest elements of a new force proposed

[14] (1) 1st Div ltr (S) to AFAF, 28 Jan 42, sub: Rpt on January Amph Exercises. 353/24 (AFAF) (S). (2) ETO and First Army ltr (C) to CG FF GHQ, 3 Feb 42, sub: Rpt on Joint Army and Navy Exercises, Cape Henry, Va. 353/28 (AFAF) (C). (3) GHQ memo (C), G–5 for Asst AG GHQ, 13 Jan 42, sub: Obsn of Amph F Exercise, Jan 12. 319.1/2 (Summary of Weekly Activities, GHQ, 1942) (C).

[15] (1) AFAF ltr (C) to CofS GHQ, 26 Jan 42, sub: Tng Dir of 1st Inf Div and Associated Army Units. (2) GHQ 1st ind (C) to preceding, AFAF, 4 Feb 42. (3) FF ltr (C) to 36th Engs, 4 Feb 42, sub: Tng. (4) FF ltr (C) to 70th Tank Bn, 4 Feb 42, sub: Tng. All in 353/27 (AFAF) (C).

for possible operations in Africa, and on its recommendation the assault element of this force was to be supplied by the 1st Division, now the most thoroughly trained of Army divisions in amphibious combat. GHQ suggested that
the place of the 1st Division in further amphibious training be taken by the 9th.
These recommendations were approved by the War Department.[16]

Training on the Pacific Coast

On the Pacific Coast the training operations outlined in the Pearl Plan of
September 1941 had been executed only in part. Working on the first phase
of the plan, the 3d Division, which had built up a large establishment of boat
crews and amphibious equipment of its own, conducted landing exercises in
Puget Sound and at the mouth of the Columbia River. The 2d Marine Division
carried on similar exercises at San Diego. The second phase of the maneuvers,
calling for a landing of both divisions in Hawaii, was not carried out because
of the outbreak of war, which also created uncertainty concerning the employment of the Second Joint Training Force.

As a means of clarifying the training program of the 3d Division, GHQ
proposed on 16 January 1942 the designation of Seattle or San Francisco, rather
than Galveston, as the embarkation point for forces which might be required
to operate in defense of the Panama Canal.[17] In response to this suggestion
G–4 of the War Department General Staff recommended that the entire Pearl
Plan be cancelled in view of the difficulties in supply and the changes in the
over-all strategic situation caused by the war. WPD ruled that before action
was taken G–4 must consult GHQ.[18]

An Army Amphibious Training Center Projected

By February 1942 GHQ had come to believe that the whole amphibious
training program should be reconsidered. In GHQ's reply to G–4 General
Clark, Deputy Chief of Staff for Training, agreed that the Pearl Plan should
be cancelled. He went on to point out, however, that General Marshall wished

[16] (1) 1st Div ltr (S) to CG AFAF, 28 Jan 42, sub: Rpt on Jan Amph Exercise. 353/24 (AFAF) (S).
(2) WD memo (S) WPD 4511–50 for CG FF, 8 Feb 42, sub: Amph Tng. 353/35 (AFAF) (S). (3) See
also item (2) of footnote 15 above.
[17] GHQ memo (S) for WPD, 16 Jan 42, sub: O'seas Movement of Army Trs. 353/9 (AFPF) (S).
[18] WD Disposition Form (S), G–4/33853, 9 Feb 42, with note by Gen Somervell. 353/25 (AFPF) (S).

the development on the Pacific Coast of an amphibious force ready for combat, and he observed that, to the best of his knowledge, a War Department order of 19 December 1941, calling upon WPD and G–3 of the General Staff to designate units for amphibious training, had not been complied with. He recommended that the composition of the Amphibious Force, Atlantic Fleet, and of the Amphibious Force, Pacific Fleet, be restudied and that the two forces be "constituted on a permanent basis to provide the attack element of whatever task forces are, or may be, designated to conduct the first major operation in the Atlantic or Pacific, respectively. The Army components of these forces should be determined, specifically designated and announced by the War Department. The necessary supplies of all classes for combat should be assembled, prepared for loading and held available in appropriate ports." [19]

Dissatisfaction with the administration and progress of amphibious training, already expressed by General Malony in his memorandum of 29 October 1941, was not removed by the landing maneuver at Cape Henry in January 1942. In mid-February GHQ received a copy of the final report on this operation, submitted by General Smith to the Commander in Chief, U. S. Atlantic Fleet. General Smith expressed with considerable candor a view largely divergent from both Army and Navy predilections. The G–5 section at GHQ, in a memorandum to WPD dated 27 February 1942, undertook to bring parts of General Smith's report to the "personal attention" of General Marshall. "The report," said this memorandum, "contains a frank criticism of Naval command, constitutes a powerful indictment of the theory and practice of Joint Action, and makes concrete recommendations for unity of command under the Commander of the Landing Force." [20]

Citing General Smith, G–5 then enumerated its grounds for complaint: the late change of locale, though justified by the submarine menace, made adequate preparation impossible, with the result that the "excellent plans" of the 1st Division miscarried; the Navy failed to provide suitable transports or adequate combatant vessels and aircraft; combatant vessels had not practiced shore bombardment in the past year; naval aircraft were untrained for cooperation with ground troops; and the Navy failed to land troops on designated beaches, so that the ship-to-shore movement was "from a tactical viewpoint, a complete failure." Results of the exercise, according to General Smith, were the

---

[19] GHQ memo (S) for G–4 WD, 23 Feb 42, sub: Amph Forces. 353/25 (AFPF) (S).

[20] For this and the following quotations see GHQ ltr (C) to WPD, 27 Feb 42, sub: Amph Force. 353/33 (AFAF) (C).

discrediting of American troops in the eyes of foreign observers, and, more important, "the loss of confidence by the first-class combat troops in the ability of responsible command echelons to place them ashore in formations that will offer a reasonable chance of success." G–5 then repeated General Smith's recommendation that unity of command in amphibious operations be vested in the commander of the landing force. In conclusion G–5 stated:

> The Army is giving whole-hearted, complete and generous support to the present Amphibious Forces, both Atlantic and Pacific. The 3d and 9th Divisions have been turned over to the Navy for tactical control and training. Action is in process to determine and provide essential non-divisional elements. . . .
>
> From the larger view, the establishment of an Army Amphibious Training Center to provide for amphibious training on the scale envisaged as essential to future operations is being investigated.

This study at GHQ, reflecting its accumulated dissatisfaction with amphibious training of Army units as conducted to date, laid the basis for plans which resulted, in June 1942, in the activation of an Army center for amphibious training. The Army Ground Forces directed this center until its dissolution in June 1943.[21]

---

[21] See AGF Historical Section, The Amphibious Training Center.

VI. The Role of GHQ in the Development of Airborne Training

The training and organization of airborne troops, whether parachutists or glider infantry, remained on a small scale throughout the life of GHQ. Nevertheless, during the months preceding March 1942 the foundation was being laid for the creation of one of the elements of the Army Ground Forces, a separate Airborne Command. In this development of airborne forces General McNair exercised an important influence, and GHQ used airborne troops in maneuvers under its direction.

For some years the United States Army had experimented with the technical possibilities of parachute and air-landing forces. The German occupation of western Europe in May–June 1940 made clear the tactical possibilities of such forces, and as a result various offices in the War Department approached the subject with renewed interest. On 5 August 1940 Maj. Gen. Henry H. Arnold urged that the projected parachute units should be assigned to the Air Corps, but General McNair, as one of his first acts at GHQ, insisted that parachute troops be included among the ground arms, since they used airplanes only for transport and actually fought on the ground. General McNair's recommendation prevailed. The Office of the Chief of Staff directed on 20 August that staff studies should be made of "the organization, equipment, and tactical employment of parachute and air-transported Infantry." [1]

---

[1] (1) Memo of Gen Arnold for DCofS USA, 5 Aug 40, sub: Prcht Trs. 322.04/1 (Inf). (2) Memo of Gen McNair for Gen Moore, 8 Aug 40, sub as above. 322.04/2 (Inf). (3) Memo OCS 21157–1 for ACofS G–3 WD from Lt Col Orlando Ward, 20 Aug 40. G–3/43293 "Aviation," AGF Requirements, TL & VA Div.

The first American parachute unit specifically organized as such was authorized on 16 September 1940 for immediate activation at Fort Benning. It was designated the 501st Parachute Battalion and its Table of Organization called for 34 officers and 412 enlisted men, all to be volunteers. GHQ played no ascertainable part in this action. The activation and training of parachute units, as of other air-landing units, remained until the dissolution of GHQ a function of the General Staff and the Chief of Infantry.[2]

The Transport Shortage
and its Effects on Organization and Training

Development of airborne units was handicapped by the severe shortage of transports. Because production of aircraft was concentrated on combat aviation, little hope existed that this shortage would soon be overcome. At the end of June 1941 the United States Army possessed, except for a few planes converted from other types, only 2 transports in Panama, 1 in the Philippines, a total of 49 used in Newfoundland and by the Office of the Chief of the Air Corps, 2 in Hawaii, and "12 planes set up separately for parachute troop and airborne infantry training" in the 50th Transport Wing, the only such wing that had been activated. Twelve transports carried merely one company with its equipment. No more planes were expected for the 50th Transport Wing until February 1942. In 1941 the need for transport planes became so great that a request was made even for the release of the plane used by GHQ and of the four allotted to the four army headquarters for the travel necessary in conducting their extensive inspections— a request to which General McNair could not accede.[3]

The air transport shortage naturally retarded the mobilization of new airborne units. In June 1941, when the size of the Army was approaching a million and a half, the 501st Parachute Battalion was its only airborne unit. Another, the 502d, was constituted on 1 July 1941, and the 503d and 504th in the next three months. As an administrative, nontactical headquarters for the parachute battalions, a Provisional Parachute Group was set up in the summer of 1941 under command of Lt. Col. William C. Lee. Meanwhile, the German

---

[2] WD ltr (C) AG 580 (9–9–40) M–C–M to CofInf, CofAC, and CG Ft Benning, 16 Sep 40, sub: Constitution of 1st Prcht Bn. AGO Records (C).

[3] (1) Chart (C) attached to AAF D/F to G–3 GHQ, 5 Aug 41, sub: Transports for Prcht Trs. Original chart in 452.1/4 (C). (2) Memo of CofS GHQ for the ACofS G–3 WD, 20 May 41, sub: Transport Airplanes for Prcht Trs. 580/14.

conquest of Crete having demonstrated the value of airborne infantry, the first air-landing (as distinguished from parachute) unit of the United States Army was constituted in Panama in July 1941. This was the 550th Infantry Airborne Battalion. A company of the 501st Parachute Battalion was sent to reinforce it. In the continental United States the first air-landing unit was the 88th Infantry Airborne Battalion, constituted on 10 September 1941.[4]

Not only mobilization but also training suffered from the shortage of transports. Only by special arrangement was the 501st Parachute Battalion able to participate in two of the eighteen air-ground tests conducted at Fort Benning, where some of the personnel of the 4th Motorized Division, who had practiced loading and unloading transports the year before, acted as air infantry. Useful lessons could be drawn from the tests, but it was felt that more thorough exploration of airborne operations was needed before plans for a full-scale development of airborne training could be made. When the commanding general of the VII Corps asked on 6 June 1941 for one company of parachutists, he was unable to obtain it for want of the twelve planes required. It was explained that all available transports were ferrying Air Corps equipment to airplane manufacturers.[5]

Airborne Elements in the GHQ-Directed Maneuvers, 1941

The request of GHQ to use airborne elements in the GHQ-directed fall maneuvers of 1941 encountered the same difficulty. The question of transports for these maneuvers had been discussed since March. In August the suggestion of the Army Air Forces that to conserve planes a battalion be moved one company at a time was rejected by General McNair, who replied that a battalion to be trained as a unit must be moved as a unit. Finally, on 3 September 1941, the Army Air Forces agreed to furnish thirteen transports for both the September

---

[4] (1) WD ltr AG 580 (2–11–41)M(Ret) M–C to CG Ft Benning, 14 Mar 41, sub: Constitution and Activation of Prcht Bns. 580/9. (2) WD ltr AG 580 (6–26–41) EA–C to CGs 8th and 9th Divs, 3 Jul 41, sub: Procurement of Enl Pers for Provisional Prcht Gp. 580/18. (3) WD ltr (C) AG 320.2 (5–14–41) MR–C to CG Panama Canal Dept, 11 Jun 41, sub: Orgn of the 550th Inf Airborne Bn, Panama Canal Dept. 320.2/1 (Inf Airborne) (C). (4) WD ltr AG 320.2 (8–21–41) MR–M–C to CG IV Corps Area, CofAAF, CofInf, and the SG, 10 Sep 41, sub: Experimental Air-Inf Bn. 320.2/27 (Inf).

[5] (1) Rpt (C) on Combined Tests to Develop Doctrine and Methods for Aviation Support of Ground Troops (no date given), pp. 21–23 and Appendix C, Tests 7 and 18. 353/27/35 (sep file) (C). (2) Ltr of Gen Smith to CofS GHQ, 6 Jun 41, sub: Proposed Field Exercise of the 501st Prcht Bn. (3) 3d ind to preceding, CofS GHQ to CG Second Army, 17 Jun 41. Both (2) and (3) in 353/1 (Prcht Trs).

and the November maneuvers and an additional twenty-six transports on two occasions during the November maneuvers.[6]

In the September maneuvers of the Second vs. Third Army the only airborne unit used was one company of the 502d Parachute Battalion. Men and equipment were dropped from different planes—a practice recognized by all as bad, since men might be landed without equipment, but unavoidable until enough suitable transports could be employed.[7] In the November maneuvers of the First Army vs. IV Corps, transports were available in considerable numbers for the first time. An airborne task force was organized under the Provisional Parachute Group. It consisted of the 502d Parachute Battalion and the 3d Battalion of the 9th Infantry, substituting for the as yet untrained 88th Airborne Battalion. Three missions were performed. One ended in a confused swarming of parachutists and defenders on the field. One was changed to a demonstration for reporters and photographers. The third resulted in a tactical accomplishment, the surprise capture and "destruction" of an important bridge. The chief recommendation made to GHQ in consequence of these operations was that transport planes should be assembled at home stations of parachute troops for training and rehearsal at least two weeks prior to the action intended. Unfortunately planes were still not available to carry out this proposal.[8]

Projects for Further Development of Airborne Troops

Nevertheless, on the level of long-range planning, thought was turning to more extensive development of airborne troops. Army journals discussed the problem, and in an outstanding article, written at a time when the Army could show nothing above the battalion, Colonel Lee envisaged the formation of special airborne divisions. In July 1941 the Army Air Forces began to experiment with gliders for transportation of men and materiel. In August G–3 of the War

[6] (1) AAF D/F (C) to G–3 GHQ, 5 Aug 41, sub: Transport of Prcht Trs. (2) Memo (C) of CofAAF for CofS GHQ, 3 Sep 41, sub as above. With attached documents. Both in 452.1/4 (C).

[7] (1) Ltr (R) of CofS GHQ to CO Provisional Prcht Gp, 29 Aug 41, sub: Prcht Tr Participation in Sep 1941 GHQ-Directed Maneuvers in Louisiana Maneuver Area. With indorsements. 353/6 (Prcht Trs). (2) Memo of CofS GHQ for CoInf, 13 Oct 41, sub: Separation of Prcht Trs and Their Equipment in Flight. With 1st ind. 353/8 (Prcht Trs).

[8] (1) Ltr of CO Provisional Prcht Gp to CofS GHQ, 4 Dec 41, sub: Participation of the Airborne Task F in the First Army vs IV Army Corps Maneuvers. 353/23 (Prcht Trs). (2) Par 12 e, ltr of Gen McNair to CG IV Army Corps, 7 Jan 42, sub: Comments on First Army vs IV Army Corps Maneuvers, Nov 16–30, 1941. 354.2/1 (IV Army Corps).

Department General Staff called upon the Air Forces to develop new cargo planes, explaining that the testing of an airborne combat team was contemplated. This force was to consist of an infantry battalion, an antitank company, a field artillery battery, and a medical detachment. Tests were conducted by the Field Artillery in dropping the 75-mm. pack howitzer by parachute. The complications arising where a new military problem had to be dealt with through the old chiefs of branches were illustrated by the organization of a parachute battery in February 1942.[9] The Chief of Field Artillery was ordered to organize this unit, which was to receive its parachute training under the Chief of Infantry, only after confirmatory tests had been carried out by the Chief of Infantry and after the necessary howitzers had been obtained from the Chief of Ordnance.

The multiplication of airborne activities raised the question of higher echelons of command. On 11 December 1941 General Twaddle, G-3 of the War Department, submitted a memorandum to GHQ. He observed:

1. When the existing parachute battalions were set up, it was believed that parachute troops would operate in small numbers, and therefore required only an administrative, not a tactical, superior headquarters. This had been provided in the "Provisional Parachute Group."

2. Subsequent experience in Europe, and in the November maneuvers, showed that in the future parachute troops would be employed in larger number, and in connection with airborne troops, glider troops and troops on the ground.

3. The November maneuvers showed the inability of the Provisional Parachute Group to operate successfully as a tactical command.

General Twaddle therefore recommended that for the four existing parachute battalions, three in the United States and one in Panama, a Parachute Group Headquarters with staff sections and a headquarters detachment be set up. General McNair concurred with reservations. He preferred a definite policy of organizing a higher headquarters for every three battalions, and he wanted the higher organization to be called a regiment.[10]

---

[9] (1) Lt Col William C. Lee, "Air Landing Divisions," *Infantry Journal*, April 1941. See also Lt Col Leo Donovan and Lt J. J. Gleason, "Division in Heaven: the Staff Work of Airborne Troops," *Military Review*, June 1941. (2) Ltr of CofAAF to CG AFCC, 7 Jul 41, sub: Orgn of Glider Units. 322.082/207. (3) WD memo G-3/40911 for CofAAF, 4 Aug 41, sub: Airplane Development for Carrying Airborne and Prcht Trs. 580/25. (4) WD ltr (C) AG 472.2 (1-8-42) MSC-C to CofInf, CofFA, CofOrd, 18 Feb 42, sub: Prcht Battery, 75-mm. Pack Howitzer. 320.2/1 (Prcht Trs) (C).

[10] (1) WD memo G-3/40911 for CofS GHQ and CofInf, 11 Dec 41, sub: Comd Echelon for Prcht Units. 320.2/37 (Inf). (2) Memo of Gen McNair for ACofS G-3 WD, 18 Dec 41, sub as in (1) above. 320.2/1 (Prcht Trs)(C).

His advice was taken in this matter. A War Department directive of 24 February 1942 constituted four parachute regiments.[11] Each regiment was to receive, as its first component, one of the four existing parachute battalions, whose numerical designation passed to the regiment. The 501st Parachute Battalion, for example, became the 1st Battalion of the 501st Parachute Infantry. No similar action was yet taken for air-landing troops, but a beginning was made in the organization of airborne troops in the usual echelons of the Army. With regiments constituted and batteries contemplated, the way was open for the creation in August 1942 of the first airborne divisions—the 82d and the 101st.[12]

In the last days of GHQ the airborne army existed largely on paper, but the basic preparations had been made for its development. Control over the 501st Parachute Battalion and the 550th Airborne Infantry Battalion was not inherited by the Army Ground Forces, since both were stationed in Panama. One of the first acts of the Army Ground Forces was to create, on 23 March 1942, an Airborne Command.[18] The headquarters of the old Provisional Parachute Group became the headquarters of the new command, and Colonel Lee the first commanding officer. The Airborne Command began its work with high enthusiasm and many projects, but with very few actual troops. Much work remained to be done before American units would be able to carry out an action similar to the German operation against Crete.

---

[11] WD ltr (R) AG 320.2 (1–20–42) MR–M–C to CofInf, 24 Feb 42, sub: Constitution, Activation and Redesignation of Prcht Units. AGF Records, 321/1 (Inf)(R).

[12] See "Reorganization of Ground Troops for Combat" and "Organization and Training of New Ground Combat Elements," in this volume, and AGF Historical Section, The Airborne Command.

[13] AGF ltr 320.2/2 (Airborne Command)–GNOPN to CO Airborne Comd, 24 Mar 42. 320.2 (A/B).

VII. GHQ and the Development of Air-Support Training and Doctrine

Responsibilities of GHQ for Air and Air-Ground Training

In its relation to the air forces GHQ passed through two periods divided by June 1941, when the Army Air Forces was recognized and established as an autonomous force within the Army.

In the first period GHQ was responsible in principle for the training of air as well as ground elements of the Army. The GHQ Air Force, somewhat confusingly so named since it long antedated the activation of GHQ, comprised all combat aviation units in the continental United States. On 19 November 1940 this force was formally put under the command of the Commanding General of the Field Forces and under the "direct control" of GHQ.[1] General McNair, as Chief of Staff, GHQ, therefore was responsible for the supervision of its training.

From the first the trend of events prevented this responsibility from being exercised, except in a very limited way. On 14 August 1940, ten days after General McNair assumed his new duties, a comprehensive training directive had been given to the Commanding General of the GHQ Air Force by the Chief of the Air Corps, General Arnold. General McNair took this to mean that the actual supervision of GHQ over air training would be limited. In a memorandum to his Air officer, Col. William E. Lynd, who had not yet reported at GHQ, he observed that General Arnold's directive appeared "to constitute a radical change of policy. Apparently the action was a personal one by the Secretary of War to the Chief of the Air Corps." At General McNair's request, Colonel Lynd, shortly after arriving, prepared a comprehensive report on the organization, training, and combat readiness of the air forces. Notwithstanding the War Department directive of 19 November explicitly placing the Commanding General of the GHQ Air Force under GHQ in the chain of

---

[1] (1) WD ltr AG 320.2 (7–25–40)M(Ret) M–OCS to CGs, etc, 26 Jul 40, sub: GHQ. 320.2/3/1. (2) WD ltr AG 320.2 (11–14–40) M–C–M to CGs, CofS GHQ, etc, 19 Nov 40, sub: Orgn, Tng and Adm of the GHQ Air Force. 320.2/26 (AF Combat Comd).

command, General McNair felt that he was called upon to do little beyond keeping himself informed regarding its training program.[2]

The second period opened with the reorganization of the air forces on 20 June 1941.[3] This action regularized the increasing autonomy of the air arm. The Army Air Forces was constituted directly under the War Department, with General Arnold as both Chief of the Army Air Forces and Deputy Chief of Staff for Air. A separate Air Staff, with the usual staff sections, soon developed. Within the Army Air Forces two major subdivisions were created: the Air Corps, charged with the control of fixed installations, individual training, supply functions, etc., and the Air Force Combat Command, which replaced the GHQ Air Force in controlling tactical aviation in the continental United States. These changes were recognized when GHQ was reorganized on the following 3 July.[4] A distinction between air forces and ground forces was clearly drawn and GHQ was relieved of responsibility for air training. It was charged with the "supervision and coordination, as at present, of the training of all ground combat forces (except those assigned to air forces) and all combined air-ground training (except training for defense against air attack) in the continental United States." This division of authority remained in effect until the reorganization of 9 March 1942, which dissolved GHQ and established the Army Ground Forces and the Army Air Forces as separate and coordinate commands.

GHQ and the air forces shared many problems in addition to the questions connected with combined air-ground training. In a general way most training activities of the ground forces were in some degree related to the development of the air forces. Ground troops on maneuvers were frequently criticized by General McNair for taking insufficient precautions against the air threat. The training of air-borne troops, though a very small-scale matter in 1940–41, directly involved the air forces. The establishment of defense commands, of which aviation was a principal component, created new organizational problems, which were finally solved in accordance with the views of General McNair, published in the field manual on air defense. The assignment of antiaircraft artillery within a defense command to the interceptor commander was gradually accepted,

[2] (1) Ltr of Gen Arnold to CG GHQ Air Force, 15 Aug 40, sub: Air Corps Tng 1940–41 (Supplementary). 353/11. (2) Memo of Gen McNair for Col Lynd, 31 Aug 40, sub: Air Corps Tng, 1940–41. (3) Memo (C) of Col Lynd for Gen McNair, 1 Oct 40, sub: The GHQ AF. 322.082/1 (C).

[3] AR 95–5, "Army Air Forces," 20 Jun 41.

[4] WD ltr AG 320.2 (6–19–41) MC–E–M to CofS GHQ, 3 Jul 41, sub: Enlargement of the Functions of GHQ. 320.2/3/34.

largely because of the influence of General McNair. Most of the relations between GHQ and the air forces, however, centered on the problem of the "combined air-ground training" over which GHQ received supervision on 3 July 1941. The problem of preparing for direct collaboration between air and ground forces in battle proved to be difficult to solve, and no final settlement had been agreed upon when the Army Ground Forces was established in 1942.

Basic Problems
in Combined Air-Ground Training

In the blitzkrieg in which the German Army swept over Belgium and France in May–June 1940 no element appeared more successful than the close support given by aviation to ground troops in combat. Other armies had lagged in developing this type of cooperation. The United States was unprepared for such warfare both in equipment and in tactical doctrine. Before large-scale air-support training could begin, it was necessary not only to procure equipment but to formulate, for the guidance both of production policies and of training programs, a new tactical doctrine for the close support of ground troops by aviation.

On 20 August 1940 General Marshall directed his G–3, Brig. Gen. Frank M. Andrews, an Air Corps officer, to initiate staff studies on this subject. The matter was turned over jointly to the Training Branch and the Miscellaneous Branch of G–3. Though Lt. Col. Harold M. McClelland, an Air Corps officer in the Miscellaneous Branch, reported that his branch had already taken sufficient action, the Training Branch nevertheless went ahead. Lt. Col. Rufus S. Ramey of that branch, after consultation with GHQ, presented on 26 September 1940 a memorandum for the Chief of Staff, signed by General Andrews.[5]

This memorandum distinguished five kinds of aviation support for ground troops:

1. Close, direct-support fire missions on the immediate front of ground forces.

---

[5] (1) Memo OCS 21157–1 of Lt Col Orlando Ward for ACofS G–3 WD, 20 Aug 40. G–3/43293, "Aviation: Misc from Sec, prior to Jan 8, 1942." AGF Rqts, TL & VA Div. (2) Memo G–3/43293 of Lt Col McClelland for the Executive, 27 Aug 40, sub: Support of Grd Trs by Avn. AGF Rqts, TL & VA Div. (3) Memo G–3/43293 of Gen Andrews for CofS USA, 26 Sep 40, sub: Avn in Support of Grd Trs. AGF Rqts, TL & VA Div. Most of the documents cited in footnotes 5 to 13 may also be found in AGO Records 353 (9–16–40) (Avn in Support of Grd Trs).

2. Air defense of friendly ground forces and installations in the combat zone.
3. Air attack against targets in hostile rear areas.
4. Support of parachute troops and air infantry.
5. Reconnaissance, liaison, and observation.

Of these items the first and second came to constitute the substance of the air-support problem. The third involved less coordination between air and ground forces in battle and was more a strategic than a tactical concern. The fourth has been described in Section VI. The fifth, aerial observation, presented relatively few administrative difficulties to GHQ and needs to be discussed only briefly.

Observation Aviation

Aerial observation, according to General Andrews' memorandum, was already well handled in the U. S. Army. Observation squadrons had been assigned in 1940 to various branches and echelons of the field forces Their training came directly under the authority of GHQ. They followed prescribed training programs in conjunction with their respective ground units, but in May 1941 an inspection by the GHQ Air Section showed that the mere issuance of instructions had not been sufficient to guarantee results. It was found that the Air officer of the Second Army had tested his observation squadrons very superficially. General McNair, privately referring to these tests as "classroom stuff," ordered further tests in the form of actual field exercises for all observation squadrons in the field forces. The tests were held in July and August 1941.[6] At that time, following the reorganization of the air forces, the observation squadrons were transferred to new air-support commands,[7] and the question of aerial observation then merged into the larger problem of air-ground cooperation.

The Problem of Air-Support Tests, 1940–41

In the use of combat aviation for air-support, General Andrews' memorandum of 26 September 1940 stated that the United States Army was inexperienced by European standards. General Andrews recommended that joint

---

[6] Draft of GHQ ltr to CGs, 3 Jul 41, sub: Test of Obsn Sqs. With supporting documents. 353/59 (AAF).

[7] See footnote 22 below.

air-ground tests be held at once and that in future maneuvers whole armies, corps, and "large elements" of the GHQ Air Force should be trained to act together.

This recommendation brought about a struggle in the War Department between a group of officers favoring immediate air-support tests and a group who believed that the GHQ Air Force should expand its equipment, enlarge its personnel, and perfect its training in strictly air matters before participating in joint training with ground arms. The struggle was not simply between air and ground officers. General Andrews, an Air officer, favored immediate tests, as did General McNair, who had concurred in the proposals of 26 September. General Arnold, Chief of the Air Corps, saw more value in air-ground combined training than did Maj. Gen. Delos C. Emmons, commander of the GHQ Air Force. In a training directive for 1940–41, issued to the GHQ Air Force shortly before the Office of the Chief of Staff initiated the studies on air-ground relations, General Arnold had expressly said: "Every opportunity will be sought to engage in field exercises with other arms." The most persistent opponent of the proposed tests was General Emmons. For a time he was supported by General Arnold, who on 25 October, in a memorandum for G–3, urgently advised against immediate tests. He declared that equipment was lacking, stated that cooperative exercises with ground troops greatly delayed the "combat crew and unit training" of air personnel, and recommended that no air-support operations be introduced into large maneuvers until 1942. The Miscellaneous Branch of G–3 and the War Plans Division shared this point of view, though somewhat less positively.[8]

In November 1940, however, the weight of authority turned in favor of the tests. General Arnold, who was Deputy Chief of Staff for Air at this time, accepted the proposed tests with certain safeguards. He obtained from General Andrews on 12 November a statement that only one squadron of combat aviation, probably the one stationed at Fort Benning, would be needed in the near future[9] and then gave instructions for the issuance of a directive ordering

[8] (1) Memo of Gen McNair for ACofS G–3 WD, 24 Sep 40, sub: Avn in Support of Grd Trs. (2) Ltr of Gen Arnold to CG GHQ AF, 15 Aug 40, sub: Air Corps Tng 1940–41 (Supplementary). 353/11. (3) Memo of CofAC (over the signature of Gen Brett) for ACofS G–3 WD, 25 Oct 40, sub as above. (4) Memo of Chief of Misc Branch GHQ for Chief of Tng Branch GHQ, 30 Sep 40, sub as above. (5) WD memo WPD for G–3 WD, 5 Nov 40, sub as above. All these documents, except (2), are in G–3/43293, "Support of Grd Trs by Avn," AGF Rqts, TL & VA Div.

[9] "Consideration of Non-Concurrences" (dated 12 Nov) appended to memo cited in footnote 5 (3) above. G–3/43293, "Support of Grd Trs by Avn," AGF Rqts, TL & VA Div.

the tests.[10] He also wrote to General Emmons announcing his decision to concur in the G–3 proposal, and assured him that the directive, when issued, would contain a clause protecting the GHQ Air Force from the obligation of large-scale training with ground troops.[11] On 20 November Colonel Ramey, charged with preparing the directive, informally notified Colonel Clark at GHQ that G–3 of the War Department favored naming GHQ as the coordinating agency for the various elements—army, corps, Armored Force, and GHQ Air Force—to be involved in the tests. G–3 seemed not to be thinking of small tests only.[12]

On 2 December Colonel Ramey finished his draft of the directive, which took the form of a War Department letter to the Chief of Staff, GHQ, ordering him to conduct tests and specifying their content. The draft reached the Office of the Chief of Staff on 4 December. It was there amended by General Arnold, Deputy Chief, who now appeared convinced of the value of the experiment. His amendments doubled the number of questions on which tests should be held. Three days later the amended draft, fully approved, left the Office of the Chief of Staff, but on 12 December Maj. Edwin B. Howard, an Air Corps officer, Chief of the Miscellaneous Branch of G–3, vehemently objected to General Arnold's extension of the scope of the tests, which, he said, the entire GHQ Air Force could not execute in the time allowed. Major Howard disclaimed responsibility and predicted a violent protest from General Emmons. These objections, however, were overruled by Colonel Twaddle, acting G–3, who observed that the Chief of Staff had already approved the directive, and on 13 December he transmitted the amended draft to The Adjutant General.[13]

The directive issued to General McNair on 17 December 1940 laid the basis for tests which lasted well into the following summer. The results of these tests were eventually incorporated in Basic Field Manual 31–35, Aviation in Support of Ground Forces, published on 9 April 1942.[14]

[10] D/S OCS 21157–1–A to ACofS G–3 WD, 15 Nov 40, for necessary action. AGO Records, 353 (9–16–40) (Avn in Support of Grd Trs).

[11] Personal ltr of Gen Arnold to Gen Emmons, 14 Nov 40. G–3/43293, "Support of Grd Trs by Avn," AGF Rqts, TL & VA Div.

[12] Informal memo of Lt Col Ramey GHQ for Lt Col Clark GHQ, 20 Nov 40, sub: Proposed Combined Tng Tests. G–3/43293, "Aviation: Misc from Sec, prior to Jan 8, 1942," AGF Rqts, TL & VA Div.

[13] (1) Memo of Col Twaddle for TAG, 2 Dec 40, sub: Combined Tests to Develop Doctrine and Methods for Aviation Support of Grd Trs. (2) Memo of Maj Howard for the ACofS G–3 WD, 12 Dec 40, sub as above, with pencilled notations of Col Twaddle. For both see G–3/43293, "Support of Grd Trs by Avn," AGF Rqts, TL & VA Div.

[14] WD ltr (C) AG 353 (9–26–40) M–C to CofS GHQ, 17 Dec 40, sub: Combined Tests to Develop Doctrine and Methods for Avn in Support of Grd Trs. 353/27/1 (C).

Within ten days of receiving the directive General McNair had assembled comments on it from his staff sections, transmitted it to the Third Army with instructions for its execution, requested the Chief of Infantry to furnish a battalion of parachute troops, and asked the Chief of the Armored Force and the Commanding General of the GHQ Air Force to state what forces they could make available.[15] Then began a period of difficulty and delay. General McNair himself, despite his prompt action, was not yet convinced that the tests should be hurried. He had been told that the air forces were not prepared, and his principle that fundamental training should take priority over training in specialized operations seemed to run contrary to the scope of the proposed tests. He therefore wrote to General Marshall on 16 January 1941 mildly criticizing "the present test at Fort Benning of air-ground cooperation, as being premature."[16]

In January 1941 new difficulties developed regarding the size of the tests. The War Department directive, following General Arnold's assurances to General Emmons, stipulated that aviation used in the tests should "be restricted to the bombardment squadron now stationed at Fort Benning, Georgia, and such additional units of other type aircraft as the Commanding General, General Headquarters Air Force, may make available without undue interference with the unit training and expansion program of the Air Corps." In order to use ground troops in the neighborhood of Fort Benning the Third Army assigned the tests to the IV Army Corps. Maj. Gen. Jay L. Benedict, Commanding General of the IV Corps, soon found that the number of planes in the squadron at Fort Benning was too small to permit worth-while tests.

To iron out this difficulty a special conference was called at the War Department on 17 January 1941. Two changes in the program, somewhat in the nature of a trade, were approved. First, General Arnold stated that by early April a whole group of light bombardment planes might become available. Second, it was agreed that responsibility for matters primarily of aviation technique should be transferred from the Third Army to the GHQ Air Force. The date for completion of the tests was deferred to 1 August 1941.[17]

[15] (1) Rpts (C) of staff sec, 20–23 Dec 40 and GHQ 1st ind to CG Third Army, 26 Dec 40, on WD ltr AG 353 (9–26–40) M–C, sub as in footnote 14. 353/27/2 (C). (2) GHQ ltrs (C) to CofInf and CG GHQ AF, 26 Dec 40, sub as in footnote 14. 353/27/7 and /8.

[16] Memo of Gen McNair for Gen Marshall, 16 Jan 41, sub: Specialized Tng. 353/136.

[17] (1) Memo of Chief of Tng Branch WD for ACofS G–3 WD, 17 Jan 41, sub: Tests in Determining Methods and Doctrines for Avn in Support of Grd Trs. G–3/43293, "Support of Grd Trs by Avn," AGF Rqts, TL & VA Div. (2) WD ltr AG 353 (1–17–41) M–C to CofS GHQ, 22 Jan 41, sub: Combined Tests. AGO Records.

Execution of Air-Support Tests, February–June 1941

The tests began on 11 February and lasted until 17 June.[18] Eighteen tests were held, becoming increasingly large as additional units of aviation were made available. Command channels were complex. The GHQ Air Force delegated its responsibilities to the Southeast Air District—renamed the Third Air Force while the tests were in progress—which in turn delegated them to the 17th Bombardment Wing. Under the 17th Wing was the 3d Light Bombardment Group and the 15th Light Bombardment Squadron, which with certain observation and pursuit units performed the exercises prescribed. The ground troops employed were the 4th Motorized Division, the 2d Armored Division, and the 501st Parachute Battalion, together with small units of other arms, all attached to the IV Corps, which itself was responsible to the Third Army and GHQ. Command over the tests was not wholly unified, since General Benedict of the IV Corps and Brig. Gen. Lewis H. Brereton of the 17th Wing occupied in some respects coordinate positions. Some misunderstanding resulted,[19] but the tests were nevertheless found by Colonel Lynd, the GHQ Air officer and observer, to be well managed.[20]

Aviation worked alternately with the 4th Motorized and 2d Armored Division in various tactical combinations involving both support and attack of ground troops. No live bombs were dropped. The Army possessed no dive bombers, and plans to employ Navy dive bombers failed to materialize. A severe shortage of radio equipment limited communications, and lack of air transport made it impossible to experiment profitably with airborne troops. All units participated at less than authorized strength.

Despite the difficulties a long list of matters was investigated during these months:

1. The minimum distance from friendly troops at which aviation might safely bomb.

[18] This and the following two paragraphs are based largely on Gen Benedict's "Report of Combined Exercises to Develop Doctrine and Methods for Aviation Support of Ground Troops" (C). 353/27/35 (separate file) (C). Gen Brereton's report is attached to Gen Benedict's account as an appendix.

[19] (1) Personal ltrs (C) of Gen Benedict to Gen McNair, 10 and 16 Apr 41. 353/27/36 (C). (2) Memo of Chief of Misc Branch WD for ACofS G-3 WD, 5 May 41, sub: Avn Support of Grd Trs. G-3/43293, "Support of Grd Trs by Avn," AGF Rqts, TL & VA Div.

[20] (1) Memo (C) of Col Lynd for CofS GHQ, 11 Apr 41, sub: Air-ground Tests to Determine Tactics, Doctrine and Technique. 353/27/36 (C). (2) *Ibid.*, 7 May 41, sub: Air-Ground Tests. 353/27/36 (C). (3) *Ibid.*, 7 May 41, sub: Additional Notes on Visit to IV Army Corps, 6 May. 333.1/7 (Ft Benning).

2. The minimum altitude at which support aviation might safely operate.

3. Methods of communication between ground and air.

4. Methods of notifying friendly ground troops when supporting air action is terminated.

5. Methods by which ground commanders might call for air support and designate targets for bombardment.

6. Methods by which fliers might distinguish friend from foe on the ground, and ground troops might distinguish between friendly and hostile aircraft.

7. Methods to secure timing of air attack in coordination with ground action.

8. Proper kinds of targets (near or distant, stationary or moving, transitory or permanent) for aviation in close support of bombardment.

9. The lapse of time between request for support and delivery of bombardment.

10. Methods for control of aircraft, whether by attachment to ground troops or otherwise.

On these and other matters General Benedict on 19 July made a thorough report, concurred in by General Brereton, who also forwarded a report for the 17th Bombardment Wing. Colonel Lynd found both reports excellent.[21] At the same time a draft for a training circular on air support was forwarded by General Benedict.

The Air-Support Commands and the 1941 Maneuvers

These reports were eagerly seized upon by both GHQ and the Army Air Forces. The Air Forces, recently constituted as an autonomous body, was engaged in reorganizing air-ground relations. A directive of 25 July 1941 created an Air Support Section in the staff of the Air Force Command, providing, however, that for liaison purposes this section should be located initially at GHQ.[22] Colonel Lynd became chief of the section. The same directive created five air-support commands to include observation and light bombardment planes formerly allotted to ground units. One air-support command was to be included in each of the four armies. The fifth air-support command was reserved for the Armored

---

[21] Memo (C) of Col Lynd for CofS GHQ, 4 Aug 41, sub: Comments on IV Army Corps and 17th Wing Rpts on Air-Ground Tests. 353/27/29 (C). The basic reports are in 353/27/35 (C) (separate file).

[22] WD ltr AG 320.2 (7–17–41) MR–M–AAF to CofAAF, 25 Jul 41, sub: Air Support Avn. With attached chart. AGO Records.

Force. To determine the functions of the new commands an Air Support Board met on 28 July.[23] It considered the reports of the IV Corps and the 17th Wing and recommended material for inclusion in the forthcoming training circular.

General McNair had long urged speedy completion of reports on the air-support tests held in the spring of 1941, since conclusions were needed in time to formulate instructions for the fall maneuvers. While recently relieved of his supervisory authority over air training, General McNair was still officially responsible for supervision and coordination of combined air-ground training.[24] He had feared that instructions for air-ground action in the coming maneuvers might be delayed by the "upheaval" going on in the Air Forces. The placing of all support aviation in air-support commands, he wrote, "is one more step in the separation of the air from the rest of the Army. What may be the result is hard to predict, but it seems quite unlikely that it will facilitate the interworking of air and ground." He was not satisfied with the results shown in General Benedict's report, which he praised as accurate and thorough. "Frankly," he wrote to General Benedict on 26 July, "I am disappointed in the capabilities of air support as indicated by your tests. It seems that aviation may intervene once in a battle—possibly at the time and place needed, possibly not. It requires a great stretch of the imagination to visualize such action as even remotely decisive, if indeed it is felt at all by the ground troops. I hope that the maneuvers may develop something more impressive in the way of speed and ferocity of air action." [25]

It was clear by July 1941 that the fall maneuvers would involve large-scale air-support operations, such as General Andrews had envisaged and General Emmons had objected to almost a year before. Though General Emmons,[26] now Commander of the Air Force Combat Command, had not changed his opinion, General Arnold ordered eight groups to take part in both the Louisiana and the Carolina maneuvers.[27] The Navy agreed to supply dive bombers.[28]

---

[23] See footnote 21.   [24] See footnote 4.

[25] Personal ltrs (C) of Gen McNair to Gen Benedict, 5 and 26 Jul 41. 353/27/31 and /37 (C).

[26] (1) Ltr of CofS GHQ to CG GHQ AF, 24 Mar 41, sub: Corps and Army Tng. 353/6 (AF Combat Comd). (2) GHQ AF 1st ind to GHQ on preceding, 3 Apr 41. 353/6 (AF Combat Comd). (3) Memo (C) of CG AFCC for CofAAF, 24 Jun 41, sub not given. 353/1 (AFCC) (C). (4) GHQ AF 2d ind to GHQ, 29 May 41, on ltr of CG First Army to GHQ, 15 May 41, sub: Corps and Army Tng. 353/55/7 (First Army). (5) GHQ AF 1st ind to GHQ, 12 Jun 41, on ltr of Gen McNair to CG GHQ AF, 5 Jun 41, sub: Air Participation in Corps and Army Tng. 353/12 (AF Combat Comd).

[27] (1) Ltr of Gen Arnold to CofS USA, 19 Jun 41, sub: Air Corps Participation in Army Maneuvers, Sep through Nov. 353/54 (AAF). (2) WD ltr AG 353 (7–3–41) MO–C to CofS GHQ, 16 Jul 41, sub: Increased Participation of Air Force Units in 1941 Maneuvers. 353/28 (AF Combat Comd).

[28] Ltr (C) OP–38–E–KB 7–16 (SC) A4–3/QA Confidential Serial 048838, Doc 32098 of Chief of Naval Opns to CofS GHQ, 17 Jul 41, sub: Dive Bomber Participation in Army Mnvrs. 353/1 (Dive Bombing) (C).

The eight-group program called for speedy preparations. Further air-ground tests were scheduled for Fort Knox in August.[29] Starting at the end of July Colonel Lynd, as well as General McNair and General Clark, worked on the Air Corps draft of an Aviation Supplement to the GHQ Umpire Manual. Much reduced in bulk by its passage through GHQ, with sentences shortened and expression clarified and with the number of air umpires cut about 30 percent, the Aviation Supplement was published on 21 August.[30] Meanwhile, Colonel Lynd substantially modified the draft training circular submitted by General Benedict, taking account of the findings of the Air Support Board. The War Department published Colonel Lynd's draft, with a number of changes, as Training Circular No. 52, 29 August 1941, entitled "Employment of Aviation in Close Support of Ground Troops." [31]

To improve the doctrine set forth in this training circular and to obtain guidance for the preparation of a field manual, General McNair on 8 September requested the principal field commanders to submit reports on air support in the light of the coming maneuvers. On 15 September GHQ was formally instructed by the War Department to prepare a field manual.[32] The stage was set for a thorough test of air-ground cooperation.

Aviation in the 1941 Maneuvers

The September maneuvers gave the most spectacular exhibition of air power ever seen in the United States. The eight Army Air Force groups took part as well as seven squadrons of Navy and Marine aviation. Even so, in pro-

---

[29] (1) Memo (C) of CofS GHQ for ACofS G-3 WD, 13 Aug 41, sub: Attack Airplanes for the Armd F. 452.1/3 (Airplanes) (C). (2) Memo No 4 of Air-Grd Tng and Test Bd, Ft Knox, Ky, 31 Aug 41, sub: Air Support (Bombardment). A tentative guide to Opns. 353/33 (AF Combat Comd).

[30] "Aviation Supplement to Umpire Manual, GHQ, U. S. Army, Aug 21, 1941, Restricted." With supporting documents. 353/19 (Tng Dirs).

[31] (1) Memo (C) of Gen Clark, G-3 GHQ for Gen McNair, 9 Aug 41, sub: Tentative Guide for the Employment of Bombardment in Close and Direct Support of Grd Forces. With supporting documents. 353/27/38 (C). (2) A Copy of Col Lynd's draft, "Tentative Guide . . .," with supporting documents, is in G-3/43293, "Support of Grd Trs by Avn," AGF Rqts, TL & VA Div. (3) "Tow Benedict and Brereton . . . in June submitted a draft of this Training Circular. It was gone over by this Headquarters and submitted to the War Department with little or no change. It emerged in quite a different form. . . ." One change was to increase the authority of the air support commander (par 4 c (4) (b)). Ltr of Maj Gen R. C. Richardson to Gen McNair, 9 Sep 41, and Gen McNair's reply, 11 Sep 41. McNair Correspondence.

[32] (1) Ltr of Gen McNair to CGs, etc, 8 Sep 41, sub: Rpts on Employment of Aviation in Close Support of Grd Trs. 353/16 (Air-Grd). (2) WD ltr AG 062.11 FM (9-9-41) PC-C to CofS GHQ, 15 Sep 41, sub: Combined Tests to Develop Doctrine and Methods for Avn Support of Grd Forces. 461/179.

portion to the 350,000 troops engaged, air strength was below the normal requirements of modern war.

In his comments General McNair confined himself to brief statements. He noted in his critique that the troops failed to respond adequately to the air threat. He pointed out that columns of men and vehicles in close order on the roads would suffer disastrously from real air attack and that for observation planes to fly for two hours at low altitudes over enemy territory was highly unrealistic. General Arnold also noted these weaknesses and others as well: poor use of radio; excessive dependence on telephones; scattering of bombers on small missions; ignoring by aircraft of danger from antiaircraft artillery; and undue length of communication channels between the ground commander's request for support and its delivery by the air unit. General Arnold found the air-support command organization vindicated in principle by the maneuvers, but requiring development in detail.[33]

In the Carolina maneuvers in November the First Army was pitted against the IV Army Corps, most of whose elements had participated in the air-support tests earlier in the year. The eight groups of Army aviation were again engaged and, theoretically, dropped fourteen thousand bombs.[34] Parachute troops also were employed.

General McNair still thought the ground troops careless in the face of the air threat. He found bombardment aviation used aggressively and effectively by the IV Corps commander, pursuit planes employed normally but too often wasted on attacks against ground objectives, observation planes still too much inclined to long leisurely flights over enemy positions, and the capabilities of aerial photography neglected. A report by an A–2 Air Staff observer dealt chiefly with matters of special interest to the Air Forces.[35]

Disagreements over Air-Ground Command Relations

After the September maneuvers attention again turned to the precise means by which air and ground units should be administratively related.

[33] (1) Ltr of Gen McNair to CG Second Army, 11 Oct 41, sub: Comments on Second vs Third Army Maneuvers, 15–30 Sep 41. 353/466 (Second Army). (2) Ltr of Gen McNair to CG Third Army, 10 Oct 41. 353/595 (Third Army). (3) Memo of Gen Arnold for CofS USA, 8 Oct 41, sub: Army Maneuvers. 354.2/1 (Rpts 1941).

[34] Memo of Col Lynd for CofS GHQ, 18 Dec 41, sub: Bombs Dropped during Carolina Maneuvers. 354.2/27 (First Army).

[35] (1) GHQ ltr to CG First Army, 22 Dec 41, sub: Comments on First Army vs IV Army Corps

The Chief of Field Artillery, not content with the new air-support commands, recommended on 8 October that at least seven observation planes be organically included in the artillery component of each division and corps. GHQ concurred with G–3 of the War Department in disapproving this proposal.[36] "I favor exhausting the possibilities of the new air-support organization," wrote General McNair on 21 October 1941, "since it gives promise of effecting a great improvement. There is grave question in my mind whether it is feasible or desirable that a ground arm attempt to operate aviation. The ground arms can and must learn to cooperate with aviation, and the process may as well begin with observation." These words mark a change, perhaps brought about by the maneuvers, from his distrust of the air-support commands at the time when they were created. He now believed that observation planes could survive only where general air superiority was maintained and that they would be wastefully used if decentralized in division commands. The recommendation of the Chief of Field Artillery had no immediate effect in this connection. A War Department order of 27 October prescribed that observation units of air-support commands should be attached to ground units as required, in peacetime by agreement between GHQ and the Air Force Combat Command—with the War Department as arbiter when agreement was impossible—and in wartime by decision of the theater commander.[37]

The Armored Force also expressed dissatisfaction with air-ground command arrangements. The commanding general of the I Armored Corps wrote on 20 October that, when a ground commander did not control his supporting air unit, he could not be certain what support he could draw on and therefore often gave less prominence to aviation in his plans than it deserved. General Devers, Chief of the Armored Force, accordingly recommended to GHQ that the 5th Air Support Command be attached to "participating elements" of the Armored Force in future maneuvers.[38]

Maneuvers, Nov 16–30, 1941. 354.2/26 (First Army). (2) GHQ ltr to CG IV Army Corps, 7 Jan 42, sub as above. 354.2/1 (IV Army Corps). (3) Memo of Capt Noland on Carolina Maneuvers, 12 Dec 41. 353/165 (AAF).

[36] Memo (C) G–3/42989 of Col Chambers for CofS USA, 28 Oct 41, sub: Air Obsn. With supporting documents. 322.082/5 (Air Corps) (C).

[37] (1) GHQ memo of Gen McNair for CofS USA, 21 Oct 41, sub: Rpt by CofFA. 354.2/2 (Rpts 1941). (2) WD ltr 320.2 (10–14–41) MO–AAF–M to CGs, CofS GHQ, etc, 27 Oct 41, sub: Control of Obstn Units. 320.2/168 (AAF).

[38] GHQ 2d and 3d inds on GHQ ltr to CofAF, 30 Sep 41, sub: Rpts on Employment of Avn in Close Spt of Grd Trs. 353/16 (Air-Grd).

When the air-support commands were created in the preceding July, the 5th Air Support Command had been specifically designed for attachment to the Armored Force, and each of the other four for attachment to one of the armies. For the duration of such attachment the army or Armored Force commander had authority over his air-support command. The present difficulty involved relations with the subordinate echelons: corps, division, or combat team under the army or Armored Force; observation, bomber, or pursuit units under the air-support command. These forward units of air and ground forces, which did the actual fighting, stood in a cooperative relation to each other. They were links in separate chains of command which converged only at the top. In the daily and hourly realities of warfare command was divided. The ground commander of a corps or lesser unit could request, but could not order, the corresponding air support officer to give support. The Air Forces insisted on maintaining these arrangements. General Emmons wrote: "Coordination is primarily the responsibility of the commander of the troops suported. To his reasonable needs and requests the air commander will conform." [39]

War Department G–2 had received reports from the Middle East which showed that the Royal Air Force had conspicuously failed to support ground troops. The British had been disastrously defeated by Rommel in the spring of 1941, and one cause of their weakness was held to be the separation, both in training and in combat, between the Royal Air Force and the Army. This separation was reported to have been bridged over only by the presence in the theater of a personal envoy of the Prime Minister, Sir Oliver Lyttleton, Minister of State. Partly in view of these reports, Colonel Kingman, Armored Force officer at GHQ, favored General Devers' recommendation for the attachment of air support to subordinate ground units. He stated that the question involved was the unity of command in a task force and that General Devers' proposal followed the German system, which had repeatedly proved successful and which gave control over aviation to subordinate field commanders within an army or theater.[40] General McNair, however, took no action on Colonel Kingman's recommendation.

---

[39] (1) WD ltr AG 320.2 (8–21–41) PC–C to CGs, CofS GHQ, CofAAF, etc, 7 Oct 41, sub: Type Orgn of Air Forces in a Theater of Opns. With attached chart. 320.2/158 (AAF). (2) AFCC ltr ACC 353 (10–31–41) Combined Tng to CofS GHQ, 15 Nov 41, sub: Rpt of Employment of Avn in Close Spt of Grd Forces. 353/18 (Air-Grd).

[40] Memo of Gen Clark for Gen McNair, 4 Nov 41, sub: Employment of 5th Air Spt Comd with Armd F Elements. With supporting documents. 353/9 (Air-Grd).

The principles of centralization and decentralization of air support strength were in conflict. Centralization would require the attachment of air forces to the highest Army commands, allotting these forces only temporarily to lower units as occasion required. This method preserved the fluidity and mobility of support aviation and made possible the assembling of mass striking power against the most important objectives. This was the principle urged by General McNair for the organization of tank destroyer units. Decentralization, through attachment of air support to lower commands, would speed up the local delivery of support. The bad feature of decentralization was that it immobilized air strength in places where it might not be needed or frittered it away on local and insignificant missions. The bad feature of centralization was that it set up long command and liaison channels and slowed down the process of getting air assistance to ground troops.

FM 31–35, Aviation in Support of Ground Forces

This issue, along with other air-ground problems, was covered in the manual, FM 31–35, Aviation in Support of Ground Forces, which was published by the War Department on 9 April 1942. From November 1941 to January 1942 GHQ had received the reports on air-ground operations in the fall maneuvers requested by General McNair on 8 September. Colonel Lynd and other officers, working with these reports, had produced a draft field manual, which was submitted by GHQ to the War Department on 31 January 1942.[41] Except for a few minor changes in wording, and with no changes in the attached organization charts, this draft was accepted by the War Department.

On air-ground command relations the doctrine was flexible. "An Air Support Command," the manual stated, "is habitually attached to or supports an army in the theater." Normally the air-support commander was to function under the army, theater, or task force commander. He would allocate, and in exceptional cases might attach, aviation units to subordinate ground units, but it was emphasized that the air-support commander was to control all participating

---

[41] (1) First Army ltr to CG FF, 8 Jan 42, sub: Rpts on Employment of Avn in Close Spt of Grd Trs. 353/26 (Air-Grd). (2) Second Army ltr to CG FF, 23 Dec 41, sub as above. 353/23 (Air-Grd). (3) Third Army ltr to CG FF, 17 Nov 41, sub as above. 353/19 (Air-Grd). (4) Rad, Devers to CG FF, 6 Jan 42. Synopsis on listing sheet. 353/25 (Air-Grd). (5) AFCC ltr ACC 353 Combined Tng (Gen) to CG FF, 9 Jan 42, sub as above. 353/27 (Air-Grd). (6) Ltr of CG FF to TAG, 31 Jan 42, sub as above. Incl draft of Field Manual. 461/179.

aviation. In general, the principle adopted was that of centralization.[42]

Various means were prescribed for achieving the advantages of decentralization. Air observation units would normally be allocated so as to permit corps and division commanders to plan their use and to call on them directly for missions. They were allotted on the basis of current Tables of Organization. Combat aviation, the manual stated, might be attached to subordinate ground units in rare and exceptional cases, when effective control of such units could not be retained by the air-support command. Normally, combat air support would be arranged at subordinate levels between air and ground officers by liaison methods. Each corps headquarters, and on occasion division headquarters, was to include an "air-support control," a group of officers in direct communication both with airdromes and with the air-support command. Lower headquarters, down to any level required by the tactical situation, might include an "air-support party," defined as "a highly mobile group composed of one or more air-support officers . . . to transmit air-support requests to air-support control." Within an army corps air-support parties would rarely be detailed to a unit headquarters below that of an infantry division. On the other hand, in armored forces and cavalry divisions they would frequently be detailed to headquarters below the divisional level to meet the requirements of rapid movement. They could transmit only requests approved by the ground unit commander and only to an air-support control.

The manual emphasized that aviation called for by ground commanders and obtained through air-support controls was not subordinate to the supported commander, but remained under the control of the air-support command. It was hoped that decentralization of liaison and communications would provide promptness and accuracy in the delivery of air support, in spite of this rigid centralization of air command. Provision for unified command was made only in the loose statement that the air-support commander "normally functions under the army, theater, or task force commander."

In other words, the manual did not decide the basic problem of centralization or decentralization. The advocates of both principles had strong arguments to support their views, but a final and realistic decision could be reached only on the basis of active combat experience of American forces. This opportunity was not offered until the Battle of Tunisia in the spring of 1943, when the Army Ground Forces, successor to GHQ, had to apply the lessons learned.

[42] For this and the two following paragraphs see particularly pars 2, 4 to 7, 52, and 109, and Figs 1 and 2 of FM 31–35, 1942.

VIII. GHQ and
the Defense Commands
in the Continental United States

In addition to all of its other functions, GHQ became involved in defense planning for the continental United States. Though this activity never became as urgent as its responsibility for certain overseas bases and never as influential as the control it exercised over training, the ideas of GHQ on the military organization of the country's defenses were a definite factor in the plans developed up to March 1942. The recommendations of GHQ regarding defense planning were governed by General McNair's fundamental belief in unity of command. The problems raised in applying this principle to the organization of defense commands in the continental United States brought to light the basic difficulties in carrying out the plans for GHQ as conceived by the Harbord Board twenty years before. The vast difference between the strategic situation of 1918 and that of 1941 was among the major causes leading to the dissolution of GHQ. This development was hastened by overlapping of planning and command responsibilities, the inability of the War Department to delegate full authority to GHQ, and the unsettled relationship between GHQ and the Air Corps in the organization for the defense of the United States established in March 1941.

The Role of GHQ in Planning the Defense of the United States

Before 3 July 1941, while still exclusively a training headquarters, GHQ had already made its influence felt in military planning. It participated in the separation of the field forces from the corps areas, a measure which made possible the creation, apart from fixed administrative establishments, of large mobile armies for tactical employment in the field. These field forces were expected to become capable of offensive warfare. The War Department's over-all strategic plan prescribed, as the primary task of the United States Army, the building of "large land and air forces for major offensive operations."[1]

But in 1940 and 1941 offensive warfare, however desirable, seemed on sober calculation of means a possibility only for the future. During most of this period, it was by no means certain that Great Britain could stand up under the hammer strokes of the Luftwaffe which were pulverizing her cities. A War Department G–2 conference in May 1941, attended by the G–2 of GHQ, attempted to estimate the military power which the United States could exert if the British should be defeated and came to the following conclusions:[2]

May–November 1941:	An unbalanced force without combat aviation could be put into the field in any area not within a thousand miles from the west coast of Europe or Africa.
November 1941–April 1942:	A small force with combat aviation could be used.
April–November 1942:	Balanced forces would be available up to the limit of ship tonnage.
After November 1942:	Shipping, equipment, and training would permit an expeditionary force of 430,000 to be put into action.

In these circumstances, the War Department had to consider above all the immediate defense of the continental United States. GHQ had no responsibility in the matter before 3 July 1941, but after that date it was responsible for the planning and after Pearl Harbor for the execution of measures to resist attack. Even before 3 July 1941, the advice of General McNair was sought and frequently accepted. Since attack was unlikely except by air, Air officers played a leading part in defense planning. Indeed, they tended to feel that the problem was exclusively theirs and to attach slight importance to collaboration with ground troops in the repelling of invasion. Nevertheless, plans for the air forces and plans for the defense of the United States became inextricably interwoven.

The Principle of Territorial Command Unity and the Air Problem

An Air Defense Command had existed since 26 February 1940, with headquarters at Mitchel Field, New York, under command of Maj. Gen. James E.

---

[1] Rainbow 5, par 15, sec IV. OPD Records (S).

[2] Memo (S), G–2 GHQ for CofS GHQ, 28 May 41, sub: Conference; Office Chief of WPD WD, 27 May 41. 381/13 (S).

Chaney.[3] It was a planning body, with authority to organize combined air-ground operations, but it had no territorial responsibility and no control over either aircraft or antiaircraft artillery except as they might be attached to it by the War Department. General Chaney repeatedly urged the organization of definite defense measures for the vital northeastern area of the United States.

In the discussions which came to a head late in 1940 General McNair was consulted. He favored the division of the continental United States into four regional defense commands. He wished to keep these distinct from the four field armies, which as mobile units might by moving away leave a region unprotected, and from the nine corps areas, which as fixed administrative organizations were not suited for combat. In each defense command, in his view, there should be unity of command over all elements of defense: pursuit aviation, antiaircraft artillery, mobile ground troops, harbor defenses, and the aircraft warning service. The area under a defense command, if invaded, would become a theater of operations, and the defense commander would become a theater commander with unified control over all military means in his theater.[4]

Fear that unity of command within a given area subject to attack might be lost caused General McNair to disapprove of certain features of the reorganization of the Air Corps effected at this time. The Air Corps, in order to create an intermediate echelon between its seventeen wings and the headquarters of the GHQ Air Force, divided the United States into four air districts. General McNair, dubious at first, was brought to accept these territorial air districts for purposes of training and administration. The Air Corps, supported by G–3 of the War Department General Staff, then proposed the creation of a bombing command and an air defense command within each air district, the former to conduct offensive operations, the latter defensive operations, "within the theater of the Air District."[5] General McNair concurred in the formation of these commands for the training and organization of mobile air units, but he demurred at the identification of air districts with theaters of operations. He maintained that, in the event of actual operations, the business of the air district was not itself to fight, but to supply appropriate bomber and pursuit aviation to the theater commander,

[3] WD ltr AG 320.2 Air Corps (2–8–40) M(Ret) M–C to CGs, etc, 26 Feb 40, sub: Creation of Air Defense Comd. AGO Records.

[4] (1) Draft memos of Gen McNair for Gen Marshall, 21 Oct and—Nov 40. 320.2/78. (2) Memo of Gen McNair for Gen Bryden, 7 Dec 40, sub: Orgn of the FF. 320.2/78.

[5] Memo (C) G–3/40679 of Acting ACofS G–3 WD for the CofS USA, 27 Nov 40, sub: Tac Orgn of GHQ Avn Air Districts and Wings. 320.2/4 (C).

Chart No. 4

Defense Commands Established 17 March 1941

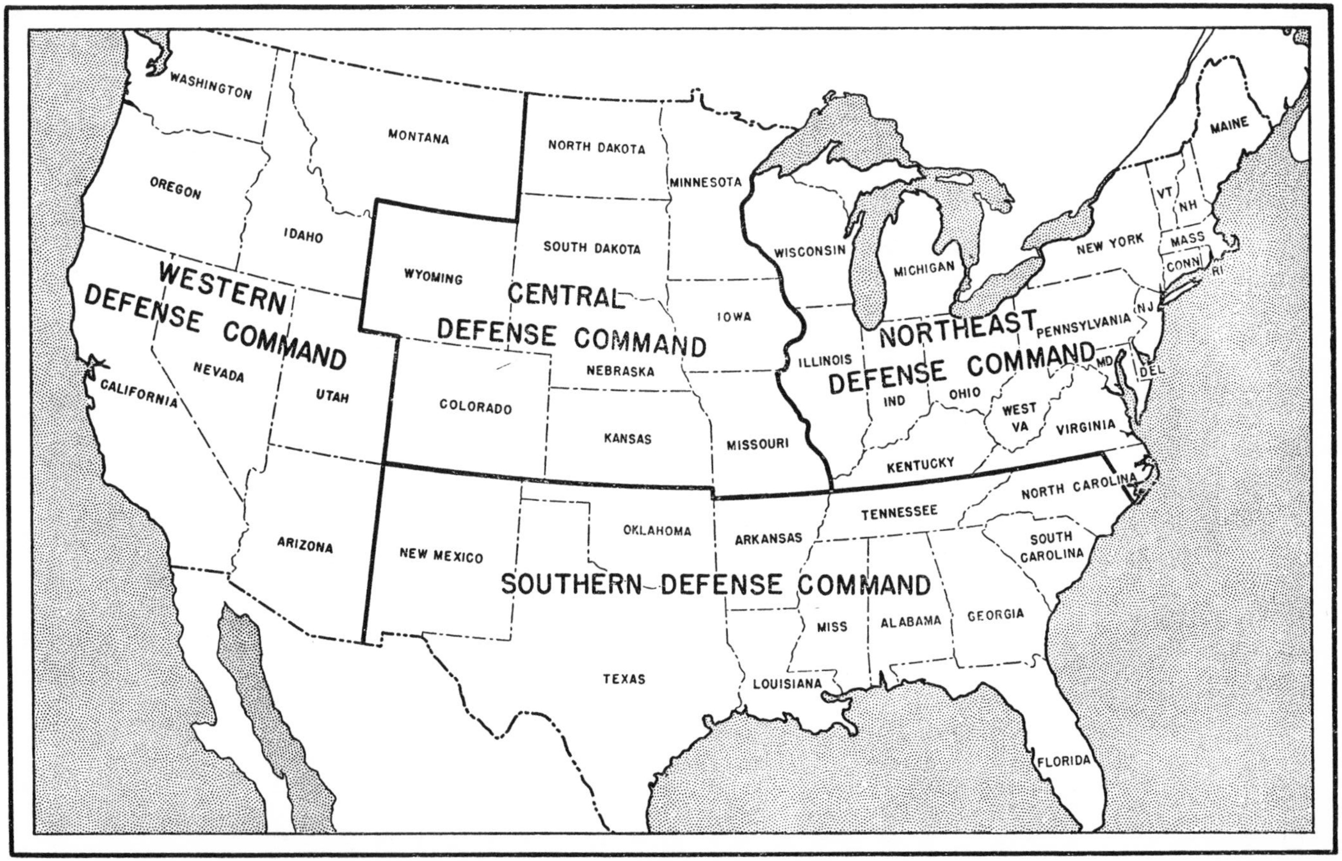

who must be placed over air and ground forces alike and be held responsible for operations as a whole.[6]

Creation of the Four Defense Commands

Action taken by the War Department in March 1941 embodied most, but not all, of General McNair's ideas. A formal order of 17 March divided the United States into four defense commands—Northeastern, Central, Southern, and Western.[7] (See Chart No. 4.) Each defense commander was to be responsible in peacetime for planning all measures against invasion of the area of his command. Should such invasion occur, he was to take charge of operations until otherwise directed by the War Department. To avoid accumulation of overhead, the commanding general of each of the four armies was designated as the commanding general of the defense command within which his headquarters was located, and the army staffs, with some reinforcement, were used as the staffs of the defense commands. GHQ was made responsible for the supervision and coordination of their planning, but not "until such time as the staff of GHQ has been expanded to undertake these additional responsibilities."

The same order of 17 March replaced the four air districts with four air forces. To prevent confusion between territorial and mobile activities, against which General McNair as well as General Chaney of the Air Corps [8] had warned, each air force was divided into a fixed and a mobile echelon. The fixed echelon would control bases, airdromes, aircraft warning services, etc. The mobile echelon would comprise a bomber command and an interceptor command. "Interceptor Command" was the name now chosen for what the proposals of the preceding fall called "Air Defense Commands" and was in turn to yield to the name "Fighter Command" in 1942. Under whatever name, pursuit (i. e., fighter) planes as distinguished from bombers were meant.

The order of 17 March did not fully provide the regional unity of responsibility desired by General McNair. The four air forces stood directly under the GHQ Air Force. They were not subordinate to the defense commands and were only roughly coterminous with them.

[6] Memo (C) of Gen McNair for ACofS G–3 WD, 14 Dec 40, sub as above. 320.2/4 (C).

[7] WD ltr (C) AG 320.2 (2–28–41) M–WPD–M to CofS GHQ, etc, 17 Mar 41, sub: Defense Plans—Continental US. With attached charts. AGO Records (C).

[8] "Plan for Organization," with pencilled note in Gen McNair's hand, "Gen Chaney's view, handed to me 3–12–41 by Maj. Saville." 320.2/4 (C).

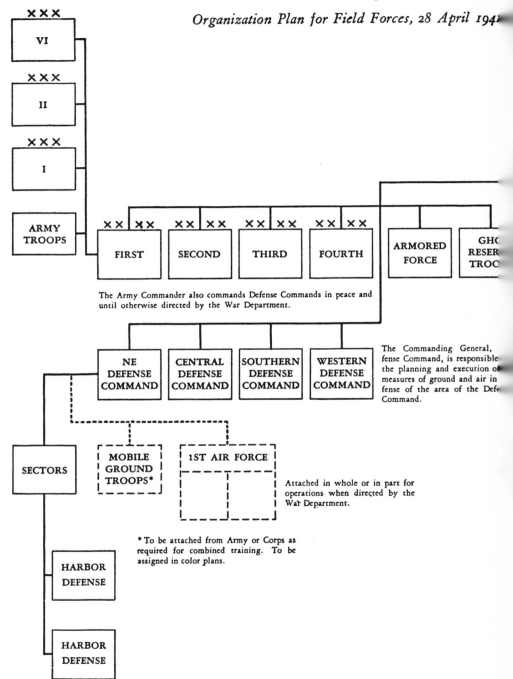

VI ✕✕✕

II ✕✕✕

I ✕✕✕

ARMY TROOPS

FIRST ✕✕ ✕✕

SECOND ✕✕ ✕✕

THIRD ✕✕ ✕✕

FOURTH ✕✕ ✕✕

ARMORED FORCE

GHC RESER TROC

The Army Commander also commands Defense Commands in peace and until otherwise directed by the War Department.

NE DEFENSE COMMAND

CENTRAL DEFENSE COMMAND

SOUTHERN DEFENSE COMMAND

WESTERN DEFENSE COMMAND

The Commanding General, fense Command, is responsible the planning and execution of measures of ground and air in fense of the area of the Def Command.

SECTORS

MOBILE GROUND TROOPS*

1ST AIR FORCE

Attached in whole or in part for operations when directed by the War Department.

* To be attached from Army or Corps as required for combined training. To be assigned in color plans.

HARBOR DEFENSE

HARBOR DEFENSE

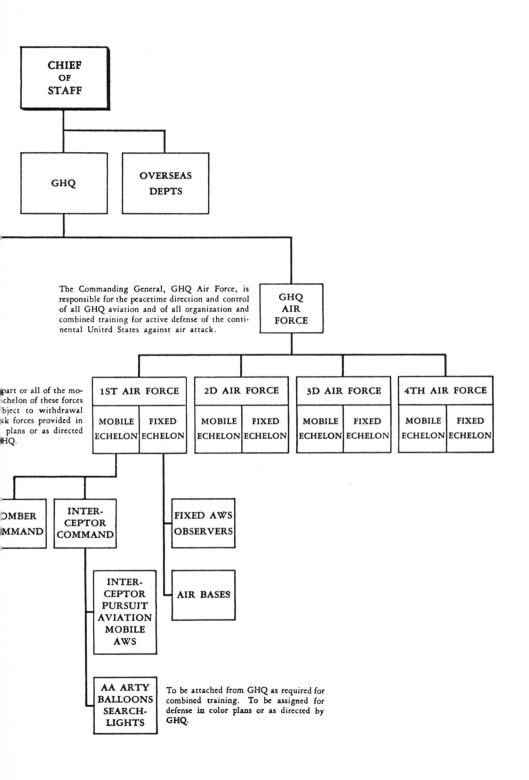

CHIEF OF STAFF

GHQ

OVERSEAS DEPTS

The Commanding General, GHQ Air Force, is responsible for the peacetime direction and control of all GHQ aviation and of all organization and combined training for active defense of the continental United States against air attack.

GHQ AIR FORCE

part or all of the mo- chelon of these forces bject to withdrawal sk forces provided in plans or as directed HQ.

1ST AIR FORCE

| MOBILE ECHELON | FIXED ECHELON |

2D AIR FORCE

| MOBILE ECHELON | FIXED ECHELON |

3D AIR FORCE

| MOBILE ECHELON | FIXED ECHELON |

4TH AIR FORCE

| MOBILE ECHELON | FIXED ECHELON |

OMBER MMAND

INTER- CEPTOR COMMAND

FIXED AWS OBSERVERS

INTER- CEPTOR PURSUIT AVIATION MOBILE AWS

AIR BASES

AA ARTY BALLOONS SEARCH- LIGHTS

To be attached from GHQ as required for combined training. To be assigned for defense in color plans or as directed by GHQ.

For peacetime planning and preparation the distribution of authority was not clear. (See Chart No. 5.) The principle of regional unity was recognized in the provision that the "planning for all measures of defense" in each area should rest with the commanding general of the defense command. But the conflicting principle of functional autonomy was recognized on the same page of the order, where responsibility for "the aviation and air defense portions of defense plans for Defense Commands" was conferred upon the commanding general of the GHQ Air Force. This provision was strengthened by additional instructions issued on 25 March, which directed that "current plans for organization of means of air defense will be transferred from the army commanders and other commanders to the commanding general, GHQ Air Force," and that the latter should nominate his own representatives on local joint planning committees.[9] In the geographical situation of the United States, with attack unlikely except by air, this was a considerable limitation on the planning powers of the regional defense commanders. The discrepancy was noted at once by General McNair as well as by others and led to prolonged discussion in the War Department. To General McNair it seemed "manifest that there must be a unified responsibility in peace for the preparation of war plans, even as there must be an undivided command within the defense command in war." [10]

The question became even further entangled in the summer of 1941. By the directive of 3 July 1941, GHQ received authority to supervise the planning of commanders of defense commands. But in June the Army Air Forces had been established as an autonomous element in the War Department, and the GHQ Air Force, renamed the Air Force Combat Command and responsible only to the Chief of the Army Air Forces, was no longer subject to even such limited authority as GHQ had exercised over it, carrying with it the power to make aviation plans for defense commands.[11] Nevertheless, General McNair continued his efforts to have planning authority transferred from the Army Air Forces to the regional commanders by whom, in case of attack, the plans would presumably be executed. On 15 August 1941 General McNair stated his position in full detail. He requested that the plans of the Air Forces for a

---

[9] (1) WD ltr cited in footnote 7. (2) WD ltr AG 320.2 (3–24–41) M–WPD–M to CGs, CofS GHQ, etc, 25 Mar 41, sub: Defense Plans—Continental US. AGO Records.

[10] (1) Memo WPD 4247–9 of Gen McNarney for CofS,—Apr 41, sub: Defense Planning—Continental US. 320.2/158/9. (2) Memo of Gen McNair for ACofS WPD, 14 May 41, sub as above, 320.2/158/9. (3) Memo G–3/45316 of Gen Twaddle for CofS USA, 10 Apr 41, sub as above. 320.2/28 (GHQ, Army and Corps) (C). (4) Memo (C) of Gen McNair for ACofS G–3 WD, 5 Jun 41, sub as above. 320.2/28 (GHQ, Army and Corps) (C).   [11] AR 95–5, 20 Jun 41.

theater be submitted to GHQ, to be embodied, if approved, in a directive from GHQ to the theater commander; that local plans proposed by a theater commander be transmitted through GHQ to the Chief of the Army Air Forces for approval or comment; and that, at the outbreak of hostilities, GHQ be given command of the air forces assigned to the theater with authority to take the necessary action to obtain such air reinforcements as might be requested.[12]

Regional unity for war operations was provided for by the directive of 17 March. As construed by the War Department, this directive prescribed in case of war the attachment of an air force to its geographically corresponding defense command. The basic War Department strategic plan stated explicitly: "When the War Department, to meet an actual or threatened invasion, activates a Theater of Operations (or similar command) in the United States contiguous territory for the combined employment of air forces and ground arms (other than antiaircraft artillery), the commander of the theater (or similar commander) will be responsible for all air defense measures in the theater." This hypothetical situation became a reality with the declaration of war the following December. The First Air Force was attached to the Northeastern Defense Command, which was now activated and renamed the Eastern Theater of Operations. The Fourth Air Force was attached to the Western Defense Command, which was in effect alerted as a theater of operations while retaining its old name. The Second and Third Air Forces, in the interior of the country, remained for training under the Air Force Combat Command. On the two coasts, the theater commanders obtained unity of command including aviation. The principle of unity, strongly advocated by General McNair, had been adopted for the potential combat zones.[13]

Coordination of Antiaircraft Weapons and Pursuit Aviation

Though in matters of higher command and planning General McNair sought to moderate the claims of the air forces, in the coordination of aviation

[12] (1) Memo of Lt Col Milburn for Lt Col Harrison, WPD, 11 Jul 41, sub: Modification of Instructions Contained in WD ltr AG 320.2 (2–28–41) M–WPD–M, 17 Mar 41, sub: Defense Planning—Continental US. 320.2/158/12. (2) GHQ memo (S) for CofS USA, 15 Aug 41, sub: Functions, Responsibilities and Authority of GHQ. AGO Records, WPD 4558 (S), Tab 11. A complete analysis of this memorandum will be found in Sections IX and X below.

[13] (1) Rainbow 5, 1941, Register No 14 (S), par 40 c (1), Sec VIII, OPD Records (S). WD ltr (S) AG 381 (12–16–41) MSC–F to CG First Army and CofAAF, 19 Dec 41, sub: Responsibility for Defense against Aircraft in Eastern US. AGO Records. (3) Min (S) Staff Conferences, GHQ, 26 Dec 41. 337 (S).

and antiaircraft artillery he found himself trying to impose on the air forces more control of ground forces than they were willing to assume.

As early as May 1940, the Air Defense Command under General Chaney began to organize southern New England into a test sector for a rehearsal of defense measures against air attack. The test sector exercise was executed in January 1941. Pursuit planes, coast artillery, regional filter boards, and the aircraft warning service, manned both by military personnel and by civilian volunteers, cooperated to resist a simulated attack by American bombers. Three observers from GHQ were present: the Air officer, Colonel Lynd, and the two Coast Artillery officers, Lt. Col. Bryan L. Milburn and Lt. Col. Morris C. Handwerk.[14]

Colonel Lynd's report to General McNair, dated 1 February 1941, concluded that the main lesson learned from the test was the need of putting antiaircraft defense under air command. This doctrine was accepted by GHQ and was incorporated in a War Department order of 7 March, assigning to the GHQ Air Force the responsibility for air defense in the continental United States. Ten days later the order of 17 March, establishing an interceptor command within each of the four air forces, provided specifically that antiaircraft artillery, searchlights, and balloon barrages should be attached to interceptor commands during operations.[15]

Precisely how the interceptor commander, always an Air officer, should exercise his control over these ground elements was a question admitting many different answers. There was agreement on the general aim. The interceptor commander must distribute local responsibilities for defense between ground elements and pursuit planes and, when both came into action in the same place, he must prevent his pursuit planes from being shot down by friendly artillery or entangled in friendly balloon barrages. Experience in England had shown that such mishaps were all too common.[16] Tactical coordination required centralization of command and intelligence together with very rapid channels of command and communication.

[14] (1) Memo (C) G–3/29400–42 of Gen Andrews for CofS, 2 Oct 40. AGO Records (C). (2) GHQ memo (C) for ACofS G–3 WD, 3 Dec 40, sub: Avn Units and Personnel for "Test Sector." 353/24 (C). (3) Tng Memo No 5, Air Defense Comd, "Test Sector" Opn, 5 Dec 40. 353/24 (C). (4) Memo (C) of Lt Col Handwerk for CofS GHQ, 29 Jan 41, sub: Rpt on Visit to CA Units and Air Defense Comd Exercises. 353/24 (C). (5) Memo (C) of Col Lynd for CofS GHQ, 1 Feb 41, sub: Test Opns for Air Defense Comd. 353/29 (C).
[15] WD ltr AG 320.2 (3–6–41) M–C–M to CGs, etc, 7 Mar 41, sub: Air Defense. 320.2/158/1. (2) WD ltr cited in footnote 7 above.
[16] Ltr ACC 354.2 (8–21–41) of CG AFCC to CofS GHQ, 21 Aug 41, sub: AAA in Interceptor Comd Exercises. 353/1 (Interceptor Comds).

As a result of experience in the test sector exercise, General Chaney recommended that the fire of all antiaircraft artillery be controlled by regional officers of the interceptor command, and G–3 of the War Department drew up a proposal to this effect. The Chief of Coast Artillery accepted the principle but made an exception for combat zones, considering it impracticable that antiaircraft batteries in the actual presence of enemy bombers should await instructions from a regional officer.[17] The question was taken up by the Air Defense Board, created in April 1941 and composed of the Chief of Coast Artillery, the Chief Signal Officer, and the Commanding General of the GHQ Air Force, General Emmons. The board agreed with the Chief of Coast Artillery, excepted combat zones from the terms of the War Department proposal, and suggested the appointment of an Antiaircraft Artillery officer on the staff of the interceptor commander.[18]

Reluctance of Air to Accept Command over Ground Forces

General McNair took issue with the findings of the Air Defense Board. On 9 July he pointed out that coordination of air defense was at least as necessary in combat zones as elsewhere. He insisted on unity of command over all air defense means. "It follows," he wrote, "that organic corps and army antiaircraft units should be abolished. All such units should be assigned or attached to interceptor commands." He recommended also that the proposed staff officer be replaced by an antiaircraft command officer, who should stand in relation to the interceptor commander somewhat as the commander of divisional artillery stood to the commanding general of a division.[19]

The issue between GHQ and the Air Forces was now reduced to two questions: (1) whether an interceptor commander should have *all* antiaircraft artillery in his area assigned or attached to his command, and (2) whether he should exercise *command* over such artillery, or only "operational control." The latter phrase, borrowed from the British, was favored by many officers in

---

[17] (1) Memo (C) G–3/40000–1 of Gen Twaddle for the CofCA, 2 Jun 41, sub: Rpt on Air Defense Comd Exercise. (2) 1st ind to preceding, CofA to CofS GHQ, 14 Jun 41. (3) GHQ 2d ind, Gen McNair to ACofS G–3, 9 Jul 41. All in 353/24 (C).

[18] Memo of Air Defense Bd for CofS USA, dated in pencil 18 Jun 41, sub: Control of Antiaircraft Units. 320.2/158/11.

[19] Memo of Gen McNair for the Air Defense Bd, 9 Jul 41, sub as above. 320.2/158/11.

the Army Air Forces. On both questions General McNair insisted on the larger powers for the air commander.

During the following months the Air Force Combat Command, under General Emmons, acting for the Chief of the Army Air Forces, prepared a draft for a Basic Field Manual, Air Defense, which was submitted to GHQ for comment in October 1941. General McNair, in consultation with General Clark, Colonels Milburn and Handwerk of the GHQ Coast Artillery Section, and Colonel Lynd, now liaison officer representing the Air Forces at GHQ, prepared comments which restated his basic views. He objected to the term "operational control" as uncertain in meaning and recommended the substitution of the word "command." Moreover, he insisted that an interceptor command should include all antiaircraft weapons in the area and urged the creation of antiaircraft commands to be placed under interceptor commanders.[20]

These recommendations, dated 22 October and repeated in a memorandum of November,[21] were eventually incorporated in training circulars published by the War Department. Training Circular No. 70, 16 December 1941, stated: "All antiaircraft artillery and pursuit aviation operating within the same area must be subject to the control of a single commander designated for the purpose." Training Circular No. 71, 18 December 1941, repeated almost word for word General McNair's language on the creation of antiaircraft commands under interceptor commanders and used the word "command" to the exclusion of "operational control."

The Air Forces was not satisfied. On 30 December General Emmons submitted to the Chief of the Army Air Forces an amended draft of the proposed Basic Field Manual on Air Defense. Though General Emmons stated that all acceptable changes had been made, some of General McNair's main criticisms made on 29 November had not been embodied.[22] In view of this development General McNair renewed his objection to the term "operational control." It is "objectionable," he wrote, "because it is unnecessary. The relation between the interceptor command and antiaircraft units operating in the same area is

---

[20] Memo of Gen McNair for CofAAF, 22 Oct 41, sub: Basic Field Manual, Air Defense, Tentative. With supporting documents. 320.2/158/15.

[21] Memo of Gen McNair for ACofS G–3 WD, 29 Nov 41, sub: Antiaircraft Units in Air Defense. 320.2/158/16.

[22] (1) Draft: Basic FM, Air Defense, Tentative. (2) AFCC memo ACC 300.7 (8–23–41) for CofAAF, 30 Dec 41, sub: Air Defense Manual. (3) AAF 1st ind to CG FF, CofCA, and CSigO, 7 Jan 42, on preceding. All in 320.2/158/15.

either command or cooperation. It cannot be something between these two." [23]

In January 1942 Brig. Gen. Clinton W. Russell became Chief of the Air Support Section of the Air Force Combat Command, which was located at GHQ. In his last post, as Chief of Staff to General Emmons, he had signed most of General Emmons' refusals to adopt General McNair's recommendations, but he now came to agree with General McNair. "The term 'operational control,'" he reported on 14 February 1942 to General McNair, ". . . is giving considerable difficulty. Action is required either to define the term explicitly or do away with it altogether and establish unity of command." [24]

The Basic Field Manual on Air Defense, when finally published on 24 December 1942, embodied General McNair's recommendations. The phrasing was less simple and clear-cut than that suggested by him, but "all" antiaircraft weapons were put under the "command" of the interceptor commander, and no use was made of the term "operational control." [25]

[23] GHQ 2d ind to CofCA and CSigO, 19 Jan 42, on memo in footnote 22 (2) above. 320.2/158/15.
[24] Memo of Gen Russell for CofS GHQ, 14 Feb 42, sub: Opn Control. 320.2/158/16.
[25] FM 1–25, Air Defense, 24 Dec 42.

IX. Failure to Develop the Plans of 1921

When authority to plan and control operations was vested in GHQ on 3 July 1941, an initial step had been taken toward putting into effect the policy for "mobilizing" the War Department laid down in the 1921 Report of the Harbord Board. That plan had been somewhat revised in 1936, but its central feature was still the transfer of the Chief of Staff, or the assignment of a commander designated by the President, to duty as commanding general of the field forces. At the outbreak of hostilities this commander was to take with him into the field as his GHQ the War Plans Division reinforced by members of other staff divisions.[1] By July 1941 the difficulties that would attend immediate execution of this feature of the mobilization plan were becoming apparent, and only the first steps were taken.

For a year before hostilities were openly declared the United States, taking over protective bases and arming friendly powers, was engaged in operations requiring centralized military direction. By June 1941 it was clear that in case of war combat operations might come quickly. But war had not begun, and with Europe occupied by the Axis and with Japan threatening in the Pacific no great single theater of operations was in sight into which, immediately or eventually, the forces being trained in the United States would be launched with an organization similar to the American Expeditionary Force of 1917–18. War was coming in a form not anticipated by the Harbord Board, which had generalized the experiences of World War I. The present emergency forced General Marshall and GHQ to remain in Washington to supervise and direct the current major task of the Army, consisting not only of the training of the troops and the procurement of equipment but also of the preparation of task forces for such operations as seemed probable in the near future. Another difficulty was raised by the possibility of hostilities in more than one major theater. In this case General

[1] See above, p. 5.

Marshall and his staff could not take the field in any one of these without defeating the plan of having the operative functions of the War Department delegated to a single agency, as they had been in the circumstances of 1917–18. Meanwhile, until the future course of events could be more clearly foreseen, WPD could not become the staff of GHQ. That division of the General Staff was more than ever needed to advise on the adjustment of strategy to the rapid shifts taking place in the world situation. All that was clear in July was that "a number of relatively minor and widely separated theaters" were developing. GHQ, with a reinforced staff, could be used to expedite action in dealing with these, and it was so used.

For several months after 3 July the 1921 plan for GHQ seems still to have been the guide to action. GHQ expected to receive command of all theaters, overseas departments, and task forces when war came or before.[2] WPD repeatedly referred to the assignment to GHQ of all active theaters as the accepted policy.[3] But, although the Eastern and Western Defense Commands were declared theaters of operations after Pearl Harbor and passed to the control of

[2] On 6 Aug 41 the Deputy Chief of Staff GHQ reported "discussion now going on toward turning over the P[hilippine] I[slands] to GHQ" (Min (S) of Staff Conferences, GHQ, 6 Aug 41. 337 (S)). The next day he notified all sections that Hawaii and the Caribbean were to be expected 1 September; Alaska, 15 September. (GHQ memo (S) to all gen and sp staff secs, 7 Aug 41, sub: Expansion of GHQ. 320.2/22 (S).) On 8 August the advance copy of a directive regarding "additional bases with projects and project officers" was announced (Diary (S), GHQ, 8 Aug 41, 314.81 (S)), and on 9 August the Deputy Chief of Staff announced that "in general, all projects and outlying bases are to be ours." (Min (S) of Staff Conferences, 9 Aug 41, 337 (S).) On 15 August General McNair specifically recommended that the planning responsibilities of GHQ be extended to include the Caribbean and Alaskan Defense Commands and its command responsibilities to include the Philippines. (See IV, *a* and *c*, GHQ memo (S) for CofS USA, 15 Aug 41, sub: Functions, Responsibilities, and Authority of GHQ. AGO Records, WPD 4558 (S), Tab II.) On 25 October the Deputy Chief of Staff announced "receipt at GHQ of WD approval of our letter to place bases, defense commands, and overseas departments under GHQ for planning." (Min (S) of Staff Conferences, 25 Oct 41. 337 (S).) On 14 November he informed the GHQ staff: "The Chief of Staff gave us a policy yesterday. He does not anticipate transfer of Hawaii, Philippine Islands and Alaska to control of GHQ before next spring." (Min (S) of Staff Conferences, 14 Nov 41. 337 (S).) As late as 5 December the GHQ conception of its prospective command mission was expressed as follows: "To serve as a command agency for the War Department for all Theaters of Operations, existing and potential, as designated by the War Department." (GHQ memo of Gen Malony for CofS GHQ, 5 Dec 41, sub: GHQ Orgn. 320.2/3/108.)

[3] (1) "In time of war, it is anticipated that GHQ will coordinate and supervise operations in all theaters and in all overseas departments and bases." Sec I, par 11, WPD memo (S) for CofS USA, undated but Aug 41, sub: Functions and Authority of GHQ. 320.2/4 (S). This policy is recommended in sec II, par 5. (2) "At such time as a theater becomes active and combat operations are indicated, GHQ can then properly act as the agency through which the Chief of Staff exercises his command functions." Par 15, sec I, memo (S) of Gen L. T. Gerow for CofS USA, 30 Aug 41, sub: Functions, Responsibilities and Authority of GHQ. AGO Records, WPD 4558 (S). (3) " . . . it is intended that GHQ will exercise superior command over all *active* theaters." WPD memo for CofS USA, 23 Sep 41, sub: Preparation of Plans. AGO Records, WPD 4175–18.

GHQ, command of any theater in which the enemy was fought was never vested in that headquarters.

The Outlook of GHQ on its Mission

The outlook and evolution of GHQ as a planning and operational headquarters was profoundly influenced by the ideas of its Deputy Chief of Staff, General Malony, who had joined GHQ on 17 June 1941. His views were dominated by the belief that there was urgent need for a single command post in the War Department and that GHQ should become that post.

His previous studies and his recent experience had brought him to this conclusion. Until 1940 he had been on a tour of duty at the War College as an instructor in the G–4 Section, and in the last year of this tour he had been chief of that section. His studies had convinced him of the fundamental importance of logistics in military planning and in war. He formulated his conclusions in axioms inspired by the writings of General Sir John Frederick Maurice: Ground governs strategy. Weapons govern tactics. Supply governs administration. When the three are in balance, war becomes a science and an art. When they are out of balance, it becomes a thing of gambles and chances.

General Malony also believed firmly in unity of command. He thought that the War Department should decide on over-all strategic plans and provide suitable types of personnel and materiel, but that the command of operations, including control of the necessary means, should be single and should be unified at the highest possible level.[4]

In 1940 he was detailed to the Devers–Greenslade Board, which made a survey of the Caribbean area, Bermuda, and Newfoundland with a view to recommending the areas to be leased from the British as bases. He was then sent to England by President Roosevelt on the Base Lease Commission, which negotiated the conditions of occupancy by the United States of the bases obtained from the British in exchange for fifty over-age destroyers.

When General Malony returned to Washington he was more than ever convinced that war was imminent. But assigned to WPD and temporarily acting as its chief, he found that the need for meeting this danger was not sufficiently reflected in the operations of the General Staff. It seemed to him that no one was in a position to take decisive action or to do more than register concurrences or

---

[4] Interview of AGF Hist Off with Gen Malony, 10 Jan 44.

nonconcurrences. General Marshall directed General Malony, who had expressed his anxiety about this situation, to take a group of topflight officers from WPD to GHQ to assist that headquarters in operational planning and in executing plans. As Deputy Chief of Staff of GHQ, he was charged by General McNair with the supervision of its new planning and operational functions.

General McNair was primarily interested in training. No evidence has been found to indicate that he welcomed the expansion given to the functions of GHQ on 3 July 1941, but he shared the basic convictions of his deputy that command should be single and should include complete control of the means necessary to its exercise. He also shared with him a sense of the extreme urgency of the crisis and the need for prompt and expeditious action. A "classic soldier"[5] in the fulfillment of his responsibilities, he gave his deputy loyal support.

Limited Powers of GHQ
as a Planning and Operational Headquarters

The functions and authority of GHQ as redefined in July 1941 were hedged about with too many restrictions to permit it to achieve the results envisaged by those who shared the views of General Malony. The basic study for the directive of 3 July 1941 laid down the premise that in delegating authority to GHQ "the War Department should be careful to avoid the relinquishment of that control which is essential to the execution of its responsibility for the Army's function in the conduct of war. To meet this responsibility, the War Department must retain strategic direction of all military operations. . . . While it must make available to GHQ all of the means required, it should retain control of the means not essential to the full execution of those operations in process."[6] By the terms of the formal directive new authority was to be delegated to GHQ only if, as, and when. GHQ was to plan "as may be directed"; to control "in those theaters assigned to its command"; to exercise command over task forces "from the date specified"; to

[5] General of the Army George C. Marshall, Address of Acceptance of the General McNair Plaque, 25 May 45. 314.7 (AGF Hist).

[6] Par 5, sec I memo (S) WPD 3209–10 for CofS USA,—Jun 41, sub: Enlargement of the Functions of GHQ. 320.2/1 (S). For the preliminary conference ("Present Colonel Ward, Colonel Brooks, and the undersigned") see "Note for Record" (S), 17 Jun 41, signed "L. T. Gerow." AGO Records, WPD 3209–11 (S)

command such forces in the United States "as shall hereafter, from time to time, be designated"; and in order to execute these missions have at its disposal "such credits . . . as may . . . be specifically allotted." [7]

Problems of Incomplete Tactical Control

GHQ immediately ran into difficulty in meeting the new responsibility assigned to it. In the first weeks of July 1941 it was given the command of Bermuda and Newfoundland bases, "tactical control" of the Greenland garrison, and the mission of preparing a task force to relieve the British in Iceland, but because of incomplete tactical control serious administrative complications quickly developed.

On 25 July General McNair tried to resolve some of these difficulties by recommending that contiguous base commands be grouped in larger defense commands.[8] Approval of this proposal would assist GHQ in exercising the required coordination and at the same time indicate the willingness of the War Department to provide GHQ with means adequate for command. Specifically, he recommended the immediate activation of a North Atlantic Defense Command to consist initially of Newfoundland, Greenland, and Iceland, with headquarters at St. Johns. He pointed out that the directive enlarging the responsibilities of GHQ violated the principle that command responsibility must carry with it control of the necessary means to fulfill it. He observed that with few exceptions the new bases acquired by the United States had been "placed under the partial command of three different agencies (one for tactical command, one for supply, and one for construction) . . . ." His proposal to group contiguous bases, as well as his further recommendation that the Alaskan and Caribbean Commands be activated at once,[9] might lessen the confusion by putting more means at the disposal of GHQ, but it is clear from the memorandum that General McNair regarded these changes only as a palliative. GHQ had not been given control of all the means necessary to perform

---

[7] WD ltr (R) AG 320.2 (6–19–41) MC–E–M, 3 Jul 41, sub: Enlargement of the Functions of GHQ. 320.2/34 (S).

[8] Memo (S) of CofS GHQ for CofS USA, 25 Jul 41, sub: Defense Comds. 320.2/32 (Gen Str) (S).

[9] WPD pointed out that the Alaskan and Caribbean Defense Commands had already been activated. Sec I, par 12, WPD memo (S) for CofS USA,—Aug 41, sub: Functions and Authority of GHQ. 320.2/1 (S). What General McNair seems to have intended was that they should be placed under GHQ.

its mission as an operational headquarters and therefore could not exercise command either promptly or effectively. General McNair later cited, as "an interesting example of superior command," the set-up in the Newfoundland Base Command: [10]

War Plans Division, WD	Personnel and material resources available.
Canadian-U. S. Permanent Defense Board	Defense Plan.
Second Corps Area	Supply other than air technical.
Middletown Depot	Air technical supply.
Chief of Engineers	Construction.
Chief of Army Air Forces through G–3 WD	Relief of the air squadrons at Newfoundland airport.
GHQ	Such inspection and coordination as is practicable under the circumstances.

The confusing position of GHQ in the chain of command is presented graphically in Chart No. 6, which was prepared by General Malony and submitted to General McNair on 5 December.[11]

The nub of the command problem of GHQ was its lack of control over material resources or supply. The arrangements for the control of logistics described above in the case of Newfoundland were essentially the same for other base commands as well as the Western and Eastern Theaters of Operations, when these were placed under GHQ in December 1941.[12] In all cases the allotment, transfer, and movement of supplies on the basis of recommendations from GHQ remained directly under the control of War Department G–4 or of the Air Corps.

---

[10] Par 3, memo (S) of CofS GHQ to ACofS WPD, 2 Sep 41, sub: Functions, Responsibility and Authority of GHQ Orgn. 320.2/1 (S).

[11] Chart attached to GHQ memo of Gen Malony for CofS GHQ, 5 Dec 41, sub: GHQ Orgn. 320.2/3/108.

[12] (1) *Bermuda*: Par 2, WD ltr (S) AG 320.2 BBC (7–8–41) MC–E–M to CofS GHQ, 8 Jul 41, sub: Comd of USA Units in Bermuda, supplemented by WD ltr (S) AG 320.2 BBC (12–8–41) MC–G–M, 11 Dec 41, sub as above. AGO Records, 320.2 (BBD) (7–8–41) (S). (2) *Greenland*: (a) WD ltr (S) AG 320.2 (7–10–41) MC–E–M, 10 Jul 41, sub: Comd of USA Units in Greenland. AGO Records, 320.2/7 (Greenland) (S); (b) WD ltr (C) AG 320.2 (11–5–41) MC–C–M, 26 Nov 41, sub: Activation of Greenland Base Comd. AGO Records, 320.2/7 (Greenland Str) (S). (3) *Western Defense Comd*: WD ltr AG 320.2 (12–13–41) MC–D–M to CG WDC, 13 Dec 41, sub: G–4 Adm Order—Designation of WDC as a TO. AGO Records (S). (4) *Eastern Theater of Opns*: WD ltr (S) AG 371 (12–19–41) MSC–E–M, 20 Dec 41, sub: G–4 Adm Order—Designation of ETO. AGO Records (S).

The Air Problem

Serious difficulties arose also from the relationship between GHQ and the Chief of the Army Air Forces, a relationship acknowledged in the War Department to be "indefinite and unsatisfactory." [13]

One source of these conflicts lay in the Air Force interpretation of the powers with which the Air arm was invested at the creation of the Army Air Forces on 20 June 1941.[14] By the terms of the basic regulation (AR 95–5, AAF, General Provisions) the Chief of the Army Air Forces, General Arnold, assisted by a fully organized staff, was given very broadly authority to plan. He was directed to issue all plans for the new Air Force Combat Command and for the Air Corps; he was to determine "the requirements" of the Air Forces, "including overseas garrisons and task forces"; he was to plan "for defense against air attack of the continental United States." [15] In regard to operations directed by the commanding general of the Air Force Combat Command, the language of the regulation was sweeping. It gave that officer "control of all aerial operations," but that control was clearly qualified by excepting from it units assigned or attached to task forces, overseas garrisons, or other commanders.[16] In general, the Army Air Forces started not only with strong convictions about air power, but also with the view that Air could not be used with maximum effect unless command was so arranged as to give full play to its unique mobility.[17] It desired a large autonomy of command in the hands of Air officers in order not to be handicapped by commanders whom it regarded as incapable of understanding the new Air problems because of their long experience and education concentrated on slow-moving ground forces. To appreciate the problem confronting GHQ it must be remembered not only that AR 95–5 recognized the Air Forces as a powerful autonomous entity, but also that General Arnold, Chief of the Army Air Forces, was Deputy Chief of Staff for Air. As such he had direct access to the Chief of Staff and did not have to obtain concurrences from the General Staff divisions of the War Department in proposing a directive. When GHQ was made an operational headquarters in July 1941, the new Chief of the Air Forces and the Chief of Staff of GHQ stood on the same footing, directly under General Marshall.

---

[13] Par 14, sec I, WPD memo (S) for CofS, undated, sub: Functions and Authority of GHQ. (Incl to GHQ memo (S) of Gen McNair for DCofS, 11 Aug 41, sub as above.) 320.2/4 (S).

[14] See above, Section VII.   [15] Par *a–b*, par 4*b*, AR 95–5, 20 Jun 41.   [16] Par 4 *a*, AR 95–5, 20 Jun 41.

[17] Memo (S) of CofAAF for CofS USA,—Nov 41, sub: Reorgn of the WD. AGO Records, WPD 4614 (S).

As soon as the new role of GHQ had been determined upon, General McNair personally sought from General Arnold his interpretation of the regulation governing the Army Air Forces. General Arnold later confirmed in writing the following definitions of his position: [18]

There is no thought of invading the established chain of command. The term "tactical operations" (in par 3 b, AR 95–5) refers to the allocation of the necessary air units and other means, and does not include their employment within the theater of operations; the term "aerial operations" (par 4 a: "control of all aerial operations") does not refer to combat operations. . . . There is no thought of aerial combat operations controlled by the Air Force Combat Command, coincident with similar operations controlled by a theater commander.

These statements are clear and definite, and no evidence has been found that General Arnold ever challenged the principle that, when a theater became active, the theater commander should be in complete command of all the means required by his mission. But GHQ was aware that the Air Forces wished to broaden the definition of powers contained in its charter. On 24 October Brig. Gen. Carl Spaatz, the Chief of the Air Staff, declared that air war planning was a function of the Chief of the Army Air Forces. He explained that the air plan for a theater, when coordinated by WPD and approved by the Chief of Staff, provided all the essentials for detailed planning by the theater commander without need of "monitoring" by GHQ. He also proposed that "an air theater of operations should be recognized, wherein the primary function of the Army Air Forces therein is to conduct air warfare, with the ground forces performing the mission of protecting the air bases." General Spaatz further declared that the air defense of the continental United States was properly to be regarded as a responsibility of the Chief of the Army Air Forces and that the commanding general of the Air Force Combat Command, acting under him, must have the powers necessary to control combat operations, presumably throughout the United States.[19] On 14 November he objected to the language of a proposed

[18] On 1 July General McNair called on General Arnold and on 5 July sent him a memorandum of "the essence of your comment," asking General Arnold "to confirm or correct them as necessary." (GHQ memo for Gen Arnold, 5 Jul 41, sub: AR 95–5, 20 Jun 41.) General Arnold as Deputy Chief of Staff for Air replied in a memorandum for the Chief of Staff GHQ, 18 Aug 41, excusing his delay on the ground of absence from his office. 320.2/52 (AAF).

[19] Par 8 a–c, par 9 a, par 10 a–b, memo (S) of CofAAF for ACofS WPD, 24 Oct 41, sub: Functions, Responsibilities and Authority of GHQ; signed by Gen Carl Spaatz, Chief of Air Staff. AGO Records, WPD 4558 (S).

AGENCY	FUNCTION	JOINT TRAINING FORCES FIRST (ATL)	JOINT TRAINING FORCES SECOND (PAC)	PUERTO RICO SECTOR PUERTO RICO	BA-HAMA	JA-MAICA	AN-TIGUA	PANAMA SECTOR PANAMA	TRINIDAD SECTOR TRINI-DAD	ST LUCIA	BRITISH GUIANA	SURI-NAM	CURA-CAO	A
G H Q	PLANNING													
	TRAINING (SUPERVISION AND COORDINATION)	Note a	Note a											
	COMMAND													
	AIR REINFORCEMENT (FURNISH ON CALL)													
	RESPONSIBILITY (EXCEPT AS INDICATED)	Note b	Note b											
COMMANDING GENERAL 1ST AIR FORCE	AIR REINFORCEMENT (FURNISH ON CALL)													
COMMANDING GENERAL 1ST AIR FORCE	TRAINING (SUPERVISE AIR UNITS ONLY)													
CHIEF AIR SERVICE COMMAND	SUPPLY (AC TECH ONLY)													
COMMANDING GENERAL 2D CORPS AREA	SUPPLY (SAME AS FOR UNITS OF FLD FORCES)													
COMMANDING GENERAL PANAMA CANAL DEPT	SUPPLY (EXCEPT AC TECH)													
COMMANDING GENERAL PUERTO RICO DEPT	SUPPLY (EXCEPT AC TECH AND ENGR CONSTR)			PLANNED										
COMMANDING GENERAL TRINIDAD BC	SUPPLY (EXCEPT AC TECH AND ENGR CONSTR)								PLANNED					
CHIEF OF ENGINEERS	CONSTRUCTION													Note d
CHIEF OF ENGINEERS	SUPPLY (ENGR CONSTR ONLY)													
US NAVY	RESPONSIBILITY (AS INDICATED)	Note c	Note c											

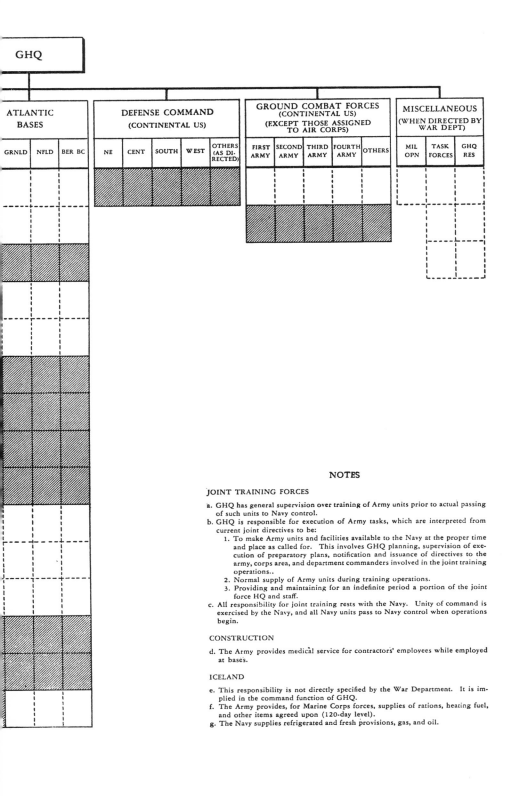

GHQ

ATLANTIC BASES			DEFENSE COMMAND (CONTINENTAL US)					GROUND COMBAT FORCES (CONTINENTAL US) (EXCEPT THOSE ASSIGNED TO AIR CORPS)					MISCELLANEOUS (WHEN DIRECTED BY WAR DEPT)		
GRNLD	NFLD	BER BC	NE	CENT	SOUTH	WEST	OTHERS (AS DIRECTED)	FIRST ARMY	SECOND ARMY	THIRD ARMY	FOURTH ARMY	OTHERS	MIL OPN	TASK FORCES	GHQ RES

NOTES

JOINT TRAINING FORCES

a. GHQ has general supervision over training of Army units prior to actual passing of such units to Navy control.

b. GHQ is responsible for execution of Army tasks, which are interpreted from current joint directives to be:
    1. To make Army units and facilities available to the Navy at the proper time and place as called for. This involves GHQ planning, supervision of execution of preparatory plans, notification and issuance of directives to the army, corps area, and department commanders involved in the joint training operations..
    2. Normal supply of Army units during training operations.
    3. Providing and maintaining for an indefinite period a portion of the joint force HQ and staff.

c. All responsibility for joint training rests with the Navy. Unity of command is exercised by the Navy, and all Navy units pass to Navy control when operations begin.

CONSTRUCTION

d. The Army provides medical service for contractors' employees while employed at bases.

ICELAND

e. This responsibility is not directly specified by the War Department. It is implied in the command function of GHQ.

f. The Army provides, for Marine Corps forces, supplies of rations, heating fuel, and other items agreed upon (120-day level).

g. The Navy supplies refrigerated and fresh provisions, gas, and oil.

directive giving GHQ command of all army forces outside the continental United States. He raised the question of airplanes that might be flown to Bermuda in defense of the continent. Under the proposed directive they would cease to be under control of the Air Force commander.[20] Finally, in November the Chief of the Army Air Forces, discussing the "priceless attributes of air power," advanced the view that these could be utilized more effectively only if "the Air Force is organized and controlled as a single entity" and placed on a footing of complete equality with the ground forces.[21]

GHQ was aware not only that such were the views of the Air Force staff but that they were shared, in part at least, by WPD. In August that division expressed the opinion that, inasmuch as GHQ was developing as a ground force command, its functions and authority should be modeled on those of the Army Air Forces. General McNair's comment was that the comparison "is inapt, since the Chief of the Army Air Forces does not command the aviation of overseas garrisons—at least not yet." [22] WPD adopted the Air Force view that the air defense of the United States was an Air Force problem and that it should be subject to air command unified under the Chief of Staff.[23]

It is not surprising, therefore, that General McNair and his staff felt it necessary to maintain a watchful defense of the authority granted to GHQ as they interpreted that authority. In June General McNair had stated his position in the following words: "There must be a unified responsibility in peace for the preparation of war plans, even as there must be undivided command within a defense command in war." [24] In a memorandum dated 15 August 1941 he dis-

[20] Par 4, memo (S) of CofAAF for ACofS WPD, 14 Nov 41, sub: GHQ Dir; signed by Gen Spaatz. AGO Records, WPD 3209–10 (S).

[21] Par a, sec I, memo (S) of CofAAF for CofS USA, — Nov 41, sub: Reorgn of the WD. AGO Records, WPD 4614 (S).

[22] Par 9, sec I, WPD memo (S) for CofS USA, — Aug 41, sub: Functions and Authority of GHQ. Incl to memo (S) of Gen McNair for DCofS GHQ, 11 Aug 41, sub: Functions and Authority of GHQ. 320.2/4 (S).

[23] Par 5 c, sec I, WPD memo (S) for CofS USA, Nov 41, sub: Orgn of the Army High Comd. 320.2/1 (S). Also, "Consideration of Nonconcurrences," WPD memo (S) for CofS USA, 5 Jul 41, sub: Rainbow 5 (OPD Records, WPD 4175–18 Rainbow No 5 to sec i (S)) where the argument is stated as follows: "WPD considers that the clear intention of AR 95–5 is to place defense against air bombardment alone (as distinct from combined operations of air and ground forces other than antiaircraft units) under the Air Force. Only thus can most effective use be made of the strategic and tactical mobility of air power. Furthermore, such arrangement conforms to the principle of unity of command for each definite task to be performed. Initially, and until an enemy gains air and naval superiority, no hostile invasion can be attempted."

[24] Comment of Gen McNair in par 2 c, Tab D, memo (C) G–3/45316 for ACofS G–3 WD, 5 Jun 41, sub: Defense Plans—Continental US. 320.2/28 (C). General McNair adhered to the same principle regarding the

cussed the problem by starting with the principle of strict accountability for command, which the Chief of the Army Air Forces had acknowledged. He defined with much care and explicit detail the position of GHQ as distinguished from that toward which the Air Forces seemed to be working:[25]

I. 5. GHQ will assume command over such air forces as are assigned to theaters, Defense Commands and task forces [under GHQ] and will prepare plans for the utilization of these forces. These plans will be submitted to the Chief of the Army Air Forces for comment. GHQ will provide the local facilities for the employment of the combat air force as set forth in the approved plans of the Chief of the Army Air Forces.

6. [Requests for air reinforcements will be made on GHQ by the theater commander.] GHQ will take the necessary action to provide [these reinforcements].

II. 1. . . . GHQ will be guided by the following concept of responsibility for air plans and air operations:

   a. That during combat operations the Chief of Army Air Forces will be a member of the Staff of the Commander of the Field Forces and will, as such, operate as a member of the GHQ Staff;

   b. That in the preparation of plans for air operations the Chief of Army Air Forces will submit to GHQ the plans for the employment of the Combat Air Forces . . . ;

   c. That [he] will submit to GHQ the plans for the employment of the Combat Air Force on independent missions . . . ;

   d. [That these plans will] in each instance specify who exercises command over air operations conducted by the Combat Air Forces.

   e. That upon receipt of [these plans] GHQ will forward these plans with a directive to the commander of each Defense command or theater. The directive will require Defense commanders to prepare and forward to GHQ the appropriate local air plans to implement the plans of the Chief of Army Air Forces.

   f. GHQ will forward local air plans to the Chief of Army Air Forces for approval or comment.

Clearly General McNair regarded the role of GHQ as more active than "monitoring" Air Force plans and directives. The views of GHQ and the Army Air Forces regarding the authority properly to be exercised by GHQ were far apart

---

overseas bases and defense commands under GHQ. See GHQ memo (S) for Air Defense Bd, 23 Jun 41, sub: Orgn of US Air Defense System. 320.2/26 (Gen Str)(S). Pars 3 a and 4 a and b of AR 95–5, 20 Jun 41, adopted in spite of nonconcurrence of General McNair, kept open the question of control over planning and even over operations. For General McNair's nonconcurrence in these paragraphs see GHQ memo (C) for CofS USA, 18 Jun 41, sub: Revision of AR 95–5. 300.3/1 (GHQ AR) (C).

[25] GHQ memo (S) for CofS USA, 15 Aug 41, sub: Functions, Responsibilities and Authority of GHQ. AGO Records, WPD 4558 (S).

and would require a definite decision by higher authority in the near future.

On the relatively minor matter of air reinforcements for base commands an agreement was reached in accord with the views of GHQ. The original directives authorized the base commanders to call on the Air Forces directly for reinforcements.[26] On 25 July General Russell, Chief of Staff of the Air Force Combat Command, requested the Chief of the Army Air Forces to see to it that air reinforcements desired by the commanding general of the Greenland Base Command be sought directly from GHQ, instead of the commanding general of the First Air Force. The Chief of Staff of GHQ naturally approved this proposal and took the opportunity to request that plans be made at once "by the proper air staff, in collaboration with this headquarters, to provide for the prompt air reinforcement of Iceland, Greenland, Newfoundland, and Bermuda Base Commands in case the need therefor should arise." Seven weeks later the Chief of the Army Air Forces expressed his willingness to comply. This action was received with much gratification at GHQ.[27]

But completely harmonious cooperation was difficult to attain. On 5 July General Emmons, Commanding General of the Air Force Combat Command, complained that he had been informed only indirectly about the plans for the task force which was being prepared for dispatch to Iceland.[28] On 10 December General Marshall, apparently in response to complaints, explained "that Gen. Arnold has not understood his position in the War Department organization; that he is Deputy for Air and in that capacity functions as other Deputies; that so far as Theaters turned over to GHQ are concerned, he will function as do other Deputies, viz., through GHQ." [29] On 28 January 1942 General McNair pointed out to General Marshall that GHQ, having been given command of United States operations in the British Isles, must be informed of "War Department plans (including air plans) pertaining to this theater," and invited his attention to the fact that the Deputy Chief of Staff for Air had sent the War Department a memorandum to implement plans for the theater without

---

[26] Par 2 *b*, WD ltr (S) AG 320.2 BBC (7–8–41) MC–E–M, 8 Jul 41, sub: Comd of USA Units in Bermuda. AGO Records (S). A similar clause appears in the directives activating other bases.

[27] ACC ltr (S) 320.2 (7–12–41) to CofAAF signed Russell, Brig Gen CofS Air Force Combat Comd, 25 Jul 41, sub: Comd of US Army Units in Greenland, with 3 inds. AGO Records, 320.2/7 (Greenland Str) (S). Pencilled notes on 3d ind of CofAAF, 3 Nov 41: (1) "Deputy. This is in line with what we planned to request!" (2) "O.K. H.J.M.[alony. DCofS]."

[28] Ltr (S) of CG AFCC to TAG, 5 Jul 41, sub: Preparation of Task Force Plans. AGO Records, 381 (7–5–41) (S).

[29] GHQ Diary (S), 10 Dec 41. 314.81 (S).

reference to GHQ.[30] Again on 11 February 1942 G–3 of the GHQ staff complained that GHQ was "having difficulty keeping up with orders affecting the American forces in the British Isles which are being issued by the Chief of the Army Air Forces." [31]

Not only in Iceland and Great Britain but also in the Caribbean difficulties arose between GHQ and the Army Air Forces. On 7 January General McNair characterized as unsatisfactory the plans submitted by the Army Air Forces for the organization of the air force in the Caribbean Defense Command, for which GHQ was then responsible. He found the "arguments advanced those used generally by the Air Corps in its efforts to detach itself from the ground arms." But, since the commanding general of the theater was an Air officer and the forces within the command were working smoothly, General McNair confined himself to an extended "memorandum for record" closing with the words: "It is to be hoped devoutly that the results may be satisfactory in case an enemy appears." [32]

Measures Taken to Improve the Position of GHQ

Despite the many difficulties encountered by GHQ in performing the missions assigned on 3 July 1941, only minor adjustments were made in the original grant of authority. GHQ obtained the right to summon theater and task force staffs to the War College for planning purposes. It obtained from General Marshall a directive ordering the Air Forces to route theater requests for air reinforcements through GHQ.[33] But on the requests in General McNair's 25 July memorandum favorable action was not taken.[34] On the fundamental ques-

---

[30] Memo (S) of Gen McNair for CG FF, 28 Jan 42, sub: Comd of US Opns in British Isles. AGO Records, 320.2/94 (NI Str BI) (S).

[31] Min (S) of Staff Conferences, 11 Feb 42. 337 (S).

[32] M/R (S), 7 Jan 42, sub: Orgn of Caribbean Air Force, with papers bearing on the question. AGO Records, 320.2/97 (CDC) (S).

[33] (1) The need is suggested in par 2, sec II, GHQ memo (S) for CofS USA, 15 Aug 41, sub: Functions, Responsibilities, and Authority of GHQ. AGO Records, WPD 4558 (S). On 23 September the Deputy Chief of Staff, GHQ, requested authority to issue directives calling in for consultation not only commanders of task forces, bases, and defense commands, but also representatives of the Projects Group of WPD and the War Plans Division of the new Army Air Forces. Memo of DCofS GHQ for CofS USA, 23 Sep 41, sub: Preparation of Plans. OPD Records, WPD 4175–18. (2) The policy was approved 21 October with the provision that representatives of WPD and the Air WPD might be too busy to appear in person when summoned for consultation, but could be consulted by arrangement. WD ltr (S) AG 381 (9–4–41) MC–E, 22 Oct 41, sub: Preparation of Plans for Task Forces, Bases and Defense Comds. AGO Records (S).

[34] For this memo see above, p. 132.

tion of the control of supplies the War Department adhered firmly to the position stated in the original directive that this control must remain in its own hands. On 21 July WPD reaffirmed and defined this position: "The directive and [the GHQ functional] chart do not contemplate that GHQ will take over functions of G–4. Rather GHQ will control only such supply credits as are specifically allotted to it by the War Department. These allotments will be made by G–4 acting for the War Department." [35] In January 1942 a *modus vivendi* was attained by establishing a procedure for coordination between WPD, G–4, GHQ, and theater commanders with regard to planning, command, and supplies.[36] After the outbreak of hostilities General Marshall directed that the following sentence be added to all orders pertaining to the movement of units and equipment: "GHQ is charged with the execution of this order." Moreover, General Arnold was instructed to forward to GHQ for transmittal all orders for activities under the control of GHQ. It was understood that the object was (1) to enable GHQ to act more expeditiously, and (2) to give it, temporarily at least, "supervision and follow-up responsibilities" with respect to all movement orders. To assist it in the latter task GHQ was presently authorized to "deal directly" with other War Department agencies.[37] In addition a grant of authority was given to GHQ on 17 December 1941 to discharge enlisted men, direct travel in overseas commands, and grant leaves of absence—an authority which had been requested on 29 August. [38]

War had come suddenly and on two fronts. The plan proposed by the Harbord Board in 1921 had to be reconsidered in the shortest time possible in the light of the new situation. A decision had to be reached whether the direction of future operations should be vested in GHQ or the General Staff of the War Department.

---

[35] Memo (S) WPD 3209–10 for CofS USA, 21 Jul 41, sub: GHQ Functional Chart. AGO Records, 320.2 (Enlargement of GHQ) (S).

[36] WD memo (S) G–4/34015 for CG FF, 24 Jan 42, sub: Coordination between WPD, G–4 WD, GHQ and Overseas Theater Comdrs. 381/94 (Gen) (S).

[37] (1) Memo (C) of Brig Gen L. T. Gerow for Col Smith, 10 Dec 41, sub: GHQ. "12/18/41. Noted— Office of Chief of Staff." AGO Records, WPD 3209–17 (C). (2) Par 2 *b*, WD ltr AG 320.2 (12–10–41) MO–C–M, 11 Dec 41, sub: Enlargement of Functions of GHQ. 320.2/3/110.

[38] WD ltr AG 210.482 (7–30–41) PC–A, 17 Dec 41, sub: Delegation of Additional Authority to GHQ and Overseas Base Comds. 320.2/3/77. The missions of GHQ in December, apparently finally defined and limited at that time, were summarized in an office memo for ACofS G–1 WD, signed J. H. Hilldring, Lt Col, Executive, 18 Dec 41, sub: Operating Procedure with Respect to the Increased Functions and Responsibilities of GHQ. 320.2/870.

X. The Dissolution of GHQ and the Establishment of Army Ground Forces

General McNair's requests in his memorandum of 25 July 1941 for the enlargement of the authority of GHQ precipitated a long and critical discussion within the War Department, terminated only by the reorganization of 9 March 1942. In the light of the strategic situation confronting the United States it was finally concluded that execution of the Harbord Board plan of 1921 was inadvisable. The training activities of GHQ were to be continued as a function of a new command, the Army Ground Forces, but its planning and operational responsibilities were transferred to agencies which received the powers never granted to GHQ.

Reform of GHQ versus Reorganization of the War Department

It was quickly seen that the proposals in General McNair's July memorandum would, if adopted, "affect both the peace and war activities of almost every agency of the War Department."[1] On 14 August General Marshall referred the issues raised to a board representing the five sections of the General Staff, the Chief of the Army Air Forces, and GHQ. Holding its first meeting on 14 and 15 August, this board concluded with only one opposing voice that "a major reorganization of the War Department was in order."[2] Thereupon WPD

---

[1] Par 4, memo (S) WPD 4558 for CofS USA, 30 Aug 41, sub: Functions, Responsibilities and Authority of GHQ. 320.2/1 (S)

[2] Par 1, memo (S) of Lt Col G. P. Hays, GHQ representative, for CofS, GHQ, 23 Aug 41, sub: Functions and Responsibilities of GHQ. 320.2/1 (S). See also pars 1–2, memo (S) of Gen McNair for Gen Bryden, DCofS WD, 21 Oct 41, sub: Functions, Responsibilities and Authority of GHQ. 320.2/1 (S). The authority for the statement that only one member of the Board opposed reorganization is par 6, memo (S) of CofAAF for ACofS WD, 24 Oct 41, sub as above. AGO Records, WPD 4558 (S).

drafted a study to implement this recommendation. It sketched an organization similar to that later put into effect in March 1942, in which GHQ was to be eliminated.[3] But its study, which was to reappear in October, was soon withdrawn, and WPD proceeded with an effort to achieve a satisfactory redefinition of the "functions, responsibilities and authority" of GHQ.[4] This effort, continued through September and October, was finally defeated by wide divergencies of opinion and interest. The two successive formulas which WPD put forward proposed too little authority for GHQ to satisfy that headquarters and too much to obtain the concurrence of G–4, G–1, and G–3 of the War Department or the Chief of the Army Air Forces.[5] In November the proposal to reorganize the entire War Department was again given the right of way.

The Point of View at GHQ on Reorganization

The criticisms at GHQ of the successive proposals to redefine its authority or to reorganize the War Department were focused on the lack of an executive agency in the War Department capable of dealing with operations comprehensively and promptly. In his 25 July memorandum General McNair did not confine himself to specific proposals, but pointed out that under existing procedure [6]

there is no War Department agency which at present can with satisfactory promptness,

    a. Coordinate the defense of contiguous bases,

    b. Operate economic supply, replacement, transportation and evacuation systems,

    c. Effect efficient administration.

[3] WPD memo (S) for CofS USA, — Aug 41, sub: Orgn of the Army High Comd. 320.2/1 (S).

[4] (1) Memo (S) WPD 4558 for CofS USA, — Aug 41, sub: Functions, Responsibilities and Authority of GHQ. 320.2/1 (S). This copy proposed to withdraw all bases from the control of GHQ; a copy dated 30 Aug 41 in AGO Records, WPD 4558 (S), left Iceland under its control. The principle observed was that GHQ was to control bases and theaters only after they became active. (2) The second attempt was embodied in memo (S) WPD 3209–10 for CofS USA,—Nov 41, sub: GHQ Directive. AGO Records, WPD 3209–10 (S).

[5] The comments and nonconcurrences of GHQ (2 Sep), of G–1 WD (15 Sep), of G–2 WD (18 Sep), of G–4 WD, and of CofAAF (24 Oct) on the memo of 30 Aug are in AGO Records, WPD 4558 (S). The substitute study was WD memo for CofS USA, — Nov 41, sub: GHQ Directive. The memo and nonconcurrences of G–3 WD (8 Nov), of G–4 WD (8 Nov), of TAG (10 Nov), of G–2 WD (12 Nov), of G–1 WD (13 Nov), and of CofAAF (14 Nov) are in AGO Records, WPD 3209–10 (S). In spite of the nonconcurrences, this memo was submitted to the Chief of Staff for approval. On 29 November it was "still on General Marshall's desk—not approved yet." Pencilled note on memo (S) of Brig Gen H. F. Loomis for Gen Bryden, 22 Nov 41, sub: GHQ Directive. WPD 3209–10 (S).

[6] Par 3, memo (S) of Gen McNair for CofS WD, 25 Jul 41, sub: Defense Comds. 320.2/32 (Gen Str) (S).

When the first plan for reorganizing the War Department was put forward by WPD in August, Lt. Col. George P. Hays, who represented GHQ in the August conferences, emphasized the same point in expressing his dissatisfaction with the reorganization proposed. He could not find the strong executive agency required and felt that the failure to provide one "shows either an unwillingness on the part of the War Plans Division to face realities or a decision to put over a study in which the element to furnish vitalization is implied rather than stated frankly." He believed that what the War Department machine needed was a "spark plug." "Responsibility should be clearly fixed in one individual, designated as chief" of the desired command group. "His authority, under the Chief of Staff, to direct action by other War Department agencies must be unquestionable." His office "must not be drawn into current business nor should any other War Department agency be allowed to usurp its authority." [7] When WPD produced its plan for increasing further the authority of GHQ, Colonel Hays returned to the charge: [8]

The basic concept underlying this study is that no real emergency exists and therefore there is no need, at this time, for the United States Army to prepare for combat operations. As long as persons in responsible positions within the War Department maintain this concept, they will successfully oppose the establishment of a command agency which can effectively prepare for and conduct combat operations. This study evades and offers no solution for the primary issue, i. e., that the United States Army now lacks an agency which is equipped to effectively prepare for and conduct combat operations, and that such an agency must be provided either in GHQ or within the War Department.

On 5 December 1941, two days before Pearl Harbor, General Malony, the Deputy Chief of Staff, GHQ, commented on the "mission of GHQ" in these words: "The international situation is critical. Equipment is lacking. No adequate reserves are available. Experience to date indicates: (1) Transportation and delivery of supplies . . . is inefficient (Iceland); (2) Joint Board procedure is ponderous and provides no direct supervision . . . ; (3) War Department retains control in such detail as to make administration confusing; (4) War Department is not organized on a war basis." [9]

---

[7] Quotations from various memos (S) of Col Hays for CofS GHQ,—Aug 41. 320.2/1 (S).

[8] Memo (S) of Col Hays for CofS GHQ, 29 Aug 41, sub not given (evidently a comment on the first draft of memo (S) WPD 4558 for CofS USA, 30 Aug 41, sub: Functions, Responsibilities and Authority of GHQ). 320.2/1 (S).

[9] Memo of DCofS GHQ for CofS GHQ, 5 Dec 41, sub: GHQ Reorgn. 320.2/3/108.

In July, when planning and operational responsibilities had been given to GHQ, it had been decided that this headquarters was to be the executive agency of the War Department for "prompt decision and expeditious action," providing effective "coordination, conduct and control" of operations.[10] Though powers were delegated to it only "if, as, and when," many officers at GHQ interpreted the step taken on 3 July as an action to implement the GHQ envisaged in the Harbord Report and embodied in the doctrine of the Army for twenty years. For several months after July 1941 the War Department, or at least the War Plans Division, adhered to that concept.[11] Nevertheless, when the War Department delayed in giving GHQ the power it needed or in creating some other "spark plug" agency, it seemed at GHQ that the difficulty "boils down to the War Department not wanting to give up any authority."[12] By December, after five months of strenuous effort, General Malony, who had been charged with making GHQ work as a planning and operational headquarters, reached the discouraging conclusions stated above.

Basic Problems Encountered in the Attempt to Strengthen GHQ, August–November 1941

The War Department was in fact faced with a situation which made GHQ as conceived by the Harbord Board a device difficult to operate. The essentials of such a GHQ were (1) power to coordinate all operations outside the continental United States, and (2) prompt executive action. But in July 1941, the war danger was developing in "a number of relatively minor and widely scattered theaters," instead of one major theater as in 1917, and coordination was an extremely difficult task. On the other hand, it was quickly seen that to make GHQ effective as a command agency, or even as a coordinating agency, it would have to be given control of supply. In his memorandum of 25 July General McNair pointed out that the command of each base theoretically under GHQ was actually divided between GHQ and two other War Department agencies.

---

[10] Pars 1–4, sec I, memo (S) WPD 3209–10 for CofS USA,—Jun 41, sub: Enlargement of the Functions of GHQ. 320.2/1 (S).

[11] See above, pp. 128–29.

[12] "Conference on GHQ functions is off on a new track and boils down to WD not wanting to give up any authority." Min (S) of Staff Conferences, GHQ, 22 Aug 41, remarks of G–3. 337 (S).

On 15 August he expressed the opinion that GHQ should be authorized to issue instructions directly to other War Department agencies in connection with the means assigned for the operation of overseas bases and theaters.[13]

The problem of supply formed the main obstacle faced by the 1921 plan for GHQ and became largely responsible for the dissolution of GHQ in 1942. Commenting on General McNair's 25 July memorandum, WPD promptly concurred in his idea "that control of supply is an essential element of command." [14] But it stated at the same time that as long as a critical shortage of equipment and shipping continued and the demands of Lend-Lease, competing with those of the Army, had to be met, "rigid control by the War Department" would be necessary. The contention was raised that to give GHQ in Washington effective command of overseas departments, bases, and theaters meant giving it powers which would place it above the War Department.[15] The Chief of the Army Air Forces granted General McNair's position that GHQ could not exercise effective command unless given control of all agencies essential thereto. But the consequence, he declared, would be that "in substance GHQ must have control of War Department agencies, Quartermaster Corps, Ordnance Department, etc." [16] This conclusion was not believed at GHQ to be necessary. The need for higher coordination between the requirements of the Army and Navy and the demands of Lend-Lease was recognized. What was desired at GHQ was a block allotment of means to GHQ on the basis of a plan approved by the General Staff. But to this G–4 of the General Staff would not consent, insisting that it must review and check the supply and transportation requirements of all operations planned by GHQ and also pass on every requisition from a base, defense, or theater commander.[17]

---

[13] GHQ memo (S) for CofS USA, 15 Aug 41, sub: Functions, Responsibilities and Authority of GHQ. AGO Records, WPD 4558 (S), Tab 11.

[14] Par 12, sec I, WPD memo (S) for CofS USA, — Aug 41, sub: Functions and Authority of GHQ. Incl to GHQ memo (S) of Gen McNair for DCofS, 11 Aug 41, sub as above. 320.2/4 (S).

[15] Pars 9 and 11, sec I, memo (S) WPD 4558 for CofS, 30 Aug 41, sub: Functions, Responsibilities and Authority of GHQ. 320.2/1 (S).

[16] Par 7, memo (S) of CofAAF for ACofS WD, 24 Oct 41, sub: Functions, Responsibilities and Authority of GHQ. AGO Records, WPD 4558 (S).

[17] (1) "GHQ does not have an organization empowered or prepared to implement a supply plan for military operations." Par 1 f, memo of Gen Brehon Somervell for CofS USA, 18 Jan 42. AGO Records, G–4/34015. (2) The matter was regulated as desired by G–4 by direction of the Chief of Staff, USA, in memo for CG, FF, 24 Jan 42, sub: Coordination between WPD, G–4 WDGS, GHQ and Overseas Theater Commanders. AGO Records, G–4/34015. (3) The statement regarding the point of view of GHQ is based on interviews of AGF Historical Officer with Maj Gen. Harry J. Malony and Brig Gen Paul McD. Robinett.

As early as 2 September General McNair himself expressed doubt as to the workability of GHQ:

Speaking broadly, superior command of the operations of two or more theaters may be by either of two methods:

> a. GHQ—on the basis that the War Department is not organized suitably for the expeditious action required. It follows inevitably that, unless GHQ can be freed from the complications of War Department organization, there is little advantage and some disadvantage in having a GHQ.
> b. A War Department streamlined in the same general manner as Gen. Pershing streamlined his own GHQ—by establishing a Services of Supply. The War Department will then exercise superior command directly.

The second alternative seemed to represent General McNair's preference for solving the problem of supply. "The views stated in the basic memorandum [a WPD memorandum of 30 August], coupled with the brief experience of this headquarters to date, indicate that serious consideration should be given to the latter method—b—in spite of the upheaval involved." [18]

On 21 October, no action having been taken in the War Department, General McNair returned to the issue, this time definitely stating his preference for reorganization: "I incline to favor the second line of action, to streamline the War Department by separating from it a zone of interior with its own commander, and absorbing GHQ into the War Department thus streamlined, and have rather indicated this view to the Chief of Staff." [19]

Development of the War Department Reorganization Plan, November 1941–March 1942

The Chief of the Army Air Forces had advocated reorganization in the Board meetings in August. On 24 October he launched a drive to realize his original recommendations. This was accompanied by a proposal to enlarge still

---

[18] Par 4, memo (S) of Gen McNair for ACofS WPD, 2 Sep 41, sub: Functions, Responsibility and Authority of GHQ. 320.2/1 (S).

[19] Par 4, GHQ memo (S) of Gen McNair for Gen Bryden, DCofS WD, 21 Oct 41, sub: Functions, Responsibilities and Authority of GHQ. 320.2/1 (S).

further the autonomy of the Air Forces by a revision of AR 95–5 as published in the previous June—a revision which, in the opinion of General McNair, would have effected a "separation of the Air Force from the rest of the Army as complete as the Commanding General, Army Air Force, chooses to make it." [20] In the first of a series of Air Force memoranda advocating reorganization of the War Department as against enlargement of the authority of GHQ, General Arnold's headquarters revived the proposals for reorganization put forth by WPD in August. [21] In the second of these memoranda the Army Air Forces outlined its own plan. It was in two parts. Part I proposed the reorganization of the Zone of Interior into three commands—air, ground, and service. Part II recommended the creation of a "Military Policy Staff" representing the Army, the Navy, the State Department, and the Economic Defense Board, under a chief of staff. General Marshall declared himself to be "favorably impressed by the basic organization proposed," but Part II was excluded from the further study now ordered. He directed WPD to develop Part I with a view to "determining its practicability and the extent to which it is an improvement over the present organization." It thus became the working basis for the reorganization put into effect on 9 March 1942. General Marshall's directive is dated 25 November 1941. [22] From that date forward there is no trace of a further attempt by the War Department to make GHQ workable for the purposes for which it had been designed in the Harbord Plan.

Both the WPD plan sketched in August and the plan now proposed by the Army Air Forces had a common central feature. [23] Both proposed the delegation of the operative functions of the War Department in the Zone of Interior to

[20] Par 1, memo of Gen McNair for the CofS USA, 10 Nov 41, sub: Proposed Revised Draft of AR 95–5. McNair Correspondence with the CofS USA.

[21] (1) Memo (S) of CofAAF for ACofS WPD, 24 Oct 41, sub: Functions, Responsibilities and Authority of GHQ. AGO Records, WPD 4558 (S). (2) Memo (S) of CofAAF for CofS USA,—Nov 41, sub: Reorgn of the WD. AGO Records, WPD 4614 (S). (3) Memo of Chief of Air Staff for ACofS WPD, 14 Nov 41, sub: GHQ Directive. AGO Records, WPD 3209–10.

[22] (1) Notes for record with memo (S) WPD 4614 for CofS USA, 18 Nov 41, sub: Orgn of the Armed Forces for War. (2) Memo (S) OCS 21278–6 for ACofS WPD, 25 Nov 41, sub not given. Both in AGO Records, WPD 4614 (Orgn of Armd Forces for War) (S).

[23] Reference to the Air Force plan will be found in footnote 21 (2), above. For the initial WPD study see memo (S) for CofS USA, — Aug 41, sub: Orgn of the Army High Comd. Copies in 320.2/1 (S) and AGO Records, WPD 4618 (S). The latter copy was probably erroneously rubber-stamped "Nov 1941," perhaps when the reorganization project was revived.

three major commands, the Army Ground Forces, the Army Air Forces, and the Services of Supply. Both accepted the Army Air Forces as established by the terms of AR 95-5, 20 June 1941. Neither was clear as to where command or supervision of the four internal defense commands was to be lodged. Neither provided for an integration of the offices of the chiefs of branches, though they were subordinated in both plans to the Zone of Interior commands. In the WPD plan they were all placed under the commanding general of the Services of Supply. In the Air Force study the chiefs of Infantry, Cavalry, Field Artillery, and Coast Artillery were placed under the commanding general of the Army Ground Forces. Furthermore, the WPD study assigned to the Services of Supply not only West Point, the general and special service schools, and officer candidate schools, but also the boards of the arms and services, civilian component training and administration, and air-raid precautions. All these agencies and functions were given a different distribution in the final reorganization.

When interviewed at a later date Army Ground Force officers who were on the staff of GHQ during the winter of 1941-42 seemed to feel that the reorganization of 9 March 1942 was "sprung" by an inner circle of planners in the War Department. This impression probably related to certain phases of the reorganization, not to the plan in its entirety.

The minutes of the daily GHQ staff conferences show that, at least until mid-October, the debate in the War Department regarding the status of GHQ was being reported to its staff. There is no indication that General McNair's conclusion, stated in his memoranda of 2 September and 21 October, that a reorganization of the War Department was probably desirable was not known to his immediate advisors at GHQ, including General Malony, if not to all members of the staff. The record shows that on 5 February 1942 General McNair discussed the plan of reorganization with Maj. Gen. Joseph T. McNarney, who had been recalled from England to take charge of it. The criticisms which General McNair submitted in writing the next day raised no serious objections.[24] On 4 March he wrote: "The new organization seems entirely sound. The experiment of having GHQ operate—which has been underway since last July—was foredoomed to failure in my estimation, since the War Department could

---

[24] Memo of Gen McNair for Gen McNarney, WPD WD, 6 Feb 42, sub: Reorgn of the WD. 320.2/1168. On 16 January a draft initialled "H[arrison]" had gone to the Plans Section, WPD, with a nonconcurrence of G–3 WD.

not turn over its responsibilities in that connection. The alternative is what is now being done—the Services of Supply—just as in the A. E. F." [25]

It is clear, therefore, that the principles underlying the plan for reorganization were known at GHQ from the first, and it can hardly be doubted that the staff was aware of the views of its chief. On the other hand, no evidence has been found to indicate that it was informed of the decision of General Marshall on 25 November to set up a committee to work on a specific plan. Certainly as late as 5 December General Malony still believed that there was a fighting chance for the enlargement of GHQ's operational authority. GHQ was not represented on the committee initially entrusted with formulating a plan of reorganization.[26] Only on 11 February was formal notice received at GHQ that the proposal to reorganize the War Department was under consideration and that an executive committee was to be created under the chairmanship of General McNarney. GHQ was directed to select a representative, and Col. James G. Christiansen was appointed.[27] At this date the contents of the plan were known at GHQ, for the minutes of the staff conference on 11 February record the following comment of its G–3: "Proposed reorganization of WD still leaves burden on General Marshall." [28]

Given these circumstances, several reasons may be conjectured for the later impression that the plan of reorganization had been sprung suddenly on the group working at GHQ. The specific plan which was adopted and which apparently was worked out between 25 November 1941 and 11 February 1942 without the knowledge of GHQ included a novel form of staff organization for Headquarters, Army Ground Forces, which that headquarters found unworkable and rejected on 12 July 1942. This probably contributed to a feeling that the plan of reorganization was excessively theoretical, and intensified the disfavor with which it was bound to be regarded by the group at GHQ

---

[25] Ltr of Gen McNair to Maj Gen E. F. McGlachlin, 4 Mar 42. McNair Correspondence.

[26] The task was given to the Plans Group, WPD, on 25 November, and on 28 November Maj C. K. Gailey, the Executive of WPD, requested that "one officer each be designated by the CofAAF and the ACofS, G–1, G–3 and G–4 to collaborate with WPD (Lt Col W. K. Harrison)." Memo (S) WPD 4614 for the Sec WDGS, 28 Nov 41. AGO Records, WPD 4614 (S). Par 3 requested the assignment of Lt. Col. Sebree, G–1, Lt. Col. Shelton, G–3, and Lt. Col. Reichelderfer, G–4, "who are already well acquainted with the subject."

[27] (1) Memo (C) OCS 16600–82 for CofS GHQ, 11 Feb 42, sub not given. 020/1 (C). (2) GHQ memo (C) for Sec WDGS, signed Hyssong, 12 Feb 42, sub: Executive Committee WD Reorganization. AGO Records, WPD 4614 (S).

[28] In 337 (S).

who had enthusiastically supported General Malony in his effort to make GHQ the driving force in the Army high command and through it to speed up and invigorate the executive action of the War Department as the United States moved into the dangers of open warfare.[29]

The reorganization adopted had three main features:[30] (1) Top control of the field forces was kept in the War Department General Staff, and the Zone of Interior functions of the War Department were delegated to three great commands, the Army Ground Forces, the Army Air Forces, and the Services of Supply—an organization designed to "follow functional (task) lines."[31] (2) The arms and services were subordinated to these commands. The technical services, together with the two combat services, the Engineers and the Signal Corps, were assigned to the Services of Supply. The arms and the new quasi arms were assigned to the Army Ground Forces. The services remained in being as organized, but their chiefs were subjected to the authority of the commanding general of the Services of Supply. In the case of the arms a different principle was followed. The chiefs of the four traditional arms disappeared. Their authority was vested in the commanding general of the Army Ground Forces, and their agencies were reassorted and integrated with the other agencies of that command. On the other hand, those of the newly developed combat arms, Armored, Tank Destroyer, and Antiaircraft Artillery (separated from the Coast Artillery), remained or became distinct commands, under the commanding general of the Army Ground Forces. (3) GHQ was liquidated, and all theaters of operations and the four defense commands of the continental United States were placed directly under the War Department General Staff. WPD, shortly to be known as OPD (Operations Division), took up the planning and operational functions which had been exercised since July 1941 by the staff of GHQ.

By these changes the War Department sought to relieve the General Staff and its Chief of operative and detailed administrative duties in order to set them free to devote themselves to planning and over-all supervision.[32] This purpose

[29] On 25 February General Malony was relieved and assigned to the Munitions Assignment Board. WD ltr AG 210.31 (2–24–42) OD–A to CG GHQ, 25 Feb 42, sub: Orders. AGO Records.

[30] Cir 59, WD, 2 Mar 42.

[31] The phrase used in par 2, sec I, WPD memo (S) for CofS USA, — Aug 41, sub: Orgn of the Army High Comd. 320.2/1 (S).

[32] Statement of Secretary of War Stimson to the press, as reported by the *New York Times,* 5 Mar 42. See also the statement of General McNarney before the Senate Committee on Military Affairs, 6 Mar 42. Hearing on S. 2092, 77th Congress, Second Session.

had also been one of the main objectives of GHQ, but had not been fully realized largely because the powers delegated were insufficient and the current international situation made it impossible to carry out the original plan of the Harbord Board.

Summary

In this reorganization of the War Department the Army Air Forces, according to the evidence available, took the lead and supplied the drive. Its motives were clearly stated in its memoranda on the subject. The authority of GHQ, as constituted on 3 July 1941, overlapped the position which the Air Forces had gained as an autonomous entity on 20 June 1941.[33] The proposed enlargement of the powers of GHQ would have limited this independence even further. Such a development did not coincide with the ideas current in the Army Air Forces, which aspired to still greater freedom of action in the belief that the effective prosecution of modern warfare required a fully autonomous air arm.[34] The Chief of the Army Air Forces sought to protect and regularize the new position of the Air Forces by a reorganization which would give the Ground Forces and the Services of Supply a similar autonomy. This objective was in general attained, though the simultaneous proposal to institute a command transcending that of the War Department was not carried out.

Though the Army Air Forces played a prominent role in the reorganization, many other factors and considerations contributed to bringing about the administrative changes in the War Department effected in March 1942. In the circumstances imposed by the course of events, a GHQ on the lines of the Harbord Plan was subject to grave disadvantages. These became evident to General McNair, as well as to other observers, as soon as the attempt was made to administer such a headquarters or develop plans for its future. War had come upon the United States in an unanticipated form, and the conclusion was

[33] (1) The functioning of GHQ as now contemplated "is restrictive of the responsibilities charged to the Army Air Forces with respect to planning for air operations pertaining to theaters of operations and task forces." Par 5, memo (S) of CofAAF for the CofS USA, 24 Oct 41, sub: Functions, Responsibilities and Authority of GHQ. AGO Records, WPD 4558 (S). (2) "An air theater of operation should be recognized. Under the present conception, such a theater is controlled by GHQ." Conflict "could be avoided only by superimposing the GHQ over the War Department." Pars 9 *a* and *b*, AGO Records, WPD 4558 (S).

[34] See the essay on the "priceless attributes of air power," par *a*, memo (S) of CofAAF for CofS USA, — Nov 41, sub: Reorgn of the WD. AGO Records, WPD 4614 (S).

reached that it had to be waged with new administrative as well as with new technical and tactical weapons.

Furthermore, new developments like armor and tank destroyers were cutting across the pattern on which the traditional arms were organized. These changes, implying refinements of specialization and new tactical combinations, brought to a head the old question of the arms and services and their relation to the General Staff. Though the chiefs of the arms and services were less independent than formerly, their actual relation to the General Staff made difficult the close command and staff planning as well as the coordination and training necessary to produce flexible and hard-hitting teams of the combined arms. The old pattern of tactical organization had to be adapted to the new type of warfare. Moreover, the existing combat arms had developed, together with a desirable branch loyalty, an aggressive and somewhat jealous branch spirit, which the new quasi arms tended to emulate. The proposed reorganization of the War Department offered a means of bringing the arms and services under firmer control.

Given these circumstances, the type of reorganization first put forward in the WPD memorandum of August made a strong appeal. General McNair favored, and the Air Forces pressed for, reorganization. The final plan, which delegated the complex Zone of Interior responsibilities of the War Department to three subordinate commands, offered the War Department General Staff an opportunity to perform its over-all planning and directive duties with greater efficiency. It effected, under these three major commands, a coordination of the services and an integration of the arms in better accord with their future use in combined operations.

In the reorganization as announced no explicit provision was made for centralized control of operations in widely scattered theaters, specifically, for "an executive group" within the War Department which "would in reality be a command section." The absorption of the operational element of GHQ into the War Department as a means of meeting this need had been rejected, and the officers composing that element in GHQ were not utilized to form a new group in the War Department. But a new group was formed in WPD, which, under its later title of Operations Division, became, in effect, the command post of General Marshall in Washington. GHQ, in its executive activities, had forecast and confirmed the need for such an agency, but was not made that agency. It is evident from the foregoing study that the motives and circumstances that led to its rejection were complex. They included organizational and personal interests and rivalries which inevitably attend the development of a new and forceful institution. The mere physical location of GHQ apart from the rest of the War Department, and the fact that at the moment there was no room in the old Munitions Building for another agency, perhaps played a part. Connected with this factor, and probably more important in determining the view taken of GHQ as a command post, was the fact that, as such, it was encased in the old conception, inherent in the plan of mobilization projected in 1921, that GHQ was destined to go overseas as the headquarters of the field forces—a conception that had promptly been antiquated by the circumstances of the oncoming emergency in 1941. GHQ had at least served a useful purpose in demonstrating the necessity of substituting for this concept that of a single agency in Washington qualified to achieve "prompt decisions and expeditious action."

General Headquarters, United States Army, closed *sine die,* and Headquarters, Army Ground Forces, opened at the Army War College on 9 March 1942. Although GHQ had not completely fulfilled the purpose for which it had been intended originally, it had been conspicuously efficient in making and implementing theater plans. It had from the outset performed with notable success the mission of training with which it had been entrusted initially. This, in general, was the view taken by representatives of the War Department in the discussion of its fate during the fall of 1941.[35] GHQ had become more than ever the command agency which directed the training and shaped the organization of the ground army for combat.[36] These were to be the two principal missions of the new command with which General McNair was now entrusted.

---

[35] Only two exceptions to this estimate of GHQ are recorded: (1) Brig. Gen. Wade H. Haislip, G–1 WD, believed that the interposition of GHQ between the Chief of Staff and corps area had broken "down the mobilization machinery of the Army. It serves no useful purpose, except to give GHQ a job." Par 2 *a* (1), memo (S) G–1/16338–8 for ACofS WPD, 15 Sep 41, sub: Functions, Responsibilities and Authority of GHQ. AGO Records, WPD 4558 (S). (2) Gen. Sherman Miles, G–2, WD, expressed his concern regarding the "general state of intelligence training of all echelons." He thought improvement of such training was a War Department function and that the training function of GHQ should be withdrawn. Memo of Gen Miles (S) for ACofS WPD, 12 Nov 41, sub: GHQ Dir. AGO Records, WPD 3209–10 (S). The comment of WPD, 22 Nov 41, was that GHQ's "training responsibilities . . . have been exercised satisfactorily since activation of that headquarters."

[36] In August 1941 WPD observed: "The duties and responsibilities of GHQ have not been clearly defined. GHQ is developing however as a Commander of Army Ground Forces." Par 9, sec I, WPD memo (S) for CofS, — Aug 41, sub: Functions and Authority of GHQ, Incl to GHQ memo (S) of Gen McNair for DCofS GHQ, 11 Aug 41, sub as above. 320.2/4 (S).

Roster of
General Staff and Special Staff, GHQ, 1941-42

General Staff

	Date of Asgmt	Rank (Aug 45)
CHIEF OF STAFF		
Brig Gen Lesley J. McNair	26 Jul 40	Lt Gen*
DEPUTY CHIEF OF STAFF		
Brig Gen Harry J. Malony	18 Jun 41	Maj Gen
Brig Gen Mark W. Clark	9 Dec 41	General
SECRETARY GENERAL STAFF		
Lt Col Floyd L. Parks	15 Jul 41	Maj Gen
ASSISTANT CHIEF OF STAFF		
G–1		
Lt Col Gordon deL. Carrington	18 Jun 41	Brig Gen*
Col Alexander R. Bolling	14 Feb 42	Maj Gen
ASSISTANT CHIEF OF STAFF		
G–2		
Lt Col Paul McD. Robinett	26 Jun 41	Brig Gen
ASSISTANT CHIEF OF STAFF		
G–3		
Lt Col Mark W. Clark	18 Jun 41	General
Lt Col George P. Hays	9 Dec 41	Maj Gen
ASSISTANT CHIEF OF STAFF		
G–4		
Lt Col Ernest N. Harmon	18 Jun 41	Maj Gen
Lt Col Willard S. Paul	3 Dec 41	Maj Gen
ASSISTANT CHIEF OF STAFF		
G–5		
Lt Col Lloyd D. Brown	9 Dec 41	Colonel

* Deceased.

Special Staff

	Date of Asgmt	Rank (Aug 45)
ADJUTANT GENERAL		
Lt Col Clyde L. Hyssong	18 Jun 41	Maj Gen
ANTIAIRCRAFT SECTION		
Lt Col Morris C. Handwerk	18 Jun 41	Brig Gen
Lt Col Charles S. Harris	1 Jul 41	Brig Gen
AVIATION SECTION		
Col William E. Lynd	18 Jun 41	Maj Gen
Col Ralph H. Wooten	18 Sep 41	Maj Gen
Brig Gen Clinton W. Russell	2 Feb 42	Brig Gen*
ENGINEER SECTION		
Maj James G. Christiansen	18 Jun 41	Maj Gen
Col William F. Tompkins	14 Jul 41	Maj Gen
FINANCE SECTION		
Lt Col Donald T. Nelson	28 Jul 41	Colonel
MEDICAL SECTION		
Lt Col Charles B. Spruit	18 Jun 41	Brig Gen
Lt Col Frederick A. Blesse	26 Jun 41	Brig Gen
QUARTERMASTER SECTION		
Lt Col Farragut F. Hall	18 Jun 41	Colonel
Lt Col Roy C. L. Graham	26 Jun 41	Brig Gen
SIGNAL SECTION		
Lt Col Richard B. Moran	18 Jun 41	Brig Gen
CIVILIAN COMPONENT		
Col Kenneth Buchanan	18 Jun 41	Colonel
HEADQUARTERS COMMANDANT		
Lt Col Ernest A. Williams	24 Jun 41	Colonel
Lt Col Thomas F. Bresnahan	18 Aug 41	Brig Gen
JUDGE ADVOCATE GENERAL		
Col Allen M. Burdett	5 Jul 41	Colonel
CHEMICAL SECTION		
Lt Col Robert W. Daniels (Actg)	12 Aug 41	Colonel
INSPECTOR GENERAL		
Col Allen M. Burdett (Actg)	12 Aug 41	Colonel
Lt Col Elliott D. Cooke	13 Oct 41	Brig Gen
ORDNANCE SECTION		
Lt Col Robert W. Daniels	13 Dec 41	Colonel
PROVOST MARSHAL		
Maj William H. Maglin	7 Jan 42	Colonel

Ground Forces in the Army

December 1941–April 1945

A Statistical Study

by

Robert R. Palmer

Contents

Table

I. Note on the Compilation of the Table

The table "Ground Forces in the Army" is a statistical presentation of the planning and mobilization of the Army, with emphasis on combatant ground forces.[1] Its aim is to show the distribution of forces within a total figure accepted as the ultimate strength of the Army in World War II. When the table was compiled the figures for 1 May 1945 were not available, but their inclusion was not regarded as necessary for the purpose of showing the scale and apportionment of strength allotted to ground forces in the mobilization of the Army.

The table was derived from successive issues of the War Department Troop Basis and from documents of the War Department General Staff and of Headquarters, Army Ground Forces, containing plans for and comments on the Troop Basis. The sources of the figures on each line of the table are given in Section III below.

The Troop Basis was issued at intervals by the War Department for general planning purposes. Its preparation and continuing revision were responsibilities of G–3, War Department General Staff, acting with advice from other agencies of the War Department and from the three major commands. The headquarters of the Army Ground Forces participated actively in discussions of the Troop Basis until the fall of 1943. After that date, as the overseas theaters were increasingly built up and as strategic plans for the employment of ground forces took more definite shape, the main influence in determining the AGF section of the Troop Basis passed to the Operations Division, War Department General Staff. Through the Operations Division the desires of theater commanders were mediated to the War Department.

The Troop Basis, while it changed considerably in form and content during the war, always served essentially the same purpose. It was primarily an outline

---

[1] The table is designed to serve as a statistical basis for the following studies in this volume: "Mobilization of the Ground Army"; "Reorganization of Ground Troops for Combat"; and "Organization and Training of New Ground Combat Elements."

of the kind of army authorized to exist. First, it stated the number of units of each type authorized to exist by a specified date in the future. This number was determined by anticipation of general war strategy and operational needs and by estimate of the manpower and equipment available and of the length of time necessary for training. Second, the Troop Basis also stated the number of units of each type already authorized to exist, that is, units already activated or mobilized. ("Active," "activated," "mobilized," and "already authorized to exist" have substantially the same meaning in the present table and its accompanying interpretation.) As the Troop Basis developed in form, it stated the number of units already mobilized on the day before the date of the Troop Basis. For example, the Troop Basis of 1 July 1943 stated the number of units, with Table of Organization strength, both as projected for 31 December 1943 and as already mobilized on 30 June 1943. The difference, for each type of unit, between the number of units already mobilized and the number authorized to exist by the future date to which the Troop Basis was projected, indicated the number of units of that type to be activated (or inactivated) during the period for which the Troop Basis of a given date was drawn up. The Troop Basis thus constituted the program of mobilization. At first it was essentially a program for the expansion of the Army. After the Army attained its contemplated strength (at the beginning of 1944) the Troop Basis was still the program of mobilization in the sense that it indicated readjustments to be made within a fixed total, stating what new units should be activated and what old units inactivated, without further enlargement of the Army, to meet current views as to changing operational needs.

The Troop Basis was thus a general budget of military manpower, indicating the needs of the Army for which manpower was required, and accounting for men in the Army, or due to be received by the Army, by showing the units and establishments to which men were allotted. The Troop Basis was not intended to be a perfect instrument of personnel accounting. It was not based on actual strengths, that is, on a counting of bodies. It was based on Tables of Organization for tactical units and on bulk allotments made by the War Department for nontactical organizations. Actual strengths varied considerably from the strength shown as mobilized in the Troop Basis. For example, divisions were understrength at the end of 1942, not having attained in actual bodies the strength of 1,056,000 enlisted men indicated in the Troop Basis as mobilized on that date. The Army was consistently overstrength after April 1944, reaching an actual strength (including commissioned and warrant officer personnel) reported as 8,157,386 for 31 March 1945, more than 300,000 in excess of the Troop Basis figure for mobilized strength on that date. The War Department therefore had to devise other methods of personnel accounting. These may be traced in the weekly Minutes of the General Council for 1944.

In its primary function, as an outline of the kind of army authorized to exist, the Troop Basis gave an accurate picture. For example, while one can obtain no actual strengths from the Troop Basis, one may accept at face value the indication of the Troop Basis of 24 November 1942 that on that date 100 divisions were authorized for mobilization by the end of 1943, or the indication in the Troop Basis of 1 April 1945 that 89 divisions were mobilized on 31 March 1945 and that their Table of Organization enlisted strength was 1,124,738. It is only in this connection, in which the Troop Basis gives a true picture, that it is used in the present table.

In form the Troop Basis went through a succession of changes, becoming with each change more elaborate and detailed. In 1942 it was issued in typescript at irregular intervals in a few copies only. By late 1944 it was compiled by machine-records methods, issued monthly, and circulated in some 200 copies. These changes are without importance for the present table. Until the last months of 1943 the Troop Basis gave detailed listing only for tactical units, showing merely rough figures for overhead, replacements, nonavailables, and other categories; and it listed tactical units of the Ground and Service Forces only, showing a bulk allotment for the Army Air Forces. After the end of 1943 Army Air Forces was listed in the same manner as Army Ground Forces and Army Service Forces, and overhead and related requirements were shown with increasing detail. These changes likewise are without significance for the present table, since the table gives only bulk figures for Army Air Forces and for overhead, etc.

Other changes in the form and content of the Troop Basis have raised problems in the preparation of the table. Until the end of 1943 the Troop Basis showed enlisted strengths only. Thereafter enlisted, warrant officer, nurse, officer, and aggregate strengths were given in separate columns. Since for purposes of the present table the figures for earlier and later dates must be comparable, and since only enlisted strengths are available for the earlier period, the table is limited to enlisted strengths throughout.

A major aim of the table is to classify the total strength of the Army, as planned and as mobilized at different dates, into combat and service troops, and to classify service troops into those employed in close conjunction with combat troops and those employed in rear-area support. At first the Troop Basis carried no indication of these classifications. By October 1944 it indicated them all. But for all dates prior to October 1944, and hence for the entire formative period of the Army, computation has been necessary, using Troop Basis figures as raw material, to obtain the figures desired for the present table on classification as between combat and service units.

Service units in 1942 were not distinguished as pertaining to the Army Service Forces (then Services of Supply) or to the Army Ground Forces. No such distinction was therefore drawn in the Troop Basis in 1942. In the months beginning with October 1942 all service units (except those of the Air Forces) were divided between the Army Service Forces and the Army Ground Forces for activation and training. Service units intended for close support of combat troops, that is, for inclusion in field armies and employment in the combat zone, were designated as pertaining to the Army Ground Forces. Service units intended for less direct support of combat troops, that is, for employment in the communications zone, were designated as pertaining to the Army Service Forces. The Troop Basis of 1 July 1943, and all succeeding Troop Bases, grouped the two types of service units separately. Henceforth the Army Ground Forces section of the Troop Basis included units of both combat and service types, and the Army Service Forces section of the Troop Basis (which included no combat units) included only those service units designated as of ASF type.

Figures in the table for ASF service units, for dates beginning with 30 June 1943, are therefore copied directly from pertinent Troop Bases without modification. Figures for ASF service units before 30 June 1943 (specifically for 24 November 1942 and 30 December 1942) have been obtained by extracting from the undifferentiated lists of service units in pertinent Troop Bases those service units designated as ASF in the Troop Basis of 1 July 1943.

Figures in the table for AGF service units, for dates beginning with 30 June 1943, cannot be copied from pertinent Troop Bases without modification, as can figures for ASF service units, because AGF service units, as listed in the Troop Basis, included some units of combat type. Figures in the table for AGF service units, for dates beginning with 30 June 1943, represent the total strength in units of service branches (chemical, engineer, medical, military police, miscellaneous, ordnance, quartermaster, and signal) allotted to the Army Ground Forces in the Troop Basis, but modified by deduction of strength in certain units (chemical, engineer, signal) considered by the War Department to be of combat type, according to definitions noted in the following paragraph. Figures for AGF service units for 24 November 1942 and 30 December 1942 represent what is left from the undifferentiated list of service units in pertinent Troop Bases after removal of both combat units and ASF units.

The Troop Basis did not identify combat units as such until October 1944, but the War Department laid down a definition of combat units for statistical purposes in Circular No. 422, 29 December 1942. This circular, as amended by Circular No. 66, 5 March 1943, has been followed in the preparation of the table. Combat units are defined as follows:

All elements of divisions . . . .(Col. 22 of the table)

All units designated as:

    Corps and Army headquarters . . . .⎫

    Infantry, cavalry, field artillery, coast artillery . . . . . .⎪

Armored, tank destroyer, amphibious, airborne . . . . . .⎪

Chemical, motorized (mortar); engineers, combat, ponton, ⎬(Col. 23 of the table)

   treadway bridge; signal, construction, operations, photo, ⎪

   pigeon, radio intelligence . . . .⎭

All antiaircraft units . . . .(Col. 25 of the table)

The totals in column 23 have been obtained by adding the figures given in the Troop Basis for (nondivisional) headquarters, armored, cavalry, coast artillery, field artillery, infantry, and tank destroyer units, and such amounts of chemical, engineer, and signal units as are appropriate after combat units of these branches are deducted from the totals for AGF units of these branches given in the Troop Basis.

Definition of combat units, when introduced into the Troop Basis on 1 October 1944, followed a new circular, No. 356, WD, 2 September 1944, which in turn followed closely, with some elaboration, the definitions laid down in Circular No. 422, 1942. Since the definitions of September 1944 were made after most of the calculations for the present table had been completed, since they varied from earlier definitions in only a minor way, and since there was no assurance that the definitions of 1944 would have more permanent significance than those of 1942, no attempt has been made to recast the present table to conform to the distinctions introduced into the Troop Basis in October 1944. And since later and earlier figures in the table must be comparable, referring at all dates to the same thing, the strength of combat and service units has been computed in the table, for dates subsequent to October 1944, in the same manner as for prior dates, no use being made of the indications as to category given in Troop Bases beginning with October 1944.

The present table would not be greatly different if the categories introduced in October 1944 had been used in its preparation, or if they had been available as far back as 1942. Seven categories, called "missions," were introduced in the Troop Basis of 1 October 1944. Only four of these applied to tactical units, the other three applying to replacements and overhead. The four applying to tactical units were substantially equivalent to the categories set up in the present table. Not counting the Air Forces, the seven categories of missions and their equivalents were as follows:

Troop Basis Beginning 1 Oct 44 (Circular 356, WD, 2 Sep 44)	Present Table (Circular 422, WD, 29 Dec 42, as Amended)
1. Combat	Total Combat Units . . . Col. 26
2. Combat Support	
3. Combat Service Support . .	AGF Service Units . . . . Col. 27
4. Service Support	ASF Service Units . . . . Col. 29
5. Training	Remainder: Overhead, Re-
6. Overhead	placements, Nonavail- Col. 33
7. Miscellaneous	ables, etc. . . . .

"Combat Support" referred mainly to certain engineer and signal units, considered as combat units in the present table; but it included also a few other units of the AGF services and all military police of AGF type, considered as service units in the present table. It likewise included a small percentage of ASF units. Hence when units whose mission was defined as "Combat" or as "Combat Support" by the War Department in September 1944 are added together, the total is somewhat larger than the total for combat units in the present table. Figures for mobilized enlisted strength for 30 March 1945, so arranged as to show the equivalence between the two systems of definition, are as follows:

Mobilized Enlisted Strength of Army,
31 March 1945

Excluding Air Forces:
1. Combat (AGF)   1,849,580
2. Combat Support (AGF)   225,464
   Combat Support (ASF)   25,372

     TOTAL   2,100,416   2,041,000 Total Combat Units
                                                   (Col. 26)

3. Combat Service Support (AGF) .   421,387
   Combat Service Support (ASF) .   25,801

     TOTAL   447,188   461,000 AGF Service Units
                                                   (Col. 27)

4. Service Support (AGF)   5,717
   Service Support (ASF)   1,044,258

     TOTAL   1,049,975   1,097,000 ASF Service Units
                                                   (Col. 29)

5. Training   575,023
6. Overhead   533,462
7. Miscellaneous   316,436

     TOTAL   1,424,921   1,422,000 Overhead, Replacements,
                                                   Nonavailables, etc. (Col. 33)

Army Air Forces   1,943,645   1,945,000 Army Air Forces (Col. 32)

     TOTAL ARMY   6,966,145   6,966,000 Total Army (Col. 34)

Aggregate strength of the entire Army was distributed on 31 March 1945, as shown by the Troop Basis of 1 April 1945, as follows:

Mobilized Aggregate Strength of Army, by Mission,
31 March 1945

Mission	AAF	AGF	ASF	Misc.	Total
Combat................	376,660	1,968,500	......	....	2,345,160
Combat Support........	343,979	238,682	26,859	....	609,520
Combat Sv Support.....	199,761	450,163	27,765	....	677,689
Service Support........	305,721	5,994	1,148,792	....	1,460,507
Training..............	327,191	342,300	47,560	211,074	928,125
Overhead..............	737,261	130,948	376,665	190,272	1,435,146
Miscellaneous..........	....	11,250	16,500	329,422	357,172
TOTAL......	2,290,573	3,147,837	1,644,141	730,768	7,813,319

Or in percentages:

Mission	AAF	AGF	ASF	Misc.	Total
Combat................	16.4	62.5	...	....	30.0
Combat Support........	15.0	7.6	1.6	....	7.8
Combat Sv Support.....	8.7	14.3	1.7	....	8.7
Service Support........	13.4	.2	69.9	....	18.7
Training..............	14.3	10.9	2.9	28.9	11.9
Overhead..............	32.2	4.1	22.9	26.0	18.4
Miscellaneous..........	....	.4	1.0	45.1	4.5
TOTAL......	100.0	100.0	100.0	100.0	100.0

Actual strength of the Army was reported to be 8,157,386 officers and men on 31 March 1945, about 4 percent in excess of Troop Basis strength. Most of the overstrength was in overhead and in replacements (classified under "Training" above). Percentage of the strength of units—combat, combat support, combat service support, and service support—would thus be somewhat less than indicated above if computed on the basis of actual strength.

Under "Action," at the left of the table, are listed in chronological order successive estimates, recommendations, and comments with respect to the Troop

Basis, together with successive versions of the Troop Basis itself as authorized by the War Department. The whole reveals the views of Headquarters, Army Ground Forces, and of the War Department General Staff on mobilization. Reading a given line horizontally shows how the "Action" of that date (estimate, recommendation, comment, or authorized Troop Basis) proposed to distribute total strength of the Army among various elements, such as types of divisions and nondivisional units, combat and service units, air and ground forces, etc. Reading a given column vertically shows successive views as to requirements for forces of the specified type. For these, estimates and recommendations figures are given where possible; where figures cannot be given, it is indicated whether the Army Ground Forces desired to raise or to reduce the strength of certain types of forces.

Figures in the table, if neither underlined nor enclosed in parentheses, represent figures used in discussions, estimates, and recommendations.

Underlined figures represent figures officially accepted and promulgated by the War Department as mobilization objectives.

Figures in parentheses, occurring at 6-month intervals, refer not to anticipated strengths (as do all other figures) but to the number of units active and the Table of Organization strength of active units on the dates concerned. Comparison of figures in parentheses with appropriate underlined figures will show the amount of further activation (or in some cases inactivation) made necessary by Troop Basis planning. Since no actual strengths are given, the table offers no information on overstrengths and shortages.

II. Analysis of the Table

Entire table.

    1. Between the planning of 1942 to the close of organized hostilities in Europe in 1945 an army of 89 divisions and supporting units was finally made available for combat.

Cols. 1, 2, 3.

    2. The planned number of divisions almost continually fell; the actual number was reduced by one in 1944.

Cols. 26, 30, 33, 34.

    3. Not as many divisions and nondivisional combat units were formed as were originally planned, partly because over-all strength of the Army became fixed at a lower figure than had been expected, partly because requirements for service troops and overhead functions proved to be larger than had been foreseen.

Col. 26:
lines 14, 16, 28, 32.

    4. Downward revision of planned strength of combat ground forces occurred especially on two occasions, in October 1942 and in June 1943.

Cols. 3, 22, 26, 32:
lines 10, 16.

    5. In October 1942, with the fixing of the Army ceiling at 7,500,000 enlisted men, the planned strength of combat ground forces, as projected by the War Department in the preceding August, was revised downward by about 14 divisions and by about 300,000 enlisted men, while planned strength of Air Forces was raised by 200,000.

Cols. 3, 22, 26, 32:
lines 16, 32.

6. In June 1943, when the Army ceiling was lowered by 529,000 (from 7,533,000 to 7,004,000 enlisted men) the strength of combat ground forces planned for 1943 was revised downward by another 12 divisions (readjusted to

Col. 32.
Col. 33.

10) and by another 337,000 enlisted men. Allotment for Air Forces was revised downward by 50,000 at this time. Allotment for overhead, etc., was revised downward by

Cols. 30, 27.

249,000. Allotment for service units was raised by 109,000, of which only 2,000 was for service units of AGF types.

Col. 2:
lines 41–45.

7. Attempts to restore in 1944 the cuts made in combat ground forces for 1943 did not succeed, in large measure because the reduction in allotment for overhead, etc., was not maintained, and because requirements for service units, of both AGF and ASF types, continued to mount.

Col. 2:
lines 41–45.

8. In particular, the attempt of the War Department at the end of 1943 to add 15 divisions to the Troop Basis, making a total of 105 divisions, was abandoned because of mounting requirements for service units and overhead, noted above, and because proposals to cut the allotment for

Col. 32:
lines 41–45.

Air Forces to 1,838,000 did not take effect. (The Air Forces were at this time developing the long-range bomber, B–29, program.)

9. In net result, therefore, on the two occasions when reduction in total planned strength of the Army was necessary, in October 1942 and in June 1943, it was accomplished mainly by reduction in planned strength of combat ground forces.

10. Not only were the cuts in combat ground forces made in October 1942 and June 1943 not restored, but also further cuts in allotment of manpower to combat ground forces were made after 1 July 1943. These cuts amounted to 433,000 by 31 March 1945. That is, the Table of Organization strength of ground combat units in existence on 31

Col. 26:
lines 32, 57.

March 1945 was 433,000 less than that allotted to ground combat units on 1 July 1943.

Col. 26:
   lines 10, 57.

11. In sum, with the reductions of October 1942 and June 1943, and with subsequent downward revisions, combat ground forces in March 1945 had about 1,000,000 fewer enlisted men than the War Department had hoped in August 1942 to attain by the end of 1943.

Col. 32:
   lines 16, 57.

12. Air Forces by 31 March 1945 had 255,000 fewer enlisted men than were allotted in November 1942, but this reduction is in part deceptive, because the percentage of enlisted men eventually commissioned, and hence not shown in this table, was far higher in the Air Forces than in other elements of the Army. In March 1945 enlisted men comprised 93.7 percent of Ground Forces but only 84.9 percent of Air Forces.

Col. 26:
   lines 19, 57.

13. In consequence of decrease in projected strength by 1,000,000, the strength of ground combat units already in existence at the end of 1942 was almost as large as the strength of such units in existence in March 1945. The figures were 1,917,000 and 2,041,000 respectively.

14. In gross figures, mobilization of combat ground forces was therefore virtually complete by the end of 1942. Thereafter increase in planned strength went to other elements of the Army, including service units of the Army Ground Forces; and development of combat ground forces was by internal readjustment within a relatively unchanging total.

Cols. 26, 34:
   lines 19, 44.

Cols. 26, 34:
   lines 44, 57.

Col. 26:
   lines 19, 57.

15. During 1943 approximately 2,000,000 men were added to the mobilized strength of the Army. Of these, only 365,000 were added to combat ground forces. During 1944 and the first quarter of 1945 there was no addition to the mobilized strength of the Army. But the strength allotted to combat ground forces was reduced by 241,000 in 1944 and the first quarter of 1945. Hence, while about 2,000,000 were added to the Army after 1942, only 124,000 were permanently added to combat ground forces.

16. The 2,000,000 men (more exactly 1,966,000) added to the authorized enlisted strength of the Army after 1942 were distributed on 31 March 1945 as follows:

	Mobilized on 31 Dec 42	Mobilized on 31 Mar 45	Added after 1942
AGF Combat Units . .	1,917,000	2,041,000	124,000
AGF Service Units. . .	243,000	461,000	218,000
ASF Service Units . . .	518,000	1,097,000	579,000
Total Service Units . .	(761,000)	(1,558,000)	(797,000)
Army Air Forces . . .	1,300,000	1,945,000	645,000
Overhead, Replacements, Nonavailables. . . .	1,022,000	1,422,000	400,000
Total Army. . .	5,000,000	6,966,000	1,966,000

Col. 30:
lines 13, 30, 47.

Col. 23:
lines 15, 30, 37, 40.

17. The Army Ground Forces repeatedly advised against further drain of manpower to noncombat functions and urged increases of allotment to combat forces. As planned on 24 November 1942, combat units were 52.7 percent of the total Army (less Air Forces). As mobilized on 31 March 1945 combat units were only 40.6 percent of the total Army (less Air Forces). Hopes of the War Department, in the months following 24 November 1942, to raise the proportion of combat units by reduction of overhead and service elements did not materialize.[1]

18. Combat ground forces, in gross numbers, were virtually mobilized as early as the end of 1942, although combat ground forces were the last elements of the Army to be employed in operations on a large scale. This difference in timing is traceable to major changes in strategic plans in 1942.

[1] See "Mobilization of the Ground Army," in this volume.

19. Development of combat ground forces after 1942 was obtained, as stated above, by readjustment within a relatively unchanging total. One form of readjustment was economy in Tables of Organization of individual units.[2] By this means additional units were formed without corresponding additional use of manpower. For example, while 1,056,000 enlisted men produced only 73½ divisions on 31 December 1942, almost exactly the same number, 1,060,000, produced 84 divisions on 30 June 1943. The 89 divisions active on 31 March 1945 required only 70,000 more men than did the 73½ divisions active on 31 December 1942. Sixteen divisions were added after 1942, with an additional quantity of manpower which would have yielded less than 5 divisions in 1942. This was because of reduction in divisional Tables of Organization in 1943. The same was true, though not demonstrable by the present table, in nondivisional units.

Cols. 4, 22:
line 19.
Cols. 3, 22:
line 31.
Cols. 1, 22:
line 57.

20. A second form of readjustment, within a relatively unchanging total for combat ground forces, was curtailment in the mobilization program of certain types of units. Curtailment took the form both of deletion of units whose activation was planned for the future and of inactivation of units already mobilized. The process was continuous through 1943 and 1944. It affected especially antiaircraft, tank destroyer, and nondivisional infantry units (also coast artillery, not shown in the present table). It went farthest in antiaircraft artillery, which on 24 November 1942 was planned to reach a total of 781 battalions with 602,000 enlisted men, but which by 31 March 1945 had only 331 battalions with 246,000 enlisted men.

Cols. 18, 20, 21.

Cols. 20, 25:
lines 16, 57.

21. Because of economies in Tables of Organization and because of deletions and inactivations, the addition of only 124,000 men to ground combat forces after 1942 produced the following increment of combat units:

[2] See "Organization and Training of New Ground Combat Elements," in this volume.

	Active 31 Dec 42	Active 31 Mar 45	Added after 1942
Infantry (including Motorized and Mountain) Divisions..........	56	67	11
Armored Divisions.................	14	16	2
Airborne Divisions................	2	5	3
Heavy Artillery Battalions..........	32	137	105
Medium Artillery Battalions........	53	113	60
Light Artillery Battalions...........	57	76	19
Tank Battalions (Nondivisional)......	26	60	34
Engineer Battalions................	69	226	157

Col. 6:
lines 5, 15, 20, 42.

Col. 9:
lines 5, 15, 40.

Col. 10:
lines 5, 15, 18, 20.

Col. 9: line 40.
Col. 11: line 35
Col. 7: lines 12–56.

Cols. 2, 8:
line 51.

22. In apportionment of strength among different types of divisions, the Army Ground Forces consistently advised a higher proportion of infantry divisions and a lower proportion of armored and motorized divisions than was originally favored by officers of the War Department General Staff. Recommendations of the Army Ground Forces to delete motorized divisions were gradually accepted. Recommendations of the Army Ground Forces to reduce the number of armored divisions in proportion to infantry divisions were accepted only in part. Recommendations of the Army Ground Forces to inactivate armored divisions already mobilized and to convert airborne divisions to light infantry were not accepted. Plans for light divisions fluctuated widely and were then abandoned. Inactivation of a cavalry division in 1944 left the number of mobilized divisions at 89.

Col. 6.

23. Because of reduction in planned numbers of armored and motorized divisions the number of infantry divisions ultimately mobilized (66) was larger than the number of infantry divisions projected in 1942, despite the falling off in the total number of divisions.

Cols. 6, 9, 11:
line 43.

24. The desirability of more infantry divisions was recognized by the War Department at the end of 1943, when, in considering an increase in total number of divi-

sions from 90 to 105, it was proposed to add 14 infantry divisions and 1 cavalry division but no armored or airborne divisions. The divisions were not added.

Cols. 13, 14:
lines 12, 15, 25,
26, 34, 42, 48, 53.

25. The Army Ground Forces, at intervals from September 1942 to March 1944, urged considerable increases of heavy and medium artillery, not accepted by the War Department in 1942, accepted in part in 1943, and accepted in 1944 (after operations at Cassino, Italy) to a degree surpassing, in heavy artillery, the highest proposals made by the Army Ground Forces at earlier dates.

Col. 17:
lines 12, 15, 21,
26, 37.

Cols. 9, 17:
line 21.

Col. 9:
line 32.

26. The Army Ground Forces urged more nondivisional tank battalions than were provided for in War Department planning. The AGF recommendation of January 1943 to obtain nondivisional tank battalions by deletion of planned armored divisions was not accepted. The number of planned armored divisions was reduced in consequence of general reduction of the Army in June 1943 rather than as a means of providing more nondivisional tank battalions. The number of nondivisional tank battalions was raised in the later months of 1943 by internal reorganization of the armored divisions.[3]

Col. 18:
line 12.

Col. 18:
line 26.

Col. 18:
lines 36, 37, 41.

Col. 18:
lines 31, 57.

27. The Army Ground Forces at first recommended tank destroyer battalions in very large numbers. It was in this item that early views of the Army Ground Forces were at widest variance with later developments. As early as 14 April 1943 (after action in North Africa) the Army Ground Forces revised its proposals for tank destroyer battalions drastically downward, confining the number to battalions already active. Inactivation was called for by the War Department Troop Basis of 4 October 1943, to a degree believed excessive by the Army Ground Forces, and subsequently modified. But 38 tank destroyer battalions were inactivated between 30 June 1943 and 31 March 1945, most of them in 1944.

[3] Figures not shown in the present table; see "Organization and Training of New Ground Combat Elements," in this volume.

Col. 20:
lines 10, 12.
Cols. 20, 25:
lines 15, 26, 30, 42.

28. In antiaircraft artillery the AGF recommendation of 811 battalions on 30 September 1942 followed allotments prescribed by the War Department. Thereafter the Army Ground Forces repeatedly advised reduction of the antiaircraft artillery program, believing that provision for Air Forces was sufficient to win general superiority in the air and that meanwhile strength allotted to ground forces should be put into units of higher combat value. The War Department hesitated to curtail the antiaircraft program. Antiaircraft artillery was in demand not only for support of combat ground forces but also for defense of fixed military and civilian installations, rear area troops, and air bases. The War Department Commit-

Cols. 22, 23, 25:
line 28.

tee on Revision of the Military Program, in June 1943, having to reduce the planned strength of the Army by 500,000, reduced the allotment for divisions by 355,000 and for nondivisional combat units other than antiaircraft by 92,000, but for antiaircraft units only by 22,000. In these proposals the planned strength of antiaircraft artillery was almost as large as the planned strength of all other nondivisional combat units and over half as large as the planned strength of divisions of all types.

Cols. 22, 23, 25:
line 32.

With some modification, these proposals were incorporated in the approved Troop Basis of 1 July 1943. Not until the Troop Basis of 4 October 1943 was the planned strength of antiaircraft artillery substantially cut. It declined rapidly in 1944. Not until 1944 did inactivation

Col. 25:
lines 44, 55.

exceed activation. Mobilized strength of antiaircraft artillery rose throughout 1943, reaching 431,000 on 31 December 1943, only to fall to 257,000 by 31 December 1944.

Col. 21:
lines 15, 18, 26,
42, 54.

29. The Army Ground Forces favored increases of nondivisional infantry units, to prevent dissipation of divisions by detachment of regiments, to provide unit replacement for relief of divisional infantry in combat, and to furnish pools of armored infantry battalions and parachute infantry regiments. Recommendations of the Army

Col. 21:
line 32.

Ground Forces were accepted in principle by the War Department in the Troop Basis of 1 July 1943, which called for 195 nondivisional infantry battalions (expressed in battalions in the table, though actually organic for the most part in nondivisional regiments). Other demands for manpower made this figure impossible to maintain. Both the number of battalions planned and the number already mobilized declined after July 1943. Deletion of infantry units, as also of tank destroyer and antiaircraft, released men for use as overseas replacements (chiefly infantry) and as fillers for new units of other types.

30. Increase of requirements for nondivisional service units beyond earlier provisions is reflected in the following percentages computed from the table:

Service Units Expressed as a Percentage of Ground Combat Units

| | Planned | | Mobilized |
	24 Nov 42	1 Jul 43	31 Mar 45
AGF Service Units (Combat Zone Services)	12%	14%	23%
ASF Units (Communications Zone Services)	27%	34%	53%
Total Service Units	39%	48%	76%

Services, as here employed, do not include engineer, signal, and chemical troops of combat types. Recommendations of the Army Ground Forces against diversion of manpower to service functions were aimed at communications-zone

Col. 27:
line 30.

services, not at combat-zone services, for which provision was believed by the Army Ground Forces to be insufficient in 1943.

Cols. 22, 29:
line 57.

In 1945 the strength of communications-zone (ASF) service units was almost equal to the strength of divisions of all types.

The actual strength of the Army in March 1945 was about what was planned before reduction of the Army ceiling by 500,000 in June 1943. Before 1 July 1943 an Army of 8,200,000 (7,500,000 enlisted) was projected. On 31 March 1945 an Army of 8,157,386 existed. Reduction in the number and strength of ground combat units effected in June 1943 to conform to the lowered ceiling remained in effect, even though the ceiling was later so far exceeded as to be restored in practice to its earlier and higher figure.

Two-thirds of the Army was overseas or en route overseas on 1 April 1945. Percentage of major elements was reported by the War Department as follows:

	Overseas and En Route Overseas	In Zone of Interior
Ground Forces	79%	21%
Miscellaneous	66%	34%
Service Forces	64%	36%
Air Forces	51%	49%
Total Army	66%	34%

Ground Forces comprised slightly less than half of all troops overseas and en route overseas—approximately 2,500,000 out of 5,400,000 (all strengths actual and aggregate). They comprised slightly less than a quarter of all troops in the Zone of Interior—630,000 out of 2,750,000. Of the 630,000 approximately 400,000 consisted of individuals in the replacement stream, and approximately 100,000 were in tactical units capable of overseas movement. The remaining 130,000 constituted the overhead personnel of schools, replacement training centers, and other Zone of Interior commands. This 130,000 represented one-tenth of all Zone of Interior personnel in the Army, since, of the 2,750,000 officers and men in the Zone of Interior on 1 April 1945, approximately 1,300,000 were in specifically Zone of Interior assignments.[4]

It may be concluded that the mission prescribed for the Army Ground Forces by the War Department in March 1942, "to provide ground force units . . . for combat operations,"[5] was accomplished by March 1945, with some 80 percent of Ground Forces overseas, another 16 percent available or becoming available for overseas duty, and 4 percent (made up with negligible exceptions of men returned from, or disqualified for, overseas service) operating the training establishment in the United States. Only a small miscellany of tactical units (aggregating 100,000) remained at home. This constituted less than 4 percent of AGF tactical forces. Over 96 percent of tactically organized Ground Forces (column 28 of the table) were overseas or en route thereto.

[4] (1) App "A," WD Gen Coun Min (S), 23 Apr 45 and App "B," 30 Apr 45. (2) "Status of Troop Basis Units as of 31 March 1945," Grd Stat Sec, Rpt No 6, 19 Apr 45.   [5] Cir 59, WD, 1942.

III. Sources of the Table

Line in Table	Description of Document	Location of Document
1.	"Division Book" kept by DCofS, AGF. See AGF Historical Section, The Building and Training of Infantry Divisions.	AGF DCofS File (S)
4.	WD memo (S) OPD 320.2 (5–10–42) (2–12–42) for G–3 WD, 23 May 42, sub: Major Troop Requirements for 1942, 1943, and 1944.	320.2/190 (S)
5.	AGF memo (S) for OPD, 28 May 42, sub as above.	320.2/190 (S)
6.	AGF M/S, Col Parks to G–3 AGF, 10 Jun 42, sub: TB for 1943.	320.2/210 (S)
7.	Same as for line 1.	
8.	WD General Council Minutes (S), 26 Aug 42.	Coordination and Records Sec, OCS.
10.	WD ltr (S) AG 320.2 (7–27–42) MS–C–M to CGs AGF, AAF, SOS, 28 Aug 42, sub: Troop Basis, 1943.	320.2/3 (TB 43) (S)
11.	WD memo (S) WDGCT 320 (9–15–42) for CofS, USA, 15 Sep 42, sub: Mobilization Plans.	OPD Record Room, 320.2 Sec IX (9) (S)
12.	AGF memo (S) for TAG, 30 Sep 42, sub: Troop Basis, 1943.	320.2/4 (TB 43) (S)
13.	Same as for line 12.	
14.	WD memo (S) WDGCT 320.2 Gen (10–25–42) for CGs AGF and SOS, 25 Oct 42, sub: Troop Basis, 1943.	320.2/5 (TB 43) (S)
15.	AGF memo (S) for G–3 WD, 29 Oct 42, sub as above.	320.2/5 (TB 43) (S)
16.	WD memo (S) WDGCT 320.2 Gen (11–21–42) for CGs AGF and SOS, 24 Nov 42, sub as above.	AGO Classified Records 320.2 (14 Jul 42) (36) Sec 1

Line in Table	Description of Document	Location of Document
18.	Memo (C) of Gen McNair for G–3 and OPD WD, 7 Dec 42, sub: Orgn of Armd Units.	320.2/18 (Armd F) (C)
19.	1943 Troop Basis, revision of 23 Feb 43.	AGF Plans Sec File 185 in GNAG Records (S)
20.	Memo (S) of Gen McNair for G–3 WD, 28 Jan 43, sub: Basis of Orgn of Mtz Div.	322/1 (Divs) (S)
21.	Memo (S) of Gen McNair for G–3 WD, 28 Jan 43, sub: Trends in Orgn of Armd Fs.	320.2/20 (Armd F)(S)
22.	WD memo (S) WDGCT 320.2 Gen (2–25–43) for G–1, G–4, OPD, CGs AGF, SOS, AAF, 25 Feb 43, sub: Troop Basis Planning.	320.2/18 (TB 43)(S)
23.	WD memo (S) WDGCT 320 (2–24–43) for CG AGF, 15 Mar 43, sub: Reorgn of Mtz Div.	322/1 (Divs)(S)
24.	WD memo (S) OPD 320.2 (2–15–43) for G–3 WD, 30 Mar 43, sub: Light Divs.	OPD Record Room 320.2 Sec IX (9) (S)
25.	Memo (S) of Gen McNair for CG ASF, 12 Apr 43, sub: Heavy Field Arty.	320.2/22 (TB 43)(S)
26.	Memo (S) of Gen McNair for G–3 WD, 14 Apr 43, sub: Modification of Mobilization Procedures.	381/177 (S)
27.	Memo (S) of Col R. T. Maddocks, Col E. W. Chamberlain, Lt Col M. S. Carter for DCofS USA, 13 Jun 43, sub: Troop Basis, 1943.	320.2/31 (TB 43)(S)
29.	AGF memo (S) for G–3 WD, 15 Jun 43, sub: 89th and 71st Light Divs, 10th Mtn Div.	322/2 (Divs)(S)
30.	Memo (S) of Gen McNair for DCofS USA, 22 Jun 43, sub: Troop Basis 1943.	320.2/31 (TB 43)(S)
31.	Troop Basis 1943, revision of 1 Jul 43.	320.2/57 (TB 43)(C)
32.	Same as for line 31.	
33.	WD General Council Minutes (S), 5 Jul 43.	Coordination and Records Sec, OCS
34.	AGF memo (S) for G–3 WD, 17 Jul 43, sub: Heavy Mobile Artillery.	320.2/22 (TB 43)(S)

Line in Table	Description of Document	Location of Document
35.	AGF memo (S) for CofS USA, 22 Sep 43, sub: Rpt of Bd on A/B Opns.	353/17 (AB)(S)
36.	Troop Basis 1943, revision of 4 Oct 43.	AGF Plans Sec File 185 (S)
37.	WD memo (S) WDGCT 320 Troop (2 Oct 43) for DCofS USA, sub: TB 43.	AGF Plans Sec File 185 (S)
40.	AGF memo for G–3 WD, 16 Oct 43, sub: Troop Basis 1944.	320.2/1 (TB 44)(S)
41.	Tentative Troop Basis 1944.	AGF Plans Sec File 185 (S)
42.	Notes (S) by Col J. B. Sherman, Plans Sec, AGF, 8 Nov 43. (Stated by CofS AGF in May 1944 to have been used by AGF in conference with War Dept.)	AGF Plans Sec File 185 (S)
43.	Draft Troop Basis 1944.	AGF Plans Sec File 185 (S)
44.	Troop Basis 1944, 15 Jan 44.	314.7 (AGF Hist)(S)
45.	Same as for line 44.	
47.	AGF memo (S) for G–4 WD, 19 Feb 44, sub: Army Maintenance Effort.	320.2/10 (TB 44)(S)
48.	AGF memo (S) for CG ASF, 20 Mar 44, sub: Revision of Army Supply Program, 1 Feb 44.	320.2/32 (TB 44)(S)
49.	AGF memo for G–3 WD, 14 Apr 44, sub: 71st and 89th Light Divs.	321/808 (Inf)
50.	AGF memo (C) for G–3 WD, 10 May 44, sub: Reorgn of 10th Light Div.	322/1 (10th Div)(C)
51.	Troop Basis, 1 Jul 44 (S).	314.7 (AGF Hist)(S)
53.	Same as for line 51.	
54.	Memo (S) of Gen Lear for G–3 WD, 23 Oct 44, sub: Separate Inf Regts.	320.2/58 (TB 44)(S)
55.	Troop Basis, 1 Jan 45 (S).	314.7 (AGF Hist)(S)
56.	Same as for line 55.	
57.	Troop Basis, 1 Apr 45 (S).	314.7 (AGF Hist)(S)

Mobilization

of the Ground Army

by

Robert R. Palmer

Contents

Tables

Chart

I. General Problems of
Mobilization

In World War II the United States mobilized 91 divisions and inactivated 2.[1] Eighty-nine divisions were employed overseas, and after entering the theaters all were maintained at or near their Table of Organization strength. The experience of World War I had been very different. At the time of the armistice in November 1918, 58 divisions had been activated but only 42 had been shipped overseas. Twelve of these 42 divisions were not functioning as combat units, having been drained for replacements or converted to other uses in France. Of the 16 divisions forming at home, 9 were at less than half-strength in November 1918, and 1 recently activated division could claim only a single enlisted man.[2] This situation in 1918 reflected the fact that the war ended before mobilization in the United States was completed. But it reflected also the fact that the War Department was unable to maintain at full strength the Army that it had projected, and that some divisions had to be dissolved, or never filled, in order that others might have enough manpower to enter or remain in combat.

It was therefore a considerable achievement, by the standards of World War I, not only to raise 91 divisions in World War II but also to maintain 89 of them at effective strength as combat units, replacing losses without dissolu-

---

[1] Changes in the status of the 2d Cavalry Division account for the two inactivated divisions. The 2d Cavalry Division was partially inactivated in July 1942 and fully reactivated in February 1943; it was completely inactivated between February and May 1944. To avoid confusion in understanding further references to the number of divisions activated and made available for combat, it should be added that 3 divisions were activated overseas—the Americal Division in New Caledonia in May 1942, and the 24th and 25th Infantry Divisions in Hawaii in February 1921 and October 1941 respectively. Eighty-eight divisions, therefore, were activated in the Zone of Interior. The partial inactivation of the 2d Cavalry Division occurred in the United States, the other after shipment overseas, in the Mediterranean Theater. Accordingly, the total number of divisions prepared for combat and shipped to theaters by the Army Ground Forces was 87.

[2] Table 2, "Personnel Statistics Report, A–21, Strength of the Army as of November 15, 1918," Statistics Branch, General Staff. AWC Library, UA 24 A554 P 1918 A 21.

tion of any divisions committed to action, although some divisions suffered heavy and continuous losses over a period of years. By 31 January 1945, 47 infantry regiments in 19 infantry divisions had lost from 100 percent to over 200 percent of their strength in battle casualties alone.[3] By May 1945 the 5 hardest-hit divisions had suffered 176 percent battle casualties in all components.[4] Yet substantially all losses were replaced.[5] To accomplish this result the Army Ground Forces trained for combat approximately 4,400,000 officers and enlisted men,[6] or about twice the number that were at any one time assigned to tactical units.

Viewed against the background of total American resources, however, a ground army of 90 divisions may seem a modest creation. It was a much smaller proportion of the total Army of the United States than the ground force mobilized in World War I. The total Army mobilized in 1945 was well over twice as large as that mobilized in November 1918. But the unit strength of combatant ground forces was not much greater than in 1918, although by the end of World War II almost twice as many men had been trained for ground combat. Because the American divisions of the later war were much smaller than those of the earlier, the 90 divisions of 1945 included only 25 percent more manpower than the divisions of 1918. (See Table No. 1.) The enemy put a larger proportion of his strength into ground forces. But the United States counted on other factors in planning its military effort. One was the strength of its allies. The Russian Army alone was estimated to have over 400 divisions in 1945 and engaged the mass of the German ground forces in addition to neutralizing the Japanese forces on the Manchurian border. Another was Allied naval strength, which made it possible for American ground forces to attack at advantageous times and places. A third was Allied air power, which enabled ground forces to attack an enemy underequipped, disrupted, and sometimes immobilized. To the strengthening of naval and air power, and to the material support of its allies, the United States devoted the larger proportion of its resources and its manpower in World War II.

[3] Figures from AGF Statistical Section.

[4] The 3d, 45th, 36th, 9th, and 4th Infantry Divisions, announced by the Under Secretary of War to have sustained combined casualties of 123,394. *New York Times*, 1 June 1945.

[5] Total reported actual strength of all divisions in the Army was over 99 percent of authorized strength as of 30 April 1945. Strength Reports of the Army (S), Vol II, 1 May 45.

[6] The Army Ground Forces trained 4,194,000 enlisted men and 203,000 officers. Army Ground Forces, *Report of Activities* (Washington, 1946), p. 38. These figures are an estimate made by Lt. Col. Seth L. Weld, from the data available to the Troop Movements Branch, G-3, AGF, in 1945.

TABLE NO. 1

The Army in Two Wars

(Aggregate Strengths)

	I	II	III	IV	V	VI	VII	VIII
	Reported Actual Strength 15 Nov 18	Troop Basis Strength (Approx. actual) 30 Apr 45	Percent of Total Army		Percent of Total Army less Air		Percent of Total Ground Combat Forces	
			1918	1945	1918	1945	1918	1945
Army Exclusive of Air Forces:								
Divisions......................	933,862	1,194,569	25.2	14.4	26.6	20.0	56.3	53.5
Nondivisional Combat (less AAA)...................	726,149	779,882	19.6	9.4	20.7	13.0	43.7	35.0
Ground Combat Forces (less AAA)...................	1,660,011	1,974,451	44.8	23.8	47.3	33.0	100.0	88.5
Antiaircraft Artillery............		259,403		3.1		4.3		11.5
Total Ground Combat Forces....	1,660,011	2,233,854	44.8	26.9	47.3	37.3	100.0	100.0
Nondivisional Service...........	945,470	1,638,214	25.5	19.8	26.7	27.4	56.9	73.5
Replacements...................	454,863	841,715	12.3	10.2	13.0	14.1	27.4	37.8
Overhead and Miscellaneous.....	453,793	1,269,709	12.3	15.3	13.0	21.2	27.4	56.9
Total Army (less Air)...........	3,514,137	5,983,492	94.9	72.2	100.0	100.0		
Army Air Forces.................	190,493	2,307,501	5.1	27.8				
TOTAL..................	3,704,630	8,290,993	100.0	100.0				

INTERPRETATION: Subject to reservations as indicated in the following note, and considering only the Army without the Air Forces, the following may be noted:

1. In 1918 almost half the Army was in combat categories, in 1945 only a little over a third. (Cols. V and VI.)

2. Within the category of combat troops, divisions and nondivisional forces (including antiaircraft) were in about the same proportion to each other in the two wars. (Cols. VII and VIII.)

3. Personnel classifiable as replacements numbered somewhat over an eighth of the Army in both wars. (Cols. V and VI.)

4. Personnel in service categories numbered somewhat over a quarter of the Army in both wars. (Cols. V and VI.)

5. Personnel in overhead and miscellaneous categories was proportionately much higher in 1945 than in 1918, approximating respectively one-fifth and one-eighth. (Cols. V and VI.) To some extent this reflects the more accurate accounting methods of 1945, by which overhead and miscellaneous functions were more carefully distinguished from tactical units than in 1918. Analysis of the overhead and miscellaneous category in the two wars appears on the following page. It may be noted that, excluding the Students Army Training Corps of 1918, which was not a form of operating overhead, the figure for 1918 scarcely exceeded 275,000, or one-thirteenth of the strength of the Army.

6. The large figure for overhead and miscellaneous in 1945 explains the relatively low proportion of combat forces, since proportion of replacements and service forces was almost the same in the two wars. (Cols. V and VI.)

7. Replacements, while forming about the same fraction of the Army in the two wars, were in higher ratio to combat forces in 1945 than in 1918, because the ratio of combat forces to the whole Army was lower. (Cols. VII and VIII.) This higher proportion of replacement to combat forces in 1945, together with the fact that they were more fully trained and that the movement of replacements was more systematically conducted, partly explains why units were kept more nearly at authorized strength in 1945 than in 1918.

8. Service troops, while forming about the same fraction of the Army in the two wars, were also in higher ratio to combat forces in 1945 than in 1918. (Cols. VII and VIII.) This reflects the fact that the combat forces of 1945, more highly mechanized and in part more distantly deployed than in 1918, required more

service support. It reflects also the fact that overhead and miscellaneous establishments required service facilities. Even if the combat troops of 1945 had received no more service support than those of 1918, the ratio of service to combat troops would have been higher in 1945, because of the need for service troops to support the overhead and miscellaneous establishments.

NOTE: While it is believed that the picture given by the above figures is accurate in its general outlines, detailed comparison of figures for the two wars is subject to serious limitations. The strength of the Army was not classified in the same way in 1918 and in 1945. The following may be noted of the categories used in the table:

Divisions. In principle the triangular divisions of 1945 had a higher percentage of combat personnel than the square divisions of 1918. In practice there was surprisingly little difference. Divisions in the AEF in November 1918 varied greatly, but the average strength of 29 effective divisions was 22,995, of which 76 percent was in infantry, field artillery and machine-gun personnel. (Tables Nos. 2 and 14 of the sources listed below.) Infantry divisions of 1945 had a T/O strength of 14,037, of which 81 percent was in infantry and field artillery. (Machine gunners were carried as infantry in 1945.) Armored divisions of 1945 had a T/O strength of 10,670, of which only 63 percent was in tank units, infantry, and field artillery. (T/O's 7 and 17, 24 January 1945.) Other divisions of 1945 (chiefly airborne) resembled infantry divisions. Weighting for the different types yields 78 percent combat strength for all divisions in 1945. Hence the proportion of combat strength in divisions of 1918 and 1945 was about the same.

Nondivisional Combat and *Nondivisional Service.* In these categories in the table the figures for 1945 include organized units only, whereas the figures given in the statistics of 1918 were not explicitly limited to organized units, and probably include some personnel which in 1945 would have been carried as "Overhead and Miscellaneous."

Antiaircraft Artillery. Refers only to units in 1945; no such category in 1918.

Replacements and *Overhead and Miscellaneous.* Principal components of these categories in 1918 and in 1945 were as follows:

Replacements

1918		1945	AGF (ARMS)	ASF (SERVICES)
Depot Brigades	196,383	Replacement Training Centers	298,100	29,600
Infantry Replacements	54,666	Replacement Depots	67,500	10,800
Machine-Gun Replacements	15,741	Emergency Replacement Stockage	17,200	2,460
Casuals and Unassigned	15,369	Officer Candidate Schools	5,000	6,000
Casuals at Ports	37,256	Officer Replacement Pools	10,000	5,000
Troops en route to Ports	250	Rotational Policy	11,250	12,500
Development Battalions	40,760	Redistribution Stations	8,300	4,150
Officers Training Schools	59,468	Casuals in Staging Areas and en route		
Casuals and Replacements in		Overseas	61,000	16,000
Europe	34,970	Other AGF and ASF	18,000	20,950
TOTAL	454,863	TOTAL AGF AND ASF	496,350	117,460

Army Specialized Training Program	16,250
Special Training Units	11,000
Overseas Replacement Depots and Training Centers	200,655
TOTAL	841,715

Overhead and Miscellaneous

1918		1945	
Headquarters of Camps, etc	16,205	Bulk Allotments to AGF (131,440) and ASF (398,467) for Zone of Interior installations, etc. (including permanent personnel of replacement agencies listed above)	529,907
Students Army Training Corps	175,872		
Recruits at Depots and Camps	32,747		
Patients in SOS Hospitals	82,013	Reception Centers (Recruits)	30,000
War Department	2,007	Hospital Population	415,000
Unclassified	116,934	War Department Groups	6,408
Other	28,015	Theater Overheads	159,726
		Repatriated Military Personnel	20,000
TOTAL	453,793	Other	108,668
		TOTAL	1,269,709

Although the ASTP of 1945 and the SATC of 1918 were alike in that their personnel were stationed on college campuses, the ASTP is here classified as "Replacements" because its trainees had had basic military training and were usable for military purposes, and the SATC is classified under "Overhead and Miscellaneous" because its trainees had had negligible military experience and were not usable for military purposes without considerable further training.

Army Air Forces. Figures for the two dates are roughly comparable, the figure for 1918 including not only the Air Service of that period but also personnel classified in 1918 under "Aircraft Production" and "Military Aeronautics"; but, since aviation in 1918 drew more heavily on services of the rest of the Army than in 1945, it is probable that the total effort expended in 1918 on aviation should be represented by a higher figure than 190,000 if comparison with 1945 is desired.

Sources: For 1918: Tables Nos. 1, 2, 4, and 14 of "Personnel Statistics Report, A–21, Strength of the Army as of November 15, 1918," dated December 5, 1918, Statistics Branch, War Department General Staff. Army War College Library, UA 24 A 554 P 68150.

For 1945: War Department Troop Basis, 1 May 1945. Ground AG Records, 320.2 Troop Basis (S). The Troop Basis, after authorizing an aggregate strength of 7,700,000 from 1 July 1943 through 1 April 1945, was raised on 1 May 1945 to cover the actual strength to which the Army had grown.

The ground forces of World War II proved to be none too large. In 1918 American troops were needed only in France. In 1942–45 they were needed on opposite sides of the globe. (See Table No. 2.) Despite the tremendous victories of the Russians, and despite control of the sea and air by the western allies, almost all American ground forces were committed before Germany surrendered in May 1945. At that time over 96 percent of the tactical troops of the Army Ground Forces were overseas, and the last divisions had been dispatched three months before. No more combat units were forming at home. No reserve, other than replacements, remained in the United States. Nor was there any significant strategic reserve of uncommitted forces in the theaters. This fact represents both a remarkably accurate planning of the minimum forces required for victory and a fairly narrow escape from disagreeable eventualities, in case general strategic plans had suffered a serious set-back.

With divisions relatively so few, their maximum battle effectiveness was at a premium. Two of the factors on which this was believed to depend were thorough training and a system for effecting relief from excessively prolonged combat strain. To provide such relief rotation of divisions, or of parts of divisions, was contemplated. Actually, the replacement problem interfered with both of the factors mentioned. The measures taken to solve it disrupted division training at home, and also melted into the stream of individual replacements separate infantry regiments and other forms of unit replacements in order to keep at full strength the divisions committed. Again, with so many other demands for ship-space, divisions were shipped to theaters rather slowly. For all of these reasons, it was difficult, and in some theaters impossible, to withdraw divisions from combat for periods of rest. During intensive combat an infantry division suffered about 100 percent losses in its infantry regiments every three months. While the

TABLE NO. 2

Deployment of the Army in 1918 and 1945

(Reported Actual Strengths)

DEPLOYMENT, 20 NOVEMBER 1918		DEPLOYMENT, 30 APRIL 1945							
Type of Troops	Europe	European Theater	Mediterranean Theater	European and Mediterranean Theaters Combined	Southwest Pacific Theater	Pacific Ocean Theater	China and India-Burma Theaters	Principal Theaters Combined	Type of Troops
Divisional Combat Troops......	678,146	819,342	102,485	921,827	183,798	80,834		1,186,459	Divisional Combat Troops
Nondivisional Combat Troops......	507,912	595,418	37,797	633,215	113,318	102,076	15,766	864,375	Nondivisional Combat Troops [a]
Total Ground Combat Troops...	1,186,058	1,414,760	140,282	1,555,042	297,116	182,910	15,766	2,050,834	Total Ground Combat Troops
Nondivisional Service Troops...	464,497	828,726	128,307	957,033	214,835	142,579	69,898	1,384,345	Nondivisional Service Troops
Air Service......	78,804	439,425	153,005	592,430	173,343	75,438	90,949	[b]932,160	Army Air Forces
Replacements......	34,970	171,933	34,551	206,484	34,203	20,371	4,365	265,423	Replacements
Patients in SOS Hospitals......	82,013	128,305	15,679	143,984	41,135	6,423	1,439	192,981	Patients
Unclassified......	116,934	54,758	17,080	71,838	29,500	19,851	10,447	131,636	Overhead
		27,598	4,972	32,570	12,372	3,380	5,966	54,288	Miscellaneous
ARMY IN EUROPE......	1,963,276	3,065,505	493,876	3,559,381	802,504	450,952	198,830	5,011,667	ARMY IN PRINCIPAL THEATERS
Percentage of Army in Europe to Total Army (3,704,630)......	53.1	37.0	6.0	43.0	9.7	5.4	2.4	60.4	Percentage of Army in Principal Theaters to Total Army (8,290,993)
Percentage of Ground Combat Troops in Europe to All Ground Combat Troops in Army (1,660,011)......	71.4	63.4	6.3	69.7	13.3	8.2	0.7	91.9	Percentage of Ground Combat Units in Principal Theaters to All Ground Combat Units in Army (2,233,854)

[a] Including as combat troops all men in engineer, signal, and chemical units of AGF type.

[b] In addition, air forces totaling approximately 200,000, under direct command of the commanding general of Army Air Forces, were engaged in overseas operations, chiefly in the Pacific, without being assigned to a theater.

Sources: For 1918: See Table No. 1. For 1945: Strength Reports of the Army, Vol. II, 1 May 1945 (S), Strength Reporting and Accounting Office, Office of the Chief of Staff.

gaps caused by these losses were generally filled by the continuous stream of replacements, divisions suffered in efficiency with such a high turnover of infantry. A severe mental strain was imposed on the individual soldier, especially the infantryman, who felt that no matter how long he fought, or how long he survived the dangers of combat, he must remain in action until removed as a casualty. Cases of battle neurosis multiplied. Or men simply became tired, and when tired were more easily killed, wounded, or captured. The stream of replacements thus flowed into somewhat leaky vessels. Army Ground Forces thought that, if more units had been available to relieve units in battle, not only would the strain on combat soldiers have been eased but some saving of manpower would probably have resulted.[7]

The present study traces the process, so far as it was known at the headquarters of the Army Ground Forces, by which the United States combatant ground army of World War II was planned, mobilized, and maintained at effective strength.[8]

The ultimate size to which the Army should be expanded was by no means the first question which had to be settled in the planning of mobilization. A more immediate problem was the timing of expansion. Under ideal conditions mobilization would synchronize on the one hand with the production of equipment, so that troops would not be organized faster than weapons became available for training or combat, and on the other hand with general strategic plans,

[7] For the evidence on which these views are based, see AGF Historical Section: The Building and Training of Infantry Divisions; Provision of Enlisted Replacements; and Procurement of Enlisted Personnel for the AGF: the Problem of Quality.

[8] Other studies prepared by the AGF Historical Section are closely related to the present study.

Three such studies appear in the present volume: (1) "Ground Forces in the Army, December 1941–April 1945: a Statistical Study," which presents the mobilization of ground elements in tabular form; (2) "Reorganization of Ground Troops for Combat," which, dealing with the internal organization of units, indicates the allotment of manpower and equipment to each type of unit set up for mobilization; and (3) "Organization and Training of New Ground Combat Elements," which presents aspects of the mobilization of armored forces, airborne units, and heavy artillery units.

Other related studies are the following: (1) Provision of Enlisted Replacements, dealing with the replacement system by which units once mobilized were kept in being; (2) The Building and Training of Infantry Divisions; (3) Problems of Nondivisional Training in the Army Ground Forces; and (4) Preparation of Units for Overseas Movement, in which details are presented regarding the effects on training of certain difficulties inherent in mobilization, such as the need of supplying cadres, the shortage of manpower and equipment, the turnover of personnel within units and the consequent need for repeated training, and the stripping of trained units for replacements; (5) Procurement of Enlisted Personnel for the AGF: the Problem of Quality; (6) The Procurement and Branch Distribution of Officers; (7) Wartime Training in the Schools of the Army Ground Forces; and (8) Training of Officer Candidates in AGF Special Service Schools, in which the effects of mobilization on the procurement and training of suitable officers, enlisted men, and specialists are treated.

so that troops would be ready in the necessary types and numbers, organized, trained and equipped, as operational requirements developed. It was wasteful of manpower to induct men before equipment was available for training, or to train them too long before they were required in operations. Another immediate problem was that of distributing the growing strength of the Army among its component parts. Apportionment had to be made between air forces and ground forces, between combat troops and service troops, and among the several branches such as Infantry, Field Artillery, Quartermaster, and Military Police. Strength had also to be distributed within each unit: in the infantry battalion, for example, among riflemen, machine gunners, clerks, and cooks. The need throughout was to achieve a balance: the right ratio of machine gunners to riflemen, of artillery to infantry units, of service to combat troops, of air forces to ground forces, and of all forces to overhead—the right ratio, or balance, being ultimately that by which the enemy could be defeated soonest.

Size and internal balance of individual units were specified in Tables of Organization (T/O's).[9] The "authorized strength" of a unit was normally its Table of Organization strength. A unit was "overstrength" if it had more men than its T/O called for, "understrength" or "short" if it had fewer. In some circumstances overstrength or understrength might be authorized.

The number of units to be mobilized was set forth in a document known as the Troop Basis, which gave the authorized strength of the entire Army as of a specified date in the future. The total figure set by the Troop Basis was the total of the Tables of Organization of all authorized units, plus allotments of manpower to allow for men in transit, hospital patients, replacements, overhead establishments, and other needs for which no set tables could be prescribed. The Troop Basis was therefore a blueprint of the Army, indicating how many bomber groups, infantry divisions, ordnance companies, etc., should be mobilized. It was a budget of manpower, showing the use to which the War Department proposed to put the manpower made available to it. It was also a plan of mobilization, showing, by successive projections several months or a year into the future, what the size and composition of the Army should be at successive future dates.[10]

The Activation Schedule was derived from the Troop Basis. The Troop Basis set up the objective and the major phases in timing. The Activation Sched-

---

[9] Treated at length below in "Reorganization of Ground Forces for Combat."

[10] For a more technical description of the Troop Basis see above, "Ground Forces in the Army, December 1941–April 1945: a Statistical Study."

ule marked out the individual steps by which the objective should be reached, showing exactly what units should be activated each month. Whether a unit called for in the Troop Basis was actually activated on a given date depended on a variety of practical and often transitory circumstances: whether men were forthcoming from Selective Service, whether a trained cadre could be obtained, whether training equipment and housing accommodations would be available. All these factors fluctuated over short periods. They were difficult to foresee. The Activation Schedule therefore had to be closely watched and frequently modified. In principle the Troop Basis was revised only for reasons of general strategy or fundamental necessity; the Activation Schedule was revised to conform to circumstances of the moment.

The broad decisions of mobilization policy that determined the total strength of the armed forces and the distribution between the War and Navy Departments were made by the highest executive authority, acting with the advice of the Joint Chiefs of Staff. Within strategical requirements as transmitted by the Joint Chiefs, the War Department determined the relative strengths of the Army Air Forces, the Army Ground Forces, and the Army Service Forces (originally called the Services of Supply). To the Army Air Forces, until the end of 1943, the War Department made a bulk allotment of manpower. The Troop Basis showed only a lump total for the Air Forces until October 1943. By that time mobilization was virtually complete.

Over the ground army, both Ground Forces and Service Forces, the War Department exercised a more immediate jurisdiction. Without explicit War Department approval the headquarters of the Army Ground Forces could not alter Tables of Organization by adding or removing a single individual. It could not modify the Troop Basis by adding or deleting a single battalion. Until September 1942 it could not change the Activation Schedule on its own authority. A few weeks after the reorganization of the War Department in March 1942 it was even proposed by G–3 of the War Department that, while the Army Air Forces and Services of Supply should continue to activate their own units, the power to activate AGF units should revert to the War Department.[11] This proposal was dropped when Army Ground Forces nonconcurred, but the War Department continued to hold the Ground Forces within a framework of central control. The Army Ground Forces had extensive powers of recommendation on matters of mobilization, but the decisions were made by the War Department General Staff.

[11] AGF Memo for G–3 WD, 9 Apr 42, sub: Agency or Agencies to Activate Units. 320.2/1915.

II. The 1942 Army

On the day before the bombing of Pearl Harbor Lt. Gen. Lesley J. McNair, then Chief of Staff, General Headquarters, estimated that an army of 200 divisions would be necessary for offensive action by the United States.[1] The expectations of the War Department General Staff ran in 1942 to somewhat the same figure.[2] A study by the Joint Chiefs on the ultimate size of the Army envisaged 334 divisions, an air force of 2,700,000, and an antiaircraft artillery force of no less than 1,102,000.[3] In the spring of 1942 the United States, ejected from the Philippines, was everywhere on the defensive. The military value of its allies was open to question; the British had been driven from Singapore and were being hard pressed in the Middle East, and the Russians were suffering defeat in the Ukraine.

The early forecasts for the U. S. Army were in the nature of preplanning estimates, and are significant mainly in illustrating the feeling at the time. Practical and specific planning could hardly look beyond a year into the future and was relatively modest in its aims.

The First Troop Basis of 1942

The plan in effect at the time of the establishment of the Army Ground Forces was the Troop Basis issued by the War Department on 15 January 1942.[4] The Army at the time of Pearl Harbor, after fifteen months of peacetime

---

[1] Memo (S) of Gen McNair for G–3 WD, 6 Dec 41, sub: Organized Reserves. GHQ Records, 320.2/58 (S).

[2] WD memo (S) OPD 320.2 (5–10–42) (2–12–42) for G–3 WD, 23 May 42, sub: Major Troop Unit Requirements for 1942, 1943, and 1944. 320.2/190 (S).

[3] Annex A (S) of JCS 57/6, 22 Oct 42. AGO Records, 322 (7–14–42) (1), Sec 1 (S).

[4] (1) WD memo (C) G–3/6457–433 for CG Field Forces, 15 Jan 42, sub: Mob and Tng Plan, Jan 42. GHQ Records, 320.2/60 (C). (2) WD ltr (C) AG 381 (1–14–42) MSC–C–M, 17 Jan 42, sub: Mob and Tng Plan 1942. GHQ Records, 320.2/62 (C).

mobilization, consisted of about 1,600,000 men. (See Table No. 3.) Some 36 divisions had been organized. The Air Corps had a personnel of only 270,000. Certain types of service units had not been developed in the proportions needed in war. The Troop Basis of January 1942 provided that by the end of 1942 the Army would reach a strength of 3,600,000 enlisted men, to include 73 divisions and an air force of 998,000. So far as ground forces were concerned, emphasis was placed on the mobilization of new divisions. The training of divisions required a year; that of nondivisional units, whether of combat or of service types, could for the most part be accomplished in six months. It was therefore believed that the nondivisional program could proceed more slowly.[5]

It was also decided in January 1942 that replacement training centers would not be expanded proportionately with the expansion of the Army. In 1941 basic training had been concentrated in replacement centers, and tactical units drew their filler personnel from graduates of the centers. General McNair believed that tactical units could be trained more rapidly and effectively under this system. But the War Department preferred not to authorize new housing for replacement centers, and to use incoming manpower to create units as rapidly as possible.[6] Units were therefore to draw filler personnel from untrained recruits at reception centers. This policy had serious effects on the mobilization of units, for it required that, in addition to training as tactical units, they function in effect as basic training centers and as replacement pools.

Many developments upset the initial program for mobilization in 1942. It proved impossible to foresee all needs, or to build the Army according to the blueprint of the January Troop Basis.[7] Units not called for in the Troop Basis were activated, and the Troop Basis was then revised to include them. With manpower thus diverted to unforeseen needs, units set up in the original Troop Basis could not be brought to authorized strength. AGF units especially suffered from chronic shortages of personnel.

Shortages were due in part to the normal process of growth.[8] Trained units had to supply personnel as cadres for the formation of new units. Some

[5] Memo (S) of Gen McNair for G–3 WD, 3 Aug 42, sub: Pers and Tng Status of Units of AGF, 320.2/283 (S).

[6] (1) WD memo G–3/6457–433 for CofS USA, 27 Dec 41, sub: Mob and Tng Plan (revised) 1942, with qualified concurrence of GHQ. AGO Records, 381 (12–27–41) (2). (2) GHQ ltr to First Army, 31 Jan 42, sub: Tng of Enl Repls Reporting Directly from Reception Centers. GHQ Records, 353/763 (First Army).

[7] (1) WD Gen Council Min (S), 21 and 29 Apr, 7 Jul, 7 Sep 42. (2) WD ltr (R) AG 320.2 (6–20–42) MS SPGAO–M to CGs, 22 Jun 42, sub: Mil Pers not Included in Current Tr Basis. 320.2/43 (R).

[8] See AGF Historical Section, The Building and Training of Infantry Divisions.

units furnished cadres more than once. All units lost enlisted men who became officer candidates or went to service schools for enlisted-specialist courses. Some men were lost as physically unfit, others as parachute volunteers. There was a large drain to the Army Air Forces, which recruited throughout the Army for aviation cadets. This attrition in units (as distinguished from supplying cadres) would have been much less had basic training remained concentrated in replacement centers, because the selective processes involved commonly occurred during the individual's first months in the service.

Foreseeing such attrition, General McNair in January 1942 recommended that new units be activated with a 10 percent overstrength, in order that they might be at T/O strength on completion of training.[9] The War Department, wishing to create a maximum number of new units with the personnel available, took the opposite course of authorizing an understrength. New units were activated at T/O strength, less basic privates. Basic privates were men included in Tables of Organization over and above all specified job assignments as an advance provision for replacements. In most units they constituted 10 percent of T/O strength. Units were supposed to be able to sustain combat without their basics, but, since it was planned to add the basics before shipment of units overseas, their absence meant a shortage which eventually had to be filled. In March 1942 a proposal was made by G-3, War Department General Staff, to authorize an additional 15 percent understrength for units in early stages of training. The proposal was not carried out. Brig. Gen. Mark W. Clark, then Chief of Staff, AGF, wrote:[10]

> It is believed that since we are at war our combat units should be trained as complete standard units, at a strength suitable for immediate combat. It is considered that to add about one-third strength to a unit approximately three months before the unit engages in battle against our well-trained adversaries, would be to place the unit on the battlefield at a disadvantage which could have been avoided without serious detriment to the war effort as a whole.

Understrength was not authorized except for the initial omission of basic privates. But it continued to exist in fact. The War Department was under heavy pressure to supply manpower to other than Ground Force organizations, and within the Ground Forces to divert manpower to other than primary combat units. The Air Forces grew more rapidly than the January Troop Basis provided.

[9] Minutes (S) GHQ staff conference, 28 Jan 42. GHQ Records, 337 (S).

[10] AGF memo (R) for G-3 WD, 19 Mar 42, sub: Reduction in Authorized Strength of Certain Units Included in Tr Basis 1942. 320.2/9 (R).

Antiaircraft units were authorized by the War Department, in this early and defensive phase of the war, beyond the numbers at first planned. The earlier plan to defer activation of nondivisional service units until after the launching of divisions on their training program broke down; service units were in fact activated in great numbers.

Operational Needs

These calls upon the War Department reflected operational needs, both in the defense commands, in which certain types of forces, especially antiaircraft, were assigned to combat stations, and in the overseas theaters, which were then beginning to be built up.

In April 1942 first priority was given to a plan to ship 1,000,000 men to the United Kingdom for employment in a cross-Channel operation in April 1943 (ROUNDUP), or in a smaller operation late in 1942 (SLEDGEHAMMER) if assistance to the Russians became absolutely imperative.[11] The plan was gradually modified as the British position in Egypt grew more critical, and in July it was postponed in favor of an operation in northwest Africa (TORCH) Meanwhile troops were shipped to Great Britain, especially service troops to prepare the way for combat forces. In August a limited offensive was mounted in the South Pacific. Other troops, chiefly in service, air, and antiaircraft units, with here and there an infantry regiment for local protection, were scattered in quiet theaters from Alaska to the Persian Gulf.

These operations had pronounced effects on mobilization and training in the Army Ground Forces. Since AGF units were generally understrength, and since the output of replacement training centers was inadequate, the filling of divisions and other units to T/O strength, in preparation for overseas movement, required transfer of trained personnel from other units destined to remain longer at home. These units in turn either remained understrength, or received untrained men from reception centers, repeated parts of their training program, and finally filled their last shortages by tapping still other units. From some old divisions whole regiments or combat teams were bodily removed. On 24 July 1942 the 30th, 31st, 33d, 38th, and 40th Divisions lacked regiments or other major parts. Thus crippled, it was difficult for them to engage in maneuvers or advanced divisional exercises. New divisions could not attain full strength on

[11] Papers (S) filed under "Bolero." AGF Plans Sec file (S).

activation because other elements of the Army had higher priority on inductees. Training of new divisions was thus delayed at the start or, once begun, was interrupted by the receipt of fillers direct from civilian life at spasmodic and unpredictable intervals. Meanwhile the attempt to create three or four new divisions a month meant that nondivisional units could not receive personnel. The Army Ground Forces preferred to pass a tactical unit as an integral whole through progressive phases of training, but it proved impossible to carry out this policy. Some small units remained at cadre strength for months after activation. Most large units, with the constant attrition and turnover of personnel, found themselves training men at different levels at the same time.[12]

Drained by the necessity of supplying cadres, officer candidates, and aviation cadets, and of furnishing personnel for overseas assignment, AGF units met difficulty in replacing their losses because of the demand of the Army Air Forces and the Services of Supply for inductees. (See Table No. 3, with Annex.) The Air Forces, which had not grown as rapidly as the ground arms in the prewar mobilization of 1941, was given high priority by the War Department in 1942. The Services of Supply, as projected in the Troop Basis of January 1942, was smaller in proportion to combat forces than it had been in 1917 and 1918. The cross-Channel plan for 1943 created new demands for port battalions, construction units, signal troops, and other service elements for use in Great Britain. In May the required proportion of service elements in the invasion force was estimated at 30 percent, a figure to which Maj. Gen. Dwight D. Eisenhower, Chief of the Operations Division, WDGS, found it necessary to consent, though he observed that with so many service troops the necessary combat troops could not be shipped.[13] But on 2 June the proportion of service troops in the force had risen to 48 percent.[14]

In May, to keep up with activation already effected or planned, the President authorized the induction of an additional 750,000 men in 1942, raising the objective set in the 1942 Troop Basis from 3,600,000 to 4,350,000.[15] Of

[12] (1) AGF M/S (S), 26 Jun 42ff. sub: Tr Unit Basis 1942. 320.2/283 (S). (2) AGF M/Ss (S), 13 Jul 42ff. 320.2/283 (S). (3) AGF memo (S) for G–3 WD, 24 Jul 42, sub: Modification of Tr Basis 1942. 320.2/2 (TB 42) (S). (4) Memo (S) of Gen McNair for G–3 WD, 3 Aug 42, sub: Pers and Tng Status of Units of AGF. 320.2/283 (S). (5) WD memo (S) WDGCT 320.2 Gen (8–3–42) for CG AGF, 7 Aug 42, sub as above. 320.2/283 (S). (6) AGF memo (S) for OPD WD, 9 Aug 42, sub: Directive for Overseas Tr Movement—Sep. 370.5/462 (S). (7) AGF memo (S) for G–3 WD, 9 Sep 42, sub as in (4) above. 320.2/283 (S).
[13] WD Gen Council Min (S), 19 May 42.   [14] Ibid., 2 Jun 42 (S).
[15] WD ltr (C) AG 320.2 (5–19–42), 20 May 42, sub: Increased Strength of the Army, Calendar Year 1942. 320.2/121/(C).

the 750,000 added, 250,000 were earmarked for the Air Forces, 250,000 were already used up by overdrafts on the Troop Basis of January, and most of the remaining 250,000 were committed to new units authorized for the Services of Supply.[16] The allotment of 4,350,000 was soon overdrawn. A revised Troop

[16] WD Gen Council Min (S), 27 May 42.

TABLE NO. 3

Growth of the Army by Branch, 1941-45

(*Reported Actual Strength and Percent of Total Army*)

BRANCH	31 December 1941		31 December 1942		31 December 1943		31 March 1945	
	Strength	Percent	Strength	Percent	Strength	Percent	Strength	Percent
Infantry, Cavalry, Field Artillery (includes Armored and Tank Destroyer) [a] ...	690,083	41.7	1,512,730	28.0	1,960,068	24.9	[b]2,423,075	29.7
Coast Artillery Corps (includes Antiaircraft) [a]	177,379	10.7	425,187	7.9	590,939	7.9	330,442	4.1
Total Ground Arms.......	867,462	52.4	1,939,917	35.9	2,451,007	32.8	2,753,517	33.8
Adjutant General..............	966	0.1	4,418	0.1	15,688	0.2	56,116	0.7
Engineers.....................	91,476	5.5	333,209	6.2	561,066	7.5	688,764	8.4
Signal........................	50,596	3.0	241,227	4.5	309,641	4.1	331,105	4.1
Medical [c]....................	129,512	7.8	469,981	8.8	622,227	8.3	670,151	8.2
Ordnance.....................	34,278	2.1	235,350	4.3	316,174	4.2	332,042	4.1
Quartermaster................	122,672	7.4	327,794	6.1	453,419	6.1	491,301	6.0
Chemical.....................	6,269	0.4	46,182	.8	66,610	.9	61,458	.7
Military Police...............	....	....	147,840	2.7	222,639	3.0	203,823	2.5
Transportation................	....	....	51,041	.9	167,612	2.2	260,260	3.2
Total Services...........	435,769	26.3	1,857,042	34.4	2,735,076	36.5	3,095,020	37.9
Air Corps...................	270,535	16.3	1,270,677	23.5	1,810,900	24.2	1,831,091	22.4
All Other (includes Women's Army Corps, Warrant and Flight Officers, and No Branch Assigned)..........	83,391	5.0	333,252	6.2	485,451	6.5	477,758	5.9
TOTAL.................	1,657,157	100.0	5,400,888	100.0	7,482,434	100.0	8,157,386	100.0

Source: "Strength of the Army," prepared monthly by Machine Records Branch, AGO.

[a] Armored, Tank Destroyer, and Antiaircraft were not reported as separate arms. Because of inclusion of these specialties in the basic ground arms, exact breakdown of the ground arms cannot be made.

[b] This figure, at this date, includes perhaps 300,000 carried in the Troop Basis as "Hospital Population," most casualties occurring in the ground arms and to a less extent in the Air Corps.

[c] Includes Army Nurse Corps, Dietitians, and Physical Therapists.

ANNEX TO TABLE NO. 3

CHART A Growth of the Army by Branch

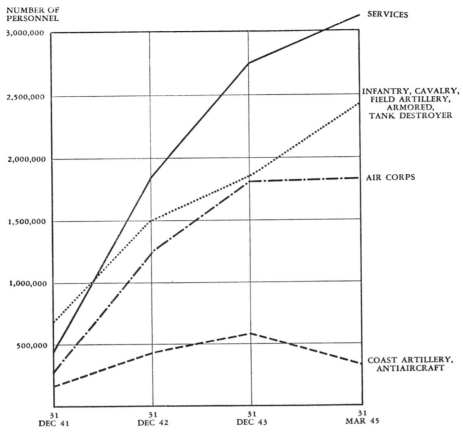

NUMBER OF
PERSONNEL

SERVICES

INFANTRY, CAVALRY,
FIELD ARTILLERY,
ARMORED,
TANK DESTROYER

AIR CORPS

COAST ARTILLERY,
ANTIAIRCRAFT

3,000,000

2,500,000

2,000,000

1,500,000

1,000,000

500,000

31 DEC 41   31 DEC 42   31 DEC 43   31 MAR 45

CHART B Percent of Each Branch in Total Army

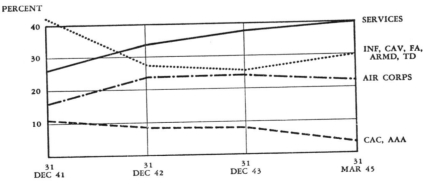

PERCENT

SERVICES

INF, CAV, FA,
ARMD, TD

AIR CORPS

CAC, AAA

40

30

20

10

31 DEC 41   31 DEC 42   31 DEC 43   31 MAR 45

CHART C   Rate of Growth of the Army by Branch

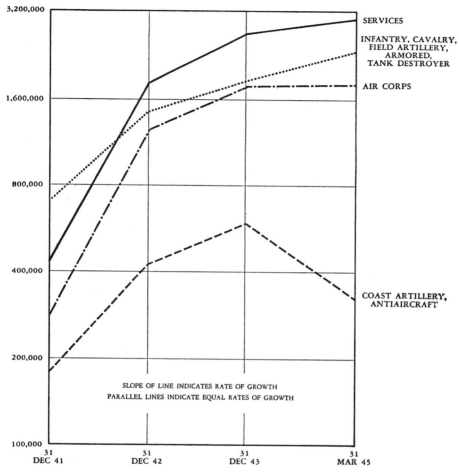

NUMBER OF
PERSONNEL

SERVICES

INFANTRY, CAVALRY,
FIELD ARTILLERY,
ARMORED,
TANK DESTROYER

AIR CORPS

COAST ARTILLERY,
ANTIAIRCRAFT

SLOPE OF LINE INDICATES RATE OF GROWTH
PARALLEL LINES INDICATE EQUAL RATES OF GROWTH

Source: Figures plotted in all three charts are those in Table No. 3.

INTERPRETATION OF A, B, AND C

1. The Air Corps and the Services expanded at the same rate in 1942 and 1943.

2. This rate was far more rapid than the rate of expansion of the Ground Arms, especially in 1942.

3. After 31 December 1943 the Ground Arms expanded more rapidly than other elements of the Army, because with the intensification of ground combat in 1944 an increased number of men in the Ground Arms were carried as replacements and as patients in hospitals.

4. The Coast Artillery Corps (mainly antiaircraft) expanded more rapidly than the other Ground Arms in 1942 and 1943, especially in 1943, when it expanded as rapidly as the Air Corps and the Services; but expansion gave way to precipitous decline in 1944 and 1945.

Basis issued in July represented an increment, for units to be mobilized in 1942, of 851,536 men over the Troop Basis of January. Of this figure, 13 percent was for combat units in the Army Ground Forces, and almost two-thirds of this 13 percent was for antiaircraft artillery.[17]

It was generally agreed in the summer of 1942 that activations, especially of service units, were getting out of hand. "There is evidence," noted G–3, WDGS, on 11 June, "that in some cases sufficient forethought is not exercised to utilize units already provided for in the Troop Unit Basis."[18] In order to build up their theaters, overseas commanders tended to request a great variety of useful but not indispensable special units; chiefs of branches wished to enlarge the usefulness of their branches to the Army; the War Department granted requests liberally, trusting in the judgment of the specialist or of the man on the spot. By September 1942 the authorized gross number of enlisted men per division had risen to 50,000, of which only 15,000 represented organic divisional strength.[19] Medical troops alone amounted to 3,500 per division in addition to the medical battalion organic in the division itself.[20] G–3, WDGS, in charge of the Troop Basis, observed that service units could not be curtailed unless American soldiers, like Japanese, would consent to live on rice.[21]

The Manpower Crisis of the Summer of 1942

By 30 June 1942 the Army Ground Forces was short 162,505 men.[22] The War Department had proposed, on 11 June, that either units be kept purposely understrength while in training (the proposal rejected by the Army Ground Forces in March) or the activation of new units be slowed down.[23]

Understrength in training units was again described by the Army Ground Forces as "unsound."[24] The request for overstrength, as a reserve against cadre

[17] Computed from WD ltr (C) AG 320.2 (7–3–42) MS–C–M, 18 Jul 42, sub: Unit Basis for Mob and Tng 1942, with other papers. 320.2/152 (C) (sep file).

[18] WD memo (C) WDGCT 320.2 (6–11–42) for CGs AGF, AAF, SOS, 11 Jun 42, sub: Tr Unit Basis 1942. (2) AGF memo (S) for G–3 WD, 26 Jun 42, sub as above. Both in 320.2/1 (TB 42) (S).

[19] WD Gen Council Min (S), 26 Aug 42.

[20] Ibid., 7 Sep 42.

[21] Ibid., 30 Jun 42.

[22] Memo (S) of Gen McNair for G–3 WD, 3 Aug 42, sub: Pers and Tng Status of Units of AGF. 320.2/283 (S).

[23] WD memo (S) WDGCT 320.2 (6–11–42) for CGs AGF, AAF, SOS, 11 Jun 42, sub: Tr Unit Basis 1942. 320.2/1 (TB 42) (S).

[24] AGF memo (S) for G–3 WD, 26 Jun 42, sub: Tr Unit Basis 1942. 320.2/1 (TB 42) (S).

losses and general attrition, was repeated.[25] The request was granted in September, when the War Department empowered the three major commands to authorize a 15 percent enlisted overstrength to such units as they might designate.[26] Overstrength, if actually attained (not merely authorized), was a protection against attrition for those units which received it. But it offered no general solution. Insofar as some units received an overstrength, one of three things had to happen: either some units had to be abnormally short, or fewer units had to be activated, or more men had to be inducted.

During June and July 1942, AGF and SOS officers considered the slowing down of the Activation Schedule. They discovered that representatives of each arm and service advised deceleration in other branches than their own. General McNair concluded that neither the Army Ground Forces nor the Services of Supply had sufficient knowledge of over-all requirements to judge conflicting claims. He urged that the War Department General Staff assume a firmer control over the Troop Basis.[27] He recommended deferment of the 97th Division, scheduled for activation in December 1942, as a means of obtaining personnel to refill the depleted older divisions.[28] The War Department approved this recommendation in August.

Further deceleration of the Activation Schedule at this time, postponing the units due for activation in July and August, would have reduced the shortages which were accumulating in the Ground Forces and would have made possible more effective training. But General McNair believed it dangerous at this time to slow down the mobilization of combat troops. He recommended instead a speeding up of inductions through Selective Service. In July the 2d Cavalry Division was partially inactivated, and the personnel were used to fill up the 9th Armored Division.[29] Although the plan for an immediate invasion of western Europe was abandoned on 25 July, it was not easy to defer activations; for an infantry division there was a preactivation process extending over three months, and involving hundreds of officers and over 1,000 enlisted cadremen. Once started,

[25] AGF memo (S) for G–3 WD, 9 Sep 42, sub: Pers and Tng Status of Units of AGF. 320.2/283 (S).

[26] WD ltr (R) AG 320.2 (9–10–42) MS–C–M to CGs AGF, AAF, SOS, 11 Sep 42, sub: Policies Concerning Mob. 320.2/80 (R).

[27] AGF memo (S) for G–3 WD, 18 Aug 42, sub: Revision of Activation Schedule. 320.2/263 (S).

[28] AGF memo (S) for G–3 WD, 24 Jul 42, sub: Modification of Tr Basis 1942. 320.2/2 (TB 42) (S).

[29] (1) Memo (S) of Gen McNair for G–3 WD, 3 Aug 42, sub: Pers and Tng Status of Units of AGF. 320.2/283 (S). (2) Information furnished by Orgn and Directory Sec, Opns Branch, Opns and Tng Div, TAGO.

this process could not be stopped without excessive waste and confusion. The War Department, unable to foresee the operations of Selective Service, and assigning inductees in large numbers to the Air Forces and the Services of Supply, could never accurately predict, three months in advance, how many inductees would be available to divisions and other AGF units on their dates of activation. The Army Ground Forces therefore proceeded with activations called for in the Troop Basis. New units were created, men failed to appear, and shortages mounted.[30]

By September 1942 the Ground Forces were short 330,000 men, or over 30 percent of authorized unit strength. (See the chart on p. 224.) The Air Forces were short 103,000, or 16 percent; the Services of Supply 34,000, or 5 percent. Shortages in the Ground Forces threatened to make proper training impossible.[31]

Change of War Plans

By this time the plan for an early attack on western Europe had been given up. An invasion of North Africa was being prepared, but major operations by United States ground troops were deferred to an undetermined but relatively distant date. Meanwhile the offensive against Germany was to be conducted chiefly by aviation.

In September 1942 a conference on personnel shortages was held at the War Department.[32] The Army Ground Forces expressed a desire to decelerate its Activation Schedule until its existing units were filled. The Army Air Forces and the Services of Supply opposed deceleration within their own commands. "It is presumed," reported the AGF representative on returning to the War College, "that AGF would postpone activations so as to make inductees available for AAF and SOS."[33] The War Department instructed each command to submit a list of "must units" for activation during the remainder of 1942. The Army Ground Forces included as "must units" only

[30] AGF memo (R) for G–3 WD, 10 Oct 42, sub: Policies Concerning Mob. 320.2/80 (R).

[31] Memo of Col Tate (Plans) for DCofS AGF, 7 Sep 42, sub: Rpt on Meeting Held under Supervision of G–3 WD on Pers Matters. 327.3/42 (LS).

[32] WD memo (C) WDGCT 320.2 Activ (9–15–42) for CG AGF, 15 Sep 42, sub: Deferment in Activation of Units. 320.2/205 (C).

[33] Memo of Col Tate (Plans) for DCofS AGF, 21 Sep 42, sub: Rpt of G–3 WD Conference on Pers Matters. AGF Plans Sec file 185 (TB 42).

two tank destroyer brigade headquarters, to supervise the training of the large number of tank destroyer battalions already in existence, and two parachute infantry regiments to absorb the personnel already graduated or about to be graduated from the parachute school.[34] Only these units, with a few others of small size, were activated by the Army Ground Forces at full strength in the last three months of 1942. Infantry and armored divisions that were planned for these months and that were too far along in the preactivation process to stop were activated at cadre strength only. Activations proceeded as planned in the Air Forces, except that certain Air Base Security Battalions (mostly Negro organizations) were deleted. Activation of SOS units continued.[35]

In September the President approved another increase, this time of 650,000, in inductions for 1942, raising the authorized enlisted strength of the Army by the end of the year to 5,000,000.[36] About a million and a half men were provided by Selective Service in the last four months of the year. Those received by the Army Ground Forces were used mainly to fill shortages in units activated before September and to bring certain units to the newly authorized 15 percent overstrengths. By March 1943 the actual and authorized strengths of the Army Ground Forces virtually balanced. But freedom from shortages proved to be temporary.[37]

Summary of Mobilization in 1942

At the close of 1942 the Army could look back on a year of unprecedented expansion. Almost 4,000,000 men had been added during the year, actual strength (including officers) having risen from 1,657,157 to 5,400,888. Thirty-seven new divisions had been called into being. Seventy-three were in existence. The pressure of growth had repeatedly broken through the plans of the Troop Basis. Growth had been uneven and inadequately controlled because of inherent difficulties in planning during a period of chaotic expansion and also because of fluctuations in strategic objectives at the highest level.

---

[34] AGF memo (S) for G-3 WD, 23 Sep 42, sub: Activations, Priorities, and RTC Pool. 320.2/352 (S).

[35] (1) WD memo (S) WDGCT 320.2 Activ (9-28-42) for CGs AAF, AGF, SOS, 28 Sep 42, sub: Activation of Units in Oct 1942. AGF Plans Sec file 185. (2) Same for units to be activated in November and December 1942. 320.2/395 (S). (3) WD Gen Council Min (S), 21 Sep and 23 Nov 42.

[36] WD Gen Council Min (S), 7 Sep 42.

[37] See the chart on p. 224.

TABLE NO. 4

Mobilization After 1942: Enlisted Strength

(*In Thousands*)

CATEGORY	Mobilized on 31 Dec 42	Mobilized on 30 Apr 45	Added after 1942	Percent Increase of Each Element	Percent of Total Increase Received by Each Element
Divisional Combat Troops........................	1,056	1,125	69	6.5	2.9
Nondivisional Combat Troops....................	861	916	55	6.4	2.3
Total Ground Combat Troops..................	1,917	2,041	124	6.5	5.2
AGF Service Troops.............................	243	461	218	89.7	9.1
Total AGF Troops............................	2,160	2,502	342	15.8	14.3
ASF Service Troops.............................	518	1,102	584	110.8	24.3
Total Service Troops..........................	(761)	(1,563)	(802)	(105.7)	(33.4)
Army Air Forces................................	1,300	1,954	654	50.3	27.1
Replacements, Overhead, and Miscellaneous.........	(1,022)	1,847	(825)	81.0	34.3
TOTAL............	5,000	7,405	2,405	48.1	100.0

In addition to a net growth of 2,405,000 in enlisted men shown above, the Army experienced a net growth of approximately 470,000 in commissioned and warrant officer personnel in this period. Such personnel numbered 885,658 on 30 April 1945, making an aggregate Troop Basis strength of 8,290,993. Only enlisted figures are shown in the above table because they are the only figures available for 31 December 1942.

Distribution of strength within the Army shifted greatly in 1942, more so than in any subsequent year of the war. (See Table No. 3, with Annex.) At the beginning of 1942 the Infantry, Cavalry, Field Artillery and Coast Artillery (branches which included tank, tank destroyer, and antiaircraft personnel) constituted 52 percent of the Army, the service branches 26 percent, and the Air Corps 16 percent. By the end of 1942 the figures were respectively 36, 37, and 24 percent. At the beginning of 1942 there were two soldiers in the ground arms for every one in the service branches, at the end of 1942 only one. During 1942 the ground arms more than doubled, but the service branches and the Air Corps multiplied more than fourfold. The Air Corps constituted only a part, though by far the largest part, of the Army Air Forces, in which elements of the service branches were also included.

TABLE NO. 5

Ground Combat Units Mobilized After 1942

UNITS	Mobilized on 31 Dec 42	Mobilized on 30 Apr 45	Added after 1942
Divisions			
Infantry..	56	*67	11
Armored...	14	16	2
Airborne...	2	5	3
TOTAL............	72	88	16
Nondivisional Battalions			
Heavy Artillery..	32	137	105
Medium Artillery..	53	113	60
Light Artillery...	57	76	19
TOTAL............	142	326	184
Engineer Battalions (Combat and Heavy Ponton)......................	69	224	155
Tank Battalions...	26	62	36

Source: Troop Bases of 23 February 1943 and 1 May 1945 (S).
For basis of computation of Table No. 4, see above,
"Ground Forces in the Army, December 1941–April 1945: a Statistical Study."

*Includes one mountain division.
These units were added with a net increase of 124,000 enlisted men for combat units of the Army Ground Forces after 1942. (See Table No. 4.) Addition of so many combat units with so little increase of total combat strength was made possible by inactivation of combat units of other types (antiaircraft, tank destroyer, coast artillery, and nondivisional infantry) and by reduction of unit Tables of Organization.

In the long run, the total authorized strength of ground combat units increased very little after 1942—by only 6.5 percent. (See Table No. 4.) Many units were added (see Table No. 5), but other units were dissolved. The number of officers and men in the combat arms other than Coast Artillery increased materially after 1942, but most of these went to fill shortages in units, or into the rising population of replacement centers, hospitals, etc., rather than to increase the total strength of combat units.

III. The 1943 Army

Planning began in the spring of 1942 for the augmentation of the Army to take place in 1943.[1] The Operations Division of the War Department General Staff wished to add 67 divisions in 1943 and 47 in 1944, bringing the total of divisions to 140 at the close of 1943 and 187 at the close of 1944.[2] The figures were admittedly very tentative. The Army Ground Forces in May 1942 pronounced such a program capable of accomplishment—before the rapid activations of the summer of 1942 raised the gross number of men per division to 50,000.[3] G–3, WD, expressed the belief that only 37 divisions should be added in 1943, in view of limitations on shipping and construction, and the undesirability of withdrawing men from industry and agriculture too long before they could be employed in military operations. The G–3 figure, involving a total of 110 divisions by the end of 1943, was accepted as the basis of further discussion.[4]

In July and August 1942 the War Department instructed the three major commands to make detailed proposals for the 1943 Troop Basis.[5] The main outlines were prescribed, although no figure on the total size of the 1943

[1] The preceding study, "Ground Forces in the Army, December 1941–April 1945: a Statistical Study," provides essential evidence for the remainder of the present study, which in turn provides a narrative explanation for the facts shown by the table; this table offers a synopsis of mobilization from the drafting of the 1943 Troop Basis to the close of the war in Europe.

[2] WD memo (S) OPD 320.2 (5–10–42) (2–12–42) for G–3 WD, 23 May 42, sub: Major Tr Unit Requirements for 1942, 1943, and 1944. 320.2/190 (S).

[3] AGF memo (S) for OPD, 28 May 42, sub as above. 320.2/190 (S).

[4] (1) WD memo G–3/6457–448 for CofS USA, 5 Feb 42, sub: Augmentation of the Army for Calendar Year 1943 (with "OK–GCM"). GHQ Records, 320.2/1242. (2) WD Gen Council Min (S), 9 June 42. (3) Memo (S) of Col Parks (DCofS AGF) for G–3 AGF, 10 Jun 42, sub: Tr Basis for 1943. 320.2/210 (S).

[5] (1) WD ltr (S) AG 320.2 (7–17–42) GS–C–M to CGs AGF, AAF, SOS, 21 Jul 42, sub: Tr Basis 1943. 320.2/2 (TB 43) (S). (2) Memo (S) of G–3 WD for CG AAF, 22 Jul 42, sub: AAF Program, 1942. 320.2/118 (AAF) (S). (3) WD ltr (S) AG 320.2 (8–27–42) MS–C–M to CGs AGF, AAF, SOS, 28 Aug 42, sub: TB 1943. 320.2/3 (TB 43) (S).

Army was yet given. A total of 2,000,000 enlisted men was allotted to the Army Air Forces. The capacity of officer candidate schools was raised to 73,000. The Army Ground Forces was to organize about 110 divisions by 31 December 1943, to increase the Antiaircraft Artillery to 610,000, and to augment the strength of other arms by certain specified percentages, which in all cases were less than the percentage increase of Antiaircraft Artillery. Brig Gen. Idwal H. Edwards, G–3, WDGS, noting that Germany had some 300 divisions and the Japanese probably 90, observed that the diversion of American military manpower to noncombat functions should be checked, that the Army in 1943 should undergo "a complete revamping," and that the gross number of men required per division should be reduced from 50,000 to 33,000 by 1944.[6] In this way he hoped that 141 divisions might be organized by the end of 1944. As it turned out, at that time there were only 89 divisions in the U. S. Army, of which the aggregate strength (not counting the Air Forces) was then approximately 5,700,000—showing a ratio of over 60,000 per division.

The Army Ground Forces submitted its detailed proposals on 30 September 1942.[7] A total of 114 divisions was recommended. Because of the inclusion of airborne and light divisions, the net divisional strength remained within the figure prescribed by the War Department. Recommendations for nondivisional units exceeded the allotments made by the War Department. The aim of the Army Ground Forces was to assure the mobilization of a balanced force, in which nondivisional troops, such as medical units, engineer battalions, ordnance maintenance companies, tank battalions, and military police, should be in a proper proportion to each other and to the number of divisions. The "type" army and "type" corps, formerly used as yardsticks to secure proper proportions, had been abandoned. For each type of unit the Army Ground Forces adopted instead a ratio per division based on anticipated requirements of operations. The strength of nondivisional combat units ("combat support") obtained by application of these ratios exceeded the War Department allotment by 122,092 men. It was mainly in heavy artillery, tanks, tank destroyers, mechanized cavalry, and nondivisional infantry that the AGF estimate of requirements for combat support exceeded that of the War Department. Recommendations for nondivisional service units ("service support")

---

[6] WD Gen Council Min (S), 26 Aug 42.
[7] AGF ltr (S) to TAG, 30 Sep 42, sub: TB 1943. 320.2/4 (TB 43) (S).

had been arrived at in conference between the Army Ground Forces and the Services of Supply. Exact demarcation had not yet been made between types of service units which the Army Ground Forces and the Services of Supply were to activate and train. Duplication and overlapping resulted. The recommendation for service support exceeded the War Department allotment by 385,752. The total excess was about 500,000.

These proposals were submitted with reservations. The Army Ground Forces recommended that if cuts were necessary they be made in armored and motorized rather than in infantry and airborne divisions, that reductions be made proportionately so as to maintain forces in balance, and that the whole question of service troops be reexamined. "Precise data," wrote the Chief of Staff, AGF, "as to the total personnel engaged in the services in the entire United States Army are not available to this headquarters for analysis. However, from the general information at hand, it appears that over-all production of services to combat forces is grossly excessive; and some definite measures to control the dissipation of manpower to these non-combatant functions must be instituted at once." [8]

The recommendations of the Army Air Forces, like those of the Army Ground Forces, exceeded the allotment made in August. At that time the War Department had allotted 2,000,000 men. The Air Forces now asked for 2,330,000.

Reduction of the AGF Program: the 100-Division Army

September and October of 1942 marked a turning point in the development of the Army. Hitherto the tendency had been toward rapid expansion of all parts of the military establishment. Now a more exact consideration of choices was made necessary by various facts of strategy, logistics, manpower, and supply.

When the plan for an early invasion of western Europe was given up, the need of mobilizing a large ground army became less immediate. Air power was to be developed first. Shipping estimates in September 1942 indicated that, at most, 4,170,000 troops could be shipped overseas by the end of 1944 and that, if the prevailing high rate of shipping losses continued, the number might not greatly exceed 3,000,000. If an air force of 1,000,000 men were placed over-

[8] Ibid., par 6.

seas (as was now suggested), the number of divisions overseas by the end of 1944 would be 88 by the most liberal estimate, and only 61 if shipping losses continued.[9] A year being allowed to train a division, it seemed premature to mobilize many more than 88 divisions by the end of 1943. As it turned out, the number of troops overseas on 31 December 1944 was 4,933,682, well above the highest estimate of 1942; this number included an air force of over 1,000,000 but only 80 divisions, though the 9 divisions remaining in the United States on 31 December 1944 were being rushed to Europe to bolster American forces depleted by the German breakthrough in the Ardennes.

In October 1942 the chairman of the War Production Board announced that the procurement program of the Army, the Navy, and the Maritime Commission for 1943, totaling $93,000,000,000, could not be met. He set the maximum at $75,000,000,000. The Joint Chiefs of Staff revised procurement plans for 1943 downward to $80,000,000,000.[10] Emphasis was kept on the aircraft program. The allotment of funds to aviation (military and naval) exceeded the combined allotments to the rest of the Army and Navy. Distribution was as follows:

Procurement Program for 1943

	Percent Reduced	New Total (in Billions)
Army Ground Program	21.0	$14.8
Army Construction (less airfields)	31.0	2.2
Navy Program	18.0	11.8
Navy Construction (less airfields)	4.2	1.1
Aircraft Program (including airfields)	10.1	33.3
Merchant Shipbuilding	22.2*	4.4
Lend Lease and U. S. S. R. Protocol	18.1	8.6
Miscellaneous	7.1	3.9
Total Procurement Program	13.7	80.1

*Increase.

In the Army Ground Program reductions were heaviest in the procurement of antiaircraft and antitank guns, tanks, mortars, and heavy artillery.

[9] (1) WD memo (S) WDGCT 320.2 Gen (9–2–42) for CGs AGF, AAF, SOS, 2 Sep 42, sub: Mob Plan, 1943. 320.2/4 (TB 43) (S). (2) Memo (S) of Joint Chiefs of Staff for the President, 30 Sep 42, sub not given. 320.2/381 (S). (3) WD memo (S) WDGCT 320.2 Gen (10–25–42) for CGs AGF, SOS, 29 Oct 42, sub: TB 1943. 320.2/5 (TB 43) (S).

[10] (1) Memo (S) JCS 134/3, 26 Nov 42, with Annex A and other papers, sub: Rpt of Joint Staff Planners. 040/8 Joint Chiefs (S). (2) Rpt (R) of the ASF for Fiscal Year 1943, p. 19.

The President authorized in October 1942 a total of 7,500,000 enlisted men for the Army (with officers, an army of about 8,200,000) by the end of 1943.[11] It seemed probable that this would remain the permanent ceiling on the strength of the Army. The Director of the Budget wished to defer the attainment of this ceiling to 30 June 1944, limiting the Army for 1943 to 6,500,000 enlisted men,[12] but the War Department obtained confirmation of the authorization of 7,500,000 for 1943.[13] It was desired to proceed with a rapid rate of mobilization, even though the need for combatant ground forces was less immediate than before, since it was believed that, with maximum over-all strength reached by the end of 1943, more divisions might be organized in 1944, if desired, by transfer of personnel within the Army.[14]

The net result of these considerations was that the War Department decided to mobilize by the end of 1943 a ground army of only 100 divisions. Fourteen divisions with supporting units were cut from the recommendations of the Army Ground Forces. This represented a reduction in planned strength of ground troops of about 450,000 below the War Department allotments of August. The recommendations of the Army Air Forces were met in part, the August allotment being raised from 2,000,000 to 2,200,000, which was 130,000 less than the Air Forces requested.[15]

In deleting 14 divisions from the proposed 1943 Troop Basis the War Department hoped to obtain a manpower reserve, which experience with mobilization in 1942 had shown to be desirable. In 1942 it had been impossible to foresee all requirements. Units had been activated which were not in the Troop Basis and for which therefore no personnel was earmarked in advance; the diversion of manpower to these unanticipated units had produced shortages throughout the Army. It was desired to have, in 1943, a pool or reserve of 500,000 not required in advance for planned and scheduled units. Hence the number of planned and scheduled units had to be kept down; the most convenient units to delete, given the state of strategic plans, shipping, and the pro-

---

[11] WD Gen Council Min (S), 12 Oct 42.

[12] AGF M/S (S), Plans to DCofS, 6 Nov 42, sub: Contemplated Reduction of Tr Basis. AGF Plans file 185 (TB 42) (S).

[13] Memo of Gen Marshall for Gen McNair, 12 Nov 42. AGF Plans Sec file 185 (Victory Program TB).

[14] WD memo (S) WDGCT 320.2 Gen (11–24–42) to CGs AGF and SOS, 24 Nov 42, sub: Tr Unit Basis 1943. AGO Records, 320.2 (14 Jul 42) (36) Sec 1 (S).

[15] WD memo (S) WDGCT 320.2 Gen (10–25–42) for CGs AGF, SOS, 19 Nov 42, sub: TB 1943. 320.2/5 (TB 43) (S).

duction of equipment, were divisions and other ground combat units.[16] As it turned out, the reserve of some 500,000 obtained by dropping these units was not available for unforeseen requirements in 1943, for before the end of 1942 130,000 were set aside for the Army Air Forces, 150,000 for the Women's Army Corps, and 150,000 for the Army Specialized Training Program. In numbers involved, that is, in the room provided for them under the fixed ceiling of Army strength, any one of these was the equivalent of the unit strength of 10 divisions.

The approved Troop Basis of 1943, calling for a 100-division Army with an enlisted strength of 7,533,000, was issued to the major commands on 25 November 1942.[17] Enlisted strength proposed for ground combat units was 2,811,000. Breakdown of this strength was regarded at Headquarters, Army Ground Forces, as unbalanced. Antiaircraft strength remained at over 600,000, not having been reduced in proportion to reductions in other arms or in anticipation of the growth of American air power. More armored divisions were retained than were believed appropriate by the Army Ground Forces in relation to infantry. The Army Ground Forces desired more tank destroyers, more nondivisional tank battalions (for employment with infantry divisions), more heavy artillery, and more separate infantry regiments, whose use in certain tasks might prevent the dismemberment of infantry divisions that had occurred in 1942.[18]

It was hoped by the Army Ground Forces that additional units of these types might be formed through transfers of personnel made surplus through certain economies which the War Department had ordered.

Reduction of Tables of Organization and Equipment

To save personnel and equipment, the War Department not only reduced the number of units in the Troop Basis but also sought to reduce the size of individual units and overhead establishments within each of the three principal commands. Units were in general controlled by Tables of Organization and Equipment, overhead establishments by special allotments in each case.

[16] (1) *Ibid.* (2) WD memo (S) WDGCT 320.2 Gen (11–2–42) for CofS USA, 2 Nov 42, sub: Unit Basis 1943, with concurring memo (S) of G–1 WD for G–3 WD, 7 Nov 42. AGO Records, 320.2 (14 Jul 42) (36) Sec 1 (S).

[17] WD memo (S) WDGCT 320.2 Gen (11–24–42) for CGs AGF and SOS, 24 Nov 42, sub: TUB 1943. AGO Records, 320.2 (14 Jul 42) (36) Sec 1 (S).

[18] (1) AGF memo (S) for G–3 WD, 29 Oct 42, sub as above. 320.2/5 (TB 43) (S). (2) WD memo (S) WDGCT 320.2 Gen (10–25–42) for CG AGF, 19 Nov. 42, sub as above. 320.2/5 (TB 43) (S).

The War Department hoped in January 1943, by reduction both of Tables of Organization and of overhead allotments, to recover 750,000 men by 1944 and to use this manpower to increase the number of tactical units of the Army by 20 percent; this would obtain in 1944, still within the 7,500,000 enlisted ceiling, a force of 120 to 125 divisions with supporting troops.[19] Some of the 750,000 men to be saved would come from reduction of individual units in size, and thus, while adding to the number of units, would not increase the number of men in units. Some of the 750,000 were to be used to form units of service, not combat, types. If only 200,000 had been added to the strength of 2,811,000 then carried in the Troop Basis for ground combat units, the enlisted strength of ground combat units in 1944 would have exceeded 3,000,000.

Tables of Organization had been thought for some time to be too liberal in providing men, vehicles, and accessories not necessary to a unit in the discharge of its mission. On 2 October 1942, as the need for economy became urgent, the War Department directed the three major commands to prepare downward revisions of their respective tables.[20] Significant economies were obtained. The infantry division, for example, even after some of the cuts proposed by the Army Ground Forces were restored by the War Department, was reduced from about 15,500 to about 14,000. Hence for every nine divisions under the old tables ten could be obtained under the new. In some types of nondivisional units the cuts were proportionately greater.

Overhead consisted for the most part of troops not organized in tactical units of the field forces but absorbed in nontactical headquarters, training installations, and Zone of Interior establishments. On 29 January 1943 the three major commands were directed to survey their overhead installations with a view to reduction.[21] Hitherto allotments to each AGF overhead installation had been made by the War Department. On 6 February 1943 the War Department undertook to make a bulk allotment for overhead to the Ground Forces, and

---

[19] (1) WD memo (C) WDGCT 320 Gen (1–29–43) to CGs AGF, AAF, SOS, 29 Jan 43, sub: Reduction of Tng Establishments and other Zone-of-Interior Activities. 320.2/262 (C). (2) WD memo (S) WDGCT-320.2 Gen (2–5–43) for CofS USA, 5 Feb 43, sub: TB Planning. 320.2/575 (S). (3) WD memo (S) WDGCT 320.2 Gen (2–25–43) to G–1, G–4, OPD, AGF, AAF, SOS, 25 Feb 43, sub as above. 320.2/18 (TB 43) (S).

[20] (1) WD ltr (S) AG 400 OB–S–C to CGs AGF, AAF, SOS, 2 Oct 42, sub: Review of Orgn and Equipment Requirements. 320.2/383 (S). (2) For the compliance of Army Ground Forces with this directive see below, "Reorganization of Ground Troops for Combat."

[21] WD memo (C) WDGCT 320 Gen (1–29–43) for CGs AGF, AAF, SOS, 29 Jan 43, sub: Reduction of Tng Establishments and Other ZI Activities. 320.2/262 (C).

General McNair received authority to suballot personnel to overhead establishments as he saw fit.[22]

Overhead in the Army Ground Forces in the spring of 1943, as calculated at that time, consisted of some 80,000 officers and enlisted men.[23] It comprised 4 percent of the total strength of the Army Ground Forces. It was mainly concentrated in the service schools, the trainer personnel of replacement training centers, and the headquarters of the Armored Force, the Antiaircraft Command, the Replacement and School Command, and other such nontactical establishments. At the headquarters of the Army Ground Forces there were about 260 officers and 750 enlisted men. General McNair believed that during 1943, with the training program at its peak and with the prospect for 1944 of training 20 percent more tactical units than were specified in the 1943 Troop Basis, little if any saving of AGF overhead would be possible. He imposed close restrictions on subordinate commands.[24] Overhead was somewhat reduced through reorganization of the Armored Force, the Airborne Command, and the Tank Destroyer Center.[25] But it was clear that if the War Department wished to make extensive recoveries from overhead it would have to look almost entirely to other elements of the Army than the Ground Forces.

In January 1943 the War Department created a Manpower Board under the presidency of Maj. Gen. Lorenzo D. Gasser. G–3, WDGS, pointed out to General Gasser various possible sources of manpower savings, including ordnance, signal and transportation troops, ports of embarkation, the Alcan Highway, the defense commands, replacement training centers, medical personnel designed to remain permanently in the United States, Zone of Interior military police, AAF hotel schools, and headquarters organizations in the Army Air Forces and the Services of Supply.[26] General McNair told General Gasser of his belief that "the Services of Supply was very, very fat, particularly in headquarters," and that the Manpower Board, since it would obtain voluntary reductions from no one, would have to institute thorough inquiries of its own.[27]

[22] WD ltr (C) AG 320.2 (2–4–43) OB–I–SP to CG AGF, 6 Feb 43, sub: Suballotment of Mil Pers for Overhead Installations and Activities of AGF. 320.2/262 (C).

[23] AGF memo (C) for G–3 WD, 17 Apr 43, sub: Reduction of Tng Establishments and Other ZI Activities. 320.2/262 (C).

[24] AGF ltr (C) to CGs, 1 Apr 43, sub: Economy of Manpower. 320.2/262 (C).

[25] See below, "Organization and Training of New Ground Combat Elements."

[26] WD memo (S) WDGCT 220 (1–21–43) for Maj Gen Gasser, sub: Possible Sources of Manpower Reductions in the Army. 320.2/575 (S).

[27] (1) AGF M/S (S), CG to Plans, 23 Feb 43. AGF Plans Sec file 224 (S). (2) Memo of Gen McNair for CofS USA, 2 Jan 43. 320.2/5761.

The principal savings obtained by the Army Ground Forces in 1943 came through reduction of T/O's of AGF units. With these reductions, a given number of units in the AGF Troop Basis could be brought to full strength with less manpower than before or, conversely, a given amount of manpower allotted to the Army Ground Forces in the Troop Basis would produce a larger number of units. The aim of the reductions, in accord with the desire of both the War Department and the Army Ground Forces, was to place a larger percentage of the Army in combat positions. This aim was not realized. The need for increasing the number of combat units was not urgent in the first part of 1943, since more such units were on hand than were intended for early employment. Paradoxically, while General McNair labored to make possible a larger number of combat units, he was also laying plans to reduce the number of combat units to be mobilized in 1943.

Further Deceleration and the AGF Pool Plan of April 1943

In the winter of 1942–43, divisions moved overseas less rapidly than had been expected. Hence they accumulated in the United States. In January the Activation Schedule for divisions was slowed down; three divisions planned for activation in May, June, and August were deferred to the last months of 1943.[28] On 5 February the War Department, foreseeing difficulty in meeting the 1943 Troop Basis, advised the Army Ground Forces that 10 of the 100 divisions planned for 1943 might have to be deferred to 1944.[29]

One difficulty was in obtaining sufficient equipment for training. Another was the crowding of housing facilities by retention of troops in the United States. The production both of equipment and of new housing for ground troops had been severely cut when the Joint Chiefs modified the procurement program.[30] In March 1943 it was also decided to furnish weapons of American manufacture to a French army of 250,000 men in North Africa.[31] The Allies thus obtained a large fighting force in a combat zone without having to ship personnel, but less equipment was available for American forces in training. Delay in providing

---

[28] WD memo (C) WDGCT 320.2 Activ (1–16–43) to CG AGF, 16 Jan 43, sub: Schedule of Activation of Divs, TB 1943. 320.2/15 (TB 43) (C).

[29] WD memo (S) WDGCT 320.2 Gen (2–5–43) to CG AGF, 5 Feb 43, sub: Tr Basis Planning. 320.2/575 (S).

[30] See AGF M/Ss (S) written between 10 Dec 42 and 27 Jan 43. 320.2/22 (TB 43) (S).

[31] AGF M/S (S), Plans to CofS, 8 Mar 43. AGF Plans Sec file 185 (Victory Program TB) (S).

equipment, observed an AGF staff study, "will continue to be reflected in press comments on the training and 'inexperience' of United States troops in action . . . . The training lag occasioned by delayed distribution of equipment will cause every intelligent soldier to conclude that his induction was premature and chargeable to poor planning." [32]

At any rate the Army Ground Forces was not satisfied with the allowances of equipment and ammunition hitherto available for training. Since early in 1942, divisions while in the United States had received only 50 percent of their authorized equipment in certain critical items, nondivisional units only 20 percent. These partial allowances had been accepted by the Army Ground Forces as unavoidable during the early stages of rapid expansion. But shortcomings shown by American troops in combat in North Africa and the Southwest Pacific were attributed by the Army Ground Forces in large measure to lack of opportunity to train with enough weapons and ammunition. [33]

On 1 March 1943 the Army Ground Forces proposed revisions of the procurement program to the War Department. [34] It requested that full allowances of equipment be made available to nondivisional units by the fourth month of training and to divisions by the sixth month, thus permitting greater realism in combined training and maneuvers. It also asked that ammunition allowances be raised to the point where all personnel might qualify in the firing of their individual weapons. Finally, it requested that procurement be modified to correspond with AGF plans to increase, out of personnel saved by reduced T/O's, the number of certain types of units in the Troop Basis believed necessary to achieve balanced forces. These were chiefly heavy and medium artillery, tank battalions, nondivisional infantry, engineers, and tank destroyer and ordnance maintenance units.

Negative replies were received to these proposals. [35] The War Department held that no general change of the procurement program was practicable in the near future. Distribution of equipment as it left the production lines was in any case controlled by the Munitions Assignment Board. The War Department preferred that personnel saved by reduction of T/O's should revert to

[32] Memo (S) of Col Winn (AGF Plans) for CofS AGF, 10 Mar 43, sub: Revision of Victory Program TB. AGF Plans Sec file 185 (Victory Program TB) (S).

[33] Ibid.

[34] AGF memo (S) for OPD, 1 Mar 43, sub: Victory Program TB. 320.2/22 (TB 43) (S).

[35] OPD memo (S) 400 WMP (3–1–43) to CG AGF, 22 Apr 43, sub: Victory Program TB. 320.2/22 (TB 43) (S).

the War Department reserve pool. This meant that it would be the War Department, rather than the headquarters of the Army Ground Forces, which decided
what units should be added to the Troop Basis to achieve a proper balance of
ground forces. In view of development of the bomber, staff officers of the War
Department expressed doubt as to the need of increases of heavy artillery. Before
authorizing additional tank battalions the War Department wished to see the
results of the reorganization of the armored divisions then under consideration.[36]
AGF headquarters concluded that the most promising way to obtain the quantity
of equipment judged necessary for units in training was to train fewer units
in 1943.

Supply of manpower also had to be considered. By March 1943 the shortages
which afflicted the Army Ground Forces in 1942 had been overcome. Units
were generally at full strength and it was desired to keep them so; but at any
moment the activation of new units, if not carefully checked against anticipated
inflow of men, might again produce shortages of manpower with their ruinous
effects on training. Recalling the crisis of the preceding September, the Deputy
Chief of Staff, AGF, on 11 February issued instructions that the staff must watch
activations "like a hawk." [37]

One danger was to receive too few men in proportion to the number of
units activated. Another was to receive too many men, and have too many
units, with respect to the dates at which they could be shipped. An officer of
the War Department General Staff observed unofficially that the Army must
reach maximum strength during 1943 for fear that, if it waited longer, the
Navy would get the men first. The Chief of Staff, AGF, thought it better to
take a chance on obtaining manpower when needed: [38]

War needs of our Army we should be able to defend. We could not defend a situation
where we had too many men away from other essential pursuits merely because we were
afraid the Navy or other agencies would gobble them up. . . . I believe in a reserve, but I
believe that you could well keep that reserve in numbers [in civilian life] and not actually
induct the men into the service until shipping indicates that we will be able to use them
when they are trained.

---

[36] Memo (S) of Col Winn, AGF Plans for CofS AGF, 10 Mar 43, sub: Victory Program TB. 320.2/22
(TB 43) (S).

[37] AGF M/S (S), DCofS to G–3, 11 Feb 43. 320.2/16 (TB 43) (S).

[38] AGF memo (S) for Col Argo, ACofS G–3 WD, 4 May 43, sub: Proposed Strength of Army. Plans
file 185 (Victory TB) (S).

All these ideas came together in a proposal made by General McNair to the War Department on 14 April 1943 for a general revision of mobilization procedures in the Ground Forces. The aim was to control the Activation Schedule by relating it more closely to shipping capacities, receipt of equipment and manpower, time necessary for training, and types of units most immediately needed for a balanced mobilization.[39]

In this plan the Army Ground Forces was considered to be a pool of troops mobilized in the United States and awaiting employment in overseas operations. The size of the pool was to be 1,500,000 (the approximate strength of AGF tactical units at this time), and was to be maintained continuously at this level until some future date when the War Department, with transfer of troops to overseas theaters and the attainment of mobilization objectives, would allow the level of the pool in the United States to decline. Meanwhile activation of new units should be suspended when the pool rose to 10 percent above its prescribed level. To activate units beyond this point, explained General McNair, would make necessary more housing construction, tie up manpower unproductively, spread training equipment too thinly among activated units, and result in having units go stale from remaining in the United States after the conclusion of their training. New units should therefore be activated only as old units were shipped. If shipments were less rapid than expected, activations would be slower. Units chosen for activation should be, not necessarily those set up in the initial 1943 Troop Basis, but those of the types judged necessary by the Army Ground Forces to obtain a proper balance of forces.

To obtain the desired balance within a total of 1,500,000 the plan included recommendations, for each type of unit in the Army Ground Forces, of the exact number which should be added to or deleted from the existing Troop Basis of 1943. Units dropped from the 1943 program might, if desired, be activated in 1944. The chief readjustments recommended were to drop 5 infantry and 4 armored divisions, adding 8 light divisions in their place, and to drop 38 tank destroyer and 118 antiaircraft battalions, adding 21 tank battalions and 32 battalions of heavy and medium artillery, together with certain engineer, signal, and quartermaster units of types which were used in close support of combat forces but which remained scarce in spite of the steady growth of the service branches. The total inductions needed to maintain a 1,500,000 pool, at the most favorable shipping rate, would be 102,000 less than were called for by the existing Troop Basis.

[39] Memo (S) of Gen McNair for G–3 WD, 14 Apr 43, sub: Modification of Mob Procedures. 381/177 (S).

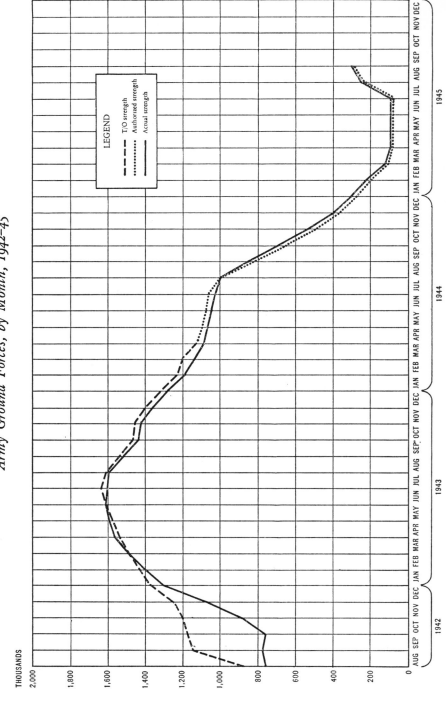

Authorized and Actual Enlisted Strength of Troop Units,
Army Ground Forces, by Month, 1942–45

LEGEND

T/O strength
Authorized strength
Actual strength

THOUSANDS

Revision of the Military Program: the 90-Division Army

The War Department took no direct action on this plan. Instead, a Committee on the Revision of the Military Program was appointed in the War Department General Staff to consider, among other matters, the dangers of overmobilization. Meanwhile the Army Ground Forces continued to activate units under the existing Troop Basis. On 21 April the Army Ground Forces, calling attention to the pool plan submitted on 14 April, and anticipating difficulties in the receipt of personnel, requested permission to defer the infantry division scheduled for activation in August. The War Department replied that no action would be taken on the AGF pool plan for over a month, and that meanwhile the preactivation process for the August division should be launched. The Chief of Staff, AGF, fearing a repetition in the summer of 1943 of the personnel crisis of 1942, took care to place this decision of the War Department in the record.[40] On 14 May the War Department announced that the pool plan would probably be approved "in principle," and that inductees would in the long run suffice to fill AGF units.[41] In June 1943 shortages began to reappear.[42] (See Chart.)

The Committee on the Revision of the Military Program reported early in June. Since the year before, when the Operations Division, WDGS, had hoped for 140 divisions by the end of 1943, the strategical picture had greatly brightened. The German advance in Russia had been checked, and bombing of Germany from Great Britain was assuming larger proportions. It was decided to reduce the strength authorized for the Army by the end of 1943 from 7,500,000 to 7,000,000 enlisted men. Ultimate size of the Army was to be determined later: "This will depend, to a large extent," observed the Committee, "on the outcome of the Russo-German operations this summer and the effectiveness of the Combined-Bomber Offensive, the trends of which should be sufficiently apparent by early September to warrant a decision."[43]

---

[40] (1) AGF memo (C) for G-3 WD, 21 Apr 43, sub: Activation of Divs in August 1943. 381/41 (C). (2) WD memo (C) WDGCT 320.2 Activ (4-21-43) for CG AGF, 29 Apr 43, sub: Activation of Divs in Aug 43. 381/41 (C).

[41] (1) Immediate Action AGF (C) memo for G-3 WD, 14 May 43, sub: Shortage of Enl Pers. (2) WD memo (C) WDGCT 220 (5-14-43) to CG AGF, 22 May 43, sub as above. Both in 320.2/36 (TB 43) (C).

[42] See papers in 320.2/42 (TB 43) (C).

[43] (1) Memo (S) of Committee on Revision of Mil Program for CofS USA, 7 Jun 43, sub: Revision of Current Mil Program. (2) WD memo (S) WDCSA (6-8-43) for G-1, G-3, G-4, OPD, AAF, AGF, ASF, 8 Jun 43, sub as above. Both in 381/177 (S).

The Committee sought to obtain the 500,000 reduction almost entirely by deleting combat ground troops from the Troop Basis. It recommended the following changes in allotments:[44]

Troop Basis as of 31 December 1943
(Enlisted Strength)

	Former Allotment	New Allotment	Reduction
Air Forces and Services	2,200,000	2,200,000	0
Divisions	1,422,918	1,067,082	355,836
Nondiv Combat Units	1,409,167	1,308,248	100,919
Nondiv Service Units	1,153,275	1,196,981	*43,706
Overhead—U. S.	503,000	458,000	45,000
Overhead—Overseas	60,000	70,000	*10,000
Trainees in Replacement Tng Ctrs	316,000	288,000	28,000
Trainees in OCS	42,000	25,000	17,000
Trainees in Army College Program	150,000	150,000	0
Office of Strategic Services	5,000	5,000	0
Unassigned	271,640	235,689	35,951
TOTAL	7,533,000	7,004,000	529,000

*Increase.

It was proposed that 12 divisions be deleted from the 1943 program, leaving 88 to be mobilized. Over 350,000 men were to be taken from divisional strength, reducing divisional strength about 25 percent, an economy made possible in part by the deletion of 12 divisions, in part by the reduction of divisional Tables of Organization. Whether the 12 divisions should be restored to the Troop Basis in 1944 was to be decided later. From "combat support" (nondivisional combat units) only 100,000 were to be taken. The proportion of combat support to divisions was to be increased, with a larger allotment for heavy artillery and for tank battalions, as desired by General McNair. In antiaircraft artillery the committee proposed no significant reductions. Allotment for service troops continued to grow. The gross number of men per division (not counting Air Forces) was about 55,000.

General McNair was willing to check the growth of the Ground Forces, though his own proposals had been less drastic, but he viewed with disfavor an

[44] Memo (S) of Committee for DCofS USA, 13 Jun 43, sub: Tr Unit Basis 1943. 320.2/31 (TB 43) (S).

economy in which all cuts were applied to combat troops. "The proposed distribution of manpower," he wrote to the War Department, "indicates a serious condition which warrants radical corrective action to effect the assignment of a much greater proportion of the manpower to units designed for offensive combat." [45] He noted that in the total ground forces intended for use against the enemy (3,642,311 men) only 29 percent was in divisions, whereas 36 percent was in combat support, 33 percent in service support, and 2 percent in theater overhead. He observed that almost half the combat support was antiaircraft artillery, "even though a strong air force is provided to combat the hostile air forces," and that the service support did "not include essential field service units in sufficient numbers for the support of 88 divisions," being predominantly in communications-zone troops. He recommended a complete reorientation of the Troop Basis in the remainder of 1943 and in 1944 to provide a larger ratio of offensive combat troops, a cut of 180,000 in antiaircraft artillery, and the taking of measures, through economy of service troops in inactive theaters and in purely Zone of Interior functions, to assure that enough medical, ordnance, signal, and quartermaster units would be at hand to maintain the combat troops, most of which were still in the United States.

On 1 July 1943 the War Department issued a new approved Troop Basis for 1943. It provided for 88 divisions and 7,004,000 enlisted men, but authorized somewhat more manpower to combat support, and somewhat less to service support, than the Committee had originally proposed. Two provisional light divisions were authorized. These soon received a permanent status. The new Troop Basis therefore projected, for 1943, a "90-Division Army."

End of Expansion of Ground Forces

The expansion of AGF tactical forces virtually terminated in the middle of 1943. The activation of 4 divisions in July and of 2 in August fulfilled the 90-division program. Thereafter no new divisions were organized and one, the 2d Cavalry Division, was inactivated overseas. Nondivisional units of AGF type continued to be activated through 1944; these included principally service units, but also certain types of combat units in large numbers, notably heavy artillery and combat engineers. But these activations were offset by inactivation of other units or by the decision not to activate units as planned.

---

[45] Memo (S) of Gen McNair for DCofS USA, 22 Jun 43, sub as above. 320.2/31 (TB 43) (S).

Individual AGF units required less manpower after the middle of 1943 than previously because of reduction in Tables of Organization. New units were added without increase of combined unit strength. When the war ended in Europe, T/O strength of all AGF type units (2,502,000 enlisted men on 31 March 1945) was about the same as for all AGF type units already mobilized on 30 June 1943 (2,471,000 enlisted men on that date). Combined strength of all AGF units of combat types only, in March 1945, was hardly greater than that of combat units already mobilized on 31 December 1942, although many combat units were added after 1942. (See Tables Nos. 4 and 5, pp. 210–11.)

It is important to keep in mind that, while the Army as a whole showed a net increase of almost 3,000,000 in 1943 and 1944, and while the combatant arms, as arms, continued to expand, the combined strength of combat units (other than the Air Forces) scarcely grew after 1942, and the combined strength of all AGF units, including service units, hardly grew after the middle of 1943.

It was not intended in July 1943 that expansion of AGF unit strength should cease. The Troop Basis of 1 July 1943 allotted an enlisted strength of 2,822,000 for all AGF units, both combat and service, by 31 December 1943. Cut from the corresponding allotment of 3,157,000 in the Troop Basis of November 1942, the new figure represented a Troop Basis reduction of 335,000. But since only 2,471,000 were as yet mobilized on 30 June, the figure of 2,822,000 called for an increase of 351,000 in AGF units in the last six months of 1943. Since AGF units were at about the same T/O strength in March 1945 as in June 1943, in the long run AGF units not only suffered a Troop Basis reduction of 335,000 on 1 July 1943 but also in net result failed to receive the increment of 351,000 which even the reduced Troop Basis of 1 July 1943 provided.

Difficulty in meeting the 1 July Troop Basis was not long in becoming apparent. Inductions did not meet stated requirements. The 42d Division, activated in July, waited until September to receive enough personnel to begin basic training. The 65th Division, activated in August (the last infantry division to be activated), waited until January 1944 for the same purpose.[46] It was this division whose activation the Army Ground Forces in the preceding April had proposed to defer. In general, Ground Force units in the United States, after a brief period at full strength in the spring of 1943, suffered from personnel shortages until August 1944, despite continuing deletion of units from the mobilization program.

---

[46] AGF G–3 files, 333.1, for 42d and 65th Divs.

On 21 September 1943, having been short-shipped 26,710 men from reception centers in August, the Army Ground Forces described its situation to the War Department.[47] Within the last few weeks, 10,817 men had been taken from infantry divisions as overseas replacements. Wholesale losses were occurring under liberal discharge policies recently adopted. Approximately 55,000 men had recently been transferred from the Ground Forces to the Army Specialized Training Program in the colleges. In the previous three months some 15,000 had been transferred to the Air Forces as aviation cadets. Hence shortages were spreading; newly activated units were short 75,000; even units alerted for overseas movement were understrength. One expected source of personnel, the surpluses left by application of reduced Tables of Organization, would yield relatively little, because with units short under the old tables little surplus would be created by reorganization under the new tables. The Army Ground Forces therefore requested full shipment of newly inducted men. The War Department replied that some of the causes of shortage were temporary (as indeed they were, though new temporary causes seemed always to be appearing), and announced that the situation would soon be relieved by a reissue of the Troop Basis, in which the number of units to be mobilized by the Army Ground Forces would again be cut.[48]

It had been planned in June to reexamine the mobilization program in September, after evaluation of the bomber offensive and the Russian summer campaign. A new Troop Basis was issued as of 4 October, again projecting the Army to 31 December 1943. Strength of combat-type units was cut by 190,000, AGF service units being somewhat increased. Despite the efforts of the Operations Division, WDGS, to impose a ceiling on service units,[49] about 125,000 enlisted men were added to forces of this type, of whom only 25,000 were for AGF service units designed for close association with combat troops. The fears felt at AGF headquarters came true; largely for want of service troops the California-Arizona Maneuver Area and other maneuver areas were gradually shut down in the winter of 1943–44, to the considerable detriment of advanced training of combat troops.

---

[47] AGF memo (C) for G–1 WD, 21 Sep 43, sub: Allocation of Reception Center Pers to AGF. 327.3/13 (C).

[48] WD memo (C) WDGAP 320.22 for CG AGF, 27 Sep 43, sub: Allocation of Reception Center Pers to AGF. 327.3/13 (C).

[49] OPD M/R (S), 24 Aug 43, sub: Percent of Serv Units in the Over-all TB. AGF Plans Sec file 185 (S).

The Troop Basis of 4 October slashed the tank destroyer program, and applied the major amputation desired by General McNair to the antiaircraft program. Units of these two arms were inactivated and their personnel converted to other branches, in which they were used, not so much to form new units, as to fill shortages in units in the United States or to furnish replacements for units overseas. The artillery objective, raised in the Troop Basis of 1 July, was now somewhat lowered; but activation of field artillery battalions had to be continued to meet even this more moderate aim, so small had been the artillery program in the earlier stages of mobilization. The combat engineer program was also cut. The program of 90 divisions for 1943 remained unchanged, all reductions in combat troops coming in nondivisional units, whose projected strength, per division, fell from about 15,270 in the Troop Basis of 1 July to about 13,000 in the Troop Basis of 4 October.

In summary, the 4 October Troop Basis, the final form of the Troop Basis for 1943, dealt with the manpower shortage by reducing the requirement for ground combat troops. Whereas on 24 November 1942 it had been planned to have 2,811,000 enlisted men in ground combat units by the end of 1943, on 4 October 1943 it was planned to have only 2,284,000. This figure was substantially realized. T/O enlisted strength of ground combat units active on 31 December 1943 was 2,282,000. Actual strength was less, because of continuing shortages. T/O strength was to be further reduced in 1944 by inactivations.

IV. The 1944-45 Army

When the detailed drafting of a Troop Basis for 1944 took place, in the later months of 1943, the role of Headquarters, Army Ground Forces, in Troop Basis planning was very much diminished. During 1943 the overseas theaters had rapidly grown, especially the North African Theater of Operations, the European Theater of Operations, and the Southwest Pacific Area. The commanding generals of these theaters estimated the size and composition of forces necessary for their respective missions. The Operations Division, WDGS, coordinating the activities of the theaters, mediating the requests of the theaters to the War Department, and scheduling the shipment of troops to theater commanders, announced operational requirements as of successive future dates. G-3, WDGS, in charge of drafting the Troop Basis, followed chiefly the expressed desires of the Operations Division. The Army Ground Forces was simply requested, in the fall of 1943, to estimate what troops it would need in 1944 for training overhead in the Zone of Interior. These overhead troops, plus Ground Force units called for by the Operations Division, plus replacements as determined by the War Department, constituted the Ground Force portion of the 1944 Troop Basis. The role of Headquarters, Army Ground Forces, was more than ever purely advisory.[1]

At the end of 1943 the War Department considered activating 15 new divisions in 1944 and reducing the allotment to the Army Air Forces to a figure in the neighborhood of 1,850,000 enlisted men. This would have given a total of 105 divisions, in place of the 120 or 125 which had been estimated early in 1943 (before total enlisted strength was cut from 7,500,000 to 7,000,000) as attainable in 1944. But the Air Forces at this time was developing its program for Very Long Range Bombers (B-29's). It was deemed impossible to reduce the Air Force allotment or to find the personnel for the new program by economies or conversions within Air Force organizations. To provide manpower for the B-29 program, and for certain lesser needs of the War Department, including continuation of the Army college program on a re-

---

[1] (1) WD memo (C) WDGCT 320 TB (21 Sep 43) for CGs AGF, ASF, AAF, 7 Oct 43, sub: TB 1943-44. 320.2/52 (TB 43) (C). (2) Memo of G-3 WD for DCofS USA, 21 Sep 43, sub: Revised TB 1943. AGO Records, 320.2 (14 Jul 42) (36) Sec 1b. (3) WD memo (C) WDGCT 320 TB (7 Oct 43) for CGs, 7 Oct 43, sub: TB 1943-44. 320.2/55 (TB 43) (C).

TABLE NO. 6

Development of the Heavy Artillery Program,
1942–44

(*Showing Number of Nondivisional Field Artillery Battalions in Successive Proposals*)

DATE	ACTION	HEAVY				MEDIUM		TOTAL
		240-mm How.	8-in. Gun	8-in. How.	155-mm Gun	155-mm How.	4½-in. Gun	
1942	(*To be Active by 31 Dec 43*)							
30 Sep	Recommended by AGF for 114 Divisions	9	4	16	72	120	20	241
25 Oct	Recommended by G–3, WDGS, for 100 Divisions	4	4	6	40	65	16	135
24 Nov	TROOP BASIS APPROVED BY WD FOR 100 DIVISIONS	4	4	6	40	65	16	135
31 Dec	(73 Divisions Active on This Date)	(2)	(0)	(6)	(24)	(53)	(0)	(85)
1943								
14 Apr	Recommended by AGF for 99 Divisions	12	4	8	48	69	26	167
30 Jun	(84 Divisions Active on This Date)	(3)	(0)	(13)	(28)	(56)	(11)	(111)
1 Jul	TROOP BASIS APPROVED BY WD FOR 88 DIVISIONS	12	4	19	42	66	16	159
17 Jul	Ideal Number Desired by AGF for 90 Divisions	36	18	90	45	135	30	354
4 Oct	TROOP BASIS APPROVED BY WD FOR 90 DIVISIONS	12	0	19	40	66	12	149
	(*To be Active by 31 Dec 44*)							
28 Oct	Tentative Troop Basis Drafted by WD for 105 Divisions	12	0	19	50	80	12	173
— Nov	Recommended by AGF for 105 Divisions	21	0	42	50	95	12	220
31 Dec	(90 Divisions Active on This Date)	(10)	(0)	(17)	(34)	(63)	(12)	(136)
1944								
15 Jan	TROOP BASIS APPROVED BY WD FOR 90 DIVISIONS	15	6	42	48	95	16	222
30 Jun	(89 Divisions Active on This Date)	(15)	(7)	(42)	(52)	(96)	(16)	(228)
	(*To be Active by 30 Jun 45*)							
1 Jul	TROOP BASIS APPROVED BY WD FOR 89 DIVISIONS	23	8	64	48	96	18	257

Sources: Same as for the table in the preceding study,
"Ground Forces in the Army, December 1941–April 1945.'

duced basis, and allowances for rotation of personnel between overseas stations and the United States, the idea of adding 15 divisions in 1944 was abandoned. The ground army would remain at 90 divisions.[2]

[2] Memo (S) of ADCofS USA for G–3 WD, 15 Jan 44, sub: TB 1944. 320.2/12 (TB 44) (S).

TABLE NO. 7

Ratios of Nondivisional to Divisional Field Artillery,
30 June 1943–1 July 1944

(*Number of Battalions, by Type, per Division*)

DATE	RATIO	HEAVY				MEDIUM		TOTAL
		240-mm How.	8-in. Gun	8-in. How.	155-mm Gun	155-mm How.	4½-in. Gun	
30 Jun 43	Actual Ratio of Active Battalions to Active Divisions	.04	.00	.15	.33	.67	.13	1.32
17 Jul 43	Ideal Ratio as Stated by AGF	.40	.20	1.00	.50	1.50	.33	3.93
28 Oct 43	Ratio in Tentative 1944 Troop Basis Drafted by WD	.11	.00	.18	.48	.76	.11	1.64
— Nov 43	Minimum Ratio Adopted by AGF for Troop Basis Planning	.20	.00	.40	.40	.90	.20	2.10
31 Dec 43	Actual Ratio of Active Battalions to Active Divisions	.11	.00	.19	.38	.70	.13	1.51
15 Jan 44	Ratio in Approved Troop Basis	.17	.07	.47	.53	1.06	.18	2.48
30 Jun 44	Actual Ratio of Active Battalions to Active Divisions	.17	.08	.47	.58	1.08	.18	2.56
1 Jul 44	Ratio in Approved Troop Basis	.26	.09	.72	.54	1.08	.20	2.89

In nondivisional units the first tentative proposals of the War Department for the 1944 Army contemplated no extensive changes from the plans for 1943, except that more combat engineers and more artillery of the lighter calibers were to be organized, certain seacoast artillery units inactivated, and an additional 125,000 enlisted men allotted to service units.

Army Ground Forces renewed, this time with success, its plea for more heavy artillery. (See Tables Nos. 6 and 7.) In 1942 and 1943 it had sought to have a considerable increase of heavy artillery incorporated in the 1943 Troop Basis as necessary to the creation of a balanced force. In September 1942 it had recommended 101 battalions (armed with 240-mm., 8-inch, and 155-mm. guns), in addition to 140 battalions of medium artillery (4.5-inch gun and 155-mm. howitzer) and the medium artillery organic in divisions.[3] The War Department, reducing the number of medium battalions to 81, was willing at that time to authorize only 54 heavy battalions.[4] In April 1943 General McNair expressed his belief that "the amount of heavy artillery in the 1943 Troop

---

[3] AGF ltr (S) to TAG, 30 Sep 43, sub: TB 1943. 320.2/4 (TB 43) (S).

[4] WD memo (S) WDGCT 320.2 Gen (11–24–42) for CGs AGF and SOS, 24 Nov 42, sub: TUB 1943. AGO Records, 320.2 (14 Jul 42) (36) Sec 1 (S).

Basis is . . . dangerously small if any major operations are to be undertaken by United States Troops prior to January 1945." He observed that "the production of such weapons is a slow process, involving an elapsed time of approximately one year after the development is completed and the numerical requirement is established." [5] After discussions with General Somervell, who shared his view, General McNair renewed his recommendation for an increase.[6] The War Department had been reluctant to plan beyond foreseeable strategic requirements, apparently influenced by a belief that the mission of heavy artillery could be performed in part by bombardment aviation.[7] But on 1 July 1943 it authorized an increase in the number of heavy battalions from 54 to 77.[8] As late as 1 January 1944 only 61 were in fact active, some of them in very early stages of training.[9] When the Troop Basis for 1944, as proposed in October 1943, provided only small increases in heavy artillery, Headquarters, Army Ground Forces, returned to the charge, believing that both OPD and overseas commanders had underestimated the amount of heavy artillery that would be needed in a major offensive. They appeared to be giving too much weight to the nature of ground operations hitherto engaged in by American forces. The War Department thereupon authorized an additional 30 battalions of heavy artillery, making a total of 111.[10] Since the number of divisions had been cut to 90, the proportion of medium and heavy artillery to divisional strength now came within the ratio which the Army Ground Forces had estimated as a necessary minimum, though still only two-thirds of the ratio which it regarded as ideal in a study published in July 1943.[11]

In April 1944 a special board of officers (Lucas Board) reviewed artillery requirements. Its recommendations were influenced by the operations at Cassino, Italy, which had indicated that reliance could not be placed on bombers

[5] Par 5, AGF M/S (S), CofS to Plans Sec, 7 Apr 43. 320.2/22 (TB 43) (S).

[6] (1) Memo (S) of Gen McNair for CG ASF, 12 Apr 43, sub: Heavy FA. 320.2/22 (TB 43) (S). (2) Memo (S) of Gen McNair for G–3 WD, 14 Apr 43, sub: Modification of Mob Proceedings. 381/177 (S).

[7] Memo (S) of Col Winn for CofS AGF, 10 Mar 43, sub: Revision of Victory Program TB, summarizing views expressed in conferences with WD staff officers. AGF Plans Sec file 185 (S).

[8] TB 1943, revision of 1 Jul 43 (S).

[9] See column 13, line 44, of the table in "Ground Forces in the Army, December 1941–April 1945: a Statistical Study," in this volume.

[10] (1) TAB I to notes (S) by Col J. B. Sherman, Plans Sec, AGF, on WD tentative 1944 TB. AGF Plans Sec file 185 (S). (2) TB 1944, 15 Jan 44 (S).

[11] See Table No. 6.

as a substitute for heavy cannon. General McNair renewed his recommendation for more heavy battalions and the War Department increased the artillery program by 32 battalions, chiefly of 8-inch and 240-mm. howitzers.[12] This brought the total number of heavy battalions authorized up to 143. Over 100 artillery battalions of calibers above 105-mm. were activated in 1944. Conversion of units of seacoast artillery and use of personnel from arms in which inactivation was in progress made the formation of new units relatively easy. The production of guns and ammunition proved to be a more difficult problem.

Implementation of the 1944 Troop Basis

The 1944 Troop Basis was published under date of 15 January 1944. It called for an army of 6,955,000 enlisted men, slightly reduced from the earlier figure of 7,004,000 to allow for passage of enlisted men into the warrant officer and commissioned grades. With officers, who were henceforth included in the Troop Basis, the authorized strength of the Army aggregated 7,700,000. This strength was attained by April 1944. But while the Army as a whole was now at its planned ultimate strength, shortages continued to exist in various components. The Army therefore continued to grow. Actual strength reached 8,000,000 by July 1944 and was approaching 8,300,000 at the time of victory in Europe in May 1945. The War Department, while obtaining special authorizations to carry this overstrength, attempted through 1944 to cut back the strength of the Army to the 7,700,000 authorized in the Troop Basis. With the continuance of war in Europe this idea was given up. In May 1945 the Troop Basis was raised to 8,290,993. Thus actual strength was finally covered with a Troop Basis authorization. This figure became the point of departure for reductions subsequent to victory in Europe.

It was doubted from the beginning whether the Troop Basis of January 1944 could be implemented, that is, whether actual needs could be met within the 7,700,000 ceiling. The main reason was that the Troop Basis made inadequate allowance for the "pipeline"—men in hospitals, in replacement centers and depots, in reassignment centers, and in transit or on furlough under policies of rotation between the United States and overseas stations. "I doubt,"

---

[12] (1) Rpt of Special Board of Offs for CofS USA, 4 May 44, sub: Adequacy of FA Program and Doctrine. 320.2/12 (TUB 44) (TS) (separate folder). (2) Memo (S) of Gen McNair for CofS USA, 30 Apr 44, sub: Increase in Medium and Heavy Artillery. 320.2/32 (TB 44) (S).

wrote General McNair in February 1944, "that the troop basis can be balanced because there is an insufficient allowance for pipeline—the invisible horde of people going here and there but seemingly never arriving."[13] With more always in the pipeline than the Troop Basis allowed for, men were not available, within the 7,700,000 ceiling, for anticipated requirements. These requirements were considerable.

Even after the idea of adding fifteen divisions was abandoned, the Troop Basis of 15 January 1944 called for new units requiring half a million men in the three major forces. The Army Ground Forces required a net increase of about 150,000 for new units—chiefly AGF service units, combat engineers, and heavy artillery. For some of these units the Army Ground Forces had been wholly unable to plan. When the Troop Basis of 15 January 1944 was delivered to headquarters of the Army Ground Forces, on 27 January, it was found to contain units on which no previous information had been received, though they were scheduled for activation by the Army Ground Forces in February and were needed for the invasion of France the following June. Certain activations scheduled for 1943, but deferred because of shortages in receipt of personnel, also remained to be carried out in 1944. Some old units were also short; divisions on the Six Months List were short almost 10,000 infantrymen; divisions not on the Six Months List were short 32,500; nondivisional engineers were short 12,000. Heavy losses overseas in 1944 were expected, for which replacements had to be made ready.[14]

In addition, further demands on the Troop Basis, not provided for in January, developed in 1944. The number of heavy artillery battalions was substantially increased, for reasons that have been previously explained.[15] Requirements for infantry replacements, in 1944 as in 1943, also exceeded all advance provisions made by the War Department.

Since the Troop Basis of January 1944 authorized no increase in the strength of the Army over that authorized for 1943 (though not attained until April 1944), and since the War Department did not intend to exceed this authorization, it was desired that manpower for new requirements in 1944 should be obtained by redistribution within the Army. Since 1942 the War Department had looked forward to a time when personnel could be redistributed to increase

---

[13] Personal ltr of Gen McNair to Maj Gen L. E. Jones, CG 10th Lt Div, 15 Feb 44. McNair Correspondence.

[14] AGF memo (S) for G–3 WD, 15 Feb 44, sub: 1944 TB. 320.2/12 (TB 44) (S).

[15] See above, pp. 232–34.

tactical forces. Measures of economy were initiated in the winter of 1942-43, including the establishment of the War Department Manpower Board. It had been hoped that the desired readjustment, within a fixed ceiling, might occur in 1944.

Plans for economy were again stated on 20 January 1944, in a memorandum of G-3, WDGS, for the Chief of Staff, U. S. Army, circulated in photostat to the headquarters of the Army Ground Forces.[16] Proposed economies included "inactivation of units rendered surplus by the changing pattern of the war" (meaning chiefly antiaircraft and tank destroyer units as far as the Army Ground Forces was concerned), "reduction in Zone of Interior activities due to decrease in the training load" (such activities were relatively small in AGF), and "the exercise of drastic economy in the use of manpower both in the United States and overseas." It was stated that considerable transfer of personnel among the major commands in the United States would be necessary, with a net balance of transfers from the Air Forces to the Ground and Service Forces. The War Department Manpower Board was to extend its investigations to overseas theaters.

Economies and Conversions in 1944

Very great economies were, in fact, accomplished in 1944. Certain luxuries of an earlier day, and installations once useful but now surplus, were stringently curtailed. Many kinds of establishments set up for other purposes tended to liquefy into the replacement stream, thus providing either combat replacements for old units or filler replacements for new units due for activation.

The Army Specialized Training Program, which held almost 150,000 partly trained troops on college campuses, was virtually dissolved. About 73,000 of its students were transferred to the Army Ground Forces.[17] Some 24,000 surplus aviation cadets were reassigned from the Air Forces to the Ground Forces in the spring of 1944.[18] The flow into the Ground Forces from these two sources did not constitute altogether a quantitative gain in manpower, since the Ground

[16] WD memo (S) WDGCT 320 TB (30 Dec 44) for CofS USA, 20 Jan 44, sub: Implementation of TB 1944. 320.2/8 (TB 44) (S).

[17] (1) Memo (S) of Gen Marshall for SW, 10 Feb 44, sub: Serious Pers Shortages. (2) AGF M/S (S), G-1 Control Div to G-1, 26 Feb 44, sub: Conference Concerning Distribution of ASTP Students. Both in 353/100 (ASTP) (S).

[18] (1) WD memo WDGCT 220.3 (24 Mar 44) for CG AGF, 29 Mar 44, sub: Almt of Pers Released by AAF. 220.3/2119. (2) AGF ltr to CGs, 6 Apr 44, sub: Distribution of Aviation Cadet Tng Pers. 220.3/2129½.

Forces surrendered some 16,000 low-caliber personnel in return, the aim being to improve the quality of combat soldiers. Toward the end of 1944 the War Department ordered the transfer to the Army Ground Forces of an additional 40,000 high-quality men from the Air Forces and 25,000 from the Service Forces.

In January 1944 the enlisted overstrength authorized at the end of 1942 (15 percent over T/O strengths) was abolished, having become less necessary with the end of expansion, when units were no longer subject to the older forms of attrition.[19] In May 1944 all Tables of Organization except for infantry rifle companies and cavalry rifle troops were reduced by removal of 50 percent of basic privates.[20] These two measures left surpluses in units from which men could be converted to new needs, or at least lowered the claims of nonrifle units for personnel.[21]

Volunteers for infantry were called for from other branches. Under this program, launched in June 1944, in addition to 66,000 parachute volunteers, 25,000 volunteers were obtained by the following February. The 25,000 were enough for the infantry of three divisions. More than half of these infantry volunteers came from sources outside the Ground Forces.[22]

Many coast artillery units were converted to heavy field artillery. Most non-divisional infantry regiments were dissolved into the replacement stream. Tank destroyer battalions were inactivated as prescribed in the January 1944 Troop Basis. Antiaircraft battalions were inactivated at a more rapid rate than the January Troop Basis envisaged. It now proved fortunate that these two arms had been so extensively built up, for they constituted storehouses of soldiers who could be used for other purposes with only a little retraining and who otherwise would not have been available in 1944. By the end of 1944 antiaircraft and tank destroyer battalions were less than half as numerous as had been anticipated in the Troop Basis of November 1942.

Service troops were saved by consolidation, closing, or reduction to a caretaker status of posts no longer required as tactical forces moved overseas. Station complements were reduced, and tactical units of the Army Ground Forces, while still in the United States, took over post housekeeping duties from which,

<hr />

[19] WD ltr (R) AG 320.2 (15 Jan 44) OB–S–C–M to CGs, 20 Jan 44, sub: Overstrength in Units in Continental U. S. 320.2/309 (R).

[20] Cir 201, WD, 22 May 44.

[21] (1) WD Gen Council Min (S), 22 May 44. (2) AGF ltr (C) to CGs, 2 Jun 44, sub: Unauthorized Overstrength in AGF Units and Installations. 320.2/436 (C). (3) AGF ltr (R) to CGs, 28 Jul 44, sub: Authorized Strengths in AGF Units and Installations. 320.2/339 (R).

[22] (1) Cir 132, WD, 6 Apr 44. (2) WD Gen Council Min (S), 19 Feb 45.

in the early period of mobilization, to speed up their training, they had been exempted.[23]

Despite these very real economies the Ground and Service Forces experienced great difficulty in meeting the activation program in 1944. So many men were needed for replacements, or disappeared into the pipeline, that although hundreds of thousands were recovered by economy, and although the Army as a whole was almost 300,000 over its Troop Basis strength by July 1944, men were not available to meet the Troop Basis of the preceding January. Troop Basis requirements were revised downward. Some Ground Force units were canceled. Between cancellation of planned activations and inactivation of units already mobilized, the total strength allotted to tactical units of the Army Ground Forces declined steadily through 1944. That is to say, activation of new units in 1944—AGF service units, combat engineers, and heavy artillery—required far less personnel than did the units which were inactivated or canceled. In the Army Ground Forces, Troop Basis strength of combat-type units only fell from 2,282,000 to 2,041,000 enlisted men between 1 January 1944 and 31 March 1945.

With such great difficulty in meeting the Troop Basis, and with the Army as a whole nevertheless 300,000 over Troop Basis strength, it was evident that the trouble was maldistribution and that concealed overstrengths must be present somewhere in the Army. The problem was complicated by methods of personnel accounting which were inadequate due to the extreme complexity of the subject. During 1944 the War Department devised improved procedures for keeping current records of both actual and authorized strengths of each theater and of each of the three major commands. But the use of Troop Basis strengths, reported actual strengths, and reported authorized strengths as distinguished from the Troop Basis, all applying to an army constantly fluctuating in size, spread over the globe, and subject to continual battle losses, presented a problem defying the most patient analysis; the problem was complicated further by the breakdown of the component branches into T/O units, replacements, and overhead, which could be defined or distinguished only with difficulty.

Searching for hidden overstrengths, the War Department discovered by September 1944 that overseas theaters were carrying overstrengths of more than 50,000 in their T/O units, especially divisions and other combat organ-

---

[23] AGF ltr to CGs, 5 Feb 44, sub: Personnel. 320.2/7001.

izations, and, in addition, reserves of replacements more than 100,000 in excess of War Department authorizations. These overstrengths, while adding to the immediate combat power of the theaters which enjoyed them, were compensated for by corresponding understrengths in units and replacements in the United States, and therefore compromised the ability of the War Department to reinforce the theaters at future dates. Broadly speaking, a theater which exceeded its authorization in combat troops was either depriving another theater of combat troops at the time or robbing itself as of a future date—except insofar as additional combat troops might be formed from noncombat organizations. But it was found that overhead was also overexpanded. "Overhead" meant troops who were neither in tactical headquarters (army, corps, etc.) nor in combat units, T/O service units, or replacement pools. Overhead in the European Theater of Operations, for which 93,227 men were authorized, actually absorbed 114,137. Overhead in the United States, authorized 1,272,323 men, absorbed 1,297,688. Gross overstrength in overhead throughout the Army was almost 50,000.[24]

Attempts to economize on overhead in the United States met with limited success. Overhead could be reduced only partly as troops moved overseas. Zone of Interior overhead, composed of officers and men in jobs which would never take them overseas, fell about 15 percent between 30 June 1943, roughly the date at which troops in the United States were at their maximum, and 31 March 1945, at which date the proportion of the Army left in the United States was approaching the minimum. Figures were as follows:[25]

Zone of Interior Military Personnel

	30 Jun 43	31 Mar 45	Number Reduced	Percent Reduced
Army Ground Forces	169,000	140,000	29,000	17.2
Army Air Forces	831,000	710,000	121,000	14.6
Army Service Forces	547,000	444,000	103,000	18.8
War Dept. Activities	13,000	23,000	*10,000	76.0
TOTAL	1,560,000	1,317,000	243,000	15.6

* Increase.

[24] Appendix "A," Chart 3, WD Gen Council Min (S), 4 Sep 44.

[25] (1) Summary of ZI Operating Pers, Changes in Str June 43–Feb 45 and Jan–Feb 45, WDMB Form, Table 1 of 8, 15 Mar 45, in Appendix "D," WD Gen Council Min (S), 26 Mar 45. (2) Same (R), Strengths 31 Mar 45, Table 1 of 8, dated 30 Apr 45, in Appendix "B," WD Gen Council Min (S), 30 Apr 45.

Over 200,000 were thus recovered for overseas assignment, whether for tactical forces, replacements, or overseas overhead; but recovery was rather slow, for reduction in Air Force Zone of Interior personnel, which comprised over half the Zone of Interior personnel in the Army, did not reach substantial proportions until the last months of 1944.

On 14 January 1944 the War Department ordered that enlisted men assigned to Zone of Interior positions be in general those not qualified for overseas service.[26] These included men disqualified by age or physical condition, or those who had already served overseas. In February 1944 there were about 600,000 enlisted men qualified for overseas duty employed in the Zone of Interior. About 400,000 were in the Air Forces, and 200,000 in the Ground and Service Forces. The latter were rapidly transferred to other positions during 1944. The 400,000 in the Air Forces remained virtually untouched until October 1944. At that time the prolongation of the war in Europe added to the drive to get able-bodied men overseas. The Air Force figure fell to 262,000, but the reduction represented for the most part transfer of physically qualified men to the category of "critical specialists," in which they became temporarily disqualified for overseas duty, and hence remained at their Zone of Interior jobs. Figures were as follows:[27]

Men Qualified for Immediate Overseas Duty But Assigned to Zone of Interior Jobs

	29 Feb 44	30 Nov 44
Army Ground Forces	41,705	6,557
Army Air Forces	397,954	262,345
Army Service Forces	158,036	4,059
War Dept. Activities	389	0
TOTAL	598,084	272,961

On 30 June 1944, during the most critical days of the Normandy beachhead operation, the number of enlisted men in the United States qualified for overseas duty but assigned to Zone of Interior jobs exceeded the number of enlisted

---

[26] WD ltr AG 220.3 (14 Jan 44) OB–C–A to CG AGF, 14 Jan 44, sub: Enl Men—Utilization of Manpower Based on Physical Capacity. 220.3/305 (LD).

[27] (1) Rpts tabulated in WD Gen Council Min (S), 14 Aug 44, p. 3. (2) Appendix "E," Chart 3, ZI Operating Pers, in WD Gen Council Min (S), 30 Nov 44. (3) WD Gen Council Min (S), 8 Jan 45.

infantrymen in the European and Mediterranean Theaters. It exceeded the number of Air Corps personnel, enlisted and commissioned, in the two theaters. It was 92 percent of the number of enlisted men in the infantry, armored and tank destroyer forces, cavalry, field artillery, coast artillery, and antiaircraft artillery in the European Theater.[28] Many combat soldiers in the theaters were physically inferior to men scheduled to remain at home. This situation was not one which the Army Ground Forces approved, but it was difficult for the War Department to correct it in 1944. Since the early days of mobilization many prime physical specimens had been trained as technicians in Zone of Interior assignments. They now occupied key positions. Under pressure of combat in 1944 the Ground and Service Forces, but not the Air Forces, generally replaced these men with men who were not qualified for overseas service or had already served overseas.

Meanwhile the War Department urged economy on overseas commanders. Attempts in this direction since 1942 had not been very successful. In April 1944 representatives of overseas theaters attended a conference in Washington. The Deputy Chief of Staff declared that in the past the War Department had liberally granted the requests of the theaters but that these requests had frequently been immoderate. He said that use of communications-zone troops had been extravagant and that waste in one theater would mean insufficiency in another. He urged the theaters to practice the same economies—inactivation, conversion, retraining—that were in progress in the United States.[29]

It became increasingly difficult for the Zone of Interior to meet the replacement needs of the theaters. The situation was recognized as critical even before

---

[28] On 30 June 1944 there were 456,032 POR-qualified enlisted men in Zone of Interior assignments. (Tabulation of G–1 Rpts on Utilization of Manpower Based on Physical Capacity, WD Gen Council Min (S), 4 Sep 44, p. 5.) On that date other figures were as follows (Strength of the Army (S) 30 Jun 44, p. 16.314.7 (AGF Hist) (S)):

		EM in Inf	Offs and EM in AC	EM in Inf, Cav, FA, CAC (Includes Armd, TD, AAA)
In ETO		291,878	312,385	496,704
In NATO		153,129	114,138	
	TOTAL	445,007	426,523	496,704
	456,032 equals:	102%	107%	92%

[29] WD Gen Council Min (S), 3 Apr 44.

the German breakthrough in the Ardennes on 16 December 1944. Officers of the War Department General Staff and Headquarters, Army Ground Forces, met in conference on 7 December.[30] Battle losses in the European Theater alone were running to 3,000 a day, or 90,000 a month, while the Army Ground Forces was receiving only 53,000 a month from reception centers. Not all these were physically fit for training as combat replacements. To raise the induction rate would raise the proportion of physically unfit. Older sources of economy were vanishing: it was stated at the conference that the Ground Forces had reached the limit of inactivation, the Service Forces in the United States were drained of physically high-grade personnel, and the Air Forces, if called on to supply more men for retraining as infantry, would have to furnish Air Force specialists in the grade of sergeant. The Chief of Staff, Army Ground Forces, was asked point-blank by G–3 of the War Department whether he believed that the War Department was providing sufficient replacements to carry on the war. He replied that he did not. He recommended that the capacity of AGF replacement training centers be raised by 160,000 infantrymen, adding that the Ground Forces, even with reduced overhead, could find means to conduct their training. It was decided that the Service and Air Forces must meet their quotas for transfers, that the AAF quota might have to be raised, that steps should be taken to raise the induction rate, and that if necessary the replacement training program should be cut to fifteen weeks.

The German counterattack of 16 December, suddenly subjecting American troops to still higher losses, therefore produced a downright emergency. The G–1 of the European Theater of Operations flew to Washington. The last divisions were rushed to Europe and hence were not available for supplying replacements. The War Department insisted that the Zone of Interior was incapable of meeting the full requirement of ETO for replacements and that the theater must greatly accelerate its own program of conversion and retraining. The bulk of the Army, it was pointed out, was now overseas, principally in Europe; such manpower resources as the Army had within itself were now in the theaters, and especially in the European Theater of Operations. It was agreed that henceforth the War Department should simply announce to each theater the number of replacements to be expected from the United States, and that each theater must meet all requirements above this number by redistribu-

---

[30] M/R (S) Enl Div G–1 AGF, sub: Overseas Repl Requirements. 320.2/170 (O'seas Repls) (S).

tion of its own strength. By sending men below desired physical standards, men with only 15 weeks' training (or with only 6 weeks' retraining in infantry), and men in the higher enlisted grades beyond the normal proportion, and by cutting the allocation of replacements to the Southwest Pacific, the War Department was able on 8 January 1945 to assure the European Theater that about 56,000 replacements a month (87 percent infantry) would arrive from the Zone of Interior from February to June. Only 43,590 a month had been allocated to ETO before the emergency of December.[31]

In January 1945 Lt. Gen. Ben Lear, who had succeeded General McNair in command of the Army Ground Forces, was transferred to the European Theater to supervise the combing of physically qualified personnel from rear-area establishments and their retraining as combat troops, principally infantry riflemen. General Lear, since the time of his command of the Second Army, had urged the assignment of the physically fit to combat positions, and the physically less fit to headquarters, service, and overhead installations. It was now his task, by conversion and retraining in Europe, to fill the gap in manpower between what the depleted Zone of Interior could supply and what the units at the front actually needed.

The Struggle to Maintain the 90-Division Army

The T/O strength of AGF units in March 1945 was not much greater than in June 1943. Indeed, the strength of ground combat units grew very little after December 1942. (See Table No. 4.) At the same time the number of men in the ground arms increased, both through inductions and through conversion and retraining. The ground arms grew more rapidly in 1944 and the first quarter of 1945 than did other elements in the Army. (See Table No. 3 and its Annex.) Increase in personnel, without increase in units, indicates that most men added to the ground arms after the middle of 1943 went into existing units as replacements or into the "pipeline." The increase of strength by arm for the most part represented, not men in units, but men who had been in units and were now in hospitals, and men who were scheduled to take their places in units but were currently at some point in the replacement stream.

---

[31] (1) Minutes of conferences at the Pentagon 23 and 28 Dec 1944. 320.2/173 (O'seas Repls) (S). (2) WD ltr (S) AGOC–E–C 320.2 (30 Oct 44) to CGs of theaters, 8 Nov 44, sub: O'seas Repls. 320.2/166 (O'seas Repls) (S). (3) WD ltr (S) AGOC–E–C 320.2 (6 Jan 45) to CGs of theaters, 8 Jan 45, sub as above. 320.2/174 (O'seas Repls) (S).

In other words, the main problem of the Ground Forces after the close of 1943 was not to activate new units but to preserve the units already active at the end of 1943, and in particular to hold together the 90 divisions already mobilized. One of these, the 2d Cavalry Division, was inactivated immediately after reaching its overseas station in 1944. In effect, the remaining 89 divisions represented the planned divisional strength of the Army. The problem was to hold together an Army of 89 divisions.

By the inactivations, conversions, and retraining described above, and by the assignment of the majority of newly inducted men to AGF replacement training centers in 1944 and 1945, the War Department succeeded in preserving the 89 divisions and avoided repeating the experience of 1918, when almost a third of the divisions then activated became hardly more than paper organizations. But the process was a complex one, in which some divisions in the United States were almost lost. The personnel needed by overseas units was not provided merely from replacement centers or from special installations for reconversion training, but to a large extent from units destined soon to enter combat themselves. Some divisions virtually went out of existence as combat organizations (as in 1918), only to be rebuilt at the latest possible moment.

The last division had hardly been activated in August 1943 when a crisis developed in the replacement system.[32] This was essentially an infantry crisis. Infantry components of divisions of the various types, by which virtually all infantry fighting was done, numbered about 700,000 officers and men, well under a tenth of the strength of the fully mobilized Army. The figure changed little after the close of 1943. But to maintain 700,000 officers and men in divisional infantry units, the strength of the Infantry as an arm rose to 1,800,000 by April 1945.

With the opening of operations in Sicily in July 1943, and the commitment of ground forces to battle in increasing numbers thereafter, a demand arose for replacements in the Infantry, which suffered most of the casualties, far beyond the capacity of infantry replacement training centers to produce. Nondivisional infantry regiments were depleted and inactivated, their personnel being sent as replacements to the Mediterranean. Divisions also were tapped. By January 1944 approximately 25,000 men had been taken from infantry divisions in the Army Ground Forces not earmarked for early ship-

---

[32] The replacements problem is dealt with in two reports prepared by the AGF Historical Section, Provision of Enlisted Replacements, and Major Developments in the Training of Enlisted Replacements.

ment.[33] These divisions in January were, on the average, 2,000 understrength in their infantry elements. As each division was earmarked in its turn, it had to be brought to T/O strength by transfer of trained personnel from divisions of lower priority. The divisions of lowest priority, generally those most recently activated, and chronically short or partly refilled with men direct from reception centers, could with difficulty proceed beyond basic training. The troubles of 1942 were repeated at the beginning of 1944.

The first weeks of 1944 were a time of extreme difficulty in replacement planning. On 4 January General McNair, reviewing the shortages in infantry divisions, expressed a fear that one or more divisions might have to be broken up.[34] On 12 January the War Department, anticipating the invasion of France, announced that within two months, in the early summer, ETO would require 50,000 more infantry and field artillery replacements than replacement training centers could produce.[35] The Army Ground Forces was directed to plan accordingly, with minimum disruption of units in the United States, minimum delay in activation of new units, and reduction of replacement training if necessary to thirteen weeks. On 19 January substantially the reverse policy prevailed: the Army Ground Forces was directed to submit a plan by which overseas combat replacements should be men with at least nine months' training, taken from all units of the Army Ground Forces not due for early shipment.[36] This directive reflected the school of thought which had long believed seventeen weeks of training insufficient to produce a good replacement. In addition, it was thought undesirable to send into combat men with only seventeen weeks of training at a replacement center, and who in many cases were 18-year-olds or "pre-Pearl Harbor fathers," while other men who had been in the Army two or three years remained in units in the United States—some of which, in an optimistic view, might never be required in battle. The justice of this policy can hardly be disputed. Its inconvenience was equally clear. The situation was an awkward one, owing to the postponement of invasion plans, as a result of which units had been ready longer than necessary before their dates of commitment.

---

[33] (1) AGF Historical Section, The Building and Training of Infantry Divisions. (2) Memo (S) of Gen McNair for CofS USA, 4 Jan 44, sub: Tng of Repls. 320.2/101 (O'seas Repls) (S).

[34] Memo (S) of Gen McNair for CofS USA, 4 Jan 44, sub: Tng of Rpls. 320.2/101 (O'seas Rpls) (S).

[35] WD memo (TS) WDGCT 370.5 (12 Jan 44) for CG AGF, 12 Jan 44, sub: Repls. 320.2 (O'seas Repls) (TS).

[36] WD memo (S) WDCSA 320.2 (16 Jan 44) for CG AGF, 19 Jan 44, sub: Combat Repls. 320.2/105 (O'seas Repls) (S).

On 25 January General McNair, in a carefully documented reply to the War Department, showed that it was mathematically impossible to hold enough divisions in the United States to give nine months' training to the required number of replacements, and at the same time to ship divisions overseas on the schedule laid down for 1944. Since 80 percent of replacements had to be infantry, it was chiefly infantry divisions that were affected. All but nine infantry divisions were due for shipment by the end of 1944. To give nine months' training, including a period within divisions, to the number of replacements estimated by the War Department as needed in 1944 would tie up sixteen divisions in the United States. For the number of replacements estimated as necessary by the Army Ground Forces (which was 50 percent higher, and nearer to the requirement that actually developed), twenty-six divisions would have to be held at home. The program proposed by the War Department, if adhered to as a continuing policy, would therefore relegate about a quarter of the infantry divisions to the status of replacement training organizations.[37]

On 7 February General McNair pointed out that, even under a seventeen-week program for training replacements, a severe shortage was to be expected. He declared that to provide overseas replacements as needed, together with their trainer personnel, and to fill shortages in units already earmarked for shipment, the Army Ground Forces would have to receive 500,000 men in the remainder of 1944. Adding requirements for new units in the troop basis, and allowing for attrition, the Ground Forces would need 1,000,000 in the remainder of 1944. If this figure could not be met, and assuming it to be correct, wrote General McNair, the only recourse would be to curtail the Troop Basis. He added: "In short we may be over-mobilized, or have an unbalanced mobilization in light of present conditions." [38] The AGF Troop Basis was in fact curtailed, as has been noted, by 250,000 between 15 January 1944 and 31 March 1945, chiefly through inactivation of antiaircraft units.

At this point, on 10 February 1944, General Marshall went directly to the Secretary of War with a proposal to liquidate the Army Specialized Training Program. Measures of economy already undertaken, he said, would provide men for units to be shipped after 31 August 1944. The need was for filling, with men already basically trained, shortages in units due for shipment before 31 August. These units were required for the forthcoming invasion of France.

---

[37] AGF memo (TS) for CofS USA, 25 Jan 44, sub: Repls. 320.2 (O'seas Repls) (TS).
[38] Memo (S) of Gen McNair for CofS USA, 7 Feb 44, sub: Repl Situation. 320.2/106 (O'seas Repls) (S).

Men basically trained were available on college campuses in the Army Specialized Training Program. General Marshall offered a choice between drastically reducing the college program and disbanding ten divisions and certain nondivisional units. The Army Specialized Training Program was immediately reduced.[39]

Of the 35 divisions among which ASTP trainees were distributed, only 7 actually went overseas before 31 August. ASTP trainees were generally assigned to lower-priority divisions, to fill vacancies caused by application of a six-month rule for overseas replacements.

The War Department abandoned the nine-month project but was still determined to draw replacements from divisions and other units before using the newcomers to the Army currently graduating from replacement training centers. On 26 February 1944 the War Department directed the Army Ground Forces to obtain overseas replacements in all the combat arms by stripping units not on the Six Months List.[40] Men chosen were to have had at least six months of service, those with the longest service to be chosen first. No 18-year-olds or pre-Pearl Harbor fathers with less than six months of training were to be sent overseas as replacements until all other sources were exhausted.

Units not earmarked were now systematically stripped. Although the six-month policy applied to replacements in all combat arms, comparatively few replacements were required except in the Infantry, so that it was mainly infantry units that lost their men. Divisions surrendered their privates and a percentage of their noncommissioned officers until a date about four months before sailing. Thus the divisions which entered combat in the latter part of 1944 were divisions which had been in training for periods averaging two years but were composed in large part of men new to the division, new to the infantry, or even new to the Army. In some ways divisions profited, for they received new men of higher quality than had been previously obtainable by the Ground Forces; but unit spirit and unit training, carefully built up in the preceding years, and generally admitted to be vital in combat, had to be recaptured at the last moment.[41]

---

[39] Memo (S) of Gen Marshall for SW, 10 Feb 44, sub: Serious Personnel Shortages. 353/100 (ASTP) (S).

[40] WD memo (C) WDGCT 200 (26 Feb 44) for CG AGF, 26 Feb 44, sub: Repls. 320.2/107 (O'seas Repls) (C).

[41] (1) AGF memo (S) for G–3 WD, 13 Mar 44, sub: Repls. 320.2/114 (O'seas Repls) (S). (2) AGF ltr (C) to CGs, 29 Mar 44, sub: O'seas Enl Repls. 320.2/110 (O'seas Repls) (C). (3) AGF ltr (R) to CGs, 30 Apr 44, sub: Refilling of Certain AGF Units 220.3/123 (R).

The six-month replacement training policy lasted for only about two months in the spring of 1944. The War Department, in view of the major offensive impending, would not decelerate the shipping schedule for divisions and other combat units. Units therefore soon became unavailable as producers of replacements. There were not enough divisions in the Army for the War Department to gain both its objectives: namely, to ship divisions to theaters as rapidly as was feasible; and to ship replacements to theaters from divisions remaining in the United States. By the summer of 1944 replacements were again being sent overseas with seventeen weeks of training. But the internal composition of infantry divisions in the United States had in the meantime been revolutionized.

While the six-month policy was given up, the 18-year-old policy was confirmed anew. On 24 June 1944 the War Department ordered categorically that no 18-year-old should be sent overseas as an infantry or armored replacement.[42] Over 20,000 18-year-olds, currently in training in infantry and armored replacement centers, were assigned to divisions on completing their course, since there was no bar on 18-year-olds going overseas as members of organized units, and since many of the men concerned would be nineteen by the time their divisions sailed. Meanwhile, to fill the void in the replacement stream, divisions lost an equal number of older men—older both in being over eighteen and in being trained members of their units. At this time about half the men being inducted into the Army were 18-year-olds. At the same time virtually all inductees were being assigned to AGF replacement centers as the Army was completely mobilized and in general needed only to replace losses, of which over 80 percent were infantry and armored. The 18-year-old rule was, therefore, difficult to apply. To find enough men over eighteen to fill infantry and armored replacement centers all available inductees over eighteen had to be used, regardless of age or physical condition. Many men received at the front as infantry and armored replacements in the later months of 1944 were therefore inadequate physically. Meanwhile the rule was abolished as unworkable. Beginning as early as August, 18-year-olds were again put into the infantry and armored replacement centers, from which, beginning in November, they were shipped overseas with seventeen weeks of training—reduced in January 1945 to fifteen.

During 1944 about 40 divisions yielded overseas replacements. Seventeen lost most of their infantry privates and many of their noncommissioned officers.

[42] WD memo (C) WDGCT 370.5 (24 Jun 44) to CG AGF, 24 Jun 44, sub: Repls. 320.2/107 (O'seas Repls) (C).

Divisions were reconstructed, in part by assignment of replacement training center graduates during the period when seventeen weeks of replacement training did not qualify a man as an overseas replacement, in part by personnel received through economies and conversions. ASTP trainees, transferred aviation cadets, and 18-year-olds from replacement training centers supplied 37 divisions, from April to July, with about 100,000 men. Men volunteering for transfer to infantry and men converted from tank destroyer and antiaircraft artillery units were also assigned to divisions, but most of these, along with men from the Air and Service Forces at the end of 1944, were assigned to special replacement centers or special infantry regiments for six weeks of infantry training.

For a time at the end of 1944 it seemed that certain infantry divisions would be broken up despite all the effort to preserve them. Operations in the European Theater, after proceeding ahead of schedule, met with strong resistance at the Siegfried Line in September. The infantry troops of divisions in action since the landings in France were desperately in need of relief. It was decided to adopt a system of unit replacement. Recommendations of the Army Ground Forces in 1943 to provide more nondivisional regiments for this purpose had not been adopted. Instead, nondivisional infantry regiments had been dissolved in considerable numbers to furnish individual replacements. Now, in October 1944, it was decided that the infantry regiments of most infantry divisions still left in the United States were to be shipped to Europe separately.[43] But the plan was altered before going fully into effect. Only certain regiments were shipped separately. In any case all division headquarters and auxiliary elements went overseas, where they were reunited with their infantry and reappeared as standard organizations. The crisis of December was likewise passed without dissolution of any divisions. The need for divisions as units was even greater than the need for their personnel as individual replacements. By February 1945 all divisions had left the Army Ground Forces.

A year earlier, in January 1944, 57 divisions were still in the United States. Most of them were more than a year old. But instead of having a stock of units from which to meet at leisure, after a long period of waiting, the calls of the Operations Division for shipment of divisions and other units to theaters, the Army Ground Forces had to make exact calculations in order to have them ready when needed. The period of waiting in 1943 was followed by a race against

---

[43] (1) AGF M/S (S), G–3 to CofS, 19 Oct 44, sub: Pers Status of Certain Divs. 320.2/760 (S). (2) Memo (S) of Gen Lear for G–3 WD, 23 Oct 44, sub: Separate Inf Regts. 320.2/58 (TB 44) (S).

time in 1944. Units scheduled to go overseas received their permanent personnel at the latest possible moment. Some went over less fully trained than the Army Ground Forces desired. Seven infantry divisions had never engaged in a division versus division maneuver. Ten had engaged in such a maneuver with from only 30 to 60 percent of the personnel which they took overseas. Not all calls of the Operations Division for nondivisional units could be met. In June 1944, for example, of 1,304 AGF-type units then put by the Operations Division on the Six Months List, 214 were reported as unavailable.[44] With the influx of new personnel, they could not be trained (or retrained) by the dates desired. The situation was like that of early 1942, when the Army Ground Forces struggled to provide units trained and at T/O strength for the invasion plan of that date.

[44] WD Gen Council Min (S), 26 Jun 44.

V. Summary

Perhaps the broadest generalization that can be made about the mobilization of combatant ground forces is that they were the first to be mobilized and the last to be used. Mobilization may be said to have begun in September 1940, with the adoption of Selective Service and induction of the National Guard. Until the declaration of war, mobilization and training were concentrated on combat-type ground forces. Air forces remained relatively small, and service units were not produced in the proportions required for war, especially for a war conducted on the far side of oceans. In 1942 the emphasis remained heavily on the formation of new divisions. By the end of 1942, divisions and other ground combat units already mobilized had an enlisted T/O strength of 1,917,000. It was planned that this figure should reach 2,811,000 by the end of 1943.

In January 1943 the War Department expressed an intention to raise, through economies of manpower, the strength of ground combat units to a figure exceeding 3,000,000 enlisted men in 1944. Although mobilization had been in progress for over two years prior to the winter of 1942–43, no significant measures were adopted to economize manpower in the Army. There was now an ambiguity in the situation. Economy was now to the fore, but the need for adding to combatant ground forces had receded. Plans for invasion of western Europe had been postponed. Combatant ground troops moved overseas very slowly in 1943. Hence reserves accumulated in the United States. With the development of air power and with Russian victories, there was no certainty that United States ground forces would be needed in large numbers. Among the many demands for military manpower those of the Army Ground Forces were judged to be of low priority in 1943. In January 1943 the activation of three divisions was deferred from the first to the last half of that year. In June 1943 twelve divisions scheduled for the last half of 1943 (including the three deferred hitherto) were deferred to 1944. But the War Department, while postponing the activation of more divisions to 1944, did not defer to 1944 the attainment of the full strength of the Army. The Troop Basis of 1943 used up the full strength which the Army could expect to reach. This strength, including officers, was 7,700,000 after June 1943, when the ceiling was lowered from the 8,200,000 set in 1942. It was largely to accommodate the Army within the lowered ceiling that activation of the twelve divisions was deferred in 1943. Despite lowering of the ceiling the Army in fact grew to a strength of over 8,200,000 as had originally been planned. Nevertheless, the deferment of divisions proved to be a postponement to the Greek calends, for the time never came when manpower was available for more divisions. The only hope of adding divisions in 1944 was through redistribution within the Army. Redistribution to divisions was not achieved for various reasons: the demand for overhead and replacements proved to be persistently in excess of estimates; the increase of service units seemed impossible to check; and certain combat requirements, such as the B–29 and heavy artillery programs, had to be met after the Army was already formed.

As a result, not only did the hope of raising ground combat strength to 3,000,000 enlisted men never materialize, but ground combat strength in the end hardly exceeded the strength already mobilized at the end of 1942. On 31 December 1942, T/O enlisted strength of ground combat units already mobilized was 1,917,000. Strength of such units mobilized on 31 March 1945 was only 2,041,000. T/O enlisted strength of divisions mobilized on 31 December 1942 was 1,056,000—on 31 March 1945 only 1,125,000. More units did exist in 1945 than at the end of 1942. Sixteen divisions were added in the first eight months of 1943, and almost 200 nondivisional field artillery battalions and over 150 engineer battalions in 1943 and 1944. (See Table No. 5.) But units were added without increase of total strength of ground combat units of all types. In other words, the added units were not obtained by redistribution and economy within the Army as a whole but principally by redistribution and economy within the combat elements of the Army Ground Forces. These redistributions and economies took the form of inactivation of ground combat units of certain types, and of decrease in the size of ground combat units of all types through downward revision of Tables of Organization. With these inactivations and reductions the total strength of ground combat units in 1945 was approximately 1,000,000 below what had been planned in the winter of 1942–43. Combat ground forces grew to only two-thirds of their anticipated strength.

Although the total strength of combat ground units did not materially rise after 1942, the total strength of the Army rose by almost 3,000,000 after that date, increasing from about 5,400,000 to almost 8,300,000. These 3,000,000 officers and men went into the Air and Service Forces, into nondivisional service units of the Army Ground Forces, into overhead in all forms, into the hospital population, and into organizations of all kinds designed for the training and storage of replacements.

Ground Combat Units in Planned Troop Basis, 1942–46

Date	Percent
August 1942	[a] 41.0
November 1942	37.3
January 1943	[a] 40.5
July 1943	35.3
January 1944	32.9
January 1945	29.4
April 1945	[b] 27.0
December 1946 (Projected for Japanese War)	22.6

[a] Estimate from pertinent War Department documents.
[b] Estimate on basis of actual strength.

Thus in the Army of over 8,000,000 in existence in April 1945 only about one-fourth were combatant ground soldiers, not counting men currently in training as replacements (approximately 500,000) who would eventually join combat units but not increase their numerical strength. Excluding the Air Forces, which numbered 2,300,000, the strength of combat units was about 37 percent of the strength of the Army. Comparison may be made with World War I. In November 1918 combat ground forces numbered 1,660,000 officers and men, within 600,000 of the corresponding figure for 1945. If from the 1945 figure one deducts the antiaircraft artillery, which scarcely existed in 1918 and which in 1945 was not all used on the battlefield, the strength of ground combat units in 1945 was only 300,000 greater than in 1918. Ground combat units in 1918, numbering 1,660,000, constituted 45 percent of the total strength of 3,700,000 then carried on the books of the War Department. Excluding aviation, which in 1918 numbered 190,000, ground combat units constituted almost half the Army. Excluding both aviation and antiaircraft artillery, the Army put half its strength into combat units in 1918 but only a third in 1945. (See Table No. 1.) Not only had strength of ground combat units fallen to 27 percent of the Army by April 1945, but according to plans then in effect for redeployment against Japan it was slated to fall to less than 23 percent by December 1946.

On 1 May 1945 Gen. Joseph W. Stilwell, Commanding General of AGF, called the attention of Gen. George C. Marshall to the "disappearing ground combat army." The trend, wrote General Stilwell, "may be pregnant with disaster if we have a tough ground fight with Japan." [1] The Operations Division WDGS, asked by General Marshall to comment, reviewed some of the main features of mobilization. It was noted that Troop Basis plans followed theater estimates of forces required. The continuing decline in the proportion of combat troops to the total Army, the Operations Division observed,[2]

is a natural result of a diminishing need in the actual numbers of assault troops due to mechanization of the Army, i. e., the great masses of armor and airplanes that prepare the way for the final assault of the foot soldier with resultant saving of human life. While decreasing the actual numbers of assault troops needed in battle, these engines of war require a large and more extensive Line of Communication. The assault trooper is still the cornerstone of the offensive. However, mechanization has made him more efficient in the carrying out of his duties and he is not now needed in the great numbers formerly demanded when assaults consisted mainly of human blows against defended positions.

With due regard for the weight of this statement, the headquarters of the Army Ground Forces felt that assault troops might be "more efficient in the carrying out of their duties" and might be employed with more "saving of human life" if certain advantages following from larger numbers could be obtained. One advantage in numbers was the ability to withdraw units before the point of fatigue at which casualties mounted. Another was the ability to concentrate decisive force at critical moments. A third was the ability to give systematic training, without the disruption and turnover within units caused by emergency demands.

That aviation and mechanization, as noted by the Operations Division, saved the lives of combat troops was not questioned by the Army Ground Forces.

[1] Memo (S) of Gen Stilwell for Gen Marshall, 1 May 45, sub: A Disappearing Ground Combat Army. 320.2/801 (S).
[2] OPD memo (S) 320.2 (1 May 45) for CofS USA, 9 May 45, sub: A Disappearing Ground Combat Army. 320.2/801 (S).

Indeed General McNair, especially in 1942 and 1943, had urged more attention to the air support of ground troops than he was able to obtain. But in Europe, despite extensive use of air and mechanized forces, a larger use of infantry had been required than had been planned. This situation might conceivably recur in the Far East. On the other hand, it could reasonably be calculated that success against Japan would depend heavily on naval and air power and on the large ground forces of foreign armies—especially those of China and the Soviet Union.

The foregoing narrative raises two general questions which reach beyond the jurisdiction of the Army Ground Forces, but on which its experience with mobilization may be of value. One question relates to the timing of mobilization, the other to its quantitative aspects.

As for timing, it is evident that if the War Department had found it possible to accelerate the preparation of air and service forces in 1940 and 1941, it would have produced a smoother mobilization in 1942 after the declaration of war. As seen in 1941, the 36 divisions mobilized before Pearl Harbor hardly seemed too many for an army totaling 1,600,000, the strength attained at the end of 1941. But they proved to be far out of proportion as the Army developed. In 1942 emphasis continued to fall on divisions; 37 divisions were activated in that year alone. It was believed that corresponding nondivisional units could be activated somewhat later than divisions, since they required less time for training. This policy proved to have serious disadvantages. Activation of divisions and of supporting nondivisional units got out of step. Since the 1942 Troop Basis at first made too little provision for service units, and since it developed that service units were in fact needed in the theaters before combat units arrived, many service units were activated in 1942 without Troop Basis authorization. Activation of service units became irregular, uncoordinated, and difficult to control. The Troop Basis, instead of forecasting mobilization, had to be changed repeatedly to authorize mobilization ex post facto. At the same time, with divisions intentionally launched some months before their corresponding nondivisional units, future commitments for nondivisional units, especially service units, were continually built up. Thus the service program always seemed to be lagging, and to find manpower for service units many combat units were kept understrength for months after activation. Meanwhile the Army Air Forces were also rapidly growing.

The timing of mobilization depended directly on strategic plans. In 1942, until mid-July, planning called for an invasion of western Europe in conjunction with the British either in the fall of 1942 or in the spring of 1943. Rapid activation of divisions in 1942 was necessary to implement this plan. Then in the summer of 1942 it was decided to confine ground operations to an invasion of North Africa, and to concentrate meanwhile on an air offensive against Germany. The date for invading western Europe with land forces was postponed. The mobilization objective for ground troops was reduced, and the rate of mobilization was slowed down. Still, two theaters had to be built up in the European area, each with a large requirement for overhead and service troops, though there was no ground fighting in the European Theater until June 1944, and in the Mediterranean Theater the number of United States divisions employed in combat seldom exceeded half a dozen.

Combatant ground forces were virtually mobilized in over-all strength by the end of 1942, and thereafter improved their striking power by economy and reorganization within themselves. Changes in war plans brought about a long period of waiting before commitment on a large scale. With three exceptions, the divisions activated after Pearl Harbor did not enter combat until 1944. For strategic plans as finally adopted and carried out, mobilization of ground forces was premature and mobilization of air forces somewhat tardy. The Army Air Forces, having to be built from the small beginnings of 1941, continued to expand rapidly while the Ground Forces essentially marked time. All types of service units, some remaining from 1942, had to be formed in 1943 and 1944. The Army Ground Forces felt that the assignment of manpower in the period following 1942, when the Army showed a net growth of almost 3,000,000, mainly to air and service units and overhead establishments, instead of combatant ground forces, might create a dangerous situation in the future.

This leads to the question of quantity. The question is essentially this: What are the decisive factors that limit the capacity of the United States to deploy combat ground forces overseas? In World War II the United States, with 12,000,000 men in its armed services including those in the Navy, produced only 95 divisions, including those in the Marine Corps. This fact must be weighed whenever ground operations overseas on any considerable scale are contemplated. The evidence surveyed in the present study indicates that the United States found its projects for ground operations overseas limited by many factors. One was the proportion of national resources needed to control the sea and the air. Another was the allocation of resources to strategic bombardment and to the support of allies. A third was the need of maintaining supply lines with streams of personnel and equipment constantly in transit over immense distances. A factor which produced problems not clearly foreseen was the demand for shipping, personnel, and overhead created by supplies which included a mass of heavy and complicated mechanical equipment, and also the materiel needed to provide American soldiers with something corresponding to the American standard of living. These demands, and the controls that seemed to be necessary to coordinate the complex of specialized units using various types of mechanical and motorized equipment, led to a prodigious growth of service and administrative units, and in part account for the unprecedented and alarming proliferation of overhead in the Army of World War II. Certain of these factors seem likely to grow with further advances in mechanization. Others, such as the pressure to enable American soldiers to take their standard of living with them, will at least not decline. The striking force that the United States can deliver in ground combat overseas is likely always to depend on the degree to which economy in these limiting factors is achieved.

How much economy of this sort was achieved in World War II is difficult to determine, but certainly by the beginning of 1945 the Army was a more economical and a leaner organization than in any previous year of the war. Indeed the fat stored up in previous years proved to be a useful reserve. It was found that much could be dispensed with under pressure: soldiers on college campuses who formed a pool over half as large as the armored forces; surpluses of aviation cadets; an antiaircraft artillery half as large as all infantry divisions combined; personnel engaged solely in post housekeeping duties; and allowances for margins of overstrength and for basic privates in tactical units. In 1944–45 troops were converted from these uses to combat jobs, with the consequence, however, that retraining had to be regrettably hasty.

These economies were produced for the most part by emergency, and men thus recaptured were used mainly as replacements, going to maintain but not to increase the number of existing units. Maintenance of units at effective strength was a considerable achievement. If only for this reason the 89 Army divisions overseas in 1945 were the equivalent, apart from superiority of fire power, of a larger number of enemy divisions. As for increase in number of combat units, all increase occurring after 1942 could be traced to economy within the Army Ground Forces rather than in the Army as a whole.

Smooth and economical mobilization, both in training and in quantitative distribution, is probably impossible to achieve in any war. It would appear to require primarily two conditions. One is a consistent strategic plan, in which successive phases of operations are foreseen well in advance and substantially adhered to. The other is an authority able to adjudicate the rival claims of ground, service, air, and naval forces, and to apportion to each of them, in the light of strategic plans, such a share of the national stock of manpower and resources as would assure to each the means for attaining maximum efficiency in its assigned role. Since no plan is infallible and no central agency omniscient, mobilization can never be perfectly smooth and perfectly economical. The problem is to find the best middle ground between rational foresight and short-run adjustments. Some of the costs and sacrifices incurred in following a course through this middle ground in World War II have been indicated in the foregoing study. The fact remains that the pursuit of that course led to victory.

Reorganization

of Ground Troops for Combat

by

Robert R. Palmer

555949 O–61—19

Contents

Tables

Chart

I. Tactical Organization
Before 8 March 1942

The mission of the Army Ground Forces, as stated by War Department Circular 59, 2 March 1942, was "to provide ground force units properly organized, trained and equipped for combat operations." Organization of units for combat, often called "tactical organization," involved two interrelated activities. One was to divide men and materials into standard parts of known and calculable capabilities, such as "the" infantry division, "the" ordnance light maintenance company, etc. The other was to combine these parts into larger wholes— task forces, corps, or armies—which were the controlling agencies of large-scale combat.

Structure of the standard parts, from the division down, but including the headquarters of corps and armies, was prescribed in Tables of Organization and Equipment. Known (1945) as "T/O&E's," these established the type units, or standard patterns, according to which actual units were formed in such numbers and at such times as mobilization policy might determine.[1] For each unit the T/O&E prescribed the number of its officers and men, the grade and job of each, the proportion of various military occupational specialists, the arrangement of command and staff and administrative personnel, the means of transport and communications, the provisions for supply, maintenance, construction, and medical care, and the kind and quantity of individual and unit armament, together with the relationship between supporting weapons and consequently the normal tactics of the unit. These features of the unit in turn determined the degree to which it was dependent, for combat or administration, on other units for support. The provision of interlocking support through association of units of various types was a principal function of corps and armies.

---

[1] In 1942 organization and equipment were expressed in T/O's and T/BA's (Tables of Basic Allowances). The T/E was substituted for the T/BA by AR 310–60, as revised on 12 October 1942. The difference, briefly, was that a T/E was set up for each standard unit, whereas there had been a single T/BA for each combat arm, covering all standard units of that arm. With the revision of AR 310–60, published on 28 August 1943, a consolidated T/O&E was issued for each standard unit.

T/O&E's prescribed the standard form of units wherever stationed, whether in the United States or overseas. It was desirable to have a uniform organization for purposes of planning and procurement and to preserve a flexible situation in which units could be dispatched to any theater at will. But the circumstances in the several theaters were widely different. It was not expected that the organization developed in the Zone of Interior would exactly meet the needs of all theaters under all conditions of combat. Theater commanders, when authorized by the War Department, were free to modify their tactical organization. Unit commanders in actual operations might rearrange their men and equipment or obtain additional men and equipment if possible, according to their best judgment of the immediate situation. The problem for the Zone of Interior was to provide basic minimum units. The standard units prescribed by T/O&E's were designed to be basic in the sense of being adequate to a reasonable variety of conditions and of requiring as little readaptation as possible by commanders charged with the actual fighting. The units were conceived as minimum in the sense of having no more men and equipment than were necessary for normal operations, so that the largest possible number of units might be formed. Requirements for basic minimum units changed with the changing experience of battle. The agencies charged with organization in the Zone of Interior received reports of battle experience, compared reports from the several theaters, balanced the requests of theater commanders against availability of men and materials, and decided whether or not to make changes in T/O&E's which would affect the structure of units in all parts of the world.

Tactical organization, while designed for combat, was indispensable to the preparatory effort as well. Tables of Organization and Equipment were the basic guides to mobilization. T/O units were the blocks out of which the Army was built. The total of all T/O units constituted the major portion of the Troop Basis.[2] The internal character of each unit, as fixed by its tables, dictated the total number of similar units required. The tabular strength and composition of each division, for example, determined the number of divisions required to make up a desired total of combat power. The internal limitations of the division likewise determined the amount of supporting field artillery, ordnance, etc. which had to be mobilized concurrently. The number of units needed to produce the required nondivisional support depended in turn on the unit tables in each arm and service.

---

[2] The use of the Troop Basis in mobilization is traced above in the study, "Ground Forces in the Army, December 1941–April 1945: a Statistical Study."

Through the medium of the Troop Basis, Tables of Organization and Equipment established procurement objectives for personnel and materiel. The number of men required for the initial filling of units, the number of replacements required to keep units at tabular strength, and the number needed for each arm and service and for every military occupational specialty were ascertained through consolidation and analysis of Tables of Organization. The listing of an item of equipment in a unit table set up an automatic demand on the appropriate supply service. Multiplication by the number of units in the Troop Basis, with the addition of factors for replacement and reserve, gave the requirement to be incorporated in the Army Supply Program.

Training also was determined by tactical organization. Basic individual training could be given apart from tactical units, and was so given in replacement training centers. But the number of men to be so trained depended on the application of loss ratios to the Tables of Organization of tactical units. Purely technical training could likewise be given apart from tactical units. Here again the number to be trained depended largely on unit tables; the technician, moreover, unless intended for rear-area assignment, was not fully proficient until he had been trained under field conditions in a tactical unit. As for students at the service schools—whether officers, officer candidates, or enlisted specialists— the content of their instruction and the number instructed, particularly in the Army Ground Forces, reflected the requirements of T/O units.

Unit and combined training and the establishment of tactical doctrine were naturally inseparable from tactical organization, since doctrine stated the proper employment of personnel and equipment, and training was essentially the inculcation of doctrine. It was a principle of the training program for units to train in the United States with the same organization, personnel, and equipment as they would have in combat. Actually, because of great turnover, recurrent shortages of personnel, and reduction of allowances of equipment, units in training were not exactly like units in combat. Nevertheless, the commander of an infantry battalion, for example, learned to handle his three rifle companies, to use the supporting fires of his antitank guns and heavy weapons company, to call for assistance from the additional weapons available in regiment and division, to carry on his administrative business with the personnel made available to him, and to draw upon agencies outside the battalion when necessary. At the same time, all personnel, from army commanders to members of antitank platoons and rifle squads, learned the part prescribed for them in the organizational scheme.

Stability was desirable in Tables of Organization and Equipment, since to change them meant changes in methods of combat, tactical doctrine, training, mobilization objectives, procurement and assignment of manpower, and procurement and issue of equipment. Yet changes were frequently necessary. Organization had to be kept abreast of combat experience. Adoption of a new weapon, substitution of one weapon for another, transfer of weapons from one echelon to another, and modifications in tactical employment, as when an increase of infantry in proportion to tanks was demanded, likewise made necessary the readjustment of tables. Tables of different types of units were interlocking, since units were planned to supply each other's needs; hence change in one might send reverberations through several others. In addition, every table represented a compromise between conflicting desiderata, such as economy, self-sufficiency, fire power, mobility, and ease of supply. In every table something was sacrificed; hence there was a constant tendency to amendment. T/O&E's were inherently unstable. They were subject to a continuing process of review and revision.

Role of the Army Ground Forces

In March 1942 the Army Ground Forces took over from the Chiefs of Infantry, Cavalry, Field Artillery, and Coast Artillery (including antiaircraft), whose offices were suspended, the task of preparing Tables of Organization for units of these arms.[3] The War Department assigned this function to the Requirements Section of the AGF headquarters staff. For armored units the Chief of the Armored Force, who survived the changes of March 1942 with functions unchanged, remained responsible for organization. Since the Armored Force, formerly independent, now became a component of the Army Ground Forces, the commanding general of the Army Ground Forces obtained authority over armored organization and equipment; but this authority was not explicitly assigned by the War Department in Circular 59 and was at first less direct than in the case of the older arms. For units of the service branches assigned to the Army Ground Forces—engineer, signal, ordnance, quartermaster, medical, chemical, and military police—responsibility for Tables of Organization and Equipment was divided in March 1942 between the Army Ground Forces and the Services of Supply. In October 1942 these powers with respect to service units

[3] (1) Cir 59, WD, 2 Mar 43. (2) WD ltr SPXPC 320.2 (3–13–42) to CGs AGF, AAF, SOS, 31 Mar 42, sub: Policies Governing T/O&E's. 320.3/123.

of types assigned to the Ground Forces were concentrated in the commanding general of the Army Ground Forces.[4] With this change, and with the elimination of the Chief of the Armored Force in 1943 and the assimilation of armor to the status of the older arms, the headquarters of the Army Ground Forces obtained a uniform degree of control over the organization and equipment of all units designated as Ground Forces. The Requirements Section, Headquarters, Army Ground Forces, became the agency responsible for reviewing about 400 Tables of Organization and Equipment, assisted in practice by other sections of AGF headquarters, the schools of the arms, the Armored, Tank Destroyer, and Airborne Centers, the Antiaircraft Command, and the relevant branches of the Army Service Forces.[5]

Before March 1942 the War Department General Staff had been responsible for coordinating and harmonizing the tables prepared by the chiefs of the various arms and services, and for developing the organization of units of the combined arms—armies, corps, and divisions. These tasks were decentralized in 1942 by delegation to the Army Ground Forces, which, however, could not effectively plan the organization of armies, corps, and divisions until, in October 1942, control was obtained over the organization of service units within these commands. In general, the work of the Army Ground Forces in tactical organization represented an integration of certain functions of the old branch chiefs and a devolution of certain functions of the War Department General Staff.

The Army Ground Forces never had final authority over organization. Approval of the War Department General Staff continued to be required for all T/O&E's before publication by The Adjutant General, and for policies of organizing T/O units into armies and corps. Final authority could hardly repose elsewhere than in the War Department itself, since organization profoundly affected all stages of the military effort from procurement to combat. The Army Ground Forces developed, prepared, planned, reviewed, and recommended. In practice, with exceptions to be seen below, the recommendations of the Army Ground Forces were almost automatically accepted by the War Department. This was because the Army Ground Forces had the skilled personnel familiar with the details of organization—a personnel originating in 1942 in the physical transfer of individuals from the offices of the chiefs and from the War Depart-

---

[4] See below, pp. 288–89.

[5] (1) AGF memo for G–4 WD, 1 Dec 43, sub: T/E's. 320.3/674. (2) AGF memo (S) for G–3 WD, 24 Jan 44, sub: Standing Operating Procedure (SOP) for Processing TO&BA's. 320.3/103 (S). The Organization Division, Requirements Section, was headed by Col. Leonard H. Frasier, GSC.

ment General Staff—and because AGF personnel, before recommending changes in tables, made the necessary study of repercussions on the Troop Basis, the supply program, and the combat value of units.

The activities of the Army Ground Forces with respect to tactical organization can be divided for convenience into four successive periods.

The first lasted from March to about October 1942. It was characterized by the incompleteness of authority exercised by the commanding general of the Army Ground Forces, by piecemeal modification of the tables of certain units, chiefly in the direction of reduction of motor vehicles, and by an increasing realization of the need for economy.

The second period, extending roughly from October 1942 to October 1943, was a year of assiduous and systematic activity in which the Army Ground Forces reviewed the organization of armies, corps, divisions, and nondivisional units, clarified the mission and functions of each, and strove to obtain an economical organization, to the end that available men and equipment might be shaped into the largest possible number of units, and that each unit, after being laboriously shipped overseas, might deliver a maximum of combat power. In this period the headquarters of the Army Ground Forces assumed a strong leadership in matters of organization. It was during the second period that the shape and structure of forces used in World War II were to a large extent determined.

In the third period, extending from the end of 1943 into 1945, the organizational changes of the second period were put increasingly to the test of combat, chiefly in Europe. Initiative in matters of tactical organization passed from the Army Ground Forces to the theater commanders. The role of the Army Ground Forces consisted largely in analyzing, comparing, evaluating, and recommending action upon theater requests for increases or modifications in allowances of personnel and equipment.

The fourth period saw organizational changes incident to redeployment for a war concentrated in the Pacific. The changes proposed in this period, reflecting the experience acquired in the third, are described in the study in this volume entitled "Reorganizing for Redeployment."

In the first two periods the great bulk of ground combat forces remained in the United States awaiting commitment to battle. The combat experience of American forces was limited in scope, and confined to the special conditions of island, desert, and mountain warfare. Planning of tactical organization could be based only in small part on recent experience of United States forces. It therefore had to be determined largely from an analysis of foreign experience, intimate understanding of the United States Army, and interpretation of the more fundamental principles of military art.

Guiding Ideas of General McNair

In these circumstances it was of the utmost importance that in the formative period the Army Ground Forces was commanded by Lt. Gen. Lesley J. McNair, who was by experience and inclination an expert in tactical organization, certainly one of the foremost experts in the Army. He personally directed his staff on this subject, and the organization with which American ground forces entered combat in World War II was to a large extent the product of his mind.

General McNair's understanding of tactical organization, while drawn from many previous experiences and from study and recollection of World War I, was especially strengthened in the field exercises of 1937 and 1939, in which War Department plans for tactical reorganization were tested. From these exercises had come the triangular infantry division used by the United States in World War II. General McNair had been chief of staff of the division which had conducted the tests. These were perhaps the most searching and thorough tests ever made of so large a unit in the United States during peacetime. They were planned to be as realistic as conditions of peace and the lack of funds and of sufficient modern equipment permitted. General McNair had determined how the general questions set by the War Department should be broken down into specific problems for testing, how personnel, armament, and equipment should be apportioned for each problem, and how the problems should be umpired and the results appraised. Beginning with the fundamental study of the infantry rifle squad, an entire divisional organization was put together piece by piece. Matters on which alternative ideas were tested included the following: frontages and fire power per man and per unit; ammunition allowances; transportation capacities; motor columns; the requirement for artillery in proportion to infantry, with consideration of calibers, ranges, trajectories, and capacities for concentration; the echeloning of automatic rifles, machine guns, and mortars in the infantry regiment, battalion, company, and platoon; the personnel, time, and equipment needed for maintenance of weapons and vehicles; the time elapsed in transmission of orders from division headquarters to front-line units; the time elapsed in hauling ammunition and supplies to front-line units from the railhead; and the amount of service support to be incorporated in the division and the degree to which the division, in the interests of its own mobility and striking power, should depend on corps and army for supporting services and reinforcing weapons. Findings on these and other questions, in the form of concrete data and statistics, were embodied in an extensive report drafted by General McNair.[6] By no means all the recommendations in this report were adopted. The War Department, while reducing the old square division of 22,000 men to a triangular division totaling about 15,000, did not reduce to the strength of 10,275 recommended in the report. (See Table No. 1.)

General McNair carried over into his command of the Army Ground Forces not only the mass of knowledge acquired in the tests of 1937 and 1939 but also a rigorous sense of what was meant by fact as distinguished from theory or speculation, a tendency to deflate claims not based on full attention to detail, and a grasp of principles of organization developed by long reflection on the subject and by having seen the application of these principles in the field. He was peculiarly qualified to assimilate into a balanced judgment the fragmentary combat experience of American forces in 1942 and 1943, the experience of foreign armies so far as it was known, and the views of specialists under his own command. He attempted to keep in proper perspective the views of the specialist and of the man on the spot, believing both too much inclined to forget the larger team. Specialists, particularly in the newer fields such as aviation, armor, psychological warfare, psychiatry, morale-building, and the more elaborate forms of military intelligence, easily exaggerated the importance of their own contribution and were frequently impatient of criticism from outside their own circles. The evaluation and control of a multitude of specialties constituted one of the most difficult and important problems of World War II. The man on the spot, locally responsible for a particular mission, likewise tended to resist control, strive for self-sufficiency, and assure the success of his mission by gathering under his own command as large a proportion of the manpower and resources of the United States as possible. The theater commanders represented this tendency on the largest scale. With so many theaters it was impossible to give any one theater commander the freedom given to General Pershing in World War I. The evaluation and control of theater demands was therefore another major problem of World War II. General McNair always insisted that the only final test of military organization, as of training and equipment, was combat. One of his first steps was to request the War Department to obtain

---

[6] "Report of the Field Service Test of the Proposed Infantry Division," with appendices A–F, 21 Mar 38. Army War College Records, McNair Papers.

detailed reports from overseas on the adequacy of organization and equipment.[7] But he was not awed by commanders who had been in combat, believing that many decisions could best be made in the Zone of Interior, especially in 1942 and 1943, when only minor elements of the enemy ground forces were being engaged by American troops. He noted for the Requirements Section of his headquarters after his visit to Africa in April 1943:[8]

> I talked to General Patton about armored organization as much as the available time permitted. At first he was against a reorganization of the armored division . . . , but after a brief explanation of our proposals he seemed to go along quite wholeheartedly. I was impressed rather forcibly and generally with the fact that the people over there are fighting and have given only fleeting consideration to organization. Even though they have the prestige born of combat experience I certainly feel that their offhand and fragmentary views are not infallible.

By 1944, as will be seen, General McNair was more willing to yield to theater opinion.

General McNair's leading idea in tactical organization was a simple and definite one: to concentrate a maximum of men and materials in offensive striking units capable of destroying the enemy's capacity for resistance. The derivatives of this idea were many. One was to have a minimum of noncombat soldiers, to hold down nontactical overhead, and to make tactical staffs small and efficient. Headquarters companies, staffs, and administrative personnel should be kept small by elimination of unnecessary links in the chain of command and by reduction of paper work through the use of verbal orders. Combat units should be streamlined for quick, decisive action; they should have only such personnel and equipment as they require at all times. What a unit needed only occasionally should be held in a reserve pool under higher headquarters. Such pools not only kept personnel and equipment from idleness but also permitted rapid massing for concentrated use. Transport and special equipment of all kinds should be assigned sparingly and pooled where possible. Weapons and units primarily defensive in character should absorb as little as possible of the national resources. Special-type units and excessively specialized personnel, useful on certain occasions only, should be discouraged. Links in the chains of supply and administration should be cut; divisions and corps should be lightened, with their overhead machinery relegated to armies.

[7] Memo of Gen McNair for OPD, 18 Apr 42, sub: Improvement of Equip and Orgn, US Army. 475/518.

[8] AGF M/S (S), CG to Rqts, 21 May 43, sub: Proceedings of Harmon Bd. 319.1/13 (NATO) (S).

TABLE NO. 1

Organic Composition of the Infantry Division, 1936–45

(Aggregate Strengths; Principal Equipment)

UNIT	Approved for Field Test by Secretary of War 13 Aug 36	Recommended by Proposed Infantry Division after Field Test —Mar 38	T/O 70 and Allied Tables as Changed to 1 Jun 41	T/O 7 and Allied Tables, 1 Aug 42	Proposed by Army Ground Forces in Revised Tables, 1 Mar 43	T/O 7 and Allied Tables, 15 Jul 43	T/O 7 and Allied Tables, 24 Jan 45
Entire Division	13,552	10,275	15,245	15,514	13,412	14,253	14,037
Division Headquarters	61	66	102	169	133	158	166
Infantry	7,416	6,987	10,020	9,999	8,919	9,354	9,204
Regiment (three)	2,472	2,329	3,340	3,333	2,973	3,118	3,068
Hq. & Hq. Company	......	167	178	132	194	108	104
Band	......	......	29	29	......	......	......
Service Company	......	89	152	132	112	114	111
Antitank Company	......	......	185	169	117	118	114
Cannon Company	......	......	......	123	......	......	......
Battalion (three)	......	691	932	916	850	871	860
Hq. & Hq. Company	......	68	52	139	112	126	121
Heavy Weapons Company	......	104	211	183	162	166	160
Rifle Company (three)	......	173	223	198	192	193	193
Field Artillery	2,529	1,818	2,656	2,479	1,949	2,160	2,111
Hq. & Hq. Battery, Division Artillery	......	128	119	116	111	114	114
Band	......	......	29	28	......	......	......
Light Artillery Battalion (three)	......	404	584	576	460	509	497
Headquarters Battery	......	122	142	165	181	132	126
Service Battery	......	......	82	78	......	77	74
Firing Battery (three)	......	94	120	111	93	100	99
Medium Artillery Battalion	......	478	785	607	458	519	506
Headquarters Battery	......	127	142	158	164	115	112
Service Battery	......	......	95	89	......	77	76
Firing Battery (three)	......	117	134	120	98	109	106
Antitank Battery	......	......	146	......	......	......	......
Auxiliary Units	3,149	1,109	2,004	2,340	1,993	2,074	2,046
Reconnaissance Troop	210	......	147	201	153	155	149
Engineer Battalion	518	175	634	745	647	647	620

	I	II	III	IV	V	VI	VII
Medical Battalion	525	420	520	504	468	465	443
Quartermaster Company	244	197	312	344	152	193	186
Ordnance Company	105	160	.....	.....	147	147	141
Signal Company	203	.....	261	322	226	226	239
Military Police Platoon	.....	103	67	80	73	73	106
Division Headquarters Company	210	54	63	144	69	110	104
Band	29	.....	.....	.....	58	58	58
Miscellaneous	1,105	.....	.....	.....	.....	.....	.....
Attached Medical	388	285	423	515	406	494	497
Infantry Regiment (three)	285	.....	106	136	112	135	136
Division Artillery	.....	.....	83	76	53	57	57
Engineer Battalion	.....	.....	14	23	17	17	17
Quartermaster	.....	.....	8	8	.....	.....	.....
Special Troops	.....	.....	.....	.....	.....	15	15
Attached Chaplain	*9*	*10*	*11*	*12*	*12*	*13*	*13*
Principal Armament:							
Rifles, cal. 30	6,284	4,509	6,942	6,233	6,465	6,518	6,349
Automatic rifles, cal. 30	314	423	375	567	243	243	405
Machine guns, cal. 30	486	.....	179	147	189	157	211
Machine guns, cal. 50	56	81	113	133	224	236	237
Mortars, 60-mm	36	18	81	81	90	90	90
Mortars, 81-mm	36	.....	36	57	54	54	54
Antitank rocket launchers	.....	.....	.....	.....	504	557	558
Antitank guns, 37-mm	24	24	60	109	63	.....	.....
Antitank guns, 57-mm	.....	.....	8	.....	.....	57	57
Guns, 75-mm	36	36	.....	.....	.....	.....	.....
Howitzers, 75-mm	.....	.....	.....	18	.....	.....	.....
Howitzers, 75-mm, self-propelled	.....	.....	.....	36	.....	.....	.....
Howitzers, 105-mm	.....	12	36	6	54	54	54
Howitzers, 105-mm, self-propelled	.....	.....	.....	.....	.....	.....	.....
Howitzers, 155-mm	12	.....	12	12	12	12	12
Vehicles, all types (except boats and aircraft)	1,868	1,249	1,834	2,149	1,640	2,012	2,114

Sources: Col. I. "Tentative Tables of Organization Approved for Field Test by the Secretary of War," 13 August 1936. Copy No. 39 in McNair Papers, Record Room, Army War College.

Col. II. Appendix C to "Report of the Field Service Test of the Proposed Infantry Division," 21 March 1938. Copy in McNair Papers, Record Room, Army War College.

Col. III. "Tables of Organization of Infantry Units, with All Changes to 1 June 1941," published by the *Infantry Journal*, August, 1941.

Col. IV. Tables of Organization published by the War Department.

Col. V. Published Tables of Organization for component units of the division; unpublished consolidated Table of Organization for the division, mimeographed copy in Organization Division, Requirements Section, Headquarters, Army Ground Forces.

Cols. VI and VII. Tables of Organization published by the War Department.

These ideas were widely accepted. They were applications of the traditional principle of economy of force. Some of them, such as the emphasis on mobile warfare, the streamlining of the division, and the use of pools, had been accepted as basic by the War Department since 1935.[9] No one advocated waste, unwieldiness, or dispersion. Disagreement arose in the judgment of concrete cases. Characteristic of General McNair was the close attention he gave to the concrete and the strictness with which he defined, interpreted, and applied the principles which no one questioned in theory. In practice there were many obstacles to successful achievement of an economy of force. There was the disposition of every unit to demand additional men and equipment. There was the habit of "empire building," the tendency of an arm, service, or specialty to multiply its functions as if in an effort to win the war alone. There was a tendency, deeply rooted in American life, to encumber the military establishment with comforts and conveniences, machines and inventions, technicians and experts, specialized services, and complex agencies of control. Effects were cumulative; an increase in the number of dentists, for example, involved an increase of dental technicians; dentists and technicians had to be fed; dentists, technicians, and cooks had to be transported; dentists, technicians, cooks, and drivers required medical care; dentists, technicians, cooks, drivers, and doctors needed clothing; hence quartermasters had to be added; since all personnel required coordination, headquarters staffs would have to be enlarged; in the end a demand for still more dentists developed. General McNair resolutely set himself against such proliferation, which added nothing to the fighting strength of the Army.

Tactical Organization in March 1942

The accepted principles of organization were announced by the War Department in a directive of 31 March 1942.[10] To guide the three major commands in the drafting of Tables of Organization certain rules were laid down which came to be called the "Ground Rules," setting ceilings on overhead personnel

[9] (1) WD ltr AG 320.2 (11–4–35) Misc F–M, 5 Nov 35, sub: Reorgn of the Div and Higher Units. (2) Army War College, Rpt of Sp Committee, 2–1936–12, Vol I, 21 Dec 35, sub as above. (3) WD staff study, 30 Jul 36, sub: Initial Rpt of the Orgn Committee on Modernization of the Army with Sp Ref to the Inf Div. All in AWC Records, 52–72.

[10] WD ltr SPXPC 320.2 (3–13–42) to CGs AAF, AGF, SOS, 31 Mar 42, sub: Policies Governing T/O&BA's. 320.3/123. Reissued memo W 310–9–43, WD, 22 Mar 43, sub as above, and memo W 310–44, WD, 26 Jan 44, sub as above.

such as cooks, orderlies, mechanics, and chaplains' assistants, and encouraging other economies such as the substitution of trailers for trucks. Everything depended on the definition and enforcement of these rules by the major commands.

Large-unit organization in March 1942 embodied the outcome of the reforming ideas of the 1930's and of the establishment of the Armored Force in July 1940. The March directive enumerated six types of divisions: infantry, motorized, armored, airborne, mountain, and cavalry.

Infantry divisions were barely emerging from a tumult of reorganization. The main features of the new plan—triangular structure through elimination of the brigade, adaptation to conditions of open warfare, and use of motor transportation only—had been discussed in the Army since the early thirties. They had in fact been urged by General Pershing in 1920, tentatively endorsed by the War Department in 1935, and tested in the field in 1937 and 1939. Not until 1940, however, after the collapse of France, did these ideas crystallize in an approved Table of Organization. The Regular Army divisions were then physically reorganized. Not until after Pearl Harbor did it prove feasible to bring the National Guard divisions into conformity with the new system. The purely wartime divisions, which began to be activated in March 1942, followed the new pattern from the start.

The infantry division was stated by the War Department on 31 March 1942 to comprise approximately 15,500 men, to be "a general purpose organization intended for open warfare in theaters permitting the use of motor transport," and to have organically assigned to it a minimum of artillery and auxiliary elements, "on the assumption that the division is part of a larger force from which it can obtain prompt combat and logistical support." The division in normal employment presupposed corps troops and army troops. It used motor transport only. It had rid itself of the mixed horse and motor transport which complicated the problem of troop movement and supply and which still characterized the German infantry division. But it did not have transportation to move all personnel and equipment simultaneously.

The motorized division was an infantry division equipped to move all of its elements simultaneously by motor. It was designed for use in conjunction with armored divisions. No actual motorized divisions existed until April 1942, at which time the 6th, 7th, 8th, and 9th Infantry Divisions were converted to motorized divisions. The 4th and 90th Infantry Divisions were motorized shortly thereafter. Motorized divisions were planned at this time in a ratio of one motorized to two armored divisions. Their organic strength was over 16,000, and they were somewhat more liberally provided with auxiliary elements than the infantry division, "on the assumption that the division may operate independently for limited periods."

The armored division, introduced into the Army in September 1940, was undergoing reorganization under the auspices of the Armored Force in March 1942. In its new form it had a strength of almost 15,000 and included 390 tanks. Six armored divisions had been activated; there were expectations of having almost fifty. The armored division was strong in auxiliary elements, "on the assumption that the division may operate independently for long periods."

Airborne and mountain divisions in March 1942 existed only on paper. The airborne division had no Table of Organization. It was viewed as a task force to be formed for a particular mission by assigning air transportation to elements of a normal infantry division reinforced by parachute troops. The mountain division, for which a T/O had been developed, was stated to consist of three mountain regiments with appropriate support, using pack transportation and numbering about 15,000 men. Cavalry divisions, of which two were active in March 1942, preserved the old square or brigade formation but were small in size, totalling about 11,000 men. It was decided in May 1942 to maintain the cavalry divisions as horse units, extending mechanization in the cavalry only to the nondivisional regiments and squadrons and to the cavalry components of infantry and armored divisions.

It was the policy of the War Department to assign organically to the division only such forces as were needed for normal operations. The concept of normal operations varied for the several types of divisions. It was thought that the armored division might normally operate at a considerable distance from the mass of the forces, the motorized division somewhat less so, the infantry division least so. Hence what the armored or motorized division needed in the way of organic elements of maintenance, supply, road repair, and other functions was more than what the infantry division needed, since the infantry division could habitually draw support from corps and army. But even the armored division was in principle held to a minimum.

The policy of minimum organic assignment to the division resulted in the accumulation of a large number of nondivisional units. The more the division was streamlined, the more nondivisional support was required. The strength of nondivisional forces, solely of types required in the combat zone, was greater than the strength of all divisions combined. By the end of 1944 it was 1,541,667 as compared with 1,174,972 for divisions of all types.

In March 1942, nondivisional units were grouped at three levels—corps troops, army troops, and the GHQ reserve. Army and corps each had a normal quota of units. As the division had an organic content set forth in its Table of Organization, so the army and corps each had an organic content set forth in Troop Lists describing the "type" army and the "type" corps. As the T/O infantry division consisted organically of three infantry regiments plus division units of other arms and services, so the type corps consisted organically of three divisions plus specified corps troops, and the type army consisted organically of three corps plus specified army troops. Units not organic in division, corps, or army constituted the GHQ reserve. Such units, relatively few in number, were available for attachment as needed to armies, which in turn might attach them to corps or divisions.

The type army and type corps were like the division in having an organic structure. Their purpose, like that of the division, was to combine dissimilar elements into balanced wholes. Unlike the division they were used chiefly for planning, to facilitate the mobilization and training of balanced forces. It was understood that in actual operations armies and corps would consist of such forces as might be assigned or attached in the immediate situation.

In addition to the normal corps there existed the cavalry corps, provided for in the tactical doctrine of the Army but never activated in World War II, and the armored corps, introduced in 1940 and physically represented by the I and II Armored Corps in March 1942. The armored corps was not a type organization for planning; it was thought of as a combat force to control the operations of two or more armored divisions, together with such supporting troops as might be provided for specific missions. The idea of an armored army, put forward from time to time by the Armored Force, had never been approved by the War Department.

Changes made by the Army Ground Forces in tactical organization, from March 1942 to the close of the formative period at the end of 1943, will be considered in the following sections in some detail. By definition, organization implies mutual and simultaneous relationships, and it does not lend itself readily to verbal presentation. In whatever manner the subject is arranged, parts of it belonging together will be separated by many pages. The basic facts in a mass of complexities may be stated in advance.

The organization developed by the Army Ground Forces represented the impact of General McNair's most firmly held convictions upon principles already basically accepted by the War Department. The aim was to obtain flexibility and economy, which were essentially the same since flexibility meant freedom to use personnel and equipment where they would produce the most effective results. The trend may be described as away from the idea of the type force and toward the idea of the task force. In other words, it was away from the organic assignment of resources to large commands according to ready-made patterns, and toward variable or *ad hoc* assignment to commands tailor-made for specific missions. The tendency away from organic assignment was evident in the disappearance of the type army and the type corps, in the dissolution of brigades and nondivisional regiments, and in the reshaping of divisions and other T/O units according to organic minima redefined at lower levels. The tendency toward tailor-made commands, that is, task forces, was evident in the emphasis placed on the idea that armies and corps should consist of whatever troops were necessary for the mission, that the division would normally enter combat reinforced by attachment of nondivisional elements according to circumstances, and that actual fighting would be carried on, not so much by the T/O infantry regiment, for example, as by a combat team made up of the infantry regiment with attached artillery, engineers, and other elements. The emphasis on attachment, the virtual disappearance of organic troops from the corps and army, and the confinement of organic troops of the division to a strictly defined minimum made necessary extensive pools of nondivisional units. These nondivisional pools became in effect GHQ reserve troops; they functioned as army troops or corps troops when specifically allotted to an army or corps. Divisions likewise became in effect GHQ reserve, since they were no longer organic in corps but were assigned as needed. The whole Army became, so to speak, a GHQ reserve pool from which task forces could be formed—whether called by this name, like the Task Force "A" which sailed for North Africa in October 1942, or called more conventionally corps or armies.

II. The Tightening Pinch, March–October, 1942

Mobility versus Transportation

The advent of war and the need of conducting operations on the far side of oceans brought to light a paradox by no means new in military history, namely that armies may be immobilized by their own means of transportation. The quantity of motor vehicles provided for combat units in prewar planning, mainly with an eye to mobility under field conditions in the United States, greatly added to the requirements of units for ship space and hence reduced the number of units that could be sent overseas. The more vehicles were used overseas the more ship space was required for fuel, lubricants, spare parts, replacement vehicles, drivers, and repair crews, and the less was available for combat personnel, weapons, and ammunition.[1]

In March 1942 a plan was adopted to send thirty divisions to the United Kingdom for a cross-Channel operation in April 1943.[2] The Army Ground Forces on 2 April 1942 informed the War Department that forces would be available.[3] The bottleneck was shipping. The number of United States troops intended for the operation had to be reduced.[4] Army Ground Forces was informed that General Marshall desired "maximum practicable reduction of motor transport

---

[1] See (1) personal ltr of Gen McNair to Brig Gen G. R. Allin, 9 Jan 41. McNair Correspondence. (2) Memo of Gen McNair for G–3 WD, 31 Jan 42, sub: Substitution of Combat Engr Regt for Gen Serv Regt in Type Army. GHQ Records, 322.11/7–5.

[2] Memo (S) of the CofS USA for the President, undated, but earlier than 2 Apr 42, sub: Basis for Prep of Attached Outline Plan for Invasion of Western Europe. AGF Plans Sec file, 20/1 (Bolero) (S).

[3] AGF memo (S) for OPD, 2 Apr 42, sub: Opns Plan—Western Europe. AGF Plans Sec file, 20/2 (Bolero) (S).

[4] Memo (S) of Col Lemnitzer, AGF for CofS AGF, 1 May 42, sub: Meeting of Bolero Committee. AGF Plans Sec file, 20/6 (Bolero) (S).

and of administrative overhead in all types of units to save cargo space." [5] In addition, it was estimated in May 1942 that because of shortages of materials, notably rubber, the expected use of motor vehicles in 1942 and 1943 would be cut 20 to 33 percent.[6]

Until October 1942 the Army Ground Forces labored under handicaps in its efforts to economize. New Tables of Organization had been approved by the War Department immediately before the reorganization of 9 March.[7] These had enlarged the infantry division and added 219 motor vehicles by expanding infantry battalion headquarters detachments into headquarters companies and by adding a cannon company to each infantry regiment. The tables just decided upon could not immediately be reconsidered. Attempts to reduce motor transport therefore went forward without a corresponding review of personnel and equipment.[8] The Army Ground Forces lacked full control even over the infantry division, since the Services of Supply shared responsibility for service elements in the division, with the chief of each technical service feeling a primary interest in units of his own branch. It was the natural ambition of each chief to supply everything requested of him with unstinting hand. Tables of Basic Allowances (T/BA's) were not closely coordinated with Tables of Organization. The Services of Supply, while it referred T/O's of AGF service units to the Army Ground Forces, for a time settled T/BA's of such units without consultation.[9] Not until 1943 was the publication of Tables of Organization and Tables of Equipment combined in a single document.

Four days after the reorganization of the War Department the Services of Supply issued a directive authorizing automotive maintenance officers on the staffs of large AGF units—one for each infantry division, two for each armored and motorized division and for each corps, four for each army, and eleven for the headquarters of the Army Ground Forces.[10] Several hundred officers were thus required. General McNair immediately protested. Such measures, he said, "go far beyond any demonstrated necessities. They are establishing a military

---

[5] Memo (S) of Col Winn, AGF for Col Parks, AGF, 11 Jun 42, sub: Bolero Conference, 11 Jun 42, AGF Plans Sec file, 20/30 (Bolero) (S).

[6] WD memo (C) WDGS 451 (5–10–42) for CGs AAF, AGF, 12 May 42, sub: Reduction in Requirements of Motor Vehicles. 451/13 (C).

[7] Published tables dated 1 Apr 42.

[8] AGF M/S (S), Rqts to G–4, G–3, CG, 27 Oct 42. 320.2/383 (S).

[9] M/R on cpy of AGF memo for CG SOS, 17 Jun 42, sub: T/O & T/BA's for units of SOS with AGF. 320.3/348.

[10] WD ltr SP 320.2 (2–20–42) OP–A–M, 13 Mar 42, sub: Allotment of Offs as Assts to G–4. 320.2/1914.

and civilian overhead, and a mass of paper work and ritual, which I know from personal experience are unwarranted." [11] General Marshall, in a personal reply, explained that the directive, prepared before the reorganization, had not originated in the Services of Supply, but he insisted that a solution for the problem of motor maintenance must be found.[12] The incident illustrated two theories of administration. One way to have new duties performed was to provide additional personnel. General McNair's way, an outgrowth of his experience and personal habits, was to assign the new duties, especially new supervisory duties, to men already on the job. He believed that most people could work harder than they did.

General McNair, who as Chief of Staff of General Headquarters, U. S. Army, had had no direct authority over organization, turned his attention to it immediately on assuming command of the Army Ground Forces. He wrote to Lt. Gen. Brehon B. Somervell, Commanding General of the Services of Supply, as follows: [13]

The triangular division was initiated some five years ago with the primary purpose of streamlining the organization and rendering it more effective in combat. Since the reorganization there has been a steady succession of changes, all in the direction of returning to the cumbersome and impracticable organization of the old square division. It is felt mandatory that every proposal which increases overhead must be resisted if the division is to be effective in combat.

The strength of the triangular division, as suggested by a War Department committee in 1936, had been 13,552; as recommended in the report drafted by General McNair in 1938, 10,275; as adopted in 1940, 14,981; as amended in 1941, 15,245; and under the new 1942 tables, 15,514.[14]

Success in trimming down the division, before October 1942, was confined largely to reduction in the infantry and artillery components, the arms over which the Army Ground Forces had control; and, within these, to reductions of motor transport, since personnel and equipment other than vehicles were not considered. Truck transport was examined in microscopic detail.

General McNair believed that the current tables were extravagant in their provision of transportation for motor maintenance, that is, of vehicles with

[11] Memo of Gen McNair for CofS USA, 17 Mar 42, sub: WD ltr SP 320.2 (2–20–42) OP–A–M–13 Mar 42. 020/28. (Correct symbol for letter discussed in memo is SP 320.2 (2–2–42) OP–A–M–13 Mar 42.)

[12] Personal memo of CofS USA for Gen McNair, 31 Mar 42, sub as above. 320.2/1914.

[13] (1) Memo of Gen McNair for CG SOS, 29 May 42, sub: Coordinated Automotive Maint. 451/666. (2) Memo of Gen McNair for CG FF, 2 Feb 42, sub: FA Orgn, Triangular Div. GHQ Records, 320.2/37 (FA)–F.

[14] See Table No. 1, pp. 474–75.

accompanying tools used for the repair and upkeep of other vehicles. He wrote
to General Somervell on 21 April 1942: [15]

> We discussed this matter briefly the other day by telephone. As a result, you designated
> one of your officers to investigate the possibility of reducing the number of trucks devoted
> to motor maintenance. The particular case studied—the infantry regiment—was brought
> to a much more rational basis, in my judgment, but I still feel that too much transportation
> is devoted to motor maintenance. The matter can be corrected only by something approaching
> a major operation. Everyone appreciates that operations now definitely in view call for
> the maximum possible use of every available ship ton. Luxuries must go, and all echelons
> of the military organization must be imbued with the idea of functioning effectively with
> reduced personnel and transportation. Especially is it apparent that each unit tends to seek
> self-sufficiency, although this procedure multiplies overhead beyond all reason.
>
> When the present triangular division was under development, not more than five years
> ago, it was found, by over two million vehicle miles of field operations, that motor mainte-
> nance could be effected properly with a ½-ton pick-up truck of parts and tools for each 64
> vehicles to be maintained. The principal difficulty in maintenance then, as now, was that
> the personnel concerned, principally motor officers and motor mechanics, did not work
> hard enough. There was complaint about tools and parts, some of it justified, but the
> principal difficulty was as stated.
>
> Admittedly the maintenance vehicles advocated by the Quartermaster Corps for proper
> motor maintenance are utilized fully. There are very complete tool equipments and sur-
> prisingly abundant stocks of parts. This superabundant equipment no doubt is the result
> of insistent demands by the using arms, and the desire of the QM Corps to meet those
> demands. They amount substantially to providing on wheels something approaching the
> motor shop in garrison. Such a conception is unreal under the conditions we face. Parts
> are sufficiently available if carried in the division. The number needed in a company or
> similar unit is limited. Many tools are a great convenience, but few are indispensable.
> The best data that I know indicate a repair in about 700 vehicle miles during tactical
> operations, and in about 3,000 vehicle miles of road movement. Under these conditions, the
> number of repairs to be made is not too formidable. Preventive maintenance calls for hard
> work, rather than elaborate equipment and transportation.

AGF and SOS officers in conference settled upon 9 trucks and 3 trailers for maintenance of the 260 vehicles in the infantry regiment. This equaled about 1 ton of
maintenance per 13 vehicles maintained, a ratio considered liberal by General
McNair, contrasting as it did with the ratio of ½ ton per 64 vehicles established in
the tests of 1937.

---

[15] Memo of Gen McNair for CG SOS, 21 Apr 42, sub: Trans for Mtr Maint. 451/464.

The transportation required for ammunition supply of the infantry regiment was scrutinized with the same minuteness. General McNair took the view, familiar to railroad men, that wheeled vehicles should be kept in circulation, not used for storage. He noted for the Requirements Section of his staff: [16]

The transportation set-up in the new tables of organization is excessive because provision is made to *carry* with the regiment what apparently is intended to be an adequate supply for one day of active combat. This procedure results in a gross waste of transportation. There can be no question that provision must be made for an abundant supply of ammunition—even a super-abundant supply—since fire dominates the battlefield. However, the reserve of ammunition, or any other supply for that matter, is mainly in the *hauling* capacity of its motor transportation.

Hauling capacity was investigated thoroughly and practically under a variety of conditions during the test of the Proposed Infantry Division in 1937. Without going into details it may be stated generally that the number of $2\frac{1}{2}$-ton trucks required is one-twelfth of the total tonnage required. The basis of this rule is:

One-way hauling distance of 30 miles to the army supply point.

Period of hauling of 20 hours—the night preceding the engagement and during the engagement itself.

Dumps near combat positions, from which the units are supplied by weapons carriers or similar vehicles.

The test referred to above, together with certain war experience, has afforded reasonably reliable data as to the ammunition consumption of the several weapons in battle. While all weapons are not used throughout a battle it is impossible to foresee which weapons will be used; hence it is necessary to provide for all weapons alike, based on the maximum consumption by every weapon. Again, it is impossible to predict the duration of an action. It may be for a few hours only, or again it may be throughout daylight hours. In order to be on the safe side, the ammunition supply considered here will be *ten times* the maximum hourly consumption. Certainly there can be no question that such a basis is superabundant—even extravagant.

Detailed computations followed, showing that about a third of the ammunition required in a day's combat by a battalion could be carried as the normal load of battalion vehicles, and that the remaining two-thirds could be hauled from supply points immediately before and during battle by battalion vehicles and regimental service trucks. General McNair estimated that twenty-five trucks could be saved from the current allotment to the infantry regiment.

Savings accomplished in April and May 1942 consisted mainly in replacement of $\frac{3}{4}$-ton trucks in the infantry by $\frac{1}{4}$-ton trucks ("jeeps") and $\frac{1}{4}$-ton trailers, on the basis of one jeep and trailer for each $\frac{3}{4}$-ton truck replaced;

[16] AGF M/S, CG to Rqts, — Apr 42. AGF Orgn Div, Rqts Sec files.

and in drastic reduction of 2½-ton trucks and 1-ton trailers in the artillery, with only partial replacement by trucks and trailers of lighter types.[17] Roughly a quarter of the 2½-ton trucks were removed from field artillery units, divisional and nondivisional. The infantry reductions saved about 6,500 pounds of rubber and 15,360 cubic feet of ship space for each regiment.[18] But the saving was offset by the recent enlargement of battalion headquarters units and addition of cannon companies to the infantry regiments. With all the effort to economize, little net progress had been made.[19]

Crucial Decisions: September–October 1942

In the later months of 1942 decisions were made which vitally affected the subsequent course of the war and brought into view more clearly than ever the need for economy in the Ground Forces. In part because of the shortage of cargo space, plans for a cross-Channel invasion of Europe were postponed in the summer of 1942. Air and Service Forces, greatly expanded, filled most of the outgoing ship space in the following year. Such restricted ground combat operations as were launched in 1942 emphasized the value of compactness in Ground Force organization. Task Force "A," dispatched from the United States to North Africa in October, was obliged to leave some of its heavy equipment behind. Action initiated in the Southwest Pacific put an unprecedented strain on shipping facilities in proportion to the number of combat troops maintained in the theater. No division left the American continent during the five months beginning with November 1942. Only seven divisions left during the ten months beginning with November 1942. No infantry or armored division formed after Pearl Harbor left the United States until December 1943—two years after the declaration of war.

On 28 September 1942 General Marshall again raised with General McNair the question of economizing motor vehicles as a means of conserving rubber and ship space.[20] "I have felt for a year or more," he wrote, "that our figures as to

[17] See published T/O's of 1 Apr 42 with changes.

[18] Incl 1 to AGF memo (S) for DCofS USA, 10 May 42, sub: Substitution of Trailers for Trucks in T/BA's. 400.34/9 (S).

[19] (1) AGF M/S (C), CG to G–4, 29 Sep 42. 451/66 (C). (2) Memo (S) of Gen McNair for OPD, 9 Jun 42, sub: Reduction of Trans and Substitution of Light for Heavy Vehicles in Bolero. 451/28 (S).

[20] Memo (C) WDCSA 451 (9–28–42) of CofS USA for Gen McNair, 28 Sep 42, sub not given. 451/66 (C).

divisional transportation were extravagant, that they represented what a division commander asked for rather than meeting the problem on the basis of over-all requirements. I might say right here that if we gave each theater commander what he asks for we would have only one theater and all the rest would have to be evacuated for lack of means." On 2 October the War Department directed the three major commands to review their Tables of Organization, eliminating unnecessary vehicles and excess noncombatant personnel. A cut of 20 percent in motor vehicles and of 15 percent in personnel was indicated as a goal.[21]

Replying to General Marshall on 8 October, General McNair noted the unfairness of levying a flat percentage reduction, since some units had already been cut. Broadening the issue of motor transport into the larger issue of tactical organization, he wrote as follows: [22]

The present regrettable excess of motor transportation is due to chiefs of arms and services seeking heavily and thinking narrowly, to field commanders who seek to make their units too self-contained, and to an over-indulgent War Department. It is futile now to exhort the same agencies as brought about the existing condition. It is believed that the remedy is one or a group of no-men empowered to:

a. Review organization and eliminate those elements—particularly headquarters and auxiliary and service units—which do not pay their way definitely in combat effectiveness. One example: there are too many echelons of reconnaissance.

b. Cut the transportation of a given organization to a minimum by prescribing the most economical type of vehicle, substituting trailers for motor vehicles, and eliminating vehicles which are not essential. One example: numerous army units need not move simultaneously, but can move by echelon.

Such a person or group will cause loud complaints from the field, and conceivably can go too far in its efforts to economize in transportation. Nevertheless, drastic countermeasures are necessary to correct present conditions, and the War Department must empower such an agency to go into all kinds of units, and back up its findings.

A reply from G–3, WDGS, to this recommendation revealed that the main hope of economy in the Army was the Army Ground Forces:[23]

Since the reorganization of the War Department, the G–3 Division has not had an organization section adequate in either numbers or experience to give Tables of Organiza-

---

[21] WD ltr (S) AG 400 (9–30–42) OB–S–C to CGs AGF, AAF, SOS, 2 Oct 42, sub: Review of Orgn and Equip Reqmts. 320.2/383 (S).

[22] Memo (C) of Gen McNair for CofS USA, 8 Oct 42, sub: Excessive Number of Mtr Vehicles. 451/66 (C).

[23] WD memo (S) WDGCT (10–8–42) for CG AGF, 30 Oct 42, sub as above. 451/66 (C).

tion the careful and detailed analysis necessary for the judicious elimination of unnecessary equipment and individuals.

As a result, its efforts in this direction are of necessity confined to general directives exhorting the major commands to review their Tables of Organization. . . . This general approach is admittedly inadequate. The three major commands, and in particular the Army Ground Forces, must be depended upon to furnish the group of "No-Men" empowered to ruthlessly and, if necessary, arbitrarily eliminate nonessential elements and equipment. G–3 will stand squarely behind your efforts to this end.

Existing Tables of Organization were apparently designed with little appreciation of the fact that every soldier and piece of equipment must be moved by ship to a combat zone.

In brief, General McNair's request for a strong central agency was deemed impossible to fulfill at this time; he must be his own "No-Man."

The War Department strengthened General McNair's hand by granting him full authority over service units in the Army Ground Forces.[24] All service units (other than those pertaining exclusively to the Air Forces) were divided between the Army Ground Forces and the Services of Supply for activation and training and for determination of organization and equipment.[25] Those intended for the combat zone were assigned to the Army Ground Forces. "This will permit you to control motor equipment," wrote General Marshall.[26] "On this basis," observed General McNair to his staff, "we are being handed the job of placing the organic transportation of the Army on a rational basis, which it is not at present."[27]

A Reduction Board was established on 7 November 1942 at AGF headquarters, composed of one officer each from the Requirements, G–3, and G–4 sections of the staff.[28] Its mission was to reduce Tables of Organization of AGF units as desired by the War Department.

The need of streamlining Tables of Organization was driven home by other policies adopted by the War Department in September and October 1942. With the postponement of plans for an early ground invasion of Europe it was decided to build up the air offensive at once. Plans were laid to place an air force of 1 million men overseas by the end of 1943. The number of ground troops to be

---

[24] (1) Memo of Gen Paul for CofS AGF, 18 Sep 42. 337/29. (2) AR 310–60, 12 Oct 42.

[25] AGF memo (with attached papers) for CG SOS, 24 Oct 42, sub: T/O&E's for SOS Units. 320.3/507.

[26] Memo (S) of Gen Marshall for Gen McNair, 21 Oct 42, sub: Reduction in Transportation. 320.2/383 (S).

[27] AGF M/S (S), CG to G–4, Rqts, 23 Oct 42. 320.2/383 (S).

[28] The Board was composed of Col. J. L. Whitelaw, Lt. Col. W. J. Eyerly, Lt. Col. A. D. MacLean. It was dissolved 23 June 1943. See 334/3 (R).

shipped in this period depended on the availability of remaining shipping.[29] It became necessary also to reduce the procurement program for 1943, which in its original form exceeded the estimated productive capacity of the United States. In view of the strategic decision to postpone the employment of ground troops, the planned procurement of AGF equipment for 1943 was cut 21 percent.[30] Procurement of heavy artillery, tanks, mortars, and antiaircraft and antitank guns was revised downward. On 25 October 1942, in connection with mobilization plans for the coming year, the War Department notified the Army Ground Forces that [31]

shipping considerations may dictate a considerable change in our strategic concept with a consequent change in the basic structure of our Army. Since from the shipping capabilities indicated above, it appears that early employment of a mass Army, which must be transported by water, is not practicable, it follows that the trend must be toward light, easily transportable units. . . . Recent indications are that a further expansion of the Air Forces may be expected which not only will reduce the number of men available for the ground forces but will complicate, if not curtail, the procurement of heavy equipment for other than the Air Forces.

Fourteen divisions were dropped from the mobilization program for 1943. Only 100 divisions were now projected for 1943. Hopes of adding more in 1944 never materialized. With the number of units in prospect diminishing, it was clear that each unit must carry a maximum of effective force.

[29] WD memo (S) WDGCT 320.2 Gen (10–25–42) for CGs of AGF, SOS, 25 Oct 42, sub: Troop Basis 1943. 320.2/5 (TB 43) (S). (2) AGF M/S (S), DCofS to staff sections, 26 Oct 42. AGF Plans Sec file 185 (TB 42) (S).

[30] (1) Annex A to memo (S) JCS 134/3, 26 Nov 42, sub: Rpt of Joint Staff Planners. 040/8 (Joint Chiefs) (S). (2) See also "Ground Forces in the Army, December 1941–April 1945: a Statistical Study," "Mobilization of the Ground Army," and "Organization and Training of New Ground Combat Elements," in this volume.

[31] WD memo (S) WDGCT 320.2 Gen (10–25–42) for CGs AGF, SOS, 25 Oct 42, sub: TB 1943. 320.2/5 (TB 43) (S).

III. The Period of Economy
October 1942 – October 1943

Although the strength of American armed forces in World War II reached approximately 12,350,000, the strength of combat units of the Army Ground Forces, including combat engineer and signal troops, never exceeded 2,300,000, and the strength of all ground units intended for the combat zones, including close-support services, never exceeded 2,700,000.[1]

There were conceivably two ways in which the headquarters of the Army Ground Forces might have sought to increase the combat strength of the ground army. One would have been to protest against ceilings set by the War Department, to demand with insistence that men and materials be furnished more liberally. General McNair, while he repeatedly recommended increased authorizations for combatant ground troops, was not one to take issue indefinitely with the decisions of higher authority. In any case more men or materials would have been difficult to obtain, so enormous were the calls of the Air Forces, the Service Forces, and the Navy upon the national stock of manpower and productive facilities, to which must be added the requirements of foreign powers for equipment produced in the United States. Until 1944, the requirements of the Ground Forces did not enjoy a high relative priority.

The other way was to organize men and materials, in the quantity provided, in such a manner as to produce a maximum of fighting power. It was the method of economy, entirely congenial to General McNair. Economy, properly understood, does not mean getting along with the least possible but getting the most out of what one has—not a minimizing of effort, but a maximizing of results. General McNair hoped, by reducing the size of units, to make it possible to mobilize and ship a large number of units. He hoped also, by pooling and by flexible organization, to make every unit available for maximum employment at all times.

The need of drastic economy was not usually clear to theater commanders,

[1] See "Ground Forces in the Army, December 1941–April 1945: a Statistical Study," and "Mobilization of the Ground Army," in this volume. As noted in the latter, the figure 2,700,000 does not include all the men trained for ground combat. In World War I, according to the Report of the Superior Board on Organization and Tactics, AEF, 1 July 1919, 3,000,000 U. S. troops were scheduled to be in France early in 1919, of which 640,000 were to be SOS troops, leaving 2,360,000 combat-zone troops.

who could not fully understand that the bottom of the barrel was in sight, at least for practical purposes, as far as combatant ground troops were concerned. Nor was General McNair's sense of urgency in the matter always fully shared by his subordinate commanders in the field or by officers of the War Department General Staff. By the close of 1942 it was evident to General McNair that every man, weapon, and ship-ton made available to the Ground Forces must be used to the utmost, at whatever strain to individuals concerned, and that economy of ground forces was vital to winning the war, insofar as large ground operations by American troops might be essential to victory. How far this might be was not clear in advance even to officers of the Army Ground Forces, but it was the business of the Army Ground Forces to assume that large-scale ground combat would develop.

The twin aspects of economy were streamlining and pooling. They were phases of the same organizational process. To streamline a unit meant to limit it organically to what it needed always, placing in pools what it needed only occasionally. A pool, in the sense here meant, was a mass of units of similar type kept under control of a higher headquarters for the reinforcement or servicing of lower commands, but not assigned to lower commands permanently and organically. Pooling occurred at all levels, from the GHQ reserve pools which reinforced armies down through army pools, corps pools, and division pools to the company pool, which, in the infantry, provided mortars and machine guns to reinforce rifle platoons. Like streamlining, pooling was a means of dealing with the overwhelming variety and specialization of equipment. It was also a corrective to standardization, providing flexibility to an army made up of standard parts. When reinforced from pools, a standard unit with a fixed Table of Organization could be shaped into the task force required in a particular situation.

One reason for pooling, as for streamlining, was wide fluctuation in requirements from day to day. No unit was organically equipped to meet peak loads. Any unit which habitually carried enough bridging equipment to cross the most broken terrain, or enough truck transport to meet rare demands for strategic movement, or enough medical and ordnance personnel to deal with the human and mechanical casualties suffered on days of intensive combat, would not only be wasteful of the national resources but so loaded down with usually unwanted appurtenances as to be disqualified to perform its normal role. Such a unit was streamlined by removal of bridging equipment, trucks, doctors, and repair men not needed normally; and those needed to meet peak loads were concentrated in pools.

Another basis for pooling was difference in the potential frontage of weapons, with the consequent possibility of massing fires. For example, 60-mm. mortars could cover more frontage than any single rifle platoon, and were therefore pooled in a weapons platoon of the rifle company, by which their fires could be shifted, distributed, or concentrated from the front of one rifle platoon to another. Similarly 81-mm. mortars and heavy machine guns were pooled in the battalion, antitank guns in the regiment, field artillery in division artillery. The longest-range artillery, which could cover more frontage than was normal for a division and hence be concentrated from various directions to support a division making a major effort, was organized in nondivisional units under corps or army control.

Differences in mobility produced the same effect. A mechanized cavalry squadron performing distant reconnaissance, which could cover a wider front than that of an infantry division, would be too restrictively employed if controlled by a division commander, and was therefore assigned to corps. Tanks, tank destroyers, and mobile antiaircraft artillery were capable of rapid concentration at any point along a wide front. They also lent themselves to employment in mass attack. General McNair therefore opposed assigning them organically to divisions. The extreme application of the same principle was in aviation, which, as the most mobile of all weapons, with a potential "frontage" extending far in all directions, was not commanded organically by even the highest ground commanders.

Units whose mobility differed on the side of slowness likewise required separate organization. Supply depots with supplies laid out, evacuation hospitals filled with patients, heavy maintenance companies surrounded by disassembled equipment, were temporarily immobile, though operating close to combat troops or even located within division areas. They were organized nondivisionally so that the division, if opportunity presented itself, could move forward freely without them. In this case higher headquarters, drawing on its pools, sent forward with the advancing division new depots, new hospitals, and new maintenance units temporarily in a mobile condition, leaving the old ones to clear themselves at leisure of the stockpiles, wounded men, and repair work which temporarily held them back.

To summarize, diversity in time and space—variations of daily need and differences in range and mobility—underlay the decision in each case as to where an item should be organically assigned. A unit was streamlined when it had no elements (personnel, weapons, or vehicles) not needed continually, no elements not primarily useful against its normal objective, no elements so slow-moving as to impair its mobility, or so fast-moving as to be frequently usable elsewhere. Pools existed to make these disparate elements available when and where they could most profitably be employed. The advantages of streamlining and pooling were economy, mobility, flexibility, and the capacity for massed employment. The disadvantage was in the dependency of commanders of streamlined units, who were obliged to call for support, in all but the most commonplace situations, on higher commanders who might not always be able to provide it. Another disadvantage was that units only temporarily associated found it difficult to develop into smoothly functioning teams. There was there-fore much disagreement on many particulars of organization; nor was it possible, with difficulties so fundamental, to find a permanent solution which all would accept. General McNair judged, in the circumstances of 1942 and 1943, that the need of economy and flexibility was paramount.

While pooling occurred at all levels, it was especially significant in the separation of nondivisional units from divisions, since the division was the primary unit of large-scale combat. In 1920 General Pershing had recommended extensive pooling under corps and army to streamline the division.[2] To obtain a division suited for open warfare, the War Department in 1936 laid down the principle that mechanized forces, motor transport, bands, reserves of supplies and ammunition, replacements, reinforcing artillery, engineers, and medical and quartermaster personnel should be pooled.[3] General McNair, and the Reduction Board working under his supervision, stood directly in this tradition.

Pooling: the Critical Cases—Tank, Tank Destroyer, and Antiaircraft Artillery

Over pooling in principle there was little or no disagreement. Differences of opinion arose over particular cases. The most controversial of these concerned tanks, tank destroyers, and antiaircraft artillery.

---

[2] 1st ind, Gen J. J. Pershing to TAG, 16 Jun 20, sub: Rpt of the Superior Bd on Orgn and Tactics, AEF. AWC Library, UA 10 U3 1919.

[3] WD staff study, 30 Jul 36, sub: Initial Rpt of the Orgn Committee on Modernization of the Orgn of the Army. AWC Records, 52–72.

555949 O-61—21

These highly mobile weapons were physically capable of assembly in large masses for a single assault, or of dispersion in close support of many small operations. It was desirable to develop a command organization capable of using such physical mobility to advantage, capable, that is, of alternately gathering together or spreading apart large quantities of tanks, tank destroyers, and antiaircraft artillery. Not only mobility but also the specialized character of these weapons called for a flexible organization. Tanks were of limited value in certain types of terrain, indispensable in others. Antiaircraft guns were useful where enemy aviation was strong, less necessary where friendly aviation was superior. It was desirable to have a command organization that could concentrate weapons in places or situations where their characteristics could be most fully exploited.

These weapons were therefore not assigned organically to divisions, with the major exception that the armored division of course had tanks, and the minor exception that the airborne division possessed a small antiaircraft battalion. The infantry division had organically no tank battalion, no tank destroyer battalion, and no antiaircraft battalion. The armored division had organically no tank destroyer or antiaircraft battalion. Both had antitank and antiair weapons of lighter types. But all tank destroyers, all antiaircraft guns except the simple .50-caliber machine gun, and all tanks not in armored divisions or mechanized cavalry were pooled in nondivisional battalions. These battalions were designed for attachment to divisions as needed.

Demand for the organic inclusion of tanks in the infantry division hardly arose until 1944. Pooling of mechanized forces was a collateral doctrine in the development of the triangular division in the 1930's; after the German victories in 1939 and 1940, and the formation of armored divisions and of the Armored Force in the United States in 1940, the idea of the tank as an auxiliary to infantry received a further setback. It was planned to attach tank battalions to infantry divisions when needed. Fewer tank battalions were formed for this purpose than were desired by the Army Ground Forces. But it was felt generally that infantry would not need tanks and that tanks should be held apart for massed armored action where possible. Use of tanks against enemy tanks was not favored. Against small-scale use of tanks by the enemy, all troops had organic antitank weapons. Against enemy tanks assembled in large numbers, the intention in 1942 was to rush tank destroyers to the threatened spot. Friendly tanks would thus be kept free for action against targets vulnerable to armor. This question did not become controversial generally until 1944.

Strong demands were made in 1942 and 1943 for the organic inclusion of tank destroyers and antiaircraft artillery in both infantry and armored divisions. General McNair resisted these demands for two reasons. First, experience indicated that the most dangerous enemy air or tank attack would occur in massed formations, against which it was impossible for every division to have individual protection, and which must be met by masses of antitank and antiaircraft artillery held in mobile pools. Second, the loading of the division with defensive "anti" weapons went counter to General McNair's desire to encourage aggressive tactics and psychology in the divisions and to avoid diversion of resources to the production of mere countermeasures. These reasons were the stronger in 1942 and 1943, since tank destroyers and antiaircraft guns had not yet developed a "secondary mission" as general-purpose artillery.

In May 1942 the Under Secretary of War urged organic assignment of antiaircraft artillery to divisions. Not convinced by General McNair's explanations, he applied to the Secretary, who requested from General McNair a statement of his views. General McNair gave his reasons, concluding that existing policy was only a starting point pending the lessons to be gained from combat.[4] The Secretary accepted this explanation.

Among the numerous officers who believed that the division required stronger antiair and antitank protection, some of the most important were armored officers, and among these a leading figure was Lt. Gen. Jacob L. Devers, then Chief of the Armored Force. General Devers questioned the length to which the pooling principle was carried. He was not simply making a plea for his specialty but advancing arguments of general application. He held that occasional attachment of nonorganic units to divisions would produce poor combined training and poor battlefield teamwork, and that it was a doubtful way of achieving either unity of command or economy of force. He wrote to General Marshall:[5]

Economy of force is not gained by having a lot of units in a reserve pool where they train individually, knowing little or nothing of the units they are going to fight with. It is

[4] (1) Memo (S) of USW for CG AGF, 18 May 42, sub: AA Protection for Inf Divs. 321/78 (CAC) (S). (2) Memos (S) of Gen McNair for SW 13 May and 29 Jul 42, sub not given. 321/78 (CAC) (S). See also AGF memo (C) for G-3 WD, 5 Nov 42, sub: AA Defense. 320.2/12 (AA) (C).

[5] Memo (C) of Gen J. L. Devers for CofS USA, 1 Nov 42, sub: Gen McNair's and Col Feller's Comments. 354.2/8 (Desert) (C).

much better to make them a part of a division or corps, even to the wearing of the same shoulder patch. If they are needed elsewhere in an emergency, they can be withdrawn easily from the division or corps and attached where they are needed. Economy of force and unity of command go together. You get little of either if you get a lot of attached units at the last moment. Team play comes only with practice.

General Devers, after a trip to North Africa, recommended in February 1943 that tank destroyer and antiaircraft equipment not only be organic in the division but also be assigned as far down as the battalion.[6]

The Secretary of War again called on General McNair for comment. At the same time, and independently, General McNair's own G–3, Brig. Gen. John M. Lentz, noted in a communication to General McNair: "I have come to believe that TD and AA equipment should be organic in divisions. The concept of attachment is sounder, but its effect has been absence of combined training." [7]

General McNair adhered to his position, writing to the Secretary as follows:[8]

General Devers raises the issue of the number and organic set-up of (1) AA guns (2) AT guns. Equally logically and pertinently he might have raised similar questions with reference to (1) GHQ tank battalions, (2) Air Base defense units, (3) Command post and train defense units.

All these items involve the basic question of whether we are building an offensive or a defensive army—whether we are going to invest our military substance in security to the last detail or in elements which can be used to defeat the enemy's armed forces.

After noting that General Devers' proposals would require 24,000 .50-caliber antiaircraft guns and 7,200 75-mm. antitank guns in addition to those provided under existing arrangements, he continued:

Our limited manpower and production facilities can be utilized to better advantage.

Having decided on the total resources to be devoted to these defensive elements there is the added question whether these resources are to be dispersed in driblets throughout our forces, or whether they are to be organized in mobile masses which can be concentrated at the decisive point under the principle of the economy of force. General Devers and his group obviously are dispersionists of the first water; I take the opposite view, believing that the artful concentration of forces at the vital point is the first essential in tactics. . . .

It goes without saying that massed guns can be dispersed either partly or wholly if desired, but guns dispersed organically cannot be massed.

The War Department supported General McNair.

[6] Rpt (S) of the mission headed by Lt Gen Jacob L. Devers to examine the problems of armored force units in the European Theater of Operations. Undated (Feb 43). 319.1/32 (Foreign Observers) (S).

[7] AGF M/S (TS), G–3 to Sec GS, 16 Feb 43. 400/4 (TS).

[8] Memo (TS) of Gen McNair for SW, 17 Feb 43, sub: Gen Devers' Rpt of His Observations Overseas. 400/4 (TS).

The question arose in different form in May 1943, when the Army Service Forces proposed changes in War Department policy on the arming of service units. Over four times as many .50-caliber machine guns as were scheduled were recommended for antiaircraft protection for installation on trucks; and 3-inch antitank cannon were proposed both for stationary depots and for truck convoys.[9] The Army Ground Forces, in a memorandum to the Army Service Forces in June 1943, pointed out that 288,134 additional .50-caliber machine guns would be required by the end of 1943 to carry out these recommendations, although only 81,683 were expected to be available by that date for combat and service units combined. Some 50,000 additional 3-inch guns would be required. The memorandum stated:[10]

At the present time the greater portion of our national resources is being used to gain air superiority. We are engaged also in building an army for offensive action, not defensive. . . . Any additions of personnel, armament or equipment for purely defensive measures must be held to the bare minimum. . . .

A hostile armored threat will be countered by massing our antitank guns at the threatened point, not by dissipating our 3-inch self-propelled antitank guns by organic assignment to service units.

The War Department continued to support General McNair.[11] The principle of pooling antiaircraft and antitank weapons was confirmed.

Streamlining: Work of the AGF Reduction Board

Streamlining of units, the obverse of pooling, was accomplished through the work of the Reduction Board created at the headquarters of the Army Ground Forces in answer to the War Department directive of 2 October 1942 calling for downward revision of Tables of Organization. The Board constituted the committee of "No-Men" desired by General McNair. It aimed to effectuate the cut of 20 percent in motor vehicles and 15 percent in personnel, set as a goal by the War Department, without lessening the combat strength of any unit or upsetting the doctrine of its tactical employment. In this task, which required

---

[9] (1) WD memo 700–9–43, 11 Feb 43, sub: Armament of Serv Trs. AGO Records. (2) Memo (S) SPOPI 470 (5–1–43) for CGs AGF, AAF, 8 May 43, sub: Armament of Serv Units. 470/16 (S).

[10] AGF memo (S) for CG ASF, 15 Jun 43, sub as above. 470/16 (S).

[11] WD memo 310–44, 23 Feb 44, restates WD memo 700–9–43, 11 Feb 43.

exact knowledge of every item and every individual in unit tables, the Board was directed and assisted by General McNair, who scrutinized every proposal of the Board down to the last jeep and the last mechanic, frequently saying "No" to his own "No-Men."

Reductions were governed by the AGF "Ground Rules," which were those set by the War Department on 31 March 1942 with certain exceptions and clarifications. The proportion of orderlies to officers was slashed; cook's helpers were eliminated where chauffeurs could help in kitchens; chauffeurs (also called light truck drivers) were to receive additional duties where possible. All "luxury" items were ruled out. Tents were withdrawn from company headquarters. Companies were limited to one portable typewriter. No chairs, tables, or safes were provided to headquarters below the division. No watches were issued to officers. Transportation was allotted for specified personnel and equipment only, with no reserve vehicles in the unit. Ammunition vehicles were provided only as necessary to haul from supply points established by higher echelons. More use of trailers was prescribed. Closely similar units were to be combined into single types. Elements whose only function was to make a unit more self-sufficient in security or supply were prohibited. But no offensive weapons were to be removed from units, and proper organization was to be developed for new weapons such as the antitank rocket launcher ("bazooka") then being issued.[12]

In the eight months of its life, from 7 November 1942 to June 1943, the Reduction Board reviewed all AGF units with a handful of exceptions, methodically squeezing out the "fat," that is, items not allowed by the Ground Rules, or considered nonessential after clarification of the mission of the unit and in view of the support provided in pools.[13] Cuts were not applied piecemeal or in a negative mood. The whole theory of army and corps organization, and hence of pooling and of inter-unit support, was undergoing constructive revision at the headquarters of the Army Ground Forces at the same time. Each unit was reshaped with an eye to its place within corps or army.

The Board found that, while basic organization was sound, there had been "many variations between tables in the men and equipment considered necessary to do a standard job," with a general tendency "to build up our

---

[12] Cpy of AGF Ground Rules in AGF Orgn Div, Rqts Sec file; also attached to AGF ltrs (C) to Armd F and TDC, 12 Nov 42, sub: Reduction of Pers and Vehicles. 320.2/340 (C).

[13] Memo of Col W. J. Eyerly for CG AGF, 26 May 43, sub: Status Rpt of the Reduction Bd. (Hereafter referred to as Red Bd.) 334/8 (AGF).

organization around a luxurious concept of operations," and a tendency "to assign single duties to personnel and equipment and thus compartmentalize personnel and equipment within sections and platoons of organizations," a procedure which led directly to unnecessary duplication.[14] The Board assumed that no unit smaller than the field army could generally be self-sufficient and that T/O units would be made sufficient for particular missions through attachments. To facilitate attachment, and as part of the army and corps reorganization, practically all nondivisional troops were placed under new Tables of Organization, with regimental and brigade tables abolished, new tables for group and other headquarters devised, and tables for separate (detachable) battalions and companies provided.

In general, the Board effected the desired cut of 15 percent in personnel and 20 percent in equipment. The tank destroyer battalion, for example, was reduced in aggregate strength from 898 to 673, and in 1/4-ton trucks from 82 to 34.

The economies proposed by the Army Ground Forces produced the "loud complaints from the field" which General McNair had predicted. Although G–3, WDGS, had promised to "stand squarely behind your efforts to this end" and attempted to do so, the proposals of the Army Ground Forces were in fact subjected to long discussion and eventual compromise. New T/O&E's were finally issued for most AGF units in July 1943. They represented for some of the most important units an upward adjustment of General McNair's recommendations.

[14] AGF M/S, Red Bd to CofS, 8 Feb 43. AGF Orgn Div, Rqts Sec, 320.30 (Red Bd).

IV. The Infantry Division

Readjustments in the infantry division in 1942 and 1943 constituted a shrinking process, not a reorganization. The conception of the division embodied in the reforms of the thirties remained basically unaltered, namely, that the division should be a compact offensive force, carrying a minimum of defensive weapons, streamlined for open warfare, and backed up by units of other types in corps and army. The infantry division was the fundamental permanent combined-arms team, intended to have the right amount of organic artillery and auxiliary elements to enable its infantry riflemen to move forward against average resistance. General McNair hoped to emphasize and clarify this conception by paring away the growth which tended to obscure it. His views were formulated in a set of Tables of Organization submitted to the War Department in February and March 1943. (See col. 5, Table No. 1, pp. 274–75.)

It should be borne in mind that at this time, in the winter of 1942–43, although the number of divisions to be mobilized in 1943 had been curtailed, it was still expected that new divisions would be mobilized as late as 1944.[1] The AGF tables outlined a division of 13,412 officers and men, over 2,000 less than the 1942 tables currently in effect. For a total of 100 infantry divisions, which still seemed a reasonable prospect, the saving of 2,000 men in each would save 200,000 men. On a 100-division basis, the saving of 150 men in every division would provide more than enough manpower for a new division.

The AGF Tables of March 1943

The smallest infantry unit, the rifle squad, remained unchanged in the new AGF tables.[2] It remained a team of twelve men, armed with ten M1 (Garand)

---

[1] (1) WD memo (C) WDGCT 320 Gen (1–29–43) for CGs AAF, AGF, SOS, 29 Jan 43, sub: Reduction of Tng Establishments and other ZI Activities. 320.2/262 (C). (2) WD memo (S) WDGCT 320.2 Gen (2–25–43) for G–1, G–4, OPD, AGF, SOS, AAF, 25 Feb 43, sub: TB Planning. 320.2/18 (TB 43) (S). The expectation is here stated of eventually having from 120 to 125 divisions within an enlisted strength of 7,500,000. Of these, some would be armored, airborne, etc., not standard infantry. See also above, "Mobilization of the Ground Army."

[2] This whole section is based mainly on comparison of published T/O's of 1 March 1943 with those of 1942, and on relevant materials in AGF files. On the infantry regiment and its components see (1) T/O 7–11 and related tables and (2) AGF memo for G–3 WD, 4 Feb 43, sub: T/O&E's, Inf Regt. 321/674 (Inf).

rifles, one automatic rifle, and one M1903 (Springfield) rifle. Three such squads formed a rifle platoon. Three rifle platoons were grouped with a weapons platoon to form a rifle company. The weapons platoon was modified slightly. It retained two .30-caliber light machine guns and three 60-mm. mortars as its primary weapons. It lost two automatic rifles but gained three antitank rocket launchers (bazookas) and one .50-caliber machine gun, the latter for antiaircraft defense. Personnel of the rifle company was cut from 198 to 192 through removal of a transportation corporal, a truck driver, a cook's helper, a messenger, an orderly, and a basic private. The 27 rifle companies of the division retained a strength of 5,184—the close-in fighters around whom the rest of the division was built. Saving 6 men in each company meant saving 162 in the division, or 16,200 if 100 infantry divisions should be mobilized.

The heavy weapons company, with which three rifle companies were grouped in the infantry battalion, was cut into more deeply than the rifle company, being reduced from 183 to 162 officers and men. Thirteen of the twenty-one men removed were truck drivers. Armament was strengthened by adding seven antitank rocket launchers and three .50-caliber machine guns to the prior quota of six 81-mm. mortars and eight .30-caliber heavy machine guns.

The headquarters company of the battalion, falling from 139 to 112, was cut proportionately more than the line companies, on the principle that headquarters overhead should be trimmed. The loss was largely in the antitank platoon, on the principle that defensive personnel should be held to a minimum. General McNair particularly frowned upon defensive weapons earmarked for the security of headquarters. The four 37-mm. antitank guns assigned to the antitank platoon were reduced to three. The 37-mm. gun was retained despite adverse reports from North Africa, on the ground that it was easier to handle than the 57-mm. gun proposed in its place, that it was effective when used within its proper range, and that in any case 57's were not yet available to replace it. Three .30-caliber machine guns, one .50-caliber machine gun, and eight anti-tank rocket launchers were added to the battalion headquarters company, which though reduced 20 percent in personnel obtained a net augmentation of armament.

By these changes, the personnel strength of the infantry battalion was reduced from 916 to 850—a saving of 66, of which only 18 were in the rifle companies.

Grouped with three infantry battalions in the infantry regiment were certain regimental units: the regimental headquarters company; the service, antitank, and cannon companies; and the medical detachment. These constituted pools of services and weapons for support of the battalions.

In the regimental headquarters company the main saving was in the communications platoon, which was relieved of eight truck drivers out of nine, five linemen out of twenty, and one switchboard operator out of three, with a net saving of 30 percent in this platoon. Armament of the company was increased by eleven antitank rocket launchers and four .50-caliber machine guns. The company emerged larger from the reorganizing process because it absorbed the cannon company.

The cannon company was a novelty in 1942, recently added to T/O's, but still existing chiefly on paper. Discussed for years, it was adopted to meet a difficulty of World War I, when advance of infantry had frequently been halted by the inability of field artillery to displace forward as rapidly as troops on foot. The cannon company of 1942 comprised 123 infantrymen manning 6 self-propelled 75-mm. howitzers and 2 self-propelled 105-mm. howitzers. Reports from the few companies in operation in North Africa were inconclusive. It was doubted at AGF headquarters that the cannon company was essential, since the regiment could be paired in a combat team with a light battalion of the division artillery.[3] The value of self-propelled artillery for this purpose was also questioned; it required more ship space than towed artillery, was more vulnerable on the battlefield, devoured more gasoline, and was too heavy for light bridges. The AGF tables of March 1943 abolished the cannon company, replacing it with three cannon platoons in the regimental headquarters company, equipped with six short-barreled, towed 105-mm. howitzers. Fifty-one men were saved in each regiment, or more than 150 in the division.

The regimental antitank company was drastically cut from 169 to 117 officers and men. Its mine-laying platoon was abolished. Basic armament of twelve 37-mm. antitank guns remained the same. One .50-caliber and four .30-caliber machine guns were added. The reorganized antitank company, with two-thirds the number of men, would handle more offensive weapons, but would be relieved of its purely defensive operation of mine laying.

In the regimental service company twenty men were saved through economy in truck drivers, clerks, and mechanics. A principal function of the service company was to transport supplies for the line battalions. With considerable

[3] AGF M/S (C), Rqts to CG, 3 Oct 42. 451/66 (C).

hesitation, because needs of the battalions had been calculated closely and reviewed as lately as the preceding April, but under extreme pressure to economize transportation, General McNair approved the replacement of 2½-ton by 1½-ton trucks in the new tables, the difference being made up by an increase in 1-ton trailers.[4] Service company personnel, currently equipped with only small arms, received ten antitank rocket launchers and eight .50-caliber machine guns in addition.

The medical detachment of the infantry regiment, divided into three battalion sections, included the aid men and litter bearers who accompanied front-line fighters into action, and the medical officers who worked at the aid stations to which casualties were first brought. General McNair believed the Medical Department very liberal in its consumption of manpower. The following case, typical of his relations with the Reduction Board, illustrates his relentless attention to detail. The Reduction Board recommended twelve litter bearers for each infantry battalion. General McNair held out for eight. The Board adhered to twelve. The Commanding General then replied: [5]

> The proposal of 8 litter bearers was not made loosely, but with a considerable factor of safety and was based on factual data. The losses assumed were the extreme maximum of the World War—15% per day of severe combat. On this basis a battalion should have about 50 litter cases. If 4 litters cannot evacuate this number from the field to the aid station there is something wrong with the set-up. The average littering distance was taken as 600 yards. Admittedly there may be cases in difficult terrain where the organic personnel will be inadequate, but reinforcements, not organic increases, are the answer in this case. Reduce 12 litter bearers to 10 as a compromise.

The Board explained that a litter team was now four men, not two. General McNair scrawled in pencil: "I give up. I was basing on two men per litter. . . . The Medical Department has run too far to change now. Fix it as you see fit. LJM." Twelve litter bearers were retained, but they operated only three litters in place of the four desired by General McNair, a disadvantage presumably offset by more rapid turnover of litters through lessening the fatigue of the bearers. The detachment as a whole was cut 18 percent through removal of 1 medical officer, 7 drivers, and 16 technicians. The regiment, for a personnel of approximately 3,000, retained 7 doctors, 2 dentists, and 103 enlisted medical men, rein-

[4] T/O 7–13 and AGF M/S, CG to Rqts, 2 Dec 42. 321/270 (MP).
[5] AGF M/S, CG to Rqts, 28 Dec 42. 320.3/636.

forced when necessary from the division medical battalion or from sources outside the division.

Total reduction in personnel of the infantry regiment was 384. Personnel was cut 11 percent; vehicles, 36 percent; ship tonnage, 14 percent. Only half the cut in the regiment was accomplished at the expense of the battalion. Half was in regimental overhead in the broad sense. In general, from the rifle platoon back the axe fell more heavily as one moved away from the front-line soldier. The same was true in the remainder of the division. Reduction in infantry alone, totalling 1,080 for the three regiments, accounted for a little over half the 2,000 saved in the division as a whole, although infantry comprised almost three-quarters of the division. The other half was in the division artillery and in division overhead.

The new tables for division artillery, as prepared by the Reduction Board, were called by General McNair "a monumental advance in de-fatting."[6] It is noteworthy that General McNair, an artilleryman by training, and hence particularly fitted to judge the requirements of that arm, attempted to reduce division artillery units by more than 20 percent both in 1938 and in 1943—both times without complete success.

Firing batteries in the artillery, like rifle companies in the infantry, lost proportionately the least. The 105-mm. batteries were each cut from 111 to 93, saving 18 men, of whom only 4 were in actual gun crews, the remainder being headquarters and maintenance personnel. The 155-mm. batteries were each cut from 120 to 98, a saving of 22 men, of whom only 8 were in gun crews, the remainder being headquarters and maintenance personnel.

In each battalion, economies in the three firing batteries accounted for less than half the saving. The main saving was accomplished through the consolidation, in each battalion, of the headquarters battery and the service battery in a combined headquarters and service battery. So trimmed down were both components that the new combined headquarters and service battery was hardly larger than the old headquarters battery alone. Twenty truck drivers, 4 mechanics, 3 cooks, and 3 orderlies were saved in the combined battery. The main saving was in the elimination of the antitank and antiaircraft platoon of fifty-two men, currently in the headquarters battery for the protection of battalion headquarters. The platoon's six 37-mm. antitank guns disappeared. Sixteen antitank

---

[6] (1) AGF M/S, CG to Rqts, 27 Nov 42. 320.3/78 (FA). (2) AGF memo for G-3 WD, 8 Feb 43, sub: T/O&E for Div Arty, Inf Div. 321/471 (FA). (3) T/O 6-10 and related tables.

rocket launchers and an increase of .50-caliber machine guns were furnished the battery for protection in emergencies, fundamental protection of artillery headquarters being left to surrounding infantry units. The medical detachment was cut almost one-third.

Primary armament of the division artillery remained unchanged—twelve 155-mm. howitzers and thirty-six 105-mm. howitzers. Personnel, including attached medical, was reduced from 2,555 to 2,002 (22 percent); vehicles, from 603 to 495 (18 percent); and ship tonnage from about 12,000 to about 9,400 (22 percent).

Infantry and artillery constituted the combat elements of the division, while everything else was in the nature of overhead. Before proceeding with a discussion of this overhead, it is well to recall that additional combat elements, held in nondivisional pools, might be attached to the division for particular operations. A division might thus be reinforced by a mechanized cavalry squadron, by one or more field artillery battalions of any appropriate caliber, by a chemical battalion manning 4.2 mortars, or by tank, tank destroyer, or antiaircraft battalions as described above. Attachment of some of these units, especially tank, tank destroyer, and antiaircraft units, became the normal practice when combat developed on a large scale in 1944, with the result that a division commander usually commanded well over 15,000 men.

A word of review is in order on protection against tanks and aircraft. These weapons, if massed, could not threaten all divisions simultaneously. A division most threatened was best protected by the pooling of counterweapons. For "normal" daily protection against occasional aircraft or small tank units the division had organic defenses. For antiair defense, 224 .50-caliber machine guns were distributed through all components. For antitank protection more than 500 rocket launchers were widely distributed, with a pooling of antitank guns in battalion headquarters and in the regimental antitank companies. In organic divisional antitank defense, the tendency was to place less reliance on special antitank units, and to provide weapons by means of which individual soldiers could rely more largely on themselves. Antitank guns were reduced in number at infantry battalion headquarters and were removed altogether from field artillery battalion headquarters. The infantry antitank company was "de-fatted." Concurrently, rocket launchers were issued as far forward as the weapons platoon of the rifle company. Individuals of the rifle platoons were equipped with antitank rifle grenades. Thus an echeloned antitank defense was set up, beginning

TABLE NO. 2

Troops in Divisions and in Nondivisional Units, by Branch, 31 December 1943 and 31 March 1945

(Authorized Aggregate Strengths: T/O Units Only; Replacements and Bulk Allotments (Overhead) Not Included)

UNITS	DIVISIONS				NONDIVISIONAL TROOPS PER DIVISION					
	Infantry Division		Armored Division		AGF Types [a]		ASF Types [b]		Total	
	31 Dec 43	31 Mar 45	31 Dec 43	31 Mar 45	31 Dec 43	31 Mar 45	31 Dec 43	31 Mar 45	31 Dec 43	31 Mar 45
Adjutant General	......	......	......	......	......	......	293	537	293	537
Antiaircraft	......	......	......	......	5,150	2,914	......	......	5,150	2,914
Armored	......	......	2,187	2,100	515	607	......	......	515	607
Cavalry	155	149	935	894	325	304	......	......	325	304
Chemical	......	......	......	......	199	276	182	153	381	429
Coast Artillery	......	......	......	......	1,059	425	......	......	1,059	425
Engineers	647	620	693	660	1,668	2,317	2,276	2,717	3,944	5,034
Field Artillery	2,160	2,111	1,623	1,625	1,404	2,197	......	......	1,404	2,197
Infantry	9,354	9,204	3,003	2,985	1,733	1,286	......	......	1,733	1,286
Medical	959	940	678	654	661	830	2,224	2,760	2,885	3,590
Military Police	73	106	91	87	139	187	872	960	1,011	1,147
Miscellaneous	......	......	......	......	107	139	126	243	233	382
Ordnance	147	141	762	732	1,486	1,811	430	530	1,916	2,341
Quartermaster	193	186	......	......	1,275	1,751	1,530	2,240	2,805	3,991
Signal	226	239	302	293	683	697	482	1,102	1,165	1,799
Tank Destroyer	......	......	......	......	787	506	......	......	787	506
Transportation	......	......	......	......	......	......	1,405	2,298	1,405	2,298
Headquarters	339	341	663	640	75	258	......	......	75	258
TOTAL	14,253	14,037	10,937	10,670	17,266	16,505	9,820	13,540	27,086	30,045

Sources: T/O 7, 15 Jul 43; T/O 17, 15 Sep 43; TB 15 Jan 44; T/O's 7 and 17, 24 Jan 45; and TB 1 Apr 45 (S).

[a] AGF types were mainly for operation in armies and corps. [b] ASF types were mainly for operation in communications zones.

with the rifleman's grenades and improvised weapons, passing through rocket launchers and antitank guns, including artillery pieces of the division, most of which could be used against tanks, and culminating in mobile tank destroyers to be attached in the event of heavy armored attack.

In passing to overhead elements of the division, it should be noted at once that the term is used with reservation, since all elements of the division were statistically classified as combat troops. All except the medical battalion were strongly armed. But the engineer, signal, ordnance, quartermaster, medical, and military police units within the division, however indispensable and however close to the fighting, were not combat troops in the same sense as the infantry and artillery. Even the mechanized reconnaissance troop was not intended primarily to fight. General McNair, following a doctrine that had been more generally preached than observed, wished to keep the proportion of these auxiliary elements to combat elements as low as possible.

This was done in two ways. First, line troops served themselves. Infantrymen of the infantry regiment and artillerymen of the field artillery battalions performed simple tasks common to all branches. Medical service was an exception in that, although all infantrymen and artillerymen were trained in first aid, each infantry regiment and artillery battalion had, as "attached medical" in its Table of Organization, a number of medical officers and enlisted men trained by and belonging to the Medical Department. Units had no attached personnel of other branches, though some (for example, the Signal Corps) had attempted in the past to have their personnel included.[7] Infantrymen and artillerymen operated their own telephones and radios without signal corps specialists, ran their own trucks and supply systems without quartermasters, engaged in rudimentary construction and mine removal without recourse to the engineers, and provided first-echelon maintenance (by the individual user) and second-echelon maintenance (by a mechanic in the using unit) for their weapons and vehicles without recourse to technicians of the Ordnance Department. The infantry regiment was virtually a small division. It served itself; it had a reconnaissance platoon; it had proportionately far more antiaircraft and antitank weapons than the division; and after the inclusion of howitzers it had its own artillery.

The other method of holding down the auxiliary elements of the division was extensive pooling of auxiliary units in corps and army. (See Table No. 2.) So pooled, they were available in the varying quantities needed from time to time

[7] "Attached Signal" troops were provided, for example, in the proposals of 1936; see staff study cited in footnote 3, p. 293.

by this or that division. In addition, for routine supply of food, gasoline, and ammunition, General McNair wished the regiments and battalions of divisions to deal directly with nondivisional service units under army control. "It is intended," read an AGF directive after the system came into effect, "that supplies move with as much freedom as possible through as few channels as necessary. *Division and corps are not in the channel of supply except in emergencies.*"[8] The using units—regiments and battalions—hauled supplies in their own trucks from army supply points expected to be from twenty to thirty miles in the rear. It was the business of army headquarters to push supply points within reach of front-line units, employing army trucks when necessary to go beyond the railhead or head of navigation. Army was also expected to provide laborers at supply points to sort supplies into unit lots and load them into unit vehicles. The using units brought no personnel except drivers to the supply points, thus avoiding waste of vehicle space by transportation of laborers. The part played by the division quartermaster, ordnance officer, engineer, and other service elements was simply to consolidate and forward unit requisitions for items supplied by his branch, determine the shares of division units when stocks were limited, and provide liaison with army headquarters when necessary. The new supply procedure, which the Ground Engineer called a "revolution," was embodied in a revision of FM 100–10, the new passages being largely written by General McNair himself.[9]

Between concentration of functions in line personnel on the one hand, and in army personnel on the other, many functions of auxiliary units within the division were squeezed out.

Reconnaissance, for example, was conducted at all levels: by patrols of the forward infantry elements; by the intelligence and reconnaissance platoon of the infantry regiment; and by mechanized cavalry squadrons in the corps. It seemed to General McNair that there were too many echelons of reconnaissance.[10] In 1938 he had not recommended any reconnaissance unit for the division at all. A mechanized cavalry troop had nevertheless been added, which from

---

[8] AGF ltr (R) to CGs, 8 Oct 43, sub: Engr Serv in the Fld. 321/212 (Engr) (R).

[9] (1) AGF M/S (R), Engr to G–4, CofS, 4 Sep 43. 321/212 (Engr) (R). (2) AGF M/S, CG to G–4, 20 Feb 43, sub: Changes in FM 100–10. 461/12 (FM 100–10). (3) Memo of G–4 AGF for CG AGF, sub: Rpt on Progress of FM 100–10. 461/12 (FM 100–10). (4) AGF memo for G–3 WD, 10 Mar 43, sub: T/O 10–17. 321/1243 (QM).

[10] Memo (C) of Gen McNair for CofS USA, 8 Oct 42, sub: Excessive No. of Mtr Vehicles. 451/66 (C).

1941 to 1942 grew in strength from 147 to 201. General McNair now proposed a troop of 153.[11]

Service units in the division occupied the narrowing gap between line units and army troops. Each, in addition to its operating functions, carried a small reserve of supplies and spare parts peculiar to its branch and provided third-echelon maintenance for equipment for which its branch was responsible.

The medical battalion included somewhat less than half the medical personnel of the division, the larger half being "attached medical" with the infantry, artillery, and combat engineers. All told, medical personnel numbered about 1,000, more than any other arm or service in the division except infantry and artillery. The division medical battalion backed up the unit detachments. The latter brought in casualties to battalion or regimental aid stations, assisted when necessary by collecting companies of the medical battalion. These companies evacuated the wounded from aid stations to clearing stations, from which those needing further treatment were transferred to evacuation hospitals operated by army. Division medical officers worked during combat at the clearing stations or reinforced medical officers attached to units farther forward. Little reduction was made in the revised table for the battalion, and there was no reduction in doctors. The veterinary officer was dropped; when the office of The Surgeon General protested, the Army Ground Forces explained that the division had no animals and that meat inspection was a function suitably relegated to army. The AGF tables likewise combined the positions of division surgeon and of commanding officer of the medical battalion, on the theory that the surgeon should not remain at division headquarters but should operate with his hospitals in the field.[12]

The combat engineer battalion of the division, between 1941 and 1942, had grown in strength from 634 to 745. The AGF tables brought it back to 647. Functions of the battalion, such as road repair, bridge building, demolition, and construction, were unchanged. A reconnaissance section was added to the battalion headquarters and service company to enable the engineer to form his own estimates of the need for bridging and road repair. Removal of certain bridging equipment from the organic impedimenta of the battalion, on the principle that it could be readily drawn from army when needed, was the principal means used to reduce the battalion. Identical battalions, kept in pools under higher

---

[11] T/O 2–27 and AGF memo for G–3 WD, 4 Feb 43, sub: T/O&E Reconnaissance Troop. 321/157 (Cav).

[12] T/O 8–15 and AGF memo for G–3 WD, 16 Feb 43, sub: T/O&E, Med Bn. 321/725 (Med), with accompanying papers.

headquarters, together with other engineer units such as light ponton companies and heavy ponton battalions, were available for support of the division when needed.[13]

The division signal company was reduced almost one-third. From a strength of 232 in 1940 it had swollen to 322 in 1942, although both infantry and artillery had radio operators, linemen, communications sergeants, and similar categories. The main function of the signal company was to construct and operate the central communications system of the division, coordinating and joining the main elements of the division with each other and with division headquarters. In part the signal company was cut by straight application of the Ground Rules; forty-five truck drivers were eliminated and their duties were assigned to various others. To some extent this company was cut by abolition of the radio intelligence platoon, whose functions were judged by the Army Ground Forces to be more appropriate for corps. A radio intelligence platoon was accordingly included in the corps signal battalion. The division signal company was brought back to a strength of 226, approximately that of 1940.[14]

The ordnance light maintenance company, made organic in the division after transfer of motor maintenance from the Quartermaster Corps to the Ordnance Department, was an especially good illustration of the economies made possible by pushing functions forward to line units or rearward to army shops. Battlefield recovery of disabled equipment and elementary repairs and maintenance were responsibilities of using units. Rather than lose control by turning over equipment to another agency for repairs, a procedure especially hazardous in combat, units were also expected to carry third-echelon maintenance to the limit of their tools and skill. No ordnance company, General McNair noted for his staff,[15]

can even make a dent in the trucks of a division, but must confine their activities to those which cannot be performed in units for lack of tools or special knowledge. There is no question in my mind that much of the so-called third echelon work in campaign must be performed by units in some degree. . . . No practicable ordnance company can be set up which will take care of motor repairs. The great mass of them must be either handled in the units or passed on to army establishments. However, it is sensible to cut out [i. e. hold, as in cutting a car out of a railroad train] at the division echelon those repairs which require not too much time but only special tools or knowledge.

[13] T/O 5–15 and AGF memo for G–3 WD, 21 Feb 43, sub: T/O&E Engr Combat Bn, Inf Div. 321/712 (Engr).
[14] T/O 11–7 and AGF memo for G–3 WD, 3 Mar 43, sub: T/O&E 11–7 Sig Co, Inf Div. 321/756 (Sig).
[15] AGF M/S, CG to Rqts, 15 Dec 42. 321/714 (Ord).

The division ordnance company, as provided in the AGF tables, was therefore intended to provide only 60 percent of the third-echelon maintenance required in the division under quiet conditions, and only 30 percent of such maintenance required during combat.[16] The company was held to a strength of 147.

The division quartermaster company retained very limited responsibilities. Motor maintenance had been transferred to ordnance. Supply of food and gasoline was decentralized to regiments and separate battalions. With trucking done by using units, the trucks of the quartermaster company constituted chiefly a reserve. Their functions were to assure water supply, to carry reserve supplies, including one reserve ration for the entire division, and to be capable of transporting tactically one battalion of infantry. Except for five trucks to which no load was assigned, kept as spare vehicles for immediate replacement of vehicle casualties, all trucks had organic loads, which they dumped when called upon to carry troops or provide reserve transportation to units. Laborers were eliminated, since sorting and loading at supply points were done by army, and unloading at receiving points by receiving units. The quartermaster company, in the March tables, was cut to 152 officers and men.[17]

By attachment of six quartermaster truck companies, kept in an army pool, the division proposed by the Army Ground Forces could be motorized completely. Six companies were sufficient because only the infantry required supplementary transportation, all other elements of the infantry division being organically motorized.[18]

The military police unit consisted of one platoon. The AGF tables of March 1943 cut it from eighty to seventy-three men. Its functions were to guide traffic, maintain straggler lines, and escort prisoners. In these functions it was supported by MP units of corps and army and could be supplemented by detail of individuals from other units of the division. To prevent detail of soldiers for this purpose was, however, one of the main reasons for having military police organic in the division.[19]

The remaining element of division overhead was the headquarters and headquarters company. Since June 1941 these had greatly expanded. Division

[16] AGF M/S, Red Bd to CG, 19 Dec 42. 321/714 (Ord). See also AGF memo for G-3 WD, 2 Feb 43, sub: T/O&E 9-8, Ord Co, Lt Maint. 321/714 (Ord).
[17] (1) AGF M/S, CG to Rqts, 2 Dec 42. 321/270 (MP). (2) AGF memo for G-3 WD, 13 Feb 43, sub: T/O&E 10-17, QM Co, Inf or Mtz Div. 321/1243 (QM), with accompanying papers.
[18] See pp. 337-38 below on the motorized division.
[19] AGF memo for G-3 WD, 16 Feb 43, sub: T/O&E 19-7, MP Plat, Inf Div. 321/270 (MP).

headquarters, on 1 June 1941, consisted of 26 officers, 2 warrant officers, and 74 enlisted men, totaling 102; on 1 August 1942, of 44 officers, 9 warrant officers, and 116 enlisted men, totaling 169. The headquarters company consisted on 1 June 1941 of 4 officers and 59 enlisted men; on 1 August 1942, of 7 officers, 3 warrant officers, and 134 enlisted men. The division headquarters establishment almost doubled in fourteen months. The general staff had grown from seven officers to twelve; the simple headquarters company of 1941 had more than doubled through addition of a transportation platoon and a defense platoon. The total increment, on a 100-division basis, took as much manpower as an entire division.

General McNair believed that the commander should work through personal contact and verbal orders, especially at the division level. Overgrown staffs, in his opinion, were the principal cause of long written orders and unnecessary paper work, through which the division lost mobility and responsiveness to command in fast-changing conditions of battle.

The AGF tables of March 1943 cut the headquarters company 50 percent, bringing it almost back to the strength of June 1941, through removal of vehicles and drivers, economy in orderlies, and abolition of the defense platoon.[20] The 56-man band was assigned, as an additional duty, the local protection of division headquarters. General McNair rejected proposals to increase postal personnel to the level authorized by the War Department (1 per 1,000 troops), despite recommendations of his own staff, The Adjutant General, and the theaters, and despite information from the Desert Training Center that division postal clerks were obliged to work day and night.[21]

Division headquarters, cut about 25 percent in both officers and enlisted assistants, remained well above the level of 1941. Commanding officers of the medical battalion and the ordnance company were required to act as special staff officers for their branches, a practice already established in the artillery, engineer, signal, and quartermaster elements of the division. Chaplains and special service officers at division headquarters were each cut from three to two. By General McNair's express order, the assistant G–4, automotive, added in 1942, was eliminated. General McNair felt that the ordnance officer could do most of the staff work connected with maintenance, an activity which, as he never tired of pointing out, profited more from elbow grease than from forms and reports.

---

[20] On Div Hq & Hq Co see (1) various AGF M/Ss, Jan 43. 320.3/166 (Inf) and (2) AGF memo for G–3 WD, 9 Mar 43, sub: T/O&E, Inf Div. 321/688 (Inf).

[21] AGF 3d ind (C) to TAG, 7 Apr 43, with attached papers. 320.3/17 (C).

To summarize, the reduced division proposed by the Army Ground Forces met the terms of the War Department directive very closely. Personnel was cut more than 13 percent, vehicles more than 23 percent. In addition, size of vehicles was reduced and number of trailers increased. Counting the ship-ton as 40 cubic feet, about 6,000 ship-tons (15 percent) were saved in tonnage needed for transport of equipment. Only a few platoons were wholly obliterated, though the infantry cannon company and the artillery service battery had been telescoped into other organizations. As the following table indicates, personnel cuts were echeloned toward the rear:

Percentage of Personnel Reduction in the Infantry Division: AGF Proposals of March 1943

Units	(105-mm.)	Percentage Reduced (155-mm.)
Infantry:		
Rifle Squad		0.0
Rifle Company		3.0
Infantry Battalion		7.2
Infantry Regiment		11.0
Field Artillery	(105-mm.)	(155-mm.)
Howitzer Section	10.0	15.4
Howitzer Battery	17.7	19.7
Field Artillery Battalion	21.2	25.4
Division Artillery		22.2
Auxiliary Units		
Reconnaissance Troop		23.9
Engineer Battalion		13.7
Medical Battalion		7.1
Signal Company		29.8
Quartermaster Company		26.2
Ordnance Company		5.2
MP Platoon		8.8
Headquarters Company (without Band)		52.1
Division Headquarters		21.3
Entire Division		13.5

Fire power was not lessened. The main loss in armament was the removal of 324 automatic rifles. Whereas formerly all units of the infantry regiment had possessed a few of these weapons, they were now confined exclusively to the rifle squad, the 243 automatic rifles remaining in the division being distributed, one each, to the 243 rifle squads. Provision of antitank guns and antitank mines was likewise cut. But more than 500 antitank rocket launchers were added, and the allotment of .50-caliber machine guns was substantially increased. Self-propelled infantry howitzers gave way to towed howitzers, in slightly reduced numbers, but the 75-mm. howitzers were replaced with 105's. In sum, increased fire power offset the reductions in weapons. With fire power the same, and with manpower cut over 13 percent, the ratio of fire power to manpower increased. Hence with a given outlay of men, food, maintenance, transportation, and administrative effort more combat power could be delivered.

Reaction to the AGF Tables

All tables prepared by the Army Ground Forces for component units of the infantry division were immediately approved by the War Department and published in April under date of 1 March 1943. When the consolidated table for the entire division was submitted it met a different fate. G–3, War Department General Staff, recommended approval, all component elements having already been approved.[22] The Chief of Staff directed that the consolidated table first be submitted to the overseas theaters for comment. General McNair wrote privately:[23]

> The Chief is reserving final decision until Edwards [G–3, War Department] and I get back from Africa, where we hope to go this week. I am not clear as to the purpose of this step, but we shall do our darnedest to check up on various features of the organization by consultation with those who have been through the mill. However, I have little hope of convincing any division commander that he can spare 450 trucks or 2,000 men.

Wounded a few days after his arrival in North Africa, General McNair missed the opportunity for a full discussion of the proposed division with officers in the theater. It is doubtful whether representatives of the War Department put the matter in quite the light in which he saw it. The positive side of economy, the possibility of increasing the number of divisions through reduction in size, was the easier to overlook since up to this time only four United States divisions had been employed in North Africa, with some sixty in training at home.

---

[22] (1) WD memo (S) WDGCT 320.2 Gen (6–4–43) for CofS USA, 8 Jun 43 sub: Revised Inf Div. AGO Records, 320.3 (8 Jun 43) (1) (S). (2) M/R on cpy of WD memo WDGCT 320.2 T/O (18 Jun 43), 18 Jun 43, sub: Revision of T/O&E's for Inf Div. AGO Records, 320.3.

[23] Personal ltr of Gen McNair to Gen F. L. Parks, 12 Apr 43. McNair Correspondence.

That the saving in personnel should be utilized for new divisions was not, indeed, the policy of the War Department at this time. In June 1943, when final decisions on the reduced division were made, the number of divisions in the mobilization program for 1943 was not raised but lowered.[24]

The North African Theater of Operations disapproved of the new division in entirety.[25] General Eisenhower reported unanimous rejection by his corps and division commanders. The division was said to be already at an absolute minimum, providing no relief for worn out personnel—a somewhat irrelevant argument since the reductions mainly affected personnel least subject to the wear of battle. The theater reported the defense platoon at division headquarters to be essential in combat; asked for more military police, not fewer; warned that reduction of the engineer, signal, and other auxiliary units would seriously impair their operations; deplored the telescoping of cannon companies and service batteries; and in general pronounced reduction anywhere to be unfeasible. Organic assignment of antiaircraft and tank destroyer battalions to the infantry division was also desired.

General McNair wrote at length to the War Department when asked to comment on the view taken by the theater. He noted that the reductions had been ordered by the War Department itself, and continued: [26]

I know of no instance where a commander has recommended a reduction of the means at his disposal—either personnel or material—and of but few cases where a commander was satisfied with what he had. Invariably commanders seek more and tend always to make their unit self-contained. It was such proclivities that brought about the present wasteful and unwieldy organization. Commanders do not consider the large picture. For example, the Commanding General, 1st Division, told me during my recent visit overseas that he needed organically a military police battalion, a reconnaissance squadron, a tank destroyer battalion, and an antiaircraft battalion. I asked him whether he would be willing to give up four infantry battalions in exchange, to which he replied No, vehemently. Nevertheless, such an addition to his division would deplete or eliminate other divisions, since the bottom of the manpower barrel is in sight.

The big question in the case of the mass of streamlined units before the War Department for decision is not what it would be nice to have in the way of a complete and perfect organization, but what is the very minimum organization which can fight effectively. It would

---

[24] See "Ground Forces in the Army, December 1941–April 1945: a Statistical Study" and "Mobilization of the Ground Army," in this volume.

[25] (1) Radio (S) CM–In–550, Algiers [Eisenhower] to WD, 1 Jun 43. (2) Radio (S) CM–In–9356, London USFOR [Devers] to WD, 14 May 43. WD Classified Message Center.

[26] Memo (S) of Gen McNair for G–3 WD, 3 Jun 43, sub: Reduced Inf Div. 322/2 (Divs) (S).

be comfortable to have 12 men in an organic gun squad, but the gun can be served readily by 8 men and 12 men certainly will not be 50% more effective than 8 men.

Our theaters now are developed sufficiently to make it quite apparent that there is gross extravagance in both human and material resources everywhere. Theater commanders naturally seek to make themselves as secure against eventualities as they possibly can. They expect the War Department to find the resources which they demand, and thus far the War Department has met their expectations obligingly. However, sooner or later, the War Department will be forced, by inadequate total resources, to decide the form and substance of theater allotments, and direct theater commanders to carry on with what is given them, not what they would like to have. There is no doubt in my mind that the total resources now in the North African theater could be changed in form with an enormous gain in fighting power.

My study of operations in the North African theater particularly, by both observation on the ground and from reports and dispatches, convinces me thoroughly that the combat forces there are too much concerned with their own security and too little concerned with striking the enemy. The infantry is displaying a marked reluctance to advance against fire, but they are masters of the slit trench—a device which is used habitually both in defense and attack. Regimental and higher commanders are not seen sufficiently in the forward areas, and battalions show the lack of this first-hand supervision. Commanders are in their command posts. I found that infantry battalions in the assault have their command posts organized in forward and rear echelons, the latter the stronger. Commanders of all echelons cry for both antiaircraft and ground defense. One high commander seized the reconnaissance company of a tank destroyer battalion for his personal guard, thereby rendering the destroyer battalion virtually ineffective. This attitude is everywhere and is undermining the offensive spirit by which alone we can win battles. I maintain that our organization must be an offensive one, not cringingly defensive. We cannot provide thousands of purely defensive weapons with personnel to man them without detracting from our offensive power. Nothing can be more unsound than to provide a headquarters guard organically for a high command post. If the commander feels so much concern for his own safety, let him withdraw a battalion from the front line for his own protection, but do not provide him with such a unit organically.

It is to be emphasized that the proposed organization, in this and other similar cases, does not weaken the fighting power of the unit, but merely strips away unessential overhead and weapons which are not usable against the enemy in offensive action. When field commentators see that the unit has been reduced in strength, they charge immediately that the revised unit is weak and lacks staying power. The facts are the reverse, since the unit has more fighting power per man than the extravagant unit which it supersedes. There will be more of the reduced unit for a given manpower, hence greater total fighting and staying power.

The reduced organizations are based on the sound fundamental that the division or other unit should be provided organically with only those means which it needs practically always. Peak loads, and unusual and infrequent demands obviously should be met from a pool—ordinarily in the army or separate corps. Such a principle is particularly applicable, for example, to engineer and medical units. In both such cases demands vary widely with the situation, and it is uneconomical in the extreme to provide the division organically with the means of meeting extreme demands which occur seldom.

General Eisenhower's comments in this case can be replied to in detail, but such discussion seems hardly appropriate. It is clear that his viewpoint is so wholly different from that upon which the reduced division is based, that it is small wonder that the reduced organization is unacceptable to him. The issue does not lie in these details but rather is, whether we are to base our military organization on comfort and convenience or on offensive fighting power.

At this very time, in June 1943, the manpower situation was so critical that 500,000 men were dropped from the proposed strength of the Army and twelve divisions were canceled from the mobilization program for 1943.[27]

A middle ground between General McNair and General Eisenhower was found by G–3 of the War Department.[28] Although the compromise, by adding over 800 men to General McNair's figures for the division, made the mobilization of any given number of divisions more difficult, it produced an individual division of considerable soundness and strength, used without substantial change in the European campaigns of 1944 and 1945. In general, the auxiliary units of the division were held down to General McNair's figures. One exception was the division headquarters company, to which the defense platoon was restored (as a guard against stray tanks, parachutists, and disaffected civilian inhabitants). Another exception was the quartermaster company, to which the service platoon was restored on the ground that the division quartermaster had no other pool of labor. In general, the combat elements of the division were modified in the direction desired by General Eisenhower. The cannon company was restored to the infantry regiment, and the service battery to the field artillery battalion. In view of developments in North Africa, the 37-mm. antitank gun was definitely abandoned in favor of the 57-mm., the mine-laying platoon was restored to the regimental antitank companies, and infantry regiments received increased allowances of mine detectors. Other questions of armament remained as decided by General McNair. Infantry regiments kept their 2½-ton trucks. About 400 vehicles were restored to the division. A medical detachment was added for the

---

[27] See the two preceding studies in this volume.

[28] (1) WD memo (S) WDGCT 320.2 Gen (6–4–43) for Cof S USA, 8 Jun 43, sub: Revised Inf Div. AGO Records 320.3 (8 Jun 43) (1) (S). (2) WD memo (S) WDGCT 320.2 T/O (18 Jun 43) to CG AGF, 18 Jun 43, sub: Revision of TO&E's for the Inf Div 321/63 (Inf) (S). (3) AGF memo for G–3 WD, 9 Jul 43, sub as above. 320.3/661. (4) AGF memo (S) for G–3 WD, 1 Jun 43, sub: Recommended Changes in T/O's. 322/3 (Divs) (S).

"special troops," or smaller auxiliaries, of the division. A division surgeon was provided in addition to the commanding officer of the medical battalion. This compromised the principle, stressed by General McNair, of reducing special staffs through combination of staff and command positions. To these amendments made by G–3, the office of the Chief of Staff added another, directing that a headquarters, special troops, be included for administration of the signal, ordnance, and quartermaster companies and the military police platoon. This headquarters, revived from the old square division, was regarded by General McNair as a wholly unnecessary piece of overhead.[29]

But for the most part the cuts made by General McNair in headquarters establishments, especially at the regimental and battalion levels, were maintained. Restorations made by the War Department were chiefly in combat elements, largely defensive, and in service elements operating in the closest conjunction with combat troops. In addition, the Army Ground Forces, acting on reports from the theaters and without instructions from the War Department, restored the medical detachment of the infantry regiment to its old figure. The disputed postal clerks were likewise added.

The division which emerged consisted of 14,253 officers and men, about 850 more than desired by General McNair, but about 1,250 fewer than currently authorized. The Army Ground Forces prepared new Tables of Organization as directed. These were published as of 15 July 1943. Infantry divisions in the United States were physically reorganized as of 1 September 1943, those overseas by installments in the following months. Since in the long run only 66 infantry divisions were mobilized, it may be said that the T/O's of 15 July 1943, saving about 1,250 in each, saved altogether 82,500 men. Conversely, the number of men formerly required for 60 divisions now produced 66.

The reorganization of the infantry division effected important economies. But to General McNair the failure of the War Department to accept his views, or to stand firmly by its own announced policies of economy, was a source of grave disappointment and concern. He saw in it an indication that the War Department would yield to the theaters to a degree which he believed destructive to central control. "Since the War Department's decisions in connection with the infantry division," he wrote on 23 June 1943, when reviewing the T/O for army headquarters, "I have much less sting in me than heretofore." [30]

[29] (1) AGF memo (S) for G–3 WD, 1 Jun 43, sub: Recommended Changes in T/O's. 322/3 (Divs) (S). (2) AGF memo for G–3 WD, 27 Nov 43, sub: Revision of FM 101–5. 322.01/5.
[30] AGF M/S, CG to Rqts, 23 Jun 43, sub: Reduc of Offs, Ord Sec, Army Hq. 320.2/191 (AGF).

V. The Armored Division

The armored division, unlike the infantry division, underwent not merely a shrinking but a thoroughgoing reorganization at the hands of the Army Ground Forces. (See Table No. 3.) The process was complicated by the semi-independent status of the Chief of the Armored Force, who was responsible for Tables of Organization for armored units. The Armored Force, established in July 1940 to do a rush job of creating armored divisions, retained a great deal of prestige and vitality after it came under the headquarters of the Army Ground Forces in March 1942. For over a year relations between AGF headquarters and Armored Force headquarters were in practice more on the level of negotiation than of military command. It was not that the two headquarters were at odds. There was considerable difference of view among General McNair's staff officers on the use of armor, and he did not insist that they present a united front during discussions with Fort Knox.[1] Armored Force officers also represented various shades of opinion on the tactics, and hence the organization, of tanks. But the differences of opinion tended to polarize in the respective points of view of the two headquarters.

Of one thing General McNair was convinced from the start: that the Armored Force, accustomed by the circumstances of its birth to doing big things in a hurry, was the most wasteful of the ground arms in its use of manpower and equipment. "Profligate," "luxurious," and "monstrous" were terms he frequently applied to armored units in 1942 and 1943.[2] "The present armored division," he wrote, "is fairly bogged down by a multiplicity of gadgets of all kinds. . . . In the matter of size, cost and complication, as compared with the number of tanks which can be used against the enemy, the armored division

---

[1] AGF M/S (S), CG to Red Bd, 10 Mar 43. 320.2/24 (Armd F) (S).

[2] For example, (1) AGF memo (C) for G–3 WD, 5 Nov 42, sub: AA Defense. 320.2/12 (AA) (C). (2) Personal ltr of Gen McNair to Col J. A. Consadine, 4 Jun 42. McNair Correspondence.

TABLE NO. 3

Organic Composition of the Armored Division, 1942–45

(Aggregate Strengths, Principal Equipment)

UNIT	1 Mar 42	15 Sep 43	24 Jan 45
Entire Division.............................	14,620	10,937	10,670
Division Headquarters........................	185	164	174
Hq. & Hq. Co., Combat Command "A"........	61	93	90
Hq. & Hq. Co., Combat Command "B"........	61	91	88
Hq., Reserve Command........................	......	8	8
Armored Component.........................	4,848	2,187	2,100
2 Armored Regiments, each..............	2,424	......	......
Hq. & Hq. Company...................	172	......	......
Reconnaissance Company..............	202	......	......
Service Company......................	191	......	......
Maintenance Company.................	188	......	......
Tank Battalion (Medium) (two)........	599	......	......
Hq. & Hq. Company................	152	......	......
Tank Company (Medium) (three)....	149	......	......
Tank Battalion (Light)................	473	......	......
Hq. & Hq. Company................	143	......	......
Tank Company (Light) (three).......	110	......	......
3 Tank Battalions, each.................	......	729	700
Hq. & Hq. Company...................	......	147	140
Service Company......................	......	119	115
Tank Company (Medium) (three)......	......	122	117
Tank Company (Light)................	......	97	94
Infantry Component.........................	2,389	3,003	2,985
Armored Infantry Regiment..............	2,389	......	......
Hq. & Hq. Company...................	138	......	......
Service Company......................	151	......	......
Armored Infantry Bn. (three)..........	700	1,001	995
Hq. & Hq. Company................	166	173	169
Service Company....................	......	75	73
Rifle Company (three)..............	178	251	251
Artillery Component.........................	2,127	1,623	1,625
Hq. Division Artillery....................	......	21	95
Armored Field Artillery Battalion (three).	709	534	510
Hq. & Hq. Battery.....................	173	111	106
Service Battery........................	152	93	89
Firing Battery (three).................	128	110	105

TABLE NO. 3—Continued

UNIT	1 Mar 42	15 Sep 43	24 Jan 45
Auxiliary Units.............................	*4,521*	*3,499*	*3,338*
Division Hq. Company..................	111	138	115
Division Service Company...............	160	......	......
Band..................................	......	58	58
Signal Company.........................	256	302	293
Reconnaissance Battalion................	872	935	894
Engineer Battalion......................	1,174	693	660
Division Trains........................	1,948	1,373	1,318
Hq. & Hq. Company..................	159	103	99
Maintenance Battalion................	873	762	732
Supply Battalion......................	414	......	......
Medical Battalion.....................	502	417	400
Military Police Platoon................	......	91	87
Attached Medical..........................	*414*	*261*	*254*
Attached Chaplain.........................	*14*	*8*	*8*
Principal Equipment:			
Medium Tanks.........................	232	186	195
Light Tanks...........................	158	77	77
105-mm. Howitzers, self-propelled.......	54	54	54
Cal. 30 Machine Guns...................	291	465	434
Cal. 50 Machine Guns...................	103	404	382
Cal. 45 Submachine Guns...............	2,160	2,803	2,811
Carbines..............................	6,042	5,286	5,051
Cal. 30 Rifles.........................	1,628	2,063	2,040
Antitank Rocket Launchers..............	......	607	609
Carriers, Half-track....................	733	501	466
Vehicles, All Types (except boats and aircraft).............................	3,630	2,653	2,276

Source: T/O 17 and allied tables, as of above dates.

presents an amazing picture of unjustified extravagance." [3] The AGF Reduction
Board went to work on the armored division in January 1943. Certain of the
division tables were pronounced by General McNair "so fat there is no place
to begin"; others were to be "combined and debunked—a major operation";
and he instructed the Board, "before I personally struggle further with these
terrible tables," to recast armored division elements along the lines of comparable
elements in the reduced infantry division. [4]

Meanwhile the question of reorganization had arisen, overshadowing the
question of mere reduction. Concurrently with the removal of "fat," the anatomy
of the division was transformed. Economy was a major objective, but changes
were also dictated by modifications in tactical doctrine.

Conceptions of the armored division passed through several stages during
the war, largely as a result of the activity of the Germans, whose successes made
it possible for various schools of American officers to get their ideas adopted.
The American armored divisions were at first modeled on the German Panzer
division of 1940 and were made up overwhelmingly of tanks with relatively
little infantry support. Virtually all tanks in the Army were placed in armored
divisions. One school thought that these heavy armored divisions would operate
well ahead of the mass of friendly forces. Divisions of foot infantry were left a
modest role. "The triangular division," wrote the Chief of the Armored Force,
on 18 July 1942, "has its place in the scheme of affairs to protect lines of communication, to hold ground, to assist the armored units in supply and the crossing of obstacles such as rivers, defiles, etc. They do not carry the spearhead of
the fight and never will when tanks and guns are present." [5] The belief that
armored divisions were a kind of elite troops, capable of peculiarly decisive
action, was the basis for furnishing them so liberally with personnel and
equipment.

But the succesful employment of antitank guns and mines, notably by the
Germans in the African campaigns from 1941 to 1943, but also by the Russians
and British, confirmed the position of those American officers, including General McNair, who had always doubted the invulnerability of the tank. It became
clear that tanks would frequently have to be escorted by foot troops sent ahead
to locate and destroy antitank defenses. It was recognized that the armored

[3] Memo (S) of Gen McNair (dictated by Gen McNair, signed by Gen J. G. Christiansen) for DCofS
USA, 20 Jul 43, sub: Comments on Maj Gen Harmon's Rpt. 319.1/13 (NATO) (S).
[4] AGF M/S, CG to Red Bd, 23 Feb 43. AGF Orgn Div, Rqts Sec (25893).
[5] Personal ltr of Gen Devers to Gen McNair, 18 Jul 42. McNair Correspondence.

division, internally, required more infantry in proportion to tanks and, externally, would usually operate in closer proximity to infantry divisions than had been supposed. The increasing rapprochement between tanks and infantry raised not only the question of the internal structure of the armored division but also that of the number of armored divisions which ought to be mobilized, as distinguished from the nondivisional tank battalions by which infantry divisions could receive tank support. General Devers, two years after making the statement quoted in the last paragraph, wrote of the Italian campaign in 1944: "Of special importance has been the work of tank battalions attached to infantry divisions. . . . Throughout the entire campaign the infantry has been the major decisive element in the advance . . . . It is team play which has assured success." [6]

Armored divisions were being reorganized, under tables prepared by the Armored Force and dated 1 March 1942, at the time when the Armored Force became a component of the Army Ground Forces.[7] The tank-infantry ratio in the new tables remained substantially as in 1940. The total strength of the division was 14,620, of which 4,848 was in tank units, 2,389 in armored infantry, and 2,127 in armored artillery. Tanks were organized in 2 regiments of 3 battalions each; infantry in a regiment of 3 battalions; artillery in 3 battalions. Armored infantry differed from foot infantry, which was not organically motorized, and from motorized infantry, which was equipped to move in trucks, in that all personnel could move simultaneously in lightly armored half-tracks. Armored artillery consisted of self-propelled 105-mm. howitzers; it was organized in 6-piece batteries, so that 3 battalions had 54 pieces. The engineer battalion of the armored division comprised 4 companies plus a treadway bridge company. A strength of 1,948 was in division trains, which included a maintenance battalion six times as large as the corresponding company in the infantry division, and a supply battalion organically included on the ground that army supply establishments would usually lag far behind the fast-moving armored division. Division headquarters included 2 "combat commands," each a subheadquarters under a brigadier general, to either of which the division commander might assign such forces as he chose for specific tactical missions. Task forces could thus be made up flexibly within the division, embodying, within limits, any desired ratio of tanks to infantry and other arms.

[6] Lt Gen J. L. Devers, Deputy Commander of the North African Theater of Operations, "Tactical Notes from the Italian Campaign," *Military Review*, XXIV (1944), 3.

[7] See Table No. 3.

General McNair in 1942, in view of the recent reorganization of the division, and considering the unsettled state of armored doctrine, wished to postpone another reorganization until combat experience had been gained.[8] In August he called the attention of General Devers to the fact that the German armored division, having been substantially reorganized since 1940, now had five times as high a ratio of infantry to tank troops as did the United States armored division.[9] General Devers, convinced of the need of more infantry, proposed that the motorized infantry divisions be "armorized," that is, that their infantry be organized and equipped as was the infantry of armored divisions.[10] Large tank masses in armored divisions would thus operate alongside large infantry masses carried in half-tracks. AGF headquarters, however, believed that the solution to the problem was not the armorizing of motorized divisions but rather the placing of small infantry units in close association with small tank units.[11]

General McNair (as though to show the semi-independent status of the Armored Force) laid General Devers' proposals before the War Department along with his own on 7 December 1942.[12] He himself, not wishing simply to put an armorized infantry division alongside armored divisions in an armored corps or simply to add infantry to the existing armored division which he believed already unwieldy, and not yet ready to break down the armored division and recombine the parts, proposed a temporary expedient pending experience to be gained in combat. He recommended that a pool of twenty-five separate armored infantry battalions be established from which armored divisions could be reinforced as necessary. He likewise recommended curtailment of the program for motorized divisions, believing that armored infantry battalions would best fill the need for close support of advancing tanks, and that other forms of infantry support, such as the taking over of positions won by armor, could be

---

[8] See (1) AGF 2d ind (S) to Armd F, 24 May 42, on AGF ltr to CofArmdF, 2 May 42, sub: Light Armd Divs. 320.2/1 (Armd F) (S). (2) Memo of 7 Dec cited in footnote 12 below.

[9] Ltr (C) of Gen McNair to CG Armd F, 24 Aug 42, sub: Proportion of Inf in Armd Div. 320.2/18 (Armd F) (C).

[10] Ltr (C) of Gen Devers to CG AGF, 6 Nov 42, sub: Grenadier Brigs of Panzer Divs. 320.2/18 (Armd F) (C).

[11] Papers, including a study by Col R. F. Ennis (item 4 of AGF M/S, CG to G–2, 12 Nov 42). 320.2/18 (Armd F) (C).

[12] Memo (R) of Gen McNair for G–3 OPD, 7 Dec 42, sub: Orgn of Armd Units. 320.2/18 (Armd F) (C).

furnished by standard infantry divisions moved when necessary by trucks from an army pool.

The fate of the motorized division is traced below. The War Department hesitated to abandon this unit but did authorize the mobilization of fifteen battalions of armored infantry. It was felt also in the War Department General Staff, after further study of foreign armies, that reorganization of the American armored division must be immediately considered.[13] The commanding general of the Army Ground Forces was instructed, on 26 January 1943, to prepare new tables at once.[14]

General McNair submitted, on 28 January, one of his most careful statements on the use of armor:[15]

1. The basic memorandum presents clearly and impressively a broad picture of tremendous significance—one which, in my view, we have not yet faced adequately.

2. It is believed that our general concept of an armored force—that it is an instrument of exploitation, not greatly different in principle from horse cavalry of old—is sound. However, some, particularly armored enthusiasts, have been led away from this concept by current events which have been misinterpreted. The German armored force of 1940 was organized for a particular situation, and was brilliantly successful for that reason. It was used at the outset as a force of exploitation, since it was well known that nothing in Europe at that time was capable of stopping it; the antitank measures then in vogue were wholly and hopelessly inadequate.

3. The struggles in Libya—particularly the battles of late May and early June, 1942—demonstrated conclusively that armor could not assault strong, organized positions except with prohibitive losses. The German 88 ruined the British armored force, which was employed unsoundly. The German armored force then exploited the success obtained and ruined the entire British force.

4. The battle of El Alamein demonstrated the correct employment of the British armor, which was held in reserve until the infantry, artillery, and air had opened a hole. The British armor then exploited the success and destroyed the German force.

5. Thus, we need large armored units to exploit the success of our infantry. We need small armored units also, in order to assist the infantry locally. The Russians appear to have devoted their armor largely to the latter principle, influenced undoubtedly by the fact that until recently they have been on the defensive strategically. It seems doubtful that they will need large armored units in the near future. If they do, such units can be formed readily.

[13] WD memo (S) MID 904 (1–11–43) for CofS USA, 11 Jan 43, sub: Trends in Orgn of Armd Fs. 320.2/20 (Armd F) (S).
[14] This paper has not been located, but is cited in General McNair's memo, 28 January 1943, and elsewhere.
[15] Memo (S) of Gen McNair for G–3 WD, 28 Jan 43, sub: Trends in Orgn of Armd Fs. 320.2/20 (Armd F) (S).

6. It is believed unwise to adopt the hybrid infantry-armored division of the British, since a division normally should contain organically only those elements which are needed in all situations. Armor is not needed on the defensive under our concept, tank destroyers being provided for the defeat of armored attacks, and having demonstrated their effectiveness for this purpose. Our GHQ tank battalions are sound for attachment to infantry divisions on the offensive where terrain and situation permit their effective employment.

7. It is believed that our 1943 troop basis has entirely too many armored divisions, considering their proper tactical employment, and too few GHQ tank battalions. It is particularly important that the latter be available in quantities to permit all infantry divisions to work with them freely and frequently. Such training has been impracticable in the past and probably will be so in 1943. This matter was brought up in connection with consideration of the 1943 troop basis, but the view presented by this headquarters was not favored by the War Department.

8. A reorganization of the armored division will be proposed in the near future, in accordance with your memorandum of January 26, 1943.

Later, General McNair wrote to the commander of the 1st Armored Division in Italy: "The big question in my mind is the relative merit of tank battalions attached to infantry divisions vs. infantry attached to armored divisions. I lean toward employing armored divisions for exploitation and tank battalions attached to infantry divisions for your present job of infighting." [16]

The work of preparing new tables for the armored division went on from January to August 1943. Numerous conferences were required to harmonize the views of the Armored Force, the Army Ground Forces, and the War Department General Staff.[17] During this period the 1st Armored Division saw action in Africa, the 2d in Sicily, but neither was employed as a unit in the type of mission for which armored divisions were intended. Combat experience, therefore, furnished only fragmentary guidance. A board of officers, convened by the Fifth Army during the African campaign, under Maj. Gen. Ernest N. Harmon, recommended many changes of detail, some of which were incorporated in the new tables, but on the whole favored no fundamental change until more armored divisions had engaged in combat.[18] New tables were nevertheless published as of 15 September 1943. All armored divisions were then physically reorganized except the 2d and 3d, which remained under the 1942 tables with modifications.

---

[16] Personal ltr of Gen McNair to Maj Gen E. N. Harmon, 3 Apr 44. McNair Correspondence.

[17] Transcript of discussion at conference between AGF and Armored Force officers on 17 March 1943 is included in file. 320.2/26 (Armd F)(S).

[18] Maj Gen E. N. Harmon, "Report on Combat Experience and Battle Lessons for Training Purposes," to AFHQ, 13 Jun 43. 319.1/13 (NATO) (S).

In redesigning the armored division, in advance of combat experience and in view of wide differences of opinion, both the Army Ground Forces and the Armored Force desired as elastic and adaptable a structure as possible.[19] The same principles of flexibility were applied as were currently being applied to nondivisional army and corps troops. The regimental echelon in the armored division was abolished. The battalion became the basic unit. The division received organically three battalions of tanks, three of armored infantry, and three of armored field artillery. Infantry strength in proportion to tanks was thereby doubled. At the same time separate tank battalions, separate armored infantry battalions, and separate armored field artillery battalions were set up in nondivisional pools. These battalions were made identical with the corresponding battalions organic in the armored division. Hence they could readily be attached to the armored division.

To make possible ready attachment and detachment all battalions of armored types—tank, infantry, and artillery, both those organic in the armored division and those which were nondivisional—were made administratively self-contained. Each received a service company (or battery) to bring supplies from army supply points, and a headquarters company (or battery) large enough to carry the burden of administration. All tank battalions became alike and hence interchangeable. Previously there had been battalions of medium tanks and battalions of light tanks; plans for the heavy tank battalion were suspended early in 1943 and in any case did not apply to the armored division. The new composite tank battalion was much stronger than the old medium battalion. Like the old medium battalion it had three companies of medium tanks; in addition it had a company of light tanks for reconnaissance or other missions requiring speed, and six medium tanks mounting 105-mm. howitzers.

"The fundamental objective," General McNair wrote to General Patton, "is to provide more infantry than at present. However, the organization is such that battalions of either armor or infantry may be added or subtracted from a division at will. Although the division organically probably will aggregate some-

---

[19] On this and following paragraphs: (1) Personal ltr of Gen Devers to Gen McNair, 1 Dec 42. 320.2/422 (Armd F). (2) Personal ltr of Gen McNair to Gen Patton, 21 Aug 43. McNair Correspondence. (3) Personal ltr of Gen McNair to Gen Harmon, 3 Apr 44. McNair Correspondence. (4) Correspondence between AGF and Armd F. 320.2/66 (Armd F) (R). (5) Armd F ltr to AGF, 11 Jun 43, sub: T/O&E's for Armd F Units. 320.2/487 (Armd F). (6) AGF memo (R) for G–3 WD, 23 Jun 43, sub: Reorgn of Armd Divs. 320.2/66 (Armd F) (R). (7) AGF memo for G–3 WD, 1 Sep 43, sub as above. 320.2–66 (Armd F) (R). (8) Published T/O 17 and related tables of 15 Sep 43.

thing like 11,000, you may make it 20,000 if you so desire, simply by adding armored or infantry battalions." [20] He might have said armored artillery battalions also, or, indeed, engineer, ordnance, or other units, since all nondivisional units in the Army Ground Forces were being reorganized in the same way. In General McNair's mind the distinction between the armored division and temporary armored formations tended to fade. He envisaged the possibility that armored groups might perform the role of armored divisions. Battalions of tanks, armored infantry, and armored artillery, taken from nondivisional pools, could, instead of being added to armored divisions, be combined with each other under group headquarters and with such service units as were needed, and thus in effect constitute small temporary armored divisions.[21]

In practice no such over-all flexibility was obtained. While some twenty separate battalions of armored artillery remained in existence, all but one of the separate armored infantry battalions were inactivated in 1943 in the face of the manpower shortage. Nor were enough separate tank battalions mobilized to provide an effective pool. The need of infantry divisions for tanks, in the campaigns in Italy, western Europe, and elsewhere, proved to be more constant than was anticipated in 1942 and 1943. Hence virtually all available tank battalions became more or less permanently attached to infantry divisions. Interchangeability broke down. Armored divisions could not be reinforced by tank or armored infantry battalions. Nor could armored battalions be combined into armored groups. The armored group in the theaters lost its functions.[22]

Flexibility within the armored division was enhanced by the reorganization. Elimination of the tank regiments and the infantry regiment, and creation of self-contained battalions, made all battalions directly attachable to the combat commands or to the "reserve command" set up as a third subheadquarters in the reorganized division. General McNair desired that the two combat commands be redesignated "groups." [23] As headquarters to which battalions could be variably attached by the division commander they strongly resembled the group headquarters then being widely introduced for flexible control of nondivisional units. Adoption of the term "group" would have emphasized the tendency for the armored division to lose divisional identity. But "combat

---

[20] Personal ltr of Gen McNair to Gen Patton, 21 Aug 43. McNair Correspondence.

[21] See below, pp. 333–35.

[22] For example, Observers Rpt M–1 (Lt Col F. Bacon on Luzon Operations), 1 Mar 45. AGF G–2 Files.

[23] (1) AGF M/S (R), CG to Rqts, 2 Feb 43. AGF Orgn Div, Rqts Sec file. (2) Items in footnote 19 above. (3) G–3 WD memo (R) for CG AGF, 22 Jul 43, Sub: Reorgn of Armd Divs. 320.2/66 (Armd F) (R).

command," preferred by the Armored Force, was favored by the War Department. It was decided also by the War Department that only one combat command should be headed by a brigadier general, the other being allotted a colonel—a "curious set-up" according to General McNair, since the functions of the two commands were the same.[24]

The Armored Force urged repeatedly that a tank destroyer battalion and an antiaircraft artillery battalion be made organic in the armored division. The argument for organic inclusion of these elements was stronger for the armored than for the infantry division; it was universally favored among overseas commanders and it was also supported by many officers of the AGF headquarters staff. Even the Reduction Board, General McNair's selected "No-men," recommended inclusion.[25] General McNair would have none of it, declining to add to "the monstrous array of transportation already encumbering" the armored division.[26] He insisted that these defensive weapons be pooled and attached as needed. The War Department supported him even against a recommendation of the European Theater of Operations.[27]

The number of tanks in the armored division was cut from 390 to 263, as compared with about 200 usually found at this time in German and British armored divisions. Thus, while tank battalions were reduced from 6 to 3, or 50 percent, and tank-unit personnel from 4,848 to 2,187, or 55 percent, the number of tanks was reduced only 30 percent. The number of M–4 medium tanks was reduced only 25 percent.

Armored infantry was greatly strengthened. The commanding general of the 1st Armored Division reported that the armored infantry regiment, under the 1942 tables, had approximately the strength of an infantry battalion as organized in the infantry division, "after the overhead including some 544 drivers have been removed." [28] He recommended the use of standard infantry in the armored division. General McNair, who generally preferred standard to specialized units

---

[24] Personal ltr of Gen McNair to Gen Harmon, 3 Apr 44. McNair Correspondence.

[25] AGF M/S (S), Col Eyerly to Rqts and CG, undated (June 1943). 319.1/13 (NATO) (S).

[26] (1) AGF memo (C) for G–3 WD, 5 Nov 42, sub: AA Defense. 320.2/12 (AA) (C). (2) Memo (S) of Gen McNair for DCofS USA, 20 Jul 43, sub: Comments on Maj Gen Harmon's Rpt. 319.1/13 (NATO) (S).

[27] (1) Radio (S) CM–In–2005, Devers to WD, 3 Jul 43. (2) Radio (S) CM–Out–1994, WD to Devers, 5 Jul 43. WD Classified Message Center.

[28] Maj Gen E. N. Harmon, par 3 g, "Report on Combat Experience and Battle Lessons for Training Purposes," to AFHQ, 13 Jun 43. 319.1/13 (NATO) (S).

The Armored Division, 1 March 1942 and 15 September 1943

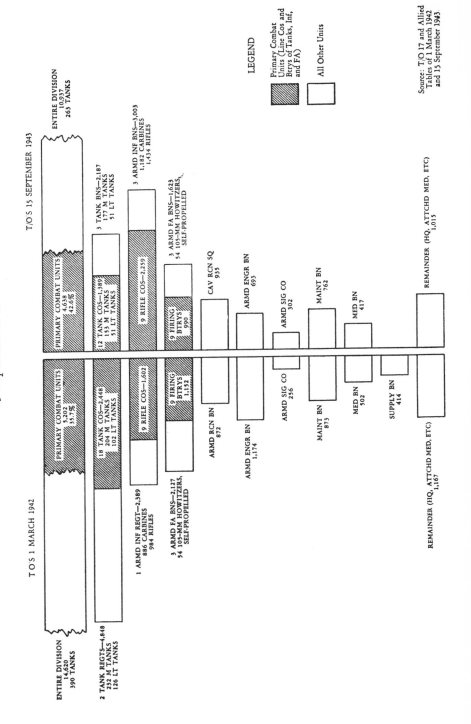

T O S 1 MARCH 1942

T/O S 15 SEPTEMBER 1943

ENTIRE DIVISION
14,620
390 TANKS

ENTIRE DIVISION
10,937
263 TANKS

PRIMARY COMBAT UNITS
5,202
35.7%

PRIMARY COMBAT UNITS
4,638
42.6%

2 TANK REGTS—4,848
232 M TANKS
126 LT TANKS

3 TANK BNS—2,187
177 M TANKS
51 LT TANKS

18 TANK COS—2,448
204 M TANKS
102 LT TANKS

12 TANK COS—1,389
153 M TANKS
51 LT TANKS

1 ARMD INF REGT—2,389
886 CARBINES
984 RIFLES

3 ARMD INF BNS—3,003
1,182 CARBINES
1,434 RIFLES

9 RIFLE COS—1,602

9 RIFLE COS—2,259

3 ARMD FA BNS—2,127
54 105-MM HOWITZERS,
SELF-PROPELLED

3 ARMD FA BNS—1,623
54 105-MM HOWITZERS,
SELF-PROPELLED

9 FIRING BTRYS
1,152

9 FIRING BTRYS
990

ARMD RCN BN
872

CAV RCN SQ
935

ARMD ENGR BN
1,174

ARMD ENGR BN
693

ARMD SIG CO
256

ARMD SIG CO
302

MAINT BN
873

MAINT BN
762

MED BN
502

MED BN
417

SUPPLY BN
414

REMAINDER (HQ, ATTCHD MED, ETC)
1,167

REMAINDER (HQ, ATTCHD MED, ETC)
1,015

LEGEND

Primary Combat Units (Line Cos and Btrys of Tanks, Inf, and FA)

All Other Units

Source: T/O 17 and Allied Tables of 1 March 1942 and 15 September 1943.

where feasible, did not favor this proposal.[29] Nor was it possible to drop many drivers from armored infantry units. The strengthening of armored infantry was accomplished by a positive increase in numbers, the battalion rising to a total of 1,001. The three battalions combined carried 750 more rifles and carbines than the regiment which they replaced, as well as a heavy increase in machine guns and bazookas. The ratio of infantrymen per tank for the division rose from 6.1 to 11.4.

Overhead was saved, as in the infantry division, by pushing some functions forward to line units and others rearward to army. Concentration of administrative activities in the battalions, and elimination of the regiment as a rigid and unnecessary barrier between battalions and combat commands, led to a great saving in personnel not intended primarily for combat. Half the strength of the two tank regiments in the 1942 tables was regimental and battalion overhead. (See chart, "The Armored Division.") Only a third of the strength of the three tank battalions in the 1943 tables was overhead. In the infantry component the proportion of personnel not in rifle companies fell from about a third to about a quarter. In the artillery battalions personnel was cut about 25 percent through drastic reduction of headquarters and service batteries.

Auxiliary elements were reduced less than in the infantry division. Indeed the reconnaissance and signal elements were enlarged. Economy was indirectly effected in reconnaissance through standardization; the battalion, hitherto a special armored organization, was now constituted as a squadron of four cavalry troops of the type organic in the infantry division, plus an assault gun troop and one light tank company of the type organic in the reorganized tank battalion. The engineer battalion was cut more than 40 percent at the personal insistence of General McNair, who believed that it should resemble the engineer battalion of the infantry division. The treadway bridge company was removed and made a nondivisional army unit. The four general engineer companies were reduced to three. General McNair found it inconsistent for armored proponents to argue that a great advantage of tracked vehicles was their ability to move off roads and at the same time to demand an exceptional complement of engineers because roads used by tracked vehicles needed frequent repair.[30]

---

[29] Memo (S) of Gen McNair for DCofS USA, 20 Jul 43, sub: Comments on Maj Gen Harmon's Rpt. 319.1/13 (NATO) (S).
[30] AGF M/S, CG to Red Bd, 31 Mar 43, sub: Armd Engr Bn. AGF Orgn Div, Rqts Sec file "Armored Division" (36560).

Much controversy developed over the division supply battalion, a quartermaster unit. The supply battalion represented the doctrine that the armored division might operate far from the mass of the forces, beyond normal support by army units. "Unquestionably," wrote General Patton from North Africa, "our original conception that we needed 250 miles of rolling supplies is erroneous. In the fighting we are now having, and did have, you were damn lucky if you got forward three miles a day. When a breakthrough occurs you can always steal enough trucks from corps or army to give you the additional rolling reserve." [31] This statement was seized upon by General McNair, who desired, for the armored division as for the infantry division, that supply should be direct from army supply points to using units, bypassing the division. General Gillem, returning from Africa and Sicily, urged that the supply battalion be retained. Officers of General McNair's staff were divided. General McNair settled the issue, noting for his Requirements Section on 10 August 1943 the following considerations: [32]

I feel definitely that we have passed the stage of arguments in connection with reorganizing the armored division. . . . I have contacted various individuals about it for a period of many months, and there are many, many views; it is impossible to meet all of them.

There is no question whatever that the division is oversupplied. Patton has admitted this categorically. Also there is no question that the army can supply the armored division as well as any other element. I am informed that Patton now has in Sicily a mere 23,000 motor vehicles, and it is not hard for me to believe it.

The supply battalion was omitted.

The new armored division, to summarize, numbered 10,937 officers and men. The main innovation was the increase in the ratio of infantry to tanks, achieved both by raising the number of infantrymen and by reducing the number of tanks. The division was cut almost 4,000 in personnel, of whom 2,661 came out of tank units. Tank units lost more than 50 percent in personnel, but only 25 percent in medium tanks. Some 500 individuals were taken from the armored artillery without loss of fire power. Other savings of personnel were mainly in the relegation of certain quartermaster and engineer functions to army. The conspicuous feature of the new division was the 3:3:3 ratio of battalions of tanks, infantry, and artillery, and the flexible command arrangements

---

[31] Personal ltr (S) of Gen Patton to Gen Gillem (cpy sent to AGF), 21 May 43. 320.2/24 (Armd F) (S).

[32] AGF M/Ss (R) written between 31 Jul and 10 Aug 1943. 320.2/78 (Armd F) (R).

by which those battalions were held together. With its auxiliaries, the new armored division was a federation of thirteen battalions led by a major general. It was intended that the federation be an open one, able to absorb by attachment tank destroyer and antiaircraft battalions, as well as additional battalions of tanks, infantry, and artillery.

Tank battalions withdrawn from the armored divisions became available as nondivisional units. Two were obtained from each of the fourteen divisions reorganized (all but the 2d and 3d Armored Divisons).[33] Theoretically the reduction from 6 to 3 tank battalions in each division should have released 3 in each; but the simultaneous enlargement of the battalions absorbed 1 battalion per division. The newly gained separate battalions, added to those already mobilized, produced for the first time a number of separate tank battalions roughly equivalent to the number of infantry divisions.[34] This ratio had long been desired by the Army Ground Forces. It was tardily reached, in the closing months of 1943, because of the time spent in redesigning the armored division, and because of the unwillingness of the War Department to authorize more tank battalions until the armored division question was settled.[35] Consequently it was only at the end of 1943 that tank battalions were available in sufficient numbers to permit infantry divisions to undergo combined training with tanks.

The net effect of the reorganization of the armored division, aside from making the armored division a more effective team of combined arms, was to shift the bulk of the tank strength of the Army from armored divisions to the support of infantry. Plans at the end of 1942 envisaged, for the end of 1943, 120 tank battalions in armored divisions and only 38 in the nondivisional pool. What the Army actually had at the end of 1943 was 54 battalions in armored divisions and 65 in the nondivisional pool.[36] Tank battalions in the nondivisional

---

[33] (1) AGF memo (C) for G–3 WD, 18 Aug 43, sub: Reorgn of Tank Bns. 321/3 (Tank Units) (C). (2) AGF memo (S) for G–3 WD, 22 Sep 43, sub: Tactical and Tng Control of GHQ Tank Bns. 320.2/36 (TB 43) (S). Thirteen divisions, from the 4th to the 20th Armored, inclusive, were reorganized by the Army Ground Forces. The 1st Armored was reorganized overseas.

[34] See above, "Ground Forces in the Army, December 1941–April 1945: a Statistical Study."

[35] WD memo (S) WDGCT 320 (1–11–43) for CG AGF, 5 Feb 43, sub: Trends in Orgn of Armd Fs, with related papers. 320.2/20 (Armd F) (S).

[36] Counting 3 tank battalions in each of 14 armored divisions, 6 in each of 2 armored divisions. The differences in totals for tank battalions were due to over-all curtailment of the mobilization program for Ground Forces. See above, "Ground Forces in the Army, December 1941–April 1945: a Statistical Study."

pool, despite projects for their employment in armored groups or in reinforcement of armored divisions, in practice became habitually attached to infantry divisions in the theaters. With the infantry division gaining tanks, and the armored division gaining infantry, the two came slightly together. But the difference remained radical: the armored division had a battalion of tanks for each battalion of infantry; the infantry division, with an attached tank battalion, had a battalion of tanks for nine battalions of infantry. The two divisions remained suited for altogether different roles, since their infantry also was differently equipped.

General McNair continued to consider the armored division an expensive military investment. The new tables had not long been published when he noted, on 9 October 1943, that the "slugging component" of the division (tanks and infantry) numbered only 5,190, the remaining 5,747 being supporting and overhead elements.[37] To maintain sixteen armored divisions seemed to him a luxury in the circumstances then obtaining, with manpower so short that planned activations were being cancelled and infantry divisions were being stripped for replacements needed in Italy. Events of 1943 had confirmed him in the belief, stated on 28 January 1943 in the memorandum quoted at length above, that the proper function of armored divisions was to exploit a success already won. For this purpose he thought, in October 1943, that an army aggregating only ninety divisions of all types needed no more than ten armored divisions. "An armored division," he wrote, "is of value only in pursuit or exploitation. For plain and fancy slugging against an enemy who is unbroken or at least intact the tank battalion or group is adequate." He thought that tank and infantry battalions could engage in close fighting with less overhead than the armored division provided. He recommended to the War Department that six armored divisions be inactivated, their tank and infantry battalions retained as nondivisional units, and their remaining personnel used either as overseas replacements or as fillers for new units in the mobilization program.[38] The War Department rejected this proposal, and the Army retained its sixteen armored divisions.

It was felt by some that General McNair took a negative and unfriendly attitude toward armor. That he was a severe critic of armored organization cannot be doubted. Challenged on these matters in February 1944, he declared flatly to the Assistant Secretary of War, speaking of the forthcoming invasion of west-

[37] AGF M/S (C), CG to Plans, 1 Oct 43. AGF Plans Sec file (C).
[38] AGF memo (S) for G–3 WD, 16 Oct 43, sub: TB 1944. 320.2/1 (TB 44) (S).

ern Europe, that "whether armor will pay its freight remains to be seen." [39] He had in mind, as of that date, the plan whereby one-third of the divisions used in the invasion would be armored. The whole question was one of ratios; it was not that General McNair scorned the armored division, but rather that he believed more infantry divisions were needed, and that ship tonnage would deliver more fighting power if the proportion of armor were reduced. As it turned out, the War Department after June 1944 was obliged to feed infantry divisions into the European Theater more rapidly than had been anticipated.

[39] Memo (S) of Gen McNair for ASW, 8 Feb 44, sub: Views Presented by Brig Gen R. E. Shugg. 330.14/100 (Criticisms) (S).

VI. Experimental Divisions

Infantry and armored divisions bore the main burden of the land fighting in World War II: they came to number eighty-two out of the eighty-nine divisions mobilized. Motorized, cavalry, airborne, mountain, and light divisions were in varying degree experimental—even more so than the armored division, although they were in substance infantry divisions, differing from standard infantry chiefly in their means of transport to the scene of combat.

Cavalry and Motorized Divisions

The cavalry division may seem an exception. Far from being a novel experiment, the cavalry division was an old organization, and its cavalrymen remained in principle horsed, not mechanized.[1] But transportation of horses was so costly in ship tonnage, and their feeding and upkeep presented such great difficulties to a motorized army, that no plans were made for shipment of cavalry divisions with their mounts. Of the two divisions mobilized, the 2d Cavalry Division was dispatched to North Africa early in 1944 only to be inactivated and broken up. Suitable employment for the 1st Cavalry Division was found in the Southwest Pacific, where it fought dismounted as infantry, under special Tables of Organization and Equipment which raised it almost to the size of an infantry division. It retained the basic square formation of the cavalry division and lacked the 155-mm. howitzer battalion found in the infantry division, but was supplied with special allowances of heavy weapons and other equipment of infantry type. It should be noted that the single cavalry

---

[1] (1) Memo of SW for USW, 21 Jul 42, sub not given. 321/99 (Cav). (2) AGF memo for G–3 WD, 5 May 42, sub: Cav Orgn. 321/51 (Cav).

division included only a fraction of cavalry units in the Army, for over 20,000 cavalrymen, all mechanized, were present in infantry and armored divisions, and almost 30,000 in nondivisional cavalry squadrons, chiefly mechanized.

The motorized division was adopted shortly after Pearl Harbor, with the intention that one be mobilized for each two armored divisions, the three to form a normal armored corps. The division in its short life went through various stages of planning, but in general it was conceived as an infantry division equipped organically with trucks for simultaneous movement without shuttling, and with large elements for reconnaissance, maintenance, and supply to give it tactical independence. From the beginning General McNair advised against this type of division, believing it wasteful to assign so much transportation organically, and preferring that improvements in infantry be made available to all infantry divisions alike.[2]

Five infantry divisions were ordered converted to motorized in 1942, and five more were planned for 1943; but in practice only the 4th Division was fully outfitted with the appropriate equipment, and it received so great an additional quantity of equipment and personnel, over the established Table of Organization, as to constitute a special task force. It was earmarked in August 1942 for overseas shipment. But it required so much ship tonnage—as much as an armored division without having the same hitting power—that no theater commander requested it in the following months.[3] Even at T/O strength, the motorized division included almost 3,000 vehicles, over 1,000 more than the reduced infantry division as planned by the Army Ground Forces. Its tires consumed almost twice as many tons of rubber—318 compared with 166. Its equipment required almost twice as much ocean tonnage—approximately 60,000 compared with 32,0000. The motorized division was, therefore, viewed with extreme disfavor by the AGF Reduction Board. General McNair recommended its abolition.[4]

The question was not whether infantry should be motorized, but how motor vehicles should be organized to motorize it most effectively. Infantry could not

[2] Memo for Gen Moore, 19 Jan 42, sub: Conservation of Mil Equip. McNair Correspondence.

[3] AGF memo (S) for G–3 WD, 4 May 1943, sub: Reorgn of the Mtz Div. 322/5 (4th Div) (S).

[4] (1) WD ltr AG 320.2 (1–19–42) PC–C, 20 Feb 42, sub: Orgn of the Mtz Div. AGO Records. (2) T/O 77, 1 Aug 42. (3) Table, undated (Jan 43) sub: Comparative figures between Mtz and Inf Divs. AGF Orgn Div, Rqts Sec files. (4) AGF M/S (S), Red Bd to CG, 23 Jan 43, sub: Mtz Div. AGF Orgn Div, Rqts Sec files. (5) Memo (C) of Gen McNair for G–3 WD, 7 Dec 42, sub: Orgn of Armd Units. 320.2/18 (Armd F) (C). (6) Memo (S) of Gen McNair for G–3 WD, 28 Jan 43, sub: Basis of Orgn of Mtz Div. 322/1 (Divs) (S).

fight from trucks; trucks were used only to put it into position for battle. It was desirable that a given number of trucks provide this form of mobility for a maximum number of troops. In 1936 the War Department, when planning to triangularize the division, had laid down the principle that motor transport for infantrymen should be pooled. General McNair clung to this principle. Shipping considerations now gave it added weight.

The standard infantry division was by no means immobile. All elements but the infantry were motorized. With its organic trucks the division could move in short bounds by shuttling, its trucks dumping their organic loads, moving the infantry, then returning to bring up the loads. As reduced by the Army Ground Forces in the months following November 1942, the division could move all personnel and equipment simultaneously if reinforced by six quartermaster truck companies, each operating forty-eight 2½-ton trucks. Six such companies, even with forty-eight 1-ton trailers apiece, required only 15,000 ship tons, roughly half the difference between the standard infantry and the motorized infantry division. With a pool of such companies an army commander could operate flexibly, either using the trucks to motorize infantry divisions at will or employing them for altogether different purposes if more urgent.

For a time the Operations Division (OPD), War Department General Staff, was unwilling to do away with the motorized division, believing it necessary as a means of giving infantry support to armored divisions. The decision to raise the infantry-tank ratio within the armored division reduced this need. OPD withdrew its objections on 18 February 1943, contingent upon reorganization of the armored division as proposed by the Army Ground Forces. All motorized divisions except the 4th were reconverted to standard infantry in March 1943.[5]

The Army Ground Forces, understanding from OPD that there was no prospective employment for a motorized division, requested permission to reconvert the 4th also.[6] OPD decided that "the 4th Motorized Division should be maintained for the present as a nucleus of personnel trained for a function, the value of which has not been conclusively disproved."[7] The European Theater, queried

---

[5] (1) WD memo (S) WDGCT 320 (12–7–42) for CofS USA, 16 Jan 43, sub: Orgn of Armd Units. AGO Records 320.2 (1–16–43) (5) (S). (2) WD memo (S) WDGCT 320 (2–24–43) to CofS USA, 24 Feb 43, sub: Reorgn of the Mtz Div. AGO Records, 320.2 (12–7–42) (S).

[6] AGF memo (S) for G–3 WD, 4 May 43, sub: Reorgn of Mtz Div. 322/5 (4th Div) (S).

[7] WD D/F (S) OPD 320.2 ETO (5–4–43) for G–3 WD, 6 May 43, sub as above. 322/5 (4th Div) (S).

on the subject, stated on 16 June 1943 that no motorized division was included in its plans for 1944 but that all infantry divisions should receive training in motor movement.[8] The 4th Division was then reconverted. A standing operating procedure for motor movement of infantry divisions was developed by the Infantry School.[9] Motor movement with attached trucks became a standard part of infantry division training.

Disappearance of the motorized division as a special unit was an incident in the reorganization of infantry and armored divisions. Its loss was not regretted later. Under stress of combat, units accomplished feats of transport not foreseen by the most economical planners. The 18th Infantry, during the rush across northern France, after having required 100 quartermaster trucks for the same type of job, found that it could move more than thirty miles a day without additional transportation, remaining at all times in condition to fight, simply by piling infantrymen on the howitzers, tanks, and tank destroyers attached to the regimental combat team.[10] By similar improvised methods the entire 36th Division passed through the city of Rome in ten hours.[11]

Airborne, Mountain, Jungle and "Light" Divisions

It was clear in 1942 that the Army must prepare itself for a variety of specialized operations, both operations under extreme conditions of climate, exemplified in Norway, Libya, and Malaysia, and operations by special means of assault, such as amphibious and airborne. The practical question was how far to go in organizing special-type units for these operations. General McNair did not wish to go very far. Following the principles of flexibility and economy, he was disinclined to organize manpower and resources for special needs which might never materialize, or which, if they did, might be less urgent than the need for standard forces. He believed that training in special-type units almost invariably taught particular skills ("tricks") at the expense of general military proficiency. He emphasized the futility of perfecting men in the techniques of skis, gliders, or

---

[8] Radio (S) CM–In–10004, 16 Jun 43 (S). WD Classified Message Center.

[9] AGF ltr to TIS, 27 Aug 43, sub: SOP for Inf Divs Provided with Mtr Trans for Foot Elements. 321/696 (Inf).

[10] "Battle Experiences Published by Hq 12th Army Group," No. 64 (R), 13 Oct 44. AGF G–2 Records.

[11] Maj Gen F. L. Walker, "Experiences with the 36th Division in Italy," *Military Review*, XXIV (1945), 15.

landing craft if after meeting the enemy they were not competent all-round soldiers. He preferred, therefore, to have the Army Ground Forces concentrate on production of standard units and give special training only to units which had completed their standard training, and only when operations requiring special training could be definitely foreseen. Much of such training, he thought, could best be given in the theaters. Training for specialized operations could be more realistic in the theater where the operations were to take place, and such operations usually required a long enough period of preparation to make appropriate training feasible.[12]

In the six months from March to September 1942 the Army Ground Forces launched four special installations: the Desert Training Center, the Airborne Command (later "Center"), the Amphibious Training Command (later "Center"), and the Mountain Training Center.[13] Each had the mission of testing equipment and formulating requirements within the field of its specialty, and of supervising the special training of such standard units as might be entrusted to it for the purpose. The Airborne Command also produced special-type troops, at first mainly parachutists but including a glider battalion. At the Mountain Training Center a few specially designated mountain units were assembled. No specially designated desert or amphibious forces developed. Airborne and mountain troops were not organized in units as large as the division.

The airborne and the mountain divisions, though not yet physically organized, were among the six types of divisions recognized by the War Department in March 1942. The mountain division was a true division, with a published Table of Organization. The airborne division was not thought of as a true division but rather as a task force to be assembled when needed by combining parachute regiments with standard forces trained in air transport for the occasion. This conception of the airborne division kept reappearing in the following years.

The strategic plans initiated in March 1942, looking to invasion of western Europe in April 1943, included the use of one United States airborne division.[14] General McNair, after consultation with the Airborne Command, became convinced of the need for a formally organized airborne division, activated and trained as such. "An airborne division should be evolved," he noted for his staff

---

[12] See for example AGF memo (S) for G–3 WD, 24 Oct 42, sub: Jungle Tng. 353/1 (Mtn & Jungle) (S).

[13] See studies of each of these installations prepared by the AGF Historical Section.

[14] Memo (S) of Col Lemnitzer for CofS AGF, 17 Jun 42, sub: A/B Div for Bolero. AGF Plans Sec file, 20/1 (Bolero) (S).

in June 1942, "with a stinginess of overhead and in transportation which has absolutely no counterpart thus far in our military establishment." [15] The War Department approved an AGF proposal to activate two such divisions, and in August 1942 the 82d and the 101st Airborne Divisions were formed by conversion of the 82d Infantry Division, with added parachute regiments.[16] A Table of Organization for the airborne division, prepared at the headquarters of the Army Ground Forces in August, was published under date of 15 October 1942.[17] Five airborne divisions were eventually activated under this table.

As conceived in 1942 (and until the end of 1944) the airborne division was a miniature infantry division, with an aggregate strength of only 8,500, but complete with all normal divisional parts plus a small organic antiaircraft battalion. Each division had one parachute infantry regiment, and two glider infantry regiments, numbering 1,958 and 1,605 men respectively, in contrast with the 3,000 troops in the standard infantry regiment. Weapons were those of the infantry division, with a predominance of the lighter types; the division artillery consisted of thirty-six 75-mm. pack howitzers. Vehicles numbered only 408 motors and 239 trailers, a total of 647, in contrast with some 2,000 in the standard infantry division. The division had no organic aircraft, depending for movement on the pool of transport planes controlled by the Army Air Forces.

Tables for the airborne division remained substantially unchanged for two years. On entering combat, however, the airborne divisions departed considerably from their tabular organization, rearranging their resources to meet the circumstances of each case.

In the summer of 1942, with an offensive in the Southwest Pacific in view, the War Department turned its attention to the preparation of mountain and jungle troops. The standard infantry division had too many heavy weapons and vehicles to move easily through roadless, mountainous, or densely wooded country. In August 1942 OPD urged consideration of a lightly equipped jungle division of some 10,000 officers and men.[18] War Department plans for mobiliza-

---

[15] (1) AGF M/S (S), CG to CofS 19 Jun 42. (2) Memo (S) of Gen McNair for G-3 WD, 2 Jul 42, sub: Policy re Tng of A/B Trs. (3) AGF memo (S) for G-3 WD, 17 Jul 42, sub: Activation of A/B Divs. All in 320.2/3 and 4 (AB) (S).

[16] AGF ltr (R) to CGs Third Army and A/B Comd, 30 Jul 42, sub: Activation of 82d and 101st A/B Divs. 320.2/9 (AB) (R).

[17] T/O 71, 15 Oct 42, and allied tables.

[18] WD memo (S) OPD 320.2 (8-7-42) for G-3 WD, 7 Aug 42, sub: Trs for Jungle Combat. 353/3 (Mtn & Jungle) (S).

tion in 1943, though not fully crystallized at this time, contemplated two or three mountain and jungle divisions.[19]

General McNair, while believing jungle training to be possible in certain parts of Florida and Louisiana, had no desire to establish a jungle center in the United States. This view received support from General MacArthur, who notified the War Department that he preferred his units to receive standard training at home, and jungle training in the Southwest Pacific under his own supervision. At the same time General MacArthur agreed that an experiment with a lightly equipped infantry division might be profitable. General McNair saw the formation of mountain and jungle units as two aspects of a single problem, namely, the creation of a unit dependent in large measure on human and animal transportation. He wished a minimum of animals in the Army's transport and advised against the formation of "light divisions," which included animal units, of unsuitable power for employment in many theaters. He thought that for the time being the whole enterprise should be kept on an experimental basis, confined to research on mountain and jungle requirements and to the special training of a few infantry regiments and supporting units. Mountain training on this scale was already beginning at the Mountain Training Center, and jungle training was conducted in Panama. By using personnel so trained as cadres and drawing on the results of research, mountain and jungle divisions could be formed in the future if and when prospects of their employment became more certain.[20]

Both the AGF G–3 Section and OPD, however, favored the formation of light divisions at once.[21] The whole problem of reducing Ground Force needs for ship space was under discussion in October 1942.[22] It was also felt that standard divisions would have to be virtually reorganized, reequipped, and retrained for amphibious operations and for mountain or jungle warfare. This had been the experience with divisions sent to England in the summer of 1942

[19] WD ltr (S) AG 320.2 (8–27–42) MS–C–M to CGs AGF, AAF, SOS, 28 Aug 42, sub: TB 1943. 320.2/3 (TB) (43) (S).

[20] See papers in 353/1 and 3 (Mtn & Jungle) (S), especially AGF memo for G–3 WD, 24 Oct 42, sub: Jungle Tng.

[21] (1) WD memo (S) WDGCT 320.2 Gen (10–1–42) for OPD, 1 Oct 42, sub: Revision of Certain Type Units in TB. (2) WD memo (S) OPD 320.2 (10–1–42) for G–3 WD, sub as above, 12 Oct 42. Both in OPD Records 320.2 Sec IX (9) (S).

[22] See above, pp. 286–89.

for the early cross-Channel plans, with divisions preparing for amphibious landings in North Africa, and with divisions initiating the offensive in the Solomon
Islands and New Guinea. OPD, to avoid such special refitting of standard divisions, proposed an all-purpose light division, to be usable in any conditions
where relatively little equipment could be carried. Such conditions were thought
by OPD to exist not only in mountain and jungle warfare but also in amphibious and airborne undertakings. It was felt by OPD that the light division, like
certain Japanese forces, should be able to operate without motor transport and
even without animals.[23]

In January 1943 the War Department directed the Army Ground Forces
to prepare tables for such a unit.[24] The light division now proposed was more
acceptable to General McNair than the light division previously envisaged. It
was less subject to the disadvantage of overspecialization. At the same time the
general program for economizing manpower and equipment had begun. The
Army Ground Forces was engrossed in the reduction of units of all types. Ship
space for ground troops was critically short. These were the months when no
divisions were leaving the United States. Without having initiated or promoted
the idea of the light division, the Army Ground Forces assumed the task of
developing it and had genuine interest in its success. It was hoped that the light
division, though admittedly weaker than the standard infantry division, would
nevertheless bring to bear, in the circumstances in which it was used, as much
fire power as would a standard division in the same circumstances. It could be
shipped overseas more readily than the standard division, would be easier to
supply and maintain, and like all divisions it could be reinforced as needed from
nondivisional pools.

Preliminary tables for a light division were submitted to the War Department on 2 March 1943.[25] The division as outlined had a total strength of about
9,000. It had the same parts as an infantry division, except that all parts were
smaller, no reconnaissance troop was provided, and field artillery was limited
to three battalions of 75-mm. pack howitzers. The division was meant to be

[23] WD memo (S) OPD 320.2 (12-30-42) for G-3 WD, 30 Dec 42, sub: Light Divs. OPD Records, 320.2
Sec IX (9) (S).

[24] (1) WD D/F (S) WDGCT 320.2 Gen (12-30-42) for CG AGF, 5 Jan 43, sub: Light Divs. (2) AGF
memo (S) for G-3 WD, 29 Jan 43, sub as above. 322/2 (Divs) (S).

[25] (1) AGF memo (S) for G-3 WD, 2 Mar 43, sub as above. 322/2 (Divs) (S). (2) T/O&E 72 T,
21 Jan 44. (3) AGF M/S (C), CG to CofS, 5 Jul 43, sub: Rpt on Winter Opns of 2d Inf Div, 1942-43.
353/1 (Winter) (C).

usable for mountain, jungle, airborne, or amphibious operations through attachment of appropriate transportation. Organic transportation was limited to handcarts (together with toboggan sleds for cold-weather mountain operations), except that the field artillery had either pack mules or 1/4-ton trucks. Other elements than the field artillery would receive transportation by attachment in the form needed—pack mules, light trucks, or native bearers—in quantity sufficient to bring supplies from army supply points (or their equivalent) five miles in the rear, or in larger quantity if supply lines were longer. For airborne operations the light division would train with gliders and would be combined with nondivisional parachute regiments to form an airborne striking force of divisional size. In mountains the division could be reenforced by the attachment of ski troops. Used amphibiously, the division would of course train with landing craft. Armament would vary slightly according to the operation, with special issues of submachine guns for jungle fighting, automatic rifles for airborne and amphibious assaults, and M1 rifles for the mountains.

Organization was now ready, but mobilization remained problematical. Whether or not to convert airborne to light divisions long remained an open question. Conversion of the cavalry divisions was likewise an issue.[26] General McNair in April 1943 recommended the formation of eight light divisions.[27] Ten light divisions were proposed in May by G–3, WDGS, to be formed by conversion of six infantry and four airborne divisions—all the airborne divisions except the 82d, which was already overseas preparing for the landing in Sicily.[28] General Eisenhower thought the light division might have a limited usefulness in such terrain as in Tunisia.[29] Col. F. D. Merrill, then representing General Stilwell in Washington, called the proposed light division almost identical with the Chinese divisions as reorganized in India and believed that light divisions would be valuable in jungles and mountains and in undeveloped countries such as China.[30] General MacArthur, for whose theater the light division had been

[26] (1) Memo (S) of Gen McNair for G–3 WD, 25 Feb 43, sub: Light Divs. 322/2 (Divs) (S). (2) WD memo OPD 320.2 (12–30–42) for G–3 WD, 3 Feb 43, sub as above. OPD Records.

[27] Memo (S) of Gen McNair for G–3 WD, 14 Apr 43, sub: Modification of Mob Procedures. 381/177 (S).

[28] WD memo (S) WDGCT 320.2 Gen (5–17–43) for CofS USA, 17 May 43, sub: Light Divs. OPD Records, 320.2 Sec IX (9) (S).

[29] Radio (S) CM–In–550, Algiers to War, 1 Jun 43. WD Classified Message Center.

[30] Memo (S) of Col F. D. Merrill for Chief, Tr Sec, Logistics Gp, OPD, 22 May 43. Written on OPD letterhead, signed "For Lt. Gen. Stilwell." OPD Records, 320.2 Sec IX (9) (S).

primarily designed, thought the proposed light division too deficient in fire power and too weak logistically for employment in the Pacific islands.[31]

Proceeding cautiously, the War Department in June 1943 authorized the formation for test purposes of only one light division, to be obtained by conversion of one of the standard infantry divisions already mobilized.[32] Attached transportation was to be trucks. The Army Ground Forces, believing that the time had come to give divisional organization to units at the Mountain Training Center, recommended the formation of a second light division, using pack mules. This was approved by the War Department.[33] Coming back to the idea of a jungle division, the Army Ground Forces also recommended and obtained approval for the formation of a third light division, to train as a pack unit.[34]

Three light divisions were therefore authorized in June 1943. The 89th Light Division (Truck) was formed by conversion of the 89th Infantry Division. The 10th Light Division (Pack, Alpine) was activated mainly from elements trained at the Mountain Training Center, centering about the 87th Mountain Infantry Regiment. The 71st Light Division (Pack, Jungle) was activated from miscellaneous elements already mobilized, mainly the 5th Infantry and 14th Infantry, which had received jungle training in Panama. Each was to engage in tests and maneuvers at the earliest practicable moment. Each was in effect a special unit, hardly embodying the flexible principles which lay behind earlier plans. Indeed, the mountaineers and ski experts now incorporated into the 10th Light Division could hardly be used in tropical warfare without excessive waste of human material.

Activation of the three light divisions added no strength to the Army, being simply a reorganization of elements already in existence. The three light divisions were included in the total of ninety divisions of all types to which the mobilization program was reduced in June 1943. With the number of standard divisions thus restricted, no more was heard of converting standard infantry to light. In September General McNair again raised the question of converting

[31] (1) WD memo (S) WDGCT 320.2 Gen (5–21–43) for CofS USA, 21 May 43, sub: Light Divs. AGO Records 322 (21 May 43) (22) (S). (2) For Gen McNair's comments on Gen MacArthur's views, see memo of Gen McNair for G–3 WD, 24 May 43, sub: Proposed Light Div. 322/2 (Divs) (S).

[32] WD memo (S) WDGCT 320.2 Gen (5–21–43) for CofS USA, 21 May 43, sub: Light Divs. AGO Records 322 (21 May 43) (22) (S).

[33] WD memo (S) WDGCT 320.2 Gen (5–21–43) for CG AGF, 3 Jun 43, sub as above, with memo for record. AGO Records 322 (21 May 43) (22) (S).

[34] AGF memo (S) for G–3 WD, 15 Jun 43, sub: 89th and 71st Light Divs, 10th Mtn Div. (Approved by DCofS USA, 21 Jun 43.) 322/2 (Divs) (S).

the airborne divisions.[35] Airborne operations in Sicily had been disappointing. Three airborne divisions were still in the United States, with their usefulness limited to special activities the value of which was currently in doubt. General McNair proposed that the airborne divisions be broken up, with their parachute elements set up as nondivisional units, and their remaining elements organized as light divisions and given a broad general training. Training for airborne operations, he proposed, should take place in the theater for each operation and should be given to combinations of parachute units and light divisions selected for the purpose. This proposal was not accepted by the War Department. In October 1943, while the idea of expanding the Ground Forces to 105 divisions was under consideration, the War Department proposed activating four more light divisions, to make a total of seven.[36] It was now General McNair who opposed an increase of light divisions.[37] He did so even before the collapse of the 105-division program, after which in any case no increase of light divisions would probably have occurred.

General McNair advised against further activation of light divisions because of opposition from the Southwest Pacific. Officers of this theater pronounced the light division useless for amphibious operations since the first landing waves had to be immediately reinforced in all possible strength. They said that heavier artillery than 75-mm. pack howitzers and more capacious vehicles than ¼-ton jeeps were indispensable at whatever cost of ocean shipping or road-building effort. The theater preferred to use the standard division, even when only a fraction of the division was committed, and to employ the remainder of the division as a source of reinforcement and supply. Commanders in the theater declared that the best policy for fighting in remote localities such as the north shore of New Guinea, at the end of long airborne and seaborne supply lines, was to put in a standard division, and use it to the point of exhaustion. The Southwest Pacific Area Command was unwilling to receive any light divisions except as additions to the standard infantry divisions allotted to it.[38]

[35] AGF memo (S) for CofS USA, 22 Sep 43, sub: Rpt of Bd on A/B Opns. 353/17 (AB) (S).

[36] Tentative TB 1944. AGF Plans Sec file 185 (S). See above, "Ground Forces in the Army, December 1941–April 1945: a Statistical Study."

[37] AGF memo (S) for G–3 WD, 17 Nov 43, sub: Proposed Light Div. 322/2 (Divs) (S).

[38] (1) Memo (S) of CofS AGF for CG AGF, 24 Mar 43, sub: Summary of Statements by Gen Sutherland. 320.2/149 (PTO) (S). (2) WD memo (S) WDGCT 320.2 Gen (5–21–43) for CofS USA, 21 May 43, sub: Light Divs. AGO Records 322 (21 May 43) (22) (S). (3) Hq USAF in Far East ltr (S) to TAG through C–in–C, SWPA, 2 Oct 43. 322/2 (Divs) (S).

General McNair believed this attitude short-sighted and wasteful. He wrote to the War Department on 17 November 1943: [39]

The Southwest Pacific Area now has a United States force aggregating some 272,000, including 124,000 service forces (46%). The maintenance of this force probably involves over 270,000 ship tons per month—one ton per man. There are five combat divisions which have reached there over a considerable period of time. These divisions are substantially equivalent to eight light divisions, without considering the supporting units required. Five standard divisions require 173,000 ship tons for equipment while eight light divisions require 54,000 tons. Thus, the light divisions would effect a saving for equipment of 119,000 tons— a fairly negligible amount in comparison with the shipping required to support the present great garrison.

Under current War Department policies allowing the theater commanders wide latitude in utilizing the shipping available to them, it is clear that the Southwest Pacific Area has no intention of accepting a light division of whatever organization, unless forced to do so by the War Department. The 1st Cavalry Division now has a reported aggregate strength of 13,258, practically the same as the standard infantry division.

. . . upon completion of the current tests of light divisions, it will be necessary to decide, not only the details of such organization, but whether theater commanders will be required to accept a light division when they prefer the heavier standard infantry division. In the meantime, it appears highly inadvisable to contemplate the activation of light divisions in addition to the three already in being.

The 10th, 71st, and 89th Light Divisions therefore remained the only units of their kind. They were experimental organizations rather than units known to be forming for combat. They continued with their tests with the outcome already partly decided against them.

Tests of the 71st and 89th Light Divisions (Pack and Truck respectively) culminated in maneuvers of the two divisions against each other from February to April 1944. The terrain chosen was the mountainous, virtually roadless, relatively warm area of the Hunter Liggett Military Reservation in California. The III Corps, which supervised the maneuvers, reported unfavorably. Handcarts, used by both divisions, were found to be inadequate and excessively fatiguing. Additional pack and truck transportation was provided during the maneuvers to permit continued action, and additional engineers were furnished to build trails needed by both mules and jeeps. Infantry regiments, only two-thirds the strength of the standard regiment to start with, employed a third or a half

[39] (1) AGF memo (S) (rewritten by Gen McNair) for G–3 WD, 17 Nov 43, sub: Proposed Light Div. 322/2 (Divs) (S). (2) Personal ltr of Gen McNair to Maj Gen C. H. White, 27 Dec. 43. McNair Correspondence.

their combat soldiers to build trails and bring up supplies. Neither division managed to deploy more than six battalions of infantry. Reconnaissance units had to be improvised. The III Corps, concluding that the light division was incapable of sustaining itself for a period of any length, recommended a return to the organization and equipment of the standard infantry division, with transfer of organic pack units (field artillery and quartermaster) to the nondivisional pool, from which they might be attached to standard divisions for mountain warfare.[40]

After these recommendations were accepted by General McNair and by the War Department General Staff, which had lost faith in the light division even before the tests were concluded,[41] the 71st and 89th were reconverted to standard divisions. Receiving additional personnel from inactivation of antiaircraft battalions, and retraining as standard divisons at the last moment, both were among the last divisions to go overseas, leaving the command of the Army Ground Forces in January 1945.[42] The 71st Division, despite its jungle background, was dispatched to the European Theater to help meet the emergency of the German breakthrough of December 1944. The incident illustrated the wisdom of avoiding overspecialization of forces.

Tests of the 10th Light Division (Pack, Alpine) produced equally negative results. Personnel and equipment were found to be insufficient in quantity. The Army Ground Forces in May 1944 recommended that the 10th Light Division also be reorganized as a standard infantry division. It was pointed out that standard infantry divisions were fighting successfully in the Italian mountains. The Army Ground Forces feared administrative complications in maintaining a single special-type mountain division, but suggested that the mountaineer and ski personnel of the 10th Light Division be kept together for use as needed and expressed a readiness to organize an enlarged mountain division if this was desired.[43] The War Department decided to retain the 10th as a special

[40] (1) Hq III Corps ltr to CG AGF, 7 Apr 44, sub: Sp Rpt on Maneuver Test, 71st and 89th Light Divs. 321/808 (Inf). (2) III Corps ltr to CG AGF, 12 May 44, sub: Final Rpt on Hunter Liggett Maneuver No. 1. 354.2/42 (Hunter Liggett 44).

[41] Memo (S) of Col R. P. Reeder, OPD, for ACofS OPD, 27 Mar 44, sub: Proposed Light Div. 322/2 (Divs) (S).

[42] (1) AGF memo for G-3 WD, 14 Apr 44, sub: 71st and 89th Light Divs. 321/808 (Inf). (2) WD memo (S) WDGCT 322 (7 Apr 44) for CG AGF, 22 Apr 44, sub as in (1). 320.2/34 (TB 44) (S).

[43] AGF memo (C) (inclosing report) for G-3 WD, 10 May 44, sub: Reorgn of 10th Light Div (Alpine). 322/1 (10th Div) (C).

mountain division. The Army Ground Forces prepared the tables, outlining a division of 14,101 officers and men, using over 6,000 mules and horses, but with motor transport for heavy hauls.[44] The new T/O 70, published as of 4 November 1944, in general resembled, in the size and structure of the division it authorized, the corresponding table of 1942 which had never been used. The 10th Mountain Division embarked for Italy in December 1944.

Airborne divisions developed in a direction opposite to that favored by General McNair in 1943. His desire to convert them to light divisions has been noted. In November 1943 General Ridgway, then commanding the battle-tested 82d Airborne Division, proposed an enlargement of the airborne division almost to the size of the infantry division.[45] The European Theater concurred. General McNair, clinging to the idea of an easily transportable airborne division and restating his doubts as to the need of airborne divisions at all, advised against the proposal, and no action was taken.[46] The European Theater continued to favor a larger airborne division, believing in the employment of airborne forces in mass. The influence of the European Theater naturally became dominant in 1944. The Organization Division, Headquarters, Army Ground Forces, processed new airborne division tables in December 1944, with such expeditiousness as to draw a commendation from the War Department.[47] The new table closely resembled the Ridgway proposal of a year earlier. Whereas the old division aggregated about 8,500, with infantry in one parachute and two glider regiments, with no artillery heavier than the 75-mm. howitzer, and with supporting elements at the barest minimum, the new division totaled 12,979, had two parachute infantry regiments, a glider regiment virtually identical with standard infantry, a battalion of 105-mm. howitzers, and more fully developed supporting units. The four airborne divisions in Europe were reorganized under the new table, the one in the Southwest Pacific remaining under the old.

To summarize, by the beginning of 1945 all the experimental and special-type divisions of 1942 had either disappeared or to a large extent lost their special

[44] (1) AGF memo for G-3 WD, 24 Oct 44, sub: T/O&E for Mtn Div. 320.3/779. (2) T/O&E 70, 4 Nov 44.

[45] WD memo (S) OPD 320.2 Afr (1 Dec 43) (with inclosures) for CG AGF, 1 Dec 43, sub: Proposed T/O for A/B Divs. 320.3/75 (S).

[46] AGF memo (S) for OPD, 17 Dec 43, sub: Changes in T/O, A/B Div. 320.3/75 (S).

[47] WD memo WDGCT 320.3 (18 Dec 44) for CG AGF, 18 Dec 44, sub: T/O&E for A/B Div. 330.13/156 (Commendations).

features. The motorized and the light division had come and gone. The jungle division had never developed except as a form of light division. The mountain division was substantially an infantry division in which motor transportation was largely replaced by mules. The cavalry division was fighting as infantry. Both the mountain division and the cavalry division were unique organizations, not types. With one exception, the airborne divisions resembled infantry divisions in strength and structure, with modifications made necessary by their mode of reaching the scene of combat. The tendency was to have only two wholly distinct types of divisions—infantry and armored. With increasing demands for organic tanks in infantry divisions, and for more infantry in armored divisions (beyond the infantry increase of 1943), even the distinction between these two types was becoming less pronounced.

VII. Army and Corps

The preceding discussion of divisions, though fundamental, refers to only a minority of troops of the Army Ground Forces. Less than half the tactical troops of the Army Ground Forces were organic in divisions. More than half were in nondivisional combat and service units. The ratio on 31 March 1945 was approximately 15 to 12—1,468,941 officers and men in nondivisional units as against 1,194,398 in divisions. There were also 1,204,976 other officers and men in ASF-type units in the communications zone. None of these figures includes replacements in training or personnel designated as overhead in the Troop Basis. In general ASF units were designed to operate in communications zones, AGF units in combat zones. It clarifies the picture to keep in mind that the total of ground troops was about 4,000,000, of which roughly 30 percent was in divisions, 40 percent in nondivisional units of AGF type intended for the combat zone, and 30 percent in nondivisional units of ASF type intended for the communications zone. Each of the 89 divisions, with an average T/O strength of about 13,400, was backed by some 30,000 in nondivisional units, of whom 16,500 were designed for close support in the combat zone and 13,500 for rear-area employment. Of the 16,500, about 11,300 were combat troops and about 5,200 service troops of AGF types, such as depot and maintenance companies of the several supply branches. Thus, toward the end of the war, each division had behind it about 11,300 nondivisional combat troops and approximately 18,700 nondivisional service troops.[1]

The present discussion deals only with nondivisional units of AGF types, numbering close to 1,500,000 troops, or 16,500 per division (as of 31 March 1945), and including units of all arms and services except the Air Corps and the Transportation Corps. The large number of these troops was a result of systematic application of the principles of streamlining and pooling, by which divisions were held to strictly defined minima and all else were centralized under higher headquarters. Examples of the methods by which nondivisional forces were increased are the policy of gathering a maximum of supply and maintenance services in the combat zone under army control, the withholding of antiaircraft and tank destroyers from organic assignment to divisions, the transfer of

[1] All figures are from the Troop Basis of 1 April 1945 (S). See Table No. 2, p. 306.

tank battalions from armored divisions to a nondivisional basis, the removal of the treadway bridge company and the supply battalion from the armored division, and the abolition of the organically motorized division, with truck transport pooled in nondivisional quartermaster companies. There are still other explanations for the growth of nondivisional units. All field artillery heavier than the 155-mm. howitzer was pooled at levels above the division, as were considerable amounts of the medium and lighter pieces. Most mechanized cavalry and all chemical troops were similarly pooled. The pool of engineers was very large, providing a strength of more than 2,300 per division, almost four times the strength of the engineer battalion organic in the division. There were three times as many signal troops in nondivisional units of the Army Ground Forces as in divisions, ten times as many quartermaster troops, and twelve times as many ordnance troops. Among the services, only the Medical Department had more personnel in divisions than in supporting medical units. These comparisons do not include ASF units in the communications zone.

The reorganization of this great mass of forces, a major problem, took place, roughly, in the year extending from October 1942 to October 1943. The process followed the same lines as with the divisions. The Reduction Board meticulously reviewed and trimmed all T/O&E's of nondivisional units. At the same time the means of combining T/O units into larger wholes was restudied. The objectives were always economy and flexibility. The problem was essentially a problem in the organization of armies and corps. Except for certain forces used to garrison small detached bases and certain antiaircraft and coast artillery used to defend airfields and fixed installations, all nondivisional troops of the Army Ground Forces were intended for assignment to armies or corps.

Abandonment of the "Type" Army and "Type" Corps

In 1942, as already explained,[2] military planning was conducted in terms of the type army and the type corps. The type army and corps had been developed in the preceding years, concurrently with the development of the triangular division, as a means of determining how many nondivisional units of various kinds would be required to supplement a given number of divisions. In the type army and the type corps, as in a T/O unit, there were elements conceived to be "organic." The organic composition of army and corps in July 1942 is indi-

[2] See above, p. 279.

cated in Table No. 4. For example, if 99 divisions were to be mobilized, it could be determined from the type organizations that 33 corps and 11 armies would be needed. Multiplying the number of nondivisional units organic in each corps by 33, and the number of nondivisional units organic in each army by 11, and adding the two products, would give the number of nondivisional units required to produce a balanced combat force of 99 divisions. By a similar calculation the composition of a task force built around any number of divisions could be projected. It would be necessary in either calculation to consider the need for GHQ reserve troops not organic in army or corps, such as parachutists, tank battalions, and certain kinds of heavy artillery and service organizations.

On 31 July 1942 the War Department directed the Army Ground Forces to present recommendations for revision of the type army and the type corps.[3] It was desired, in the interests of economy, that the necessity of all organic units be reviewed. The Army Ground Forces was instructed to consult with the Army Air Forces and the Services of Supply. The Army Air Forces was concerned because observation aviation was organic at this time in both army and corps; the Services of Supply, because it shared the responsibility at this time for service units assigned to the Army Ground Forces. The idea of separate air command had already developed to the point where organic assignment of air units to ground commands in practice was not contemplated. In October 1942 the Services of Supply was to lose its authority over the organization, equipment, and training of service units operating within corps and armies. Hence army and corps organization soon became a problem to be dealt with by the Army Ground Forces alone, subject to War Department approval.

The Army Ground Forces on 21 September 1942 proposed that the concept of the type army and type corps be abandoned.[4] General McNair believed that the type army and corps, though avowedly used only for planning, set up false preconceptions with regard to tactics and logistical operations. It was understood that an army or corps in combat would contain such forces as were deemed necessary in the immediate situation. General McNair believed that the same flexibility should govern planning and training, especially with the Army facing operations in widely different theaters still unknown. He cited German tactical organization, by which task forces could be formed at will from standard parts. He feared that, just as manpower and equipment might be wasted by organic

---

[3] WD memo WDGCT 320.2 (T/O) (7–31–42) for CGs AAF, AGF, SOS, 31 Jul 42, sub: Revision of Type Army Corps and Army Troops. 320.2/5816.

[4] AGF memo for G–3 WD, 21 Sep 42, sub as above. 320.2/5816.

TABLE NO. 4

Composition of the "Type" Army and "Type" Corps, 31 July 1942

BRANCH	TYPE ARMY (NON-CORPS)	TYPE CORPS		
		Corps "A"	Corps "B"	Corps "C"
	No Divisions	3 Inf Divs	3 Inf Divs	3 Inf Divs
Antiaircraft	1 Brig	1 Regt	1 Regt	1 Regt
Armored	None	None	None	None
Cavalry	None	1 Regt, Mecz	1 Regt, Mecz	1 Regt, Mecz
Chemical	1 Maint Co	None	None	None
	1 Depot Co			
	1 Impreg Co			
	1 Lab Co			
	3 Decon Cos			
Engineers	3 Gen Serv Regts	2 Combat Regts	2 Combat Regts	2 Combat Regts
	6 Bns Sep	1 Top Co, Corps	1 Top Co, Corps	1 Top Co, Corps
	1 Depot Co			
	1 Top Bn			
	1 Water Supply Bn			
	4 Lt Pont Cos			
	2 Dump Truck Cos			
	1 Cam Bn			
	1 Maint Co			
	2 Hv Pont Bns			
Field Artillery	None	1 Brig	1 Brig	1 Brig
Infantry	None	None	None	None
Medical	3 Medical Regts	1 Medical Bn	1 Medical Bn	1 Medical Bn
	1 Vet Co Sep			
	4 Surg Hosps			
	10 Evac Hosps			
	1 Conv Hosp			
	1 Lab			
	1 Supply Depot			
Military Police	1 MP Bn	1 MP Co	1 MP Co	1 MP Co
Ordnance	2 Am Bns	1 Maint Bn	1 Maint Bn	1 Maint Bn
	1 Maint Bn			
Quartermaster	3 MM Bns	2 Trk Cos	2 Trk Cos	2 Trk Cos
	1 MT Supply Co	1 MM Co	1 MM Co	1 MM Co
	1 Trk Regt	1 Gas Supply Co	1 Gas Supply Co	1 Gas Supply Co
	6 Serv Bns	1 Serv Co	1 Serv Co	1 Serv Co
	1 Gas Sup Co			
	1 Car Co			
	1 Ster Bn			
	1 Depot Co			
Signal	1 Const Bn	1 Sig Bn	1 Sig Bn	1 Sig Bn
	1 Photo Co			
	1 Pigeon Co			
	1 Rad Intell Co			
	1 Opn Bn			
	1 Depot Co			
Tank Destroyer	3 TD Bns	1 TD Gp	1 TD Gp	1 TD Gp
		(5 Bns)	(5 Bns)	(5 Bns)
Aviation	1 Obsn Gp	4 Obsn Sqds	4 Obsn Sqds	4 Obsn Sqds

Source: Memo WDGCT 320.2(T/O) to AGF, AAF, SOS, Sub: Revision of Type Army Corps and Army Troops, 31 Jul 1942. In 320.2/5816.

assignment to divisions, so they might also be wasted by organic assignment to a type corps or a type army. He wished to have no elements frozen, by faulty organization, in places where maximum employment was not possible. Given the limitations on shipping, and the heavy requirements of the Army Air Forces and the Services of Supply for ship space, he wished every unit sent overseas by the Army Ground Forces to be readily available for use at the decisive spot.

The organization advanced by the Army Ground Forces did away with organic army troops and corps troops and made all nondivisional units organically GHQ Reserve. Army and corps retained no organic elements except those necessary for command—chiefly headquarters and signal units. Troops were organized in interchangeable parts, in permanent units of the smallest size compatible with efficiency. For combat units this was judged to be the battalion. From the mass of battalions, all organically GHQ Reserve, forces would be assigned or attached to armies and corps as needed. There would be two kinds of permanent T/O units—divisions and separate battalions. A corps would be a variable combination of divisions and battalions; an army, a combination of corps with additional battalions and perhaps divisions. The brigade disappeared as a fixed nondivisional unit, as it had already disappeared from the division. The fixed regiment likewise ceased to exist as a nondivisional unit; it was soon to disappear from the armored division as well, and remain, in general, as an echelon known only to infantry, mainly in infantry divisions. In its place was put the group.

This plan, before its submission to the War Department on 21 September 1942, was strongly advised against by some officers of General McNair's staff.[5] They held that team training would suffer if units were so highly interchangeable; that, with so much basic equipment removed from the division by streamlining, a definite and fixed corps pool was necessary as a form of insurance; and that confusion would result from such radical departure, during mobilization, from the organization, functions, and nomenclature made familiar in the years of peace. They argued that in the planning of balanced forces planners must have in mind, whether consciously or not, some large-scale "type" organization; and that with so many persons involved in planning there must be some pattern generally understood and agreed upon. These arguments, though recognized as cogent, were outweighed in General McNair's judgment by the economy and flexibility obtainable under the system proposed.

[5] See the staff studies and M/S in 320.2/5816 and in AGF Plans Sec file 95, 320.2/111.

The proposal of 21 September was returned without action by the War Department.[6] OPD stressed the arguments against it.[7] General McNair was unwilling to push the matter at this time, although, as he said, the existing organization had never been tested in war or peace, and the need of economizing in organization and equipment had been repeatedly stated by the Chief of Staff.[8] Indeed, at this very time the War Department dispatched a letter to all overseas commanders urging economy upon them. It was here affirmed that a wasteful service organization had resulted in some overseas establishments from use of the type army and corps (and type air force and communications zone) in the planning of overseas forces.[9]

Although never approved formally and explicitly as a whole, the system as outlined above went into effect piecemeal during 1943.

The Battalion-and-Group System

One feature of the AGF proposal of 21 September 1942 was immediately approved. The War Department on 24 December 1942 granted permission to convert nondivisional regiments in antiaircraft artillery, field artillery, mechanized cavalry, and combat engineers to separate battalions, and to activate group headquarters in each of these arms in a ratio of one to each four battalions.[10] The group was a form of organization already employed with certain newer weapons, notably tank and tank destroyers. It differed from the regiment in that component battalions were self-sufficient for supply and administration (in the manner described above for battalions of the reorganized armored division), and that the battalions were not assigned organically to the group, but attached to and detached from it as circumstances dictated. The group was not a T/O unit. It might contain, at a given moment, no battalions or a half-dozen battalions, though three or four were considered normal. Group headquarters were sup-

[6] WD memo WDGCT 320 (12–17–42) for CG AGF, 24 Dec 42, sub: Reorgn of Units of the Army. 320.2/5816.

[7] WD memo OPD 320.2 (9–21–42) for G–3 WD, 16 Nov 42, sub: Revision of Type Corps & Army Troops. 320.2/5816.

[8] (1) AGF M/S, CG to DCofS, 3 Dec 42, sub as in note 7. (2) AGF M/S, DCofS to G–3, 31 Dec 42, sub: Reorgn of Units of the Army. Both in 320.2/5816.

[9] WD ltr (C) AG 320.2 (12–7–42) OB–S–D–M to theater comdrs, 10 Dec 42, sub: Economy of Forces. 320.2/233 (C).

[10] See footnote 6 above.

posed to avoid administration, to be tactical only, to control battalions in combat, and to supervise their training. Battalions in principle dealt directly with army on administrative matters and brought their own supplies from army supply points.

The conversions authorized by the War Department on 24 December 1942 were gradually effected in 1943. They involved not merely the dissolution of regiments but also the internal reorganization of battalions to provide administrative self-sufficiency. With antiaircraft artillery, field artillery, cavalry, and combat engineers converted, and tanks and tank destroyers already so organized, the result was to place all nondivisional units of the combat arms except infantry on the flexible battalion-and-group system. Since very little infantry was nondivisional the exception was minor. Nor was the further exception of coast artillery significant. The same principles, as explained above, were applied within the armored division.[11]

Service units were similarly reorganized. On 29 December 1942 General Marshall informally expressed the opinion that the organization of service troops was wasteful.[12] He noted that large organic units, such as the regiment, were satisfactory for large missions, but that there was no economical means of sending small units on small missions, for example to island bases, and no means, except through excessive headquarters overhead, of controlling numerous small service units of diverse types. "It seems to me," he wrote, "that we should have these service units so set up that we can put together composite battalions, composite regiments and composite brigades." The system proposed by the Army Ground Forces on the preceding 21 September had been designed to provide the flexibility desired by General Marshall. In addition, in connection with ordnance units, the Army Ground Forces had recently proposed that a battalion headquarters be created for control of variable numbers of ordnance companies of dissimilar types such as heavy maintenance, evacuation, and depot. Such a battalion was in effect a "group" of companies. General McNair recommended that this scheme be generalized to meet the problem raised by General Marshall.[13]

During 1943 the regiment virtually disappeared from the organization of service troops. Truck regiments formerly organic in the type army were

[11] AGF ltr 35 (R), 20 Jan 43, sub: Orgn & Asgmt of Gp Hq and Bns. 320.2/165 (R).

[12] Memo of Gen Marshall for Gens McNair, Somervell, Edwards, 29 Dec 42, sub not given. 320.2/5773.

[13] See unused draft and AGF memo to CofS USA, 5 Jan 43, sub: Orgn of Serv Trs. 320.2/5773.

broken up into administratively self-sufficient separate battalions. Medical regiments formerly organic in the type army were broken up into administratively self-sufficient companies of various types such as collecting, clearing, and depot. Quartermaster and ordnance troops, and some engineer and signal troops, were likewise organized in separate companies. In general, in the services the company became the basic T/O unit, as was the battalion in the arms. For command over several companies, within the same service though of different types if desired, battalion headquarters and headquarters detachments were created to which companies could be attached as needed. There were thus two kinds of nondivisional battalions: fluid battalions for ordnance, quartermaster, and medical troops; fixed battalions for combat troops and for certain kinds of medical, signal, engineer, and military police units. For command over several battalions of either type, group headquarters were provided in all arms and services of the Ground Forces except chemical, military police, and signal, in which so large a massing by branch was considered unnecessary, and except in the infantry, where the regiment survived to perform this function.[14]

For command over several groups it was the intention of the Army Ground Forces to provide brigade headquarters. The old T/O brigade, with an organic component of regiments, found in antiaircraft artillery, field artillery, and cavalry, was abolished. The troops of these brigades were reorganized in self-sustaining battalions and squadrons. The new brigade, like the group, was organically only a headquarters and headquarters company, to which subordinate units could be flexibly attached. It was expected that such brigades could be formed in any arm or service in which a demand for so large a single-branch organization might arise. In fact, the Army Ground Forces organized brigades on the new plan only for antiaircraft, field artillery, and tank destroyer units. One infantry airborne brigade was also created. Actually only one tank destroyer brigade went overseas; field artillery brigades were not needed in quantity because groups were attached directly to corps artillery headquarters; and brigades became common only in the antiaircraft artillery, in which their number declined as antiaircraft battalions were inactivated.[15]

[14] The system was formally explained, in answer to a request by G–4 WD, in AGF memo for G–4 WD, 25 May 43, sub: Comd for Nondiv Units. 320.2/6009. See also the AGF ltrs to the field on the use of service units of each branch: (1) 30 Mar 43, sub: Ord Serv in the Fld, AGF. 321/74 (Ord). (2) 8 Oct 43, sub: Engr Serv in the Fld, AGF. 321/212 (Engr) (R). (3) 14 Oct 43, sub: Sig Orgn. 321/786 (Sig). (4) 16 Oct 43, sub: QM Serv in the Fld. 321/266 (QM) (R). (5) 22 Oct 43, sub: Med Orgn. 321/766 (Med).

[15] Annex IX to AGF ltr (R) to CGs, 21 Jul 43, sub: Orientation with Ref to Revised Orgn. 320.2/242 (R).

The breaking up of nondivisional forces into T/O battalions or companies, held together in temporary non-T/O combinations under flexible group and brigade command, or under flexible battalion command in the case of the service companies, in effect produced the revolution of organic army troops and corps troops which the Army Ground Forces had originally proposed. If there was no such thing as an organically constituted regiment or brigade, there could hardly be, within reason, an organically constituted corps or army. The principle of flexibility had prevailed.

Higher Headquarters

One of General McNair's principal goals was to hold down the size of headquarters staffs. Substitution of the group for the regiment, with the group headquarters handling four battalions and passing administrative matters on to army, was intended to economize headquarters overhead. The same objective was aimed at in elimination of the regiment from the armored division, in the general cutting of division staffs by the Reduction Board, and in the paring of headquarters companies at all levels.

General McNair's reasons for cutting all staffs applied especially to the staffs of higher headquarters—those of armies and corps. One reason was to conserve manpower, the other to speed up operations. Higher staffs tended to absorb large numbers of the most experienced officers. By 1943 only one officer in fifty was a professional soldier. "I wish we could give green divisions more experienced officers," General McNair wrote to General Patton, "but they are just not available. One primary reason—almost the only one—is the great mass of Regular Army officers who are serving in the unimaginable array of command echelons with their staggering large staffs." [16] Moreover, large staffs, in General McNair's opinion, produced a mass of paper work, liaison, and unnecessary coordination which threatened to block the very rapidity of action for which modern armies were physically equipped. "Operations cannot possibly be swift and effective if staffs are large and clumsy. Lack of staff training and fitness cannot be compensated for by increasing size." [17] General McNair limited his own staff to about 250 commissioned officers, in a headquarters controlling at the maximum some two million troops.

[16] Personal ltr (S) Gen McNair to Gen Patton, 23 Oct 43. McNair Correspondence (S).

[17] AGF ltr (R) to CGs, 21 Jul 43, sub: Orientation with Ref to Revised Orgn. 320.2/242 (R).

One method by which he hoped to reduce army and corps headquarters was to combine staff and command positions in the manner well established in the division artillery.[18] Here the artillery commander was at the same time the artillery officer on the staff of the division commander. General McNair believed that special staffs could be greatly reduced by general application of this plan. He held that if a corps, for example, had no tank destroyers attached to it, it needed no antitank section on the corps staff; if it did possess tank destroyers, then the senior commander of attached tank destroyer units (probably a colonel commanding a group) was better qualified than anyone else to act as staff adviser to the corps commander on antitank matters. Similarly, at the army level, the brigadier general commanding the antiaircraft brigade, if the army possessed one, and the brigade or group commander in every other arm and service represented among army troops, would be the special staff officer for matters of his branch. But because the duties of certain officers were multiplied to a point considered impracticable by some, with consequent doubt as to whether real economy would result, the plan met with resistance both in the War Department and in the field and was not systematically followed in practice.

Another means of economizing staffs was to limit their work to strictly defined essentials. General McNair wished the corps to be a combat unit only, with administrative activities concentrated in army. He held down his own staff by leaving a maximum of administrative work to the War Department.

But the more the principle of flexible organization of army and corps troops was adopted the heavier was the work load imposed on army and corps head-quarters. These headquarters, under combat conditions, carried the major responsibility for shifting separate battalions and companies about, combining and recombining them in temporary formations, attaching them to divisions, detaching and attaching them elsewhere, determining where they could best be used, ordering their movement, and keeping the record of their whereabouts and availability at all times. With nondivisional units dissolved organically into bat-

---

[18] See draft written by General McNair for directive of 21 Jul 1943, sub: Orientation with Reference to Revised Orgn, par beginning, "The revised organization places command above staff." This paragraph did not appear in the directive, because the principle involved was not fully enough accepted by the War Department to justify its inclusion. Draft in 322/1 (Corps) (R). See also (1) AGF memo (C) for G–3 WD, 13 Apr 43, sub: A/T Pers. 321/6 (TD) (C). (2) AGF M/S (S), G–3 to CofS, 20 Apr 43, sub: A/T Sec for Div Corps and Army Hq. 320.2/23 (NATO) (S). (3) AGF M/S, CG to G–3, 7 Sep 42, sub: Revision of Type Army Corps and Army Trs. 320.2/5816.

talions and companies, under lieutenant colonels and captains (in contrast to the division with its major general), and with the intermediate group and brigade headquarters exercising no administrative functions, a great deal of assistance and control of many small units by army and corps headquarters was required.

TABLE NO. 5

Evolution of Corps Headquarters, 1942–45

ITEM	1 JUL 42	29 MAR 43	15 JUL 43	27 DEC 43	19 JAN 45
Headquarters, Corps:					
Commissioned Officers:					
Commanding General	3	3	3	3	3
General Staff	20	16	21	26	29
Adjutant General	4	3	3	4	4
Antiaircraft	3				
Artillery	8				
Chaplain	3	2	2	2	2
Chemical	2	2	2	2	2
Engineer	6	3	3	4	4
Finance	2	2	2	2	2
Inspector General	4	1	2	3	3
Judge Advocate	1	1	1	2	2
Medical	5	2	3	4	4
Ordnance	2	4	4	5	5
Quartermaster	6	2	2	4	4
Signal	3		3	4	4
Special Service		2	2	2	1
Total Commissioned	72	43	53	67	69
Warrant Officers	12	5	5	7	7
Enlisted Men	150	88	93	106	109
Total Headquarters, Corps	234	136	151	180	* 185
Headquarters Company, Corps	137	96	96	98	95
Headquarters & Headquarters Co	371	232	247	278	280

Source: T/O's 100–1 and 100–2

* Augmentation of 14 officers, 1 warrant officer, 17 enlisted men provided in T/O when authorized by theater commander.

It was therefore difficult to reduce higher headquarters as much as General McNair desired.

In view of the difficulties the Table of Organization for army headquarters was not materially modified in 1943. Corps headquarters was drastically reduced by the Army Ground Forces in March 1943, though the reductions did not last.[19] (See Table No. 5.) The principle adopted was that the corps consisted essentially of its commander and a small headquarters, with an organic headquarters company, an organic signal battalion, and an organic headquarters and headquarters battery for the corps artillery, which in turn possessed organically only a field artillery observation battalion. Thus the means of corps command were organic; troops would be put in and taken out according to the shifting needs of combat. The brigadier general commanding the corps artillery and the colonel commanding the corps signal battalion would function as corps staff officers; hence the artillery and signal sections of the old headquarters were dropped. The antiaircraft section was dropped also, the commanding officer of corps antiaircraft troops (if any) being expected to discharge staff duties. Staff advice on armored, tank destroyer, or other matters pertaining to a single arm would be procured in the same way. Since the corps was intended to be tactical only, the staff sections for technical and administrative services were reduced. Column 1 of Table No. 5 shows the corps headquarters of 1942; column 2, the reductions desired by the Army Ground Forces in March 1943; column 3, the less drastic reductions approved by the War Department and incorporated in a Table of Organization in July 1943. Corps in the Army Ground Forces were reorganized according to this table in August. They received an augmentation for training since it was believed by the Army Ground Forces that corps in training carried a greater burden of inspection and supervision than they should carry in combat. Protests against the new table were received from the theaters. General McNair was accused of proposing for overseas use a smaller corps headquarters than he would himself use in training. The War Department ordered an upward revision of the table, with results shown in column 4.[20]

---

[19] AGF memo for G–3 WD, 20 Mar 43, sub: T/O&E Corps. 320.2/5983, and published T/O 100–1, 29 Mar 43.

[20] (1) AGF memo (C) for OPD, 10 Aug 43, sub: Reorgn of Corps Hq and Organic Trs. 320.2/247 (C). (2) WD memo (R) WDGCT 320.3 (1 Oct 43) for CG AGF, 5 Oct 43, sub: T/O&E's for Corps. 322/4 (Corps) (R). (3) Personal memo (S) of Gen McNarney for Gen McNair, 17 Dec 43, sub: T/O's for Type Corps Hq. McNair Correspondence (S).

Before submitting the revisions called for, General McNair wrote to the War Department on 15 October 1943: [21]

The present strength can be increased to any figure desired by the War Department. This headquarters is opposed to such increase.

The overhead of headquarters in this war is viewed as staggering. We have the advantage of the most modern equipment in communications and transportation, which should operate to reduce overhead but actually is operating to increase overhead instead. General Bradley stated to me recently that the present corps headquarters was too small because he required each of his staff sections to visit the troops daily. Thus he was demanding in substance a double corps headquarters. General Fredendall stated that the present corps headquarters is more than adequate. General Patch expressed the same view. . . . The last two commanders voiced the view that large corps headquarters not only were unnecessary but would hinder mobile active operations. I concur in such views.

If commanders are allowed to indicate their own needs, experience has shown repeatedly and almost invariably that there will be no end to the increases demanded. Headquarters will go on increasing so long as this policy is followed. The results are apparent in our theaters all over the world.

The reply of G–3, WDGS, made no comment on these remarks. The corps, as again reorganized, was about as large in commissioned strength as in 1942.

Theory of Army and Corps

The division, the largest T/O unit, was the largest unit shipped to the theaters in the form in which it was made up in the United States. Armies and corps were not shipped as such. What was shipped were the elements—divisions, separate battalions and companies, group headquarters, corps headquarters, and army headquarters. Overseas commanders made up their armies and corps from these elements as they chose. Armies and corps (also groups) were simply so many containers, between which the actual contents of the Army—T/O divisions, battalions, and companies—were passed back and forth at will. Units were taken out of containers in the United States, shipped overseas, and put into new containers on arriving in the theater. Armies and corps were shipped separately.

With a few exceptions, all the armies and corps were supplied by the Army Ground Forces. The Fifth, Sixth, and Seventh Armies were activated overseas.

---

[21] Memo (R) of Gen McNair for G–3 WD, 15 Oct 43, sub: T/O&E's for Corps. 322/4 (Corps) (R).

So too were all army groups and the First Allied Airborne Army. The First Army went to Europe directly from the Eastern Defense Command, never having been under the commanding general of the Army Ground Forces. These were the only exceptions. All corps were trained by the Army Ground Forces or its predecessor, GHQ, and all those activated after 9 March 1942 were activated by the Army Ground Forces. By 1945 there were twenty-four corps, of which only one remained in the United States.

On the matter of armies General McNair proceeded slowly. He rejected advice of his staff, in 1942, to activate additional armies under his own command.[22] Using the principle of flexibility to its utmost, he employed only the Second and Third Armies (and four independent corps) even when troops under his command reached their maximum, in August 1943, of sixty-seven divisions with corresponding nondivisional units. For a short time at the end of 1943 the Second, Third, and Fourth Armies were in the Army Ground Forces. The Third (that is, its headquarters) then proceeded overseas. No new armies were activated by the Army Ground Forces until 1944, when the Eighth, Ninth, Tenth, and Fifteenth Armies were activated and shipped in quick succession. Meanwhile the Second and Fourth Armies remained in the United States in the Army Ground Forces. The identity of these armies persisted in name only, for it was largely their headquarters personnel, trained in army functions, which went overseas under new army designations. By January 1945 not a single division was left in the Second and Fourth Armies, which, virtually exhausted of troops of every kind, remained as empty containers awaiting the return of units to the United States.

The Army Ground Forces, though it shipped no armies or corps as such, nevertheless largely determined the form taken by armies and corps in the theaters. Theater commanders could build armies and corps as they pleased, but they worked with prefabricated materials. Every unit, whether troop unit or headquarters unit, was shaped by its T/O&E to perform certain functions and stand in a certain relation to other units, and it was for these functions and these relations that its personnel were trained in the United States.

The idea insisted upon by General McNair was that the army was both a combat and an administrative agency, the corps a combat agency only, unless operating independently, in which case it should be reinforced to function as a

---

[22] AGF M/S (S) DCofS to G–1, G–3, G–4, 28 Oct 42, sub: Revision of AGF Orgn. AGF Plans Sec file 132 (S).

small army.[23] In administration and supply the army was intended to bypass the corps and, to a certain extent, the division. For supply of food, fuel, and ammunition, in the words of an AGF directive already quoted, "division and corps are not in the channel of supply, except in emergencies." [24] Nondivisional battalions and separate companies, and the regiments and battalions within divisions, were provided with supply machinery expected to mesh directly with that of army. Army was to push forward supply points to positions accessible to the trucks of small using units. Army personnel sorted supplies into unit lots and loaded the trucks arriving at supply points. To enable army to discharge this role the Troop Basis included a great mass of units for assignment to armies or independent corps as needed—quartermaster truck, railhead and gasoline supply companies, ordnance ammunition companies, and depot companies of the several services. Similarly, army provided third-echelon maintenance for both divisions and nondivisional units, a function for which a mass of ordnance maintenance, engineer maintenance, chemical maintenance, and signal repair companies were provided. Army likewise evacuated disabled or captured equipment, provided hospitals, and furnished reinforcing medical collecting and clearing companies for units whose needs exceeded their organic means. Facilities for major undertakings in bridge building, water supply, map making, photography, and other functions were likewise provided in engineer and signal units assigned to army.

The corps was conceived as consisting essentially of a commander and a handful of staff officers who gave unity of direction and continuity of purpose to a mass of units in combat, however much the individual units might be used up, exchanged, or replaced. All combat units in an army, except those in army reserve, were intended to be passed on to the several corps, shifting from one corps to another at the discretion of the army commander. Corps operated the pools of nondivisional combat units—corps artillery, cavalry squadrons, engineers, tanks, tank destroyers, chemical battalions, etc.—distributing them to divisions by attachment, using them to support a division most in need, assembling them for mass action, or holding them in reserve. With the divisions lacking many weapons organically, and held down by T/O's to the minimum required for "normal" operations, the corps became the key headquarters for employing all combat elements in proper tactical combinations.

---

[23] AGF ltr (R) to CGs, 21 Jul 43, sub: Orientation with Reference to Revised Orgn. 320.2/6031 (R).
[24] AGF ltr (R), 8 Oct 43, sub: Engr Serv in the Fld. 321/212 (Engr) (R).

Composition of the Third Army, 1 October 1942

(Illustrative of Army and Corps Organization in the Army Ground Forces)

BRANCH	ARMY TROOPS (NON-CORPS)	CORPS IN THIRD ARMY		
		IV Corps	VIII Corps	X Corps
	2 Infantry Divisions 1 Cavalry Division	6 Infantry Divisions	2 Infantry Divisions 1 Motorized Division	4 Infantry Divisions
Antiaircraft				
Armored				
Cavalry	1 Brig 1 Regt	1 Regt, Mecz	1 Regt, Mecz	
Chemical	3 Chemical Bns 7 Decontaminating Cos 2 Depot Cos 3 Maintenance Cos			
Engineers	7 Gen Serv Regts 1 Water Supply Bn 1 Camouflage Bn 2 Hv Pont Bns 1 Bn Sep 2 Lt Pont Bns 1 Dep Trk Co 5 Dep Cos 3 Maint Cos 1 Top Co, Corps	1 Top Co, Corps	2 Combat Regts 1 Top Co, Corps	2 Combat Regts 1 Top Co, Corps

Field Artillery	1 Brg, including
	  1 155-mm
	    Gun Regt
	  2 155-mm
	    How Regts
	1 155-mm How Regt
	1 105-mm How Regt
	4 105-mm How Bns
		1 Brig, including
		  1 155-mm
		    Gun Regt
		  2 155-mm
		    How Regts
		1 FA Obsn Bn
			1 Brig, including
			  1 155-mm
			    Gun Regt
			  2 155-mm
			    How Regts
			1 FA Obsn Bn
				1 Brig, including
				  1 155-mm
				    Gun Regt
				  2 155-mm
				    How Regts

Infantry				
Medical	4 Medical Regts 1 Medical Bn 1 Amb Bn 1 Gas Treat Bn 1 Conv Hosp 11 Evac Hosps, Mtz 2 Evac Hosps 1 Vet Evac Hosp 1 Vet Gen Hosp 1 Vet Co Sep 8 Labs 4 Supply Depots 1 Gen Disp 1 Aux Surg Grp	1 Medical Bn	1 Medical Bn	
Military Police	1 MP Bn 1 MP Co	1 MP Co	1 MP Co	1 MP Co

BRANCH	ARMY TROOPS (NON-CORPS)	CORPS IN THIRD ARMY		
		IV Corps	VIII Corps	X Corps
Ordnance	17 Hv Maint Cos 4 Hv Maint Cos (Field Army) 4 Med Maint Bns 3 Med Maint Cos 8 Mot Transp Cos 3 Mot Transp Sup Cos 2 Am Cos 2 Dep Cos	1 Maint Bn	1 Maint Bn	1 Maint Bn
Quartermaster	5 Serv Bns 1 Ster Bn 14 Trk Cos 2 Car Cos 6 Ldry Cos 7 Bkry Cos 2 Remount Trps 1 Graves Regis Co 2 Sales Cos 4 Railhead Cos 1 Refrig Co (Fixed) 1 Salv Repr Co 4 Salv Coll Cos 3 Dep Cos	1 Serv Co	1 Serv Co 1 Gas Sup Bn 2 Trk Cos	1 Serv Co 1 Trk Co
Signal	1 Sig Bn 1 Const Bn 2 Oprn Cos 2 Const Cos 1 Rad Int Co 2 Repr Cos 3 Dep Cos 1 Pigeon Co 1 Phot Lab GHQ	1 Sig Bn		1 Sig Bn
Tank Destroyer	2 Group Hq 22 Bns			
Miscellaneous	10 ABS Bns 1 MRU (Mob) 5 Hq & Hq Det Sp Trps	1 MRU (Mob)	1 MRU (Mob)	1 MRU (Mob)

Source: 320.2 Assignment Lists (R).

TABLE NO. 7   *Composition of the Third Army, 10 November 1943*

(Illustrative of Army and Corps Organization in the Army Ground Forces)

BRANCH	ARMY TROOPS (NON-CORPS)	CORPS IN THIRD ARMY				
		IX Corps	X Corps	XVIII Corps	XIX Corps	VIII Corps
	1 Cav Div	6 Inf Divs	4 Inf Divs 1 Armd Div	2 Inf Divs 1 Armd Div	2 Inf Divs 2 Armd Divs	
Antiaircraft	2 Brig Hq 4 Gp Hq 8 Bns					
Armored	1 Tank Gp Hq 3 Tank Bns	1 Tank Gp Hq 1 Tank Bn	2 Tank Bns	5 Tank Bns	2 Tank Bns	
Cavalry	1 Brig		1 Regt, Mecz 1 Rcn Sq, Mecz	1 Regt, Mecz	1 Regt, Mecz	
Chemical	5 Decon Cos 1 Depot Co 3 Maint Cos			2 Chem Bns, Mtz		
Engineers	2 Combat Gp Hq 1 Bn Sep 5 Combat Bns 5 Hvy Pont Bns 1 Top Bn 1 Water Supply Bn 2 Cam Cos 1 Depot Co 1 Dep Trk Co 2 Lt Equip Cos 2 Maint Cos 1 Top Co, Corps 1 Treadway Bridge Co	3 Combat Gp Hq 9 Combat Bns 1 Combat Co, Sep 3 Lt Equip Cos 1 Lt Pont Co 2 Maint Cos 1 Top Co, Corps	2 Combat Gp Hq 6 Combat Bns 1 Lt Equip Co 2 Lt Pont Cos 1 Maint Co 1 Top Co, Corps 1 Treadway Bridge Co	2 Combat Gp Hq 4 Combat Bns 2 Lt Pont Cos 1 Treadway Bridge Co	1 Top Co, Corps 1 Treadway Bridge Co	
Field Artillery	1 Gp Hq 2 155-mm How Bns	1 Hq IX Corps Arty 2 Gp Hq 1 Obsn Bn 4 155-mm Gun Bns 1 155-mm How Bn 5 105-mm How Bns	1 Hq X Corps Arty 4 Gp Hq 1 Obsn Bn 4 155-mm Gun Bns 8 155-mm How Bns 2 105-mm How Bns	1 Hq XVIII Corps Arty 2 Gp Hq 1 Obsn Bn 2 155-mm Gun Bns 2 155-mm How Bns 4 4.5″ Gun Bns	1 Hq XIX Corps Arty 4 Gp Hq 2 155-mm Gun Bns 4 155-mm How Bns	1 Hq VIII Corps Arty 1 Obsn Bn
Infantry	2 Inf Regts	2 Inf Regts			2 Armd Inf Bns	
Medical	4 Gp Hq 2 Amb Bns 9 Med Bns 1 Gas Treat Bn 1 Amb Co 13 Clearing Cos 26 Coll Cos	1 Bn Hq 1 Amb Co 1 Clearing Co 2 Coll Cos				

	1 Depot Co 1 Sanitary Co 3 Vet Cos 6 Evac Hosps SM 2 Labs 2 Vet Evac Hosps				
Military Police	3 MP Bns			2 MP Cos	
Ordnance	2 Am Bns 1 Ord Bn 20 Hq Ord Bn 8 Am Cos 8 Dep Cos 2 Evac Cos 7 Hv Auto Maint Cos 10 Hv Maint Cos (Field Army) 4 Hv Maint Cos (Tank) 1 Lt Maint Co 1 Maint Co (AA) 19 Med Auto Maint Cos 13 Med Maint Cos				
Quartermaster	1 Trk Regt 2 Hq Trk Regts 2 Hq QM Bns 5 Hq QM Bns (Mob) 4 Hq Tr Trans Bns 2 Gas Supply Bns 1 Serv Bn 1 Ster Co 4 Bkry Cos 3 Car Cos 4 Depot Cos 2 Ldry Cos 6 Pk Trs 5 Railhead Cos 1 Salvage Coll Co 24 Troop Trans Cos 33 Trk Cos				
Signal	1 Armored Sig Bn 2 Cons Bns 2 Opn Bns 1 Cons Co 1 Dep Co 2 Opn Cos 2 Pigeon Cos 1 Photo Co 2 Repr Cos	2 Sig Bns 1 Rad Int Co	1 Sig Bn	2 Sig Bns 1 Rad Int Co	
Tank Destroyer	1 Brig Hq	1 Gp Hq 5 TD Bns	2 Gp Hq 6 TD Bns	2 Gp Hq 5 TD Bns	1 Gp Hq 5 TD Bns
Miscellaneous	7 Bands 14 Hq Special Troops 1 MRU (Fixed)	1 MRU (Mob)	1 MRU (Mob)	1 MRU (Mob)	1 MRU (Mob)

Source: 3? 07 ~~~ment Lists (R)

With all corps made flexible and the type corps abolished, the armored corps became an unnecessary special unit. General McNair in 1943 assigned armored divisions, as they completed their training under the Armored Force, to ordinary army corps as well as to armored corps, in order that all higher commanders might gain experience with armor. At the same time the abolition of the motorized division, designed for use in an armored corps, and the concentration of service functions in army, including the servicing of armor, deprived the armored corps of its specific functions. As a result, although four armored corps had been activated, they were not very different from ordinary army corps. The armored corps was abolished as a special unit in August 1943.[25] Under the flexible system, any corps could be made into an armored corps by assignment of officers experienced in armor to its headquarters, and by assignment of armored divisions, truck companies to motorize its infantry divisions, and other suitable units. It was believed that services necessary to armored and fast-moving forces—gasoline supply, bridging, and maintenance—could be moved forward by army with sufficient speed.

The Army Ground Forces, to obtain the structure in training which was intended to be used in combat, carried out a general reorganization of its army and corps troops in 1943, at which time the great bulk of combat units and close-support services was under AGF command. In 1942 the headquarters of the Army Ground Forces had assigned some units, but merely attached others, to its subordinate armies and corps. Assigned units had generally been those organic in the type organizations. Beginning in January 1943 the Army Ground Forces assigned all units to its subordinate commands, which in turn might attach them to their own subordinate echelons.[26] Virtually all nondivisional service units were assigned by the Army Ground Forces to armies and separate corps, virtually all combat units to corps. The ordnance battalion and the medical battalion formerly assigned to corps disappeared. Their places were taken by self-sustaining ordnance and medical companies, grouped in flexible battalions and assigned to armies (or separate corps). Reassignment became general in August 1943. At this time a mass of new T/O&E's was published, consummating the work of the Reduction Board, and reshaping units in the light of

[25] (1) Staff studies in 320.2/16 (Armd F) (S). (2) AGF memo (C) (with related papers) for G–3 WD, 17 Aug 43, sub: Redesignation of Armd Corps. 320.2/247 (C).

[26] AGF ltr (R) to CGs, 16 Jan 43, sub: Asgmt and Attachment of Units. 320.2/167 (R).

their intended position within armies and corps. At one sweep, as of midnight 8–9 August, about 200 nondivisional combat units were reassigned from armies to corps. Corps commanders were instructed not to attach these units to divisions except for specified periods for combined training, but to hold them in corps pools.[27]

Effects of army and corps reorganization are illustrated in Tables Nos. 4,[28] 6, and 7, which show, first, the type organizations of 1942, second, the actual composition of the Third Army as of 1 October 1942, and, third, the composition of the Third Army as of 10 November 1943, after readjustments as described above had been made. Attention is called particularly to Table No. 7. The concentration of service elements under army is evident, as is also the distribution of combat elements to corps. The use of brigade and group headquarters can be seen, as well as that of the flexible battalion for medical, ordnance, and quartermaster companies. The cavalry brigade and the mechanized cavalry and quartermaster regiments were survivals of the older organization, due for gradual elimination. The assignment of separate tank battalions to corps in significant numbers was at this date a new phenomenon: to the great detriment of combined infantry-tank training of smaller units, few such battalions had previously been available. The mixing of infantry and armored divisions in the same corps for combined training at higher levels can be noted. The fact that the XIX Corps had until recently been the III Armored Corps is indicated by the presence in this corps of two armored divisions and of a treadway bridge company and two separate armored infantry battalions. It will be observed that the VIII Corps had virtually no troops whatsoever. This was because the VIII Corps had been alerted for overseas movement and was awaiting shipment as an empty container.

---

[27] (1) AGF ltr (C) to CGs, 5 Aug 43, sub: Asgmt of Combat Units to Corps. 320.2/300 (C). (2) AGF ltr (R) to CGs, 29 Oct 43, sub: Asgmt of Combat-Type Units. 320.2/267 (R).

[28] See above, p. 354.

VIII. Summary

The principles underlying the new tactical organization, in all aspects of their application to armies, corps, divisions, and nondivisional units, were set forth in a letter on "Orientation with Reference to Revised Organization" which General McNair himself wrote and issued to his commanders on 21 July 1943. No summary can take the place of this letter, the fullest statement on organization made by him during his command of the Army Ground Forces. Since it is indispensable to a thorough understanding of the subject, it is reproduced in its entirety at the end of this study.

Reduction of unit personnel and equipment had many implications. It undoubtedly increased the combat power delivered per ton of shipping. It lightened the problem of supplying fuel, spare parts, and replacements of men and vehicles. Forces became more compact and maneuverable by loss of impedimenta. But operation at minimum levels naturally produced stresses and strains. Tables of Organization and Equipment received piecemeal augmentations, the pendulum thus swinging again in the opposite direction. Fundamental tables (for example, those of the infantry and armored divisions) remained substantially unchanged until the end of the war in Europe. There were many cases, however, of augmentation by special allowance, outside the T/O&E's, but in effect enlarging the units.

Application of the new organization in the theaters after 1943 brought new developments.[1] In general, a reaction set in against the extreme emphasis on flexibility and economy. Nor did it prove possible to confine corps and group headquarters to tactical functions only.

Great economies were accomplished by the Army Ground Forces in consumption of manpower. Because of reduction in division tables, the 89 divisions active in 1945 required only 70,000 more enlisted men than the 73 divisions active at the end of 1942. Sixteen divisions were thus obtained with an outlay

---

[1] See below, "Reorganizing for Redeployment."

of manpower which in 1942 would have produced less than five. In nondivisional field artillery the 142 battalions mobilized at the end of 1942 required almost exactly 100,000 enlisted men for themselves and their overhead of higher artillery command. In February 1945 the 329 mobilized battalions required only 182,000. Under the 1942 tables 182,000 men would have produced approximately 260 battalions. Hence 69 battalions were gained without use of additional manpower.[2]

But it cannot be said that the economies achieved by General McNair were used as he preferred and intended, that is, to increase the number of ground combat units. In general, no more ground units, but in fact fewer, were mobilized under the reduced tables than had been set up for mobilization under the unreduced tables. In June 1943, as the work of unit reduction neared its completion, more than 300,000 men were cancelled from the AGF Troop Basis.[3]

Given conditions and expectations prevailing in the summer of 1943, it is probable that the total planned strength of ground forces would have been cut at that time whether AGF units were reduced or not. With still further cuts, and with the failure of expected restorations to materialize, the authorized strength of all AGF-type units on 31 March 1945 was approximately 1,000,000 less than had been projected two years before. The fact that units were reduced in size meant that this loss in number of men did not produce a corresponding loss in number of units. This was of immeasurable importance, for certainly the total number of ground combat units finally mobilized was none too many. By producing a fighting army out of a shrinking stock of allotted manpower the most extreme policies of economy would seem to have been abundantly justified.

[2] Calculations based on Troop Basis (S).

[3] See "Ground Forces in the Army, December 1941–April 1945: a Statistical Study" and "Mobilization of the Ground Army," in this volume.

AGF Letter on Revised Organization, 21 July 1943

HEADQUARTERS
ARMY GROUND FORCES
ARMY WAR COLLEGE
WASHINGTON 25, D. C.

320.2/6031 (R) (21 Jul 43) GNGCT   21 July 1943

Subject: Orientation with Reference to Revised Organization.

TO: Commanding Generals,
            Second and Third Armies,
            IV and XIII Corps,
            II Armored Corps,
            Airborne Command,
            Antiaircraft Command,
            Armored Command,
            Desert Training Center,
            Replacement and School Command,
            Tank Destroyer Center.

General

1. The following information and comments are transmitted by way of orientation in connection with pending revision of the organization of large units.

2. The organization of combat and supporting service units is being revised extensively and necessary Tables of Organization and Tables of Equipment will be issued in near future. See paragraph 2, letter, Hq AGF, 320.2/185 (R) (3 Mar 43) GNGCT, 3 March 1943, Subject: "Reorganization of Units under New Tables of Organization." The purposes of this revision may be stated generally as follows:

   a. To economize manpower, in order that the overall needs of armed forces, of industry, and of agriculture may be met in the maximum degree.

b. To permit available shipping to transport overseas a maximum of fighting power.

c. To provide a more flexible organization, permitting full application of the principle of economy of force and massing of military might at the decisive point.

d. To reduce headquarters and other overhead to speed up command. Command functions must keep pace with fast transportation and signal communication.

e. To devote strength as fully as possible to elements which can be made effective offensively against the enemy and reduce those elements which are passively defensive.

Organization of Large Units

3. The army is a tactical and administrative unit. The revised organization contemplates that administrative functions be more extensive and complete than at present. In exercise of such administrative functions, the army should by-pass the corps in every way possible in order that the corps may devote itself so far as practicable to tactical and training functions. Corps currently in training in the United States are in general occupying themselves too much with administration. Army commanders must take the steps necessary to correct this condition. The reduced administrative procedure applied in some headquarters and headquarters detachments, special troops, could well be applied to corps. A separate corps will have a status similar to that of an army.

4. *a.* The corps will consist essentially of a headquarters and headquarters company, a signal battalion, headquarters and headquarters battery, corps artillery, and a field artillery observation battalion. Its functions will be primarily tactical. It will be reinforced according to the combat situation by divisions, groups of artillery, antiaircraft, tank battalions, tank destroyer battalions, engineer battalions, engineer companies, and reconnaissance squadrons. In combat, according to the situation, non-divisional units (except reconnaissance squadrons) may be put under division control. In principle, they are passed on to divisions unless they may be employed effectively for more or less simultaneous support of more than a single division. Grouping battalions for training provides essential supervision by higher commanders. Such training must not preclude close association of battalions, and perhaps groups, with divisions for combined training. However, permanent attachments of battalions to divisions

is undesirable since such action will prevent training in mass employment. See letter, Hq AGF, 353/2209 (1 Apr 43) GNGCT, 1 April 1943, Subject: "Assignment and Training of Group Headquarters and Battalions of Tank, Tank Destroyer, and Antiaircraft Artillery."

b. The artillery commander commands all reinforcing artillery received and not passed on to divisions and has the additional function of corps artillery officer. The corps artillery headquarters has a large staff. For training purposes, it will be advisable to use part of it to perform training functions of present corps artillery section, thereby permitting the artillery commander to devote his attention during training periods to considerable number of groups and separate battalions attached to the corps. In this way, the existing satisfactory organization for training may continue. (See paragraph 12, below.)

5. Orders to reorganize infantry and armored divisions under new Tables of Organization and Equipment will issue at a later date. The following information is furnished on the new organizations.

a. The motorized division as a distinct organization has been eliminated. An infantry division can be transported by the attachment of a troop transport battalion consisting of six truck companies. It follows that the training of all infantry divisions will include development of a Standard Operating Procedure for motor movement and the execution of such movements.

b. The infantry division has been reduced in aggregate strength by approximately 8 per cent and in fuel consuming motor vehicles by 14 per cent.

c. The armored division will be reorganized into two combat commands or groups of flexible composition of self-sustaining tank and armored infantry battalions. The organic total strength includes three tank battalions and three armored infantry battalions. The artillery strength remains at three battalions. The infantry and artillery strength of the division, in comparison with the tank strength, will be increased greatly.

d. It is planned that all tank battalions with certain exceptions will be interchangeable—including those of armored divisions and of General Headquarters Reserve. The battalion will include three medium companies and one light company. Thus there will be a pool of tank battalions available for both support of the infantry and as replacement units of armored divisions. Similarly, a pool of armored infantry battalions is being organized so that replacement and reinforcing infantry units will be available for armored divisions. Again the reconnaissance squadrons of armored divisions and separate reconnaissance squadrons will be identical except for the number of reconnaissance troops, permitting interchange of such units as necessary.

e. A new light division, suitable for amphibious, airborne, mountain and jungle operation is being tested. The aggregate strength of this light division is approximately 9,000 and its equipment varies with the type of operations in which it is to engage. There will be a minimum of transportation. The division will be on foot, with hand carts, except for those essential loads which cannot be transported in this manner. Such loads will be handled by pack animals or ¼-ton trucks. Approximately 400 men will be subtracted from strength of the division when motor transportation is used.

f. The radio intelligence platoon is being removed from division signal companies because it is felt that such activities pertain more properly to the corps signal battalion, at least until equipment for such operation has been developed more fully, its capacities measured and operational needs determined more completely than at present. Trained traffic analysts have been provided in the corps signal battalion to evaluate information obtained by the radio intelligence platoons. An effort is being made to reduce and simplify the set-up of signal equipment without sacrificing the essential effectiveness of signal operations.

g. The division engineers will hold to a strength which some commanders may regard as too small. There is no lack of appreciation of the number of engineering functions or of the considerable overall strength of engineers needed. However, a division of whatever type is supposedly a mobile unit and nature and extent of engineer operations under such conditions necessarily must be limited. If and when operations do not move so rapidly, it is readily possible to introduce engineers from the corps and army, reinforcing or relieving the division engineers of functions which are beyond their capabilities. Bridge trains are excluded from division engineers because they are not needed under all conditions. The need of bridges can be foretold from maps, air photographs and ground reconnaissance and bridges can be provided by companies and battalions from the army.

Comments on Organization

6. Staffs are being revised downward. They are to be provided solely for combat needs. Operations cannot possibly be swift and effective if staffs are large and clumsy. Lack of staff training and fitness cannot be compensated for by

increasing size. The development of suitable Standard Operating Procedures lightens the burden of staffs and expedites operations. In general, field orders in maneuvers still are far too lengthy. The average formal mimeographed field order, prepared under conditions which would be impractical in service, can be replaced by messages of a few lines, expediting operations greatly and largely eliminating the frequent capture of elaborate orders by the opposing forces. Field orders should be oral or in message form habitually for all elements of divisions and frequently for the corps. The practice of assembling subordinate commanders for issuance of orders is pernicious, since it takes commanders away from their units at critical times and delays operations intolerably. Liaison officers should be used for dissemination of orders.

7. *a.* The revised organization takes extensive advantage of the pooling principle. For example, there are General Headquarters pools of artillery battalions, tank destroyer battalions, reconnaissance squadrons, antiaircraft battalions, engineer companies and battalions, armored infantry battalions, tank battalions; group headquarters for artillery, tank destroyer, engineer, cavalry, antiaircraft, armored infantry, and tank units; necessary and appropriate brigade headquarters; and service units. In general, group headquarters will be provided in the ratio of one to every three or four battalions; brigade headquarters in appropriate cases one to every three or four groups.

b. Unlike the old regiment and brigade, which had organic battalions and regiments, the new groups and brigades have no organic units. Battalions, of any or various types, and in any number, may be attached to a group headquarters; varying number of groups to a brigade headquarters. The flexibility of the new organization makes it readily possible to form task forces to meet particular needs, thus effecting economy and permitting massing of means according to the situation. Except in the infantry regiment, battalions are self-sustaining, that is they are self-administering in the same sense as the regiment heretofore.

8. Organic antiaircraft and antitank defense of divisions is a moot question. It is entirely natural that division commanders desire such defensive means in strength sufficient to defeat all attacks. Provisions of this kind are impractical and unsound from the standpoint of economy of force. At the same time it is reasonable to furnish a limited defense organically and provide a pool of means sufficient to reinforce threatened points so as to afford full protection. The infantry has antitank guns, but the pool of tank destroyer units affords a more powerful reserve to meet a massed tank attack. Similarly, all units have organic

antiaircraft protection in the form of caliber .50 machine guns on ring mounts of vehicles, but the major antiaircraft protection is in the form of self-propelled or mobile, automatic weapons, antiaircraft battalions assigned organically to a General Headquarters pool, which are highly suitable for this purpose. The employment of special pool units is a command decision, according to the situation.

Supply and Maintenance

9. All organic provisions for supply are based on the principles of paragraph 38, FM 100–10, 9 December 1940. The following comments are made:

a. The army is being provided with abundant and flexible means of placing supplies within convenient reach of the transportation of using units, regiments, self-sustaining battalions, and small separate units.

b. The army handles all supplies upon their arrival in the combat zone, using army personnel and transportation. It establishes and mans all supply points down to include those which deliver to using units. The using units need no personnel specifically detailed for loading the supplies and bring only transportation and personnel normally assigned to the vehicle to the supply point.

c. Unit reserves of rations and water normally are confined to kitchen trucks and trailers. Resupply of both rations and water is by any available unit transportation.

d. Unit transportation generally includes no provisions for a reserve of fuel and lubricants, except in the case of tanks or similar vehicles consuming large quantities. Motor vehicles in general have an adequate reserve in fuel tank and cans carried in vehicles. Resupply of fuel and lubricants is by any available unit transportation, in the discretion of the unit commander.

e. There is no change in the present system of ammunition supply. The reserve of ammunition of a unit consists primarily of hauling capacity of its vehicles. In general, the number of ammunition vehicles assigned a unit is based on hauling, rather than carrying capacities. The unit commander must see that ammunition vehicles are employed actively and continuously to the extent necessary to insure an adequate supply of ammunition at all times.

10. Adequate provision is made for motor maintenance, provided that all echelons are employed effectively. Admittedly, third echelon maintenance of divisions is inadequate of itself to handle all third echelon repairs under severe operating conditions. The excess of such repairs must be made by third echelon

shops of army and when practical, by second echelon shops of units. When time permits and when scheduled maintenance services are not interrupted, it is greatly to the advantage of units to make all possible repairs within units, in order to avoid evacuating a vehicle with the attendant temporary loss of effectiveness. Accordingly, it is emphasized that maintenance echelons of units should be trained and practiced in making all repairs to the limit of their capacity in tools, parts, and skill. Unserviceable vehicles beyond third echelon repairs should be freely evacuated for replacement. The commanding officer of the third echelon maintenance unit of a division is ex officio motor officer of the division. His activities should extend beyond his own unit and include inspection of all maintenance elements of the division.

Augmentation of Corps Headquarters

11. Orders are issuing directing reorganization of certain corps headquarters under Table of Organization 100–1, 15 July 1943. This reorganization will cause considerable reduction in corps headquarters. It is appreciated that corps headquarters in training in the United States have problems and responsibilities other than those of an army or corps in combat. Their units are comparatively dispersed geographically and there is a continuing need for close supervision and tests of training.

12. In order to meet the training requirements of corps assigned to armies, the following allotment is being provided:

	INF	FA	ENGR	ARMD–TD	AA–AS
Colonel	1				
Lt Colonel	2	2 (1)	*1	*1	*1
Major	2	1 (1)	*1	*1	*1
Captain	1	(3)			
TOTAL Off	6	**3 (5)	*2	*2	*2
TOTAL EM	4	6 (4)	*3	*3	*3

( ) Armored Corps.
* Only when no group headquarters of the type indicated is present. If one or more type group headquarters are present, corps commander may assign special staff functions to one or more officers of a group headquarters.
** Five officers for headquarters and headquarters battery, corps artillery can augment three allotted officers to continue existing training section of eight officers and current procedure.

13. The following allotment, in addition to training allotment, is being furnished in order to provide adequate personnel for administrative requirements for corps operating directly under Army Ground Forces.

	ENGR	SIG	AG	IG	JA	FIN	MED	ORD	QM	TOTAL
Major	1	1	1	1	1	1	1	1	2	10
Captain	1	1	1				1	1	1	6
TOTAL Off	2	2	2	1	1	1	2	2	3	16
TOTAL EM	3	4	7	2	2	3	3	4	7	35

Functions of Army and Corps

14. The following conception of functions is believed the most suitable under the pending organization and in view of the problems of armies and corps in the United States:

a. In general, combat units in training in the United States will be assigned or attached to corps, service units to armies and separate corps.

b. The army should absorb the maximum of administration, endeavoring in every possible manner to simplify procedures and eliminate paper work and reports. The army's role in connection with training should be general supervision of all units without duplicating or interfering with the more detailed supervision by subordinate headquarters.

c. In accordance with letter, Hq AGF, 320.2/93 (R) (15 Oct 42) GNGCT, 15 October 1942, Subject: "Headquarters and Headquarters Detachments, Special Troops, Army and Corps," (as amended), each army and separate corps has been authorized certain headquarters and headquarters detachments, special troops, to direct and supervise both tactical and administrative instruction and training of its component units, with the exception of divisions, brigades and groups. Each group commander is charged with supervising training of individual units of the group, as well as of the combination as a team. Groups will not be attached to headquarters and headquarters detachments, special troops.

d. The corps has the primary function of as close and frequent supervision of training as is possible in view of size of its headquarters and number and dispersion of its units. The more important training tests preferably should be conducted by the corps staff. See paragraph 7a, letter, Hq AGF, 319.22/22

(1 Jan 43) GNGCT, 1 January 1943, Subject: "Conduct of Training." A separate corps combines the functions of army and corps.

e. The tabular organization of army and corps staffs should be disregarded in connection with training inspections in whatever degree is necessary in order to utilize the entire staff as wholly as possible for training supervision. Activities of the headquarters should be reduced to a minimum, and all personnel sent to the field in connection with training and in capacities best suited to meet training needs. Particularly in the corps, it is important that organic staff compartmentation be overridden with this end in view and major proportion of all personnel be kept in the field. See paragraph 1, "Conduct of Training" referred to in d, above.

15. Paragraph 2, letter Hq AGF, 320.2/187 (R) (1 Mar 43) GNGAP–A, 1 March 1943, Subject: "Personnel Administration in 'Assigned' and 'Attached' Units," and all other instructions in conflict with the principles stated above are rescinded.

By command of LT. GEN. McNAIR:

Signed: J. R. DRYDEN,
Lt. Col., A. G. D.,
Ass't Ground Adjutant General.

Organization and Training

of New Ground Combat Elements

by

Robert R. Palmer

Contents

Tables

Charts

I. New Weapons and
Old Principles

This study examines the principles and policies followed by the Army Ground Forces in dealing with ground combat elements which, singly or in combination, were relatively new and untried at the outbreak of World War II. In general, their development represented the application to war of the results of scientific, mechanical, and industrial progress in the interval between World War I and World War II. Such progress profoundly affected the traditional arms—Infantry, Cavalry, Field Artillery—and the new Air arm, but these are treated only incidentally in the present study. The study is focused on the development of new types of ground forces which were tending to become arms, specifically on tank forces, antitank forces, airborne forces, and antiaircraft artillery. The rapid development which continued to take place within the area thus defined raised some of the most controversial questions faced by the Army and the War Department during the progress of the war. Officers on the staff of the Army Ground Forces, as well as qualified soldiers in the various components of the Army, inevitably held divergent views, and current solutions had to be found by trial and error. Lt. Gen. Lesley J. McNair, while taking positive positions necessary to effective command, frequently and freely recognized that views might honestly differ, since appeal to extensive experience was impracticable.

The net effect of technical innovations in World War II was a tremendous increase in the speed and mobility with which fire power could be brought to bear. Physical mobility was increased by motorization, which, remarkably developed in the preceding two decades, made possible improved self-propelled or truck-drawn guns, rapid movement of troops by plane, half-track, and truck, and new uses for tanks and aircraft. Tactical mobility, or the use of physical mobility for reasoned objectives, was enhanced by parallel progress in communications, partly in wire, chiefly in radio, which in various forms from the "walkie-talkie" to new developments in short wave could furnish commanders of all echelons with immediate information.

The Germans, in the air-tank blitz of 1939 and 1940, used the new devices to effect what seemed at the time a revolution in tactics. Americans were easily persuaded, both within and outside the armed services, that modern war required a profusion of machines and that personnel employing the machines must receive highly specialized training in their use. It was more difficult to hold steadily in view the end for which the machines existed, and the total combined effect to which forms of specialization were meant to contribute.

The problem resolved itself into the integration of new techniques of warfare with the old, but still basic, principles of tactics and strategy. Many, including General McNair, insisted on keeping such principles constantly in mind. Greater mobility gave new meaning to the old tactical ideas of surprise, flexibility, and concentration. The old idea of balanced forces became more important, rather than less, because of technical specialization and interdependence in the armed services. The need of unity of over-all command was more urgent, rather than less, because of the freedom which had to be granted to specialists for the promotion of their chosen arms. Unity of command was also the more necessary as forces became more mobile, if all were to be engaged in fighting the same war. Economy of force remained a basic necessity even for a country priding itself on the superiority of its resources.

The Idea of Balance in AGF Policy

General McNair stated his basic views on the "Evaluation of Modern Battle Forces" in an exchange of papers with G–2 of the War Department General Staff in March 1941. G–2 had suggested that the infantry-artillery team might be rendered obsolete by the air-tank team employed by the Germans.[1] In reply, General McNair expressed a continuing belief in the central importance of infantry. He doubted whether aviation would replace field artillery, however much it might extend the depth of attack. He stated his views as follows:[2]

---

[1] WD memo G–2/2016–1297 for CofS USA, 1 Mar 41, sub: Evaluation of Modern Battle Forces. GHQ Records, 059/1.

[2] Memo of Gen McNair for CofS USA, 12 Mar 41, sub as above. GHQ Records, 059/1.

March 12, 1941

MEMORANDUM FOR THE CHIEF OF STAFF:

Subject: Evaluation of Modern Battle Forces.

The following comments are submitted in connection with G–2 memorandum, March 1, 1941, this subject, as directed by your memorandum of March 3:

1. G–2 is to be congratulated on this study.

2. It is felt that the picture presented is hardly a balanced one. The German mechanized army was not alone and supported only by aviation, as might be inferred, for example, from the second paragraph of the G–2 memorandum. It is my understanding that over twenty infantry divisions formed a long finger from Sedan to Abbeville along the Aisne, backing up the armored force, protecting its communications, and thus making possible its headlong rush. In making this comment, there is no thought of detracting from the brilliancy and importance of the operation of the armored force.

3. As to the weapons which are heralded as supplanting infantry and artillery:

a. The tank was introduced to protect against automatic small arms fire, which was developed so greatly during and since the World War. Its answer is fire against which the tank does not protect—the antitank gun. That this answer failed was due primarily to the pitifully inadequate number and power of French and British antitank guns, as well as their incorrect organization. The tank is a conspicuous target and cannot cope with a sufficiently powerful gun in position. The antitank mine also is a thoroughly effective antitank weapon.

b. Air support of armored elements depends on air superiority, which the Germans possessed overwhelmingly.

4. The picture to be studied is not alone that presented by the G–2 memorandum, but rather one in which tanks are met by reasonably adequate countermeasures, and in which the aviation supporting the tanks is unable to drive its adversaries from the air. In such a picture, armored legions quite conceivably might emerge from such an all-out attack an almost total loss. It is unsafe to stake the national defense on such an uncertain prospect.

5. As to action to meet the situation presented:

a. With reference to the air threat, sufficient aviation is the primary need, and is being procured. Antiaircraft fire to protect ground troops also is needed in a mobile mass sufficient to meet concentrated air attacks, but is not being procured.

b. The need of a greatly expanded *mobile* force of suitable antitank guns has been pointed out repeatedly, but is not being procured.

c. An armored force is being developed as rapidly as possible. It is unnecessary to decide now where this development should stop, with reference to infantry divisions. Subsequent war experience should throw further light on this question.

d. The operation in question and others in the present war do not point to an increase in the number of cavalry divisions.

6. Given proper action along the foregoing lines, the infantry division will continue to be the backbone of an army.

In short, in General McNair's opinion, the infantry division, backed by artillery, would remain the basic instrument of warfare if the proper new forces were developed to support it and if a degree of air superiority could be obtained. Balance between different weapons was the essential. Details of the balance should be determined by experience.

This remained General McNair's view. In 1941, when he felt that the balance inclined too little to the new forces, he strongly urged their development. In 1942, when the United States had fully entered the war, and the balance seemed to swing toward an undue development not only of aviation but also of antiaircraft artillery, armored and motorized divisions, and specialized units of many types, General McNair frequently appeared in a more conservative position, urging the importance of the foot soldier and the field gun.

By the time of the establishment of Army Ground Forces in March 1942, the War Department had taken steps to provide the forces enumerated by General McNair in paragraph 5 of his memorandum of March 1941.[3] The Army Air Forces was created under that name in June 1941. The developmental functions of older ground arms were grouped under the Replacement and School Command of the Army Ground Forces. Newer tactical elements, because of their special problems of development and expansion, were each given an independent organization directly subordinate to Headquarters, Army Ground Forces.[4]

These newer tactical elements—armored, tank destroyer, antiaircraft, and airborne—trained their personnel and developed their equipment and tactics in special establishments, known variously (in an order of descending importance) as a force, command, or center. Each establishment, since its function was to develop the maximum possibilities of given weapons, was operated by officers who believed strongly in these possibilities, who spent their whole time in exploring them, and who therefore developed branch spirit to a high degree. The commanding generals—Lt. Gen. Jacob L. Devers of the Armored Force (not the first commander, but the first under Army Ground Forces), Maj. Gen. John A. Green of the Antiaircraft Command, Maj. Gen. Andrew D. Bruce of the Tank Destroyer Center, and Maj. Gen. William C. Lee of the Airborne Command—were all officers who had struggled to get their programs more

---

[3] (1) See above, "Origins of the Army Ground Forces: General Headquarters, United States Army, 1940–42," especially Sections III and VII. (2) See also AGF Historical Section, A General History of the Army Ground Forces.

[4] Ibid.

fully incorporated into the Army. Each organization had a spirit of enthusiasm for its own role, a valuable and creative spirit, but one which General McNair wished to direct toward the over-all interests of the Army as he understood them.

One aim of the reorganization of 9 March 1942 was to subdue the spirit of branch independence. The trend of AGF policy with respect to the Air Forces was to cooperate on matters of common interest; with respect to the older arms (Infantry, Cavalry, Field Artillery, and Coast Artillery), to administer them centrally through the Replacement and School Command or directly through the AGF headquarters staff; and with respect to the newer establishments or quasi arms (Armored, Tank Destroyer, Antiaircraft, and Airborne), at first to allow a degree of independence, later to assimilate them to the status of the older arms by subordinating them more fully to AGF headquarters, either directly or through the Replacement and School Command. The fulfillment of this policy took about two years, except that cooperation with the headquarters of the Army Air Forces was never as complete as General McNair desired. The aim of the policy was to secure a balance of forces: first, a balance in mobilization, for example, between armored and infantry troops (the higher balance between aviation and ground forces being of necessity left to the War Department); second, a balanced training in the sense of combined training to weld the several arms into teams; and consequently, third, the production on the battlefield of a complex but unified fighting force.

In this way each arm would be developed in the most useful ratio to other arms. None would grow simply for its own advantage or in an enthusiastic belief in the peculiar decisiveness of its operations. None would consume resources which might more effectively be assigned to another. Balance meant an economy of force, or a maximizing of the military power of the United States.

Mobilization Planning in 1942

Mobilization policy in 1942 inclined heavily toward the expansion of newer tactical specialties, and toward the endowment of all units with a great array of mechanical equipment, especially in motor transportation. The inadequacy of prewar provisions made such a program necessary. There was also a tendency to build heavily equipped units and to furnish American troops with a quantity of conveniences corresponding to the living habits of the American people. Toward the end of 1942, after the first rush of rearmament, the basic problem of logistics inherent in the situation of the United States asserted itself. American military power was not a mere matter of what could be assembled in the United States but rather of what force could be exerted at distances of from three to twelve thousand miles.[5] However much the world may have shrunk with the development of aviation or the course of political thinking, for logistical purposes the oceans were about as wide in 1942 as in 1917. The bulkier the equipment, the less could be sent overseas. The more auxiliary personnel and materiel put on shipboard, the less was the offensive power which could be delivered.

In May 1942 the War Department had ordered the conversion of 7 infantry divisions provided in the 1942 Troop Basis into 4 armored and 3 motorized divisions.[6] The Operations Division (OPD), War Department General Staff, estimated that, by the end of 1943, 46 armored and 23 motorized divisions out of a total of 140 divisions should be mobilized.[7] Army Ground Forces pronounced this program feasible but judged the proportion of armored and motorized to infantry divisions excessive and "not in consonance with existing transportation shortages."[8] Army Ground Forces advised against mechanization of the two cavalry divisions, holding that the nondivisional cavalry regiments, which were all mechanized (with light tanks, armored cars, self-propelled howitzers, and trucks), were sufficient.[9] Two airborne divisions were organized in the summer of 1942. Tank destroyer battalions were rapidly activated. Antiaircraft battalions were activated even more rapidly, frequently outrunning the 1942 Troop Basis. General McNair doubted the value of antiaircraft artillery as an offensive weapon, since much of it was used to protect rear-area installations or airfields, and since those units which operated with mobile ground forces were useful primarily only so long as American air power was undeveloped.[10]

[5] WD memo (C) WDGCT 451 (10-8-42) for CG AGF, 30 Oct 42, sub: Excessive Number of Motor Vehicles. 451/66 (C).

[6] WD memo (S) WDGCT 320.2 (4-28-42) for CG AGF, 4 May 42, sub: Armd and Mtzd Divs. 320.2/165 (S).

[7] WD memo (S) OPD 320.2 (5-10-42) (2-12-42) for G-3 WD, 23 May 42, sub: Maj Tr Unit Reqts for 1942, 1943, 1944. 320.2/190 (S).

[8] AGF memo (S) for OPD WDGS, 28 May 42, sub: Maj Tr Unit Reqts for 1942, 1943, 1944. 320.2/190 (S).

[9] (1) AGF memo for G-3 WD, 5 May 42, sub: Cav Orgn. 321/51 (Cav). (2) See also memo, SW for ASW, 21 Jul 42. 321/99 (Cav).

[10] (1) See above, in "Ground Forces in the Army, December 1941–April 1945: a Statistical Study," cols 16 and 21 of the table. (2) See above also, "Mobilization of the Ground Army."

By the fall of 1942 the need of economy became evident. Estimates obtained by the War Department disclosed the limits in the capacity of the United States to produce war material,[11] and for the first time the ceiling on the manpower available to the Army came into view. The limitations on shipping capacity were felt as the submarine menace continued unabated. In addition, and in part because of these limitations, the strategic plans of the Combined Chiefs of Staff had changed; the idea of early ground operations in western Europe had been abandoned. The War Department dispatched a long memorandum to the commanding generals of the Army Ground Forces and the Services of Supply, reading in part as follows:[12]

The above shipping considerations may dictate a considerable change in our strategic concept with a consequent change in the basic structure of our Army. Since, from the shipping capabilities indicated above, it appears that the early employment of a mass Army, which must be transported by water, is not practicable, it follows that the trend must be toward light, easily transportable units rather than units of the heavier type. Likewise, the proportion of Air Forces may have to be increased. . . .

Indications are that the 7,500,000 men allotted to the Army for 1943 approaches the maximum manpower level that the Army is going to be able to reach. If this is the case, it is highly necessary that we not commit the type of Army which we shall build in 1943 too definitely to a single strategic concept such as 5440 [the now postponed plan for the invasion of Europe] which may prove impracticable of accomplishment. Recent indications are that a further expansion of the Air Forces may be expected which not only will reduce the number of men available for the ground forces but will complicate, if not curtail, the procurement of heavy equipment for other than the Air Forces.

In other words, it was decided to push the development of air power rather than a fuller development of the ground army.

In considering how to reduce the originally planned strength of the ground army for 1943, Army Ground Forces and the War Department agreed that shipping capacity should be a governing factor. The Army Ground Forces favored reduction in those units, whether light or heavy, whose shipment added the least to combat power overseas. The War Department favored reduction in the heavy units which were the most difficult to transport. Army Ground Forces recommended that reduction be made preferably in antiaircraft and

---

[11] Rpt (R) of ASF for Fiscal Year 1943, p. 19.

[12] WD memo (S) WDGCT 320.2 Gen (10–25–42) for CGs AGF, SOS, 25 Oct 42, sub: TB 1943. 320.2/5 (TB 43) (S).

service units and in armored and motorized divisions rather than in infantry and airborne divisions. By late 1942 there were strong tactical reasons for reviewing the ratio of armored to infantry strength. Army Ground Forces also recommended that an appropriate balance among units of different types (whether light or heavy) be maintained in the reductions.[13]

The War Department, applying cuts chiefly in heavier units, reduced the originally proposed number of armored and motorized divisions, though not as much as the Army Ground Forces desired. Cuts were made also in the planned number of other heavy units: nondivisional tank battalions (more useful than armored divisions for close support of infantry); tank destroyer battalions; and nondivisional field artillery, especially heavy artillery. The figures adopted for these units were well below those recommended by the Army Ground Forces— in the case of heavy artillery 50 percent below what the Army Ground Forces believed necessary. The planned strength of antiaircraft artillery (half the strength contemplated for infantry) remained virtually unchanged for another year. Nor was the expansion of service units effectively checked. The resulting mobilization program, embodied in November 1942 in the first version of the 1943 Troop Basis, was regarded by the Army Ground Forces as seriously unbalanced.[14]

Tactical Reorganization for Economy and Balance

When, in October 1942, the War Department empowered General McNair to reorganize the ground forces on a basis of the strictest economy, he took advantage of the opportunity to apply his conceptions of a properly balanced force. The application and its effect on the composition of the ground forces at successive stages of World War II have been described in the two preceding studies,[15] and need be only briefly summarized here.

Carrying out with rigor his mandate to cut back the number of vehicles in the ground army, which in his opinion had become excessive to the point of

[13] (1) *Ibid.* (2) AGF memo (S) for G–3 WD, 29 Oct 42, sub as above. (3) WD memo (S) WDGCT 320.2 Gen (10–25–42) for CG AGF, 19 Nov 42, sub as above. All in 320.2/4 and 5 (TB 43) (S). (4) See above, "Mobilization of the Ground Army."

[14] See above, "Mobilization of the Ground Army," p. 217.

[15] See above, "Reorganization of Ground Troops for Combat," pp. 297–99, and "Mobilization of the Ground Army," pp. 217–220. For earlier developments, see above, "Origins of the Army Ground Forces: General Headquarters, United States Army, 1940–42," pp. 51 ff.

impairing mobility, General McNair also reduced the proportion of units in categories that were not only difficult to ship because of their massive equipment, but which he believed had been developed to a point in excess of tactical requirements. The two most important of these categories were motorized and armored divisions. He sought, with less success, to cut down the proportion of antiaircraft artillery, not only because of its mass of specialized equipment but also because antiaircraft artillery was primarily a defensive arm. At the same time, to offset the effect of these cuts, he proposed a reorganization of the whole structure of tactical command in the ground forces, with the object of introducing a maximum of economy and flexibility into the employment of all categories of specialized and mobile units so that they could be brought into action when and where most critically needed. The recommendations of General McNair for a reduction in the proportion of armored and antiaircraft units and for an increase in the proportion of field artillery were, in general, followed, after delays and debates which are described in the preceding studies. Motorized divisions disappeared. The organic motor transportation of all ground units was cut to the bone. The twin principles of streamlining and pooling were put into effect in a drastic reorganization of tactical commands. The net result was a ground army whose parts were less self-sufficient, but which was lighter in equipment and more flexible in its capacity to mass its fire power at critical points on a wide front. Its fire power as a whole was increased, without reducing that of its front line units. It was not a force built around motorized and armored units, as some had anticipated and desired, but one whose main strength was in infantry, backed by guns of all kinds which could be massed or detailed to support in attack, and supplemented by less encumbered armored divisions designed to exploit a breakthrough. The infantry division continued to be the backbone of the United States ground army as organized in World War II.

II. Organization for Training

The armored, tank destroyer, antiaircraft, and airborne elements of the Army, which had grown up as separate enterprises in 1940 and 1941, each possessed or received, on coming under the Army Ground Forces in 1942, a special establishment (called a "force," "command," or "center") for the development of its equipment and doctrine and the training of its enlisted and officer personnel.[1] In exercising these functions the new establishments resembled the "arms"—infantry, cavalry, etc.—but they could not become arms because of restrictions in legislation governing the Army. In some respects, however, they were more than arms. Whereas the true arms had been gathered under the Replacement and School Command, the new establishments, or quasi arms, enjoyed an independent existence within the Army Ground Forces. The true arms exercised no command authority; the new establishments were military commands, charged with the training of tactical units. Whereas units of the older arms were trained from the moment of activation under armies, corps, and divisions, units of the new forces, in which a new and special knowledge was needed, were trained initially under their respective force, command, or center, passing later to armies, corps, or divisions for combined training.

The policy of the Army Ground Forces was to allow a degree of independence to the special establishments while development and expansion were the foremost needs, but later to check their independence by assimilating them to the status of the older arms.

Growth of the Special Establishments

At first, by the War Department reorganization of 9 March 1942, only the Armored Force and the Antiaircraft Command (the term "Antiaircraft Force" had been considered but rejected) had the full features of a quasi arm. Each

---

[1] Each of these commands has written its own history under the direction of the AGF Historical Section. The present study attempts only a very brief over-all survey.

possessed a service board and a service school, including an officer candidate school, and each trained individual replacements for its units. Each exercised jurisdiction over personnel administration, operated replacement pools, and controlled assignments. Each had command of tactical units: virtually all armored units in the United States were assigned to the Armored Force, and all antiaircraft units in the United States except those in defense commands were assigned to the Antiaircraft Command.[2] (See Tables Nos. 1 to 4.)

The Armored Force enjoyed also certain other powers. Unlike other ground arms, it dealt directly with War Department agencies and private manufacturers in matters of procurement. It controlled the distribution of tanks to the motorized divisions, the mechanized cavalry, and the few armored units which in 1942 were not under its own command. It helped to establish the Desert Training Center and sought to share in its control. In May 1942 it was confirmed in its authority over the promotion and assignment of all armored officers in the Army Ground Forces. Requisitions for enlisted personnel of other ground arms were filled in 1942 by The Adjutant General, but requisitions for armored personnel were filled by the Chief of the Armored Force.[3]

Because of this wide jurisdiction and for various other reasons—the fact that the tank was a prime offensive weapon, that the units under its command were as large as divisions and corps, and that its chief (from September 1942 to May 1943) held, like General McNair, the rank of lieutenant general—the Armored Force was by far the strongest and most autonomous of the special establishments in the Army Ground Forces. With a strength ranging from 100,000 to 200,000, it compared to a field army in size. There was a tendency among armored officers to believe that large armored units could operate tactically alone, far ahead of more slowly moving ground troops. The habit of the Armored Force in 1941 of comparing itself to the Air Forces has already been noted.[4] This ambition had been dampened by the War Department.

---

[2] (1) AGF ltr to Maj Gen J. A. Greene, CofCA, 9 Mar 42, sub: Advance Directive, Activation of AA Comd. 320.2/2 (AA). (2) For the Armored Force see above, "Origins of the Army Ground Forces: General Headquarters, United States Army, 1940–42," Sec. III.

[3] (1) See papers in 470.8/143. (2) See AGF Historical Section, The Desert Training Center and C–AMA. (3) AGF ltr to CGs, 20 May 42, sub: Admin Jurisdiction over Offs of Armd Force Units While Under Temp Control of Other Comdrs. 320.2/121 (Armd F). (4) See AGF Historical Section, Provision of Enlisted Replacements.

[4] See above, "Origins of the Army Ground Forces: General Headquarters, United States Army, 1940–42," p. 72.

TABLE NO. 1

Assignment of Armored Divisions in the Army Ground Forces, 1942–44

ASSIGNED TO:	1 MAY 42	1 SEP 42	1 FEB 43	1 JUL 43	10 NOV 43	1 MAY 44
Armored Force (exclusive of Corps)	5	10	6	3	2	...
Armored Corps under Armored Force:						
II Armored Corps.............	2	...	...	...	...	...
III Armored Corps............	...	...	2	...	...	...
IV Armored Corps............	...	...	...	2	...	...
Total in Armored Force......	7	10	8	5	2	...
Desert Training Center............	...	1	2	2	1	...
II Armored Corps (directly under AGF)............	...	...	2	2	...	...
III Armored Corps (under Third Army)............	...	...	...	2	...	...
Second Army......................	...	...	...	1	...	...
Fourth Army......................	...	...	...	...	2	...
III Corps.........................	...	...	...	...	1	1
VIII Corps........................	...	...	...	1	...	...
IX Corps.........................	...	...	...	...	...	1
X Corps..........................	...	...	...	...	1	...
XII Corps........................	...	...	...	...	1	...
XIII Corps.......................	...	...	...	1	1	...
XVI Corps........................	...	...	...	...	...	1
XVIII Corps......................	...	...	...	...	1	...
XIX Corps........................	...	...	...	...	2	...
XX Corps.........................	...	...	...	...	1	...
XXI Corps........................	...	...	...	...	...	2
XXII Corps.......................	...	...	...	...	...	2
XXIII Corps......................	...	...	...	...	...	2
Total in Armored Force..........	7	10	8	5	2	0
Total not in Armored Force......	0	1	4	9	11	9
TOTAL IN ARMY GROUND FORCES......................	7	11	12	14	13	9

Source: AGF records, 320.2 Assignment Lists (C).

TABLE NO. 2

Assignment of Tank Battalions (Other Than in Armored Divisions) in the Army Ground Forces, 1942–44

ASSIGNED TO:	1 MAY 42	1 SEP 42	1 FEB 43	1 JUL 43	10 NOV 43	1 MAY 44
Armored Force....................	10	8	19	16	14	2
Tank Destroyer Center.............	1	2	3	3	3	...
Desert Training Center............	3	2	2	2	2	...
Second Army......................	...	1	1	...	...	...
Third Army.......................	...	...	...	2	3	...
Fourth Army......................	...	...	...	...	6	1
Replacement & School Command...	...	...	...	1	1	7
I Corps...........................	1	...	...	...	...	...
III Corps.........................	...	...	...	...	...	...
VII Corps.........................	...	1	...	...	1	3
IX Corps..........................	...	...	...	...	...	...
X Corps...........................	...	...	...	...	1	2
XII Corps.........................	...	...	...	...	2	...
XIII Corps........................	...	...	...	...	2	...
XVI Corps.........................	...	...	...	1	3	1
XVIII Corps.......................	...	...	...	...	...	2
XIX Corps.........................	...	...	...	...	5	...
XX Corps..........................	...	...	...	...	2	...
XXI Corps.........................	...	...	...	...	2	1
XXII Corps........................	...	...	...	...	...	3
XXIII Corps.......................	...	...	...	...	...	5
Total in Armored Force..........	10	8	19	16	14	2
Total not in Armored Force......	5	6	6	9	33	25
TOTAL IN ARMY GROUND FORCES.....................	15	14	25	25	47	27

Source: AGF records, 320.2 Assignment Lists (C).

TABLE NO. 3

Assignment of Tank Destroyer Battalions in the Army Ground Forces, 1942–44

ASSIGNED TO:	1 MAY 42	10 NOV 42	1 MAY 43	10 NOV 43	1 MAY 44
Tank Destroyer Center......................	1	28	56	27	...
Armored Force.............................	6	3	2	...	...
Second Army...............................	20	14	9	...	...
Third Army................................	13	17	12	...	...
Fourth Army...............................	...	...	...	7	1
Desert Training Center.....................	1	2	6	6	...
II Armored Corps..........................	...	4	1	...	...
III Corps.................................	...	...	...	5	1
IV Corps..................................	...	...	4	...	...
VI Corps..................................	3	2	...	...	...
VII Corps.................................	4	...	...	...	...
VIII Corps................................	...	...	...	...	...
IX Corps..................................	5	4	...	5	9
X Corps...................................	...	...	...	6	...
XI Corps..................................	...	...	...	5	...
XII Corps.................................	...	...	...	5	...
XIII Corps................................	...	...	3	1	1
XV Corps..................................	...	...	...	...	...
XVI Corps.................................	...	...	...	...	3
XVIII Corps...............................	...	...	...	5	...
XIX Corps.................................	...	...	...	5	...
XX Corps..................................	...	...	...	7	...
XXI Corps.................................	...	...	...	...	1
XXII Corps................................	...	...	...	...	5
XXIII Corps...............................	...	...	...	...	16
Replacement & School Command..............	...	...	...	...	4
Total at Tank Destroyer Center............	1	28	56	27	0
Total not at Tank Destroyer Center........	52	46	37	57	41
TOTAL IN ARMY GROUND FORCES.....	53	74	93	84	41

Source: AGF records, 320.2 Assignment Lists (C).

TABLE NO. 4

*Assignment of Antiaircraft Artillery Battalions
in the Army Ground Forces, 1942–44*

ASSIGNED TO:	1 MAY 42	10 NOV 42	1 MAY 43	10 NOV 43	1 MAY 44
Antiaircraft Command.........................	48	137	238	186	147
Armored Force...............................	...	...	2	...	...
Second Army................................	...	...	9	1	1
Third Army.................................	...	...	2	8	...
Fourth Army................................	...	...	...	6	5
Desert Training Center.......................	1	...	4	7	...
II Armored Corps...........................	...	...	3	...	...
III Corps..................................	...	...	...	...	11
IX Corps..................................	...	...	...	...	2
X Corps...................................	...	...	...	...	...
XI Corps..................................	...	...	...	1	...
XII Corps.................................	...	...	...	3	...
XIII Corps................................	...	...	1	12	8
XVI Corps................................	...	...	...	...	3
XVIII Corps...............................	...	...	...	...	...
XX Corps.................................	...	...	...	1	...
XXI Corps................................	...	...	...	...	4
XXII Corps...............................	...	...	...	...	...
XXIII Corps...............................	...	...	...	...	...
Total in Antiaircraft Command.........	48	137	238	186	147
Total not in Antiaircraft Command.....	1	0	21	39	34
TOTAL IN ARMY GROUND FORCES	49	137	259	225	181

Source: AGF records, 320.2 Assignment Lists (C).

By 1943, with the detachment of armored units from its command, and with the tremendous expansion of antiaircraft artillery, the Armored Force was not as large as the Antiaircraft Command. Nor was it ever as geographically extensive, being concentrated at Fort Knox, Ky., whereas the Antiaircraft Command, from its headquarters at Richmond, Va., controlled at one time as many as eleven training centers throughout the United States.

The Airborne Command was not provided for in the War Department reorganization, but it was activated by the Army Ground Forces on 23 March 1942, replacing the Provisional Parachute Group organized in 1941.[5] The Parachute School was transferred from the Infantry School to the new command, as were all airborne units then existing in the United States—two incomplete parachute infantry regiments and one glider infantry battalion.[6] Airborne divisions, when later activated, were placed under the Airborne Command for training only, under army headquarters for administration and supply.[7] No replacement training center, board, or school (other than for parachutists) was created for the Airborne Command; these functions, along with personnel administration, were performed for airborne troops by other agencies of the Ground Forces.[8] The Airborne Command remained primarily a training center and did not develop as far as the other special establishments in the direction of being an arm.

The status of tank destroyers remained undecided for several months. The War Department reorganization placed a Tank Destroyer Command directly under Headquarters, Army Ground Forces. This command possessed only the limited functions of the Tank Destroyer Tactical and Firing Center activated in the preceding December.[9] Many officers questioned whether the tank destroyer was a weapon around which a separate organization should be built. General Devers wished to annex the training of tank destroyers, as well as that of

[5] (1) Memo of Gen McNair for CofS USA, 17 Mar 42, sub: A/B Comd. 320.2/1 (AB). (2) AGF ltrs to A/B Comd, 23 and 24 Mar 42, sub as above. 320.2/1 (AB). (3) AGF ltr (R) to CO A/B Comd, 8 Apr 42, sub as above. 320.2/1 (AB) (R).

[6] (1) AGF ltr to A/B Comd and R&SC, 6 May 42, sub: Pcht Sch. 320.2/21 (AB). (2) A/B Comd ltr (C) to CG AGF, 18 Apr 42, sub: A/B Comd Tng Situation. 353/1 (AB) (C).

[7] (1) AGF ltr (C) to CGs A/B Comd, Second and Third Armies, 21 Oct 42, sub: Directive for Tng A/B Divs. 353/11 (AB) (C). (2) Personal ltr (S) of Brig Gen F. L. Parks, CofS AGF to Brig Gen M. B. Ridgway, 29 Jul 42, 322.98 (S).

[8] The request of the Airborne Command for establishment of a service board was disapproved. AGF 1st ind, 7 Jun 43, to AB Comd ltr, 15 May 43, sub: A/B Bd. 320.2/225 (AB).

[9] TDC Info Bull 10, a statement by TDC of its own functions, 30 Mar 42. 020/34.

mechanized cavalry, to the Armored Force.[10] This transfer of the tank destroyers was favored by the chief of the Operations Section, Headquarters, Army Ground Forces; he also recommended that airborne training should be conducted by the field armies, believing that Army Ground Forces was dealing with too many directly subordinate headquarters.[11] General McNair had long thought that antitank and antiaircraft training in their initial phases should be separate from the Armored Force and from the Air Force, largely on psychological grounds.[12] But he had not yet decided how far the separate organization of tank destroyer training should go. On 11 July 1942, observing that the Tank Destroyer Command hardly constituted more than a service school, having no command authority like that of the Armored and Antiaircraft establishments, he recommended to the War Department that it be placed with the schools of the older arms and under the Replacement and School Command.[13]

There were at this time about seventy tank destroyer battalions in various parts of the country, attached principally to the field armies. They were in different stages of incompleteness in organization and equipment, most of them being lineal descendants of the provisional antitank battalions created in 1941 by a redistribution of artillery weapons. AGF staff officers, after inspecting these battalions, reported on 13 July 1942 that all were confused by uncertainty of organization, that none had a good firing range, and that since tank destroyer tactics were not crystallized each battalion followed its own ideas of training. The report urged the necessity of a unit training center through which battalions could be rotated for standardization at the highest level.[14]

Instead, therefore, of being curtailed, the Tank Destroyer Command was expanded in the latter half of 1942. An advanced unit training center was established for the battalions already active, together with a basic unit training center for the numerous new battalions called for in the Troop Basis. Step by step, General Bruce received full command authority over the tank destroyer bat-

[10] Memo (C) of CofArmdF for CG AGF, 21 Mar 42, sub not given. 320.2/7 (Armd Center) (C).

[11] Memo of Col Ott, Opns Div AGF for CG AGF, 27 May 42, sub: Orgn of Hq and Fld Elements of AGF. 020/73.

[12] (1) See above, "Origins of the Army Ground Forces: General Headquarters, United States Army, 1940–42," p. 81. (2) Memo of Gen McNair for G–3 WD, 2 Sep 41, sub: Orgn of AT Units in the Army. GHQ Records, 353/15 (AT).

[13] (1) Memo of Gen McNair for G–3 WD, 11 Jul 42, sub: Change in Status of TDC. Approved by WD. 320.2/69 (TDC). (2) AGF 4th ind (C) to CG SOS, 1 May 42. 320.2/2 (TDC) (C).

[14] Incl to memo of Maj F. T. Unger, 13 Jul 42, sub: Summary of Inspection of TD Bns. 353/42 (TDC).

talions sent to him for training. His requests for a replacement training center and an officer candidate school were granted. With these enlargements the Tank Destroyer Command, although redesignated as a "Center," and although its school and replacement center was put under the Replacement and School Command, nevertheless reached the stature of a quasi arm.[15]

In October 1942 the Tank Destroyer Center was empowered to inspect, as an agency of Army Ground Force headquarters, all tank destroyer battalions attached to armies and other subdivisions of the Army Ground Forces. The purpose of these inspections was to maintain uniform standards of training, acquaint field units with the latest doctrine, and estimate status of equipment, degree of combat efficiency, and readiness for overseas shipment. The Tank Destroyer Center was the first of the special establishments to receive this authority to inspect units not under its own command. The others in 1942 had virtually no units attached to the field forces.[16]

While the powers of the Tank Destroyer Center expanded in 1942, those of the Armored Force were gradually restricted. General McNair came increasingly to believe that the Armored Force, as he said, "should join the Army." In this respect the Armored Force presented, in accentuated form, a problem raised by all the special establishments. Since the Armored Force was the oldest and strongest of these establishments, it was the first to feel the restrictions imposed by the Army Ground Forces on branch independence. On 19 March 1942 the I Armored Corps was transferred from the Armored Force to the Desert Training Center.[17] The complete separation of the Desert Training Center from the Armored Force was effected. Plans were launched for increasing the infantry strength within the armored division, and for assigning armored corps, divisions, and battalions to nonarmored higher command. In December 1942 the Armored Force yielded to the Army Ground Forces its jurisdiction over the distribution of tanks.[18]

By the end of 1942 the operations of the special establishments had become very similar. The armored, antiaircraft, and tank destroyer organizations gave

[15] (1) AGF ltr to R&SC, 14 Aug 42, sub: Opn of TDC. 320.2/87 (TDC). (2) AGF ltr to CGs, 16 Aug 42, sub as above. 320.2/69 (TDC). (3) Papers in 320.2/4 (TDC) (C), 320.2/14 (TDC) (R), 353/72 (S), and 320.2/69 (TDC).

[16] AGF ltr to CGs, 21 Oct 42, sub: Tng Inspections, TD Units. 331.1/9 (TDC).

[17] AGF ltr (C) to CGs, 19 Mar 42, sub: Asgmt of I Armd Corps. 320.2/4 (Armd Center)(C).

[18] AGF ltr (R) to CGs, 27 Dec 42, sub: Allocation and Distribution of Tks. With related papers. 570.8/133 (R).

basic training, officer and specialist training, and other forms of individual instruction. The Armored Force and Antiaircraft Command controlled assignment of their personnel, a function assumed by the Tank Destroyer Center, by delegation from the Replacement and School Command, in March 1943.[19] All three activated units of their respective types and provided the cadres and unit training programs. The three, together with the Airborne Command, acted as unit training centers, giving initial or branch training to their respective battalions and divisions. All four were responsible for the progress of tactical doctrine, training methods, and equipment in their several fields.

For combined training, by plans made late in 1942, units were to be detached from their special establishments on the completion of their branch training, and attached (later assigned) to armies and corps.[20] The question presented itself of how the special establishments should exercise their functions with regard to personnel, doctrine, and equipment after their units were withdrawn from their respective commands. Airborne units were so few, and the functions of the Airborne Command so restricted, as to present no problem. For the Armored Force, Antiaircraft Command, and Tank Destroyer Center, identical solutions were adopted.

In personnel administration, these three retained the responsibility for maintaining the records necessary to classify and assign personnel of their arms. In procuring cadres for new units which they activated, and for other purposes of their own, they were forbidden, without the approval of Army Ground Forces, to withdraw personnel of their arms from units attached to tactical commanders for combined training. In the interest of unity of authority commanders of these tactical units received jurisdiction over personnel administration of the attached units, except where permanent transfer or change of station was involved.[21]

To link the training establishments with the field forces in matters of training, doctrine, and equipment, the system of inspections originally applied to the tank destroyer battalions was extended to armored and antiaircraft units. Like

[19] R&SC ltr to CG AGF, 15 Mar 43, sub: Asgmt of TD Off and Enl Men. 320.2/211 (TDC). (2) See papers in 320.2/7 (TDC) (C).

[20] (1) Memo (S) of Col Winn for Gen McNair, 2 Oct 42, sub: Revision of AGF Comd Orgn. 320.2/493 (S). (2) AGF M/S, CG to G–1 and G–4, 5 Nov 42, with related papers. 320.2/396. (3) Papers in AGF Plans Sec file 154.

[21] (1) AGF ltr (R) to CGs, 16 Jan 43, sub: Pers Administration in "Assigned" and "Attached" Units. 320.2/167 (R). (2) AGF ltr (R) to CGs, 1 Mar 43, sub as above. 320.2/187 (R).

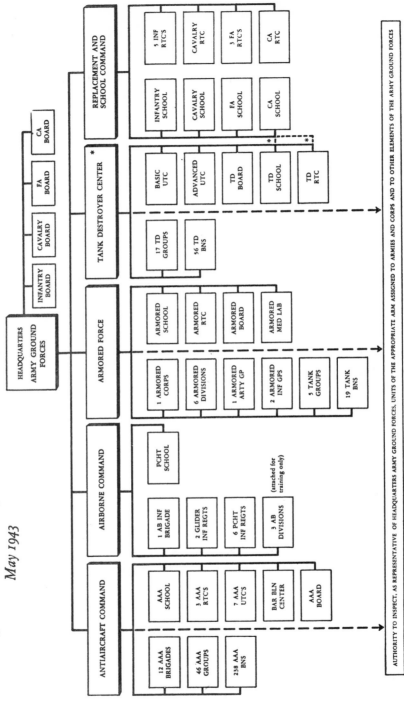

Chart No. 1

Arms and Quasi Arms in the Army Ground Forces,
May 1943

HEADQUARTERS ARMY GROUND FORCES

INFANTRY BOARD | CAVALRY BOARD | FA BOARD | CA BOARD

ANTIAIRCRAFT COMMAND
- 12 AAA BRIGADES
- 46 AAA GROUPS
- 238 AAA BNS
- AAA SCHOOL
- 3 AAA RTC'S
- 7 AAA UTC'S
- BAR BLN CENTER
- AAA BOARD

AIRBORNE COMMAND
- 1 AB INF BRIGADE
- 2 GLIDER INF REGTS
- 6 PCHT INF REGTS
- 3 AB DIVISIONS (attached for training only)
- PCHT SCHOOL

ARMORED FORCE
- 1 ARMORED CORPS
- 6 ARMORED DIVISIONS
- 1 ARMORED ARTY GP
- 2 ARMORED INF GPS
- 5 TANK GROUPS
- 19 TANK BNS
- ARMORED SCHOOL
- ARMORED RTC
- ARMORED BOARD
- ARMORED MED LAB

TANK DESTROYER CENTER *
- 17 TD GROUPS
- 56 TD BNS
- BASIC UTC
- ADVANCED UTC
- TD BOARD
- TD SCHOOL *
- TD RTC *

REPLACEMENT AND SCHOOL COMMAND
- INFANTRY SCHOOL
- CAVALRY SCHOOL
- FA SCHOOL
- CA SCHOOL
- 5 INF RTC'S
- CAVALRY RTC
- 3 FA RTC'S
- CA RTC

AUTHORITY TO INSPECT, AS REPRESENTATIVE OF HEADQUARTERS ARMY GROUND FORCES, UNITS OF THE APPROPRIATE ARM ASSIGNED TO ARMIES AND CORPS AND TO OTHER ELEMENTS OF THE ARMY GROUND FORCES

* For the administration of its school and replacement training center the Tank Destroyer Center was subordinate to the Replacement and School Command.

Chart No. 2

Arms and Quasi Arms in the Army Ground Forces,
May 1944

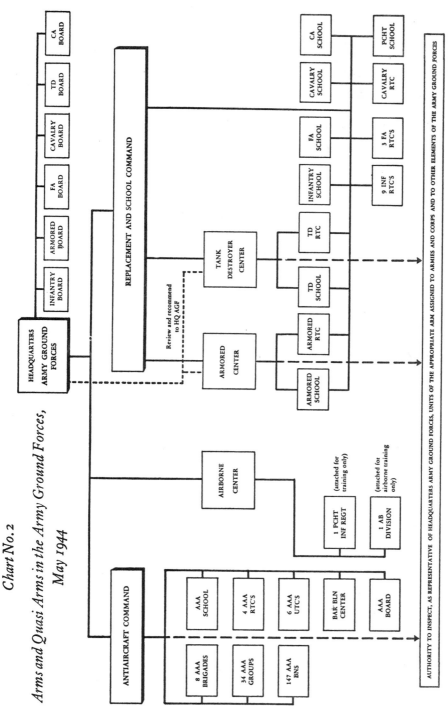

Source: AGF Records, 320.2 (Assignment Lists) (C).

AUTHORITY TO INSPECT, AS REPRESENTATIVE OF HEADQUARTERS ARMY GROUND FORCES, UNITS OF THE APPROPRIATE ARM ASSIGNED TO ARMIES AND CORPS AND TO OTHER ELEMENTS OF THE ARMY GROUND FORCES

the Tank Destroyer Center, the Armored Force and the Antiaircraft Command became inspecting agencies for Headquarters, Army Ground Forces.[22] Officers of the three organizations—preferably general officers according to General Mc-Nair's intention[23]—were to inspect units of their respective arms in the field armies or separate corps and to submit comments in the form of letters to be dispatched by Army Ground Forces to the tactical commanders concerned. The system did not work well at first; inspections were infrequent (except those of the Antiaircraft Command), or were conducted by junior officers, or turned into technical inspections of equipment, notably in the case of the Armored Force.[24] Since armies would conduct their own technical inspections after reaching theaters of operations, General McNair wished them to do the same in training. A new directive was issued in August 1943, clarifying the aims of the inspections desired.[25]

Throughout 1943 the functions of the special establishments remained generally stabilized as described above. (See Chart No. 1.) However, activation and unit training became less important in practice because activation of combat units in the Ground Forces (except in the Field Artillery) virtually ceased with the revision of the Troop Basis in July 1943. Units produced and trained by the special establishments passed in increasing numbers to the field forces for combined training. (See Tables Nos. 1–4.) As time went on, the special establishments were less busy as unit training centers and proportionately more occupied with inspections and with the functions which they shared with the older arms—the perfection of equipment and doctrine, individual training, and administration of personnel.

Decline of the Special Establishments

The first to feel the change was the Armored Force, which in June 1943 was redesignated the Armored Command.[26] The new name, implying a greater degree of subordination, was an indication of a process long in development

---

[22] AGF ltr to CGs, 10 Dec 42, sub: Tng Inspections, AA, Armd, and TD Units. 333/82.

[23] AGF ltr to CGs AA Comd, Armd F, TDC, 21 Feb 43, sub as above. 333/82.

[24] Series of AGF M/Ss in 333/82 and 333.1/1504.

[25] AGF ltr to CGs, 22 Aug 43, sub: Tng Inspections, AA, Armd, and TD Units. 333.1/1504.

[26] (1) AGF M/S (C), CG to CofS, 11 May 43, sub: Armd Force Reorgn. (2) Memo (C) of Gen Lear for CofS USA, 14 May 43, sub as above. Both in 320.2/30 (Armd Center) (C).

and still not finished. Contact between officers of the AGF staff and of the Armored Force became closer. Army Ground Forces began to cut down at Fort Knox what General McNair regarded as excessive overhead.[27] It was at this time that the armored corps was abolished and the long discussions of the armored division were brought to an end. The training of armored divisions and of separate and armored infantry battalions was coordinated with the general Army Ground Forces training program.[28] Army Ground Forces now provided (what the Armored Force had provided before) week-by-week training programs and tests for armored units. They were modeled on the programs and tests which had been effective since November 1942 for other units of the ground arms. Armored artillery, a component of armored divisions, was required to meet all field artillery tests, including the test for unobserved fires from which it had previously been exempted.[29] Tests were also issued by Army Ground Forces for the improvement of tank gunnery.[30] The Armored Command continued to be responsible for the inspections and for the developmental and personnel functions performed by the Armored Force.

In February 1944, after some months of planning, the armored and tank destroyer establishments were eliminated from the chain of tactical command.[31] (See Chart No. 2.) However, because of continuing difficulties in antiaircraft training and the need of liaison with the Army Air Forces, the Antiaircraft Command remained untouched. The Airborne Command was not greatly modified, never having developed as far as the other special establishments. Its designation was changed to the Airborne Center. The Parachute School was withdrawn from it and placed with other schools under the Replacement and School Command. During the activations of parachute regiments, the Parachute School had tended to become a unit training center; henceforth it operated in effect as a replacement training center, supplying individual parachutists as requisitioned by units. The Airborne Center continued to give airborne training to such units as might be attached to it for the purpose. The Airborne Center also reviewed the equipment, doctrine, tactics, and training literature of para-

---

[27] AGF ltr (R) to Armd Comd, 21 Aug 43, sub: Revision of Almt of Pers to the Armd Comd. 320.2/77 (Armd F) (R).

[28] AGF ltr to CGs, 16 Aug 43, sub: Tng Directive Effective 1 Nov 42. 353/52 (Tng Dir).

[29] AGF ltr to CGs, 29 Aug 43, sub: Revision of AGF FA and TD Tests. 353/52 (Tng Dir).

[30] AGF ltr to GCs, 24 Nov 43, sub: Tng Directive Effective 1 Nov 42, 353/52 (Tng Dir).

[31] AGF M/S (C), CG to CofS, 6 Dec 43, sub: Reorgn of TDC, Armd Comd, and A/B Comd. 320.2/100 (AB) (C).

chute and airborne units, and acted as the agency of the Army Ground Forces in dealing with the Troop Carrier Command of the Army Air Forces.[32]

The armored and tank destroyer organizations, which had been respectively the strongest and the weakest of the special establishments two years before, became identical in February 1944.[33] Both were placed under the Replacement and School Command, which, together with the Antiaircraft Command, remained the only developmental agency in the Ground Forces enjoying the status of a command. The Armored Command was redesignated the Armored Center. Only about thirty officers were allotted to it. About twenty officers were allotted to the Tank Destroyer Center.

The Armored and Tank Destroyer Centers ceased to function in unit training. Each lost control of its service board. Both boards were placed, as were the boards of the older arms, directly under the Requirements Section of the Army Ground Forces General Staff. In plans drafted by the AGF staff it was at first proposed that the two Centers should lose control over their respective service schools and replacement installations as well. They would in this event have been left with no subordinate echelons at all. General McNair preferred that each center under the Replacement and School Command retain jurisdiction over its service school and replacement center.[34] On routine matters of training and assignment the Replacement and School Command bypassed the two Centers and dealt directly with the Armored School, Armored Replacement Training Center, Tank Destroyer School, and Tank Destroyer Replacement Training Center in the same way that it dealt with the schools and replacement centers of the older arms in which no Center intervened. On questions of policy involving armored or tank destroyer affairs, the Replacement and School Command consulted the center concerned.

In some matters the Armored and Tank Destroyer Centers retained a vestige of their old separate identity, reporting directly to Headquarters, Army

[32] (1) AGF M/S (C), CG to G–3, 4 Oct 43. 320.2/12 (AB) (C). (2) AGF M/S (C), CG to G–3, 23 Oct 43, sub: A/B Comd. 320.2/12 (AB) (C). (3) WD D/F (C) 322 (7 Feb 44) to CG AGF, 11 Feb 44, sub: Redesignation of A/B Comd. 320.2/101 (AB) (C). (4) AGF ltr (C) to CG A/B Comd, 22 Feb 44, sub: Reorgn of A/B Comd. 320.2/100 (AB) (C). (5) AGF memo (S) for G–3 WD, 23 Feb 44, sub: Pcht Repl. 320.2/112 (O'seas Repls) (S).

[33] (1) AGF ltr (R) to CG Armd Comd, 13 Feb 44, sub: Reorgn of Armd Comd. 320.2/87 (Armd Comd) (R). (2) AGF ltr (R) to CG TDC, 13 Feb 44, sub: Reorgn of TDC. 320.2/34 (TDC) (R). (3) Papers in 320.2/12 (TDC) (S) and 320.2/100 (Armd Center) (C).

[34] AGF M/S (C), CG to CofS, 7 Jan 44. 320.2/100 (AB) (C).

Ground Forces. They continued to inspect armored and tank destroyer units and to submit comments in the form of drafts of letters to be dispatched by Army Ground Forces to tactical commanders. They continued also to review and make recommendations on the tactics, doctrine, and training literature of their arms.

After the reorganization of February 1944 the Army Ground Forces administered its armored, tank destroyer, and airborne elements in almost exactly the same way as it administered the older arms. All schooling and replacement training (except antiaircraft) were conducted through the Replacement and School Command. All service boards (except antiaircraft) were direct projections of the Requirements Section of the Ground Force headquarters staff. The AGF staff had always included officers responsible for training literature, visual aids, review of doctrine and organization, and similar matters, for all the arms. For the armored, tank destroyer, and airborne "arms" they were assisted by officers at the three centers. AGF staff officers had always inspected units in the field and submitted reports in the form of comments to be incorporated in letters to tactical commanders. For armored and tank destroyer units these officers were supplemented by others at the Armored and Tank Destroyer Centers. The officers at the Armored and Tank Destroyer Centers were in effect Ground Force staff officers stationed in the field, with the additional role of advising the Replacement and School Command, which itself was hardly more than a large annex to Headquarters, Army Ground Forces.

Organization for Combined Training

In the best of circumstances the integration of the new forces into a tactics of combined arms would have presented an exceptionally difficult problem of training. The relative novelty of the new forces, together with the rapid change to which their doctrine and equipment were constantly subject, meant that higher commanders often did not understand how best to employ them in conjunction with other arms. Units trained initially in special branch establishments were in danger of acquiring a somewhat parochial outlook. Organization on a nondivisional basis or in divisions of special type (armored and airborne) meant that even after a unit passed to the field forces it might have infrequent contact with other elements of the Army.

Moreover, until late in 1943 the circumstances were unfavorable. Prior to the reorganization of the armored divisions in September 1943 there were never enough separate tank battalions for combined training with infantry divisions.[35] Combined training of antiaircraft and airborne units was gravely handicapped by lack of airplanes.[36] Shortages of equipment and manpower, common to all the ground arms, delayed the initial branch training of units, postponing the date at which such units could be assigned to tactical organizations for combined training. Some units, especially antiaircraft, had to be hurriedly shipped overseas in the first year of hostilities, and even later, with no combined training at all.[37]

As a consequence, by the late summer of 1943, after the campaigns in North Africa and Sicily, it was generally agreed that combined training had been unsatisfactory. Antiaircraft artillery shot down friendly planes; airborne operations were confused; infantry and armored officers told AGF observers that their training in each other's operations had been wholly inadequate. Higher commanders and staffs showed inexperience in the planning and coordinating of operations, sometimes unnecessarily employing tanks, tank destroyers, or airborne troops in inappropriate missions, or using them in such driblets that their effectiveness was lost.[38]

For combined training in the United States various means were at hand. One was simply to bring together, for lectures, discussions, and demonstrations, the commanders and staff officers of armies, corps, and divisions. Many such conferences were held: at the Tank Destroyer Center in 1942 for the initiation of higher commands in the newest antitank doctrines; at Fort Benning in 1942 for the exhibition of air support of ground troops; and again at Fort Benning in April 1944 to review and improve the teamwork of infantry, tanks, and artillery. These conferences, however realistically the demonstrations might simulate combat, and however thorough the explanations and discussions might be, were believed by General McNair to have only a limited value.[39] Except for small selected units, the troops played no part; the assembled officers enlarged their knowledge but had no chance to practice it.

---

[35] For the number of tank battalions in AGF see above, Table No. 2.

[36] (1) AGF memo (C), G–3 to CofS, 18 Jan 43, sub: Rpt of Inspection of A/B Installations. 353.02/7 (AGF) (C). (2) AGF memo (S) for G–3 WD, 23 Jun 43, sub: Plans for A/B Tng for Balance of 1943. 353/15 (AB) (S). (3) See AGF Historical Section, The Antiaircraft Command and Center.

[37] See below, pp. 425–26.

[38] See rpts of AGF obsrs in 319.1 (Foreign Obsrs) (C) and (S).

[39] See AGF Historical Section, The Procurement and Branch Distribution of Officers.

Another means was provided by the inspections of units in the field forces conducted by higher officers of the various special establishments, acting as representatives of Headquarters, Army Ground Forces. The system opened channels of understanding and information between tactical commanders and the agencies concerned with development, and it had the advantage of always functioning in reference to particular units which were actually passing through the combined phase of their training cycle.

Maneuvers offered a third method. Maneuver areas, especially the Desert Training Center, were the schools in which higher commanders learned to handle complex forces under tactical conditions, and in which individual units obtained practical experience in meeting their responsibilities to other units and in turn received their support. For large operations, maneuvers were the closest approximation to combat. But there were disadvantages: an individual or unit could not correct mistakes immediately or drill repeatedly in weak points; live ammunition was generally not used; and the maneuver period was short.

A fourth means of combined training, for which none of the others was an adequate substitute, was the close and habitual association of special-type units in larger units of combined arms. The division was the primary combined-arms unit, but none of the units here under discussion was organic in the standard division. The problem was, therefore, essentially a problem in the organization of army and corps.

In August 1942 General McNair directed the Plans Section of his staff to draft a scheme for the attachment of nondivisional tank battalions to armies and corps for combined training. The scheme was broadened to include tank destroyer battalions, antiaircraft units, and nondivisional field artillery. "Nondivisional units," observed the Plans Section, "should be distributed so as to place all types at or near every division. They can then be used by one or more divisions in combined training. The supporting units should be available to each division about five months after activation of the division." [40] This seemingly obvious arrangement had to be dismissed except as an ideal aim. The stationing of a unit depended on many considerations other than convenience of combined training—on place of activation, imminence of overseas shipment, railroad facilities, housing accommodations, and other factors. In practice, as mobilization developed, no one could anticipate how far a division would have progressed

[40] (1) Memo (S) of Col Winn for Gen McNair, 2 Oct 42, sub: Revision of AGF Comd Orgn. With related papers. 320.2/493 (S). (2) See AGF Plans Sec files 154 (S) and 320.2/167 (R).

in its training five months after activation. In any case the matter was of little practical urgency in 1942, since most units of the types in question either were still undergoing branch training in their respective special establishments or were shipped overseas before combined training could be given.

In March 1943, with an increasing number of units graduating from their special establishments, General McNair again raised the question of their combined training. A difficulty peculiar to the newer arms was that their units had to be trained not only for close combined operations with divisions but also for mass action with other units of their own type. The higher commander must be left free to disperse or assemble such units at will—to attach them locally to divisions or to gather them for a unified blow. To neglect combined training with divisions would be bad—so bad that Brig. Gen. John M. Lentz, AGF G-3, came to doubt the wisdom of the nondivisional organization. But to neglect the possibility of concentrated action of mobile forces would be to ignore one of the main lessons of the war. General McNair had in mind not only the comparatively small actions hitherto engaged in by American ground forces but also the needs of an ultimate major offensive. He repeated his fundamental conceptions in a note for General Lentz dated 10 March 1943:[41]

It appears that the question is arising more or less generally as to the policy in assigning and training TD—also AA—battalions and groups after they leave the training centers and before they go overseas.

The underlying principle, it seems to me, is that such units organically are a pool from which tactical needs can be met where and when they arise. Since such flexibility of employment may and probably will require massed employment of battalions and groups, it follows that such employment must be included in training as a primary requisite.

The foregoing . . . must not preclude the close association of battalions, and perhaps groups, with divisions for combined training. It must not be overlooked, however, that the permanent attachment of battalions to divisions will prevent training in massed employment, hence is *inadvisable*. It is deemed far preferable—in fact, *imperative*—that the battalions be trained together most of the time, and that combined training with divisions be arranged as appropriate according to what the division is doing. It is not too frequently that division training will lend itself to combined training with TD and AA battalions.

These views were embodied in a directive to commanders of armies and separate corps in the Army Ground Forces, dated 1 April 1943, governing the advanced training not only of tank destroyer and antiaircraft battalions but also of non-

---

[41] AGF M/S, CG to G-3, 10 Mar 43. 353.02/103 (AGF).

divisional tank battalions, to which the same principles applied.[42] The directive was largely anticipatory in nature, since the number of tank and antiaircraft battalions available for assignment to higher tactical commands in the Ground Forces continued to be small. Tank destroyer battalions were available in larger numbers.

A new army and corps organization, after a year of preparation at AGF headquarters, was announced in July 1943.[43] The "type" army and "type" corps disappeared. Armies and corps were henceforth to consist of such divisions and other units as might be assigned for specific purposes. The army remained both tactical and administrative. The corps became primarily a fighting organization. Service troops formerly assigned to corps were transferred to armies. Combat troops formerly assigned to armies were transferred to corps.[44] At the same time, with the abolition of the armored corps, there remained only one kind of corps. The corps commanders became the officers immediately responsible for the combined training of armored divisions with infantry divisions, and of all types of nondivisional combat units with both armored and infantry divisions. The corps, in training as in combat, was supposed to be a balanced force in which a variable number of divisions was supported by appropriate proportions of field artillery, mechanized cavalry, combat engineers, tanks, tank destroyers, and antiaircraft units, all organized flexibly in battalions and groups.

Not until some months after announcement of the new organization were enough units of all types available to implement it. In the fall of 1943 antiaircraft units for the first time became available in significant numbers for combined training with other elements of the Army Ground Forces. It was also in the fall of 1943, with the reorganization of the armored divisions, that the Army Ground Forces for the first time obtained separate tank battalions in numbers approximately equivalent to the number of infantry divisions, making it possible to pair battalions and infantry divisions for combined training. At the same time the last of the armored divisions completed their initial organization and training under the Armored Command, and the last of the tank destroyer battalions passed through the Advance Unit Training Center at Camp Hood.

---

[42] AGF ltr to GSs, 1 Apr 43, sub: Asgmt and Tng of Gp Hq and Bns of Tk, TD, and AAA. 353/2209.

[43] AGF ltr (R) to CGs, 21 Jul 43, sub: Orientation with Reference to Revised Orgn. 320.2/242 (R).

[44] (1) AGF ltr (C) to CGs, 5 Aug 43, sub: Asgmt of Combat Units to Corps. 320.2/300 (C). (2) AGF ltr (R) to CGs, 29 Oct 43, sub: Asgmt of Combat-type Units. 320.2/267 (R). (3) See AGF Historical Section, Problems of Nondivisional Training in the Army Ground Forces.

The net effect is apparent in Tables Nos. 1–4 above, showing the assignment of armored, tank destroyer, and antiaircraft units at successive dates in the history of the Army Ground Forces. The tendency is clear in the physical massing of the figures in each table from upper left to lower right. There is a kind of natural history to which each type of unit conforms with variations: first, a period of concentration under the special training establishments; second, a period in which assignment to armies was common; and third, a period of distribution among corps. For reasons already made clear, the second period precedes the first in the case of the tank destroyers. In general, the third period was not clearly present until 1944, by which time the armored and tank destroyer unit training centers were closed down and units were widely distributed to the corps still remaining in the Army Ground Forces.

Combined training improved toward the close of 1943, both because of the new organization and because equipment and ammunition had become somewhat less scarce. Special considerations affecting the antiaircraft and tank destroyer arms are set forth below. Of the mechanized weapons, the principal one was the tank.

An AGF directive of 16 October 1943 outlined the duties of corps commanders in combined training of tanks with infantry.[45] Shortcomings observed in both maneuvers and combat were summarized: tanks had failed to give full fire support to infantry advancing in front, or had been used as stationary "pill boxes," or had been committed without proper support by other arms; and infantry had failed to engage antitank guns, or to follow tanks closely, or to consolidate gains. Each corps commander was instructed to have tank battalions train with infantry divisions in both the combined-training and the post-maneuver phases of the divisional cycle. In maneuvers each infantry division was to have one or more tank battalions in support. The Armored Command in February 1944, on the basis of its inspections, declared that attachment of tank battalions to infantry divisions was not receiving enough emphasis, and recommended a conference of high commanders at Fort Knox.[46] Army Ground Forces arranged instead a conference under the combined auspices of the Armored Command, the Infantry School, and the Field Artillery School.[47]

---

[45] AGF ltr (R) to CGs, 16 Oct 43, sub: Inf-Tk Tng. 353/9 (Inf) (R).

[46] Ltr (C) of CG Armd Cen to CG AGF, 16 Feb 44, sub: Inf-Tk Cooperation. 353/100 (Armd Cen) (C).

[47] (1) AGF ltr (C) to CG Armd Cen, 4 Mar 44, and to CG R&SC, 5 Mar 44. 353/100 (Armd Cen) (C). (2) AGF ltr to CGs, 24 Mar 44, sub: Conference on Inf-Arty-Tk Cooperation. 337/415.

This conference, held in April at Fort Benning, and centering about realistic demonstrations of the three arms in coordinated action, was so successful that it drew a commendation from General McNair and approval from G–3 of the War Department General Staff.[48]

A new AGF directive was issued on 14 June 1944. It applied to tank destroyers as well as to tanks.[49] The attachment of battalions to infantry divisions, hitherto left to the discretion of higher commanders, was now explicitly ordered, for periods not to exceed two months for each battalion. Divisions were to conduct combat firing of infantry, artillery, tanks, and tank destroyers together as far as possible. The directive not only provided that whole battalions should operate with whole divisions, but for the first time stipulated that tank destroyer units as small as the company, and tank units as small as the platoon, should engage in close teamwork with small units of infantry. Such localization reflected combat conditions in Italy and the Pacific islands.

General McNair had long held that tank units must be trained in two ways: first, for action in armored masses, second for close combination with other arms. The whole tactical organization of armor was designed to make possible rapid shifting from one role to the other. Through 1943, as is shown in the directive of 1 April 1943 cited above, the emphasis had tended to fall on massed employment. This tendency, since not all things are possible simultaneously, had perhaps impeded combined training. With the directive of 14 June 1944 the emphasis moved toward the close association of armor, tank for tank, with small groups of men on foot. Carried to an extreme conclusion, this would mean a tactical organization of armor of the kind which went down in France in 1940 before the German armored divisions, and which the United States abandoned in 1940 with the establishment of the Armored Force. It was carried to no such conclusion; in training, the attachment of tank battalions to divisions for more than two months was forbidden. Massed employment was not forgotten. The balance was simply a little less in its favor.

---

[48] (1) Ltr of Gen McNair to CG R&SC, 29 Apr 44, sub: Inf-Arty-Tk Conferences and Demonstrations. 337/415. (2) WD Gen Council Min (S), 25 Apr 44.

[49] AGF ltr to CGs, 14 Jun 44, sub: Combined Tng for Tk and TD Units with Inf Divs. 353/2311.

III. Problems of Weapons and Equipment

The Antiaircraft Question

Special difficulties presented themselves in the training of antiaircraft artillery. Gen. George C. Marshall frequently expressed dissatisfaction with this phase of the training program, and in October 1943 directed General McNair to make it, together with the replacements question, the object of his concentrated attention.[1] On two occasions a movement to transfer antiaircraft training to the Army Air Forces gained considerable headway in the War Department.

Most of the shortcomings could be traced to the fact that Antiaircraft Artillery faced an exceptionally large program of expansion while having at the same time to provide numerous units for operational needs. In the three years following 31 December 1940 the Infantry increased by 600 percent, the Field Artillery by 500 percent, but Antiaircraft Artillery increased by 1,750 percent, and if plans in effect until October 1943 had been carried out the increase would have been over 2,400 percent. While the other newly developed arms also expanded many times, no other ground arm had to ship its units to combat areas as rapidly as antiaircraft. In the earlier and defensive phase of the war the demand for antiaircraft artillery was exceptionally heavy both in overseas theaters and bases and in defense commands in the United States. Units were shipped after acquiring a minimum proficiency with their weapons and before receiving combined training with other Ground arms or with aviation. Throughout 1942 it was usual for antiaircraft batteries to reach combat stations after only twelve weeks of unit training and with individual members who, because of personnel turnover com-

[1] Memo (C) of Gen Marshall for Gen McNair, 13 Oct 43, sub not given. 353/123 (C).

mon to all the ground arms, had had even less than twelve weeks. Improperly trained themselves, these units nevertheless removed from the Army Ground Forces much of the best personnel from which cadres could be drawn. They also took much of the best equipment.[2]

In these circumstances new units had to start with small and half-trained cadres. The proportion of novice officers was even higher than in other ground arms. Equipment for training had to be spread very thin. In addition, command supervision was generally less effective than, say, in an infantry division, both because antiaircraft units were small, and because the background of higher antiaircraft officers lay in the Coast Artillery, in which opportunity to gain command experience had been less extensive than in other arms.[3] A further difficulty was that the Army Air Forces, which controlled the aviation on which the Antiaircraft Command was dependent for realistic training, could never in 1942 and 1943 supply enough tow-target missions, particularly in view of the quantity of antiaircraft units which the War Department had decided to mobilize.[4]

The Antiaircraft Command was handicapped in its supervision over training by the wide dispersion of its training centers, made necessary in turn by the large number of its units. Having to meet urgent calls in the earliest period of the war, the Antiaircraft Command failed to regularize and stabilize its training policies to the degree achieved by most other elements of the Ground Forces. The shortest possible training period, a 13-week Mobilization Training Program, was adhered to throughout 1942. A notable system of inspections was worked out by the Antiaircraft Command; but for a long time no standard tests at the close of unit training, similar to those given in other arms, were developed.[5] Combined training remained a rare luxury until late in 1943.

These facts were well known at AGF headquarters. In November 1942 G–3, Army Ground Forces, urged various modifications. General McNair at first felt that in view of the needs of expansion the training program should not be lengthened, and that in any case antiaircraft units, because their functions were

---

[2] (1) See AGF Historical Section, The Antiaircraft Command and Center. (2) AGF M/S (S), AA Br to G–3, 17 Oct 43. 353/195 (S). (3) AGF memo, CofS to Gen McNair, 23 Sep 42, sub: SW's Council Meeting.

[3] Memo (C) of Gen McNair for CofS USA, 22 Oct 43, sub: Tng of Repls and AA Units. 353/123 (C).

[4] See AGF Historical Section, Air-Ground Cooperation.

[5] (1) AGF M/S, G–3 to CofS, 3 Nov 42, sub: Visit to AATC's. 353.02/1 (AGF). (2) AGF M/S (S), Tng Div to G–3, 20 Oct 43. 353/195 (S).

technical and relatively limited, could if necessary get along with an abbreviated training.[6] But in December 1942 the unit training period (including basic) was nevertheless lengthened to eighteen weeks, and in July 1943 to twenty-two weeks. By the latter date the functions of antiaircraft artillery were becoming more varied and the training problem correspondingly more complex, as combat experience showed the value of antiaircraft guns in their "secondary role" against ground targets. Attempts were made in 1942 to give antiaircraft units combined training,[7] but until October 1943 the majority of antiaircraft units went overseas without combined training with either ground arms or aviation.[8]

In the theaters antiaircraft guns brought down a gratifying number of enemy planes,[9] but also fired too frequently on friendly craft. The effects were felt not only of hurried training at home but also of the lack of satisfactory training in the theaters during the long periods of inaction. Command organization in the theaters was deficient both for the supervision of antiaircraft training and for the coordination of antiaircraft guns with friendly fighter aviation in combat.

A proposal therefore gained ground in Washington for the transfer of the Antiaircraft Command to the Army Air Forces. The issue first came to a head in February 1943. G–3, War Department General Staff, made the proposal, supported by G–1 and G–4 and by Lt. Gen. Henry H. Arnold.[10] The main argument was that antiaircraft artillery and fighter aircraft should be trained together because they should operate as a team in combat. General McNair had himself, in 1941, strongly urged upon the Army Air Forces that antiaircraft artillery, when used in area defense in conjunction with fighter aviation, should be under the command of the fighter commander. Air officers had finally consented to the inclusion of this point in FM 1–25, which, however, was not being generally observed in the theaters in 1943.[11] Of the need for combined training of antiaircraft units with air units General McNair had no doubt; but he believed

[6] AGF M/S, CG to G–3, 12 Nov 42. 353.02/1 (AGF).

[7] (1) WD memo (C) WDGCT 353 (6–17–42) for CG AGF, 17 Jun 42, sub: Tng of AA Units. With indorsements. 353/55 (C). (2) AGF memo (C) for CofS USA, 31 Oct 42, sub: Attachment of AA AW Bns to Div for Joint Tng. 321/75 (CA) (C).

[8] See AGF Historical Section, The Antiaircraft Command and Center.

[9] For statistics see AGF Historical Section, The Antiaircraft Command and Center.

[10] WD memo (S) for CGs AGF, AAF, 8 Feb 43, sub: Integration of AAA with AAF. With concurrences. 321/224 (CA) (S).

[11] See above, "Origin of the Army Ground Forces: General Headquarters, United States Army, 1940–42," pp. 121–27.

also that there was a need for combined training with mobile ground troops, though the need was obscured by the fact that few ground troops had yet been engaged in mobile operations. In any case General McNair could not see how the branch or unit training of antiaircraft artillery, a necessary preparation for combined training of any kind, would be improved by a transfer of the Antiaircraft Command to the Air Forces.[12] The Operations Division, War Department General Staff, agreed, and the proposal was dropped.[13]

It arose again in September 1943, when the War Department, after American planes had been shot down by friendly antiaircraft guns in the Sicilian campaign, appointed a board under Maj. Gen. Homer L. Oldfield to survey the antiaircraft problem. The board submitted a number of findings, among them the following: (1) that air commanders, in the defense of fixed installations in the theaters, should exercise command over their supporting antiaircraft units (which General McNair had urged since 1941); (2) that air commanders should control the allocation of all antiaircraft units (to which Army Ground Forces could not agree, since many antiaircraft units were needed for support of mobile ground troops); (3) that the Army Ground Forces regarded antiaircraft artillery as a defensive weapon (which was true, but was a belief held even more positively by theorists of air power); (4) that combined training had been bad (the causes for this have been mentioned above); and (5) that the dissemination of technical knowledge and training doctrine in the theaters had been inadequate (a fact which was regarded as outside the jurisdiction of the Army Ground Forces). The board recommended as a remedy the transfer of antiaircraft training to the Army Air Forces.[14]

The War Department disregarded the board's recommendation [15] but did bring pressure on the Army Ground Forces for improvement.[16] "The CofS, USA, lacks confidence, to put it mildly, in the antiaircraft training that we are giving," General McNair noted for his chief of staff on 15 October 1943.[17] The

---

[12] Memo (S) of Gen McNair for G–3 WD, 19 Feb 43, sub: Integration of AAA with AAF. 321/224 (CA) (S).

[13] OPD memo for G–3 WD, 23 Feb 43, sub as above. 321/224 (CA) (S).

[14] Memo (S) of Maj Gen H. L. Oldfield and others for G–3 WD, 27 Sep 43, sub: AAA. 321/224 (CA) (S).

[15] WD memo (S) WDCSA 353.17 (13 Oct 43) of Gen McNarney for Gen McNair, 13 Oct 43, sub as above. 321/224 (CA) (S).

[16] Memo of Gen Marshall for Gen McNair, 13 Oct 43, sub not given. 353/123 (C).

[17] AGF M/S (S), CG to CofS, 15 Oct 43. 321/224 (CA) (S).

Inspector General was at this time rejecting about 25 percent of the antiaircraft units presenting themselves for overseas movement.[18]

General McNair, while believing that the Chief of Staff had been given an unduly unfavorable impression of antiaircraft training, directed officers of his own staff and of the Antiaircraft Command to consider reforms.[19] Training tests of the kind used in the field artillery had been introduced by the Antiaircraft Command in the preceding July. In response to criticisms made by AGF headquarters these tests were now made more factual, searching, and detailed. They were published in January 1944 as AGF tests appended to the general AGF training directive in effect since 1 November 1942.[20] Readiness tests were also developed by which commanders of antiaircraft unit training centers could apply to units scheduled for overseas shipment the same standards that The Inspector General employed.[21] On the whole the situation tended to correct itself. By the end of 1943 equipment for training was somewhat more plentiful and the supply of antiaircraft units was coming into a more favorable ratio to overseas demand; in consequence an increasing number of units could remain in the United States long enough to receive training with other ground arms or with the Air Forces. Many proposed changes were rejected by General McNair as irrelevant or useless. He continued to believe that the existing system was workable, given the conditions without which no system would work; and he continued to place confidence in General Green.[22]

General Green proposed that the Army Ground Forces, through the Antiaircraft Command, have agents in the theaters to supervise the training of antiaircraft units, the testing of equipment, the dissemination of training literature, and other matters.[23] General McNair considered such action "wrong in principle, and contrary to Circular 59 as I see it."[24] It violated the basic idea of the War Department reorganization of March 1942, to which General McNair still adhered. To obtain the results aimed at, general officers were exchanged between the Antiaircraft Command and the theaters. Responsibility was left with the

---

[18] AA Comd ltr (C) to CGs Tng Centers, 8 Nov 43, sub: Deficiencies Reported by TIG. 321/410 (CA) (Sep binder) (S).

[19] AGF M/S (C), CG to G–3 and G–1, 15 Oct 43, sub: Tng of Repls and AA Units. 353/123 (C).

[20] AGF ltr to CGs, 30 Jan 44, sub: Tng Directive Effective 1 Nov 42. 353.01/107.

[21] See footnote 18 above.

[22] AGF M/S (C), CG to G–3 and G–1, 15 Oct 43, sub: Tng of Repls and AA Units. 353/195 (S).

[23] Memo (S) of Gen Green for Gen McNair, 30 Oct 43, sub not given. 321/410 (CA) (Sep binder) (S).

[24] AGF M/S (S), CG to CofS, 2 Nov 43. 321/410 (CA) (S).

theater commanders. Following another of General Green's recommendations, a War Department circular of November 1943 provided that each theater or task force headquarters should include an Antiaircraft Officer, "of appropriate rank," who would function as staff adviser on antiaircraft matters, supervising training, inspecting equipment, determining requirements, and advising on the allocation of units within the command.[25]

Combined training of antiaircraft units with other elements of the Army Ground Forces was regularized by an AGF directive of 8 May 1944.[26] To improve combined training with aircraft the War Department instructed Army Ground Forces and Army Air Forces, at the end of 1943, each to appoint a general officer as Antiaircraft Artillery Liaison Officer. Brig. Gen. Rupert E. Starr was assigned to this position by the Army Ground Forces.

While efforts to improve training proceeded, the number to be trained declined.[27] At first over 800 battalions of antiaircraft artillery had been planned. In October 1943, simultaneously with its criticism of antiaircraft training, the War Department reduced the planned figure to 575, thus checking the expansion which was the main cause of training deficiencies. Even after this reduction the antiaircraft units active at the end of 1943 had an authorized strength almost four times that of the nondivisional field artillery, and over two-and-a-half times that of all armored divisions and tank battalions combined. About 100 battalions were inactivated, until the total fell to 460 in 1944. Many of the antiaircraft troops whose training caused such concern wound up in the infantry.

The Tank Destroyer Question

The problem of tank destroyers, like that of antiaircraft artillery, became critical in 1943. After the German offensive of 1940 the stopping of tanks became one of the most serious problems faced by the Army. There were in general two schools. One held that the best antitank weapon was another tank. Officers who had devoted themselves to armored development tended to favor this school. The other school, of which General McNair was a founder and moving spirit,

---

[25] Tng Cir 124, WD, 13 Nov 43, sub: AAA. 321/410 (S).

[26] AGF ltr (S) to CGs, 8 May 44, sub: Combined Tng of AAA Units with Other Elements of AGF. 353.01/116. See also papers in 353/208 (S).

[27] See above, "Ground Forces in the Army, December 1941–April 1945: a Statistical Study."

held that one's own tanks should be kept free for action against unarmored enemy troops and that enemy tanks should be opposed chiefly by a mobile mass of unarmored guns.

In 1941, under pressure from General McNair, then at GHQ, and on the strong initiative of General Bruce, then lieutenant colonel in the War Department General Staff, the War Department tooks steps to realize the ideas of the second school. Artillery usable against tanks was withdrawn from organic assignment to armies, corps, and divisions, organized into GHQ antitank battalions, and employed experimentally in maneuvers. The effectiveness of the gun as an antitank weapon was demonstrated. Work began on the development of self-propelled mounts, toward which General McNair maintained an attitude of suspended judgment, detecting a degree of faddism in the enthusiasm for self-propelled artillery, and doubting that enough was gained in useful mobility to offset the disadvantages of greater size and less accurate fire. The guns were organized in GHQ battalions to permit concentration in mobile masses when necessary to meet massed formations of tanks. Throughout the maneuvers of 1941 General McNair insisted that the antitank battalions be employed more aggressively. His aim was to dispel the defensive psychology which the German successes had created. At the end of 1941 the antitank battalions were redesignated tank destroyer battalions, the new name savoring more of the offensive.[28]

In 1942 the Tank Destroyer Center, under General Bruce, developed step by step, as described above, into one of the new mechanized quasi arms, despite moves to annex it to the Armored Force or the Replacement and School Command, and despite the skepticism still felt by officers of the "tank vs. tank" school, who regarded the antitank gun as at best a defensive weapon around which no separate organization should be built. By the end of 1942 the strength of the new arm was almost 100,000; 80 battalions were active and 64 more were planned.

General Bruce made it his business to inculcate a spirit of fearlessness in the presence of tanks. The tank, together with the dive bomber, had created terror bordering on panic in the German campaigns of 1940. The exorcising of the feeling of helpless terror was perhaps in the long run the main achievement of the

---

[28] See above, "Origins of the Army Ground Forces: General Headquarters, United States Army, 1940–42," Sec. IV. For Gen McNair's views on the towed vs. the self-propelled gun see (1) GHQ 1st ind to G–3 WD, 16 Jan 41, on memo of Col Kingman for CofS GHQ, 13 Jan 41, sub: Mechanized AT Orgn. GHQ Records, 322.091/5 (Armd F). (2) Memo of Gen McNair for G–3 WD, 2 Sep 41, sub: Orgn of AT Units in the Army. GHQ Records, 353/15 (AT). (3) Memo (C) of Gen McNair for CofS USA, 27 Oct 42, sub: Col Fellers' Comments on DTC. 354.1/8 (DTC) (C).

Tank Destroyer Center. General Bruce taught his men to fight tanks with every means at their disposal—to move boldly ahead with their destroyers and shoot it out with cannon, or on occasion to use "dismounted action," creeping forward in "tank-hunting parties" to dispatch the monsters with antitank grenades.[29] At the Tank Destroyer Center General McNair's desire for offensive antitank tactics was more than fulfilled.

As tanks put on heavier armor, tank destroyer battalions adopted heavier guns. The 37-mm. antitank gun had shown itself to possess only limited usefulness. During 1942 the three types of tank destroyer battalions with which the year opened were converted to a single type—heavy self-propelled, armed primarily with twenty-four 75-mm. guns mounted on half-tracks. The Tank Destroyer Center confined its instruction to the operations of this standard battalion.[30]

By the beginning of 1943 the tank destroyers were receiving their first real combat test in North Africa. Reports were unfavorable. "The tank destroyers have proved disappointing," declared one high-ranking observer flatly.[31] Lt. Gen. George S. Patton, an armored officer by background, pronounced the tank destroyers unsuccessful in the conditions of the theater.[32] General Devers, in the report to the War Department mentioned above, affirmed that "the separate tank destroyer arm is not a practical concept on the battlefield." [33]

Commenting in February 1943 on General Devers' report, General McNair outlined for the Secretary of War his own conception of tank destroyer tactics, and elaborated what he meant by offensive tank destroyer action. He noted that the tank, though slow and ponderous, was bound to advance if it was to perform its mission.[34]

---

[29] FM 18–5, 16 Jun 42, sub: Orgn and Tactics of TD Units, e. g., pars 38ff., 176, 182, 210.

[30] (1) Ltr (C) of Gen Bruce to TAG, 6 Mar 42, sub: Amendment of Tr Unit Mobilization and Tng Schedule, Jan 42, by Elimination of Light TD Bns and Substitution of Heavy TD Bns. 320.2/1 (TD (C). (2) AGF 2d ind on above to TDC. 320.2/1 (TD) (C). (3) WD ltr (R) AG 320.2 (5–29–42) MR–M–GN to CGs, 31 May 42, sub: Reorgn of TD Units. 320.2/1 (TD) (R). (4) See AGF Historical Section, The Tank Destroyer History, Sec. III.

[31] (1) Rpt (C) of Maj Gen W. H. Walker, 12 Jun 43. 319.1/26 (Foreign Obsrs) (S). (2) Rpt (S) of Lt Gen Fredendall, 10 Mar 43. 319.1/1 (NATO) (S).

[32] Personal ltr (S) of Gen Patton to Gen McNair, 26 Mar 43. 319.1/1 (NATO) (S).

[33] "Conclusions," #7, of rpt (S) of the mission headed by Lt Gen Jacob L. Devers to examine the problems of armored force units in the ETO. [Undated but Feb 43.] 319.1/32 (Foreign Obsrs) (S).

[34] Incl to memo (TS) of Gen McNair for SW, 17 Feb 43, sub not given. 400/4 (TS).

Since the tank must advance, the TD need only to maneuver for a favorable position, conceal itself thoroughly and ambush the tank. It is correct to think of the TD as acting offensively, in that it does not sit passively on the chance that a tank may come its way, but on the contrary seeks out the tank and places itself where it can attack the tank effectively. However, the destroyer would be foolish indeed to act offensively in the same manner as the tank, for such tactics would place the destroyer at a disadvantage, and would sacrifice unnecessarily the advantages which the destroyer has by the very nature of things.

The trouble in North Africa was that the tank destroyers, instead of firing from concealed positions, maneuvered too freely during combat. Instead of being aggressive in their reconnaissance and preparatory dispositions, they were aggressive in the face of the tanks themselves, and suffered severe casualties because of their virtual lack of armor. Concealment was in any case difficult. The heavy destroyer, with its 75-mm. gun on a self-propelled mount, proved to have too high a silhouette to be easily adaptable to a tactics of concealment and ambush. But the excessive use of maneuver during combat was due in large part to the orders of higher commanders to whom the tank destroyer battalions were attached. Because of the novelty of the tank destroyer and insufficiency of combined training at home, and because some commanders were unsympathetic to the tank destroyer idea, battalions were assigned missions for which they were unsuited. On 21 March 1943 Allied Force Headquarters (AFHQ) at Algiers, in its Training Memorandum No. 23, attempted to clarify the subject both for tank destroyer personnel and for higher commanders. The memorandum restated the doctrine of tank destroyer employment, putting emphasis on rapid reconnaissance, thorough concealment in prepared positions, and avoidance of premature fire.[35]

Army Ground Forces immediately directed the Tank Destroyer Center to rewrite its manual governing tactical employment, FM 18–5, in the light of AFHQ Training Memorandum No. 23.[36] For guidance in the meantime, Army Ground Forces published Training Circular No. 88, 1943. The rewriting of FM 18–5 was described as urgent. Officers at the Tank Destroyer Center were inclined to believe that the fault lay in the application, not the substance, of their published doctrine. In any case the developing uses of tank destroyer battalions in the theaters had to be studied. Changes of command at the Tank

---

[35] AFHQ Tng Memo 23 (S), 21 Mar 43, sub: Employment of TD Units. 319.1/1 (NATO) (S). See also observers' report cited in footnote 33 above.

[36] (1) AGF 1st ind (S) to TDC, 23 Apr 43, on TDC ltr 353 (TD)—GNGCT (4–3–43). 353/1 (TDC) (S). (2) Ltr (S) of Gen McNair to CG TDC, 7 Apr 43, sub: Visit to TDC. 353.02/6 (AGF) (S).

Destroyer Center caused much rewriting. Over a year was consumed in revising FM 18–5 to the satisfaction of all concerned.

The high silhouette of the self-propelled destroyer led many participants in the North African operations, including Maj. Gen. Lloyd R. Fredendall and Maj. Gen. Omar N. Bradley, to prefer the towed gun for tank destroyer battalions, since the towed gun could be dug in with only its muzzle protruding. As early as 1 January 1943 Army Ground Forces directed the Tank Destroyer Center to organize an experimental battalion with towed 3-inch guns.[37] General McNair believed that the Tank Destroyer Center underrated the mobility, for practical purposes, of towed weapons.[38] Self-propelled battalions in the United States were gradually converted to towed.[39] No towed battalions were used in combat in 1943. Following the requests of theater commanders (probably influenced by British example) it was decided in November 1943 to have half the battalions self-propelled and half of them towed.[40]

The total number of battalions to be mobilized was cut down. General McNair in 1942 had pressed for a large program, recommending 222 battalions (in an army of 114 divisions) for the Troop Basis of 1943.[41] He anticipated a need of concentrating as many as twenty battalions at a time against massed attack by enemy armor, and accordingly urged upon the War Department the activation of a tank destroyer brigade headquarters for each field army.[42] General Bruce envisaged a brigade for every corps.[43] But massed armor was scarcely used against American forces in 1943. No demand for tank destroyer brigades came from the theaters; even the group headquarters was scarcely

---

[37] AGF ltr to TDC, 1 Jan 43, sub: Formation of Towed TD Bn for Test Purposes. 320.2/180 (TDC).

[38] (1) Ltr (S) of Gen McNair to CG TDC, 7 Apr 43, sub: Visit to TDC. 353.02/6 (AGF) (S). (2) AGF M/S, 5 May 43, note by "LJM." 320/8 (TDC).

[39] AGF memo (S) for OPD WD, 13 Apr 43, sub: Towed TD Bns. 321/11 (TD) (S). Other papers in 321 (TD) (C), 321 (TD) (R), and 321 (TD).

[40] (1) Memo (S) of Gen McNair for OPD, 8 Oct 43, sub: Ratio of Towed to Self-propelled TD Units. (2) WD memo (S) OPD 320.2 (1 Nov 43) for CG AGF, 5 Nov 43, sub as above. Both in 321/13 (TD) (S). (3) AGF M/S, CG to G–3, Rqts, and G–1, 16 Nov 43, sub: Ltr from Gen Hester to Gen McNair. 320.2/226 (TDC).

[41] See above, "Ground Forces in the Army, December 1941–April 1945: a Statistical Study."

[42] (1) AGF M/S, CG to Rqts, 18 Aug 42, sub: TD Orgn. 320.2/99 (TDC). (2) AGF memo for CofS USA, 19 Sep 42, sub as above. 320.2/99 (TDC). (3) AGF ltr (R) to TDC, 21 Nov 42, sub: Activation of Hq and Hq Companies, 1st and 2d TD Brigs. 320.2/18 (TDC) (R). (4) AGF memo for CofS USA, 4 Mar 43, sub: T/O and T/E for Hq and Hq Co, TD Brig. 321/3 (TDC). (5) WD D/F 320.2 (2–10–43) for CG AGF, 18 Mar 43, sub as above. 321/3 (TDC).

[43] TDC ltr to CG AGF, 11 Aug 42, sub: TD Orgn. 320.2/99 (TDC).

used overseas, tank destroyer battalions being commonly attached to divisions in the African and Italian campaigns, and little used in the Pacific. The War Department authorized only two brigades, of which one was inactivated early in 1944, the other shipped to the European Theater of Operations.

In place of the 222 battalions first suggested by Army Ground Forces, the War Department authorized only 144. In the changed circumstances of the early part of 1943 General McNair altered his position and assumed the initiative in checking the growth of an enterprise which was in many ways his own child. On the one hand, it became clear from the limited operations in Tunisia that increases of field artillery, tank battalions, and combat engineers were desirable and that tank destroyer units would not be requested by theater commanders in anything like the numbers that were becoming available. On the other hand, with the continuing postponement of a major ground offensive, troops were crowding the training centers in the United States to such a degree that the tempo of mobilization had to be slowed down. In proposing measures for dealing with this situation, General McNair on 14 April 1943 recommended a curtailment of the tank destroyer program to 106 battalions.[44] This was substantially the number already active or in process of activation. In October the War Department planned to cut the number to 64, which would require the inactivation of 42 battalions.This reduction was believed excessive by Army Ground Forces, and wasteful of training and equipment.[45] Yet there were many trained men in tank destroyer units, as in antiaircraft, coast artillery, and other primarily defensive arms, who could be better employed elsewhere. On 29 October 1943 Army Ground Forces, observing that 39 divisions had a total shortage of 45,293 (due mainly to the need of replacements in Italy), asked authority from the War Department to inactivate 25 tank destroyer battalions, using most of the personnel to fill depleted divisions.[46] This authority was immediately obtained. Inactivation went on into 1944 until only 78 tank destroyer battalions were left.

Though the tank destroyer development did not turn out exactly as anticipated by the school which promoted it, it played an important part in the mobili-

---

[44] (1) Memo (S) of Gen McNair for G–3 WD, 14 Apr 43, sub: Modification for Mobilization Procedures. 381/177 (S). (2) Ground Force Combat Units, TB 43, 23 Feb 43. Incl to WD memo (C) WDGCT 320.2 Gen (3–8–43) for WDGS and CGs, 8 Mar 43, sub: Ground TB 43. AGF Plans Sec file 185 (S).

[45] WD memo (S) WDGCT 320 TB (2 Oct 43) for DCofS USA, sub: Troop Basis 1943. AGF Plans Sec file 185 (S).

[46] AGF memo (C) for G–3 WD, 29 Oct 43, sub: Inactivation of TD Units. 321/12 (TD) (C).

zation of the Army to meet the situation presented in 1940. The Tank Destroyer Center exercised an influence beyond the special-type battalions which it trained. As the center of antitank activity and research it was the main agency, as far as the United States was concerned, by which the tank menace of 1940 was overcome, the idea of the invulnerability of armored forces exploded, and armored forces consequently reintegrated into a tactics of combined arms. Special tank destroyer battalions became proportionately less necessary as armored forces lost their ability (insofar as they had ever had it) to fight as a separate arm. As tanks came to be less commonly employed in armored masses there was less need for tank destroyer battalions capable of rapid concentration. In general, the success of antitank developments by 1943 was as great as anyone would have dared to expect in the dark days of 1940.

More particularly, the tank destroyer battalions, though not activated in the numbers originally planned, were fast and hard-hitting fighting units. They were among the most heavily mechanized units in the Army. The completely motorized battalion of 1944, with a strength of less than 800 men, occupied ten miles of road space, was largely self-sufficient for maintenance and administration, included strong elements of reconnaissance, radio, and antiaircraft protection, and carried thirty-six 3-inch or 76-mm. guns (towed or self-propelled)—the same number of light field pieces as in the three light artillery battalions of a division. The battalions adopted, in addition to their primary antitank functions, a general role of supporting artillery. As higher commanders gained skill in tank destroyer employment, the battalions were put to a variety of aggressive uses, such as destroying of antitank guns as well as of tanks, acting as an advance guard and covering withdrawals, assisting in the clearing of mine fields, and laying of interdiction and harassing fires in conjunction with division artillery.[47]

Here again the development was not exactly what was expected. It was in fact better; for it was always better, in General McNair's view, for a combat unit to escape from the limitations of too specialized a role. In a sense also the two antitank schools were reconciled. That the tank destroyer was a useful weapon none could reasonably deny. But those who had argued that the tank destroyers should not be a separate arm could draw comfort from the thought

---

[47] For a vivid picture see "The TD Battalion in Action," a report prepared by Lt Col J. P. Barney, FA, CO, 776th TD Bn, received by AGF through the AGF Board, NATO, and circulated by Dissemination Division, Hq, AGF, under date of 24 May 44. AGF Board NATO file A Misc 21.

that they were successful in proportion as they took on the characteristics of highly mobile artillery.

Tanks, Tank Destroyers, and Antiaircraft Guns as Field Artillery

The tendency of tank destroyers, tanks, and antiaircraft guns to function as auxiliary field artillery was one of the most interesting developments of 1943 and 1944. To a certain degree the new special arms were broadened and strengthened by a recourse to more traditional methods of warfare. The older arm began to absorb the new quasi arms.

The tendency may be said to have first appeared in a practical way about the middle of 1943, at which time Allied Force Headquarters informed the War Department that battle commanders wished the tank destroyer battalions to develop their capacities for indirect fire.[48] Army Ground Forces enlarged the suggestion to include tanks, for which no similar demand had arisen, but which General McNair regarded in principle as a special form of artillery.[49] Early in September a board was convened at the Army War College, composed of Maj. Gen. Orlando Ward, successor to General Bruce in command of the Tank Destroyer Center, Brig. Gen. Roland P. Shugg, Artillery Officer of the Armored Command, and Brig. Gen. Jesmond D. Balmer, Commandant of the Field Artillery School. Difficulties in the way of "artillerizing" the tanks and tank destroyers were considerable. Indirect fire would necessitate more refined equipment, more mathematical training, and more complex arrangements for observation, communication, and liaison. The board recommended a minimum of innovation.[50] General Lentz, AGF G-3, believed that tanks should remain as they were but that tank destroyers should be virtually assimilated to field artillery. General McNair was cautious. While disappointed in the board, he was inclined to share its conclusion. He noted for General Lentz:[51]

Our war experience in this connection has been misleading thus far, in that we have not yet met the German Army in serious combat. . . . Thus it seems unwise to conclude that the tank and tank destroyer will be unoccupied in their primary roles and can be used as artillery.

---

[48] Armd F ltr (C) to TAG, 5 Aug 43, sub: Reorgn of TD Bns. 321/9 (TD) (C).

[49] AGF memo (C) for CofS USA, 31 Aug 43, sub as above. 321/9 (TD) (C).

[50] Rpt (S) of Maj Gen Orlando Ward and others, 8 Sep 43. 353/194 (S).

[51] AGF M/S, CG to G-3, 9 Oct 43, sub: Arty Tng in TDs and Tks. 353/194 (S).

On the other hand, their fire power collectively is great and should be utilized wherever practicable. . . . However, since I am unconvinced that such occasions will be other than rare when the big show starts, I feel that for the present equipment and personnel and use of these weapons as artillery should be confined to the barest minimum in quantity and to the simplest terms generally. . . .

In general I believe that my view does not go so far as yours toward the employment of these weapons as Field Artillery. However, I am willing, as always, to argue.

The question was, as usual, one of finding a proper balance between courses of action each of which presented advantages. A directive issued by Army Ground Forces on 6 November 1943 sought to gain the advantages of versatility without losing those of specialization. A War Department Training Circular conveyed the same doctrine to the Army as a whole.[52]

The emphasis in the action of tanks and tank destroyers was kept by this directive on their respective primary missions. Each was recognized to have a secondary mission of reinforcing field artillery in circumstances where no need of the primary mission could be foreseen. Decision in particular cases was left to the higher commander.

Training in the secondary role was made additional to, and distinct from, training in the primary role. Each tank and tank destroyer unit, before receiving any field artillery instruction, had to proceed through its normal individual and unit training program, then participate in combined training or in maneuvers in its primary capacity, demonstrating by firing tests its proficiency in tank or tank destroyer functions. This accomplished, a month of intensive training as reinforcing artillery followed under the supervision of army and corps commanders. A training program was supplied by the Field Artillery School, in collaboration with the Tank Destroyer Center and the Armored Command. The coordination of fires, designation of targets, maintenance of telephones, and similar matters were left to the field artillery unit, normally division or corps artillery, which the tanks or tank destroyers reinforced. Training was prescribed only in such types of artillery missions as tanks and tank destroyer units could accomplish with minor additions of small items of equipment and with no addition of personnel. Units were kept streamlined for their primary functions.

---

[52] (1) AGF ltr to CGs, 6 Nov 43, sub: Employment of Tks and TDs as Arty. (2) Tng Cir 125, WD, 13 Nov 43. (3) AGF ltr to CGs, 28 Feb 44, sub as in (1) above. Both in 353/2233.

In antiaircraft artillery, tactical and training doctrine had long recognized a secondary mission of fire against tanks, which were vulnerable to the high-velocity antiaircraft guns. In existing circumstances little such training had been feasible. In April 1944 an AGF directive (generalized by a War Department training circular) expanded the secondary role of antiaircraft guns to include auxiliary field artillery functions. The same conditions and limitations were set as for tanks and tank destroyers, except that a modicum of field artillery instruction was introduced into the antiaircraft gun unit training program, which was extended from twenty-four to twenty-six weeks for the purpose. After functioning successfully in their primary role in combined training, antiaircraft units were to receive, when practicable, a month of field artillery training under army or corps command.[53]

Meanwhile, in the winter of 1943–44, the secondary roles were actively developed in the theaters. As enemy air power declined, antiaircraft units that were attached to mobile ground troops looked increasingly to surface targets. The tank destroyers, in the temporarily static conditions of the Italian front, and in the mountainous Italian terrain where massed armor could not be used, increasingly operated as reinforcing artillery.[54] Tanks clung more to their primary role, though they had to be used in driblets. In the United States the Army Ground Forces, while incorporating the new development, kept it definitely subordinate to the primary missions of the three arms, in preparation for the "big show" to come.

[53] (1) AGF ltr to CGs, 15 Apr 44, sub: Employment of AAA Gun Units (Mobile and Semimobile) in Secondary Roles. 353/610 (CA). (2) Tng Cir 23, WD, 8 Apr 44.
[54] (1) Incl 1 to AGF Bd NATO Rpt 105, 8 Jan 44. (2) OPD Information Bull, Vol I, No 8, 24 Apr 44. Both in 314.7 (AGF Hist).

IV. Summary

Certain generalizations can be derived from the preceding account of the policies of Headquarters, Army Ground Forces, toward the new combat forces during the formative period of the Army from 1942 to 1944. The problem, in general terms, was the handling of new and specialized arms. The general solution adopted was to promote the new arms while keeping them within a framework within which the older arms retained their due importance. Tactically, the new arms were organized flexibly to prevent overloading of the standard division and to enable higher commanders to employ units of the new arms as circumstances might demand, either in masses of the same arm or separately in conjunction with other arms and with the standard division.

For training, each new combat force received a branch organization with more independence than in the older arms as long as rapid development was a major aim. Later, as the new forces became well established and as a branch training of their units was accomplished, their branch organization was assimilated to that of the older arms, all arms being subordinated to the interests of the Army Ground Forces as a whole. For combined training, units of the new arms, as of the old, were assigned to the field forces—armies and corps. But combined training of the new forces, though essential as a means of integrating the new with the old, was never altogether satisfactory in practice. It suffered not only from difficulties in personnel and timing which afflicted the whole Army, but also from certain handicaps due to organization: the fact that until late in 1943 the tank strength of the Army was for the most part locked up in armored divisions, so that infantry divisions could with difficulty train with armor; and the fact that the nondivisional organization of antiaircraft artillery, tank destroyers, and tanks (except for tanks in armored divisions) had only limited opportunities for combined training. In addition, theaters sometimes required that shipment take place before combined training could be undertaken. Mobilization likewise was uneven, producing more antiaircraft and tank destroyer units and fewer heavy artillery units than proved to be necessary.

As time went on more emphasis fell on the use of antiaircraft and tank destroyer weapons, and to a lesser extent on tanks, in the role of field artillery. With this development the tendency to specialization subsided, and more flexibility and economy in the use of artillery pieces were obtained.

In the organization and training of the new forces, the Army Ground Forces aimed at securing the advantages without the disadvantages of specialization and branch spirit, keeping in mind the need of balanced forces and combined arms training, as well as economy, flexibility, and over-all unity in planning and command.

Reorganizing

for

Redeployment

by

Bell I. Wiley

Contents

Tables

Chart

I. Basic Redeployment Problems

In its earliest stages, planning with reference to the disposition of personnel at the termination of hostilities was focused on demobilization. The first draft of the basic War Department program, issued in November 1943, was captioned "Demobilization Regulations 1–1";[1] not until about February 1944 was the title changed to "Readjustment Regulation 1–1."[2] The initial emphasis on demobilization was due to the fact that planners were thinking at first in terms of World War I, when an armistice brought an abrupt end to hostilities everywhere and when a speedy and orderly conversion of soldiers to civilians was both the immediate and the ultimate problem. As policy makers of World War II proceeded with their plans, they soon realized that the situation was different from that of 1918: that the fighting would probably cease in Europe before victory was won in the Pacific, that demobilization after the defeat of Germany would be only partial, and that demobilization must be conditioned by the requirements for conquering Japan. Hence, after the first few months, emphasis in planning shifted from demobilization to readjusting the Army for Pacific needs and redeploying forces in Europe for an all-out effort against the Japanese.[3]

Personnel Readjustment Planning

At first it appeared that the Army Ground Forces might play a leading role in the formulation of readjustment policy. Early in 1943, before receipt of any instructions from the War Department, the Mobilization Division of the Ground G–3 Section initiated studies of World War I experience in

---

[1] This draft is filed in 320.2/1 (Redepl) (separate binder) (R).

[2] Special Planning Division WDSS, Monthly Progress Report (S) on Demobilization Planning, Feb 1944. 314.7 (AGF Hist) (S).

[3] These statements are based on a study of the following sources: (1) Monthly Progress Report on Demobilization Planning (S) submitted by the Special Planning Division WDSS, June–December 1943. AGF Plans Sec file 157 (S). (2) Memo of Col Herbert B. Powell for Col H. T. Todd, 1 Mar 43, sub: Demob Study. 314.7 (AGF Hist). (3) Memo (S) of Col Clinton I. McClure for G–1 AGF, 21 Jun 43, sub: Methods of Demob. With related papers. 314.7 (AGF Hist) (S). (4) Memo (S) of Brig Gen Wm. F. Tompkins, Spec Planning Div WDSS for CG AGF, attn Brig Gen J. C. Christiansen, 6 Aug 43, sub: Demob Planning. With related papers. AGF Plans Sec file 158 (Demob) (S).

demobilization as recorded in monographs prepared by classes at the Army War College and in other pertinent sources.[4]

In April 1943 basic demobilization planning was made the responsibility of the Army Service Forces and delegated to the Project Planning Division of the office of the Deputy Chief of Staff for Service Commands.[5] This division was headed by Brig. Gen. William F. Tomkins. Col. Clinton I. McClure of the Ground G–1 Section was appointed to a subcommittee charged with drawing up recommendations as to the basis of demobilization—whether by unit, civilian skill, length of service, or a combination of various factors.[6] Colonel McClure, after an extensive survey of the experience of the United States and other countries in World War I, and after consulting G–3 and other interested staff sections, recommended for the Army Ground Forces that "demobilization in general should be by units."[7] The subcommittee accepted this view and recommended to General Tompkins in July 1943 that for either partial or final demobilization, tactical and administrative units be released *in toto.*

The Army Ground Forces strongly advocated unit demobilization because it was simple, flexible, more rapid than any individual plan, and, during the period of partial demobilization, would interfere less with the prosecution of the war against Japan than would an individual "selection-out" plan. Moreover, the United States had used the unit plan with success both in the Civil War and in World War I, while British experience with an individual selection-out scheme in World War I had not been satisfactory. For these reasons, Lt. Gen. Lesley J. McNair strongly favored demobilization by unit.[8]

The Tompkins group, which on 22 July 1943 became the nucleus of the Special Planning Division of the War Department Special Staff, was at first favorably inclined toward the idea of unit demobilization but eventually re jected the subcommittee's recommendation and adopted instead a plan which

[4] Memo of Col H. B. Powell for Col. H. T. Todd, 1 Mar 43, sub: Demob Study. 314.7 (AGF Hist).

[5] (1) Project Planning Division Office of DCofS for Service Comds, ASF, Progress Report on Demob Planning, 30 Jun 43 (S). AGF Plans Sec file 157 (S). (2) WD memo (S) for Spec Planning Div WDSS, 22 Jul 43, sub: Orgn and Functions, Spec Planning Div, WD. AGF Plans Sec file 157 (S).

[6] (1) Memo (S) of Col Clinton I. McClure for G–1 AGF, 25 Jun 43, sub: Demob. 314.7 (AGF Hist) (S). (2) Memo (S) of Brig Gen J. N. Dalton, Director Pers ASF for DCofS Serv Comd, 14 Jul 43, sub: Basis for Demob. WD G–1 file, binder marked "Basis of Demob" (S).

[7] Memo (S) of Col Clinton I. McClure for G–1 AGF, 21 Jun 43, sub: Methods of Demob. 314.7 (AGF Hist) (S).

[8] AGF M/S (R), G–1 to Plans, 16 Dec 43, sub: Demob Regulations No. 1–1. With related papers. AGF Plans Sec file 153 (Demob Regulation No 1–1) (S).

called for demobilization by a selection-out of individuals, based on length of service, dependency, combat, and other factors.[9] The occasion for this shift was apparently a report of the National Resources Planning Board, published on 30 June, which advocated demobilization by individuals.[10]

It was argued in favor of the individual selection-out plan that experience after World War I was not a safe guide for World War II because of the difference in the composition of units and the necessity in World War II of continuing the fight in the Pacific after it had ended in Europe. A second consideration was that unit demobilization was unfair to the individual, since in consequence of the replacement system there was a great variation in length of service within each organization. It was believed that public opinion would not support a plan which did not give preference to individuals who had a record of long service. For these reasons the National Resources Planning Board in June 1943, the Joint Chiefs of Staff in September 1943, and the War Department itself in 1943 decided in favor of an individual selection-out plan of demobilization.[11]

When the draft of "Demobilization Regulations 1-1" was submitted to the Army Ground Forces for comment in December 1943, the Plans Section, which in August 1943 had been designated as the coordinating agency for demobilization matters in the Army Ground Forces,[12] drew up a nonconcurrence because the draft failed to provide for demobilization by unit. But when it was called to the attention of the AGF Chief of Staff that both the Joint Chiefs of Staff and General of the Army George C. Marshall were firm in their support of an individual selection-out plan rather than a unit plan of demobilization, the nonconcurrence was withdrawn.[13]

After creation of the Special Planning Division in the War Department Special Staff, and after failure to secure acceptance of the unit plan of demobilization, the Army Ground Forces made no attempt to take the initiative in the shaping of high-level policies for personnel readjustment. But through representation on War Department committees charged with preparation of the Readjustment Regulation (RR) series and through comment on successive

[9] AGF M/S (R), Plans to G-1, 20 Dec 43, sub: Demob Regulation No 1-1. 320.2/1 (Redepl) (R).

[10] See AGF Historical Section, The Demobilization Period.

[11] History of the Personnel and Administration Branch, SPD WDSS, 7 Dec 41-1 Sep 45. (Draft prepared by Col Alan Richardson.) SPD WDSS Records.

[12] M/S (S), Gen Staff Sec to Plans, 4 Aug 43, sub: Orgn and Functions, Spec Planning Div. AGF Plans Sec file 158 (Demob) (S).

[13] AGF M/S (S), Plans to CofS AGF, 28 Dec 43, sub: Proposed Demob Regulation No. 1-1, 30 Nov 43. With related papers. AGF Plans Sec file 153 (Demob Regulation No. 1-1) (S).

drafts of this series, General McNair and, after his transfer to Europe for the
OVERLORD Operation, his successors, Lt. Gen. Ben Lear and Gen. Joseph
W. Stilwell, were able to secure inclusion of some of their principles in the
basic War Department program.[14]

Early in 1944 an officer of the Control Division of the Ground G–1 Section
was directed to maintain liaison with the War Department in personnel aspects
of redeployment. From that time until V-J Day this officer, accompanied frequently by representatives of other interested sections and The Adjutant General,
sat almost daily in conferences sponsored by the Special Planning Division for
the formulation of War Department directives for personnel readjustment.[15]
In May 1945, when the War Department directed creation of an *ad hoc* committee composed of representatives of the three major commands to facilitate
bulk transfers of personnel called for by Readjustment Regulations, a G–1 officer
moved to the Pentagon to represent the Army Ground Forces on this committee.[16]

The principal AGF contributions to the War Department program were
as follows: [17]

1. *Adjustment of critical score multiples in such a way as to safeguard
military necessity and at the same time give ample recognition for participation
in ground combat.*

Maj. Gen. Frederick H. Osborn, who originated the service score plan in
May 1944, recommended a weighting of credits as follows: [18]

    a. Service credit—1 point for each month in the service after the beginning
       of the emergency.

    b. Overseas credit—2 points for each month overseas.

---

[14] The complete series, filed in 300.8/1 (Redepl), is as follows:
    RR 1–1 Readjustment of Personnel
    RR 1–2 Personnel Procedure for Readjustment Movements
    RR 1–3 Athletic and Recreation Program
    RR 1–4 Army Education Program
    RR 1–5 Readjustment of Officers
    RR 1–6 Demobilization of Category IV Elements
    RR 1–1 and RR 1–5 deal primarily with personnel.
[15] Statement of Lt Col J. U. Parker, AGF G–1 Sec to AGF Hist Off, 29 Aug 45.
[16] Statement of Maj H. T. Sears to AGF Hist Off, 15 Jan 46.
[17] This summary of AGF contributions is based mainly on an interview by the AGF Hist Off of
Lt Col J. U. Parker, AGF G–1 Section, 29 Aug 45. Colonel Parker performed the liaison functions of
the Army Ground Forces with the War Department in personnel aspects of redeployment from May 1944
until his departure from Headquarters, AGF, late in 1945.
[18] ASF memo (R) SPMSD 327.02 for WD SPD, 31 May 44, sub: Suggested Changes in WD Plan
for Readjustment of Pers of the Army after the Defeat of Germany. 320.2/4 (Redepl) (R).

c. Combat credit—3 points for each month in combat zone.

d. Number of wounds—6 points for each wound (as recognized by award of Purple Heart).

e. Number of children—12 points per child under 18 years.

The Army Ground Forces was of the opinion that the heavy weighting given for overseas and combat service by General Osborn's plan would take from the Army so vast a number of seasoned soldiers that it would endanger the effectiveness of operations against Japan. On AGF recommendation, overseas credit combined with combat zone credit was reduced to 1 point per month.[19] The Army Ground Forces was also responsible for the inclusion of credit for battle participation, consisting of 5 points for each campaign star.[20] When in the course of discussions it was proposed that all battle decorations be included in the computation of combat credit, the Army Ground Forces demurred on the ground that such a plan would give undue advantage to Army Air Forces personnel. It withdrew its objection when War Department representatives stated that the Army Air Forces might be given a higher eligibility score than Ground Forces—a prediction which did not materialize. Believing that the point system as originally drawn would favor a man with many children over one with few children and much battle experience, the Army Ground Forces also secured adoption of a provision limiting parenthood credit to a maximum of 36 points. An AGF suggestion that, in computing service credit, time lost for misconduct should be deducted, while at first rejected "because of the complications which might arise and because the man would be punished twice for one offense," was subsequently included in RR 1-1.[21]

2. *Location of initial assignment jurisdiction over surplus officers returned from overseas in the major command with which they last served (commonly known as the "Source Major Force" plan).*

Before adoption of the Readjustment Regulations all officers returning to the United States for reassignment, regardless of their overseas connection, reverted to the assignment jurisdiction of the branch (or more properly the major command controlling the branch) in which they had been originally commissioned. Thus, ordnance officers released for any reason from overseas

[19] AGF M/S (S), Control to G-1, 6 Jun 44, sub: Changes in WD Plan for Readjustment of Pers after the Defeat of Germany. 314.7 (AGF Hist) (S).

[20] AGF memo (R) for CofS USA [undated, but about 6 Jun 44], sub: Suggested Changes in WD Plan for Readjustment of Pers of the Army after the Defeat of Germany, 320.2/4 (Redepl) (R).

[21] (1) AGF M/S (S), Control for G-1, 6 Jun 44, sub: Changes in WD Plan for Readjustment of Pers after the Defeat of Germany. 314.7 (AGF Hist) (S). (2) RR 1-1, par 12c.

service with AGF units passed on arrival in a U. S. port to the control of the Chief of Ordnance, and an infantry officer returned from overseas service with an Air Force unit reverted to the control of the Army Ground Forces.

When the War Department proposed that all overseas officers who became surplus in redeployment be returned to the United States for disposition, the Army Ground Forces became apprehensive as to the effect of current reassignment policies on AGF units. It did not relish the idea of getting back from the Army Service Forces large numbers of officers whose basic branch was one of the AGF arms, because it was thought that many of them while in the Army Service Forces would have become so "rusty" in their original duties as to require considerable retraining—and this was deemed undesirable and uneconomical. Moreover, it was believed that some of these officers, because of great aptitudes in technical specialties, had attained grades which they could not satisfactorily fill in command positions with Ground troops—and demotion was not considered desirable.[22]

But even more disturbing was the prospect of losing to the Army Service Forces large numbers of officers whose basic branch was one of the services but who had served for long periods in Ground units. There was no source within the Army Ground Forces for the procurement of service officers, and it was feared that requisitions on branch chiefs would not yield the highest-type officers; even if personnel of the highest quality were obtained, considerable training and indoctrination would be necessary to fit them for their Ground duties.[23]

Prompted by these considerations, the Army Ground Forces proposed in November 1944 that the Source Major Force plan be written into RR 1–5. This suggestion elicited a strong protest from the Army Service Forces, which maintained that the Source Major Force plan "would allow the AGF to divert any [ASF] officers so desired to other duties and to send the least desirable officers back to the command of origin. Examples of this would be capable engineers or quartermaster officers whom the AGF might desire to utilize as infantry officers or [in] branch immaterial positions." Moreover, the Army Service Forces contended that it was better able to determine the professional qualifications and abilities of officers trained by the services, and that the Source Major Force policy "creates an opportunity for unnecessary waste of training,

---

[22] AGF M/S (S), G–1 to CofS, AGF, 18 Nov 44, sub: Return of Offs to Source Major Force 370.01/150 (Demob) (S).
[23] *Ibid.*

skills, and manpower and lowering of morale through misassignment of officers possessed of special technical abilities." [24]

War Department G-1, G-3, Operations Division, and Special Planning Division supported the position of the Army Ground Forces, and the Source Major Force plan was incorporated in RR 1-5. In registering its nonconcurrence with the Army Service Forces, the War Department General Staff cited those provisions of RR 1-5 that required the Army Ground Forces to pass on to the Army Service Forces, for determination of essentiality, such officers of the services as were surplus to the needs of the Army Ground Forces, as well as provisions that call for liaison between the forces for disposition of officers in whom there was a joint interest.[25]

Application of the Source Major Force plan may be illustrated as follows. An officer whose basic branch was one of the services but whose most recent assignment had been in an AGF organization (as listed in the current "Analysis of the Present Status of the War Department Troop Basis"), on return from overseas or on release as surplus by a continental defense command, came first under the control of the Army Ground Forces for assignment. If needed there, he was assigned to an AGF unit or installation. If deemed surplus to AGF needs, he was turned over to the Army Service Forces, who either gave him an assignment or declared him unessential and separated him from the service. In special cases of joint interest, either command might relinquish initial assignment jurisdiction by arrangements satisfactory to both.[26]

There was some sentiment in Headquarters, Army Ground Forces, for applying the Source Major Force principle to enlisted men, but the matter was not strongly pressed. The plan as finally adopted provided that surplus service personnel (that is, personnel whose basic branch was one of the services) re-

---

[24] ASF memo (R) SPOPD 370.01 for WD SPD, 26 Mar 45, sub: Par 8c RR 1-5 Tab B to memo (R) of SPD for CofS USA, 30 Mar 45, sub: RR 1-5. SPD WDSS Records, binder RR 1-5 (R).

[25] Memo (R) of WD SPD for CofS USA, 30 Mar 45, sub: RR 1-5. SPD WDSS Records, binder RR 1-5 (R).

[26] (1) Statement of Lt Col J. U. Parker, AGF G-1 Sec to AGF Hist Off, 29 Aug 45. (2) Record (S) of Conf on Redepl Policies and Procedures, Hq AGF, 27-28 Mar 45. 337/1 (Redepl) (Separate binder) (S). (3) In May 1945 the Army Ground Forces requested authorization "to retain an overstrength of engineer, ordnance, signal, quartermaster and chemical warfare officers—not to exceed 25 percent of the number of the officers authorized Army Ground Forces at any time" in order to facilitate the preparation of Ground service-type units for redeployment. The War Department approved the request, but the end of the war came before the plan could be put into operation. Statement of Lt Col J. U. Parker, AGF G-1 Sec to AGF Hist Off, 20 Sep 45. See in this connection AGF memo (S) for CofS USA, 31 May 45, sub: Authorization for Overstrength of Ground Serv Type Offs. 320.2/11 (Redepl) (S).

turned from overseas, whether from Ground or Service type organizations, should go to appropriate ASF training centers for refresher training. The Army Service Forces was to supply the requisitions of the Army Ground Forces for service personnel, the requisitions specifying needs per month according to military occupational specialties (MOS).[27]

In addition to assisting in the preparation and revision of the War Department's personnel program, the Army Ground Forces issued instructions of its own, known as Readjustment Memoranda (RM), to implement applicable Readjustment Regulations. RM 1-1, Personnel Readjustment, prepared in the G-1, G-3, and AG (C&RD) Sections in the latter part of 1944 and the early months of 1945, after passing through several draft stages, was issued to subordinate commands on 8 May 1945. A brief document, RM 1-3, Athletic and Recreation Program, was issued on 19 March 1945 to implement RR 1-3. RM 1-5, Readjustment of Officers, was published on 5 June 1945.[28] Army Ground Forces did not prepare memoranda on the other War Department Readjustment Regulations, since they concerned subjects not essentially a part of AGF operations.[29]

The RM series, while requiring much time and effort in preparation, was devoted largely to details of administrative procedure. Its principal function was to adapt to Ground uses applicable portions of the War Department Readjustment Regulations.

Redeployment Movements

Procedure for the return of units to the United States was laid down in two War Department documents: Annex B, Redeployment Movements, published as an inclosure to a War Department letter dated 29 November 1944, and Readjustment Regulation 1-2, dated 15 September 1944.[30] Representatives of the Army Ground Forces who participated in War Department conferences called in connection with the preparation of these documents, and Headquarters, Army Ground Forces, commented on successive drafts submitted prior to their

---

[27] Statement of Col J. U. Parker, AGF G-1 Sec to AGF Hist Off, 29 Aug 45.

[28] These documents are filed as follows: RM 1-3: 300.6/1 (RM 1-3) (Redepl)
          RM 1-1: 300.6/1 (RM 1-1) (Redepl)   RM 1-5: 300.6/2 (RM 1-5) (Redepl)

[29] Par 11, AGF Info Ltr No 3 (R), 25 Jun 45. 300.6/3 (AGF Info Ltrs) (R).

[30] (1) Incl to WD ltr AG 370.5 (24 Nov 44) OB-S-E-M, 29 Nov 44, sub: WD Policies and Procedures Governing the Redeployment of the Army upon Cessation of Hostilities in Europe. (Revised edition dated 20 Apr 45 issued on 2 May 45.) 370.5/05 (Redepl) (R). (2) RR 1-2, Personnel Procedure for Readjustment Movements, 15 Sep 44. (Revised 11 Apr 45.) 300.8/1 (Redepl).

publication. While the return of units to stations in the United States was primarily an ASF responsibility, the Army Ground Forces made two important contributions to movement procedure.[31]

The first of these was the adoption of the reception-station method of processing units. In the course of redeployment planning, the following four methods were discussed:[32]

1. *The port method.* Units would be broken up at staging areas, personnel would be processed by the port commanders, and individuals would travel to their homes on furlough or to new stations at their own expense.

2. *Permanent-station method.* Units would proceed directly from port to new permanent stations, where the training agency would process personnel. Individuals would proceed home and back to permanent stations at their own expense.

3. *Intermediate-station method.* Units would proceed from port to intermediate stations, where the training agency (AGF, ASF, or AAF) would process personnel, and individuals would go home and back to intermediate stations at government expense. Units after assembly would proceed to permanent stations.

4. *Reception-station method.* Units would move by groups (designated by theater commanders on the basis of residence) from port to the reception station nearest the homes of men in the group, at government expense. Individuals, after processing at reception stations, would proceed home and back to reception stations at their own expense, and then to permanent stations in groups.

The Army Service Forces favored the intermediate-station method, as this plan brought Ground units under AGF control as soon as they arrived at the intermediate stations and thus made the Army Ground Forces responsible for issuance of furlough orders, checking of records, and other details of processing. War Department directives published in November and December 1944 prescribed this method.[33] The Army Ground Forces raised a strong objection and urged instead that the reception-station method be adopted. It presented these arguments in support of its position:[34]

[31] Statement of Lt Col J. A. Hanson, G–4 Task Force Div to AGF Hist Off, 3 Jan 46.

[32] (1) Statement of Lt Col C. W. Siegert, Installations and Movements Div AGF G–3 Sec to AGF Hist Off, 3 Jan 46. (2) M/R (S) Task Force Div G–4, 17 Nov 44, sub: WD Conf on 7 Nov 44, Draft Redepl Movements. G–1 Control Div file (Redepl) (S).

[33] Statement of Lt Col C. W. Siegert to AGF Hist Off, 3 Jan 46.

[34] See footnote 32 (2) above.

1. Delay in granting furloughs until after movement to the intermediate station would have an adverse effect on morale.

2. The intermediate-station method required more rail travel and extra handling of individual equipment, which would have to be unloaded at the intermediate station and then reshipped to the training station.

3. In processing personnel at intermediate stations, the Army Ground Forces would have to duplicate the work and overhead of a staging area.

4. For processing large units the Army Ground Forces would have to maintain one or more division camps. No such camp was available for use as an intermediate station in the vicinity of the New York Port of Embarkation, Camp Pickett, Va., being the nearest.

In order to resolve the matter, the War Department directed the three major commands to test the two methods. AGF representatives participated in observing and reporting on the processing of several units under each of the plans through eastern ports in the latter part of 1944 and the early weeks of 1945. As a result of these experiments, the War Department in March 1945 ordered adoption of the reception-station method.[35]

The second contribution of the Army Ground Forces to redeployment movement procedure was the suggestion that advance detachments be provided for ground units returning from overseas. Believing that early and direct contact with units was essential to effective planning, the Army Ground Forces requested in April 1945 that theater commanders be directed to order such detachments to the United States about one month in advance of their units. The detachments were to be composed as follows:

Type of Unit	Officers	Enlisted Men
Army	20	67
Corps	20	54
Infantry Division	42	144
Armored Division	35	109
Airborne Division	40	130
Separate Regiments	7	28
Separate Battalions	3	7
Evacuation and Convalescent Hospitals	3	7

---

[35] (1) AGF memo (S) for CofS USA, 14 Feb 45, sub: Redepl Movements. (2) AGF M/S (S), G-3 to CofS, 2 Apr 45, sub: Selection of a Method of Moving Units after Arrival in the U. S. during Redepl. Both in 370.5/1 (Redepl) (S).

The Army Ground Forces proposed to use the advance groups (1) to act as a planning staff for training purposes, (2) to furnish necessary information regarding personnel and equipment information of the unit, and (3) to provide personnel for feeding and housing individuals during the period when they were assembling at the permanent station following their recuperation furloughs.[36]

The Operations Division questioned the necessity of advance detachments for units as small as the battalion, but the original recommendation was finally approved by the War Department on 7 May 1945 with only minor modifications.[37]

Equipment

The War Department Supply Plan for the period after V-E Day provided that units redeployed through the United States take with them from Europe only the minimum essential equipment needed to preserve unit integrity.[38] Additional equipment required for redeployment training in the United States was to be provided in the Zone of Interior.[39]

In the early stages of redeployment planning the Army Ground Forces, fearing that the period for retraining would be inadequate, began to insist that each unit be given a 100-percent allowance of equipment for redeployment training, that the equipment be in combat-serviceable condition, and that it be laid down at training stations before the return of personnel from recuperation furloughs. Only thus, it was argued, could full advantage be taken of the time available for redeployment training. ASF authorities questioned the necessity of providing full allowances of equipment for redeployment training. They took the position that units had been trained originally with partial allowances and that retraining could be accomplished under a similar system. The

[36] AGF memo (C) for CofS USA, 18 Apr 45, sub: Advance Dets for Units Returning to the U. S. 370.5/2 (Redepl) (C).

[37] (1) WD D/F (C) OPD 370.5 (18 Apr 45) to CG AGF, 26 Apr 45, sub: Advance Dets for Units Returning to the U. S. (2) AGF memo (C) for CofS USA, 2 May 45, sub as in (1). (3) WD D/F (C) OPD 270.5 (18 Apr 45) to CG AGF, 7 May 45, sub: Advance Dets for Units Returning to the U. S. All in 370.5/2 (Redepl) (C).

[38] The WD Supply Plan was published in annex A to WD ltr AG 400 (30 Oct 44) OB–S–E–M, 4 Nov 44, sub: WD Policies and Procedures Governing the Redepl of the Army upon the Cessation of Hostilities in Europe. 370.5/15 (Redepl) (R).

[39] Record (S) of Conference on Redepl Policies and Procedures, Hq AGF, 27–28 Mar 45. Remarks of Lt Col J. H. Hanson. 337/1 (Redepl) (S).

Army Service Forces also objected to the requirement that equipment be combat-serviceable and advocated instead that training serviceability should be the standard prescribed. The Army Ground Forces countered this argument with the statement that no clear-cut definition of training serviceability had ever been established and that if any standard short of combat serviceability were specified units would lose precious training time in repairing and maintaining their equipment.[40]

After a considerable period of argument, during which Ground officers pushed their case aggressively, the War Department upheld the position of the Army Ground Forces. In May 1945 G–3 of the War Department agreed to assign an equipment priority of "A–2a" to units in redeployment, a priority previously given only to units alerted for overseas movement. If this should be found inadequate to insure a complete supply of authorized allowances, the War Department G–3 proposed to give redeployed units a theater priority, the highest of all equipment priorities.[41]

The Redeployment Troop Basis

The Army Ground Forces was not called on to assist in preparing the redeployment Troop Basis.[42] But when the first edition of this document, dated 15 March 1945, was issued to the major commands for guidance in planning, the Army Ground Forces submitted to the War Department a brief of recommended changes.

The redeployment Troop Basis prescribed a total of 65 divisions; infantry divisions were reduced from 65 to 50, and airborne divisions from 5 to 3. The Army Ground Forces, assuming that the number of divisions had been established "according to a definite plan," made no comment as to the aggregate specified in the redeployment Troop Basis. But it did recommend that two infantry divisions be substituted for the two airborne divisions that were scheduled for inactivation. The basis of this suggestion was the high degree of effectiveness demonstrated by airborne units in Europe. Not only did an airborne division have "fighting ability comparable to an infantry division," according to the Army Ground Forces, but the mere presence of an airborne

---

[40] AGF M/S, G–4 for CofS, 30 Apr 45, sub: Equip for Redepl Tng. G–4 TF files, binder "Chief of Staff."

[41] AGF M/S, G–4 for CofS, 30 May 45, sub: Conference on Equip Priority. G–4 TF files, binder "Chief of Staff."

[42] Statement of Col H. T. Todd, AGF Mob Div G–3 Sec to AGF Hist Off, 12 Oct 45.

division was "a constant threat which required the enemy to hold out deep reserves when such reserves may be needed on the active front." [43] The War Department thereupon restored one of the deleted airborne divisions to the Troop Basis.

Believing that provisions of the redeployment Troop Basis covering combat support and replacements ran counter to some of the basic lessons of experience in ground combat, the Army Ground Forces made its strongest representations on these points. For example, the redeployment Troop Basis called for large reductions in engineering units. Combat engineer battalions were reduced from 211 to 129, treadway bridge companies from 31 to 17, and technical combat engineer teams from 20 to 4. The Army Ground Forces urged a less drastic reduction, citing the fact that 35 percent of the force used in the Leyte operations were engineers and that in some other operations engineers constituted as high as 40 percent of the participating strength. The War Department modified the original provisions only slightly: 3 of the deleted combat battalions, 1 treadway bridge company, and 10 technical combat teams were restored. Action with reference to engineer categories for which the Army Ground Forces recommended increases is summarized below: [44]

Unit	Prescribed in Current TB (1 Apr 45)	Prescribed in Redepl TB (15 Mar 45)	Recommended by AGF for Redepl TB (27 Apr 45)	Prescribed in Revised Redepl TB (1 Jul 45)
Combat Gp Hq	77	36	59	40
Combat Bn	211	129	151	132
Hvy Ponton Bn	15	13	19	15
Light Equip Co	38	33	67	38
Treadway Bridge Co	31	17	34	18
Tech Combat Team	20	4	12	14
Tech Int Research Team	5	4	5	6

The Army Ground Forces also urged an upward revision of ordnance support, particularly of ordnance maintenance. But the War Department did not accept the AGF recommendation; instead, it specified further reductions in

[43] AGF memo (S) for CofS USA, 27 Apr 45, sub: WD Redepl TB. With related papers. 320.2/1 (Redepl TUB) (S).

[44] (1) *Ibid.* (2) WD Redepl TB (S), 15 Mar. 45. AGF G-3 Mob Div files. (3) WD TB (S), 1 Apr 45. 320.2/78 (TUB) (Separate binder) (S). (4) WD TB (S), 1 Jul 45. 320.2/88 (TUB) (S). The remainder of this section on the redeployment Troop Basis is based on the same sources.

all types of ordnance support. Action with reference to ordnance units of categories in which the Army Ground Forces recommended increases is tabulated below:

Unit	Prescribed in Current TB (1 Apr 45)	Prescribed in Redepl TB (15 Mar 45)	Recommended by AGF for Redepl TB (27 Apr 45)	Prescribed in Revised Redepl TB (1 Jul 45)
Gp Hq	19	22	27	19
Bn Hq	155	141	180	128
Am Co	172	152	155	128
Depot Co	110	100	105	92
Evac Co	50	24	31	15
Heavy Auto Maint Co	139	109	162	87
Heavy Maint, FA	58	42	43	38
Maint, Tank	49	46	77	39
Maint Co, AA	45	32	43	29
Med Auto Maint Co	172	135	217	129

Recommendations for increases of certain categories of medical and signal units met with similar results.

There was wide divergence of opinion as to chemical mortar battalions: the regular Troop Basis of 1 April 1945 provided for 25 of these units; the redeployment Troop Basis of 15 March 1945 raised the number to 29; the Army Ground Forces on 27 April recommended 55; the 1 July revision of the redeployment Troop Basis authorized 32.

In the arms the story was about the same as in the services. The regular Troop Basis of 1 April 1945 called for 68 tank destroyer battalions; the redeployment Troop Basis, 15 March 1945, cut the number back to 28; the Army Ground Forces on 27 April recommended 59; the July revision of the redeployment Troop Basis authorized 48. The regular Troop Basis provided for 3 field artillery rocket battalions; the first edition of the redeployment Troop Basis, 15 March 1945, authorized 6; the Army Ground Forces on 27 April recommended 17; the 1 July revision of the redeployment Troop Basis left the figure at 6. The Army Ground Forces wanted the number of tank battalions raised from 43, as prescribed in the redeployment Troop Basis of 15 March, to 65 and recommended that one of these units be made an organic part of each infantry division. This recommendation was turned down, and the number of tank battalions was reduced to 36 in the 1 July revision.

The Army Ground Forces thought that the War Department had erred on the side of generosity in estimating redeployment needs in antiaircraft artillery units. While not proposing a specific figure, it took the position that "based on the superiority of air power in the Pacific, substantial reductions can be effected." The Army Ground Forces also recommended that the proportion of mobile battalions be increased so as to facilitate the use of antiaircraft units in the secondary role of supporting field artillery. The War Department in the 1 July revision of the redeployment Troop Basis reduced the number of antiaircraft artillery units 19 percent, but it did not adopt the AGF suggestion for increasing the proportion of mobile battalions. Details of adjustment are summarized in the following table:

Unit	Prescribed in Current TB (1 Apr 45)	Prescribed in Redepl TB (15 Mar 45)	Recommended by AGF for Redepl TB (27 Apr 45)	Prescribed in Revised Redepl TB (1 Jul 45)
AAA A Wpns, Mbl	79	46	49	16
AAA A Wpns, SP	30	18	30	25
AAA A Wpns, Sem	76	50	35	56
AAA Gun Bn, Mbl	38	20	37	17
AAA Gun Bn, Sem	76	62	55	64
AAA MG Btry, A/B (T/O&E 44–217)	14	14	0	11
AAA MG Btry, A/B (T/O&E 44–278)	15	15	0	2
AAA MG Btry, A/B (T/O&E 44–278T)	0	0	29	0
TOTAL	328	225	235	191

The redeployment Troop Basis as first published on 15 March 1945 prescribed reductions of the AGF replacement training center (RTC) capacity from 370,000 to 180,000, a cut of 51 percent as against a reduction of only 26 percent in the arms that were to be maintained by the replacement system. Calling attention to the fact that in the past "the inadequacy of the RTC program . . . has necessitated many expedients to increase the number of replacements in an attempt to meet requirements," the Army Ground Forces urged the War Department to consider raising the specified RTC capacity. The 1 July revision of the redeployment Troop Basis raised the figure from 180,000 to 245,000.

II. Changes in Organization

Redeployment Tables of Organization and Equipment (T/O&E's), commonly referred to as "R" tables, had their origin in January 1945. At that time the War Department abandoned for planning purposes the policy of rejecting, on account of limitations of manpower, recommendations for increase in T/O&E's, however strong the evidence of their need. Instead, a policy was adopted which provided for the construction of new tables, based on operational experience. These tables were to be suspended until such time as the manpower situation permitted putting them into effect—which presumably would be in the period following the defeat of Germany. Each table prepared under the new policy was to be distinguished by addition of the letter "R" following the number (e. g., T/O&E 11–7R) and prefaced with the statement: "This table will not become effective except upon notification from the War Department." [1]

On 7 February 1945 the War Department informed the Army Ground Forces that the infantry division would be considered the basic unit for application of the "R" tables and directed that initial recommendations for changes in the infantry division be submitted in chart form by 20 February. The War Department stated further that tables for other units would be prepared subsequently, in the following order: (1) units which normally support the division, (2) units which support corps, and (3) units which support army. The directive of 7 February also provided that the "R" tables would be prepared with a view to use, insofar as practicable, in the postwar army. [2]

The War Department directed specifically that two provisions be written into the "R" tables: (1) elimination of dual assignments which required personnel to perform secondary duties to the detriment of their primary mission—for example, cook's helpers and switchboard operators were not to be charged with the driving of vehicles; and (2) inclusion in T/O&E's of certain items ordinarily provided to theaters in "special lists of equipment," but which experi-

[1] WD ltr (R) AG 320.3 (12 Jan 45) OB–I–WDGCT–M to CGs, 20 Jan 45, sub: Redepl T/O&E's. 320.3/1 (Redepl) (R).

[2] WD memo (S) WDGCT 320.3 (7 Feb 45) for CG AGF, 7 Feb 45, sub: Redepl T/O&E's. 320.3/1 (Redepl) (S).

ence had shown to be required in normal operations of units, together with such personnel as were needed for manning the equipment in question. The War Department also specified that consideration be given to inclusion in the new tables of the following changes repeatedly recommended by overseas commanders: (1) provision of adequate communication in the signal company, artillery, infantry regiment, and the other components of the division; (2) replacement of the military police platoon by a company; (3) substitution in the cannon company of a self-propelled weapon for the towed howitzer; and (4) provision of a more effective weapon in the antitank company. The directive of 7 February 1945 stated further: "If the consensus of opinion of theaters favors retention of the Cannon and Antitank Companies organically in the Infantry Regiment . . . [AGF's] comments are desired on the inclusion of Tank, Tank Destroyer and Antiaircraft Artillery Battalions organically in the division as contrasted either with the present method of attachment or a proposed method of assignment." [3]

Subsequent instructions from the War Department stated that the new tables were "not intended to be special tables for operations in the Pacific" and that changes proposed by the Army Ground Forces should therefore not be based on recommendations from the Pacific alone but on suggestions of all theaters.[4] Supplementary directives also provided that the AGF recommendations in chart form be submitted in three categories, as follows: [5]

Plan 1. Changes generally agreed upon by theaters, which did not involve reorganization of the division and which (1) eliminated dual functions and (2) provided for addition of adequate communication, personnel, and other modifications previously directed by the War Department.

Plan 2. Same as Plan 1, plus recommended changes in the organization of units in the division, such as substitution of a military police company for the platoon, and changes in the cannon company to include self-propelled weapons.

Plan 3. Same as Plans 1 and 2, plus such over-all changes of the divisional organization as were deemed desirable, including addition of a tank battalion and other units with corresponding increases in the service units.

---

[3] *Ibid.*

[4] WD memo (S) 320.3 (7 Feb 45) for CG AGF, 22 Feb 45, sub: Redepl T/O&E's. 320.3/1 (Redepl) (S).

[5] (1) *Ibid.* (2) AGF M/S (S), Rqts–3 to Gen Staff Secs and CofS AGF, 27 Feb 45, sub: Redepl T/O&E's. 320.3/1 (Redepl) (S).

In sum, the War Department wanted three plans ranging from generally approved minimum increases within the existing frame of the infantry division to a remolding of the division into an organization that would reflect the accepted lessons of World War II.

The AGF "R" Tables

Spade work on the three plans was done in the Requirements Section, whose cumulative files of theater comments (broken down by T/O's and weapons) afforded excellent background material for the task at hand.[6] Information already available was supplemented by cable communications with theater commanders and by conference with high-ranking personnel who had returned to the United States after tours of duty overseas. Commanding generals of subordinate centers and commands and commandants of the AGF schools were also called on for suggestions; in addition, a group of AGF officers visited Fort Benning to discuss in detail with the commandant, Maj. Gen. Fred Walker, who had led the 36th Division in Italy, and with his staff proposed changes in the organization and weapons of the division.[7]

In late February a special AGF committee of 9 officers (4 from Requirements, 1 from each of the other General Staff Sections, and 1 from the Signal Section), using data compiled in the Requirements Section as a basis, made an intensive study of proposed changes in divisional T/O&E's. This committee on 1 March submitted to the AGF Chief of Staff three plans, which were transmitted on 8 March to the War Department.[8]

Plan 1, following War Department instructions, maintained the existing structure of the division and provided only such increases in strength and equipment as were generally agreed on by theater commanders. Personnel changes called for by this plan are shown in Table No. 1.

---

[6] Statement of Maj R. N. Nye to AGF Hist Off, 15 Nov 45.

[7] (1) *Ibid.* (2) Replies to questions sent to local and theater commanders are filed in 320.3 (Redepl) (S) and 320.2 (Redepl) (S).

[8] (1) Memo of Col J. P. Donnovin, Orgn and Equip Div for Brig Gen R. S. Ramey, 31 Oct 45, sub not given. Files of Orgn and Equip Div, AGF G-3 Sec. (2) Rpt (S) of Committee on "R" T/O's for the Inf Div. 320.3/1 (Redepl) (S). (3) AGF M/S (S), Rqts-3 to CofS AGF, 1 Mar 45, sub: "R" T/O's for Inf Div. 320.3/1 (Redepl) (S). (4) AGF memo (S) for CofS USA, attn G-3 Div, 8 Mar 45, sub: "R" T/O's for Inf Div. 320.3/1 (Redepl) (S).

TABLE NO. 1

Changes in the Division Proposed by AGF Plan 1, 28 February 1945

UNIT	T/O&E's IN EFFECT 1 MARCH 1945			PLAN 1			DIFFERENCE		
	OFF	WO	EM	OFF	WO	EM	OFF	WO	EM
Entire Division	763	44	13,230	775	44	15,175	+12	0	+1,945
Hq & Hq Co	46	8	207	49	8	243	+3	0	+36
Hq Sp Trs	2	0	7	2	0	7	0	0	0
MP Plat	4	0	102	4	0	104	0	0	+2
Ord Co	9	1	131	9	1	137	0	0	+6
QM Co	10	0	176	10	0	179	0	0	+3
Sig Co	9	4	226	11	4	315	+2	0	+89
Engr Bn	27	3	590	28	3	632	+1	0	+42
Med Bn	34	2	407	34	2	483	0	0	+76
Cav Recon Tr	6	0	143	6	0	146	0	0	+3
Inf Regt (each)	140	5	2,923	134	5	3,330	−6	0	+407
Div Arty	143	9	1,959	163	9	2,377	+20	0	+418
Atchd Med	40	0	457	44	0	506	+4	0	+49
Atchd Ch	13	0	0	13	0	0	0	0	0
Atchd Band	0	2	56	0	2	56	0	0	0

Source: Proposed T/O&E 7R and allied tables (mimeographed, tentative), Plan 1, 28 Feb 45. Files of Orgn and Equip Div, AGF G–3 Sec.

The principal augmentations were as follows:

1. Addition of truck drivers, so as to eliminate dual assignments for truck drivers, radio operators, and cook's helpers.

2. Additional communications personnel for wire teams, switchboard operators, and radio operators.

3. Additional postal personnel.

4. Additional ammunition bearers.

One of the significant changes was the addition of a squad of seven men to each rifle company to operate rocket launchers and flame throwers. The principal change in equipment under Plan 1 was the addition to each company, battery, or similar unit of a truck (¾- or 1½-ton) for headquarters and supply.[9]

Plan 2 included all the increases of personnel and equipment provided in Plan 1 and specified additional augmentations. (See Table No. 2.)

---

[9] AGF memo (S) for CofS USA, attn G–3 Div, 8 Mar 45, sub: "R" T/O's. With related papers. 320.3/1 (Redepl) (S). The charts setting forth the details of the three plans listed as inclosures 2 and 3 of this memo are not filed with the memo, but copies are on file in the Orgn and Equip Div of the AGF G–3 Sec.

TABLE NO. 2

Comparison of Changes in the Division Proposed by AGF Plans 1 and 2,
26–28 February 1945

UNIT	PLAN 1			PLAN 2			DIFFERENCE		
	OFF	WO	EM	OFF	WO	EM	OFF	WO	EM
Entire Division	775	44	15,175	812	47	16,622	+37	+3	+1,447
Hq & Hq Co	49	8	243	52	8	247	+3	0	+4
Hq Sp Trs	2	0	7	2	0	7	0	0	0
MP Plat (or Co)	4	0	104	7	0	169	+3	0	+65
Ord Co	9	1	137	11	2	218	+2	+1	+81
QM Co	10	0	179	10	0	236	0	0	+57
Sig Co (or Bn)	11	4	315	12	6	328	+1	+2	+13
Engr Bn	28	3	632	33	3	804	+5	0	+172
Med Bn	34	2	483	52	2	551	+18	0	+68
Cav Recon Tr	6	0	146	14	0	235	+8	0	+89
Inf Regt (each)	134	5	3,330	137	5	3,617	+3	0	+287
Div Arty	163	9	2,377	163	9	2,377	0	0	0
Atchd Med	44	0	506	32	0	543	−12	0	+37
Atchd Ch	13	0	0	13	0	0	0	0	0
Atchd Band	0	2	56	0	2	56	0	0	0

Source: Proposed T/O&E 7R and allied tables (mimeographed, tentative),
Plans 1 and 2, dated respectively 28 and 26 Feb 45. Files of Orgn and Equip Div, AGF G–1 Sec.

It substituted a military police company for the platoon, and a signal battalion for the company; moreover, it stipulated important changes in the organization and armament of the cannon and antitank companies of the infantry regiment. Details of these organizational changes will be presented below in the discussion of Plan 3. In general, the new plan called for replacement of the six towed 105-mm. M–3 howitzers of the cannon company by nine M–4 tanks armed with 105-mm. howitzers, and substitution in the antitank company of medium tanks carrying 90-mm. guns in lieu of the towed 57-mm. antitank guns.

Plan 3 included the changes outlined in Plans 1 and 2, called for additional augmentations of personnel and equipment, and provided for the addition of a tank battalion as an organic part of the infantry division. The strength of the division contemplated in Plan 3 was 18,285 (867 officers, 50 warrant officers, and 17,368 enlisted men), an increase of 4,248 (104 officers, 6 warrant officers, and 4.138 enlisted men) over the Division T/O&E in effect on 1 March 1945. (See Table No. 3 for details of Plan 3 and comparison with the other two plans and that currently in effect.)

TABLE NO. 3

Comparison of Changes in the Division Proposed by AGF Plans 1, 2, and 3, 26–28 February 1945

UNIT	T/O&E's IN EFFECT 1 MAR 45			PLAN 1			PLAN 2			PLAN 3		
	OFF	WO	EM	OFF	WO	EM	OFF	WO	EM	OFF	WO	EM
Entire Division	763	44	13,230	775	44	15,175	812	47	16,622	867	50	17,368
Hq & Hq Co	46	8	207	49	8	243	52	8	247	52	8	247
Hq Sp Trs	2	0	7	2	0	7	2	0	7	2	0	7
MP Plat (or Co)	4	0	102	4	0	104	7	0	169	7	0	169
Ord Co	9	1	131	9	1	137	11	2	218	11	2	252
QM Co	10	0	176	10	0	179	10	0	236	10	0	236
Sig Co (or Bn)	9	4	226	11	4	315	12	6	328	12	6	353
Engr Bn	27	3	590	28	3	632	33	3	804	33	3	804
Med Bn	34	2	407	34	2	483	52	2	551	53	2	552
Cav Recon Tr	6	0	143	6	0	146	14	0	235	14	0	235
Inf Regt (each)	140	5	2,923	134	5	3,330	137	5	3,617	137	5	3,617
Div Arty	143	9	1,959	163	9	2,377	163	9	2,377	176	9	2,407
Tank Bn										37	3	624
Atchd Med	40	0	457	44	0	506	32	0	543	36	0	575
Atchd Ch	13	0	0	13	0	0	13	0	0	13	0	0
Atchd Band	0	2	56	0	2	56	0	2	56	0	2	56

Source: Proposed T/O&E 7R and allied tables (mimeographed, tentative), Plans 1, 2, and 3, dated respectively 28, 26, and 26 Feb 45. Files of Orgn and Equip Div, AGF G–3 Sec. Plan 3 as drawn on 26 Feb provided a chemical mortar battalion (36 officers, 1 warrant officer, 639 enlisted men) in the division artillery, but since this battalion was later deleted it was not included in the above tabulation.

Since Plan 3 incorporated the provisions of the other two plans and since it was the one which the Army Ground Forces recommended to the War Department for adoption, on the ground that it embodied most fully the experience of World War II, it will be considered in detail.[10] Comparisons, unless otherwise indicated, will be with organizations as prescribed in T/O&E's in effect 1 March 1945. (For brevity the former will be referred to as "new" and the latter as "old.")

No changes were made in the rifle squad, but a rocket squad of seven men, armed with bazookas or flame throwers, was added to the rifle platoon to make the platoon more effective in operations against armor and pillboxes.

[10] The discussion of Plan 3 which follows, unless otherwise indicated, is based on the following sources: (1) AGF memo (S) for CofS USA, attn G–3 Div, 8 Mar 45, sub: "R" T/O&E's. With related papers. 320.3/1 (Redepl) (S). (2) Inf Sch ltr (S) to CG AGF, 17 Feb 45, sub: Redepl T/O&E's. 320.3/1 (Redepl) (S). (3) Proposed T/O&E 7R and allied tables (mimeographed, tentative), Plan 3, 26 Feb 45. Orgn and Equip Div, AGF G–3 Sec files.

The weapons platoon of the rifle company was augmented by a special weapons section of 17 men (1 leader, 1 messenger, and 3 squads of 5 men each) whose principal weapon was the 57-mm. recoilless rifle. The light machine-gun section of the weapons platoon was increased from 2 to 3 squads; this not only gave added fire power but also permitted the attachment of 1 light machine gun squad to each rifle platoon. The new rifle company had 6 officers and 241 enlisted men as against 6 officers and 187 enlisted men in the old company; it was better balanced and more effective.

The heavy weapons company, whose position in the infantry battalion was coordinate with that of the weapons platoon in the rifle company, was modified considerably. To increase flexibility and to provide a scheme that would conform to the triangular organization of the infantry battalion, the 2 heavy machine gun platoons, each having 4 squads, were combined into 1 machine gun platoon of 3 sections, each having 2 squads. Under the old organization 2 officers and 70 enlisted men manned 8 water-cooled machine guns; under the new plan 2 officers and 63 enlisted men manned 6 water-cooled machine guns and 6 light machine guns. Thus the reorganization of the heavy machine gun platoons yielded more fire power per man, at the same time providing increased flexibility.

Another change designed to increase flexibility and fire power was the transfer of the antitank platoon from the headquarters company of the infantry battalion to the heavy weapons company, and replacement of the three towed 57-mm. guns by six 75-mm. recoilless rifles. It was thought that the somewhat cumbersome, primarily defensive 57-mm. guns were not fully effective in a fast-moving attack; moreover, it was deemed desirable to place all of the battalion's supporting weapons in one company. In its new location the antitank platoon was redesignated as a gun platoon. The new heavy weapons company was a triangular organization, consisting of a machine gun platoon, a gun platoon, and a mortar platoon, with a strength of 7 officers and 197 enlisted men.

The infantry battalion headquarters company received additional radio operators and wiremen. Moreover, an intelligence and reconnaissance section of 16 enlisted men was added to fulfill demands for a trained unit in the battalion for intelligence and reconnaissance missions. Total strength of the battalion (officers and enlisted men) was increased from 860 to 1,060.

One of the most important changes on the regimental level was that affecting the cannon company. This unit had been added to the infantry regiment in 1942 to provide close-in direct-fire support for ground troops, particularly in fast-moving operations. Original plans had called for arming the cannon company with self-propelled howitzers (six 75-mm. and two 105-mm. howitzers per company), but in the revisions of organization of 1943, various considerations, including economy of shipping space, led to the adoption of short-barreled towed 105-mm. howitzers (six per company—two in each platoon) as the principal weapon.[11]

Later reports from the theaters indicated that the cannon company in actual operations was used only occasionally in its intended role. The towed howitzers were not sufficiently maneuverable for close support of rapidly advancing rifle units. In many if not in most instances normal employment was by indirect fire; in such cases it was common practice to tie the cannon company in with the field artillery communications system and to use it as an additional battery of artillery. To a large extent direct-fire missions were performed by attached tank and/or tank destroyer units. Still, there was no indication that divisions would willingly give up their cannon companies.[12]

Polling of theaters in 1944 and early 1945 on the question of changing the equipment and organization of the cannon company produced a variety of responses. Preponderant opinion seemed to favor the self-propelled over the towed mount. As to calibers, some commanders favored the 75-mm., some the 105-mm., and some the 3-inch; one report from the Southwest Pacific Area (SWPA) favored the 37-mm. gun. The commanding general of the Mediterranean Theater of Operations, U. S. Army (MTOUSA), offered this comment:[13]

It is not expected that a unanimous opinion concerning the best type of weapon for use by infantry cannon companies in their normal role will be forthcoming in the immediate future. . . . It appears, as a general observation, that the most recent important engagement sometimes unduly influences the opinions of the participating commanders with respect to what may be termed average or normal requirements necessitating a permanent change in T/O&E's.

The AGF committee appointed in February to suggest changes in organization and equipment adopted after considerable discussion the recommenda-

[11] See above, "Reorganization of Ground Troops for Combat."

[12] (1) AGF M/S (S), (GNRQT–3 15197), Rqts–3 to G–3, 9 Feb 45, sub: Redepl Tables of Orgn and Equip. With attached papers. Orgn and Equip Div, AGF G–3 Sec files. (2) ETO ltr (C) AG 322.34 OPGC to TAG, 15 Feb 45, sub: Inf Cannon Co. 320.3/1 (Redepl) (S).

[13] MTOUSA 1st ind (S), 16 Dec 44, on AGF ltr (R) 350.05/110, 7 Dec 44, sub: Self-Propelled TD Bn Organic to Divs. Orgn and Equip Div, AGF G–3 Sec files, binder marked "R" Tables (S).

tion of the Infantry School that the cannon company be organized and equipped as a standard tank company (to be designated "Tank Company, Infantry Regiment"), with its principal weapon the 105-mm. howitzer mounted on tank T26E2 (17 tanks in all—5 in each platoon and 2 in company headquarters). In his review of the committee's recommendations, Maj. Gen. Albert W. Waldron, Chief of the Requirements Section, rejected the proposal to convert the cannon company into a standard tank company and specified instead a company of 9 tanks (3 platoons, each equipped with 3 tanks T26E2, 105-mm. howitzers). General Waldron based his action primarily on the fact that the maximum number of tanks for the cannon company recommended by theater commanders was nine. To go beyond this he deemed a violation of a principle long followed by the Army Ground Forces of proposing no revision of T/O&E's which were not backed by theater recommendations.[14]

The AGF committee also accepted as its own the recommendation of the Infantry School that the 57-mm. gun be given up as the primary weapon of the antitank company, that the name of this unit be changed to "Infantry Destroyer Company," and that it be organized as a standard tank company equipped with seventeen T26E1 tanks carrying 90-mm. guns.[15] As in the case of the cannon company, General Waldron substituted for the committee's recommendation of a standard tank company a unit of 9 tanks (T26E1, 90-mm. gun) organized into 3 platoons of 3 sections each.[16]

One of General Waldron's reasons for reducing the number of tanks in the cannon and antitank companies was his belief that the War Department would not agree to placing in the infantry division the number of tanks provided for in the committee's recommendations.[17] For when the 34 tanks in each of the infantry regiments (17 in the cannon company and 17 in the antitank company) were added to the 71 in the tank battalion (made organic in the infantry division under Plan 3) the total number of tanks in the

[14] Statement of Maj Gen A. W. Waldron to AGF Hist Off, 27 Nov 45.

[15] During the course of its study the committee considered a proposal to delete the antitank company and to convert the cannon company into a combined cannon-antitank organization consisting of three platoons each having five tanks—three armed with 105-mm. howitzers and two with 90-mm. guns. See Rpt of Committee on "R" T/O's for the Inf Div in 320.3/1 (Redepl) (S). This proposal was rejected on two grounds: (1) the missions of the antitank and cannon companies were inherently distinct and should not be combined in a single unit; (2) such an organization was without precedent and had no theater indorsement. Statement of Maj Gen A. W. Waldron to AGF Hist Off, 27 Nov 45.

[16] Rpt (S) of Committee on "R" T/O's for the Inf Div. 320.3/1 (Redepl) (S).

[17] Statement of Maj Gen A. W. Waldron to AGF Hist Off, 27 Nov 45.

division was 173. This was almost two-thirds the number of tanks authorized the armored division, for which T/O&E 17, dated 24 January 1945, authorized 195 medium tanks and 77 light tanks.[18] General Waldron's reduction of tanks in the cannon and antitank companies from 17 to 9 cut down the total number of tanks in the infantry division from 173 to 125.

The mission envisioned for the new cannon and antitank companies as stated by the Infantry School and accepted by the Army Ground Forces was as follows:[19]

Cannon Company (redesignated Tank Company) . . . will take on the role of an assault company, and should in addition be capable of destroying enemy armor. It is intended that it should normally engage, by direct fire, targets which are too tough for battalion weapons, to include personnel, pill boxes, and other targets of opportunity, fire on which is desirable before it can be obtained from the artillery.

Antitank Company . . . its primary role will be to destroy enemy armor and its secondary [mission] will be similar to that of the Tank Company. The regimental commander will have his choice, according to the situation, as to whether the destroyer company or the tank company should lead.

The service company of the infantry regiment was changed very little except for an increase in enlisted strength from 96 to 141 to meet the enlarged responsibilities resulting from the addition of tanks and other complicated items of equipment to the regiment.

The principal changes in the regimental headquarters and headquarters company were as follows:

1. Addition of a countermortar section of 1 officer and 23 enlisted men equipped with instruments for the electronic location of enemy weapons.

2. Addition of the mine platoon transferred from the regimental antitank company as a result of the conversion of the latter unit to a tank company. It was contemplated that when not engaged in their primary activity personnel of the mine platoon would be used to supplement defense of the regimental command post.

3. Increase of intelligence and communications personnel.

These and other augmentations gave the regimental headquarters and headquarters company a strength of 14 officers and 182 enlisted men as against 12 officers and 91 enlisted men in the old organization.

---

[18] See above, Table No. 3 in "Reorganization of Ground Forces for Combat."

[19] Infantry Sch ltr (S) to CG AGF, 17 Feb 45, sub: Redepl T/O&E's. 320.3/6 (Redepl) (S).

A 1½-ton cargo truck was added to all companies of the regiment to meet the need demonstrated by combat experience for an additional vehicle to transport baggage, headquarters supplies, and kitchen. Another change affecting the regiment as a whole was the changing of the MOS numbers for Basics to Riflemen; this action stemmed from the belief that the minimum qualification for Basics in any organization was the ability to perform the functions of the primary crewmen, which in the Infantry was, of course, the rifleman.[20]

The Infantry School recommended that an air-liaison section, equipped with two Cub-type airplanes, be added organically to each regiment so that the regimental commander would always have at hand air reconnaissance and observation. The AGF committee went along with the Infantry School, but General Waldron was bound by the rule to reject all changes that had not been advocated by a theater commander.[21]

The new regiment was larger by 719 men, including attached medical personnel and chaplains, than was the old. Details of the changes in strength and weapons are summarized in Table No. 4.

It is apparent from this table that the new regiment was not only stronger in men but also more mobile, better balanced, and (in view of the adoption of recoilless weapons) harder-hitting than the old organization. Increase of communications and intelligence personnel and addition of tanks and other new weapons also made the regiment more self-sufficient than formerly. In fact, it was almost a division in miniature.

No major change was made in the organization of the division artillery. Personnel, less attached medical and chaplain, was increased from 2,111 to 2,592 officers and enlisted men. Augmentations were mainly in the following categories: communications (wiremen, switchboard operators, and radio operators), fire-direction personnel, ammunition bearers, and forward observers. Since reports from theaters had indicated that the number of pilots for liaison planes was insufficient to provide necessary rotation and relief, two additional pilots were provided for division artillery headquarters and two for each of the four battalions. Another significant change provided for deletion of the forward observer section from the battalion headquarters and the inclusion of a forward observer section in each of the firing batteries.

---

[20] Statement of Maj H. T. Sears, C&RD, GAG Sec, to AGF Hist Off, 31 Nov 45.

[21] Statement of Maj Gen A. W. Waldron to AGF Hist Off, 27 Nov 45.

TABLE NO. 4

Changes in the Infantry Regiment Proposed by AGF Plan 3, 26 February 1945
Personnel

UNITS	NEW REGIMENT (Proposed in Plan 3, 26 Feb 45)			OLD REGIMENT (T/O&E 7, 24 Jan 45)			DIFFERENCE		
	OFF	WO	EM	OFF	WO	EM	OFF	WO	EM
3 Rifle Companies (each)........................	6	0	241	6	0	187	0	0	+54
Heavy Weapons Co............................	7	0	197	8	0	152	−1	0	+45
Battalion Hq & Hq Co.........................	10	0	105	9	0	112	+1	0	−7
Total 3 Bns (each)..........................	35	0	1,025	35	0	825	0	0	+200
Regimental Hq Co............................	14	1	182	12	1	91	+2	0	+91
Service Co..................................	8	4	141	11	4	96	−3	0	+45
Antitank Co.................................	5	0	100	7	0	152	−2	0	−52
Cannon Co..................................	5	0	119	5	0	109	0	0	+10
Total Regiment............................	137	5	3,617	140	5	2,923	−3	0	+694
Attached Medical............................	8	0	151	10	0	126	−2	0	+25
Attached Chaplain...........................	3	0	0	3	0	0	0	0	0
TOTAL.................................	148	5	3,768	153	5	3,049	−5	0	+719

Transportation and Weapons (Less Medical)

TYPE OF WEAPON OR VEHICLE	NEW REGIMENT	OLD REGIMENT	DIFFERENCE
Carbine, cal .30..................................	967	836	+131
Gun, machine, cal .30, heavy, flexible...............	18	24	−6
Gun, machine, cal .30, light, flexible................	45	36	+9
Gun, machine, HB, cal .50, flexible..................	33	35	−2
Gun, submachine, cal .45..........................	69	63	+6
Gun, 57-mm, towed...............................	0	18	−18
Howitzer, 105-mm................................	0	6	−6
Launcher, rocket, AT, 2.36-in......................	110	112	−2
Mortar, 60-mm...................................	27	27	0
Mortar, 81-mm...................................	18	18	0
Pistol, auto, cal .45..............................	353	293	+60
Rifle, auto, cal .30...............................	135	135	0
Rifle, M1, cal .30................................	2,268	1,831	+437
Rifle, M1C, cal .30...............................	27	27	0
Rifle, 57-mm, recoilless...........................	27	0	+27
Rifle, 75-mm, recoilless...........................	18	0	+18
Tank, medium, w-arm (105-mm How)................	9	0	+9
Tank, medium, w-arm (90-mm T26E1)..............	9	0	+9
Trailer, ¼-ton...................................	92	77	+15
Trailer, 1-ton...................................	63	28	+35
Truck, ¼-ton...................................	147	146	+1
Truck, ¾-ton, WC...............................	12	15	−3
Truck, 1¼-ton, cargo............................	36	31	+5
Truck, 1½-ton, CP..............................	4	0	+4
Truck, 2½-ton, cargo............................	39	33	+6
Vehicle, tank recovery............................	2	0	+2

Sources: (1) AGF M/S (S), Rqts–3 to CofS, 1 Mar 45, sub: "R" Tables of Orgn for Inf Div. 320.3/1 (Redepl) (S).　(2) T/O&E 7 and allied tables, 24 Jan 45.

Of special units in the division the reconnaissance troop received the greatest increase. The basis of the increase was reports from theaters, particularly from ETO, that the troop as currently organized was not adequate for performance of its primary mission. The Cavalry School recommended the addition of a rifle platoon and a reconnaissance platoon to the old organization, but Headquarters, Army Ground Forces, deeming an additional reconnaissance platoon not essential, added only the rifle platoon. An air section of 4 officer pilots and 2 enlisted mechanics, equipped with 2 liaison planes, was added to extend the reconnaissance capabilities of the troop. To increase its punch, a mortar platoon of three sections, each armed with an 81-mm. mortar, was added in lieu of the 60-mm. mortars previously included in the reconnaissance platoon. Trailers and trucks were added for transportation of mortars, mortar crews, and ammunition. The over-all strength of the new reconnaissance troop was 14 officers and 235 enlisted men as against 6 officers and 143 enlisted men of the old organization.[22]

Plan 3, like Plans 1 and 2, as stated above, called for substitution of a company of military police for the old platoon. This change accorded with the experience of commanders in all theaters who had found the platoon inadequate for police and traffic work and the handling of prisoners of war. The new organization consisted of 1 military police platoon and 3 traffic platoons and had a strength of 7 officers and 169 enlisted men, compared with 4 officers and 102 enlisted men of the old platoon.

The division quartermaster company was augmented by 60 enlisted men (old company—10 officers, 176 enlisted men; new company—10 officers, 236 enlisted men). Theater experience had indicated the absolute necessity of providing relief drivers for 2½-ton trucks, and 24 of the men added were for this purpose. The augmentation also included an additional service section for breaking down supplies into unit lots, guarding division dumps, and assisting in the registration of graves.

Reports of AGF observers in the various theaters had frequently registered complaint against the inadequacy of the division's engineer facilities and indicated that it was common practice to augment the organic battalion by more or less permanent attachment of a corps battalion.[23] To meet partially at least

[22] (1) Cav Sch ltr (S) to CG AGF, 27 Feb 45, sub: Proposed Changes in Redepl T/O&E's. 320.3/2 (Redepl) (S). (2) AGF M/S (S), Rqts–3 to CofS, 1 Mar 45, sub: "R" T/O's for Inf Div. 320.3/1 (Redepl) (S).

[23] (1) Statement of Col J. B. Hughes, AGF Engr Off to AGF Hist Off, 28 Apr 45. (2) AGF M/S (S), Rqts–3 to CofS, 1 Mar 45, sub: "R" T/O's for Inf Div. 320.3/1 (Redepl) (S).

the engineer needs demonstrated by combat experience, the Army Ground Forces advocated the addition of a fourth company to the engineer battalion. It was contemplated that this extra unit would support the three engineer companies normally attached to the regimental combat teams and provide general engineer service for other troops of the division. A sufficient number of equipment operators was added to the battalion to permit the running of equipment on a 24-hour basis. The strength of the engineer battalion, less attached medical, was increased from 620 to 840 officers and enlisted men.

Theater commanders had also found divisional signal facilities inadequate for normal operating requirements. To meet this deficiency the signal company was changed to a battalion, with an increase in strength from 9 officers, 4 warrant officers, and 226 enlisted men to 12 officers, 6 warrant officers, and 353 enlisted men. Personnel added to the signal organization consisted mainly of relay switchboard operators, wire teams, and radio operators.

In furtherance of the idea of triangularization, and to provide essential augmentation of organic medical service, an additional clearing platoon was added in the clearing company of the division medical battalion; this modification made a clearing platoon available for attachment to each of the three regimental combat teams. Other changes in medical personnel provided for consolidation of all division dental officers under the control of the medical battalion (to be attached to divisional units for dental service as required) and transfer of the neuropsychiatrist from the medical section of division headquarters to the clearing company, where combat experience had indicated that his services were most needed. The new medical battalion had 53 officers, 2 warrant officers, and 552 enlisted men as against 34 officers, 2 warrant officers, and 407 enlisted men in the old.

The adding of vehicles and weapons to various elements of the division increased the maintenance load of the ordnance company. This unit received additional men to meet its enhanced responsibilities in third-echelon maintenance and ordnance supply. Moreover, to fill a need revealed by combat experience, a contact platoon was added, the mission of which was to provide immediate and limited ordnance service in forward areas. The word "light" was deleted from the title of the company. The strength of the new unit was 11 officers, 2 warrant officers, and 252 enlisted men as compared with 9 officers, 1 warrant officer, and 131 enlisted men in the old organization.

The principal changes in division headquarters were as follows: (1) inclusion organically of photo interpreters and order-of-battle personnel who in common theater practice had served on an attached basis; (2) increase of the G–3 and G–4 staffs each by a captain to provide the additional assistance which combat experience had indicated to be necessary; and (3) addition of a captain to the special services section to act as post exchange officer and to assist in athletic and recreational activities. The division headquarters company was increased by 28 enlisted men to eliminate dual functions and to provide additional cooks and orderlies.

The AGF committee on the "R" tables also recommended inclusion of a chemical mortar (4.2-inch) battalion (36 officers, 1 warrant officer, and 639 enlisted men) as an organic part of the infantry division. Theater experience had indicated that the 4.2-inch mortars, when attached to the division, provided valuable close-in support for infantry units. The AGF committee deemed it desirable in the interest of teamwork to make a mortar battalion an integral part of the division.[24] In his review of the committee's recommendations General Waldron proposed that the mortar battalion be assigned to the division artillery in order to take full advantage of the artillery's communication and fire-direction facilities. At first, G–3 of the Army Ground Forces would not support the plan to include the chemical battalion organically in the division, but after considerable discussion he withdrew the nonconcurrence. When Plan 3 was submitted to the AGF Chief of Staff, he struck out the chemical battalion. The reason for the deletion, according to General Waldron, was the belief that the division provided in Plan 3 was too large and that it was more practicable to eliminate the chemical battalion than to make other reductions.[25]

Another change which the Army Ground Forces recommended in Plan 3 was the inclusion of a medium tank battalion as an organic part of the infantry division. Reports from theaters indicated that the normal procedure in combat was to attach a tank battalion to the division and that combat commanders were practically unanimous in urging that the armored unit be made an integral part of the division to the end that, in training as well as in fighting, a division might work with the same units. Only thus, they held, could the necessary teamwork between tank, infantry, and artillery units be developed. The following comments are typical:[26]

---

[24] Rpt (S) of Committee on "R" T/O's for the Inf Div. 320.3/1 (Redpl) (S).

[25] Statement of Maj Gen A. W. Waldron to AGF Hist Off, 27 Nov 45.

[26] AGF Bd MTOUSA Rpt 339 (S), 14 Mar 45, sub: Current Questions Regarding Inf Opns. Files of Dissemination Br, AGF G–2 Sec.

Lt. Col. Elmore D. Beggs, G–3, 88th Division: In the 88th Division the tanks did not always have an opportunity to work together before going into action but when there was a lull, and infantry and tanks did get a chance to work together in the rear area, it paid big dividends. Many times in our attacks north of the Arno we had tank units assigned to the division that we had never seen before or had never worked with and thus the team play was not smooth and likewise the success of the operation. It is my belief that when it is practical, no operation should be undertaken, in which tanks are used without first giving the infantry and the tank unit a chance to work together before going into action. Combined training is a prerequisite to the success of an infantry-tank operation.

Lt. Col. Mark T. Martin, Jr., G–3, 34th Division: Combined training is a prerequisite to the success of an infantry-tank operation. It cannot be expected that, infantry knowing the armor draws enemy fire, will work successfully with tanks without being familiar with them. At Anzio the 135th Infantry Regiment had an opportunity to work with the 1st Armored Division before going into action and later, when they broke out of the Anzio Beachhead, they suffered only eighty-seven (87) casualties in three days of tank action and took three hundred (300) prisoners. Perfect coordination between infantry platoon and tank platoon was responsible for this great success. Again, at the crossing of the Rapido River, the 168th Infantry Regiment forced a successful crossing due to the perfect coordination between this regiment and the 756th Tank Battalion which supported it. These units had had an opportunity to work together before going into action.

AGF Observer, MTOUSA: In my talk with corps and division commanders in this theater, I find that whenever the tactical situation is such as to permit divisions to work with supporting tank units before going into action, it is generally done. The time is not always as long as it should be but in most cases it is generally from one (1) to two (2) days. What the division commanders would like, if it is possible, is to have the same tank unit that they train with, and get to know, support them during the operation. In some cases this has not always happened and you have a division attacking in the morning with a tank unit it has never seen before or has never worked with. This is hard on both infantry and tank commanders and the perfect coordination that is so responsible for success is not there.

Tabulations of the opinion of 21 high commanders (1 army commander, 2 corps commanders, and 18 infantry division commanders) in ETO in early 1945 showed only one, a division commander, who was opposed to making the tank battalion a part of the division.[27]

The War Department on 5 April 1945 disapproved inclusion of the tank battalion in the infantry division, along with most of the other augmentations proposed by the Army Ground Forces in Plan 3, on the ground of limitations of

[27] A photostatic copy of this tabulation (C), sub: What Weapons Does the RCT Normally Require in Combat, is filed in 320.3/1 (C).

personnel available to the Army.[28] On 13 April 1945 the AGF Chief of Staff wrote to his G–3: [29]

> The Commanding General [Stilwell] believes that we should go back to the War Department with a strong letter urging the inclusion of a tank battalion as an organic part of the division. Please prepare, with Requirements, a memo for submission to War Department G–3 stating somewhat as follows:
>
> Practically all reports we get from theaters indicate the desirability of having at least one organic tank battalion in a division. Experience to date is overwhelmingly indicative of this. Infantry troops need and should have tanks to go forward in the attack and those tanks should be organic so that combined training may be continuous.

The Chief of Staff also directed that figures should be prepared showing the cost in personnel of including the tank battalions in the division and at the same time providing an adequate GHQ reserve.[30]

The Army Ground Forces submitted its plea for reconsideration of the tank battalion question in two communications for the War Department, both dated 27 April 1945. One, commenting on the redeployment Troop Basis, pointed out that sufficient tank battalions were active to include one in each division and provide a GHQ reserve of approximately fifteen battalions.[31] The other stated the case for the organic battalion in greater detail, along the lines directed by the AGF Chief of Staff: [32]

> Such procedure [shifting of tank battalions from division to division] as confirmed in reports received from the Pacific has in many cases resulted in a lack of necessary infantry-tank coordination. Infantry troops need and should have tank support. In order that combined infantry-tank training may be continuous, it is believed that the only way to obtain satisfactory coordination is to provide a tank battalion as an organic part of the infantry division.

On 7 June 1945 the War Department G–3 replied that "advice from the theaters has indicated their desire to retain the Tank Battalions as separate units

---

[28] WD memo (R) WDGCT 320.3 (5 Apr 45) for CG AGF, 5 Apr 45, sub: "R" T/O&E's for Inf Div. 20.3/2 (Redepl) (R).

[29] AGF M/S (R), CofS to G–3, 13 Apr 45, sub: "R" T/O&E's for Inf Div. 320.3/2 (Redepl) (R).

[30] *Ibid.*

[31] AGF memo (S) CofS USA, attn G–3 Div., 27 Apr 45, sub: WD Redepl TB. 320.2/1 (Redepl UB) (S).

[32] AGF memo (C) for CofS USA, attn G–3 Div, 27 Apr 45, sub: "R" T/O&E's for Inf Divs. 320.3/1 Redepl) (C).

and not to provide for them as an organic part of the Infantry Division." [33] This statement came as a distinct surprise to the Army Ground Forces, since comments previously received from the commanders of ETO and MTOUSA had strongly indorsed organic tank battalions in infantry divisions. General MacArthur added his indorsement to the others early in June 1945, but his cablegram apparently was not received in the War Department before its disapproval of the AGF recommendation to make tank battalions organic parts of infantry divisions. [34]

About 20 June 1945 Maj. Gen. James G. Christiansen, Chief of Staff, Army Ground Forces, paid a visit to Maj. Gen. Idwal H. Edwards, G-3, War Department, and urged him, in view of the nearly unanimous advocacy of organic tank battalions by high combat commanders, to reconsider his disapproval of the plan. General Edwards indicated his willingness to reopen the matter and suggested that the Army Ground Forces present additional evidence to support its recommendation. [35]

Meanwhile, on 26 June 1945, the War Department sent General MacArthur a cable in substance as follows: [36]

1. Bearing these facts in mind, should 34 Infantry Divisions now in or scheduled for the Pacific each include an organic tank battalion?

a. Currently 21 tank battalions are in or scheduled for the Pacific. Additional battalions to bring the total to 34, plus any desired for use with corps or army, can be made available by stripping Pacific reserve and utilizing divisional units.

b. No additional tank battalions over those now set up for the Pacific can be lifted prior to March 1946 unless a corresponding setback in units and cargo space is nominated by you.

---

[33] WD memo (S) WDGCT 320 TB (27 Apr 45) for CG AGF, 7 Jun 45, sub: WD Redepl TB. 320.2/1 (Redepl TUB) (S). This was in reply specifically to the AGF memo referred to in footnote 31 above. The communication referred to in footnote 32 was not answered until 31 Jul 45. (See WD memo (C) WDGCT 320.3 (27 Apr 45) for CG AGF, 31 Jul 45, sub: Tk Bns in the Inf Div. 320.3/5 (Redepl) (C).) This memo of 31 Jul 45 rejected the organic tank battalions on the ground that (1) General MacArthur did not favor it and (2) not enough tanks were available to permit inclusion of a tank battalion in each company and division and at the same time equip the cannon and antitank companies with tanks as provided in the recently adopted "R" Tables of Organization and Equipment.

[34] (1) AGF M/S (S), Rqts-3 to CofS, 15 Jun 45, sub: Organic Tk Bns for Inf Div. With attached papers. (2) Paraphrase of rad (S) CM-In-7954 (9 Jun 45), signed MacArthur. Both in files of Orgn and Equip Div, AGF G-3 Sec files (S).

[35] AGF M/S (S), CofS to G-3, 21 Jun 45, sub: Organic Tk Bns for Inf Divs. 320.2/1 (Redepl TUB) (S).

[36] Paraphrase of rad (S) CM-Out-22195, 26 Jun 45. Orgn and Equip Div, AGF G-3 Sec files (S).

When confronted with the alternative of leaving the tank battalions out of the infantry divisions or putting them in at the expense of depleting his general reserve and breaking up some of his armored divisions, General MacArthur chose the former.[37] The War Department G–3 interpreted this as a withdrawal by General MacArthur of his previous indorsement of the organic tank battalion in the infantry division.[38] Believing further agitation futile, the Army Ground Forces let the matter lie.[39]

The AGF committee considered the advisability of recommending the inclusion of tank destroyer and antiaircraft battalions as organic parts of the infantry division.[40] Reports from theaters indicated that attachment of these units to divisions was not uncommon, and some commanders favored making them an integral part of the division. Sentiment for inclusion of the tank destroyer battalions apparently was stronger than for antiaircraft artillery, but in neither case was it as strong as support for the organic tank battalions.[41] The Tank Destroyer Center favored making the tank destroyer battalion part and parcel of the infantry division, and the Antiaircraft Command took a similar view with respect to the antiaircraft artillery battalions.[42] But the AGF committee and Headquarters, Army Ground Forces, took the position that the placing of tanks in the cannon and antitank companies of the infantry regiment and the addition of recoilless weapons to the division's armament, as provided in Plan 3, lessened the need of having the tank destroyers and antiaircraft guns habitually in support. Further objections were found in the size which the division would attain if antiaircraft and tank destroyer battalions were added to it.[43]

The Army Ground Forces sent Plans 1, 2, and 3 to the War Department on 8 March 1945 and recommended the adoption of Plan 3.[44] The division which

[37] Paraphrase of rad (S) CM–In–28225 (29 Jun 45), signed MacArthur, 29 Jun 45. Orgn and Equip Div, AGF G–3 Sec files (S).

[38] WD memo (C) WDGCT 320.3 (27 Apr 45) for CG AGF, 31 Jul 45, sub: Tk Bns in the Inf Div. 320.3/5 (Redepl) (Ç).

[39] Pencilled notation dated 1 Jul 45 by Col H. S. Schrader on AGF M/S (S), G–3 to CofS, 29 Jun 45, sub: Organic Tk Bns for Inf Div. 320.2/1 (Redepl TUB) (S).

[40] Rpt (S) of Committee on "R" T/O's for the Inf Div. 320.3/1 (Redepl) (S).

[41] See tabulation (C) of opinion of combat commanders, "What Weapons Does the RCT Normally Require in Combat?" 320.2/1 (Redepl TUB) (S).

[42] (1) TDC ltr (S) to CG AGF, 16 Feb 45, sub: Redepl T/O&E's. 320.3/1 (Redepl) (S). (2) AAC ltr (S) to CG AGF, 17 Feb 45, sub: Redepl T/O&E's. 320.2/1 (Redepl TUB) (S).

[43] Statement of Maj Gen A. W. Waldron to AGF Hist Off, 27 Nov 45.

[44] AGF memo (S) for CofS USA, attn G–3 Div, 8 Mar 45, sub: "R" T/O's for Inf Div. 320.3/1 (Redepl) (S).

the Army Ground Forces proposed after weeks of study covering the combat experience of all theaters was a much stronger unit than had been employed until then. In the first place, it was a large division—18,285 officers and men—larger by 2,771 than the division at the height of its expansion in 1942 prior to trimming by the Reduction Board, and approaching in size the square division—21,134 officers and men—of prewar days.[45] In the second place, it was a powerful division—stronger in fire power than the division which it was intended to supplant, thanks to the replacement of the 57-mm. antitank guns by larger-caliber 75-mm. recoilless rifles and higher velocity 90-mm. guns, addition of 57-mm. recoilless rifles to rifle companies, and increase of the proportion of 81-mm. mortars and heavy machine guns in heavy weapons companies. In the third place, it was a mobile division. The substitution of self-propelled for towed guns in the cannon and antitank companies and the replacement of the cumbersome truck-drawn 57-mm. guns in the antitank platoons by 57-mm. recoilless rifles, so light that they could be carried by one man, made for more rapid displacement than had been possible before. Fourth, the division proposed in Plan 3 was relatively free of the more flagrant deficiencies of the division which it was designed to replace, namely, inadequacy of communications, engineer, maintenance, transportation, and military police personnel to perform the services normally required in a division in combat. Finally, it was a more self-sufficient division than that provided by prior tables. With its organic tanks and its powerful recoilless rifles, it was better able to cope with enemy armor, machine-gun nests, pillboxes, and other strong points; with its enlarged reconnaissance troop, additional liaison planes, electronic countermortar facilities, and more ample communications set-up, it was better able to keep informed of enemy disposition and strength and to maintain contact with adjacent units; with its augmentations of trucks, drivers, cooks, medical assistants, quartermaster personnel, engineer-equipment operators, and ordnance-maintenance personnel, it had to depend less upon higher headquarters for services and was better prepared therefore to take care of itself for limited periods of independent or semi-independent operations.

In recommending such a division, the Army Ground Forces was saying in effect that the organization adopted in 1943 had been found wanting on the battlefield and that the Reduction Board had gone too far in its pruning. Reports from the theaters showed that the division prescribed in the 1943 tables was

---

[45] (1) T/O 7, 1 Nov 40. Files of Orgn and Equip Div, AGF G–3 Sec. (2) See above, Table No. 1 in "Reorganization of Ground Troops for Combat."

incapable of meeting the demands habitually required of it in combat and that as a result additional elements had to be attached on a more or less permanent basis. It was found that attachment had these disadvantages: (1) Service elements of the division (particularly ordnance, quartermaster, and medical units), already taxed to the limit by the demands of organic units, were incapable of handling the increased load of work. (2) Attached organizations could not be absorbed as completely in the team as units molded into the division by training and continuing combat association.

In 1943 General McNair had been following instructions from the War Department in reducing the division, but from the time of his experimentation with the proposed infantry division in 1937 he had shown his belief in the type of division set up by his Reduction Board. His basic concept in reorganizing the division in 1943 had been to give it self-sufficiency only for normal situations. In his program of training, a basic concept had been the division as a battle team. The verdict of division commanders after the experience of combat, backed by that of the theater commanders and ratified by his own headquarters, was that the infantry division as reorganized in 1943 could not meet normal situations in combat without the habitual attachment of certain other elements; in other words, that it had been so reduced in 1943 as to deprive it of maximum effectiveness as a battle team. In any case the final decision of the War Department in 1945, as in 1943, was that the lack of manpower available for combat made anything but a lean infantry division impracticable.[46]

One suggestion made by the Infantry School in connection with the "R" tables deserves special mention, namely, the addition of certain commissioned personnel, and the upgrading of others, in the division. The Infantry School recommended, in view of the heavy casualties among lieutenants, that a second lieutenant, second in command, be assigned to each rifle platoon. The Infantry School proposed further that rifle, heavy weapons, tank, antitank, service, and regimental headquarters companies should be commanded by majors; the infantry battalion by a colonel, with a lieutenant colonel as executive; and the infantry regiment (combat team) by a brigadier general with a colonel as executive (S–1 and S–2 of the regiment to be majors; S–3 and S–4 to be lieutenant colonels). In support of the recommendation to make the regimental com-

---

[46] For sources of this discussion of the division proposed under Plan 3 see (1) footnote 10 above; (2) statement of Col J. S. Sauer, Orgn and Equip Div, AGF G–3 Sec to AGF Hist Off, 13 Nov 45; and (3) statement of Maj Gen A. W. Waldron to AGF Hist Off, 27 Nov 45.

manders brigadier generals the Infantry School submitted the following argument: [47]

There is no reason why the commander of the infantry regiment or combat team of more than 3,000 men (the rough equivalent of four battalions) should be discriminated against in rank. The commander of the division artillery is a Brigadier General. He commands four battalions and less than 2,500 men. The fact that the infantry regimental commander must supervise and direct, under most difficult conditions, not only his own regiment, but attached units, a command greater in strength and in responsibility than that of the divisional artillery, should entitle him to equal rank with that of a division artillery commander.

The Infantry School also proposed elimination of the position of assistant division commander (stating that "there is no real need for the Brigadier General as assistant division commander") and increase of the divisional chief of staff's rank to brigadier general.[48]

The AGF committee did not concur in the proposals to assign additional lieutenants to the platoon and to increase the grade of company and battalion officers. However, it accepted and forwarded the recommendations for eliminating the assistant division commander, raising the grade of the regimental executive to colonel, and making the regimental commanders and division chief of staff brigadier generals.[49] All these proposals were disapproved by General Waldron, who gave as the primary reason for his disapproval the lack of any theater recommendation to support them. Referring specifically to the matter of regimental command, the Requirements Chief observed: [50]

The agitation to make the regimental commander a general was based on the assumption that it was normal for him to lead a combat team in overseas operations. This assumption was erroneous. Actually the employment of the division by regimental combat teams was the exception rather than the rule.

The Ground Chief of Staff supported the position of General Waldron, and none of the increases in rank proposed by the Infantry School was included in Plan 3 as forwarded to the War Department.

---

[47] Inf Sch ltr (S) to CG AGF, 17 Feb 45, sub: Redepl T/O&E's. 320.3/6 (Redepl) (S).
[48] *Ibid.*
[49] Rpt (S) of Committee on "R" T/O's for the Div. 320.3/1 (Redepl) (S).
[50] Statement of Maj Gen A. W. Waldron to AGF Hist Off, 27 Nov 45.

The WD "R" Tables

On 5 April 1945 the War Department notified the Army Ground Forces that the three plans submitted on 8 March had been studied and that "if personnel limitations were less critical, one of the plans or a modification thereof could well be adopted to provide a sound Infantry Division." But, stating its belief that the manpower situation would continue to be critical during redeployment, the War Department laid aside all three plans (though directing continuation of study of changes that might be made at a later date) and ordered submission of tables at the earliest practicable date providing the following specific changes: [51]

1. *Signal Company*—Addition of two construction teams and essential operation and maintenance personnel (total augmentation—40 enlisted men).
2. *Hq and Hq Co. Infantry Regiment*—Addition of communications personnel, counter-mortar section, and antitank mine platoon (total augmentation per regiment—2 officers and 61 enlisted men).
3. *Cannon Company*—Replacement of towed howitzers, by 9 tanks carrying 105-mm howitzers (strength—5 officers and 119 enlisted men).
4. *Antitank Company*—Redesignation as Infantry Destroyer Company, equipped with 9 tanks armed with 90-mm guns (strength—5 officers and 100 enlisted men).
5. *Rifle Company*—Addition of one rocket squad (7 enlisted men) to each rifle platoon (total augmentation—189 enlisted men per regiment).
6. *Heavy Weapons Company*—Transfer of antitank platoons from battalion head-quarters to heavy weapons company with no increase of personnel.
7. *Military Police Platoon*—To be replaced by a company (total augmentation—3 officers and 67 enlisted men).
8. *Hq & Hq Battery, Division Artillery*—Addition of counter-mortar personnel (total augmentation in division artillery—4 officers and 47 enlisted men).
9. *Field Artillery Battalion 105-mm Howitzer*—Addition of communications and counter-mortar personnel; inclusion in an augmentation column of personnel and equipment for increasing the firing battery from 4 to 6 guns if/and when specifically directed by the War Department.
10. *Field Artillery Battalion, 155-mm Howitzer*—Addition of communications personnel (17 enlisted men).

The increases directed by the War Department on 5 April amounted to approximately 900 officers and men for the whole division, which was slightly

[51] WD memo (R) 320.3 (5 Apr 45) for CG AGF, 5 Apr 45, sub: "R" T/O&E's for Inf Div. 320.3/2 (Redepl) (R).

less than half of the augmentation proposed by the Army Ground Forces under Plan 1—a plan which included only those increases deemed most essential on the basis of combat reports.[52] Moreover, the instructions of 5 April did not include certain changes previously directed by the War Department such as (1) elimination of dual functions, (2) increased intelligence personnel in the infantry regiment, and (3) additional fire-direction personnel, ammunition handlers, and forward observers in the field artillery. Furthermore, no maintenance personnel was added to the ordnance company to meet the increased load resulting from the placing of tanks in the cannon and antitank companies.[53]

The action of the War Department in trimming "R" tables to fit current personnel resources came as a surprise to Headquarters, Army Ground Forces, since earlier instructions from the War Department had indicated that in revamping the division permanent postwar needs were to be considered. Even previously declared minimum essential increases were now disallowed.[54]

During the weeks immediately preceding and following V-E Day, the War Department modified the restrictions laid down in the letter of 5 April to permit the setting up of a division approximately the size of that prescribed in Plan 1. Tables for the new division were submitted to the War Department on 14 May and published shortly thereafter. The "R" tables were dated 1 June 1945, but the specific War Department authority required for putting them into effect was withheld until October, when the 2d and 4th Divisions were directed to reorganize under the new tables.[55]

The tables as published on 1 June 1945 incorporated the changes outlined by the War Department in the letter of 5 April mentioned above and provided additional augmentations as follows: [56]

1. Postal personnel (1 officer and 5 enlisted men) and transport quartermaster teams in division headquarters.

---

[52] AGF M/S (R), Rqts–3 to CofS AGF, 19 Apr 45, sub: "R" T/O&E's for Inf Div. 320.3/2 (Redpl) (R).

[53] (1) *Ibid.* (2) AGF M/S (R), G–4 to G–2, 20 Apr 45, sub: "R" T/O&E's for Inf Div. 320.3/2 (Redpl) (R).

[54] These statements are based mainly on the following sources: (1) AGF M/S (R), Rqts–3 to CofS AGF, 19 Apr 45, sub: "R" T/O&E's for Inf Div. 320.3/2 (Redpl). (2) AGF M/S (R), G–4 to G–2, 20 Apr 45, sub and location as in (1). (3) Statement of Maj Gen A. W. Waldron to AGF Hist Off, 27 Nov 45.

[55] (1) Statement of Col J. S. Sauer to AGF Hist Off, 13 Nov 45. (2) AGF memo for CofS USA, 16 Oct 45, sub: Reorgn of Inf Divs. With related papers. 320.3/452 (Inf).

[56] AGF memo (R) for CofS USA, attn G–3 Div, 14 May 45, sub: "R" T/O&E's for Inf Div. 320.3/2 (Redpl) (R).

TABLE NO. 5

*Comparison of "R" Table Infantry Division with Old Division
and That Proposed by AGF Plan 3*

Personnel

UNIT	"R" TABLE DIVISION (1 Jun 45)			OLD DIVISION (1 Mar 45)			PLAN 3 (Proposed Div) (8 Mar 45)		
Division Headquarters.........	162			157			175		
Infantry........................	10,686			9,204			11,277		
Regiment (three).........		3,562			3,068			3,759	
Hq & Hq Co.........			175			104			197
Sv Co................			143			111			153
AT Co...............			101			159			105
Cn Co...............			101			114			124
Bn (three)...........			1,014			860			1,061
Hq & Hq Co......				93			121			115
HW Co..........				195			160			204
Rifle Co (three)...				242			193			247
Field Artillery.................	2,273			2,111			2,592		
Hq & Hq Btry, Div Arty...		130			114			150	
Light Arty Bn (three)......		538			497			609	
Hq Btry..............			158			126			159
Sv Btry..............			74			74			90
Firing Btry (three).....			102			99			120
Medium Arty Btry.........		529			506			615	
Hq Btry..............			126			112			142
Sv Btry..............			76			76			95
Firing Btry (three).....			109			106			126
Auxiliary Units................	2,226			2,055			2,953		
Cav Recon Tr.............		149			149			249	
Engr Bn..................		621			620			840	
Med Bn...................		467			443			607	
QM Co...................		186			186			246	
Ord Co...................		150			141			265	
Sig Co...................		306			239			371	Bn
MP Plat..................		176			106			176	Co
Div Hq Co...............		104			104			132	
Hq Sp Trs...............		9			9			9	
Band.....................		58			58			58	
Tank Battalion...............							664		
Hq & Sv Co..............								204	
Tk Co (four)..............								115	
Attached Medical.............	478			497			611		
Attached Chaplain............	13			13			13		
Entire Division................	15,838			14,037			18,285		

2. Enlargement of the ordnance maintenance company by 9 enlisted men to provide maintenance for the tanks in the cannon and antitank companies.

3. Addition of 27 enlisted men to the signal company and setting up of augmentation teams in the "Remarks" column to provide radio and message-center facilities for unusual operations.

TABLE NO. 5—Continued

Equipment

TYPE	"R" TABLE DIVISION (1 Jun 45)	OLD DIVISION (1 Mar 45)	PLAN 3 (Proposed Div) (8 Mar 45)
Rifle, cal. 30, M1................	7,223	6,349	7,975
Gun, machine, cal .30..........	229	211	268
Gun, machine, cal .50..........	244	237	243
Rifle, auto, cal .30..............	405	405	405
Mortar, 60-mm.................	81	90	81
Mortar, 81-mm.................	57	54	57
Launcher, rocket, antitank, 2.36-in	585	558	596
Gun, 57-mm....................	......	57	3
Gun, submachine, cal .45......	122	......	795
Howitzer, 105-mm.............	36	54	36
Howitzer, 105-mm, self-propelled......................	27	......	27
Howitzer, 155-mm.............	12	12	12
Carbine, cal .30...............	5,720	5,158	6,317
Pistol, cal .45.................	1,687	1,228	1,446
Rifle, recoilless, 57-mm........	81	......	81
Rifle, recoilless, 75-mm........	57	......	57
Gun, 90-mm...................	27	......	27
Vehicles (except boats and aircraft).....................	2,564	2,113	2,620

Sources: (1) T/O&E 7R, 1 Jun 45.
(2) T/O&E 7, 24 Jan 45.
(3) Proposed T/O&E 7R and allied tables (mimeographed, tentative), Plan 3, dated 26 Feb 45. In files of Orgn and Equip Div, AGF G–3 Sec.

4. Consolidation of all the division's dentists in the medical battalion, for attachment to units as required, and increase of the medical battalion by 5 enlisted men (first sergeant, cook, mechanic, and 2 dental technicians).

The strength of the division prescribed in the 1 June tables was 15,838 (787 officers, 44 warrant officers, and 15,007 enlisted men). Details of personnel and equipment are set forth in Table No. 5. A breakdown of components is given in the Chart "Organization and Equipment of Infantry Division, 1 June 1945." [57]

The division which finally emerged on 1 June after months of study and planning was an improvement over that which it supplanted in that it had

[57] The discrepancy between the aggregate strength of the division indicated by the chart (15,868) and the total of 15,838 indicated by Table No. 5 is due to the fact that attached medical personnel were reduced by thirty enlisted men after preparation of the chart and before issuance of the printed table (T/O&E 7R) on which the chart is based.

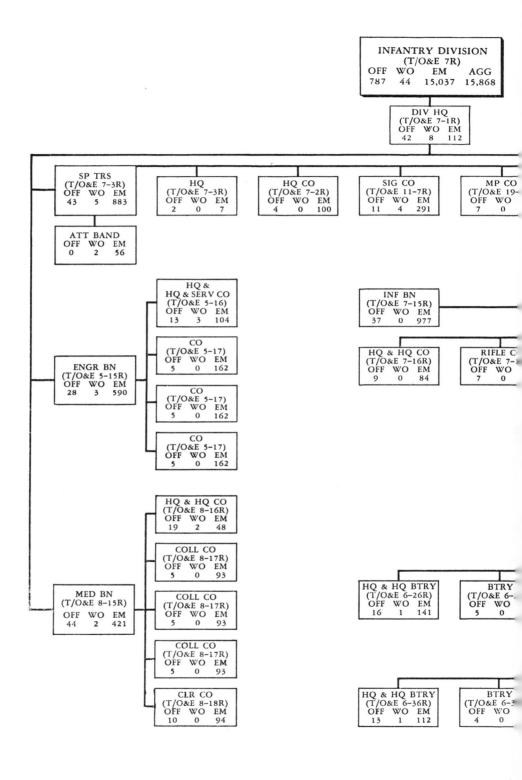

INFANTRY DIVISION
(T/O&E 7R)

OFF	WO	EM	AGG
787	44	15,037	15,868

DIV HQ
(T/O&E 7–1R)

OFF	WO	EM
42	8	112

SP TRS
(T/O&E 7–3R)

OFF	WO	EM
43	5	883

HQ
(T/O&E 7–3R)

OFF	WO	EM
2	0	7

HQ CO
(T/O&E 7–2R)

OFF	WO	EM
4	0	100

SIG CO
(T/O&E 11–7R)

OFF	WO	EM
11	4	291

MP CO
(T/O&E 19-)

OFF	WO
7	0

ATT BAND

OFF	WO	EM
0	2	56

HQ &
HQ & SERV CO
(T/O&E 5–16)

OFF	WO	EM
13	3	104

INF BN
(T/O&E 7–15R)

OFF	WO	EM
37	0	977

CO
(T/O&E 5–17)

OFF	WO	EM
5	0	162

HQ & HQ CO
(T/O&E 7–16R)

OFF	WO	EM
9	0	84

RIFLE C
(T/O&E 7–)

OFF	WO
7	0

ENGR BN
(T/O&E 5–15R)

OFF	WO	EM
28	3	590

CO
(T/O&E 5–17)

OFF	WO	EM
5	0	162

CO
(T/O&E 5–17)

OFF	WO	EM
5	0	162

HQ & HQ CO
(T/O&E 8–16R)

OFF	WO	EM
19	2	48

COLL CO
(T/O&E 8–17R)

OFF	WO	EM
5	0	93

COLL CO
(T/O&E 8–17R)

OFF	WO	EM
5	0	93

HQ & HQ BTRY
(T/O&E 6–26R)

OFF	WO	EM
16	1	141

BTRY
(T/O&E 6–)

OFF	WO
5	0

MED BN
(T/O&E 8–15R)

OFF	WO	EM
44	2	421

COLL CO
(T/O&E 8–17R)

OFF	WO	EM
5	0	93

CLR CO
(T/O&E 8–18R)

OFF	WO	EM
10	0	94

HQ & HQ BTRY
(T/O&E 6–36R)

OFF	WO	EM
13	1	112

BTRY
(T/O&E 6–3)

OFF	WO
4	0

Organization and Equipment of Infantry Division,
1 June 1945 (Proposed T/O&E 7R)

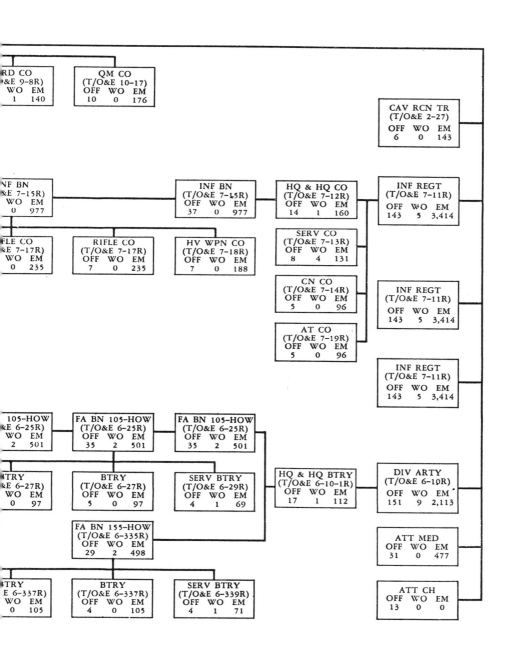

more adequate communications, postal, and military police facilities; was less vulnerable, in view of the radar teams, to enemy mortars; was more mobile and possessed of more striking power by virtue of its tanks and recoilless guns. But it fell far short of the division which the Army Ground Forces envisioned in Plan 3. Dual assignment was not eliminated; intelligence facilities of the infantry regiment were not augmented; and only small increases were made in the strength of the ordnance and medical organizations and none at all in the reconnaissance troop, the quartermaster company, and the engineer battalion.[58] In short, the division set up in June 1945 incorporated to only a limited extent the lessons learned on the field of combat.[59]

On 27 May 1945 the Army Ground Forces invited the War Department's attention to the fact that personnel resources under Ground control were not adequate to supply the additional officers and men (1,801 for each division) required for reorganizing under the "R" Tables.[60] Two days later the War Department directed ETO and MTO either to reorganize the divisions under the new tables prior to their departure from Europe or to ship the required augmentations in separate detachments, in order that reorganization might be effected in the United States.[61] In July plans were changed to provide the following: (1) piecemeal reorganization of divisions already in the Pacific as equipment and personnel became available and as operations permitted; (2) shipment of the first divisions redeployed through the United States with 1,800 overstrength, for reorganization by General MacArthur; and (3) reorganization in the United States of the last five divisions redeployed from personnel provided by ETO and MTO. But on account of delay in the departure of "augmentation packets" from Europe, it was necessary just before V-J Day to change plans again and to order shipment of the first redeployed divisions to the Pacific without additional strength.[62]

While the "R" Tables were in preparation the War Department approved a recommendation made by the Army Ground Forces in January 1945 to add a

---

[58] (1) AGF memo (R) for CofS USA, attn G–3 Div, 14 May 45, sub: "R" Tables of Orgn and Equip for Inf Div. 320.3/2 (Redepl) (R).

[59] AGF M/S, Inf Branch to Col Frasier, 11 May 45, sub: "R" T/O&E's for Inf Div. Orgn and Equip Div, AGF G–3 Sec files.

[60] AGF memo (C) for CofS USA, attn G–3 Div, 27 May 45, sub: Pers for "R" Tables. 320.3/2 (Redepl) (C).

[61] WD D/F (C) WDGCT, 320.3 to CG AGF, 6 Jun 45, sub: Pers for "R" Tables. 320.3/2 (Redepl) (C).

[62] AGF M/S (S) for Rqts. 8 Aug 45, sub: CM–Out–37395. 370.5/25. (Redepl) (S).

fourth regiment to each infantry division scheduled for redeployment.[63] This change was based on the necessity of giving infantry more respite from front-line duty than had previously been practicable. It was intended that the four regiments should be rotated in such a way as to permit each to spend about one-fourth of the time in rest and recuperation.

In May 1945 the Army Ground Forces proposed that the first of the twenty-nine additional regiments required for implementation of the new plan be formed from the separate infantry regiments that had been used for training replacements and that others be organized from the replacement stream as personnel became available. The basis of the suggestion was the belief that some regiments should be sent immediately to General MacArthur to provide relief for units suffering from battle weariness and that others should be available for redeployment training with the first divisions returning from Europe.[64]

The War Department disapproved the proposal to utilize the separate infantry regiments for rotational purposes and directed instead that the regiments required for implementation of the plan be taken from divisions constituting the strategic reserve.[65] The War Department justified this action on the ground that it would cause less disruption to supply phases of redeployment than the AGF plan and that regiments taken from reserve divisions would be better fitted for relief missions than units formed from replacement personnel in the United States.[66] In June 1945 the Army Ground Forces noted with concern that the War Department plan would reduce to three the number of reserve infantry divisions; but because of the victory over Japan in August the War Department proposal was not carried out.[67]

---

[63] (1) AGF memo (C) for CofS USA, 6 Jan 45, sub: Improvement of Inf Fighting Power. (See particularly Tabs B & I.) Separate inclosure. 000.7/121 (Inf Prog) (C). (2) AGF memo (S) for CofS USA, 13 Mar 45, sub: Combat Tour of Inf Men. 000.7/12 (Inf Prog) (S). (3) AGF memo (S) for CofS USA, 10 May 45, sub: Inf Rqts for Rotation. 320.2/14 (Redepl) (S). (4) WD D/F (S) WDGCT 322 (10 May 45) to CG AGF, 23 May 45, sub: Inf Rqts for Rotation. 320.2/14 (Redepl) (S).

[64] During the Italian campaign General Lucian Truscott reported: "The division [3d Infantry Division] was relieved from action on 17 November after 59 consecutive days of offensive action against German forces employing delaying and defensive action. During this period of 59 days, the division sustained 3,144 battle casualties and 5,446 nonbattle casualties, a total loss of 8,590." See AGF memo (S) for CofS USA, 1 Feb 44, sub: Inf Strength in the Inf Div. 000.7/5 (Inf Prog) (S).

[65] WD D/F (S) WDGCT (10 May 45) to CG AGF, sub: Inf Regts for Rotation. 320.2/14 (Redepl) (S).

[66] Memo (S) of Gen J. E. Hull, OPD for Gen Handy, DCofS USA, 30 May 45, sub: 4th Inf Regt per Div. 322/7 (Divs) (S).

[67] AGF M/S (S), G-3 to CofS AGF, 18 Jun 45, sub: 4th Inf Regt Proposed for Rotation in Inf Divs. 320.2/4 (Redepl TUB) (S).

III. AGF Liaison
at War Department and ASF
Installations

Readjustment following the defeat of Germany called for an unprecedented amount of collaboration between the major commands. To represent AGF interests in collaborative activities, the Army Ground Forces appointed liaison officers at ports of embarkation and debarkation and at War Department personnel centers (consolidated agencies operated by the Army Service Forces for execution of certain Army-wide personnel functions), and extended liaison previously established at hospitals and redistribution stations.

Port Liaison

A gesture toward AGF liaison at ports of embarkation had been made in the fall of 1942, when at General Marshall's direction a small command group representing each of the major forces but commanded by the port commander was established at each staging area to assist in the supervision of nondivisional units; the major forces were directed to maintain liaison with their respective command groups. For various reasons, but mainly because he was averse to entering activities which he did not command, General McNair did not designate AGF personnel for port-command groups, choosing instead to let port commanders fill the positions with ASF personnel. Moreover, the liaison specified by General Marshall was delegated by the Army Ground Forces to commanders of armies and corps, who were instructed "to render such assistance as may be required by the port commanders as may be practicable." The liaison maintained under this system was largely nominal. To all practical effect, AGF units lost contact with the Army Ground Forces when they boarded the troop trains at camp and headed for a staging area.[1]

The "hands-off-after-they-leave-our-command-attitude" of General McNair was not shared by some of the officers of his staff, particularly those whose activities brought them in close touch with units during their final days under AGF control.[2] After General McNair departed from the Army Ground Forces, the Task Force Division of the Ground G–4 Section began to urge the establishment of permanent liaison at ports of embarkation, largely on the basis of its experience in maintaining liaison with ASF authorities at the Elmira Holding and Reconsignment Point and of visits of G–4 officers to ports to instruct AGF personnel in cold-weather equipment. G–4 of the Army Ground Forces in February 1945 recommended the assignment of AGF liaison detachments at each of the principal ports of embarkation.[3]

He proposed not only that these detachments be charged with assisting outgoing units through ports of embarkation but also that they serve AGF personnel returning from overseas in redeployment. G–4 noted in passing that the Army Air Forces had for some time maintained command groups at each port to advise and assist outgoing and incoming AAF personnel. The Chief of Staff of the Army Ground Forces on 21 March approved in principle the establishment of liaison detachments but directed that action be suspended until V-E Day could be definitely predicted.[4]

A few days after the AGF Chief of Staff made this decision, the port liaison plan received support from a source outside the Army Ground Forces. On 25 March 1945 General Marshall, who had been greatly disturbed by reports that returnees from overseas were being treated in such a way as to cause them to feel that they were "not wanted," wrote a personal letter to General Stilwell, Commanding General of the Army Ground Forces, stating:[5]

From the moment the man reaches the United States, Ground Force influence should become apparent to him and should continue until he is separated from the service or

---

[1] (1) See AGF Historical Section, Preparation of Units for Overseas Movement. (2) AGF M/S, G–4 to CofS AGF, 22 Feb 45, sub: Ln Det at PE's. 322/4 (AGF Ln Dets).

[2] Statement of Lt Col J. A. Hanson, G–4 TF Div to AGF Hist Off, 2 Jun 45.

[3] (1) *Ibid.* (2) AGF M/S, G–4 to CofS AGF, 22 Feb 45, sub: Ln Det at PE's. 322/4 (AGF Ln Dets).

[4] AGF M/S, CofS AGF to G–4, 21 Mar 45, sub: Ln Det at PE's. 322/4 (AGF Ln Dets).

[5] Personal ltr of Gen G. C. Marshall to Gen J. W. Stilwell, 25 Mar 45. 220.3/19 (O'seas Return).

becomes a permanent responsibility of another command. Effective orientation and care in assignment are of evident importance. . . . Many of these returnees will be discharged during the redeployment period and it is highly desirable that the final months of their military service should leave no basis for bitterness in the years to come, as was so frequently the case in 1919.

General Marshall concluded his note with this important statement:

The responsibilities placed on the Army Ground Forces when the army was reorganized in 1942 were essentially those pertaining to training. It may be that to accomplish the purpose I have in mind your responsibilities should be restated. Please look into this matter and if you need modification of any War Department instructions let me have your suggestions.

General Stilwell, believing a restatement of AGF responsibilities unnecessary, immediately took steps to accomplish the object sought by General Marshall. On 29 March the Army Ground Forces wrote to the Army Service Forces asking for concurrence in the establishment of AGF liaison detachments at ports of embarkation and debarkation. The Army Service Forces promptly gave a favorable response.[6]

Stationing of liaison personnel at ports was initiated in May 1945.[7] While separate staffs were commonly set up for embarkation and debarkation liaison at a given port, both were under the supervision of the senior AGF liaison officer stationed at that port, and there was considerable exchange of assistance between the two staffs.[8]

On 10 May Headquarters, Army Ground Forces, instructed port liaison officers in their duties. Their mission with reference to debarking personnel consisted mainly of the following matters: welcoming returnees; impressing upon them the interest of the Army Ground Forces in their welfare; providing them with available information concerning leaves or furloughs, new stations, and plans for reequipping units upon arrival at assembly station; obtaining and forwarding to Headquarters, Army Ground Forces, information on status of personnel, equipment, and training; and furnishing publicity material on Ground personnel to port public relations officers and to the AGF Special Information Section. The mission with respect to outgoing personnel included making recommendations on training in staging areas (in coordination with the AGF Command Group); filling equipment and personnel shortages that

[6] AGF ltr to ASF, 29 Mar 45, sub: Ln Dets at Ports of Embarkation and Debarkation. With attached papers. 322/4 (AGF Ln Dets).

[7] AGF ltr to CG ASF, 4 May 45, sub: Asgmt of AGF Ln Off. 322/4 (AGF Ln Dets).

[8] Statement of Maj H. T. Sears, AGF AG Sec to AGF Hist Off, 15 Jan 46.

developed after departure from the home station; correcting deficiencies noted in The Inspector General's Preparation for Overseas Movement (POM) inspection report; and assuring officers and men of the Ground commander's interest in their future well-being. Liaison personnel were reminded that while representing the Commanding General, Army Ground Forces, they were subject to the command jurisdiction of port authorities. They were warned specifically against imposing any delay in the processing or movement of units of individuals.[9]

Original plans called for the stationing of two AGF officers at each port, but, as redeployment movement increased, liaison detachments were enlarged.[10] On 31 August 1945 port liaison officers totaled forty-eight.[11]

Liaison at Personnel Centers

Liaison at War Department personnel installations had its origin in October 1943, with assignment of AGF officers at reception stations.[12] In May 1944 liaison was established at reception centers;[13] but liaison staffs at these installations were small and their functions were limited largely to matters of classification and assignment.[14] After the War Department established personnel centers by bringing reception centers and other personnel agencies under small supervisory

---

[9] AGF ltr to Port Ln Offs, 10 May 45, sub: Instructions to Ln Offs of AGF at Ports of Embarkation and Debarkation. 322/12 (AGF Ln Dets).

[10] (1) AGF M/S, G–4 to CofS, 22 Feb 45, sub: Ln Dets at PEs. (2) AGF ltr to CG ASF, 4 May 45, sub: Asgmt of AGF Ln Offs. Both in 322/4 (AGF Ln Dets).

[11] Roster of officers assigned to Hq AGF, 31 Aug 45. 330.3 (AGF). Distribution of officers was as follows:

Port	No. of Officers
New York	14
San Francisco	8
Boston	7
Seattle	7
Los Angeles	4
Hampton Roads	3
New Orleans	2
Miami (Port of Aerial Embarkation)	1
New York (Port of Aerial Embarkation)	1
Washington (Port of Aerial Embarkation)	1

[12] Information provided AGF Hist Off by Maj H. T. Sears, AGF AG Sec, 15 Jan 45.

[13] AGF M/S, G–1 to CofS, 15 May 44, sub: Physical Profile Plan. With attached papers, 220.01/3 (Phys Prof.

[14] Statement of Maj H. T. Sears, AGF AG Sec to AGF Hist Off, 15 Jan 46.

headquarters, the Army Ground Forces extended liaison functions to separation centers and brought the previously established liaison activities at reception centers and reception stations under the senior liaison officer, known as "the AGF Liaison Officer," stationed by War Department directive at each personnel center.[15]

The War Department on 1 March 1945 prescribed in general terms the functions to be performed by liaison staffs of the three major commands at personnel centers.[16] The Army Ground Forces on 2 May 1945 outlined in detail the duties of its own liaison teams.[17] The effect of these directives was to extend liaison activities considerably beyond classification and assignment into larger matters of preparing returnees psychologically for further and effective participation in the war, or return to civilian life, as the case might be.[18]

Liaison functions may best be presented by describing the operations of the AGF liaison staff at a hypothetical but typical War Department center as of early July 1945.[19]

Trains coming directly from port unloaded the returnees at the reception station. After the men had cleaned up, turned in their uniforms for laundry or salvage, and donned fatigue suits (which they were to wear until processing was completed), they were divided into groups, according to major command. The group belonging to the Army Ground Forces was escorted to an assembly room in the Ground area of the reception station, where the AGF liaison officer, a lieutenant colonel, speaking on behalf of the Commanding General, Army Ground Forces, delivered a brief address of welcome. Following this talk each

---

[15] (1) Cir 329, WD, 10 Aug 44. (2) AGF ltr to TAG, 13 Apr 45, sub: Liaison Pers of the AGF at WD Pers Cens. 322/5 (AGF Ln Dets). (3) AGF ltr to AGF Ln Offs, 2 May 45, sub: Ln Pers of AGF at WD Pers Cens. 322/9 (AGF Ln Dets). (4) Statement of Maj H. T. Sears, AGF AG Sec, to AGF Hist Off, 15 Jan 46.

[16] Cir 67, WD, 1 Mar 45.

[17] AGF ltr to AGF Ln Offs, 2 May 45, sub: Ln Pers of the AGF at WD Pers Cens. 322/9 (AGF Ln Dets).

[18] Ordinarily the Ground liaison staff at a personnel center was divided into three sections, one each for the reception station, separation center, and reception center. Since processing of returnees constituted the major activity, most of the liaison staff served the reception station. If, for example, a staff consisted of six officers, four would have their desks at the reception station, one at the reception center, and one at the separation center. But there was a considerable amount of collaboration among all elements of the liaison staff. Statement of Maj H. T. Sears, AGF AG Sec to AGF Hist Off, 15 Jan 46, and of Lt Col John G. Bennett, AGF Ln Off, WD Pers Cen, Cp Shelby, Miss, 6 Jul 45.

[19] This account of liaison operations is based primarily on personal observations of the AGF Historical Officer at War Department Personnel Centers, Camp Chaffee, Ark., 3 July 45, and Camp Shelby, Miss., 5–6 July 45, and statements on those dates of members of the liaison staffs of these centers to the AGF Historical Officer.

man was given a mimeographed letter of welcome which it was presumed he would read during the course of his processing.[20]

[20] The following is a copy of the letter of welcome issued by the AGF Liaison Officer at the War Department Personnel Center, Camp Shelby, Miss., as of 6 July 45:

ARMY GROUND FORCES WELCOMES YOU HOME

On behalf of General Jacob L. Devers, Commander of Army Ground Forces, I welcome you to Reception Station #5. Your stay here will be brief; less than 24 hours. The more you cooperate in the processing, the faster you will leave. We want you to get out on furlough, have a swell time, forget your worries. But there are a few helpful hints and reminders for your furlough.

SECURITY. We are still at war with Japan and our buddies are over there fighting. Talk of troop movements, new equipment, strength of units, training and the like, can be of great aid to the enemy and may even kill one of your own friends. So keep buttoned up as far as specific facts go. If you are asked to make any sort of public statement, first clear it with an Army Public Relations Officer.

CONDUCT. Act like a man and a soldier! You can still have all the fun you want and stay out of trouble. Your family and friends are proud of you! Don't let them down. Play square with the MP's and you will find they're your friends. They'll give you help if you need it. Carry your orders with you at all times. Don't waste your money on unauthorized uniforms—in most places, you won't be allowed to wear them. Stick to GI clothing—it's the best there is. Wear those decorations and stripes— you've earned them.

COMPLIANCE WITH ORDERS. Your orders will tell you where to report and the date of reporting. Make sure you get there on time. If you should lose all your money and need transportation, turn into the nearest military post for transportation. This *will* be charged against your three cents per mile, if you are paying your own way.

ILLNESS. If you are taken ill while en route or at home, report to the nearest military hospital and have them notify your next station. Your furlough will be extended for the length of time you are in the hospital. If serious emergency prevents your getting to a military hospital, have the military authorities notified at the first possible time. A word about extensions of furlough:—extensions will be granted only when cleared through the Red Cross. *DO NOT* wire this station direct for an extension, but have your local Red Cross contact the Red Cross at the station to which you are to report at the end of your furlough.

FURLOUGH ADDRESS. Any mail coming to this station will be forwarded to the furlough address you give us. However, you may travel anywhere in the United States as long as you have a copy of your orders with you. But keep in touch with your furlough address.

VENEREAL DISEASE. You all know the story on VD—it's trouble any way you look at it. Play it safe, the way you've been taught in the Army. *Don't let VD ruin your furlough!*

RATIONING. Rationing is a big word in civilian life today. Shoes, gasoline and food are rationed. Here's the way we help you out. You can get a ration coupon for one pair of shoes before you leave here. This coupon is good for 30 days in any civilian store or PX. Your local ration board will give you a gallon of gasoline for each day of furlough and a full civilian allowance of food ration points upon presentation of your orders. Cigarettes are not rationed in civilian life, but like many other luxuries, you usually can't get them. You will be given a tobacco ration card here before you leave, so stock up at the PX.

If you have any further questions, don't hesitate to ask any of the officers or men in the AGF Liaison Office. We're here to help you and make your furlough as pleasant as possible. Have a fine furlough and—   *GOOD LUCK!*

JOHN G. BENNETT, Lt. Colonel, Infantry, AGF Liaison Officer

After the address of welcome the men were lined up for interview by a crack corps of enlisted liaison assistants, most of whom were veterans of several campaigns. The principal purpose of this interview was to examine the returnees' service records—the Form 20 (which had been turned over to the liaison staff as soon as the train came in)—to see that their Specification Serial Numbers (SSN) had been properly listed and to check the accuracy of Adjusted Service Rating (ASR) scores. Returnees whose status was such as to require special attention were sent to one of the liaison officers for interview.

At the conclusion of the interviews, soldiers who had ASR scores of 85 (the current "critical score") or above, and who did not fall into one of the 17 "scarce categories" listed by the Army Ground Forces, were escorted in groups of about 50 to the separation center, which was about a half-mile distant from the reception station. There the Ground returnees were received by the AGF officer allotted to that installation. This officer made known his availability for assistance in all phases of the separation process. As the men waited their turn for medical examination, checked their souvenirs for safekeeping, lined up for final payment, and performed various other details of the separation process, they were visited occasionally by the liaison officer, who circulated among them making inquiry as to their progress and demonstrating in sundry ways the interest of the Army Ground Forces in their well-being. When bottlenecks slowed the flow of proceedings, the AGF officer did not hesitate to call the situation to the attention of responsible separation-center officers. At the conclusion of the processing, the men turned in their fatigues and drew a clean uniform, a new pair of shoes, and a ration check for a pair of civilian shoes. They were en route home within forty-eight hours of their arrival at the reception station.[21]

[21] Personal ltr of Lt Col John G. Bennett to AGF Hist Off, 17 Jul 45. 314.7 (AGF Hist).
SSN's listed as scarce in July 1945 were as follows:

187—Repeaterman Telephone	790—Weather Observer-Teletype Technician
077—Powerhouse Engr (Minimum 2 Years Power or Substation Opr Experience)	798—Transmitter Attendant, Fixed Station
080—Marine Engineer	801—Cryptographic Repairman (Designated Equipment)
267—Translator (Asiatic Language)	808—Cryptanalysis Technician
320—Interpreter (Asiatic Language)	953—Radar Repairman, Reporting Equipment (Designated Set) (Instr)
366—Orthopedic Mechanic	Acoustic Technican (College Graduate with Maj in Speech or Acoustics Plus Experience in Fitting Hearing Aids)
538—Voice Interpreter (Asiatic Language)	
543—Radio Intelligence Control Chief	
709—Traffic Analyst (Radio)	Electro Encephalographic Specialist
739—Intercept Operator, J	

Men not eligible for separation went from their interview with the AGF liaison staff to adjoining rooms occupied by ASF reception-station personnel. Here they received furlough orders and pay. The final step in their processing was the exchange of the fatigue suits for two clean uniforms. If the men belonged to units undergoing redeployment, their orders required their return to the reception station at the end of the recuperation furlough. If they were casuals they were directed to proceed from their homes to an appropriate AGF camp for temporary assignment to a casual battalion.

Liaison officers at the reception station, as at the separation center, made it a practice to move about among the men throughout the processing so that they would be readily available in case assistance was desired. The stay of most redeployees at reception stations did not exceed twenty-four hours.

On V-E Day AGF liaison officers at War Department personnel centers aggregated 80.[22] By 25 August 1945 the number had increased to 119.[23]

Liaison at Hospitals and Redistribution Centers

Liaison at hospitals had its inception in September 1944 when a small group of officers and men from Headquarters, Army Ground Forces, made an informal visit to AGF patients at Walter Reed General Hospital. Reactions to this and subsequent calls were so favorable that the Army Ground Forces in February 1945 obtained permission of the Commanding General, Army Service Forces, to station an AGF liaison team of one officer and one enlisted man at each general and convalescent hospital to assist Ground patients in matters of pay, allotments, promotions, decorations, recovery of personal effects, and other personal affairs.[24]

A Personal Affairs Branch was set up in the G–1 Section of AGF headquarters to administer the new program. In addition, two officers were allotted to each of the subordinate armies, and one to the 1st Headquarters and Headquarters Detachment, Special Troops, Army Ground Forces, to inspect and report on the

---

[22] AGF ltr to AGF Ln Offs, 2 May 45, sub: Ln Pers of the AGF at WD Pers Cens. 322/9 (AGF Ln Dets).

[23] Information furnished AGF Historical Officer by Capt F. Docky, AGF AG Sec, 28 Jan 46.

[24] (1) "History of Miscellaneous Division, G–1 Section AGF." Prepared in November 1945 by Lt Col P. J. Kopcsak, Chief of the Personal Affairs Branch, Misc Div, G–1 Section; this study will be cited hereafter as Hist of Misc Div. Files of Misc Div, AGF G–1 Sec. (2) AGF ltr to CG ASF, 21 Feb 45, sub: AGF Ln Pers to ASF Gen Hospitals and Independent Convalescent Hospitals. With related papers. 322/1 (AGF Ln Dets).

liaison activities in their respective areas. In April 1945, eighty selected officers and eighty enlisted men, all of whom were combat veterans, were assigned to Headquarters, Army Ground Forces, and sent to the ASF School for Personnel Services at Lexington, Va., for a month of instruction in personal affairs guidance. By a special arrangement officers of Headquarters, Army Ground Forces, gave orientation lectures to Ground liaison personnel attending this school. In May 1945, 69 officers and 37 enlisted men, all of whom were graduates of the school for personnel services, were assigned to 63 general hospitals and 5 convalescent hospitals. In June liaison was extended to the 26 Regional Hospitals in the United States. To assist liaison staffs in accomplishing their mission the Personal Affairs Branch of Headquarters, Army Ground Forces, prepared a manual known as the Hospital Liaison SOP which incorporated data from the personal affairs course given at Lexington, Va., and from War Department policies pertinent to hospitalized and returned personnel. Liaison officers were authorized to supplement their staffs by selecting officers from ambulatory patients to act as their assistants. All in all, 438 patients were used as assistants during the period June through August.[25]

AGF liaison officers were busy people. They were called on for assistance on questions ranging from marital difficulties to fleecings by used-car dealers. It was not uncommon for their assistance to be invoked by patients whose principal need was the companionship of a friendly listener. Because of their service in confessor roles, some of the liaison officers referred to themselves as assistant chaplains. They were kept busy with such problems as obtaining full credit for awards, decorations, and battle participation, since the part played by those items in computation of ASR scores made patients particularly anxious to have them complete; location of baggage and personal effects delayed or lost in transit; conversion of insurance; adjustment of pay and allotments; securing of veterans benefits; and determination of the patient's status and disposition. In June, July, and August 1945, liaison officers counselled 132,153 AGF patients out of a total of 510,297 AGF personnel hospitalized during this period.[26]

---

[25] Hist of Misc Div. Files of Misc Div, AGF G–1 Sec.

[26] (1) AGF ltr (R) to CGs Second and Fourth Armies and 1st Hq and Hq Dets, Sp Trs, AGF, 12 May 45, sub: Personal Affairs. 322/2 (AGF Ln Dets) (R). (2) Personal observations of the AGF Hist Off at the Hospital Cen, Cp Carson, Colo, 29 Jun 45, and statement on that date of Capt Paul W. Smith, AGF Ln Off Hosp Cen, Cp Carson, to AGF Hist Off. (3) Hist of Misc Div. Files of Misc Div, AGF G–1 Sec.

Headquarters, Army Ground Forces, decided in July 1944 to place liaison officers at AGF–ASF redistribution stations.[27] These, like the personnel centers, were War Department installations operated by the Army Service Forces. They were established in the summer of 1944 as a result of General Marshall's expressed desire to provide recuperation and reassignment facilities for AGF and ASF returnees comparable to those previously provided at his direction for AAF personnel.[28] The mission of the AGF–ASF redistribution stations as prescribed by the War Department was "to obtain maximum utilization of personnel of the Army Ground Forces and Army Service Forces returned to the United States from overseas stations for reassignment, by painstaking occupational and physical classification, mental and physical reconditioning, orientation, reindoctrination and reassignment carried on without haste in an environment characterized by mental and physical relaxation and comfort." [29]

Redistribution stations superseded the War Department Personnel Reassignment Centers created early in 1944. Ground liaison staffs at these centers were transferred to redistribution stations, and additional personnel was procured from other sources as required by expansion of the redistribution system.[30] At the peak of its growth this system consisted of six hotel-type stations and two post installations.[31]

Work of AGF liaison personnel at redistribution stations consisted largely of greeting AGF returnees, advising them in the adjustment of their personal affairs, answering inquiries as to AGF assignment policies, and in sundry other ways seeking to impress upon them the pride of the AGF commander in their past achievement and his interest in their future well-being.[32]

All returnees earmarked for service under the Army Ground Forces by redistribution station authorities were turned over to AGF liaison officers, who in turn referred them to Headquarters, Army Ground Forces, (officers to G–1,

[27] AGF M/S, G–1 to CofS, 8 Jul 44, sub: Ln Offs for AGF–ASF Redist Stations. 354.1/3 (Redist Sta).

[28] (1) Memo of Gen G. C. Marshall for Gen L. J. McNair, 12 Apr 44, sub not given. 354.1/1 (Redist Cens) (C). (2) Cir 303, WD, 17 Jul 44. 353.02/666 (AGF).

[29] (1) WD memo (C) for CG ASF, 6 May 44, sub: Establishment of Redist Cens. 354.1/4 (Redist Cens) (C). (2) Cir 303, WD, 17 Jul 44. 353.02/666 (AGF).

[30] AGF M/S, G–1 to CofS AGF, 8 Jul 44, sub: Ln Offs at AGF–ASF Redist Stations. 354.1/3 (Redist Sta).

[31] (1) ASF memo SPGAA 210.3 Gen (7 Aug 44)—300 for CG AGF, 7 Aug 44, sub: AGF and ASF Redist Stations. 354.1/5 (Redist Sta). (2) ASF memo SPGAH 210.3 Gen (26 Feb 44)—300 for WD G–1, 5 Mar 45, sub: Redist Stations. 354.1/13 (Redist Sta).

[32] Organizational and Functional Chart (as of 24 May 45), AGF Ln Sec, Hot Springs, Ark. 354.1/16 (Redist Sta).

enlisted men to the Classification and Replacement Division) for assignment.[33]

Officers of Headquarters, Army Ground Forces, who visited the redistribution stations at Miami and Asheville in March 1945 reported that cooperation between AGF liaison officers and redistribution station personnel was good. They found deficiencies, however, in liaison administration: liaison personnel were not in sufficiently close touch with Headquarters, Army Ground Forces, to answer adequately the questions put to them by returnees; and at Miami not all returning AGF officers were interviewed by the liaison staff. Steps were taken to correct these deficiencies.[34]

On 19 May 1945, G–1 of the Army Ground Forces reported that the average monthly flow of AGF personnel through all AGF–ASF redistribution stations for the previous six months had been as follows: [35]

Rotational Personnel	5, 138
Battle Casualties	1, 409
Casual Returnees	161
Escaped Prisoners	11
TOTAL	6, 719

In May 1945 the War Department suspended rotation of AGF and ASF personnel for all theaters.[36] Because of this action and because it was deemed impracticable to route the flood of individuals returning from overseas in redeployment through redistribution stations, steps were taken in the summer gradually to close down AGF–ASF redistribution facilities.[37] On 25 August 1945 the War Department ceased issuing orders directing personnel to hotel-type stations, in order to permit closing of these installations by 15 October 1945. Army Ground Forces recommended that post-type stations be kept in operation until a later date to process prisoners of war and low-score hospital convalescents.[38]

[33] (1) *Ibid.* (2) Statement of Maj Dwight F. Emmel, C&RD AGF AG Sec, 25 Jan 46.

[34] AGF memo of G–1 for CofS AGF, 15 Mar 45, sub: Visit to AG and SF Redist Stations at Miami Beach, Fla, and Asheville, N. C. With related papers. 353.02/988 (AGF).

[35] AGF M/S (S), G–1 to CofS, 19 May 45, sub: Redist Cens. 354.1/1 (Redist Cens) (S).

[36] Memo of WD G–1 for MPD ASF, 21 May 45, sub: Redist Stations. 354.1/17 (Redist Sta).

[37] (1) AGF memo for CofS USA, 19 Mar 45, sub: Redist Stations. 354.1/13 (Redist Sta). (2) AGF M/S, C&RD to G–1, 24 May 45, sub: Redist Stations. With related papers. 354.1/17 (Redist Sta).

[38] M/R, Enlisted Div G–1 Sec AGF, 21 Aug 45, sub not given. 354.1/18 (Redist Sta).

Administration of Liaison Activities

Until the spring of 1945 liaison personnel at all installations were assigned to the Replacement and School Command. With the extension of liaison activities in April and May 1945, it was deemed advisable to centralize administration of liaison personnel at Headquarters, Army Ground Forces. To this end, orders were issued in April assigning all liaison personnel to that headquarters.[39]

In May 1945 a liaison personnel control division was established in the Ground Adjutant General's Section to coordinate supervision of liaison activities and to exercise administrative control over liaison personnel. This division assigned liaison officers and their assistants, issued periodic letters of information for their guidance, and collected and processed reports of their activities. Promotions, efficiency ratings, and other administrative details were coordinated with installation commanders.[40]

Contact with liaison activities was maintained by occasional visits of Headquarters officers to the field and by personal and official correspondence with liaison officers.[41] As previously noted, immediate supervision of liaison officers at hospitals was delegated to subcommands.

At its peak the liaison system was an extensive establishment. Shortly after V-J Day AGF liaison officers at ports, personnel centers, redistribution stations, and hospitals, all of whom were carried on the roster of Headquarters, Army Ground Forces, aggregated 337—40 percent of the total commissioned personnel assigned to that headquarters at the time and slightly more than twice the total number of officers on duty at Headquarters, Army Ground Forces, at its inception in March 1942.[42]

---

[39] AGF M/S, AG Pers to C&RD, 13 Apr 45, sub: Asgmt of AGF Ln Offs. With related papers. 210/21 (AGF Ln Offs).

[40] (1) Hist of Misc Div. Files of Misc Div, AGF G–1 Sec. (2) AGF ltr to Ln Offs, 3 May 45, sub: Admin of AGF Ln Pers. 322/6 (AGF Ln Dets).

[41] (1) For correspondence see the following files:

    210   (AGF Liaison Offs)
    322   (AGF Liaison Dets)
    354.1 (Redist Sta)
    354.1 (Personnel Cens)

(2) For reports of inspection see 353.02 (AGF). (3) AGF Info ltrs are filed in 300.6 (AGF Info Ltr) (R).

[42] (1) Roster of Officers assigned to Hq AGF, 31 Mar 45. 330.3 (AGF). (2) See AGF Historical Section, A General History of the Army Ground Forces. The number of officers initially assigned to Headquarters, AGF, in March 1942 was 164.

IV. Redeployment of "D" Division

Note: "D" Division is a hypothetical unit whose experience is detailed to summarize the impact of redeployment policies on units selected for the final assault on Jápan, after a period of rest and retraining in the United States. For the sake of definiteness and accuracy the experience of a real unit, the 5th Infantry Division, was used as a guide in tracing the course of redeployment. But materials from other sources have been included to round out the narrative when these materials were considered representative.[1]

The end of hostilities in Europe on 8 May 1945 found "D" Division holding a line in Czechoslovakia near the Austrian border. On 24 May the division assumed occupational duties in the vicinity of Passau in Bavaria.

Shortly after V-E Day the division began to transfer out men having ASR scores of 85 and above, selecting for earliest removal those having the highest scores. Replacements were requisitioned by MOS, but this was of little avail on account of the depleted condition of available replacement stocks; losses

---

[1] The account of the Redeployment of "D" Division, unless otherwise indicated in subsequent reference notes, is based mainly on the following sources:

  (1) Interview by the AGF Historical Officer (on dates indicated) of the following:
    Brig Gen A. D. Warnock, Asst Div Comdr, 5th Inf Div, 20 Nov 45.
    Col W. M. Breckinridge, CO 10th Regt, 5th Inf Div, 5 Feb 46.
    Lt Col R. C. Dickens, G–3, 5th Inf Div, 5 Feb 46.
    Lt Col V. M. Thackeray, G–2, 5th Inf Div, 5 Feb 46.
    Lt Col M. L. Rosen, Asst Liaison Officer, New York Port of Embarkation, 6 Feb 46. (Colonel Rosen witnessed the redeployment processing of the 5th Division at the New York PE.)
  (2) Status Report on 5th Inf Div (prepared by Hq 3d Army, ETO) dated 12 Jun 45. 319.1/51 (R).
  (3) AGF memo (R) of Maj L. A. Twomey for ACofS G–3, 10 Sep 45, sub: WD IG Inspections. With related papers. 353/836 (Readiness) (R). (4) Second Army ltr, Asst G–4 to G–4, 23 Aug 45, sub: Functioning of Automatic Supply for Redepl Tng Units, Cp Campbell, Ky. 333.1/221 (2d Army) (Sep binder). (5) ETO ltr (C) AG 370.5 OPGC (49) to CGs 12th Army Group, etc, 16 Jun 45, sub: Movement Orders, Shipment 10197. Files of G–3 Mob Div (C). (6) Newspaper report of arrival of 86th Infantry Division, *New York Times*, 18 Jun 45. (7) Colonel Breckinridge, Lt. Col. Thackeray, and Lt. Col. Dickens read the present narrative in draft form and accepted it as representative in general of their experience in the redeployment of the 5th Infantry Division.

were replenished by such odds and ends as reinforcement depots happened to have at hand. By the middle of June the division had lost about 1,800 men. On 16 June 3,700 more men, all having ASR scores of 85 or above, were sent to another division, a unit which was to be returned to the United States for in-activation, in exchange for an equal number of low-score men. This brought the total number of losses between V-E Day and 20 June to 5,500. Early in July the division commander was informed that his unit was entitled to credit for two additional campaigns. This required the release of about 600 more men, bringing total losses in Europe to 6,100. Officer losses between V-E Day and reassembly in the United States aggregated 103.

These losses stripped the division of most of its key specialists and noncom-missioned officers. Replacements received from another division, while usually furnished in equivalent MOS's, fell far below the men whose posts they inherited in grade, experience, leadership, and general "know-how." Unit headquarters from division to company were virtually swept clean of experienced clerks, leaving to novices the keeping of records and the performance of other admin-istrative functions at a time when these activities, in view of impending redeploy-ment, were of particular importance. For example, in the first round of discharge the G–3 Section of Division Headquarters lost two master sergeants of more than two years' experience in their current duties, and in a second round a short time later had to give up a staff sergeant with similar qualifications. These men were replaced by T/4's and T/5's, none of whom had had more than two months' experience in the type of work required of them in their new positions.

Field artillery, engineer, signal, and service elements of the division were hardest hit by the turnover, for these units, by virtue of their relatively low casualty rates, had a much greater percentage of high-point men than the regi-ments. Because of the nature of their duties, they also had a considerably higher proportion of technical specialists. Release of men having 85 or more points took away 91 percent of the quartermaster company, 86 percent of the ordnance company, 77 percent of the signal company, and 71 percent of the field artillery, as against 37 percent of the infantry.

Serious as it was, the loss in experience and technical proficiency was not as damaging to the division as the injury done to teamwork and *esprit de corps* by the turnover of personnel. With more than a hundred of its veteran officers and almost half of its battle-seasoned men replaced by newcomers, and with many of the remainder having joined only a short time before V-E Day, the division as it stood at the threshold of redeployment training was a team only in name. So disruptive, indeed, was the turnover that the division commander estimated, on the basis of losses suffered prior to departure for the port of Le Havre, that a minimum of four months' training would be required before the division could be well enough integrated to operate efficiently on the field of battle.

On 25 May the division received warning that it was to be moved from Europe in July. Immediately it began shedding excess equipment accumulated by one means or another during its long period of combat service. On 13 June it relinquished its occupational duties to another division and began preparing trucks and other organizational equipment for delivery to supply depots in France, since orders from higher headquarters directed that movement from Europe was to be made with minimum essential equipment only.

On 16 June orders were received directing immediate dispatch to the United States of an advance party of 42 officers and 144 men to prepare the way for the remainder of the division.[2] The orders specified that the party was to include the assistant division commander, representatives from the general and special staff sections, and 1 officer and 7 enlisted men from each of 20 "provisional battalions" into which units of the division were grouped for housekeeping purposes; of the 7 enlisted men, 4 were cooks, 1 a 1st sergeant, 1 a mess sergeant, and 1 a supply sergeant.[3]

The advance party sailed from Le Havre on 27 June and arrived at Camp Shanks, New York Port of Embarkation, on 5 July. As the ship steamed into New York harbor it was boarded by the AGF Port Liaison Officer (a colonel) and his first assistant (a lieutenant colonel), both veterans of ETO, who extended greetings and welcome for the Commanding General, Army Ground Forces, and briefly oriented the assistant division commander and key members of the party in their mission. Two questions were uppermost in the minds of the group: (1) where is the division to be stationed, and (2) how long a training period will it have. The liaison officer specified Camp Campbell as the station but was indefinite about the training period; under the pressure of questioning, he ventured "one or two months" as a guess—a statement that in view of their knowledge of the personnel situation was most disturbing to the advance party. When the assistant division commander inquired about the

---

[2] WD ltr (C) AG 370.5 (4 Jun 45) OB–S–E SPMOT–M to CGs ETO, AGF, ASF, 8 Jun 45, sub: Return of the 5th Inf Div to the U. S. 370.5/1 (5th Inf Div) (C).

[3] ETO ltr (S) AG 370.5 OPGC (49) to CGs 12th Army Group, etc, 16 Jun 45, sub: Movement Orders Shipment 10197. Files of G–3 Mob Div.

training program, the liaison officer showed him AGF Training Memorandum No. 1—the basic directive prepared several months before for guidance in redeployment training.[4] This was the first copy of the document that anyone in the division had seen, but since the liaison officer had no other he was not willing to part with it. Only after his arrival at Camp Campbell a month later did the assistant division commander obtain a copy of this directive.

The assistant division commander gave such information as was currently available about the division's personnel, equipment, and training status to the liaison officer, who passed it on to Second Army, the headquarters charged with supervising the redeployment training of "D" Division. The value of the information was limited considerably by the fact that the division continued to lose personnel after departure of the advance group from Europe.

Following a brief processing at the staging area, members of the advance party went in groups to reception stations, whence they proceeded individually on a 30-day furlough to their respective homes or other points which they chose for recuperation.

The advance party, reassembling at Camp Campbell August 10–12, immediately launched preparations for the arrival two weeks later of the remainder of the division. This was a time of unrelenting activity, save only for a brief pause on August 14 to celebrate V-J Day. One of the most pressing tasks was the sorting of three truckloads of mail, official and personal, that had accumulated during the recuperation period. Awaiting disposal also were several hundred telegrams addressed to officers and men of the division. The principal activities were checking with post authorities on the status of supplies; drawing and unpacking of essential equipment, which current directives required to be shipped to camp ahead of the division; keeping of morning reports; inspecting barracks; preparing food for the advance group; and setting up messes for the main body of the division.

Post authorities and the 13th Headquarters and Headquarters Company, Special Troops, Second Army, assisted in the preparations; nevertheless, activities were hindered by an inadequacy of personnel—particularly of drivers and clerks—and a deficiency of transportation. Manpower was so sparse, indeed, that officers of the advance party had to drive trucks, and the assistant division commander found it necessary personally to delve into the mountain of mail bags in search of essential training directives.

[4] See AGF Historical Section, Redeployment Training, Sec. I.

A fundamental source of difficulty was the composition of the enlisted element of the advance party. Drawing, checking, and conditioning of supplies and equipment proved to be the most important responsibility of the advance group; only a few of the members, however, were supply personnel, and because of the turnover resulting from release of high-point men a large portion of those falling in supply categories were inexperienced in their duties. One of the consequences of this circumstance was that equipment and supply matters were not in good shape when the main body of the division arrived in camp. The experience at Camp Campbell indicated that it would have been better to have substituted supply personnel for some of the cooks in the advance party. Cooks could have been borrowed from local agencies, but supply personnel proved unobtainable in anything like the numbers required.

In the meantime the division proper, which the advance party left in Bavaria in mid-June, had troubles of its own. Shortly after turning over its sector to another division on 13 June, "D" Division, which up to that time had been completely absorbed in occupational duties, attempted to initiate a program of training. But the continual screening of personnel and the packing and delivery of organizational equipment to remote and scattered depots were so distracting as to limit training largely to drill, lectures on military courtesy, orientation discussions, and physical-fitness exercises. Even in these subjects, training was scanty.

Between 23 and 28 June the division moved to an assembly area at Camp St. Louis. Here small arms and other nonorganizational equipment not to be taken on shipboard by individuals were turned in for equivalent items already packed for shipment. Here also an attempt was made to resume training, but with disappointing results. In fact, at no time during the two months spent in Europe after V-E Day was the division able to participate in anything worthy of the designation of redeployment training, as the term was understood in the Army Ground Forces.

On 4 July the division started moving from Camp St. Louis to the staging area at Camp Lucky Strike. Here it was necessary to make out a second shipping list, as the staging area commander required a different procedure from that prescribed for the first listing by the base section commander; at port the laborious listing had to be done a third time, because the port commander followed a form different from that used in the first two instances. Preparation of the list was the more onerous on account of the dearth of experienced clerks in the division. An attempt was made to check Form 20's and other individual records at port, but results, mainly on account of lack of experienced clerks, left much to be desired.

Movement to the staging area was completed on 7 July, and to port four days later. The first ship, carrying an infantry regiment, left Le Havre on 11 July; three other transports, two of which carried a regiment each, and the third of which carried the field artillery and miscellaneous elements, sailed during the following week.

Congestion and poor facilities made the passage unpleasant for most of the division. One of the regiments, less fortunate than the other units, was transported on a boat which had been seriously damaged on D Day by a mine and which had been pressed into redeployment service without adequate rehabilitation. The ship had some 3,300 men on board; but it was equipped to bunk only about 2,700, and its messing facilities provided full accommodation at one sitting for no more than 250. The men were served two hot meals a day, but hot food was limited to stewed and boiled items, as kitchens were not equipped for baking or frying; cooks were unable to prepare fresh bread of any sort during the eight-day voyage. But personnel generally bore the privations without complaint, mainly because home, with comfortable beds and plentiful food, lay at the end of the journey.[5]

Activities on all the ships were greatly restricted by lack of space. An organized program of physical exercise, for example, was not even attempted. One essential matter attended to on the ship, which Redeployment Regulations contemplated would be completed much earlier, was the breakdown of personnel into reception-station groups. The main reasons for the postponement were the disruption and confusion caused by turnover of personnel, absorption in other duties, and lack of information as to procedure.

The three boats transporting the regiments reached New York during the period July 19–21; the ship carrying the artillery went to Boston, arriving 27 July. Experiences of the division from the time of entering home port and arrival at the assembly area may be summarized by following the activities of "R" Regiment. The boat carrying this regiment arrived in New York Harbor on 19 July. As the ship steamed up the bay a small craft laden with WAC musicians and dancers came out to escort it to the pier. The returning soldiers hailed this reception with a thunderous tumult of shouting and whistling and prolonged waving of caps. After the cheering subsided an official reception party consisting of representatives of the New York Port of Embarkation and

[5] Statement of Col W. M. Breckinridge, CO 10th Regt, 5th Inf Div to AGF Hist Off, 8 Feb 46.

the AGF liaison detachment went aboard (Ground liaison representatives numbered 5—3 officers and 2 enlisted men). Both the senior port officer and the AGF liaison officer, the latter speaking for the Commanding General, Army Ground Forces, broadcast a "Hello, Welcome Home!" over the ship's amplifying system, after which they assembled key officers for a short orientation conference. At this meeting port authorities outlined high points of processing through the staging area, and the AGF liaison officer oriented the group as to their activities after arrival at reception stations. The liaison officer was swamped with questions about furloughs, pay, clothing, ration coupons, training programs, and similar details. Returnees noted with approval the cooperative attitude of the liaison representatives, but later they expressed disappointment that answers to their inquiries were not more definite and complete.

After the conference the liaison staff moved about on deck for a while, extending greetings and answering questions, and then left the ship to prepare for meeting the groups at the piers and in the staging area.

When the transport docked, the men debarked by units in accordance with instructions issued at the conference. After a brief stop on the pier for coffee and doughnuts they proceeded to trains which took them to Camp Shanks, one of the staging areas for the New York Port of Embarkation. On arrival at Camp Shanks they threw their duffle bags on trucks and marched to theaters—a train load to a theater—where they were greeted by port and liaison representatives. The AGF liaison officer addressed the returnees as follows: [6]

FELLOW SOLDIERS:

The Army Ground Forces, which trained most of you and watched with pride and admiration your magnificent achievements overseas, is happy to see you back and wants to do everything it can to make your return home pleasant. General Stilwell, commanding the Army Ground Forces, has sent me to give his personal greetings to all of you. The General has assigned Army Ground Force representatives to this area, and to the reception station to which you will go from here, with a specific mission—to help you get home quicker, to help you with your problems, and to absorb some of your gripes.

Here at Camp Shanks we are in Building X.

You can easily recognize us by our Army Ground Force Shoulder Patch, and our AGF name card.

We are not magicians, but we're willing to try almost anything to give a hand. Whether you need us or not, welcome home. And the best of luck to you all.

---

[6] Incl 2 to ltr of Col John E. Adkins, AGF Ln Off NYPE to Lt Col Louis H. Coxe [undated, but about 25 Jun 45], sub not given. 322/219 (AGF Ln Dets).

Following the theater meeting the returnees were directed to their barracks and then to mess halls where they were served "steak with all the trimmings." After this surfeiting, the men were issued one clean suit of summer clothing—a welcome exchange for the woolen clothes which they wore on the homeward voyage—and assembled into reception station groups of about twenty-five persons, in accordance with the breakdown accomplished on shipboard. Within twenty-four hours of debarkation the returnees were boarding trains for their respective reception stations.

Excepted from the groups ordered to reception stations were organization detachments (usually one officer and one enlisted man per detachment) from each regiment, each artillery battalion, and each of the other principal components of the division, who were sent directly from port to Camp Campbell with unit records deemed essential to planning for the administration and training of the division after its reassembly. When the records had been deposited with responsible authorities at camp, members of the detachments proceeded directly to their homes on furlough.

Processing of the main body of the division at the reception stations was rapid and smooth.[7] One incident of the processing which brought considerable grief to officers of the division was the separation from the service by personnel centers of scores of high-point men who had indicated a desire to go with the division to the Pacific; a large portion of those released were men of Regular Army background holding key positions in their units. To make matters worse, the division commander was not informed of the separations. As late as 17 October 1945 the division reported to Second Army that it was still carrying on its rolls the names of 335 men who did not report to duty after their recuperation furlough and that "it was thought that they were discharged" at reception stations.[8]

V-J Day came during the recuperation furlough. Partly because of this fact, the assembly of the men at Camp Campbell extended over an unduly long period.

Trains coming into camp were met by members of the post personnel and the division's advance party, who by means of loud speakers and placards directed returnees to unit assembly areas (one area for each of the three regiments, one for the artillery, and one for miscellaneous organizations), where

---

[7] See the preceding section, "AGF Liaison at War Department and ASF Installations."

[8] 5th Div ltr to CG Second Army, 17 Oct 45, sub: Disposition of EM. With related papers. 220.3/1 (5th Div).

they were broken down into companies or other groups and were headed for their respective barracks.

Training was initiated on 5 September, but because of prevailing circumstances the program was greatly restricted. As previously mentioned, the equipment situation left much to be desired: some items, including 57-mm. guns and general-purpose vehicles, had not been received by post authorities. Others were not available for use because of the inability of the advance detachment and local agencies to get them unpacked and in condition. Uncertainty as to the mission of the unit was also a hindering factor. Division authorities made persistent inquiries of higher headquarters as to modifications of the basic redeployment training directive, but replies were perforce indefinite. A third deterrent was the continuous turnover of personnel which came with the further lowering of points after V-J Day. The attitude of men remaining in the division was not conducive to effective training. Those anticipating discharge had little heart for any sort of training and low-point men were unfavorably disposed towards a program which had patently been designed for a shooting war in the Pacific.

In view of these circumstances it was decided to restrict training, until things settled down, largely to athletic games and firing exercises. The men liked to shoot, and shoot they did for days upon end. Not until 1946 did conditions become sufficiently stable to permit launching of a balanced program of training.

Glossary of Abbreviations *

AA	Antiaircraft
AAA	Antiaircraft Artillery
AAF	Army Air Forces
A/B	Airborne
AFHQ	Allied Force Headquarters
AG(C&RD)	Adjutant General (Classification and Replacement Division)
AGF	Army Ground Forces
ASF	Army Service Forces
ASR	Adjusted service rating
ASTP	Army Specialized Training Program
AT	Antitank
ETO	European Theater of Operations
FA	Field Artillery
GHQ	General Headquarters
MG	Machine gun
MOS	Military occupational specialty [specification serial number]
MP	Military police
MTO	Mediterranean Theater of Operations
MTOUSA	Mediterranean Theater of Operations, U. S. Army
MTP ·	Mobilization Training Program
OPD	Operations Division [War Department General Staff]
POM	Preparation for Overseas Movement
QM	Quartermaster
RM	Readjustment Memorandum
ROTC	Reserve Officers' Training Program
RR	Readjustment Regulation
RTC	Replacement training center

*See also War Department, Dictionary of United States Army Terms (TM 20–205).

SOP	Standing operating procedure
SOS	Services of Supply
SSN	Specification serial number
SWPA	Southwest Pacific Area [Command]
TB	Troop Basis
T/BA	Table of Basic Allowances
TD	Tank destroyer
T/O	Table of Organization
T/O&E	Table of Organization and Equipment
WAC	Women's Army Corps
WD	War Department
WDGS	War Department General Staff
WPD	War Plans Division [War Department General Staff]

Guide to Footnotes

No generally accepted practice for citing War Department documents exists. In the present series of studies on the Army Ground Forces the method adopted is designed to realize three main objectives: (1) to furnish the reader essential information on the character, the source, the addressee, the date, and the subject matter of the document; (2) to assist the reader who may wish to consult the source; and (3) to make citations as brief as possible.

In general, abbreviations conform to TM 20–205, Dictionary of United States Army Terms, issued by the War Department on 18 January 1944. The file symbols used are those of the decimal filing system compiled by The Adjutant General in *War Department Decimal File System* (Washington, Government Printing Office, 1943).

The following may serve as an example:

> WD ltr (S) AG 353 (9–3–41) MC–E to CofS GHQ, 23 Sep 41, sub: Tng of 1st Div and Supporting Army Units for Landing Opns. 353/1 (AFAF) (S).

The meaning of the above citation is as follows:

1. The document is an official War Department directive (WD ltr), classified originally as Secret (S) and signed by The Adjutant General or one of his assistants (AG).

2. It was given the file number 353, which is assigned to training activities of the Army.

3. In this file it can be located under the date of 3 September 1941 (9–3–41), the day on which the basic policy decision authorizing the issue of the directive was made.

4. The final copy of the directive was prepared for signature and distribution by the War Plans Group of the Miscellaneous Division, Adjutant General's Office, and originated in the Operations Division, War Department General Staff (MC–E).[1]

---

[1] Explanations of this type of symbol may be found in War Department circulars issued periodically whenever major changes in organization occur.

5. It was addressed to the Chief of Staff, General Headquarters (CofS GHQ), on 23 September 1941, and discussed the training of the 1st Division and supporting Army units for amphibious operations.

6. At GHQ the letter was filed with a group of related papers, all numbered 1, in the training file (353/1) under the cut-off heading "Amphibious Force, Atlantic Fleet (AFAF)." The entire file is or was classified Secret.

At all times the classification indicated is that given to the document when issued: (S) for Secret, (C) for Confidential, and (R) for Restricted. Reclassification of documents, a continuous process accelerated since the termination of hostilities, has not been taken into consideration. The classification of information in the text that has been derived from classified documents has been removed by authority of the Commanding General, Army Ground Forces, or of the War Department.

The file symbol at the end of the note is given only as an aid to further investigation. It shows where the document, or a copy of it, was located when last consulted by the authors in late 1945. When this symbol is not preceded by the initials of a War Department office, as in the example given above, it refers in the first study of this volume to the files of General Headquarters, U. S. Army, maintained by the Adjutant General of that headquarters; in all other studies, to the records of the Army Ground Forces. When the symbol is preceded by "AGO Records," it means that the document has been consulted in the files of the Adjutant General's Office of the War Department. In the case of documents originating in neither General Headquarters, U. S. Army, nor the Army Ground Forces, the original file symbol has generally been incorporated in the title, and the location at the time of consultation has been indicated at the end of the citation.

The following list of the types of documents used in the footnotes is added to assist the reader unfamiliar with War Department and Army usage:

AR. Army Regulations are issued by the War Department and include basic policies and rules for the governing of the Army. They have the force and effect of law to the Army.

FM. Field Manuals are official handbooks containing information and instructions for guidance in training and in the operation and maintenance of materiel and equipment.

Cir. Circulars are more temporary directives issued by the War Department or specific headquarters. War Department Circulars may later be incorporated into Army Regulations. Even less permanent instructions are frequently transmitted as memoranda or letters, addressed respectively to all or a selected group of agencies within a command.

GO. General Orders include announcements of official acts of the Secretary of War or the commanding officer of a headquarters.

Bull. Bulletins contain matter which is informative or advisory in nature. They are usually employed for transmitting legislative or executive actions of importance to the Army.

Memo. The memorandum form of correspondence is normally employed within a headquarters for the transmittal of orders, advice, or information. The term "memorandum" is also used for the publication of instructions in place of circulars (see above, *Cir.*). In this case the memorandum is cited in the footnotes as a memo of the agency in question, for example, "WD memo."

Ltr. The letter form of correspondence is used for the transmittal of orders, advice, or information between different headquarters or field agencies. When the term "letter" is used in place of circular, the document is cited as "WD ltr," etc. (see above, *Cir.*). Personal letters, when consulted, are indicated as such.

Ind. An indorsement is used as a reply or forwarding note to a military communication and is added to the original communication.

M/S. A Memorandum Slip is used for informal interoffice communication.

WD D/F. The War Department Disposition Form is the cover sheet for the routing of a staff paper and may contain instructions or comments. For more informal transmittal Disposition or Routing Slips are used.

Telg, Rad, TWX. These refer respectively to telegrams, radiograms, and teletype messages. Usually no subject matter is indicated. *Radre* is used to indicate replies to radiograms ("reference your radiogram").

Bibliographical Note

The studies in this volume are based almost entirely on documents. No previous study of GHQ has been published. The AGF Command has been treated in *What You Should Know About Army Ground Forces,*[1] written by Col. Joseph I. Greene, editor of the *Infantry Journal,* to meet the needs of readers as yet unfamiliar with the 1942 reorganization. After the death of General McNair in July 1944 the *New Yorker,* in its issues for 14 and 21 October 1944, published a "Profile" written by CWO E. J. Kahn, Jr., then a member of the staff of Headquarters, Army Ground Forces. In revised form this was brought out as a little book entitled *McNair: Educator of an Army,*[2] which included the first general account of the activities of the Army Ground Forces to the date of General McNair's death. A more extensive record of the functions and achievements of that command, covering the whole period of the war, is to be found in *Army Ground Forces, Report of Activities,*[3] submitted to the Chief of Staff by the Commanding General, Army Ground Forces, 10 January 1946. The two last-named publications were based in part on materials contained in draft studies of the history of the Army Ground Forces, prepared by its Historical Section, six of which are published in the present volume.

Research for the studies in this volume was devoted principally to the papers in the central records files of GHQ and AGF, maintained by the Adjutants General of those headquarters. This research was supplemented when necessary by resort to the files of the staff sections of Headquarters, AGF, or their divisions, or to the central or staff section files of the War Department General Staff.

The central files of GHQ and AGF, maintained to furnish the basis for current staff and command action, present a remarkably complete record of the

---

[1] W. W. Norton and Co., New York, 1943.

[2] *Infantry Journal,* Washington, 1944.

[3] Published by Headquarters, Army Ground Forces.

operations and decisions of the two commands, of the steps leading to their decisions, and of the information on which decisions were based. In general, the central records in both cases contain the following types of documents:

1. Carbon copies of letters, memoranda, and messages dispatched from the two headquarters.

2. Drafts of such letters, memoranda, or messages, often annotated by hand, which were not used or were issued in a revised form.

3. Originals of staff memoranda or memorandum slips circulated only within the headquarters staff, and usually bearing dated notes or comments of the staff officers concerned, the Chief of Staff, or the Commanding General—invaluable for tracing the course of a discussion and the ideas and influences that were brought to bear on a decision.

4. Originals of letters, memoranda, or disposition forms addressed to the headquarters by other agencies of the War Department or by coordinate or subordinate headquarters.

5. Copies of papers received at the headquarters for information, concurrence, or action.

6. Carbons or typed copies of papers originating elsewhere, received by the headquarters for action, and returned to the sender or indorsed to a new addressee.

7. Mimeographed directives, generally letters, issued by The Adjutant General, GHQ, or Headquarters, AGF, or the armies and other subordinate commands.

In the papers relating to a given course of action most or all of the categories listed above will be found. The central files also contain staff studies, the reports of boards responsible to the headquarters, and annotated drafts of training circulars, manuals, and the like submitted to the War Department for approval.

In the records of both headquarters the papers relating to a certain course of action were filed together in a group. Each paper in the group was given the same number. This appears after the diagonal following the file classification symbol, for example, 320.2/135 or 335/9 (S). The series of related papers in the group may cover a considerable period of time and in such cases often breaks the chronological sequence of the papers in a given binder of the general series within which it appears. But within each binder the groups are arranged in chronological order in accordance with the dates of the basic papers through which the course of action was initiated. In general, each group contains, if not the documents themselves, clues to the documents needed for a study of the action.

Such records of staff sections of Headquarters, AGF, or their subdivisions as were consulted in the preparation of the history or were believed by the Historical Section to be of possible value for further research, and which were not in the central records, have been transferred as far as practicable to the Historical Records Branch of the Adjutant General's Office. Included with these are memoranda of the interviews conducted by the historical officers. Neither GHQ nor Headquarters, AGF, was an office of record. Before their central files were transferred to the Adjutant General's Office, mimeographed letters issued by the War Department or its major commands for general distribution were by order screened out of the records. Also removed were the cross-index sheets which had originally been inserted to facilitate reference for staff use. A reference to the papers removed can usually be found by using the listing sheets on the face of each of the series of binders into which the papers in a given classification are assembled. These sheets list the individual papers originally contained in the groups described above. The date of each paper appears in a separate column. These dates are not in exact chronological order but are of assistance in finding a paper the date of which is known, and are often the only practicable method of finding such a paper.

The bulk of the central records of both headquarters is to be found in its General Correspondence files. Each also kept files for subordinate commands, for example, the Armored Command or the Third Army. In addition the records of GHQ originally included files for base and defense commands, representing its operational responsibilities. Under each of these categories papers were filed in the appropriate decimal classifications, for example, 320.2 (for papers relating to organization and strength), or 353 (for papers relating to training). Within each of these classifications "cut-off" series appear for important subjects, for example, 353 (Training Directives), or 353 (Air-Ground). The listing sheets on the binders of the general series furnish references to all papers in the cut-off series.

The classifications richest in material for the history of both headquarters are 320.2 and 353 and their various cut-offs. They contain half or more of the records of primary historical or administrative significance. Together these two series constitute the nearest approach to a master or policy file of both commands. In addition, the Records Division of the Adjutant General, AGF, collected in a Policy File copies of papers regarded by that office as defining the policies of the Command. While useful as an initial guide, this series is not a substitute for research in the 320.2 and 353 series.

Besides these two important series, files likely to repay research regarding the central development and main policies of GHQ and AGF are the following:

210   —Officers
311   —Telephone Conversations
314.7 —Histories
319.1 —Reports
319.1 —(Overseas Observers)
333   —Inspections
337   —Conferences
352   —Schools
353.01—Training Directives
353.02—Instruction Visits
354.1 —RTC's
354.2 —Maneuvers
381   —War Plans
461   —Publications

To assist further research, certain characteristics of the two sets of central records may be mentioned. First, both headquarters, in filing papers received from outside, assigned their own file numbers irrespective of the file numbers which these papers might already bear. Second, the central records of AGF are, in general, in much better order than those of GHQ, which had to depend on a small and untrained Records Division working under the pressure of emergency and rapid expansion. Some confusion resulted. Furthermore the Division resorted to a certain amount of improvisation, and some scattering of related papers resulted. To curb the rapidly increasing bulk of certain series, new files were opened or the old broken down into subheadings. The dispersion was controlled, but only in part, by cross-indexing.

One unconventional device used by GHQ to control bulky series must be mentioned. In certain cases in which the papers in a group within a classification series became numerous, the group was put in a separate binder and the papers in it were assigned an additional number. The result was such designations as 320.2/158/27 and 353/27/14 (C).

A student desiring to trace a special or technical question in either the GHQ or AGF records will find the following procedure helpful:

1. Locate, in the alphabetical subject index to the file manual, the decimal symbol there assigned to the subject.

2. Consult this number in the records.

3. Work by cross reference, or by means of the listing sheet on the face of each binder, to other parts of the records which were given different decimal classifications.

Studies Prepared During the War
by the Historical Section, Army Ground Forces

*Origins of the Army Ground Forces: General Headquarters, United States
    Army, 1940–42 (R)
A General History of the Army Ground Forces (R)

Mobilization of the Ground Forces

*Ground Forces in the War Army: A Statistical Study (R)
*Mobilization of the Ground Army (R)
**Procurement of Enlisted Personnel for the AGF: the Problem of
    Quality (R)
**The Procurement and Branch Distribution of Officers (R)
**The Provision of Enlisted Replacements (R)

Organization of the Ground Forces

*Reorganization of Ground Troops for Combat (R)
*Organization and Training of New Ground Combat Elements (R)

Unit Training

**The Building and Training of Infantry Divisions (R)
**Problems of Nondivisional Training in the Army Ground Forces (R)
The Desert Training Center and C—AMA (R)
History of the Second Army (R)
History of the Third Army (R)
History of the Fourth Army (R)
History of the Activation of Headquarters of the Fifteenth Army (R)
**Preparation of Units for Overseas Movement (R)

Special Training of Units

The Amphibious Training Center (R)
Training in Mountain and Winter Warfare (R)
The Mountain Training Center (R)

Training of Specialized Units

The Airborne Command and Center (R)
The Antiaircraft Command and Center (R)
The Armored Force, Command, and Center (R)
History of the Tenth Light Division (Alpine) (R)
The Tank Destroyer History (R)

Individual Training

**Wartime Training in the Schools of the Army Ground Forces (R)
**Training of Officer Candidates in AGF Special Service Schools (R)
**Major Developments in the Training of Enlisted Replacements (R)
The Replacement and School Command (R)

Equipment

The Role of the Army Ground Forces in the Development of Equipment (R)

Special Problems of Organization and Training

Air-Ground Cooperation (R)
The Training of Negro Troops (C)

Redeployment

*The Role of Army Ground Forces in Redeployment (R)
**Redeployment Training (R)

*Revised and published in this volume.
**To be revised and published in the next volume in the AGF series.

THE UNITED STATES ARMY IN WORLD WAR II

Tentative List of Subseries

	Approximate Number of Volumes
The War Department	8
The Army Air Forces	7
The Army Ground Forces	4
The Army Service Forces	6
The European Theater of Operations	8
The War in the Mediterranean	7
The War in the Pacific	12
The China-Burma-India Theater	3
The Middle East Theater	2
The Defense of the Americas	2
The Technical Services	28
The Administrative Services	4
Special Projects	8
TOTAL	**99**

555949 O–61—35

Index

O

U.S. GOVERNMENT PRINTING OFFICE : 1961 O—555949